GW00670443

ISBN: 9781314366907

Published by:
HardPress Publishing
8345 NW 66TH ST #2561
MIAMI FL 33166-2626

Email: info@hardpress.net
Web: http://www.hardpress.net

ROBERT BROWNING

Drawn at Rome in 1859 by Field Talfourd

OXFORD EDITION

THE
RING AND THE BOOK

BY

ROBERT BROWNING

WITH AN INTRODUCTION BY EDWARD DOWDEN

AND FOUR FACSIMILES

HENRY FROWDE

OXFORD UNIVERSITY PRESS

LONDON, EDINBURGH, GLASGOW, NEW YORK

TORONTO, MELBOURNE AND BOMBAY

1912

CONTENTS

ILLUSTRATIONS

INTRODUCTION

A LOVER of poetry who desired to make acquaintance with Browning's work once inquired of him which poem he should read first, and straightway came the reply—'*The Ring and the Book*, of course.' Browning's advice was prompted less by a comprehension of what would win and what might throw off a friendly reader than by the sense that the whole of his own mind was more fully represented in this than in any other of his writings. Certainly he had shown his thews in *The Ring and the Book*; it is his largest and most sustained achievement. But a volume or sequence of volumes comprising more than twenty thousand lines of verse—equal in number to those of *Paradise Lost* twice told—can hardly be regarded as an introduction to his work; it is perhaps the chief, the ultimate thing to master. Browning's friend, John Forster, when in early days he made the first selection from the poetical works, knew better than did the poet himself how to awaken the faith and hope and courage which are needed before we venture on a considerable enterprise. Yet it remains true that the whole mass of the poet's mind thrusts itself forward with more domineering force in his story of the Roman murder-case than in such lyric pieces and dramatic fragments as are best fitted to gain from the outset believers in the genius of Robert Browning. Nowhere else is his search for truth more impassioned or more persistent; nowhere else are the abstractions of his brain more adequately embodied in concrete forms of art; nowhere else is there a finer play of that intellectual casuistry, which, after a web of sophistries has been spun, is severed by one swift sword-stroke of the spirit. We find here at its highest his feeling for the power which one soul can wield over another ; we find here his delight in the radiance of innocence in its greatest intensity; we find here his deepest ponderings of moral wisdom, and his uttermost indignation against whatever is treacherous and cruel. Veiled memories of his past and eager hopes for the future are here. Nor do we miss Browning's characteristic humour, a thing rather of a robust temperament, like that of his own Herakles, than of any subtle mingling of laughter with tenderness. Finally, if the right to lay—not without a purpose—a burden of weariness on the reader is sometimes claimed by the poet, he assuredly claims that right in abundant measure in *The Ring and the Book*, when the advocates of the culprit and of his victim perorate and cite their precedents.

Browning's father is said to have taken unusual interest in the investigation of complex criminal cases. The son inherited a like curiosity in the study of facts and motives connected with crime. The late Mr. Kegan Paul told in his *Memories* of a dinner-party where the conversation turned on murder ; Browning surprised him by showing his acquaintance to the minutest detail with every *cause célèbre* of that kind within living memory.

It was on a blazing day of June 1860, when Browning had passed his forty-eighth birthday, that he found—pushed by the 'Hand' of 'predestination' above his shoulder—in the Piazza di San Lorenzo, Florence, and purchased for a lira the ' square old yellow book ' which supplied him with the ' crude fact ' from which his poem was fashioned. In the opening section of that poem he tells us how his imagination was instantly seized by the story of the long-forgotten murder of two centuries since; how, as he walked towards Casa Guidi, his eyes were fastened upon the pages until the heart of the old pamphlets had been plucked out, and how, when darkness fell, as he stood upon the terrace, breathing

.The beauty and the fearfulness of night,

he saw the whole tragedy of Arezzo and of Rome rise before his eyes and enact itself again.

'When I had read the book', Browning said to Mr. Rudolf Lehmann, 'my plan was at once settled. I went for a walk, gathered twelve pebbles from the road, and put them at equal distances on the parapet that bordered it. Those represented the twelve chapters into which the poem is divided, and I adhered to that arrangement to the last.' After a time, however, he must have hesitated and faltered. He offered the story as early as the winter of 1860 to his friend Miss Ogle as the subject for a novel. He suggested to another friend, Mr. W. C. Cartwright, that he should write an account of it, and even proposed to give him the book—the book of 'pre-destination'. Possibly the shock of Mrs. Browning's death in June 1861 may have caused him to doubt his ability to carry through so vast an undertaking. But in 1862 he wrote from Biarritz as if he had decided to convert 'the Roman murder-story' into a poem, and had already been shaping it in his imagination. Two years later he had, while staying in the south of France, defined his scheme. He wrote —so Browning told Mr. W. M. Rossetti—on a regular systematic plan, making use of the early hours of each day: 'He has written', Mr. Rossetti noted in his diary, 'his forthcoming work all consecutively—not some of the later parts before the earlier.' Such was what Browning styles his 'smithcraft', and no smith could hammer his work upon the anvil with a steadier hand. In 1868 the poem was completed. Addressing the ' old yellow book ' in the last section of his work he asks—

> How will it be, my four-years'-intimate, ·
> When thou and I part company anon ?

Four years carries us back to the date when Browning visited the Pas de Roland. The poem was published in four monthly volumes during the winter of 1868-9.

In addition to the collection of pamphlets, pleadings, and manuscripts bound together in the volume found by Browning in the Piazza di San Lorenzo, he had as a secondary and minor source an Italian manuscript discovered in London and communicated to him by one of his acquaintances ; this was printed by Sir John Simeon in *Miscellanies XII*, 1868-9, of the Philobiblion Society. It tells the story of Guido and Pompilia briefly, adding certain scraps of information which are not given in the poet's primary sources. Here Browning found the name of Pompilia's infant son—Gaetano ; here he read of the exposure of the bodies of Pietro and Violante in the church of San Lorenzo, with other details which he was not slow to utilize. Yet another manuscript account of the trial and death of Franceschini and his companions came to light in a library of Rome too late to be of service to the poet ; a translation was printed by Browning's biographer, W. Hall Griffin, in the *Monthly Review*, November 1900. It tends to confirm the interpretation of the facts which is presented in *The Ring and the Book*.

The ' Book ' itself has found a resting-place, in accordance with Browning's desire, in the library of Balliol College, Oxford. The College possesses also the portrait of the poet painted by his son, and here the Book is represented as supported by Browning's hands. A photographic reproduction of the contents of the volume, with translation, notes, and much subsidiary matter, was edited by an American student of Browning, Mr. Charles W. Hodell, and was issued by the Carnegie Institution of Washington in 1908. The volume, which is formidable in size, contains a valuable essay by the editor, comparing the treatment of the story as found in the poem with the ' crude fact ' as disclosed by the original documents. The same editor has supervised a reprint of the documents in a popular form, but without his elaborate essay ; all who study the poem must acknowledge themselves debtors to Mr. Hodell.

' My stress lay on the incidents in the development of a soul,' Browning wrote of his Sordello : ' little else is worth study.' It was in like manner the probing and the exposition of character that interested him before all else in his dealing with the Roman murder-case of 1698. But little of this was to be found in the pamphlets and legal documents that lay before him. Even the crude fact was here presented as in dispute. Browning, like his Pope, had to pronounce on the whole matter, to interpret the various allegations in his own way, and to fashion the characters in accordance with the view which he had taken. If we are to accept his metaphor of the ring shaped from untempered gold with the help of alloy, we are compelled to reverse the meaning of the metaphor as set forth by the poet ; the gold is contributed by Browning's imagination ; the alloy is the fact or the alleged fact as contributed by the Book. In the course of his repeated perusals of the documents he selected with scrupulous care every detail that was in harmony with his design ; but his own imaginative interpretation of the affair supplied the test by which he valued the assertions of the several parties. His conception of the characters in large measure determined his appraisement of the documentary statements. 'It is a wonderful book,' said Carlyle to Browning, ' one of the most wonderful poems ever written. I re-read it all through—all made out of an Old Bailey story that might have been told in ten lines, and only wants forgetting.' And Carlyle was right. We could not tolerate the recital of the Old Bailey story, from different points of view, by speaker after speaker, if the story were the chief thing. But Guido, Pompilia, Caponsacchi, the Pope, are of perennial interest; innocence and guilt, pure chivalry, faith and love, spiritual wisdom, are things that for ever concern us. Browning had already made the dramatic monologue his chief medium for presenting the complexities of character. He lacked the true dramatic instinct which makes dialogue a living thing ; but he could exhibit character in position. It was natural that he should now employ the monologue, summoning each of his leading personages to the task of self-revealment. And in the process the story itself changes, assuming new meanings and new colours in accordance with the temperament and character of each successive speaker. Ten times it is told, and yet it is not told once :

> Our human speech is naught,
> Our human testimony false, our fame
> And human estimation words and wind.

The truth of each speech is relative to him who speaks.

How much Browning obtained from his sources and how little he obtained are alike and almost equally remarkable. A multitude of petty details found in the documents is incorporated in the poem ; but the poet can recreate an incident or alter its significance, or can develop a few words or lines into a full and continuous narrative. The incident, for example, of confetti-throwing in the theatre is mentioned in the affidavit of Pompilia ; but all its deeper meaning, when

> She turned,
> Looked our way, smiled the beautiful sad strange smile,

is of the poet's invention. Again, the flight of Pompilia and Caponsacchi from Arezzo is, of course, dealt with in the original statements, but the breathless and entrancing narration of that flight assigned by Browning to the Canon—once ' fribble and coxcomb and light-o'-love ', now a kind of solemn soldier-saint— is not to be found outside the poem.

It is especially the characters of the actors in these tragic events that Browning has created or re-fashioned and developed. The Guido Franceschini of the Book has not the distinction of being an interesting villain. His cruelty, cunning, greed for gain can be inferred from the documents ; but Browning's Guido is a man of intellect, capable of self-control after his sufferings in the torture-chamber, ingenious in sophistry, keen in irony, clear-sighted and cool enough to take advantage of every point that may tell in his favour. Browning felt with his Pope that our imperative duty is to rid the earth of such a miscreant. And yet he is God's creature. To God must be left his ultimate destiny ; truth may be flashed upon Guido's eyes by one fierce blow ; he may even yet see and be saved :

> Else I avert my face, nor follow him
> Into that sad obscure sequestered state
> Where God unmakes but to remake the soul
> He else made first in vain ; which must not be.

Pompilia had prayed that, though Guido could not behold the light on God's face, he yet might touch God's shadow and be healed; and the last word on Guido's lips, in which the climax passes beyond the name of God, is a cry for help to the innocence and purity which he had outraged.

'I found Pompilia in the book just as she speaks and acts in my poem'—so declared Browning to an acquaintance. The truth is that he found in the Book whatever he needed and desired to find. Another reader of the documents might fail to discover the Pompilia of Browning. The advocate on the side of the murderer was justified in making much of the fact that Pompilia stated that the fugitives reached Castelnuovo in the dawn, whereas her companion Caponsacchi and the other witnesses declared that it was in the evening, and that the night was spent at the inn. She lied from policy, declared her counsel; she swooned, says Browning, and lost count of time. If anything in the original sources shadowed forth the Pompilia of the poem it is the sworn testimony of the Augustinian, Fra Celestino Angelo, and others who attended her on her death-bed. 'I have discovered and marvelled at an innocent and saintly conscience', he avers, 'in that ever-blessed child.' She condoned, according to another witness, 'with superhuman generosity the offences of the one who had caused her innocent death.' And again—'She was often asked by her confessor and other persons whether she had committed any offence against Guido, her husband . . . and she always responded that she had never committed any offence against him, but had always lived with all chastity and modesty.' The poet was certainly not without a certain suggestion in the Book for his image of Pompilia as the flawless rose, gathered, as his Pope expresses it, for the breast of God. But, as has been noticed by Mr. Hodell, two important features of her characterization are wholly of Browning's invention. ' In the Book there is not a hint of Pompilia's sense of motherhood, which according to the poet was the real motive of Pompilia's flight from Arezzo, and was the quickener of her new trust in God, that came with the impulse to save her babe. In her monologue this sense of motherhood is one of the tenderest human traits of Pompilia as her motherly faith and motherly solicitude dwell on the thought of the little Gaetano.' Again, the idea of her exalted spiritual love for Caponsacchi we owe altogether to Browning. Apart from the forged letters there is no proof in the Book of her love (if we should not rather call it worship) of the man who had been a saviour in her distress. As Mr. Hodell observes, Browning might have made the defence of Pompilia and Caponsacchi easier in the eyes of the world if he had not imagined this mutual devotion of spirit to spirit. But he dared to represent a real, if almost a supernatural thing, and he has lifted up the reader's heart so that what is highest in the love of man and woman becomes credible. When Browning himself first wrote words to his future wife which were meant to lead to marriage, he had seen her only once and he believed that she was suffering from some disease of the spine that would keep her always a prostrate invalid. In such an enthusiasm of admiration and pity as he felt then lay perhaps the germ of not a little that found development in his future art.

The central event in Caponsacchi's life, as we find it in the poem, is that which has a certain resemblance to sudden religious conversion—the passing away at the command of what he calls ' faith ', but what we may as truly name ' love ', of the ' fribble and cox-

comb ', and his translation into a kind of armed
St. George, a soldier-saint.   Nothing of this is to be
discovered in the Book.   The hint from which the
Caponsacchi of earlier days is imagined comes indeed
from Pompilia's affidavit.   The Canon was accustomed
to pass, with other young men of Arezzo, before
Count Guido's house, ' and stop to talk with certain
hussies who were standing there.'   According to
Pompilia, when she begged him to bring her to Rome,
to her father and mother, ' he replied that he did not
wish to meddle at all in such an affair, as it would
be thought ill of by the whole city.'   It is only at last
that he is induced to promise that he will deliver
her from the house which has grown a prison.   In
Browning's rehandling of the theme, when Pompilia,
stirred by the consciousness of motherhood, implores
Caponsacchi's aid, there is not a moment of hesitation.   She sees the same ' silent and solemn face'
which she had first descried in the theatre, and when
her entreaty has been made :

<blockquote>
He replied—
The first word I heard ever from his lips,
All himself in it—an eternity
Of speech, to match the immeasurable depth
O' the soul that then broke silence—' I am yours.'
</blockquote>

This is nobly imagined.   It would be to inquire too
curiously if we were to ask whether this passion of
the deliverer had suddenly taken possession of the
future author of *The Ring and the Book* when, on his
first visit to the house in Wimpole Street, he saw
a little figure, chained, as he believed, to the sofa,
a pallid face and the great, eager, wistful eyes.   It is
certain that at that moment the words ' I am yours '
were spoken within his heart.

Of the Pope only the barest mention is found in the
Book.   ' There is no proof,' writes Mr. Hodell, ' that

he took any personal interest in the story, nor even that he did anything else than deny Guido the protection of clerical privilege. The sentence against the murderers was by the court, and not by the Pope. The Pope merely took the negative attitude of non-interference.' From the pages of history Browning doubtless learnt that Innocent XII was a wise and disinterested ruler of the Church. He called the poor his ' nephews ' and distributed among them the bene-fits which some of his predecessors had reserved for favourites or kinsfolk. Browning spoke of his Pope to the Rev. John Chadwick with special affection. But in truth he is not the historical Antonio Pignatelli of 1698. He is the spokesman of the poet's own ideas —a brother, as Mr. Hodell names him, of Rabbi Ben Ezra and the Apostle John. He is a ' grey ultimate decrepitude ', and yet through him we hear the voices of the invisible world pronouncing judgement on the persons and the incidents of earth, while yet he remains entirely human, and uses an old man's sagacity to the full in the discrimination of deeds and motives.

To the Book, of course, the pleadings of the advocates, with their many Latin citations, are directly due. The American critic has fortitude enough to enjoy these pleadings. No doubt excellent reasons can be assigned to account for their presence; but excellent reasons can be assigned for many things that we endure. I confess I bear the Book a grudge because it seemed to make necessary the presence in the poem of Dominus Hyacinthus de Archangelis and Doctor Johannes-Baptista Bottinius. The diversions occasioned by the eight-years-old Cinone's birthday feast are Browning's addition ; but the birthday feast, with its fried liver and fennel, is itself somewhat of a weariness to the flesh. Resting-places in the poem, one admits, are needed ; some level ground is required in order that we may perceive aright the abysses and the mounts of vision. The smoke of Half-Rome and his fellows may serve as a necessary contrast to the fire that issues from the heart and soul of Caponsacchi. Every vast poem has perhaps its tracts of weariness. We do not venture to say that Browning was wrong in his general design ; but we cannot help wishing that his touch were lighter and that our period of trial were less prolonged. A robust critic, resolved to admire, may smile at such a confession of human infirmity. But except the robust critic, who that has floundered through the legal pleadings has ever willingly returned to them ? Half-Rome and The Other Half-Rome may serve as a huge prologue ; but was it absolutely essential that the speaker of Tertium Quid should dissertate to ' Eminence This ' and ' All-Illustrious That ' ? It is, however, only just to remember that the same passionate interest in his theme and in every part of it which made Browning comprehend the gallantry, the purity, the spiritual wisdom, of his central characters led him to deal in the same unfaltering way with the minor personages who played their part in the tragic story, or who were conceived as representatives of the popular opinion of the day.

EDWARD DOWDEN.

THE

RING AND THE BOOK

I

THE RING AND THE BOOK

Do you see this Ring ?
    'T is Rome-work, made to match
(By Castellani's imitative craft)
Etrurian circlets found, some happy morn,
After a dropping April ; found alive
Spark-like 'mid unearthed slope-side figtree-roots
That roof old tombs at Chiusi : soft, you see,
Yet crisp as jewel-cutting. There 's one trick,
(Craftsmen instruct me) one approved device
And but one, fits such slivers of pure gold   10
As this was,—such mere oozings from the mine,
Virgin as oval tawny pendent tear
At beehive-edge when ripened combs o'erflow,—
To bear the file's tooth and the hammer's tap :
Since hammer needs must widen out the round,
And file emboss it fine with lily-flowers,
Ere the stuff grow a ring-thing right to wear.
That trick is, the artificer melts up wax
With honey, so to speak ; he mingles gold
With gold's alloy, and, duly tempering both,   20
Effects a manageable mass, then works.
But his work ended, once the thing a ring,
Oh, there 's repristination ! Just a spirt
O' the proper fiery acid o'er its face,
And forth the alloy unfastened flies in fume ;
While, self-sufficient now, the shape remains,
The rondure brave, the lilied loveliness,
Gold as it was, is, shall be evermore :
Prime nature with an added artistry—
No carat lost, and you have gained a ring.   30

What of it ?   'T is a figure, a symbol, say ;
A thing's sign : now for the thing signified.

Do you see this square old yellow Book, I toss
I' the air, and catch again, and twirl about
By the crumpled vellum covers,—pure crude fact
Secreted from man's life when hearts beat hard,
And brains, high-blooded, ticked two centuries since ?
Examine it yourselves !   I found this book,
Gave a *lira* for it, eightpence English just,
(Mark the predestination !) when a Hand,   40
Always above my shoulder, pushed me once,
One day still fierce 'mid many a day struck calm,
Across a Square in Florence, crammed with booths,
Buzzing and blaze, noontide and market-time ;
Toward Baccio's marble,—ay, the basement-ledge
O' the pedestal where sits and menaces
John of the Black Bands with the upright spear,
'Twixt palace and church,—Riccardi where they lived,
His race, and San Lorenzo where they lie.
This book,—precisely on that palace-step   50
Which, meant for lounging knaves o' the Medici,
Now serves re-venders to display their ware,—
'Mongst odds and ends of ravage, picture-frames
White through the worn gilt, mirror-sconces chipped,
Bronze angel-heads once knobs attached to chests,
(Handled when ancient dames chose forth brocade)
Modern chalk drawings, studies from the nude,
Samples of stone, jet, breccia, porphyry
Polished and rough, sundry amazing busts
In baked earth, (broken, Providence be praised !) 60
A wreck of tapestry, proudly-purposed web
When reds and blues were indeed red and blue,
Now offered as a mat to save bare feet
(Since carpets constitute a cruel cost)
Treading the chill scagliola bedward : then
A pile of brown-etched prints, two *crazie* each,
Stopped by a conch a-top from fluttering forth
—Sowing the Square with works of one and the same
Master, the imaginative Sienese
Great in the scenic backgrounds—(name and fame 70
None of you know, nor does he fare the worse :)
From these . . . Oh, with a Lionard going cheap
If it should prove, as promised, that Joconde

Whereof a copy contents the Louvre !—these
I picked this book from. Five compeers in flank
Stood left and right of it as tempting more—
A dogseared Spicilegium, the fond tale
O' the Frail One of the Flower, by young Dumas,
Vulgarized Horace for the use of schools,
The Life, Death, Miracles of Saint Somebody,   80
Saint Somebody Else, his Miracles, Death and Life,—
With this, one glance at the lettered back of which,
And ' Stall ! ' cried I : a *lira* made it mine.

Here it is, this I toss and take again ;
Small-quarto size, part print part manuscript :
A book in shape but, really, pure crude fact
Secreted from man's life when hearts beat hard,
And brains, high-blooded, ticked two centuries since.
Give it me back ! The thing 's restorative
I' the touch and sight.   90

                         That memorable day,
(June was the month, Lorenzo named the Square)
I leaned a little and overlooked my prize
By the low railing round the fountain-source
Close to the statue, where a step descends :
While clinked the cans of copper, as stooped and rose
Thick-ankled girls who brimmed them, and made place
For marketmen glad to pitch basket down,
Dip a broad melon-leaf that holds the wet,
And whisk their faded fresh. And on I read   100
Presently, though my path grew perilous
Between the outspread straw-work, piles of plait
Soon to be flapping, each o'er two black eyes
And swathe of Tuscan hair, on festas fine :
Through fire-irons, tribes of tongs, shovels in sheaves,
Skeleton bedsteads, wardrobe-drawers agape,
Rows of tall slim brass lamps with dangling gear,—
And worse, cast clothes a-sweetening in the sun :
None of them took my eye from off my prize.
Still read I on, from written title-page   110
To written index, on, through street and street,
At the Strozzi, at the Pillar, at the Bridge ;
Till, by the time I stood at home again
In Casa Guidi by Felice Church,
Under the doorway where the black begins

With the first stone-slab of the staircase cold,
I had mastered the contents, knew the whole truth
Gathered together, bound up in this book,
Print three-fifths, written supplement the rest.
' *Romana Homicidiorum* '—nay,   120
Better translate—' A Roman murder-case :
' Position of the entire criminal cause
' Of Guido Franceschini, nobleman,
' With certain Four the cutthroats in his pay,
' Tried, all five, and found guilty and put to death
' By heading or hanging as befitted ranks,
' At Rome on February Twenty Two,
' Since our salvation Sixteen Ninety Eight :
' Wherein it is disputed if, and when,
' Husbands may kill adulterous wives, yet 'scape   130
' The customary forfeit.'

                            Word for word,
So ran the title-page : murder, or else
Legitimate punishment of the other crime,
Accounted murder by mistake,—just that
And no more, in a Latin cramp enough
When the law had her eloquence to launch,
But interfilleted with Italian streaks
When testimony stooped to mother-tongue,—
That, was this old square yellow book about.   140

Now, as the ingot, ere the ring was forged,
Lay gold, (beseech you, hold that figure fast !)
So, in this book lay absolutely truth,
Fanciless fact, the documents indeed,
Primary lawyer-pleadings for, against,
The aforesaid Five ; real summed-up circumstance
Adduced in proof of these on either side,
Put forth and printed, as the practice was,
At Rome, in the Apostolic Chamber's type,
And so submitted to the eye o' the Court   150
Presided over by His Reverence
Rome's Governor and Criminal Judge,—the trial
Itself, to all intents, being then as now
Here in the book and nowise out of it ;
Seeing, there properly was no judgment-bar,
No bringing of accuser and accused,
And whoso judged both parties, face to face

Posizione
Di tutta La Causa Criminale
Contro
Guido Franceschini Nobile
Aretino, e suoi Sicarij Stati
fatti morire in Roma il dì 22.
Febb.^{io} 1698.
Il primo con la decollazione d'altri
quattro di Forca

Romana Homicidiorum

Disputatur an et quando Maritus
possit occidere Vxorem
Adulteram
absque incursu pœnæ Ord.^{riæ}

FACSIMILE TITLE-PAGE OF THE 'BOOK'

Before some court, as we conceive of courts.
There was a Hall of Justice ; that came last :
For justice had a chamber by the hall   160
Where she took evidence first, summed up the same,
Then sent accuser and accused alike,
In person of the advocate of each,
To weigh that evidence' worth, arrange, array
The battle. 'T was the so-styled Fisc began,
Pleaded (and since he only spoke in print
The printed voice of him lives now as then)
The public Prosecutor—' Murder 's proved ;
' With five . . . what we call qualities of bad,
' Worse, worst, and yet worse still, and still worse yet ;
' Crest over crest crowning the cockatrice,   171
' That beggar hell's regalia to enrich
' Count Guido Franceschini : punish him ! '
Thus was the paper put before the court
In the next stage, (no noisy work at all,)
To study at ease. In due time like reply
Came from the so-styled Patron of the Poor,
Official mouthpiece of the five accused
Too poor to fee a better,—Guido's luck
Or else his fellows', which, I hardly know,—   180
An outbreak as of wonder at the world,
A fury-fit of outraged innocence,
A passion of betrayed simplicity :
' Punish Count Guido ? For what crime, what hint
' O' the colour of a crime, inform us first !
' Reward him rather ! Recognize, we say,
' In the deed done, a righteous judgment dealt !
' All conscience and all courage,—there 's our Count
' Charactered in a word ; and, what 's more strange,
' He had companionship in privilege,   190
' Found four courageous conscientious friends :
' Absolve, applaud all five, as props of law,
' Sustainers of society !—perchance
' A trifle over-hasty with the hand
' To hold her tottering ark, had tumbled else ;
' But that 's a splendid fault whereat we wink,
' Wishing your cold correctness sparkled so ! '
Thus paper second followed paper first,
Thus did the two join issue—nay, the four,
Each pleader having an adjunct. ' True, he killed
' —So to speak—in a certain sort—his wife,   201

' But laudably, since thus it happed ! ' quoth one :
Whereat, more witness and the case postponed.
' Thus it happed not, since thus he did the deed,
' And proved himself thereby portentousest
' Of cutthroats and a prodigy of crime,
' As the woman that he slaughtered was a saint,
' Martyr and miracle ! ' quoth the other to match :
Again, more witness, and the case postponed.
' A miracle, ay—of lust and impudence ;   210
' Hear my new reasons ! ' interposed the first :
' —Coupled with more of mine ! ' pursued his peer.
' Beside, the precedents, the authorities ! '
From both at once a cry with an echo, that !
That was a firebrand at each fox's tail
Unleashed in a cornfield : soon spread flare enough,
As hurtled thither and there heaped themselves
From earth's four corners, all authority
And precedent for putting wives to death,
Or letting wives live, sinful as they seem.   220
How legislated, now, in this respect,
Solon and his Athenians ?   Quote the code
Of Romulus and Rome !   Justinian speak !
Nor modern Baldo, Bartolo be dumb !
The Roman voice was potent, plentiful ;
Cornelia de Sicariis hurried to help
Pompeia de Parricidiis ; *Julia de*
Something-or-other jostled *Lex* this-and-that ;
King Solomon confirmed Apostle Paul :
That nice decision of Dolabella, eh ?   230
That pregnant instance of Theodoric, oh !
Down to that choice example Ælian gives
(An instance I find much insisted on)
Of the elephant who, brute-beast though he were,
Yet understood and punished on the spot
His master's naughty spouse and faithless friend ;
A true tale which has edified each child,
Much more shall flourish favoured by our court !
Pages of proof this way, and that way proof,
And always—once again the case postponed.   240

Thus wrangled, brangled, jangled they a month,
—Only on paper, pleadings all in print,
Nor ever was, except i' the brains of men,
More noise by word of mouth than you hear now—

Till the court cut all short with ' Judged, your cause.
' Receive our sentence ! Praise God ! We pronounce
' Count Guido devilish and damnable :
' His wife Pompilia in thought, word and deed,
' Was perfect pure, he murdeed her for that :
' As for the Four who helped the One, all Five— 250
' Why, let employer and hirelings share alike
' In guilt and guilt's reward, the death their due ! '

So was the trial at end, do you suppose ?
' Guilty you find him, death you doom him to ?
' Ay, were not Guido, more than needs, a priest,
' Priest and to spare ! '—this was a shot reserved ;
I learn this from epistles which begin
Here where the print ends,—see the pen and ink
Of the advocate, the ready at a pinch !—
' My client boasts the clerkly privilege, 260
' Has taken minor orders many enough,
' Shows still sufficient chrism upon his pate
' To neutralize a blood-stain : *presbyter,*
' *Primæ tonsuræ, subdiaconus,*
' *Sacerdos,* so he slips from underneath
' Your power, the temporal, slides inside the robe
' Of mother Church : to her we make appeal
' By the Pope, the Church's head ! '

                        A parlous plea,
Put in with noticeable effect, it seems ; 270
' Since straight,'—resumes the zealous orator,
Making a friend acquainted with the facts,—
' Once the word " clericality " let fall,
' Procedure stopped and freer breath was drawn
' By all considerate and responsible Rome.'
Quality took the decent part, of course ;
Held by the husband, who was noble too :
Or, for the matter of that, a churl would side
With too-refined susceptibility,
And honour which, tender in the extreme, 280
Stung to the quick, must roughly right itself
At all risks, not sit still and whine for law
As a Jew would, if you squeezed him to the wall,
Brisk-trotting through the Ghetto. Nay, it seems,
Even the Emperor's Envoy had his say
To say on the subject ; might not see, unmoved,

Civility menaced throughout Christendom
By too harsh measure dealt her champion here.
Lastly, what made all safe, the Pope was kind,
From his youth up, reluctant to take life,   290
If mercy might be just and yet show grace;
Much more unlikely then, in extreme age,
To take a life the general sense bade spare.
'T was plain that Guido would go scatheless yet.

But human promise, oh, how short of shine!
How topple down the piles of hope we rear!
Now history proves . . . nay, read Herodotus!
Suddenly starting from a nap, as it were,
A dog-sleep with one shut, one open orb,
Cried the Pope's great self,—Innocent by name   300
And nature too, and eighty-six years old,
Antonio Pignatelli of Naples, Pope
Who had trod many lands, known many deeds,
Probed many hearts, beginning with his own,
And now was far in readiness for God,—
'T was he who first bade leave those souls in peace,
Those Jansenists, re-nicknamed Molinists,
('Gainst whom the cry went, like a frowsy tune,
Tickling men's ears—the sect for a quarter of an hour
I' the teeth of the world which, clown-like, loves to chew
Be it but a straw 'twixt work and whistling-while,
Taste some vituperation, bite away,   312
Whether at marjoram-sprig or garlic-clove,
Aught it may sport with, spoil, and then spit forth)
' Leave them alone,' bade he, ' those Molinists!
' Who may have other light than we perceive,
' Or why is it the whole world hates them thus ? '
Also he peeled off that last scandal-rag
Of Nepotism ; and so observed the poor
That men would merrily say, ' Halt, deaf and blind,
' Who feed on fat things, leave the master's self   321
' To gather up the fragments of his feast,
' These be the nephews of Pope Innocent !—
' His own meal costs but five carlines a day,
' Poor-priest's allowance, for he claims no more.'
—He cried of a sudden, this great good old Pope,
When they appealed in last resort to him,
' I have mastered the whole matter : I nothing doubt.
' Though Guido stood forth priest from head to heel,

' Instead of, as alleged, a piece of one,—   330
' And further, were he, from the tonsured scalp
' To the sandaled sole of him, my son and Christ's,
' Instead of touching us by finger-tip
' As you assert, and pressing up so close
' Only to set a blood-smutch on our robe,—
' I and Christ would renounce all right in him.
' Am I not Pope, and presently to die,
' And busied how to render my account,
' And shall I wait a day ere I decide
' On doing or not doing justice here ?   340
' Cut off his head to-morrow by this time,
' Hang up his four mates, two on either hand,
' And end one business more ! '

         So said, so done—
Rather so writ, for the old Pope bade this,
I find, with his particular chirograph,
His own no such infirm hand, Friday night ;
And next day, February Twenty Two,
Since our salvation Sixteen Ninety Eight,
—Not at the proper head-and-hanging-place   350
On bridge-foot close by Castle Angelo,
Where custom somewhat staled the spectacle,
('T was not so well i' the way of Rome, beside, ·
The noble Rome, the Rome of Guido's rank)
But at the city's newer gayer end,—
The cavalcading promenading place
Beside the gate and opposite the church
Under the Pincian gardens green with Spring,
'Neath the obelisk 'twixt the fountains in the Square,
Did Guido and his fellows find their fate,   360
All Rome for witness, and—my writer adds—
Remonstrant in its universal grief,
Since Guido had the suffrage of all Rome.

This is the bookful ; thus far take the truth,
The untempered gold, the fact untampered with,
The mere ring-metal ere the ring be made !
And what has hitherto come of it ? Who preserves
The memory of this Guido, and his wife
Pompilia, more than Ademollo's name,
The etcher of those prints, two *crazie* each,   370
Saved by a stone from snowing broad the Square

With scenic backgrounds ?   Was this truth of force ?
Able to take its own part as truth should,
Sufficient, self-sustaining ?   Why, if so—
Yonder 's a fire, into it goes my book,
As who shall say me nay, and what the loss ?
You know the tale already : I may ask,
Rather than think to tell you, more thereof,—
Ask you not merely who were he and she,
Husband and wife, what manner of mankind,   380
But how you hold concerning this and that
Other yet-unnamed actor in the piece.
The young frank handsome courtly Canon, now,
The priest, declared the lover of the wife,
He who, no question, did elope with her,
For certain bring the tragedy about,
Giuseppe Caponsacchi ;—his strange course
I' the matter, was it right or wrong or both ?
Then the old couple, slaughtered with the wife
By the husband as accomplices in crime,   390
Those Comparini, Pietro and his spouse,—
What say you to the right or wrong of that,
When, at a known name whispered through the door
Of a lone villa on a Christmas night,
It opened that the joyous hearts inside
Might welcome as it were an angel guest
Come in Christ's name to knock and enter, sup
And satisfy the loving ones he saved ;
And so did welcome devils and their death ?
I have been silent on that circumstance   400
Although the couple passed for close of kin
To wife and husband, were by some accounts
Pompilia's very parents : you know best.
Also that infant the great joy was for,
That Gaetano, the wife's two-weeks' babe,
The husband's first-born child, his son and heir,
Whose birth and being turned his night to day—
Why must the father kill the mother thus
Because she bore his son and saved himself ?

Well, British Public, ye who like me not,   410
(God love you !) and will have your proper laugh
At the dark question, laugh it !   I laugh first.
Truth must prevail, the proverb vows ; and truth
—Here is it all i' the book at last, as first

There it was all i' the heads and hearts of Rome
Gentle and simple, never to fall nor fade
Nor be forgotten. Yet, a little while,
The passage of a century or so,
Decads thrice five, and here 's time paid his tax,
Oblivion gone home with her harvesting,   420
And all left smooth again as scythe could shave.
Far from beginning with you London folk,
I took my book to Rome first, tried truth's power
On likely people. ' Have you met such names ?
' Is a tradition extant of such facts ?
' Your law-courts stand, your records frown a-row :
' What if I rove and rummage ? ' '—Why, you'll waste
' Your pains and end as wise as you began ! '
Everyone snickered : ' names and facts thus old
' Are newer much than Europe news we find ,   430
' Down in to-day's *Diario.* Records, quotha ?
' Why, the French burned them, what else do the
      French ?
' The rap-and-rending nation ! And it tells
' Against the Church, no doubt,—another gird
' At the Temporality, your Trial, of course ? '
' —Quite otherwise this time,' submitted I ;
' Clean for the Church and dead against the world,
' The flesh and the devil, does it tell for once.'
' —The rarer and the happier ! All the same,
' Content you with your treasure of a book,   440
' And waive what 's wanting ! Take a friend's advice !
' It 's not the custom of the country. Mend
' Your ways indeed and we may stretch a point :
' Go get you manned by Manning and new-manned
' By Newman and, mayhap, wise-manned to boot
' By Wiseman, and we'll see or else we won't !
' Thanks meantime for the story, long and strong,
' A pretty piece of narrative enough,
' Which scarce ought so to drop out, one would think,
' From the more curious annals of our kind.   450
' Do you tell the story, now, in off-hand style,
' Straight from the book ? Or simply here and there,
' (The while you vault it through the loose and large)
' Hang to a hint ? Or is there book at all,
' And don't you deal in poetry, make-believe,
' And the white lies it sounds like ? '
                        Yes and no !

From the book, yes ; thence bit by bit I dug
The lingot truth, that memorable day,
Assayed and knew my piecemeal gain was gold,— 460
Yes ; but from something else surpassing that,
Something of mine which, mixed up with the mass,
Made it bear hammer and be firm to file.
Fancy with fact is just one fact the more ;
To-wit, that fancy has informed, transpierced,
Thridded and so thrown fast the facts else free,
As right through ring and ring runs the djereed
And binds the loose, one bar without a break.
I fused my live soul and that inert stuff,
Before attempting smithcraft, on the night   470
After the day when,—truth thus grasped and gained,—
The book was shut and done with and laid by
On the cream-coloured massive agate, broad
'Neath the twin cherubs in the tarnished frame
O' the mirror, tall thence to the ceiling-top.
And from the reading, and that slab I leant
My elbow on, the while I read and read,
I turned, to free myself and find the world,
And stepped out on the narrow terrace, built
Over the street and opposite the church,   480
And paced its lozenge-brickwork sprinkled cool ;
Because Felice-church-side stretched, a-glow
Through each square window fringed for festival,
Whence came the clear voice of the cloistered ones
Chanting a chant made for midsummer nights—
I know not what particular praise of God,
It always came and went with June.   Beneath
I' the street, quick shown by openings of the sky
When flame fell silently from cloud to cloud,
Richer than that gold snow Jove rained on Rhodes,
The townsmen walked by twos and threes, and talked,
Drinking the blackness in default of air—   492
A busy human sense beneath my feet :
While in and out the terrace-plants, and round
One branch of tall datura, waxed and waned
The lamp-fly lured there, wanting the white flower.
Over the roof o' the lighted church I looked
A bowshot to the street's end, north away
Out of the Roman gate to the Roman road
By the river, till I felt the Apennine.   500
And there would lie Arezzo, the man's town,

The woman's trap and cage and torture-place,
Also the stage where the priest played his part,
A spectacle for angels,—ay, indeed,
There lay Arezzo ! Farther then I fared,
Feeling my way on through the hot and dense,
Romeward, until I found the wayside inn
By Castelnuovo's few mean hut-like homes
Huddled together on the hill-foot bleak,
Bare, broken only by that tree or two   510
Against the sudden bloody splendour poured
Cursewise in his departure by the day
On the low house-roof of that squalid inn
Where they three, for the first time and the last,
Husband and wife and priest, met face to face.
Whence I went on again, the end was near,
Step by step, missing none and marking all,
Till Rome itself, the ghastly goal, I reached.
Why, all the while,—how could it otherwise ?—
The life in me abolished the death of things,   520
Deep calling unto deep : as then and there
Acted itself over again once more
The tragic piece. I saw with my own eyes
In Florence as I trod the terrace, breathed
The beauty and the fearfulness of night,
How it had run, this round from Rome to Rome—
Because, you are to know, they lived at Rome,
Pompilia's parents, as they thought themselves,
Two poor ignoble hearts who did their best
Part God's way, part the other way than God's,   530
To somehow make a shift and scramble through
The world's mud, careless if it splashed and spoiled,
Provided they might so hold high, keep clean
Their child's soul, one soul white enough for three,
And lift it to whatever star should stoop,
What possible sphere of purer life than theirs
Should come in aid of whiteness hard to save.
I saw the star stoop, that they strained to touch·
And did touch and depose their treasure on,
As Guido Franceschini took away   540
Pompilia to be his for evermore,
While they sang ' Now let us depart in peace,
' Having beheld thy glory, Guido's wife ! '
I saw the star supposed, but fog o' the fen,
Gilded star-fashion by a glint from hell ;

Having been heaved up, haled on its gross way,
By hands unguessed before, invisible help
From a dark brotherhood, and specially
Two obscure goblin creatures, fox-faced this,
Cat-clawed the other, called his next of kin   550
By Guido the main monster,—cloaked and caped,
Making as they were priests, to mock God more,—
Abate Paul, Canon Girolamo.
These who had rolled the starlike pest to Rome
And stationed it to suck up and absorb
The sweetness of Pompilia, rolled again
That bloated bubble, with her soul inside,
Back to Arezzo and a palace there—
Or say, a fissure in the honest earth
Whence long ago had curled the vapour first,   560
Blown big by nether fires to appal day :
It touched home, broke, and blasted far and wide.
I saw the cheated couple find the cheat
And guess what foul rite they were captured for,—
Too fain to follow over hill and dale
That child of theirs caught up thus in the cloud
And carried by the Prince o' the Power of the Air
Whither he would, to wilderness or sea.
I saw them, in the potency of fear,
Break somehow through the satyr-family   570
(For a grey mother with a monkey-mien,
Mopping and mowing, was apparent too,
As, confident of capture, all took hands
And danced about the captives in a ring)
—Saw them break through, breathe safe, at Rome again,
Saved by the selfish instinct, losing so
Their loved one left with haters. These I saw,
In recrudescency of baffled hate,
Prepare to wring the uttermost revenge   579
From body and soul thus left them : all was sure,
Fire laid and cauldron set, the obscene ring traced,
The victim stripped and prostrate : what of God ?
The cleaving of a cloud, a cry, a crash,
Quenched lay their cauldron, cowered i' the dust the crew,
As, in a glory of armour like Saint George,
Out again sprang the young good beauteous priest
Bearing away the lady in his arms,

Saved for a splendid minute and no more.
For, whom i' the path did that priest come upon,
He and the poor lost lady borne so brave,   590
—Checking the song of praise in me, had else
Swelled to the full for God's will done on earth—
Whom but a dusk misfeatured messenger,
No other than the angel of this life,
Whose care is lest men see too much at once.
He made the sign, such God-glimpse must suffice,
Nor prejudice the Prince o' the Power of the Air,
Whose ministration piles us overhead
What we call, first, earth's roof and, last, heaven's floor,
Now grate o' the trap, then outlet of the cage :   600
So took the lady, left the priest alone,
And once more canopied the world with black.
But through the blackness I saw Rome again,
And where a solitary villa stood
In a lone garden-quarter : it was eve,
The second of the year, and oh so cold !
Ever and anon there flittered through the air
A snow-flake, and a scanty couch of snow
Crusted the grass-walk and the garden-mould.
All was grave, silent, sinister,—when, ha ?   610
Glimmeringly did a pack of were-wolves pad
The snow, those flames were Guido's eyes in front,
And all five found and footed it, the track,
To where a threshold-streak of warmth and light
Betrayed the villa-door with life inside,
While an inch outside were those blood-bright eyes,
And black lips wrinkling o'er the flash of teeth,
And tongues that lolled—Oh God that madest man !
They parleyed in their language. Then one whined—
That was the policy and master-stroke—   620
Deep in his throat whispered what seemed a name—
' Open to Caponsacchi ! ' Guido cried :
' Gabriel ! ' cried Lucifer at Eden-gate.
Wide as a heart, opened the door at once,
Showing the joyous couple, and their child
The two-weeks' mother, to the wolves, the wolves
To them. Close eyes ! And when the corpses lay
Stark-stretched, and those the wolves, their wolf-work
    done,
Were safe-embosomed by the night again,
I knew a necessary change in things ;   630

As when the worst watch of the night gives way,
And there comes duly, to take cognizance,
The scrutinizing eye-point of some star—
And who despairs of a new daybreak now ?
Lo, the first ray protruded on those five !
It reached them, and each felon writhed transfixed.
Awhile they palpitated on the spear
Motionless over Tophet : stand or fall ?
' I say, the spear should fall—should stand, I say ! '
Cried the world come to judgment, granting grace
Or dealing doom according to world's wont,   641
Those world's-bystanders grouped on Rome's cross-
    road
At prick and summons of the primal curse
Which bids man love as well as make a lie.
There prattled they, discoursed the right and wrong,
Turned wrong to right, proved wolves sheep and sheep
    wolves,
So that you scarce distinguished fell from fleece ;
Till out spoke a great guardian of the fold,
Stood up, put forth his hand that held the crook,
And motioned that the arrested point decline :   650
Horribly off, the wriggling dead-weight reeled,
Rushed to the bottom and lay ruined there.
Though still at the pit's mouth, despite the smoke
O' the burning, tarriers turned again to talk
And trim the balance, and detect at least
A touch of wolf in what showed whitest sheep,
A cross of sheep redeeming the whole wolf,—
Vex truth a little longer :—less and less,
Because years came and went, and more and more
Brought new lies with them to be loved in turn.   660
Till all at once the memory of the thing,—
The fact that, wolves or sheep, such creatures were,—
Which hitherto, however men supposed,
Had somehow plain and pillar-like prevailed
I' the midst of them, indisputably fact,
Granite, time's tooth should grate against, not graze,—
Why, this proved sandstone, friable, fast to fly
And give its grain away at wish o' the wind.
Ever and ever more diminutive,
Base gone, shaft lost, only entablature,   670
Dwindled into no bigger than a book,
Lay of the column ; and that little, left

By the roadside 'mid the ordure, shards and weeds.
Until I haply, wandering that way,
Kicked it up, turned it over, and recognized,
For all the crumblement, this abacus,
This square old yellow book,—could calculate
By this the lost proportions of the style.

This was it from, my fancy with those facts,
I used to tell the tale, turned gay to grave,   680
But lacked a listener seldom ; such alloy,
Such substance of me interfused the gold
Which, wrought into a shapely ring therewith,
Hammered and filed, fingered and favoured, last
Lay ready for the renovating wash
O' the water.   ' How much of the tale was true ? '
I disappeared ; the book grew all in all ;
The lawyers' pleadings swelled back to their size,—
Doubled in two, the crease upon them yet,
For more commodity of carriage, see !—   690
And these are letters, veritable sheets
That brought posthaste the news to Florence, writ
At Rome the day Count Guido died, we find,
To stay the craving of a client there,
Who bound the same and so produced my book.
Lovers of dead truth, did ye fare the worse ?
Lovers of live truth, found ye false my tale ?

Well, now ; there 's nothing in nor out o' the world
Good except truth : yet this, the something else,
What 's this then, which proves good yet seems untrue ?
This that I mixed with truth, motions of mine   701
That quickened, made the inertness malleolable
O' the gold was not mine,—what 's your name for this?
Are means to the end, themselves in part the end ?
Is fiction which makes fact alive, fact too ?
The somehow may be thishow.
                              I find first
Writ down for very A. B. C. of fact,
' In the beginning God made heaven and earth ; '
From which, no matter with what lisp, I spell   710
And speak you out a consequence—that man,
Man,—as befits the made, the inferior thing,—
Purposed, since made, to grow, not make in turn,
Yet forced to try and make, else fail to grow,—

Formed to rise, reach at, if not grasp and gain
The good beyond him,—which attempt is growth,—
Repeats God's process in man's due degree,
Attaining man's proportionate result,—
Creates, no, but resuscitates, perhaps.
Inalienable, the arch-prerogative   720
Which turns thought, act—conceives, expresses too !
No less, man, bounded, yearning ' free,
May so project his surplusage of soul
In search of body, so add self to self
By owning what lay ownerless before,—
So find, so fill full, so appropriate forms—
That, although nothing which had never life
Shall get life from him, be, not having been,
Yet, something dead may get to live again,
Something with too much life or not enough,   730
Which, either way imperfect, ended once :
An end whereat man's impulse intervenes,
Makes new beginning, starts the dead alive,
Completes the incomplete and saves the thing.
Man's breath were vain to light a virgin wick,—
Half-burned-out, all but quite-quenched wicks o' the
      lamp
Stationed for temple-service on this earth,
These indeed let him breathe on and relume !
For such man's feat is, in the due degree,
—Mimic creation, galvanism for life,   740
But still a glory portioned in the scale.
Why did the mage say,—feeling as we are wont
For truth, and stopping midway short of truth,
And resting on a lie,—' I raise a ghost ' ?
' Because,' he taught adepts, ' man makes not man.
' Yet by a special gift, an art of arts,
' More insight and more outsight and much more
' Will to use both of these than boast my mates,
' I can detach from me, commission forth
' Half of my soul ; which in its pilgrimage   750
' O'er old unwandered waste ways of the world,
' May chance upon some fragment of a whole,
' Rag of flesh, scrap of bone in dim disuse,
' Smoking flax that fed fire once : prompt therein
' I enter, spark-like, put old powers to play,
' Push lines out to the limit, lead forth last
' (By a moonrise through a ruin of a crypt)

' What shall be mistily seen, murmuringly heard,
' Mistakenly felt : then write my name with Faust's !
Oh, Faust, why Faust ?   Was not Elisha once ?—
Who bade them lay his staff on a corpse-face.   761
There was no voice, no hearing : he went in
Therefore, and shut the door upon them twain,
And prayed unto the Lord : and he went up
And lay upon '`   _orpse, dead on the couch,
And put his mouth upon its mouth, his eyes
Upon its eyes, his hands upon its hands,
And stretched him on the flesh ; the flesh waxed
     warm :
And he returned, walked to and fro the house,
And went up, stretched him on the flesh again,   770
And the eyes opened.   'Tis a credible feat
With the right man and way.
                         __Enough of me !
The Book ! I turn its medicinable leaves
In London now till, as in Florence erst,
A spirit laughs and leaps through every limb,
And lights my eye, and lifts me by the hair,
Letting me have my will again with these
—How title I the dead alive once more ?

Count Guido Franceschini the Aretine,   780
Descended of an ancient house, though poor,
A beak-nosed bushy-bearded black-haired lord,
Lean, pallid, low of stature yet robust,
Fifty years old,—having four years ago
Married Pompilia Comparini, young,
Good, beautiful, at Rome, where she was born,
And brought her to Arezzo, where they lived
Unhappy lives, whatever curse the cause,—
This husband, taking four accomplices,
Followed this wife to Rome, where she was fled   790
From their Arezzo to find peace again,
In convoy, eight months earlier, of a priest,
Aretine also, of still nobler birth,
Giuseppe Caponsacchi,—and caught her there
Quiet in a villa on a Christmas night,
With only Pietro and Violante by,
Both her putative parents ; killed the three,
Aged, they, seventy each, and she, seventeen,
And, two weeks since, the mother of his babe

First-born and heir to what the style was worth   800
O' the Guido who determined, dared and did
This deed just as he purposed point by point.
Then, bent upon escape, but hotly pressed,
And captured with his co-mates that same night,
He, brought to trial, stood on this defence—
Injury to his honour caused the act ;
That since his wife was false, (as manifest
By flight from home in such companionship,)
Death, punishment deserved of the false wife
And faithless parents who abetted her   810
I' the flight aforesaid, wronged nor God nor man.
' Nor false she, nor yet faithless they,' replied
The accuser ;   ' cloaked and masked this murder
      glooms ;
' True was Pompilia, loyal too the pair ;
' Out of the man's own heart this monster curled,
' This crime coiled with connivancy at crime,
' His victim's breast, he tells you, hatched and reared ;
' Uncoil we and stretch stark the worm of hell ! '
A month the trial swayed this way and that
Ere judgment settled down on Guido's guilt ;   820
Then was the Pope, that good Twelfth Innocent,
Appealed to : who well weighed what went before,
Affirmed the guilt and gave the guilty doom.

Let this old woe step on the stage again !
Act itself o'er anew for men to judge,
Not by the very sense and sight indeed—
(Which take at best imperfect cognizance,
Since, how heart moves brain, and how both move
      hand,
What mortal ever in entirety saw ?)
—No dose of purer truth than man digests,   830
But truth with falsehood, milk that feeds him now,
Not strong meat he may get to bear some day—
To-wit, by voices we call evidence,
Uproar in the echo, live fact deadened down,
Talked over, bruited abroad, whispered away,
Yet helping us to all we seem to hear :
For how else know we save by worth of word ?

Here are the voices presently shall sound
In due succession.   First, the world's outcry

Around the rush and ripple of any fact   840
Fallen stonewise, plumb on the smooth face of things ;
The world's guess, as it crowds the bank o' the pool,
At what were figure and substance, by their splash :
Then, by vibrations in the general mind,
At depth of deed already out of reach.
This threefold murder of the day before,—
Say, Half-Rome's feel after the vanished truth ;
Honest enough, as the way is : all the same,
Harbouring in the centre of its sense
A hidden germ of failure, shy but sure,   850
Should neutralize that honesty and leave
That feel for truth at fault, as the way is too.
Some prepossession such as starts amiss,
By but a hair's breadth at the shoulder-blade,
The arm o' the feeler, dip he ne'er so brave ;
And so leads waveringly, lets fall wide
O' the mark his finger meant to find, and fix
Truth at the bottom, that deceptive speck.
With this Half-Rome,—the source of swerving, call
Over-belief in Guido's right and wrong   860
Rather than in Pompilia's wrong and right :
Who shall say how, who shall say why ? 'T is there—
The instinctive theorizing whence a fact
Looks to the eye as the eye likes the look.
Gossip in a public place, a sample-speech.
Some worthy, with his previous hint to find
A husband's side the safer, and no whit
Aware he is not Æacus the while,—
How such an one supposes and states fact
To whosoever of a multitude   870
Will listen, and perhaps prolong thereby
The not-unpleasant flutter at the breast,
Born of a certain spectacle shut in
By the church Lorenzo opposite. So, they lounge
Midway the mouth o' the street, on Corso side,
'Twixt palace Fiano and palace Ruspoli,
Linger and listen ; keeping clear o' the crowd,
Yet wishful one could lend that crowd one's eyes,
(So universal is its plague of squint)   879
And make hearts beat our time that flutter false :
—All for the truth's sake, mere truth, nothing else !
How Half-Rome found for Guido much excuse.

Next, from Rome's other half, the opposite feel
For truth with a like swerve, like unsuccess,—
Or if success, by no more skill but luck :
This time, through rather siding with the wife,
However the fancy-fit inclined that way,
Than with the husband.   One wears drab, one, pink ;
Who wears pink, ask him ' Which shall win the race,
' Of coupled runners like as egg and egg ? '   890
' —Why, if I must choose, he with the pink scarf.'
Doubtless for some such reason choice fell here.
A piece of public talk to correspond
At the next stage of the story ; just a day
Let pass and new day bring the proper change.
Another sample-speech i' the market-place
O' the Barberini by the Capucins ;
Where the old Triton, at his fountain-sport,
Bernini's creature plated to the paps,
Puffs up steel sleet which breaks to diamond dust,
A spray of sparkles snorted from his conch,   901
High over the caritellas, out o' the way
O' the motley merchandizing multitude.
Our murder has been done three days ago,
The frost is over and gone, the south wind laughs,
And, to the very tiles of each red roof
A-smoke i' the sunshine, Rome lies gold and glad :
So, listen how, to the other half of Rome,
Pompilia seemed a saint and martyr both !

Then, yet another day let come and go,   910
With pause prelusive still of novelty,
Hear a fresh speaker !—neither this nor that
Half-Rome aforesaid ; something bred of both :
One and one breed the inevitable three.
Such is the personage harangues you next ;
The elaborated product, *tertium quid* :
Rome's first commotion in subsidence gives
The curd o' the cream, flower o' the wheat, as it were,
And finer sense o' the city.   Is this plain ?
You get a reasoned statement of the case,   920
Eventual verdict of the curious few
Who care to sift a business to the bran
Nor coarsely bolt it like the simpler sort.
Here, after ignorance, instruction speaks ;
Here, clarity of candour, history's soul,

The critical mind, in short : no gossip-guess.
What the superior social section thinks,
In person of some man of quality
Who,—breathing musk from lace-work and brocade,
His solitaire amid the flow of frill,   930
Powdered peruke on nose, and bag at back,
And cane dependent from the ruffled wrist,—
Harangues in silvery and selectest phrase
'Neath waxlight in a glorified saloon
Where mirrors multiply the girandole :
Courting the approbation of no mob,
But Eminence This and All-Illustrious That
Who take snuff softly, range in well-bred ring,
Card-table-quitters for observance' sake,
Around the argument, the rational word—   940
Still, spite its weight and worth, a sample-speech.
How quality dissertated on the case.

So much for Rome and rumour ; smoke comes first :
Once the smoke risen untroubled, we descry
Clearlier what tongues of flame may spire and spit
To eye and ear, each with appropriate tinge
According to its food, pure or impure.
The actors, no mere rumours of the act,
Intervene.   First you hear Count Guido's voice,
In a small chamber that adjoins the court,   950
Where Governor and Judges, summoned thence,
Tommati, Venturini and the rest,
Find the accused ripe for declaring truth.
Soft-cushioned sits he ; yet shifts seat, shirks touch,
As, with a twitchy brow and wincing lip
And cheek that changes to all kinds of white,
He proffers his defence, in tones subdued
Near to mock-mildness now, so mournful seems
The obtuser sense truth fails to satisfy ;
Now, moved, from pathos at the wrong endured,
To passion ; for the natural man is roused   961
At fools who first do wrong, then pour the blame
Of their wrong-doing, Satan-like, on Job.
Also his tongue at times is hard to curb ;
Incisive, nigh satiric bites the phrase,
Rough-raw, yet somehow claiming privilege
—It is so hard for shrewdness to admit
Folly means no harm when she calls black white !

—Eruption momentary at the most,
Modified forthwith by a fall o' the fire,   970
Sage acquiescence ; for the world 's the world,
And, what it errs in, Judges rectify :
He feels he has a fist, then folds his arms
Crosswise and makes his mind up to be meek.
And never once does he detach his eye
From those ranged there to slay him or to save,
But does his best man's-service for himself,
Despite,—what twitches brow and makes lip wince,—
His limbs' late taste of what was called the Cord,
Or Vigil-torture more facetiously.   980
Even so ; they were wont to tease the truth
Out of loath witness (toying, trifling time)
By torture : 'twas a trick, a vice of the age,
Here, there and everywhere, what would you have ?
Religion used to tell Humanity
She gave him warrant or denied him course.
And since the course was much to his own mind,
Of pinching flesh and pulling bone from bone
To unhusk truth a-hiding in its hulls,
Nor whisper of a warning stopped the way,   990
He, in their joint behalf, the burly slave,
Bestirred him, mauled and maimed all recusants,
While, prim in place, Religion overlooked ;
And so had done till doomsday, never a sign
Nor sound of interference from her mouth,
But that at last the burly slave wiped brow,
Let eye give notice as if soul were there,
Muttered ' 'Tis a vile trick, foolish more than vile,
' Should have been counted sin ; I make it so :
' At any rate no more of it for me—   1000
' Nay, for I break the torture-engine thus ! '
Then did Religion start up, stare amain,
Look round for help and see none, smile and say
' What, broken is the rack ?   Well done of thee !
' Did I forget to abrogate its use ?
' Be the mistake in common with us both !
' —One more fault our blind age shall answer for,
' Down in my book denounced though it must be
' Somewhere.   Henceforth find truth by milder
       means ! '
Ah but, Religion, did we wait for thee   1010
To ope the book, that serves to sit upon,

And pick such place out, we should wait indeed !
That is all history : and what is not now,
Was then, defendants found it to their cost.
How Guido, after being tortured, spoke.

Also hear Caponsacchi who comes next,
Man and priest—could you comprehend the coil !—
In days when that was rife which now is rare.
How, mingling each its multifarious wires,   1019
Now heaven, now earth, now heaven and earth at once,
Had plucked at and perplexed their puppet here,
Played off the young frank personable priest ;
Sworn fast and tonsured plain heaven's celibate,
And yet earth's clear-accepted servitor,
A courtly spiritual Cupid, squire of dames
By law of love and mandate of the mode.
The Church's own, or why parade her seal,
Wherefore that chrism and consecrative work ?
Yet verily the world's, or why go badged
A prince of sonneteers and lutanists,   1030
Show colour of each vanity in vogue
Borne with decorum due on blameless breast ?
All that is changed now, as he tells the court
How he had played the part excepted at ;
Tells it, moreover, now the second time :
Since, for his cause of scandal, his own share
I' the flight from home and husband of the wife,
He has been censured, punished in a sort
By relegation,—exile, we should say,
To a short distance for a little time,—   1040
Whence he is summoned on a sudden now,
Informed that she, he thought to save, is lost,
And, in a breath, bidden re-tell his tale,
Since the first telling somehow missed effect,
And then advise in the matter.   There stands he,
While the same grim black-panelled chamber blinks
As though rubbed shiny with the sins of Rome
Told the same oak for ages—wave-washed wall
Whereto has set a sea of wickedness.
There, where you yesterday heard Guido speak,   1050
Speaks Caponsacchi ; and there face him too
Tommati, Venturini and the rest
Who, eight months earlier, scarce repressed the smile,
Forewent the wink ; waived recognition so

Of peccadillos incident to youth,
Especially youth high-born ; for youth means love,
Vows can't change nature, priests are only men,
And love needs stratagem and subterfuge :
Which age, that once was youth, should recognize,
May blame, but needs not press too hard against. 1060
Here sit the old Judges then, but with no grace
Of reverend carriage, magisterial port.
For why ?   The accused of eight months since,—the
      same
Who cut the conscious figure of a fool,
Changed countenance, dropped bashful gaze to ground,
While hesitating for an answer then,—
Now is grown judge himself, terrifies now
This, now the other culprit called a judge,
Whose turn it is to stammer and look strange,
As he speaks rapidly, angrily, speech that smites :
And they keep silence, bear blow after blow,   1071
Because the seeming-solitary man,
Speaking for God, may have an audience too,
Invisible, no discreet judge provokes.
How the priest Caponsacchi said his say.

Then a soul sighs its lowest and its last
After the loud ones,—so much breath remains
Unused by the four-days'-dying ; for she lived
Thus long, miraculously long, 't was thought,
Just that Pompilia might defend herself.   1080
How, while the hireling and the alien stoop,
Comfort, yet question,—since the time is brief,
And folk, allowably inquisitive,
Encircle the low pallet where she lies
In the good house that helps the poor to die,—
Pompilia tells the story of her life.
For friend and lover,—leech and man of law
Do service ; busy helpful ministrants
As varied in their calling as their mind,
Temper and age : and yet from all of these,   1090
About the white bed under the arched roof,
Is somehow, as it were, evolved a one,—
Small separate sympathies combined and large,
Nothings that were, grown something very much :
As if the bystanders gave each his straw,
All he had, though a trifle in itself,

Which, plaited all together, made a Cross
Fit to die looking on and praying with,
Just as well as if ivory or gold.
So, to the common kindliness she speaks,   1100
There being scarce more privacy at the last
For mind than body : but she is used to bear,
And only unused to the brotherly look.
How she endeavoured to explain her life.

Then, since a Trial ensued, a touch o' the same
To sober us, flustered with frothy talk,
And teach our common sense its helplessness.
For why deal simply with divining-rod,
Scrape where we fancy secret sources flow,
And ignore law, the recognized machine,   1110
Elaborate display of pipe and wheel
Framed to unchoke, pump up and pour apace
Truth in a flowery foam shall wash the world ?
The patent truth-extracting process,—ha ?
Let us make all that mystery turn one wheel,
Give you a single grind of law at least !
One orator, of two on either side,
Shall teach us the puissance of the tongue
—That is, o' the pen which simulated tongue
On paper and saved all except the sound   1120
Which never was. Law's speech beside law's thought ?
That were too stunning, too immense an odds :
That point of vantage, law let nobly pass.
One lawyer shall admit us to behold
The manner of the making out a case,
First fashion of a speech ; the chick in egg,
And masterpiece law's bosom incubates.
How Don Giacinto of the Arcangeli,
Called Procurator of the Poor at Rome,
Now advocate for Guido and his mates,—   1130
The jolly learned man of middle age,
Cheek and jowl all in laps with fat and law,
Mirthful as mighty, yet, as great hearts use,
Despite the name and fame that tempt our flesh,
Constant to that devotion of the hearth,
Still captive in those dear domestic ties !—
How he,—having a cause to triumph with,
All kind of interests to keep intact,
More than one efficacious personage

To tranquillize, conciliate and secure,   1140
And above all, public anxiety
To quiet, show its Guido in good hands,—
Also, as if such burdens were too light,
A certain family-feast to claim his care,
The birthday-banquet for the only son—
Paternity at smiling strife with law—
How he brings both to buckle in one bond ;
And, thick at throat, with waterish under-eye,
Turns to his task and settles in his seat
And puts his utmost means to practice now :   1150
Wheezes out law and whiffles Latin forth,
And, just as though roast lamb would never be,
Makes logic levigate the big crime small :
Rubs palm on palm, rakes foot with itchy foot,
Conceives and inchoates the argument,
Sprinkling each flower appropriate to the time,
—Ovidian quip or Ciceronian crank,
A-bubble in the larynx while he laughs,
As he had fritters deep down frying there.
How he turns, twists, and tries the oily thing   1160
Shall be—first speech for Guido 'gainst the Fisc.

Then with a skip as it were from heel to head,
Leaving yourselves fill up the middle bulk
O' the Trial, reconstruct its shape august,
From such exordium clap we to the close ;
Give you, if we dare wing to such a height,
The absolute glory in some full-grown speech
On the other side, some finished butterfly,
Some breathing diamond-flake with leaf-gold fans,
That takes the air, no trace of worm it was,   1170
Or cabbage-bed it had production from.
Giovambattista o' the Bottini, Fisc,
Pompilia's patron by the chance of the hour,
To-morrow her persecutor,—composite, he,
As becomes who must meet such various calls—
Odds of age joined in him with ends of youth.
A man of ready smile and facile tear,
Improvised hopes, despairs at nod and beck,
And language—ah, the gift of eloquence !
Language that goes as easy as a glove   1180
O'er good and evil, smoothens both to one.
Rashness helps caution with him, fires the straw,

In free enthusiastic careless fit,
On the first proper pinnacle of rock
Which happens, as reward for all that zeal,
To lure some bark to founder and bring gain :
While calm sits Caution, rapt with heavenward eye,
A true confessor's gaze amid the glare,
Beaconing to the breaker, death and hell.
' Well done, thou good and faithful ! ' she approves :
' Hadst thou let slip a faggot to the beach,   1191
' The crew had surely spied thy precipice
' And saved their boat ; the simple and the slow,
' Who should have prompt forestalled the wrecker's
        fee :
' Let the next crew be wise and hail in time ! '
Just so compounded is the outside man,
Blue juvenile pure eye and pippin cheek,
And brow all prematurely soiled and seamed
With sudden age, bright devastated hair.
Ah, but you miss the very tones o' the voice,   1200
The scrannel pipe that screams in heights of head,
As, in his modest studio, all alone,
The tall wight stands a-tiptoe, strives and strains,
Both eyes shut, like the cockerel that would crow,
Tries to his own self amorously o'er
What never will be uttered else than so—
To the four walls, for Forum and Mars' Hill,
Speaks out the poesy which, penned, turns prose.
Clavecinist debarred his instrument,
He yet thrums—shirking neither turn nor trill,   1210
With desperate finger on dumb table-edge—
The sovereign rondo, shall conclude his *Suite*,
Charm an imaginary audience there,
From old Corelli to young Haendel, both
I' the flesh at Rome, ere he perforce go print
The cold black score, mere music for the mind—
The last speech against Guido and his gang,
With special end to prove Pompilia pure.
How the Fisc vindicates Pompilia's fame.

Then comes the all but end, the ultimate   1220
Judgment save yours.   Pope Innocent the Twelfth,
Simple, sagacious, mild yet resolute,
With prudence, probity and—what beside
From the other world he feels impress at times,

Having attained to fourscore years and six,—
How, when the court found Guido and the rest
Guilty, but law supplied a subterfuge
And passed the final sentence to the Pope,
He, bringing his intelligence to bear
This last time on what ball behoves him drop   1230
In the urn, or white or black, does drop a black,
Send five souls more to just precede his own,
Stand him in stead and witness, if need were,
How he is wont to do God's work on earth.
The manner of his sitting out the dim
Droop of a sombre February day
In the plain closet where he does such work,
With, from all Peter's treasury, one stool,
One table and one lathen crucifix.
There sits the Pope, his thoughts for company ;   1240
Grave but not sad,—nay, something like a cheer
Leaves the lips free to be benevolent,
Which, all day long, did duty firm and fast.
A cherishing there is of foot and knee,
A chafing loose-skinned large-veined hand with hand,—
What steward but knows when stewardship earns its
      wage,
May levy praise, anticipate the lord ?
He reads, notes, lays the papers down at last,
Muses, then takes a turn about the room ;
Unclasps a huge tome in an antique guise,   1250
Primitive print and tongue half obsolete,
That stands him in diurnal stead ; opes page,
Finds place where falls the passage to be conned
According to an order long in use :
And, as he comes upon the evening's chance,
Starts somewhat, solemnizes straight his smile,
Then reads aloud that portion first to last,
And at the end lets flow his own thoughts forth
Likewise aloud, for respite and relief,
Till by the dreary relics of the west   1260
Wan through the half-moon window, all his light,
He bows the head while the lips move in prayer,
Writes some three brief lines, signs and seals the same,
Tinkles a hand-bell, bids the obsequious Sir
Who puts foot presently o' the closet-sill
He watched outside of, bear as superscribed
That mandate to the Governor forthwith :

Then heaves abroad his cares in one good sigh,
Traverses corridor with no arm's help,
And so to sup as a clear conscience should.   1270
The manner of the judgment of the Pope.

Then must speak Guido yet a second time,
Satan's old saw being apt here—skin for skin,
All a man hath that will he give for life.
While life was graspable and gainable, free
To bird-like buzz her wings round Guido's brow,
Not much truth stiffened out the web of words
He wove to catch her : when away she flew
And death came, death's breath rivelled up the lies,
Left bare the metal thread, the fibre fine   1280
Of truth, i' the spinning : the true words come last.
How Guido, to another purpose quite,
Speaks and despairs, the last night of his life,
In that New Prison by Castle Angelo
At the bridge-foot : the same man, another voice.
On a stone bench in a close fetid cell,
Where the hot vapour of an agony,
Struck into drops on the cold wall, runs down
Horrible worms made out of sweat and tears—
There crouch, well nigh to the knees in dungeon-straw,
Lit by the sole lamp suffered for their sake,   1291
Two awe-struck figures, this a Cardinal,
That an Abate, both of old styled friends
Of the part-man part-monster in the midst,
So changed is Franceschini's gentle blood.
The tiger-cat screams now, that whined before,
That pried and tried and trod so gingerly,
Till in its silkiness the trap-teeth join ;
Then you know how the bristling fury foams.
They listen, this wrapped in his folds of red,   1300
While his feet fumble for the filth below ;
The other, as beseems a stouter heart,
Working his best with beads and cross to ban
The enemy that comes in like a flood
Spite of the standard set up, verily
And in no trope at all, against him there :
For at the prison-gate, just a few steps
Outside, already, in the doubtful dawn,
Thither, from this side and from that, slow sweep
And settle down in silence solidly,   1310

Crow-wise, the frightful Brotherhood of Death.
Black-hatted and black-hooded huddle they,
Black rosaries a-dangling from each waist ;
So take they their grim station at the door,
Torches alight and cross-bones-banner spread,
And that gigantic Christ with open arms,
Grounded. Nor lacks there aught but that the group
Break forth, intone the lamentable psalm,
' Out of the deeps, Lord, have I cried to thee ! '—
When inside, from the true profound, a sign   1320
Shall bear intelligence that the foe is foiled,
Count Guido Franceschini has confessed,
And is absolved and reconciled with God.
Then they, intoning, may begin their march,
Make by the longest way for the People's Square,
Carry the criminal to his crime's award :
A mob to cleave, a scaffolding to reach,
Two gallows and Mannaia crowning all.
How Guido made defence a second time.

Finally, even as thus by step and step   1330
I led you from the level of to-day
Up to the summit of so long ago,
Here, whence I point you the wide prospect round—
Let me, by like steps, slope you back to smooth,
Land you on mother-earth, no whit the worse,
To feed o' the fat o' the furrow : free to dwell,
Taste our time's better things profusely spread
For all who love the level, corn and wine,
Much cattle and the many-folded fleece.
Shall not my friends go feast again on sward,   1340
Though cognizant of country in the clouds
Higher than wistful eagle's horny eye
Ever unclosed for, 'mid ancestral crags,
When morning broke and Spring was back once more,
And he died, heaven, save by his heart, unreached ?
Yet heaven my fancy lifts to, ladder-like,—
As Jack reached, holpen of his beanstalk-rungs !

A novel country : I might make it mine.
By choosing which one aspect of the year
Suited mood best, and putting solely that   1350
On panel somewhere in the House of Fame,
Landscaping what I saved, not what I saw :

—Might fix you, whether frost in goblin-time
Startled the moon with his abrupt bright laugh,
Or, August's hair afloat in filmy fire,
She fell, arms wide, face foremost on the world,
Swooned there and so singed out the strength of things.
Thus were abolished Spring and Autumn both,
The land dwarfed to one likeness of the land,
Life cramped corpse-fashion. Rather learn and love
Each facet-flash of the revolving year !—   1361
Red, green and blue that whirl into a white,
The variance now, the eventual unity,
Which make the miracle. See it for yourselves,
This man's act, changeable because alive !
Action now shrouds, now shows the informing thought;
Man, like a glass ball with a spark a-top,
Out of the magic fire that lurks inside,
Shows one tint at a time to take the eye :
Which, let a finger touch the silent sleep,   1370
Shifted a hair's-breadth shoots you dark for bright,
Suffuses bright with dark, and baffles so
Your sentence absolute for shine or shade.
Once set such orbs,—white styled, black stigmatized,—
A-rolling, see them once on the other side
Your good men and your bad men every one,
From Guïdo Franceschini to Guy Faux,
Oft would you rub your eyes and change your names.

Such, British Public, ye who like me not,   1379
(God love you !)—whom I yet have laboured for
Perchance more careful whoso runs may read
Than erst when all, it seemed, could read who ran,—
Perchance more careless whoso reads may praise
Than late when he who praised and read and wrote
Was apt to find himself the self-same me,—
Such labour had such issue, so I wrought
This arc, by furtherance of such alloy,
And so, by one spirt, take away its trace
Till, justifiably golden, rounds my ring.

A ring without a posy, and that ring mine ?   1390

O lyric Love, half-angel and half-bird
And all a wonder and a wild desire,—
Boldest of hearts that ever braved the sun,

C

Took sanctuary within the holier blue,
And sang a kindred soul out to his face,—
Yet human at the red-ripe of the heart—
When the first summons from the darkling earth
Reached thee amid thy chambers, blanched their blue,
And bared them of the glory—to drop down,
To toil for man, to suffer or to die,— 1400
This is the same voice : can thy soul know change ?
Hail then, and hearken from the realms of help !
Never may I commence my song, my due
To God who best taught song by gift of thee,
Except with bent head and beseeching hand—
That still, despite the distance and the dark,
What was, again may be ; some interchange
Of grace, some splendour once thy very thought,
Some benediction anciently thy smile :
—Never conclude, but raising hand and head 1410
Thither where eyes, that cannot reach, yet yearn
For all hope, all sustainment, all reward,
Their utmost up and on,—so blessing back
In those thy realms of help, that heaven thy home,
Some whiteness which, I judge, thy face makes proud,
Some wanness where, I think, thy foot may fall !

HALF-ROME

WHAT, you, Sir, come too ?   (Just the man I'd meet.)
Be ruled by me and have a care o' the crowd :
This way, while fresh folk go and get their gaze :
I'll tell you like a book and save your shins.
Fie, what a roaring day we've had !   Whose fault ?
Lorenzo in Lucina,—here's a church
To hold a crowd at need, accommodate
All comers from the Corso !   If this crush
Make not its priests ashamed of what they show
For temple-room, don't prick them to draw purse
And down with bricks and mortar, eke us out   11
The beggarly transept with its bit of apse
Into a decent space for Christian ease,
Why, to-day's lucky pearl is cast to swine.
Listen and estimate the luck they've had !
(The right man, and I hold him.)
                                        Sir, do you see,
They laid both bodies in the church, this morn
The first thing, on the chancel two steps up,
Behind the little marble balustrade ;   20
Disposed them, Pietro the old murdered fool
To the right of the altar, and his wretched wife
On the other side.   In trying to count stabs,
People supposed Violante showed the most,
Till somebody explained us that mistake ;
His wounds had been dealt out indifferent where,
But she took all her stabbings in the face,
Since punished thus solely for honour's sake,
Honoris causâ, that 's the proper term.
A delicacy there is, our gallants hold,   30
When you avenge your honour and only then,
That you disfigure the subject, fray the face,
Not just take life and end, in clownish guise.
It was Violante gave the first offence,
Got therefore the conspicuous punishment :

While Pietro, who helped merely, his mere death
Answered the purpose, so his face went free.
We fancied even, free as you please, that face
Showed itself still intolerably wronged ;
Was wrinkled over with resentment yet,   40
Nor calm at all, as murdered faces use,
Once the worst ended : an indignant air
O' the head there was—'tis said the body turned
Round and away, rolled from Violante's side
Where they had laid it loving-husband-like.
If so, if corpses can be sensitive,
Why did not he roll right down altar-step,
Roll on through nave, roll fairly out of church,
Deprive Lorenzo of the spectacle,
Pay back thus the succession of affronts   50
Whereto this church had served as theatre ?
For see : at that same altar where he lies,
To that same inch of step, was brought the babe
For blessing after baptism, and there styled
Pompilia, and a string of names beside,
By his bad wife, some seventeen years ago,
Who purchased her simply to palm on him,
Flatter his dotage and defraud the heirs.
Wait awhile !   Also to this very step
Did this Violante, twelve years afterward,   60
Bring, the mock-mother, that child-cheat full-grown,
Pompilia, in pursuance of her plot,
And there brave God and man a second time
By linking a new victim to the lie.
There, having made a match unknown to him,
She, still unknown to Pietro, tied the knot
Which nothing cuts except this kind of knife ;
Yes, made her daughter, as the girl was held,
Marry a man, and honest man beside,
And man of birth to boot,—clandestinely   70
Because of this, because of that, because
O' the devil's will to work his worst for once,—
Confident she could top her part at need
And, when her husband must be told in turn,
Ply the wife's trade, play off the sex's trick
And, alternating worry with quiet qualms,
Bravado with submissiveness, quick fool
Her Pietro into patience : so it proved.
Ay, 'tis four years since man and wife they grew,

This Guido Franceschini and this same   80
Pompilia, foolishly thought, falsely declared
A Comparini and the couple's child :
Just at this altar where, beneath the piece
Of Master Guido Reni, Christ on cross,
Second to nought observable in Rome,
That couple lie now, murdered yestereve.
Even the blind can see a providence here.

From dawn till now that it is growing dusk,
A multitude has flocked and filled the church,
Coming and going, coming back again,   90
Till to count crazed one.   Rome was at the show.
People climbed up the columns, fought for spikes
O' the chapel-rail to perch themselves upon,
Jumped over and so broke the wooden work
Painted like porphyry to deceive the eye ;
Serve the priests right !   The organ-loft was crammed,
Women were fainting, no few fights ensued,
In short, it was a show repaid your pains :
For, though their room was scant undoubtedly,
Yet they did manage matters, to be just,   100
A little at this Lorenzo.   Body o' me !
I saw a body exposed once . . . never mind !
Enough that here the bodies had their due.
No stinginess in wax, a row all round,
And one big taper at each head and foot.

So, people pushed their way, and took their turn,
Saw, threw their eyes up, crossed themselves, gave
     place
To pressure from behind, since all the world
Knew the old pair, could talk the tragedy
Over from first to last : Pompilia too,   110
Those who had known her—what't was worth to them !
Guido's acquaintance was in less request ;
The Count had lounged somewhat too long in Rome,
Made himself cheap ; with him were hand and glove
Barbers and blear-eyed, as the ancient sings.
Also he is alive and like to be :
Had he considerately died,—aha !
I jostled Luca Cini on his staff,
Mute in the midst, the whole man one amaze,
Staring amain and crossing brow and breast.   120

' How now ? ' asked I.   ' 'Tis seventy years,' quoth he,
' Since I first saw, holding my father's hand,
' Bodies set forth : a many have I seen,
' Yet all was poor to this I live and see.
' Here the world's wickedness seals up the sum :
' What with Molinos' doctrine and this deed,
' Antichrist 's surely come and doomsday near.
' May I depart in peace, I have seen my see.'
' Depart then,' I advised, ' nor block the road
' For youngsters still behindhand with such sights ! '
' Why no,' rejoins the venerable sire,   131
' I know it 's horrid, hideous past belief,
' Burdensome far beyond what eye can bear ;
' But they do promise, when Pompilia dies
' I' the course o' the day,—and she can't outlive
       night,—
' They'll bring her body also to expose
' Beside the parents, one, two, three a-breast ;
' That were indeed a sight which, might I see,
' I trust I should not last to see the like ! '
Whereat I bade the senior spare his shanks,   140
Since doctors give her till to-night to live
And tell us how the butchery happened.   ' Ah,
' But you can't know ! ' sighs he, ' I'll not despair :
' Beside I'm useful at explaining things—
' As, how the dagger laid there at the feet,
' Caused the peculiar cuts ; I mind its make,
' Triangular i' the blade, a Genoese,
' Armed with those little hook-teeth on the edge
' To open in the flesh nor shut again :
' I like to teach a novice : I shall stay ! '   150
And stay he did, and stay be sure he will.

A personage came by the private door
At noon to have his look : I name no names :
Well then, His Eminence the Cardinal,
Whose servitor in honourable sort
Guido was once, the same who made the match,
(Will you have the truth ?) whereof we see effect.
No sooner whisper ran he was arrived
Than up pops Curate Carlo, a brisk lad,
Who never lets a good occasion slip,   160
And volunteers improving the event.
We looked he'd give the history's self some help,

Treat us to how the wife's confession went
(This morning she confessed her crime, we know)
And, may-be, throw in something of the Priest—
If he 's not ordered back, punished anew,
The gallant, Caponsacchi, Lucifer
I' the garden where Pompilia, Eve-like, lured
Her Adam Guido to his fault and fall.
Think you we got a sprig of speech akin   170
To this from Carlo, with the Cardinal there ?
Too wary, he was, too widely awake, I trow.
He did the murder in a dozen words ;
Then said that all such outrages crop forth
I' the course of nature, when Molinos' tares
Are sown for wheat, flourish and choke the Church :
So slid on to the abominable sect
And the philosophic sin—we've heard all that,
And the Cardinal too, (who book-made on the same)
But, for the murder, left it where he found.   180
Oh but he 's quick, the Curate, minds his game !
And, after all, we have the main o' the fact :
Case could not well be simpler,—mapped, as it were,
We follow the murder's maze from source to sea,
By the red line, past mistake : one sees indeed
Not only how all was and must have been,
But cannot other than be to the end of time.
Turn out here by the Ruspoli ! Do you hold
Guido was so prodigiously to blame ?
A certain cousin of yours has told you so ?   190
Exactly ! Here 's a friend shall set you right,
Let him but have the handsel of your ear.

These wretched Comparini were once gay
And galiard, of the modest middle class :
Born in this quarter seventy years ago,
And married young, they lived the accustomed life,
Citizens as they were of good repute :
And, childless, naturally took their ease
With only their two selves to care about
And use the wealth for : wealthy is the word,   200
Since Pietro was possessed of house and land—
And specially one house, when good days were,
In Via Vittoria, the aspectable street
Where he lived mainly ; but another house
Of less pretension did he buy betimes,

The villa, meant for jaunts and jollity,
I' the Pauline district, to be private there—
Just what puts murder in an enemy's head.
Moreover,—and here 's the worm i' the core, the germ
O' the rottenness and ruin which arrived,—   210
He owned some usufruct, had moneys' use
Lifelong, but to determine with his life
In heirs' default : so, Pietro craved an heir,
(The story always old and always new)
Shut his fool's-eyes fast on the visible good
And wealth for certain, opened them owl-wide
On fortune's sole piece of forgetfulness,
The child that should have been and would not be.

Hence, seventeen years ago, conceive his glee
When first Violante, 'twixt a smile and a blush,   220
With touch of agitation proper too,
Announced that, spite of her unpromising age,
The miracle would in time be manifest,
An heir's birth was to happen : and it did.
Somehow or other,—how, all in good time !
By a trick, a sleight of hand you are to hear,—
A child was born, Pompilia, for his joy,
Plaything at once and prop, a fairy-gift,
A saints' grace or, say, grant of the good God,—
A fiddle-pin's end !   What imbeciles are we !   230
Look now : if some one could have prophesied,
' For love of you, for liking to your wife,
' I undertake to crush a snake I spy
' Settling itself i' the soft of both your breasts.
' Give me yon babe to strangle painlessly !
' She'll soar to the safe : you'll have your crying out,
' Then sleep, then wake, then sleep, then end your
        days
' In peace and plenty, mixed with mild regret,
' Thirty years hence when Christmas takes old folk '—
How had old Pietro sprung up, crossed himself,   240
And kicked the conjuror !   Whereas you and I,
Being wise with after-wit, had clapped our hands ;
Nay, added, in the old fool's interest,
' Strangle the black-eyed babe, so far so good,
' But on condition you relieve the man
' O' the wife and throttle him Violante too—
' She is the mischief ! '

We had hit the mark.
She, whose trick brought the babe into the world,
She it was, when the babe was grown a girl,　　　250
Judged a new trick should reinforce the old,
Send vigour to the lie now somewhat spent
By twelve years' service ; lest Eve's rule decline
Over this Adam of hers, whose cabbage-plot
Throve dubiously since turned fools'-paradise,
Spite of a nightingale on every stump.
Pietro's estate was dwindling day by day,
While he, rapt far above such mundane care,
Crawled all-fours with his baby pick-a-back,
Sat at serene cats'-cradle with his child,　　　260
Or took the measured tallness, top to toe,
Of what was grown a great girl twelve years old :
Till sudden at the door a tap discreet,
A visitor's premonitory cough,
And poverty had reached him in her rounds.

This came when he was past the working-time,
Had learned to dandle and forgot to dig,
And who must but Violante cast about,
Contrive and task that head of hers again ?
She who had caught one fish, could make that catch
A bigger still, in angler's policy :　　　271
So, with an angler's mercy for the bait,
Her minnow was set wriggling on its barb
And tossed to the mid-stream ; that is, this grown girl
With the great eyes and bounty of black hair
And first crisp youth that tempts a jaded taste,
Was whisked i' the way of a certain man, who snapped.

Count Guido Franceschini the Aretine
Was head of an old noble house enough,
Not over-rich, you can't have everything,　　　280
But such a man as riches rub against,
Readily stick to,—one with a right to them
Born in the blood : 'twas in his very brow
Always to knit itself against the world,
So be beforehand when that stinted due
Service and suit : the world ducks and defers.
As such folks do, he had come up to Rome
To better his fortune, and, since many years,
Was friend and follower of a cardinal ;

C 3

Waiting the rather thus on providence,   290
That a shrewd younger poorer brother yet,
The Abate Paolo, a regular priest,
Had long since tried his powers and found he swam
With the deftest on the Galilean pool :
But then he was a web-foot, free o' the wave,
And no ambiguous dab-chick hatched to strut,
Humbled by any fond attempt to swim
When fiercer fowl usurped his dunghill-top—
A whole priest, Paolo, no mere piece of one
Like Guido tacked thus to the Church's tail !   300
Guido moreover, as the head o' the house,
Claiming the main prize, not the lesser luck,
The centre lily, no mere chickweed fringe.

He waited and learned waiting, thirty years ;
Got promise, missed performance—what would you
    have ?
No petty post rewards a nobleman
For spending youth in splendid lackey-work,
And there 's concurrence for each rarer prize ;
When that falls, rougher hand and readier foot
Push aside Guido spite of his black looks.   310
The end was, Guido, when the warning showed,
The first white hair i' the glass, gave up the game,
Determined on returning to his town,
Making the best of bad incurable,
Patching the old palace up and lingering there
The customary life out with his kin,
Where honour helps to spice the scanty bread.

Just as he trimmed his lamp and girt his loins
To go his journey and be wise at home,
In the right mood of disappointed worth,   320
Who but Violante sudden spied her prey
(Where was I with that angler-simile ?)
And threw her bait, Pompilia, where he sulked—
A gleam i' the gloom !

             What if he gained thus much,
Wrung out this sweet drop from the bitter Past,
Bore off this rose-bud from the prickly brake
To justify such torn clothes and scratched hands,
And, after all, brought something back from Rome ?

Would not a wife serve at Arezzo well   330
To light the dark house, lend a look of youth
To the mother's face grown meagre, left alone
And famished with the emptiness of hope,
Old Donna Beatrice ?   Wife you want
Would you play family-representative,
Carry you elder-brotherly, high and right
O'er what may prove the natural petulance
Of the third brother, younger, greedier still,
Girolamo, also a fledgeling priest,
Beginning life in turn with callow beak   340
Agape for luck, no luck had stopped and stilled.
Such were the pinks and greys about the bait
Persuaded Guido gulp down hook and all.

What constituted him so choice a catch,
You question ?   Past his prime and poor beside ?
Ask that of any she who knows the trade.
Why first, here was a nobleman with friends,
A palace one might run to and be safe
When presently the threatened fate should fall,
A big-browed master to block door-way up,   350
Parley with people bent on pushing by
And praying the mild Pietro quick clear scores :
Is birth a privilege and power or no ?
Also,—but judge of the result desired,
By the price paid and manner of the sale.
The Count was made woo, win and wed at once :
Asked, and was haled for answer, lest the heat
Should cool, to San Lorenzo, one blind eve,
And had Pompilia put into his arms
O' the sly there, by a hasty candle-blink,   360
With sanction of some priest-confederate
Properly paid to make short work and sure.

So did old Pietro's daughter change her style
For Guido Franceschini's lady-wife
Ere Guido knew it well ; and why this haste
And scramble and indecent secrecy ?
' Lest Pietro, all the while in ignorance,
' Should get to learn, gainsay and break the match :
' His peevishness had promptly put aside
' Such honour and refused the proffered boon,   370
' Pleased to become authoritative once.

' She remedied the wilful man's mistake—'
Did our discreet Violante. Rather say,
Thus did she, lest the object of her game,
Guido the gulled one, give him but a chance,
A moment's respite, time for thinking twice,
Might count the cost before he sold himself,
And try the clink of coin they paid him with.

But passed, the bargain struck, the business done,
Once the clandestine marriage over thus,   380
All parties made perforce the best o' the fact ;
Pietro could play vast indignation off,
Be ignorant and astounded, dupe alike
At need, of wife, daughter and son-in-law,
While Guido found himself in flagrant fault,
Must e'en do suit and service, soothe, subdue
A father not unreasonably chafed,
Bring him to terms by paying son's devoir.
Pleasant initiation !

                The end, this :   390
Guido's broad back was saddled to bear all—
Pietro, Violante, and Pompilia too,—
Three lots cast confidently in one lap,
Three dead-weights with one arm to lift the three
Out of their limbo up to life again :
The Roman household was to strike fresh root
In a new soil, graced with a novel name,
Gilt with an alien glory, Aretine
Henceforth and never Roman any more,
By treaty and engagement : thus it ran :   400
Pompilia's dowry for Pompilia's self
As a thing of course,—she paid her own expense ;
No loss nor gain there : but the couple, you see,
They, for their part, turned over first of all
Their fortune in its rags and rottenness
To Guido, fusion and confusion, he
And his with them and theirs,—whatever rag
With a coin residuary fell on floor
When Brother Paolo's energetic shake
Should do the relics justice : since 'twas thought,
Once vulnerable Pietro out of reach,   411
That, left at Rome as representative,
The Abate, backed by a potent patron here,

And otherwise with purple flushing him,
Might play a good game with the creditor,
Make up a moiety which, great or small,
Should go to the common stock—if anything,
Guido's, so far repayment of the cost
About to be,—and if, as looked more like,
Nothing,—why, all the nobler cost were his   420
Who guaranteed, for better or for worse,
To Pietro and Violante, house and home,
Kith and kin, with the pick of company
And life o' the fat o' the land while life should last.
How say you to the bargain at first blush ?
Why did a middle-aged not-silly man
Show himself thus besotted all at once ?
Quoth Solomon, one black eye does it all.

They went to Arezzo,—Pietro and his spouse,
With just the dusk o' the day of life to spend,   430
Eager to use the twilight, taste a treat,
Enjoy for once with neither stay nor stint
The luxury of lord-and-lady-ship,
And realize the stuff and nonsense long
A-simmer in their noddles ; vent the fume
Born there and bred, the citizen's conceit
How fares nobility while crossing earth,
What rampart or invisible body-guard
Keeps off the taint of common life from such.
They had not fed for nothing on the tales   440
Of grandees who give banquets worthy Jove,
Spending gold as if Plutus paid a whim,
Served with obeisances as when . . . what God ?
I'm at the end of my tether ; 'tis enough
You understand what they came primed to see :
While Guido who should minister the sight,
Stay all this qualmish greediness of soul
With apples and with flagons—for his part,
Was set on life diverse as pole from pole :
Lust of the flesh, lust of the eye,—what else   450
Was he just now awake from, sick and sage,
After the very debauch they would begin ?—
Suppose such stuff and nonsense really were.
That bubble, they were bent on blowing big,
He had blown already till he burst his cheeks,
And hence found soapsuds bitter to the tongue.

He hoped now to walk softly all his days
In soberness of spirit, if haply so,
Pinching and paring he might furnish forth
A frugal board, bare sustenance, no more,   460
Till times, that could not well grow worse, should
    mend.

Thus minded then, two parties mean to meet
And make each other happy. The first week,
And fancy strikes fact and explodes in full.
' This,' shrieked the Comparini, ' this the Count,
' The palace, the signorial privilege,
' The pomp and pageantry were promised us ?
' For this have we exchanged our liberty,
' Our competence, our darling of a child ?
' To house as spectres in a sepulchre   470
' Under this black stone heap, the street's disgrace,
' Grimmest as that is of the gruesome town,
' And here pick garbage on a pewter plate
' Or cough at verjuice dripped from earthenware ?
' Oh Via Vittoria, oh the other place
' I' the Pauline, did we give you up for this ?
' Where 's the foregone housekeeping good and gay,
' The neighbourliness, the companionship,
' The treat and feast when holidays came round,
' The daily feast that seemed no treat at all,   480
' Called common by the uncommon fools we were !
' Even the sun that used to shine at Rome,
' Where is it ?   Robbed and starved and frozen too,
' We will have justice, justice if there be ! '
Did not they shout, did not the town resound !
Guido's old lady-mother Beatrice,
Who since her husband, Count Tommaso's death,
Had held sole sway i' the house,—the doited crone
Slow to acknowledge, curtsey and abdicate,—
Was recognized of true novercal type,   490
Dragon and devil.   His brother Girolamo
Came next in order : priest was he ?   The worse !
No way of winning him to leave his mumps
And help the laugh against old ancestry
And formal habits long since out of date,
Letting his youth be patterned on the mode
Approved of where Violante laid down law.
Or did he brighten up by way of change ?

Dispose himself for affability ?
The malapert, too complaisant by half   500
To the alarmed young novice of a bride !
Let him go buzz, betake himself elsewhere
Nor singe his fly-wings in the candle-flame !

Four months' probation of this purgatory,
Dog-snap and cat-claw, curse and counterblast,
The devil's self had been sick of his own din ;
And Pietro, after trumpeting huge wrongs
At church and market-place, pillar and post,
Square's corner, street's end, now the palace-step
And now the wine-house bench—while, on her side,
Violante up and down was voluble
In whatsoever pair of ears would perk
From goody, gossip, cater-cousin and sib,
Curious to peep at the inside of things
And catch in the act pretentious poverty
At its wits' end to keep appearance up,
Make both ends meet,—nothing the vulgar loves
Like what this couple pitched them right and left,—
Then, their worst done that way, they struck tent,
      marched :
—Renounced their share o' the bargain, flung what
      dues   520
Guido was bound to pay, in Guido's face,
Left their hearts'-darling, treasure of the twain
And so forth, the poor inexperienced bride,
To her own devices, bade Arezzo rot
And the life signorial, and sought Rome once more.

I see the comment ready on your lip,
' The better fortune, Guido's—free at least
' By this defection of the foolish pair,
' He could begin make profit in some sort
' Of the young bride and the new quietness,   530
' Lead his own life now, henceforth breathe unplagued.'
Could he ?   You know the sex like Guido's self.
Learn the Violante-nature !

                              Once in Rome,
By way of helping Guido lead such life,
Her first act to inaugurate return
Was, she got pricked in conscience : Jubilee

Gave her the hint. Our Pope, as kind as just,
Attained his eighty years, announced a boon
Should make us bless the fact, held Jubilee—   540
Short shrift, prompt pardon for the light offence,
And no rough dealing with the regular crime
So this occasion were not suffered slip—
Otherwise, sins commuted as before,
Without the least abatement in the price.
Now, who had thought it ?   All this while, it seems,
Our sage Violante had a sin of a sort
She must compound for now or not at all :
Now be the ready riddance !   She confessed
Pompilia was a fable not a fact :   550
She never bore a child in her whole life.
Had this child been a changeling, that were grace
In some degree, exchange is hardly theft ;
You take your stand on truth ere leap your lie :
Here was all lie, no touch of truth at all,
All the lie hers—not even Pietro guessed
He was as childless still as twelve years since.
The babe had been a find i' the filth-heap, Sir,
Catch from the kennel !   There was found at Rome,
Down in the deepest of our social dregs,   560
A woman who professed the wanton's trade
Under the requisite thin coverture,
Communis meretrix and washer-wife :
The creature thus conditioned found by chance
Motherhood like a jewel in the muck,
And straightway either trafficked with her prize
Or listened to the tempter and let be,—
Made pact abolishing her place and part
In womankind, beast-fellowship indeed—
She sold this babe eight months before its birth   570
To our Violante, Pietro's honest spouse,
Well-famed and widely-instanced as that crown
To the husband, virtue in a woman's shape.
She it was, bought and paid for, passed the thing
Off as the flesh and blood and child of her
Despite the flagrant fifty years,—and why ?
Partly to please old Pietro, fill his cup
With wine at the late hour when lees are left,
And send him from life's feast rejoicingly,—
Partly to cheat the rightful heirs, agape,   580
Each uncle's cousin's brother's son of him,

For that same principal of the usufruct
It vext him he must die and leave behind.

Such was the sin had come to be confessed.
Which of the tales, the first or last, was true ?
Did she so sin once, or, confessing now,
Sin for the first time ?   Either way you will.
One sees a reason for the cheat :   one sees
A reason for a cheat in owning cheat
Where no cheat had been.   What of the revenge ?
What prompted the contrition all at once,   591
Made the avowal easy, the shame slight ?
Why, prove they but Pompilia not their child,
No child, no dowry ;   this, supposed their child,
Had claimed what this, shown alien to their blood,
Claimed nowise :   Guido's claim was through his wife,
Null then and void with hers.   The biter bit,
Do you see !   For such repayment of the past,
One might conceive the penitential pair
Ready to bring their case before the courts,   600
Publish their infamy to all the world
And, arm in arm, go chuckling thence content.

Is this your view ?   'Twas Guido's anyhow
And colourable :   he came forward then,
Protested in his very bride's behalf
Against this lie and all it led to, least
Of all the loss o' the dowry ;   no !   From her
And him alike he would expunge the blot,
Erase the brand of such a bestial birth,
Participate in no hideous heritage   610
Gathered from the gutter to be garnered up
And glorified in a palace.   Peter and Paul !
But that who likes may look upon the pair
Exposed in yonder church, and show his skill
By saying which is eye and which is mouth
Thro' those stabs thick and threefold,—but for that—
A strong word on the liars and their lie
Might crave expression and obtain it, Sir !
—Though prematurely, since there 's more to come,
More that will shake your confidence in things   620
Your cousin tells you,—may I be so bold ?

This makes the first act of the farce,—anon

The stealing sombre element comes in
Till all is black or blood-red in the piece.
Guido, thus made a laughing-stock abroad,
A proverb for the market-place at home,
Left alone with Pompilia now, this graft
So reputable on his ancient stock,
This plague-seed set to fester his sound flesh,
What did the Count ?   Revenge him on his wife ?
Unfasten at all risks to rid himself 631
The noisome lazar-badge, fall foul of fate,
And, careless whether the poor rag was ware
O' the part it played, or helped unwittingly,
Bid it go burn and leave his frayed flesh free ?
Plainly, did Guido open both doors wide,
Spurn thence the cur-cast creature and clear scores
As man might, tempted in extreme like this ?
No, birth and breeding, and compassion too
Saved her such scandal. She was young, he thought,
Not privy to the treason, punished most 641
I' the proclamation of it ; why make her
A party to the crime she suffered by ?
Then the black eyes were now her very own,
Not any more Violante's : let her live,
Lose in a new air, under a new sun,
The taint of the imputed parentage
Truly or falsely, take no more the touch
Of Pietro and his partner anyhow !
All might go well yet. 650

    So she thought, herself,
It seems, since what was her first act and deed
When news came how these kindly ones at Rome
Had stripped her naked to amuse the world
With spots here, spots there and spots everywhere ?
—For I should tell you that they noised abroad
Not merely the main scandal of her birth,
But slanders written, printed, published wide,
Pamphlets which set forth all the pleasantry .
Of how the promised glory was a dream, 660
The power a bubble and the wealth—why, dust.
There was a picture, painted to the life,
Of those rare doings, that superlative
Initiation in magnificence
Conferred on a poor Roman family

By favour of Arezzo and her first
And famousest, the Franceschini there,
You had the Countship holding head aloft
Bravely although bespattered, shifts and straits
In keeping out o' the way o' the wheels o' the world,
The comic of those home-contrivances   671
When the old lady-mother's wit was taxed
To find six clamorous mouths in food more real
Than fruit plucked off the cobwebbed family-tree,
Or acorns shed from its gilt mouldered frame—
Cold glories served up with three-pauls' worth' sauce.
What, I ask,—when the drunkenness of hate
Hiccuped return for hospitality,
Befouled the table they had feasted on,
Or say,—God knows I'll not prejudge the case,—   680
Grievances thus distorted, magnified,
Coloured by quarrel into calumny,—
What side did our Pompilia first espouse ?
Her first deliberate measure was, she wrote,
Pricked by some loyal impulse, straight to Rome
And her husband's brother the Abate there,
Who, having managed to effect the match,
Might take men's censure for its ill success.
She made a clean breast also in her turn ;
She qualified the couple handsomely !   690
Since whose departure, hell, she said, was heaven,
And the house, late distracted by their peals,
Quiet as Carmel where the lilies live.
Herself had oftentimes complained : but why ?
All her complaints had been their prompting, tales
Trumped up, devices to this very end.
Their game had been to thwart her husband's love
And cross his will, malign his words and ways,
So reach this issue, furnish this pretence
For impudent withdrawal from their bond,—   700
Theft, indeed murder, since they meant no less
Whose last injunction to her simple self
Had been—what parents'-precept do you think ?
That she should follow after with all speed,
Fly from her husband's house clandestinely,
Join them at Rome again, but first of all
Pick up a fresh companion in her flight,
Putting so youth and beauty to fit use,
Some gay, dare-devil. cloak-and-rapier spark

Capable of adventure,—helped by whom   710
She, some fine eve when lutes were in the air,
Having put poison in the posset-cup,
Laid hands on money, jewels and the like,
And, to conceal the thing with more effect,
By way of parting benediction too,
Fired the house,—one would finish famously
I' the tumult, slip out, scurry off and away
And turn up merrily at home once more.
Fact this, and not a dream o' the devil, Sir !
And more than this, a fact none dare dispute,   720
Word for word, such a letter did she write.
And such the Abate read, nor simply read
But gave all Rome to ruminate upon,
In answer to such charges as, I say,
The couple sought to be beforehand with.

The cause thus carried to the courts at Rome,
Guido away, the Abate had no choice
But stand forth, take his absent brother's part,
Defend the honour of himself beside.
He made what head he might against the pair,   730
Maintained Pompilia's birth legitimate
And all her rights intact—hers, Guido's now—
And so far by his tactics turned their flank,
The enemy being beforehand in the place,
That, though the courts allowed the cheat for fact,
Suffered Violante to parade her shame,
Publish her infamy to heart's content,
And let the tale o' the feigned birth pass for proved,—
Yet they stopped there, refused to intervene
And dispossess the innocents, befooled   740
By gifts o' the guilty, at guilt's new caprice :
They would not take away the dowry now
Wrongfully given at first, nor bar at all
Succession to the aforesaid usufruct,
Established on a fraud, nor play the game
Of Pietro's child and now not Pietro's child
As it might suit the gamester's purpose.   Thus
Was justice ever ridiculed in Rome :
Such be the double verdicts favoured here
Which send away both parties to a suit   750
Nor puffed up nor cast down,—for each a crumb
Of right, for neither of them the whole loaf.

Whence, on the Comparini's part, appeal——
Counter-appeal on Guido's,—that's the game :
And so the matter stands, even to this hour,
Bandied as balls are in a tennis-court,
And so might stand, unless some heart broke first,
Till doomsday

          Leave it thus, and now revert
To the old Arezzo whence we moved to Rome.   760
We've had enough o' the parents, false or true,
Now for a touch o' the daughter's quality.
The start's fair henceforth—every obstacle
Out of the young wife's footpath—she's alone—
Left to walk warily now : how does she walk ?
Why, once a dwelling's doorpost marked and crossed
In rubric by the enemy on his rounds
As eligible, as fit place of prey,
Baffle him henceforth, keep him out who can !
Stop up the door at the first hint of hoof,   770
Presently at the window taps a horn,
And Satan's by your fireside, never fear !
Pompilia, left alone now, found herself ;
Found herself young too, sprightly, fair enough,
Matched with a husband old beyond his age
(Though that was something like four times her own)
Because of cares past, present and to come :
Found too the house dull and its inmates dead,
So, looked outside for light and life.

              And lo   780
There in a trice did turn up life and light,
The man with the aureole, sympathy made flesh,
The all-consoling Caponsacchi, Sir !
A priest—what else should the consoler be ?
With goodly shoulderblade and proper leg,
A portly make and a symmetric shape,
And curls that clustered to the tonsure quite.
This was a bishop in the bud, and now
A canon full-blown so far : priest, and priest
Nowise exorbitantly overworked,   790
The courtly Christian, not so much Saint Paul
As a saint of Cæsar's household : there posed he
Sending his god-glance after his shot shaft,
Apollos turned Apollo, while the snake
Pompilia writhed transfixed through all her spires.

He, not a visitor at Guido's house,
Scarce an acquaintance, but in prime request
With the magnates of Arezzo, was seen here,
Heard there, felt everywhere in Guido's path
If Guido's wife's path be her husband's too.   800
Now he threw comfits at the theatre
Into her lap,—what harm in Carnival ?
Now he pressed close till his foot touched her gown,
His hand brushed hers,—how help on promenade ?
And, ever on weighty business, found his steps
Incline to a certain haunt of doubtful fame
Which fronted Guido's palace by mere chance ;
While—how do accidents sometimes combine !
Pompilia chose to cloister up her charms
Just in a chamber that o'erlooked the street,   810
Sat there to pray, or peep thence at mankind.

This passage of arms and wits amused the town.
At last the husband lifted eyebrow,—bent
On day-book and the study how to wring
Half the due vintage from the worn-out vines
At the villa, tease a quarter the old rent
From the farmstead, tenants swore would tumble
     soon,—
Pricked up his ear a-singing day and night
With ' ruin, ruin ' ;—and so surprised at last-
Why, what else but a titter ? Up he jumps.   820
Back to mind come those scratchings at the grange,
Prints of the paw about the outhouse ; rife
In his head at once again are word and wink,
Mum here and *budget* there, the smell o' the fox,
The musk o' the gallant. ' Friends, there 's falseness
     here ! '

The proper help of friends in such a strait
Is waggery, the world over.   Laugh him free
O' the regular jealous-fit that 's incident
To all old husbands that wed brisk young wives,
And he'll go duly docile all his days.   830
' Somebody courts your wife, Count ?   Where and
     when ?
' How and why ?   Mere horn-madness : have a care !
' Your lady loves her own room, sticks to it,
' Locks herself in for hours, you say yourself.

' And—what, it's Caponsacchi means you harm ?
' The Canon ?   We caress him, he's the world's,
' A man of such acceptance,—never dream,
' Though he were fifty times the fox you fear,
' He'd risk his brush for your particular chick,
' When the wide town's his hen-roost ! Fie o' the
    fool ! '   840
So they dispensed their comfort of a kind.
Guido at last cried ' Something is in the air,
' Under the earth, some plot against my peace :
' The trouble of eclipse hangs overhead,
' How it should come of that officious orb
' Your Canon in my system, you must say :
' I say—that from the pressure of this spring
' Began the chime and interchange of bells,
' Ever one whisper, and one whisper more,
' And just one whisper for the silvery last,   850
' Till all at once a-row the bronze-throats burst
' Into a larum both significant
' And sinister : stop it I must and will.
' Let Caponsacchi take his hand away
' From the wire !—disport himself in other paths
' Than lead precisely to my palace-gate,—
' Look where he likes except one window's way
' Where, cheek on hand, and elbow set on sill,
' Happens to lean and say her litanies
' Every day and all day long, just my wife—   860
' Or wife and Caponsacchi may fare the worse ! '

Admire the man's simplicity, ' I'll do this,
' I'll not have that, I'll punish and prevent ! '—
'Tis easy saying.   But to a fray, you see,
Two parties go.   The badger shows his teeth :
The fox nor lies down sheep-like nor dares fight.
Oh, the wife knew the appropriate warfare well,
The way to put suspicion to the blush !
At first hint of remonstrance, up and out
I' the face of the world, you found her : she could
    speak,   870
State her case,—Franceschini was a name,
Guido had his full share of foes and friends—
Why should not she call these to arbitrate ?
She bade the Governor do governance,
Cried out on the Archbishop,—why, there now,

Take him for sample ! Three successive times,
Had he to reconduct her by main-force
From where she took her station opposite
His shut door,—on the public steps thereto,
Wringing her hands, when he came out to see,   880
And shrieking all her wrongs forth at his foot,—
Back to the husband and the house she fled :
Judge if that husband warmed him in the face
Of friends or frowned on foes as heretofore !
Judge if he missed the natural grin of folk,
Or lacked the customary compliment
Of cap and bells, the luckless husband's fit !

So it went on and on till—who was right ?
One merry April morning, Guido woke
After the cuckoo, so late, near noonday,   890
With an inordinate yawning of the jaws,
Ears plugged, eyes gummed together, palate, tongue
And teeth one mud-paste made of poppy-milk ;
And found his wife flown, his scrutoire the worse
For a rummage,—jewelry that was, was not,
Some money there had made itself wings too,—
The door lay wide and yet the servants slept
Sound as the dead, or dosed which does as well.
In short, Pompilia, she who, candid soul,
Had not so much as spoken all her life   900
To the Canon, nay, so much as peeped at him
Between her fingers while she prayed in church,—
This lamb-like innocent of fifteen years
(Such she was grown to by this time of day)
Had simply put an opiate in the drink
Of the whole household overnight, and then
Got up and gone about her work secure,
Laid hand on this waif and the other stray,
Spoiled the Philistine and marched out of doors
In company of the Canon who, Lord's love,   910
What with his daily duty at the church,
Nightly devoir where ladies congregate,
Had something else to mind, assure yourself,
Beside Pompilia, paragon though she be,
Or notice if her nose were sharp or blunt !
Well, anyhow, albeit impossible,
Both of them were together jollily
Jaunting it Rome-ward, half-way there by this,

While Guido was left go and get undrugged,
Gather his wits up, groaningly give thanks   920
When neighbours crowded round him to condole.
' Ah,' quoth a gossip, ' well I mind me now,
' The Count did always say he thought he felt
' He feared as if this very chance might fall !
' And when a man of fifty finds his corns
' Ache and his joints throb, and foresees a storm,
' Though neighbours laugh and say the sky is clear,
' Let us henceforth believe him weatherwise ! '
Then was the story told, I'll cut you short :
All neighbours knew : no mystery in the world.   930
The lovers left at nightfall—over night
Had Caponsacchi come to carry off
Pompilia,—not alone, a friend of his,
One Guillichini, the more conversant
With Guido's housekeeping that he was just
A cousin of Guido's and might play a prank—
(Have not you too a cousin that's a wag ?)
—Lord and a Canon also,—what would you have ?
Such are the red-clothed milk-swollen poppy-heads
That stand and stiffen 'mid the wheat o' the Church !—
This worthy came to aid, abet his best.   941
And so the house was ransacked, booty bagged,
The lady led downstairs and out of doors
Guided and guarded till, the city passed,
A carriage lay convenient at the gate.
Good-bye to the friendly Canon ; the loving one
Could peradventure do the rest himself.
In jumps Pompilia, after her the priest,
' Whip, driver ! Money makes the mare to go,
' And we've a bagful. Take the Roman road ! ' '950
So said the neighbours. This was eight hours since.

Guido heard all, swore the befitting oaths,
Shook off the relics of his poison-drench,
Got horse, was fairly started in pursuit
With never a friend to follow, found the track
Fast enough, 'twas the straight Perugia way,
Trod soon upon their very heels, too late
By a minute only at Camoscia, at
Chiusi, Foligno, ever the fugitives
Just ahead, just out as he galloped in,   966
Getting the good news ever fresh and fresh,

Till, lo, at the last stage of all, last post
Before Rome,—as we say, in sight of Rome
And safety (there's impunity at Rome
For priests, you know) at—what's the little place ?
What some call Castelnuovo, some just call
The Osteria, because o' the post-house inn,
There, at the journey's all but end, it seems,
Triumph deceived them and undid them both,
Secure they might foretaste felicity   970
Nor fear surprisal : so, they were surprised.
There did they halt at early evening, there
Did Guido overtake them : 'twas day-break ;
He came in time enough, not time too much,
Since in the courtyard stood the Canon's self
Urging the drowsy stable-grooms to haste
Harness the horses, have the journey end,
The trifling four-hours'-running, so reach Rome.
And the other runaway, the wife ?   Upstairs,   979
Still on the couch where she had spent the night,
One couch in one room, and one room for both.
So gained they six hours, so were lost thereby.

Sir, what's the sequel ?   Lover and beloved
Fall on their knees ?   No impudence serves here ?
They beat their breasts and beg for easy death,
Confess this, that and the other ?—anyhow
Confess there wanted not some likelihood
To the supposition so preposterous,
That, O Pompilia, thy sequestered eyes   989
Had noticed, straying o'er the prayerbook's edge,
More of the Canon than that black his coat,
Buckled his shoes were, broad his hat of brim :
And that, O Canon, thy religious care
Had breathed too soft a *benedicite*
To banish trouble from a lady's breast
So lonely and so lovely, nor so lean !
This you expect ?   Indeed, then, much you err.
Not to such ordinary end as this
Had Caponsacchi flung the cassock far,
Doffed the priest, donned the perfect cavalier ;   1000
The die was cast : over shoes over boots :
And just as she, I presently shall show,
Pompilia, soon looked Helen to the life,
Recumbent upstairs in her pink and white,

So, in the inn-yard, bold as 't were Troy-town,
There strutted Paris in correct costume,
Cloak, cap and feather, no appointment missed,
Even to a wicked-looking sword at side,
He seemed to find and feel familiar at.
Nor wanted words as ready and as big   1010
As the part he played, the bold abashless one.
' I interposed to save your wife from death,
' Yourself from shame, the true and only shame :
' Ask your own conscience else !—or, failing that,
' What I have done I answer, anywhere,
' Here, if you will ; you see I have a sword :
' Or, since I have a tonsure as you taunt,
' At Rome, by all means,—priests to try a priest.
' Only, speak where your wife's voice can reply ! '
And then he fingered at the sword again.   1020
So, Guido called, in aid and witness both,
The Public Force. The Commissary came,
Officers also ; they secured the priest ;
Then, for his more confusion, mounted up
With him, a guard on either side, the stair
To the bed-room where still slept or feigned a sleep
His paramour and Guido's wife : in burst
The company and bade her wake and rise.

Her defence ? This. She woke, saw, sprang upright
I' the midst and stood as terrible as truth,   1030
Sprang to her husband's side, caught at the sword
That hung there useless, since they held each hand
O' the lover, had disarmed him properly,
And in a moment out flew the bright thing
Full in the face of Guido,—but for help
O' the guards who held her back and pinioned her
With pains enough, she had finished you my tale
With a flourish of red all round it, pinked her
        man
Prettily ; but she fought them one to six.
They stopped that,—but her tongue continued free :
She spat forth such invective at her spouse,   1041
O'erfrothed him with such foam of murderer,
Thief, pandar—that the popular tide soon turned,
The favour of the very *sbirri*, straight
Ebbed from the husband, set toward his wife,
People cried ' Hands off, pay a priest respect ! '

And ' persecuting fiend ' and ' martyred saint '
Began to lead a measure from lip to lip.

But facts are facts and flinch not ; stubborn things,
And the question ' Prithee, friend, how comes my
    purse   1050
' I' the poke of you ? '—admits of no reply.
Here was a priest found out in masquerade,
A wife caught playing truant if no more ;
While the Count, mortified in mien enough,
And, nose to face, an added palm in length,
Was plain writ ' husband ' every piece of him :
Capture once made, release could hardly be.
Beside, the prisoners both made appeal,
' Take us to Rome ! '
                Taken to Rome they were ;   1060
The husband trooping after, piteously,
Tail between legs, no talk of triumph now—
No honour set firm on its feet once more
On two dead bodies of the guilty,—nay,
No dubious salve to honour's broken pate
From chance that, after all, the hurt might seem
A skin-deep matter, scratch that leaves no scar :
For Guido's first search,- -ferreting, poor soul,
Here, there and everywhere in the vile place
Abandoned to him when their backs were turned,
Found,—furnishing a last and best regale,—   1071
All the love-letters bandied twixt the pair
Since the first timid trembling into life
O' the love-star till its stand at fiery full.
Mad prose, mad verse, fears, hopes, triumph, despair,
Avowal, disclaimer, plans, dates, names,—was nought
Wanting to prove, if proof consoles at all,
That this had been but the fifth act o' the piece
Whereof the due proemium, months ago
These playwrights had put forth, and ever since
Matured the middle, added 'neath his nose.   1081
He might go cross himself : the case was clear.

Therefore to Rome with the clear case ; there plead
Each party its best, and leave the law do right,
Let her shine forth and show, as God in heaven,
Vice prostrate, virtue pedestalled at last,
The triumph of truth ! What else shall glad our gaze

When once authority has knit the brow
And set the brain behind it to decide
Between the wolf and sheep turned litigants ?   1090
' This is indeed a business ' law shook head :
' A husband charges hard things on a wife,
' The wife as hard o' the husband : whose fault here ?
' A wife that flies her husband's house, does wrong :
' The male friend's interference looks amiss,
' Lends a suspicion : but suppose the wife,
' On the other hand, be jeopardized at home—
' Nay, that she simply hold, ill-groundedly,
' An apprehension she is jeopardized,—
' And further, if the friend partake the fear,   1100
' And, in a commendable charity
' Which trusteth all, trust her that she mistrusts,—
' What do they but obey the natural law ?
' Pretence may this be and a cloak for sin,
' And circumstances that concur i' the close
' Hint as much, loudly—yet scarce loud enough
' To drown the answer " strange may yet be true : "
' Innocence often looks like guiltiness.
' The accused declare that in thought, word and deed,
' Innocent were they both from first to last   1110
' As male-babe haply laid by female-babe
' At church on edge of the baptismal font
' Together for a minute, perfect-pure.
' Difficult to believe, yet possible,
' As witness Joseph, the friend's patron-saint.
' The night at the inn—there charity nigh chokes
' Ere swallow what they both asseverate ;
' Though down the gullet faith may feel it go,
' When mindful of what flight fatigued the flesh
' Out of its faculty and fleshliness,   1120
' Subdued it to the soul, as saints assure :
' So long a flight necessitates a fall
' On the first bed, though in a lion's den,
' And the first pillow, though the lion's back :
' Difficult to believe, yet possible.
' Last come the letters' bundled beastliness—
' Authority repugns give glance to twice,
' Turns head, and almost lets her whip-lash fall ;
' Yet here a voice cries " Respite ! " from the clouds—
' The accused, both in a tale, protest, disclaim,   1130
' Abominate the horror : " Not my hand "

'　Asserts the friend—" Nor mine " chimes in the wife,
'　" Seeing I have no hand, nor write at all."
'　Illiterate—for she goes on to ask,
'　What if the friend did pen now verse now prose,
'　Commend it to her notice now and then ?
'　'Twas pearls to swine : she read no more than wrote,
'　And kept no more than read, for as they fell
'　She ever brushed the burr-like things away,
'　Or, better, burned them, quenched the fire in smoke.
'　As for this fardel, filth and foolishness,　　　1141
'　She sees it now the first time : burn it too !
'　While for his part the friend vows ignorance
'　Alike of what bears his name and bears hers :
'　'Tis forgery, a felon's masterpiece,
'　And, as 'tis said the fox still finds the stench,
'　Home-manufacture and the husband's work.
'　Though he confesses, the ingenuous friend,
'　That certain missives, letters of a sort,
'　Flighty and feeble, which assigned themselves　　1150
'　To the wife, no less have fallen, far too oft,
'　In his path : wherefrom he understood just this—
'　That were they verily the lady's own,
'　Why, she who penned them, since he never saw
'　Save for one minute the mere face of her,
'　Since never had there been the interchange
'　Of word with word between them all their life,
'　Why, she must be the fondest of the frail,
'　And fit, she for the " apage " he flung,
'　Her letters for the flame they went to feed.　　1160
'　But, now he sees her face and hears her speech,
'　Much he repents him if, in fancy-freak
'　For a moment the minutest measurable,
'　He coupled her with the first flimsy word
'　O' the self-spun fabric some mean spider-soul
'　Furnished forth : stop his films and stamp on him !
'　Never was such a tangled knottiness,
'　But thus authority cuts the Gordian through,
'　And mark how her decision suits the need !
'　Here's troublesomeness, scandal on both sides,
'　Plenty of fault to find, no absolute crime :　　1171
'　Let each side own its fault and make amends !
'　What does a priest in cavalier's attire
'　Consorting publicly with vagrant wives
'　In quarters close as the confessional,

' Though innocent of harm ? 'Tis harm enough :
' Let him pay it, and be relegate a good
' Three years, to spend in some place not too far
' Nor yet too near, midway twixt near and far,
' Rome and Arezzo,—Civita we choose,   1180
' Where he may lounge away time, live at large,
' Find out the proper function of a priest,
' Nowise an exile,—that were punishment,
' But one our love thus keeps out of harm's way
' Not more from the husband's anger than, mayhap
' His own . . . say, indiscretion, waywardness,
' And wanderings when Easter eves grow warm.
' For the wife,—well, our best step to take with her,
' On her own showing, were to shift her root
' From the old cold shade and unhappy soil   1190
' Into a generous ground that fronts the south :
' Where, since her callow soul, a-shiver late,
' Craved simply warmth and called mere passers-by
' To the rescue, she should have her fill of shine.
' Do house and husband hinder and not help ?
' Why then, forget both and stay here at peace,
' Come into our community, enroll
' Herself along with those good Convertites,
' Those sinners saved, those Magdalens re-made,
' Accept their ministration, well bestow   1200
' Her body and patiently possess her soul,
' Until we see what better can be done.
' Last for the husband : if his tale prove true,
' Well is he rid of two domestic plagues—
' The wife that ailed, do whatsoever he would,
' And friend of hers that undertook the cure.
' See, what a double load we lift from breast !
' Off he may go, return, resume old life,
' Laugh at the priest here and Pompilia there
' In limbo each and punished for their pains,   1210
' And grateful tell the inquiring neighbourhood—
' In Rome, no wrong but has its remedy.'
The case was closed.   Now, am I fair or no
In what I utter ? Do I state the facts,
Having forechosen a side ? I promised you !

The Canon Caponsacchi, then, was sent
To change his garb, re-trim his tonsure, tie
The clerkly silk round, every plait correct,

Make the impressive entry on his place
Of relegation, thrill his Civita,   1220
As Ovid, a like sufferer in the cause,
Planted a primrose-patch by Pontus : where,
What with much culture of the sonnet-stave
And converse with the aborigines,
Soft savagery of eyes unused to roll,
And hearts that all awry went pit-a-pat
And wanted setting right in charity,
What were a couple of years to while away ?
Pompilia, as enjoined, betook herself
To the aforesaid Convertites, the sisterhood   1230
In Via Lungara, where the light ones live,
Spin, pray, then sing like linnets o'er the flax.
' Anywhere, anyhow, out of my husband's house
' Is heaven,' cried she,—was therefore suited so.
But for Count Guido Franceschini, he—
The injured man thus righted—found no heaven
I' the house when he returned there, I engage,
Was welcomed by the city turned upside down
In a chorus of inquiry.   ' What, back—you ?
' And no wife ?   Left her with the Penitents ?   1240
' Ah, being young and pretty, 'twere a shame
' To have her whipped in public : leave the job
' To the priests who understand !   Such priests as
      yours—
' (Pontifex Maximus whipped Vestals once)
' Our madcap Caponsacchi : think of him !
' So, he fired up, showed fight and skill of fence ?
' Ay, you drew also, but you did not fight !
' The wiser, 'tis a word and a blow with him,
' True Caponsacchi, of old Head-i'-the-Sack
' That fought at Fiesole ere Florence was :   1250
' He had done enough, to firk you were too much.
' And did the little lady menace you,
' Make at your breast with your own harmless sword ?
' The spitfire ! Well, thank God you're safe and sound,
' Have kept the sixth commandment whether or no
' The lady broke the seventh : I only wish
' I were as saint-like, could contain me so.
' I am a sinner, I fear I should have left
' Sir Priest no nose-tip to turn up at me ! '
You, Sir, who listen but interpose no word,   1260
Ask yourself, had you borne a baiting thus ?

Was it enough to make a wise man mad ?
Oh, but I'll have your verdict at the end !

Well, not enough, it seems : such mere hurt falls,
Frets awhile, and aches long, then less and less,
And so is done with. Such was not the scheme
O' the pleasant Comparini : on Guido's wound
Ever in due succession, drop by drop,
Came slow distilment from the alembic here
Set on to simmer by Canidian hate,   1270
Corrosives keeping the man's misery raw.
First fire-drop,—when he thought to make the best
O' the bad, to wring from out the sentence passed,
Poor, pitiful, absurd although it were,
Yet what might eke him out result enough
And make it worth his while he had the right
And not the wrong i' the matter judged at Rome.
Inadequate her punishment, no less
Punished in some slight sort his wife had been ;
Then, punished for adultery, what else ?   1280
On such admitted crime he thought to seize,
And institute procedure in the courts
Which cut corruption of this kind from man,
Cast loose a wife proved loose and castaway :
He claimed in due form a divorce at least.

This claim was met now by a counterclaim :
Pompilia sought divorce from bed and board
Of Guido, whose outrageous cruelty,
Whose mother's malice and whose brother's hate
Were just the white o' the charge, such dreadful depths
Blackened its centre,—hints of worse than hate,   1291
Love from that brother, by that Guido's guile,
That mother's prompting. Such reply was made,
So was the engine loaded, wound up, sprung
On Guido, who received the bolt in breast ;
But no less bore up, giddily perhaps.
He had the Abate Paolo still in Rome,
Brother and friend and fighter on his side :
They rallied in a measure, met the foe
Manlike, joined battle in the public courts,   1300
As if to shame supine law from her sloth :
And waiting her award, let beat the while
Arezzo's banter, Rome's buffoonery,

On this ear and on that ear, deaf alike,
Safe from worse outrage.   Let a scorpion nip,
And never mind till he contorts his tail !
But there was sting i' the creature ; thus it struck.
Guido had thought in his simplicity—
That lying declaration of remorse,
That story of the child which was no child   1310
And motherhood no motherhood at all,
—That even this sin might have its sort of good
Inasmuch as no question could be more,
Call it false, call the story true, no claim
Of further parentage pretended now :
The parents had abjured all right, at least,
I' the woman still his wife : to plead right now
Were to declare the abjuration false :
He was relieved from any fear henceforth
Their hands might touch, their breath defile again
Pompilia with his name upon her yet.   1321
Well, no : the next news was, Pompilia's health
Demanded change after full three long weeks
Spent in devotion with the Sisterhood,—
Rendering sojourn,—so the court opined,—
Too irksome, since the convent's walls were high
And windows narrow, nor was air enough
Nor light enough, but all looked prison-like,
The last thing which had come in the court's head.
Propose a new expedient therefore,—this !   1330
She had demanded—had obtained indeed,
By intervention of whatever friends
Or perhaps lovers—(beauty in distress,
In one whose tale is the town-talk beside,
Never lacks friendship's arm about her neck)—
Not freedom, scarce remitted penalty,
Solely the transfer to some private place
Where better air, more light, new food might be—
Incarcerated (call it, all the same)
At some sure friend's house she must keep inside,
Be found in at requirement fast enough,—   1341
Domus pro carcere, in Roman style.
You keep the house i' the main, as most men do
And all good women : but free otherwise,
Should friends arrive, to lodge and entertain.
And such a *domum*, such a dwelling-place,
Having all Rome to choose from, where chose she ?

What house obtained Pompilia's preference ?
Why, just the Comparini's—just, do you mark,
Theirs who renounced all part and lot in her   1350
So long as Guido could be robbed thereby,
And only fell back on relationship
And found their daughter safe and sound again
So soon as that might stab him : yes, the pair
Who, as I told you, first had baited hook
With this poor gilded fly Pompilia-thing,
Then caught the fish, pulled Guido to the shore
And gutted him,—now found a further use
For the bait, would trail the gauze wings yet again
I' the way of what new swimmer passed their stand.
They took Pompilia to their hiding-place—   1361
Not in the heart of Rome as formerly,
Under observance, subject to control—
But out o' the way,—or in the way, who knows ?
That blind mute villa lurking by the gate
At Via Paulina, not so hard to miss
By the honest eye, easy enough to find
In twilight by marauders : where perchance
Some muffled Caponsacchi might repair,
Employ odd moments when he too tried change,   1370
Found that a friend's abode was pleasanter
Than relegation, penance and the rest.

Come, here's the last drop does its worst to wound,
Here's Guido poisoned to the bone, you say,
Your boasted still's full strain and strength : not so !
One master-squeeze from screw shall bring to birth
The hoard i' the heart o' the toad, hell's quintessence.
He learned the true convenience of the change,
And why a convent wants the cheerful hearts
And helpful hands which female straits require,   1380
When, in the blind mute villa by the gate,
Pompilia—what ? sang, danced, saw company ?
—Gave birth, Sir, to a child, his son and heir,
Or Guido's heir and Caponsacchi's son.
I want your word now : what do you say to this ?
What would say little Arezzo and great Rome,
And what did God say and the devil say
One at each ear o' the man, the husband, now
The father ? Why, the overburdened mind
Broke down, what was a brain became a blaze.   1390

In fury of the moment—(that first news
Fell on the Count among his vines, it seems,
Doing his farm-work,)—why, he summoned steward,
Called in the first four hard hands and stout hearts
From field and furrow, poured forth his appeal,
Not to Rome's law and gospel any more,
But this clown with a mother or a wife,
That clodpole with a sister or a son :
And, whereas law and gospel held their peace,
What wonder if the sticks and stones cried out ?   1400

All five soon somehow found themselves at Rome,
At the villa door : there was the warmth and light—
The sense of life so just an inch inside—
Some angel must have whispered ' One more chance ! '

He gave it : bade the others stand aside :
Knocked at the door,—' Who is it knocks ? ' cried one.
' I will make,' surely Guido's angel said,
' One final essay, last experiment,
' Speak the word, name the name from out all names
' Which, if,—as doubtless strong illusions are,   1410
' And strange disguisings whence even truth seems
      false,
' And, for I am a man, I dare not do
' God's work until assured I see with God,—
' If I should bring my lips to breathe that name
' And they be innocent,—nay, by one touch
' Of innocence redeemed from utter guilt,—
' That name will bar the door and bid fate pass.
' I will not say " It is a messenger,
' " A neighbour, even a belated man,
' " Much less your husband's friend, your husband's
      self : "   .   1420
' At such appeal the door is bound to ope.
' But I will say '—here's rhetoric and to spare !
Why, Sir, the stumbling-block is cursed and kicked,
Block though it be ; the name that brought offence
Will bring offence : the burnt child dreads the fire
Although that fire feed on a taper-wick
Which never left the altar nor singed fly :
And had a harmless man tripped you by chance,
How would you wait him, stand or step aside,
When next you heard he rolled your way ? Enough.

' Giuseppe Caponsacchi ! ' Guido cried ;   1431
And open flew the door : enough again.
Vengeance, you know, burst, like a mountain-wave
That holds a monster in it, over the house,
And wiped its filthy four walls free again
With a wash of hell-fire,—father, mother, wife,
Killed them all, bathed his name clean in their blood,
And, reeking so, was caught, his friends and he,
Haled hither and imprisoned yesternight
O' the day all this was.   1440
                    Now the whole is known,
And how the old couple come to lie in state
Though hacked to pieces,—never, the expert say,
So thorough a study of stabbing—while the wife
Viper-like, very difficult to slay,
Writhes still through every ring of her, poor wretch,
At the Hospital hard by—survives, we'll hope,
To somewhat purify her putrid soul
By full confession, make so much amends
While time lasts ; since at day's end die she must.

For Caponsacchi,—why, they'll have him here,   1451
The hero of the adventure, who so fit
To tell it in the coming Carnival ?
'Twill make the fortune of whate'er saloon
Hears him recount, with helpful cheek, and eye
Hotly indignant now, now dewy-dimmed,
The incidents of flight, pursuit, surprise,
Capture, with hints of kisses all between—
While Guido, the most unromantic spouse,
No longer fit to laugh at since the blood   1460
Gave the broad farce an all too brutal air,
Why, he and those our luckless friends of his
May tumble in the straw this bitter day—
Laid by the heels i' the New Prison, I hear,
To bide their trial, since trial, and for the life,
Follows if but for form's sake : yes, indeed !

But with a certain issue : no dispute,
' Try him,' bids law : formalities oblige :
But as to the issue,—look me in the face !—
If the law thinks to find them guilty, Sir,   1470
Master or men—touch one hair of the five,
Then I say in the name of all that's left

Of honour in Rome, civility i' the world
Whereof Rome boasts herself the central source,—
There's an end to all hope of justice more.
Astræa's gone indeed, let hope go too !
Who is it dares impugn the natural law ?
Deny God's word ' the faithless wife shall die ' ?
What, are we blind ?　How can we fail to see,
This crowd of miseries make the man a mark,　1480
Accumulate on one devoted head
For our example, yours and mine who read
Its lesson thus—' Henceforward let none dare
' Stand, like a natural in the public way,
' Letting the very urchins twitch his beard
' And tweak his nose, to earn a nickname so,
' Of the male-Grissel or the modern Job ! '
Had Guido, in the twinkling of an eye,
Summed up the reckoning, promptly paid himself,
That morning when he came up with the pair　1490
At the wayside inn,—exacted his just debt
By aid of what first mattock, pitchfork, axe
Came to hand in the helpful stable-yard,
And with that axe, if providence so pleased,
Cloven each head, by some Rolando-stroke,
In one clean cut from crown to clavicle,
—Slain the priest-gallant, the wife-paramour,
Sticking, for all defence, in each skull's cleft
The rhyme and reason of the stroke thus dealt,
To-wit, those letters and last evidence　1500
Of shame, each package in its proper place,—
Bidding, who pitied, undistend the skulls,—
I say, the world had praised the man.　But no !
That were too plain, too straight, too simply just !
He hesitates, calls law forsooth to help.
And law, distasteful to who calls in law
When honour is beforehand and would serve,　justice
What wonder if law hesitate in turn,
Plead her disuse to calls o' the kind, reply
Smiling a little ' 'Tis yourself assess　1510
' The worth of what's lost, sum of damage done :
' What you touched with so light a finger-tip,
' You whose concern it was to grasp the thing,
' Why must law gird herself and grapple with ?
' Law, alien to the actor whose warm blood
' Asks heat from law whose veins run lukewarm milk,—

'What you dealt lightly with, shall law make out
'Heinous forsooth ? '
                        Sir, what's the good of law
In a case o' the kind ? None, as she all but says.   1520
Call in law when a neighbour breaks your fence,
Cribs from your field, tampers with rent or lease,
Touches the purse or pocket,—but wooes your wife ?
No : take the old way trod when men were men !
Guido preferred the new path,—for his pains,
Stuck in a quagmire, floundered worse and worse
Until he managed somehow scramble back
Into the safe sure rutted road once more,
Revenged his own wrong like a gentleman.
Once back 'mid the familiar prints, no doubt   1530
He made too rash amends for his first fault,
Vaulted too loftily over what barred him late,
And lit i' the mire again,—the common chance
The natural over-energy : the deed
Maladroit yields three deaths instead of one,
And one life left : for where's the Canon's corpse ?
All which is the worse for Guido, but, be frank—
The better for you and me and all the world,
Husbands of wives, especially in Rome.
The thing is put right, in the old place,—ay,   1540
The rod hangs on its nail behind the door,
Fresh from the brine : a matter I commend
To the notice, during Carnival that's near,
Of a certain what's-his-name and jackanapes
Somewhat too civil of eves with lute and song
About a house here, where I keep a wife.
(You, being his cousin, may go tell him so.)

*Natural Law would have passed
But waiting & inactivity
brought Guido's downfa*

THE OTHER HALF-ROME

ANOTHER day that finds her living yet,
Little Pompilia, with the patient brow
And lamentable smile on those poor lips,
And, under the white hospital-array,
A flower-like body, to frighten at a bruise
You'd think, yet now, stabbed through and through
    again,
Alive i' the ruins. 'T is a miracle.
It seems that, when her husband struck her first,
She prayed Madonna just that she might live
So long as to confess and be absolved;   10
And whether it was that, all her sad life long,
Never before successful in a prayer,
This prayer rose with authority too dread,—
Or whether, because earth was hell to her,
By compensation, when the blackness broke
She got one glimpse of quiet and the cool blue,
To show her for a moment such things were,—
Or else,—as the Augustinian Brother thinks,
The friar who took confession from her lip,—
When a probationary soul that moves   20
From nobleness to nobleness, as she,
Over the rough way of the world, succumbs,
Bloodies its last thorn with unflinching foot,
The angels love to do their work betimes,
Staunch some wounds here nor leave so much for God.
Who knows ? However it be, confessed, absolved,
She lies, with overplus of life beside
To speak and right herself from first to last,
Right the friend also, lamb-pure, lion-brave,
Care for the boy's concerns, to save the son   30
From the sire, her two-weeks' infant orphaned thus,
And—with best smile of all reserved for him—
Pardon that sire and husband from the heart.
A miracle, so tell your Molinists !

There she lies in the long white lazar-house.
Rome has besieged, these two days, never doubt,
Saint Anna's where she waits her death, to hear
Though but the chink o' the bell, turn o' the hinge
When the reluctant wicket opes at last,
Lets in, on now this and now that pretence,   40
Too many by half,—complain the men of art,—
For a patient in such plight. The lawyers first
Paid the due visit—justice must be done ;
They took her witness, why the murder was ;
Then the priests followed properly,—a soul
To shrive ; 't was Brother Celestine's own right,
The same who noises thus her gifts abroad :
But many more, who found they were old friends,
Pushed in to have their stare and take their talk
And go forth boasting of it and to boast.   50
Old Monna Baldi chatters like a jay,
Swears—but that, prematurely trundled out
Just as she felt the benefit begin,
The miracle was snapped up by somebody,—
Her palsied limb 'gan prick and promise life
At touch o' the bedclothes merely,—how much more
Had she but brushed the body as she tried !
Cavalier Carlo—well, there 's some excuse
For him—Maratta who paints Virgins so—
He too must fee the porter and slip by   60
With pencil cut and paper squared, and straight
There was he figuring away at face—
' A lovelier face is not in Rome,' cried he,
' Shaped like a peacock's egg, the pure as pearl,
' That hatches you anon a snow-white chick.'
Then, oh that pair of eyes, that pendent hair,
Black this, and black the other ! Mighty fine—
But nobody cared ask to paint the same,
Nor grew a poet over hair and eyes
Four little years ago when, ask and have,   70
The woman who wakes all this rapture leaned
Flower-like from out her window long enough,
As much uncomplimented as uncropped
By comers and goers in Via Vittoria : eh ?
'Tis just a flower's fate : past parterre we trip,
Till peradventure someone plucks our sleeve—
' Yon blossom at the briar's end, that 's the rose
' Two jealous people fought for yesterday

' And killed each other : see, there 's undisturbed
' A pretty pool at the root, of rival red ! '   80
Then cry we, ' Ah, the perfect paragon ! '
Then crave we, ' Just one keepsake-leaf for us ! '

Truth lies between : there 's anyhow a child
Of seventeen years, whether a flower or weed,
Ruined : who did it shall account to Christ—
Having no pity on the harmless life
And gentle face and girlish form he found,
And thus flings back : go practise if you please
With men and women : leave a child alone
For Christ's particular love's sake !—so I say.   90

Somebody, at the bedside, said much more,
Took on him to explain the secret cause
O' the crime : quoth he, ' Such crimes are very rife,
' Explode nor make us wonder now-a-days,
' Seeing that Antichrist disseminates
' That doctrine of the Philosophic Sin :
' Molinos' sect will soon make earth too hot ! '
' Nay,' groaned the Augustinian, ' what 's there new ?
' Crime will not fail to flare up from men's hearts
' While hearts are men's and so born criminal ;   100
' Which one fact, always old yet ever new,
' Accounts for so much crime that, for my part,
' Molinos may go whistle to the wind
' That waits outside a certain church, you know ! '

Though really it does seem as if she here,
Pompilia, living so and dying thus,
Has had undue experience how much crime
A heart can hatch. Why was she made to learn
—Not you, not I, not even Molinos' self—
What Guido Franceschini's heart could hold ?   110
Thus saintship is effected probably ;
No sparing saints the process !—which the more
Tends to the reconciling us, no saints,
To sinnership, immunity and all.

For see now : Pietro and Violante's life
Till seventeen years ago, all Rome might note
And quote for happy—see the signs distinct
Of happiness as we yon Triton's trump.

What could they be but happy ?—balanced so,
Nor low i' the social scale nor yet too high,   120
Nor poor nor richer than comports with ease,
Nor bright and envied, nor obscure and scorned,
Nor so young that their pleasures fell too thick,
Nor old past catching pleasure when it fell,
Nothing above, below the just degree,
All at the mean where joy's components mix.
So again, in the couple's very souls
You saw the adequate half with half to match,
Each having and each lacking somewhat, both
Making a whole that had all and lacked nought ;   130
The round and sound, in whose composure just
The acquiescent and recipient side
Was Pietro's, and the stirring striving one
Violante's : both in union gave the due
Quietude, enterprise, craving and content,
Which go to bodily health and peace of mind,
But, as 't is said a body, rightly mixed,
Each element in equipoise, would last
Too long and live for ever,—accordingly
Holds a germ—sand-grain weight too much i' the
     scale—   140
Ordained to get predominance one day
And so bring all to ruin and release,—
Not otherwise a fatal germ lurked here :
' With mortals much must go, but something stays ;
' Nothing will stay of our so happy selves.'
Out of the very ripeness of life's core
A worm was bred—' Our life shall leave no fruit.'
Enough of bliss, they thought, could bliss bear seed,
Yield its like, propagate a bliss in turn
And keep the kind up ; not supplant themselves
But put in evidence, record they were,   151
Show them, when done with, i' the shape of a child.
' 'T is in a child, man and wife grow complete,
' One flesh : God says so : let him do his work ! '

Now, one reminder of this gnawing want,
One special prick o' the maggot at the core,
Always befell when, as the day came round,
A certain yearly sum,—our Pietro being,
As the long name runs, an usufructuary,—
Dropped in the common bag as interest   160

Of money, his till death, not afterward,
Failing an heir : an heir would take and take,
A child of theirs be wealthy in their place
To nobody's hurt—the stranger else seized all.
Prosperity rolled river-like and stopped,
Making their mill go ; but when wheel wore out,
The wave would find a space and sweep on free
And, half-a-mile off, grind some neighbour's corn.

Adam-like, Pietro sighed and said no more :
Eve saw the apple was fair and good to taste,   170
So, plucked it, having asked the snake advice.
She told her husband God was merciful,
And his and her prayer granted at the last :
Let the old mill-stone moulder,—wheel unworn,
Quartz from the quarry, shot into the stream
Adroitly, should go bring grist as before—
Their house continued to them by an heir,
Their vacant heart replenished with a child.
We have her own confession at full length
Made in the first remorse : 't was Jubilee   180
Pealed in the ear o' the conscience and it woke.
She found she had offended God no doubt,
So much was plain from what had happened since,
Misfortune on misfortune ; but she harmed   ,
No one i' the world, so far as she could see.
The act had gladdened Pietro to the height,
Her husband—God himself must gladden so
Or not at all—(thus much seems probable
From the implicit faith, or rather say
Stupid credulity of the foolish man   190
Who swallowed such a tale nor strained a whit
Even at his wife's far-over-fifty years
Matching his sixty-and-under.)   Him she blessed,
And as for doing any detriment
To the veritable heir,—why, tell her first
Who was he ?   Which of all the hands held up
I' the crowd, would one day gather round their gate,
Did she so wrong by intercepting thus
The ducat, spendthrift fortune thought to fling   199
For a scramble just to make the mob break shins ?
She kept it, saved them kicks and cuffs thereby.
While at the least one good work had she wrought,
Good, clearly and incontestably !   Her cheat—

What was it to its subject, the child's self,
But charity and religion ?   See the girl !
A body most like—a soul too probably—
Doomed to death, such a double death as waits
The illicit offspring of a common trull,
Sure to resent and forthwith rid herself
Of a mere interruption to sin's trade,   210
In the efficacious way old Tiber knows.
Was not so much proved by the ready sale
O' the child, glad transfer of this irksome chance ?
Well then, she had caught up this castaway :
This fragile egg, some careless wild bird dropped,
She had picked from where it waited the foot-fall,
And put in her own breast till forth broke finch
Able to sing God praise on mornings now.
What so excessive harm was done ?—she asked.

To which demand the dreadful answer comes—   220
For that same deed, now at Lorenzo's church,
Both agents, conscious and inconscious, lie ;
While she, the deed was done to benefit,
Lies also, the most lamentable of things,
Yonder where curious people count her breaths,
Calculate how long yet the little life
Unspilt may serve their turn nor spoil the show,
Give them their story, then the church its group.

Well, having gained Pompilia, the girl grew
I' the midst of Pietro here, Violante there,   230
Each, like a semicircle with stretched arms,
Joining the other round her preciousness—
Two walls that go about a garden plot
Where a chance sliver, branchlet slipt from bole
Of some tongue-leaved eye-figured Eden tree,
Filched by two exiles and borne far away,
Patiently glorifies their solitude,—
Year by year mounting, grade by grade surmounts
The builded brick-work, yet is compassed still,
Still hidden happily and shielded safe,—   240
Else why should miracle have graced the ground ?
But on the twelfth sun that brought April there
What meant that laugh? The coping-stone was reached;
Nay, a light tuft of bloom towered above
To be toyed with by butterfly or bee,

Done good to or else harm to from outside :
Pompilia's root, stem and a branch or two
Home enclosed still, the rest would be the world's.
All which was taught our couple though obtuse,
Since walls have ears, when one day brought a priest,
Smooth-mannered soft-speeched sleek-cheeked visitor,
The notable Abate Paolo—known   252
As younger brother of a Tuscan house
Whereof the actual representative,
Count Guido, had employed his youth and age
In culture of Rome's most productive plant—
A cardinal : but years pass and change comes,
In token of which, here was our Paolo brought
To broach a weighty business. Might he speak ?
Yes—to Violante somehow caught alone   260
While Pietro took his after-dinner doze,
And the young maiden, busily as befits,
Minded her broider-frame three chambers off.

So—giving now his great flap-hat a gloss
With flat o' the hand between-whiles, soothing now
The silk from out its creases o'er the calf,
Setting the stocking clerical again,
But never disengaging, once engaged,
The thin clear grey hold of his eyes on her—
He dissertated on that Tuscan house,   270
Those Franceschini,—very old they were—
Not rich however—oh, not rich, at least,
As people look to be who, low i' the scale
One way, have reason, rising all they can
By favour of the money-bag : 't is fair—
Do all gifts go together ?   But do n't suppose
That being not so rich means all so poor !
Say rather, well enough—i' the way, indeed,
Ha, ha, to better fortune than the best,
Since if his brother's patron-friend kept faith,   280
Put into promised play the Cardinalate,
Their house might wear the red cloth that keeps warm,
Would but the Count have patience—there's the point!
For he was slipping into years apace,
And years make men restless—they needs must see
Some certainty, some sort of end assured,
Sparkle, tho' from the topmost beacon-tip
That warrants life a harbour through the haze.

In short, call him fantastic as you choose,
Guido was home-sick, yearned for the old sights 290
And usual faces,—fain would settle himself
And have the patron's bounty when it fell
Irrigate far rather than deluge near,
Go fertilize Arezzo, not flood Rome.
Sooth to say, 't was the wiser wish : the Count
Proved wanting in ambition,—let us avouch,
Since truth is best,—in callousness of heart,
Winced at those pin-pricks whereby honours hang
A ribbon o'er each puncture : his—no soul
Ecclesiastic (here the hat was brushed) 300
Humble but self-sustaining, calm and cold,
Having, as one who puts his hand to the plough,
Renounced the over-vivid family-feel—
Poor brother Guido ! All too plain, he pined
Amid Rome's pomp and glare for dinginess
And that dilapidated palace-shell
Vast as a quarry and, very like, as bare—
Since to this comes old grandeur now-a-days—
Or that absurd wild villa in the waste
O' the hill side, breezy though, for who likes air, 310
Vittiano, nor unpleasant with its vines,
Outside the city and the summer heats.
And now his harping on this one tense chord
The villa and the palace, palace this
And villa the other, all day and all night
Creaked like the implacable cicala's cry
And made one's ear-drum ache : nought else would
  serve
But that, to light his mother's visage up
With second youth, hope, gaiety again,
He must find straightway, woo and haply win 320
And bear away triumphant back, some wife.
Well now, the man was rational in his way—
He, the Abate,—ought he to interpose ?
Unless by straining still his tutelage
(Priesthood leaps over elder-brothership)
Across this difficulty : then let go,
Leave the poor fellow in peace ! Would that be wrong ?
There was no making Guido great, it seems,
Spite of himself : then happy be his dole !
Indeed, the Abate's little interest 330
Was somewhat nearly touched i' the case, they saw :

Since if his simple kinsman so were bent,
Began his rounds in Rome to catch a wife,
Full soon would such unworldliness surprise
The rare bird, sprinkle salt on phœnix' tail,
And so secure the nest a sparrow-hawk.
No lack of mothers here in Rome,—no dread
Of daughters lured as larks by looking-glass !
The first name-pecking credit-scratching fowl
Would drop her unfledged cuckoo in our nest   340
To gather greyness there, give voice at length
And shame the brood . . . but it was long ago
When crusades were, and we sent eagles forth !
No, that at least the Abate could forestall.
He read the thought within his brother's word,
Knew what he purposed better than himself.
We want no name and fame—having our own :
No worldly aggrandizement—such we fly :
But if some wonder of a woman's-heart
Were yet untainted on this grimy earth,   350
Tender and true—tradition tells of such—
Prepared to pant in time and tune with ours—
If some good girl (a girl, since she must take
The new bent, live new life, adopt new modes)
Not wealthy—Guido for his rank was poor—
But with whatever dowry came to hand,
There were the lady-love predestinate !
And somehow the Abate's guardian eye—
Scintillant, rutilant, fraternal fire,—
Roving round every way had seized the prize   360
—The instinct of us, we, the spiritualty !
Come, cards on table ; was it true or false
That here—here in this very tenement—
Yea, Via Vittoria did a marvel hide,
Lily of a maiden, white with intact leaf
Guessed thro' the sheath that saved it from the sun ?
A daughter with the mother's hands still clasped
Over her head for fillet virginal,
A wife worth Guido's house and hand and heart ?
He came to see ; had spoken, he could no less—   370
(A final cherish of the stockinged calf)
If harm were,—well, the matter was off his mind.

Then with the great air did he kiss, devout,
Violante's hand, and rise up his whole height

(A certain purple gleam about the black)
And go forth grandly,—as if the Pope came next.
And so Violante rubbed her eyes awhile,
Got up too, walked to wake her Pietro soon
And pour into his ear the mighty news
How somebody had somehow somewhere seen   380
Their tree-top-tuft of bloom above the wall,
And came now to apprise them the tree's self
Was no such crab-sort as should feed the swine,
But veritable gold, the Hesperian ball
Ordained for Hercules to haste and pluck,
And bear and give the Gods to banquet with—
Hercules standing ready at the door.
Whereon did Pietro rub his eyes in turn,
Look very wise, a little woeful too,
Then, periwig on head, and cane in hand,   390
Sally forth dignifiedly into the Square
Of Spain across Babbuino the six steps,
Toward the Boat-fountain where our idlers lounge,—
Ask, for form's sake, who Hercules might be,
And have congratulation from the world.

Heartily laughed the world in his fool's-face
And told him Hercules was just the heir
To the stubble once a corn-field, and brick-heap
Where used to be a dwelling-place now burned.
Guido and Franceschini ; a Count,—ay :   400
But a cross i' the poke to bless the Countship ? No !
All gone except sloth, pride, rapacity,
Humours of the imposthume incident
To rich blood that runs thin,—nursed to a head
By the rankly-salted soil—a cardinal's court
Where, parasite and picker-up of crumbs,
He had hung on long, and now, let go, said some,
But shaken off, said others,—in any case
Tired of the trade and something worse for wear,
Was wanting to change town for country quick,   410
Go home again : let Pietro help him home !
The brother, Abate Paolo, shrewder mouse,
Had pricked for comfortable quarters, inched
Into the core of Rome, and fattened so ;
But Guido, over-burly for rat's hole
Suited to clerical slimness, starved outside,
Must shift for himself : and so the shift was this !

What, was the snug retreat of Pietro tracked,
The little provision for his old age snuffed ?
' Oh, make your girl a lady, an you list,   420
' But have more mercy on our wit than vaunt
' Your bargain as we burgesses who brag !
' Why, Goodman Dullard, if a friend must speak,
' Would the Count, think you, stoop to you and yours
' Were there the value of one penny-piece
' To rattle 'twixt his palms—or likelier laugh,
' Bid your Pompilia help you black his shoe ? '

Home again, shaking oft the puzzled pate,
Went Pietro to announce a change indeed,
Yet point Violante where some solace lay   430
Of a rueful sort,—the taper, quenched so soon,
Had ended merely in a snuff, not stink—
Congratulate there was one hope the less
Not misery the more : and so an end.

The marriage thus impossible, the rest
Followed : our spokesman, Paolo, heard his fate,
Resignedly Count Guido bore the blow :
Violante wiped away the transient tear,
Renounced the playing Danae to gold dreams,
Praised much her Pietro's prompt sagaciousness,   440
Found neighbours' envy natural, lightly laughed
At gossips' malice, fairly wrapped herself
In her integrity three folds about,
And, letting pass a little day or two,
Threw, even over that integrity,
Another wrappage, namely one thick veil
That hid her, matron-wise, from head to foot,
And, by the hand holding a girl veiled too,
Stood, one dim end of a December day,
In Saint Lorenzo on the altar-step—   450
Just where she lies now and that girl will lie—
Only with fifty candles' company
Now—in the place of the poor winking one
Which saw,—doors shut and sacristan made sure,—
A priest—perhaps Abate Paolo—wed
Guido clandestinely, irrevocably
To his Pompilia aged thirteen years
And five months,—witness the church register,—
Pompilia, (thus become Count Guido's wife

Clandestinely, irrevocably his,)   460
Who all the while had borne, from first to last,
As brisk a part i' the bargain, as yon lamb,
Brought forth from basket and set out for sale,
Bears while they chaffer, wary market-man
And voluble housewife, o'er it,—each in turn
Patting the curly calm inconscious head,
With the shambles ready round the corner there,
When the talk 's talked out and a bargain struck.

Transfer complete, why, Pietro was apprised.
Violante sobbed the sobs and prayed the prayers
And said the serpent tempted so she fell,   471
Till Pietro had to clear his brow apace
And make the best of matters : wrath at first,—
How else ? pacification presently,
Why not ?—could flesh withstand the impurpled one,
The very Cardinal, Paolo's patron-friend ?
Who, justifiably surnamed ' a hinge ',
Knew where the mollifying oil should drop
To cure the creak o' the valve,—considerate
For frailty, patient in a naughty world,   480
He even volunteered to supervise
The rough draught of those marriage-articles
Signed in a hurry by Pietro, since revoked :
Trust 's politic, suspicion does the harm,
There is but one way to brow-beat this world,
Dumb-founder doubt, and repay scorn in kind,—
To go on trusting, namely, till faith move
Mountains.

                    And faith here made the mountains move.
Why, friends whose zeal cried ' Caution ere too late !'—
Bade ' Pause ere jump, with both feet joined, on
        slough ! '—   491
Counselled ' If rashness then, now temperance ! '—
Heard for their pains that Pietro had closed eyes,
Jumped and was in the middle of the mire,
Money and all, just what should sink a man.
By the mere marriage, Guido gained forthwith
Dowry, his wife's right ; no rescinding there :
But Pietro, why must he needs ratify
One gift Violante gave, pay down one doit
Promised in first fool's-flurry ? Grasp the bag   500

Lest the son 's service flag,—is reason and rhyme,
Above all when the son 's a son-in-law.
Words to the wind ! The parents cast their lot
Into the lap o' the daughter : and the son
Now with a right to lie there, took what fell,
Pietro's whole having and holding, house and field,
Goods, chattels and effects, his worldly worth
Present and in perspective, all renounced
In favour of Guido.   As for the usufruct—
The interest now, the principal anon,   510
Would Guido please to wait, at Pietro's death :
Till when, he must support the couple's charge,
Bear with them, housemates, pensionaries, pawned
To an alien for fulfilment of their pact.
Guido should at discretion deal them orts,
Bread-bounty in Arezzo the strange place,—
They who had lived deliciously and rolled
Rome's choicest comfit 'neath the tongue before.
Into this quag, ' jump ' bade the Cardinal !
And neck-deep in a minute there flounced they.   520

But they touched bottom at Arezzo : there—
Four months' experience of how craft and greed
Quickened by penury and pretentious hate
Of plain truth, brutify and bestialize,—
Four months' taste of apportioned insolence,
Cruelty graduated, dose by dose
Of ruffianism dealt out at bed and board,
And lo, the work was done, success clapped hands.
The starved, stripped, beaten brace of stupid dupes
Broke at last in their desperation loose,   530
Fled away for their lives, and lucky so ;
Found their account in casting coat afar
And bearing off a shred of skin at least :
Left Guido lord o' the prey, as the lion is,
And, careless what came after, carried their wrongs
To Rome,—I nothing doubt, with such remorse
As folly feels, since pain can make it wise,
But crime, past wisdom, which is innocence,
Needs not be plagued with till a later day.

Pietro went back to beg from door to door,   540
In hope that memory not quite extinct
Of cheery days and festive nights would move

Friends and acquaintance—after the natural laugh,
And tributary ' Just as we foretold—'
To show some bowels, give the dregs o' the cup,
Scraps of the trencher, to their host that was,
Or let him share the mat with the mastiff, he
Who lived large and kept open house so long.
Not so Violante : ever a-head i' the march,
Quick at the bye-road and the cut-across,   550
She went first to the best adviser, God—
Whose finger unmistakably was felt
In all this retribution of the past.
Here was the prize of sin, luck of a lie !
But here too was the Holy Year would help,
Bound to rid sinners of sin vulgar, sin
Abnormal, sin prodigious, up to sin
Impossible and supposed for Jubilee' sake :
To lift the leadenest of lies, let soar
The soul unhampered by a feather-weight.   560
' I will ' said she ' go burn out this bad hole
' That breeds the scorpion, baulk the plague at least
' Its hope of further creeping progeny :
' I will confess my fault, be punished, yes,
' But pardoned too : Saint Peter pays for all.'

So, with the crowd she mixed, made for the dome,
Through the great door new-broken for the nonce
Marched, muffled more than ever matron-wise,
Up the left nave to the formidable throne,
Fell into file with this the poisoner   570
And that the parricide, and reached in turn
The poor repugnant Penitentiary
Set at this gully-hole o' the world's discharge
To help the frightfullest of filth have vent,
And then knelt down and whispered in his ear
How she had bought Pompilia, palmed the babe
On Pietro, passed the girl off as their child
To Guido, and defrauded of his due
This one and that one,—more than she could name,
Until her solid piece of wickedness   580
Happened to split and spread woe far and wide :
Contritely now she brought the case for cure.

Replied the throne—' Ere God forgive the guilt,
' Make man some restitution ! Do your part !

' The owners of your husband's heritage,
' Barred thence by this pretended birth and heir,—
' Tell them, the bar came so, is broken so,
' Theirs be the due reversion as before !
' Your husband who, no partner in the guilt,
' Suffers the penalty, led blindfold thus   590
' By love of what he thought his flesh and blood
' To alienate his all in her behalf,—
' Tell him too such contract is null and void !
' Last, he who personates your son-in-law,
' Who with sealed eyes and stopped ears, tame and
      mute,
' Took at your hand that bastard of a whore
' You called your daughter and he calls his wife,—
' Tell him, and bear the anger which is just !
' Then, penance so performed, may pardon be ! '

Who could gainsay this just and right award ?   600
Nobody in the world : but, out o' the world,
Who knows ?—might timid intervention be
From any makeshift of an angel-guide,
Substitute for celestial guardianship,
Pretending to take care of the girl's self :
' Woman, confessing crime is healthy work,
' And telling truth relieves a liar like you,
' But what of her my unconsidered charge ?
' No thought of, while this good befalls yourself,
' What in the way of harm may find out her ? '   610
No least thought, I assure you : truth being truth,
Tell it and shame the devil !
                          Said and done :
Home went Violante and disbosomed all :
And Pietro who, six months before, had borne
Word after word of such a piece of news
Like so much cold steel inched through his breast-
      blade,
Now at its entry gave a leap for joy,
As who—what did I say of one in a quag ?—
Should catch a hand from heaven and spring thereby
Out of the mud, on ten toes stand once more.   621
' What ? All that used to be, may be again ?
' My money mine again, my house, my land,
' My chairs and tables, all mine evermore ?
' What, the girl's dowry never was the girl's,

'And, unpaid yet, is never now to pay ?
'Then the girl's self, my pale Pompilia child
'That used to be my own with her great eyes—
'He who drove us forth, why should he keep her
'When proved as very a pauper as himself ?   630
'Will she come back, with nothing changed at all,
'And laugh " But how you dreamed uneasily !
'" I saw the great drops stand here on your brow—
'" Did I do wrong to wake you with a kiss ? "
'No, indeed, darling !   No, for wide awake
'I see another outburst of surprise :
'The lout-lord, bully-beggar, braggart-sneak,
'Who not content with cutting purse, crops ear—
'Assuredly it shall be salve to mine
'When this great news red-letters him, the rogue !
'Ay, let him taste the teeth o' the trap, this fox,   641
'Give us our lamb back, golden fleece and all,
'Let her creep in and warm our breasts again !
'What care for the past ?—we three are our old selves,
'Who know now what the outside world is worth.'
And so, he carried case before the courts ;
And there Violante, blushing to the bone,
Made public declaration of her fault,
Renounced her motherhood, and prayed the law
To interpose, frustrate of its effect   650
Her folly, and redress the injury done.

Whereof was the disastrous consequence,
That though indisputably clear the case
(For thirteen years are not so large a lapse,
And still six witnesses survived in Rome
To prove the truth o' the tale)—yet, patent wrong
Seemed Guido's ; the first cheat had chanced on him :
Here was the pity that, deciding right,
Those who began the wrong would gain the good.
Guido pronounced the story one long lie   660
Lied to do robbery and take revenge :
Or say it were no lie at all but truth,
Then, it both robbed the right heirs and shamed him
Without revenge to humanize the deed :
What had he done when first they shamed him thus ?
But that were too fantastic : losels they,
And leasing this world's-wonder of a lie,
They lied to blot him though it brand themselves.

So answered Guido through the Abate's mouth.
Wherefore the court, its customary way,   670
Inclined to the middle course the sage affect—
They held the child to be a changeling,—good :
But, lest the husband got no good thereby,
They willed the dowry, though not hers at all,
Should yet be his, if not by right then grace—
Part-payment for the plain injustice done.
But then, that other contract, Pietro's work,
Renunciation of his own estate,
That must be cancelled—give him back his goods,
He was no party to the cheat at least !   680
So ran the judgment :—whence a prompt appeal
On both sides, seeing right is absolute.
Cried Pietro ' Is Pompilia not my child ?
' Why give her my child's dowry ? '—' Have I right
' To the dowry, why not to the rest as well ? '
Cried Guido, or cried Paolo in his name :
Till law said ' Reinvestigate the case ! '
And so the matter pends, unto this day.

Hence new disaster—that no outlet seemed ;
Whatever the fortune of the battle-field,   690
No path whereby the fatal man might march
Victorious, wreath on head and spoils in hand,
And back turned full upon the baffled foe,—
Nor cranny whence, desperate and disgraced,
Stripped to the skin, he might be fain to crawl
Worm-like, and so away with his defeat
To other fortune and the novel prey.
No, he was pinned to the place there, left alone
With his immense hate and, the solitary
Subject to satisfy that hate, his wife.   700
' Cast her off ?   Turn her naked out of doors ?
' Easily said !   But still the action pends,
' Still dowry, principal and interest,
' Pietro's possessions, all I bargained for,—
' Any good day, be but my friends alert,
' May give them me if she continue mine.
' Yet, keep her ?   Keep the puppet of my foes—
' Her voice that lisps me back their curse—her eye
' They lend their leer of triumph to—her lip
' I touch and taste their very filth upon ? '   710

In short, he also took the middle course
Rome taught him—did at last excogitate
How he might keep the good and leave the bad
Twined in revenge, yet extricable,—nay
Make the very hate's eruption, very rush
Of the unpent sluice of cruelty relieve
His heart first, then go fertilize his field.
What if the girl-wife, tortured with due care,
Should take, as though spontaneously, the road
It were impolitic to thrust her on ?   720
If, goaded, she broke out in full revolt,
Followed her parents i' the face o' the world,
Branded as runaway not castaway,
Self-sentenced and self-punished in the act ?
So should the loathed form and detested face
Launch themselves into hell and there be lost
While he looked o'er the brink with folded arms ;
So should the heaped-up shames go shuddering back
O' the head o' the heapers, Pietro and his wife,
And bury in the breakage three at once :   730
While Guido, left free, no one right renounced,
Gain present, gain prospective, all the gain,
None of the wife except her rights absorbed,
Should ask law what it was law paused about—
If law were dubious still whose word to take,
The husband's—dignified and derelict,
Or the wife's—the . . what I tell you.   It should be.

Guido's first step was to take pen, indite
A letter to the Abate,—not his own,
His wife's,—she should re-write, sign, seal and send.
She liberally told the household-news,   741
Rejoiced her vile progenitors were fled,
Revealed their malice—how they even laid
A last injunction on her, when they fled,
That she should forthwith find a paramour,
Complot with him to gather spoil enough
Then burn the house down,—taking previous care
To poison all its inmates overnight,—
And so companioned, so provisioned too,
Follow to Rome and all join fortunes gay.   750
This letter, traced in pencil-characters,
Guido as easily got retraced in ink
By his wife's pen, guided from end to end,

As it had been just so much Hebrew, Sir :
For why ? That wife could broider, sing perhaps,
Pray certainly, but no more read than write
This letter ' which yet write she must,' he said
' Being half courtesy and compliment,
' Half sisterliness : take the thing on trust ! '
She had as readily re-traced the words   760
Of her own death-warrant,—in some sort 't was so.
This letter the Abate in due course
Communicated to such curious souls
In Rome as needs must pry into the cause
Of quarrel, why the Comparini fled
The Franceschini, whence the grievance grew,
What the hubbub meant : ' Nay,—see the wife's own
    word,
' Authentic answer ! Tell detractors too
' There 's a plan formed, a programme figured here
' —Pray God no after-practice put to proof,   770
' This letter cast no light upon, one day ! '

So much for what should work in Rome,—back now
To Arezzo, go on with the project there,
Forward the next step with as bold a foot,
And plague Pompilia to the height, you see !
Accordingly did Guido set himself
To worry up and down, across, around,
The woman, hemmed in by her household-bars,—
Chased her about the coop of daily life,
Having first stopped each outlet thence save one
Which, like bird with a ferret in her haunt,   781
She needs must seize as sole way of escape
Though there was tied and twittering a decoy
To seem as if it tempted,—just the plume
O' the popinjay, and not a respite there
From tooth and claw of something in the dark,—
Giuseppe Caponsacchi.
                Now begins
The tenebrific passage of the tale :
How hold a light, display the cavern's gorge ?   790
How, in this phase of the affair, show truth ?
Here is the dying wife who smiles and says
' So it was,—so it was not,—how it was,
' I never knew nor ever care to know—'
Till they all weep, physician, man of law,

Even that poor old bit of battered brass
Beaten out of all shape by the world's sins,
Common utensil of the lazar-house—
Confessor Celestino groans ' 'T is truth,
' All truth and only truth : there 's something else,
' Some presence in the room beside us all,   801
' Something that every lie expires before :
' No question she was pure from first to last.'
So far is well and helps us to believe :
But beyond, she the helpless, simple-sweet
Or silly-sooth, unskilled to break one blow
At her good fame by putting finger forth,—
How can she render service to the truth ?
The bird says ' So I fluttered where a springe   809
' Caught me : the springe did not contrive itself,
' That I know : who contrived it, God forgive ! '
But we, who hear no voice and have dry eyes,
Must ask,—we cannot else, absolving her,—
How of the part played by that same decoy
I' the catching, caging ? Was himself caught first ?
We deal here with no innocent at least,
No witless victim,—he 's a man of the age
And a priest beside,—persuade the mocking world
Mere charity boiled over in this sort !
He whose own safety too,—(the Pope 's apprised—
Good-natured with the secular offence,   821
The Pope looks grave on priesthood in a scrape)
Our priest's own safety therefore, may-be life,
Hangs on the issue ! You will find it hard.
Guido is here to meet you with fixed foot,
Stiff like a statue—' Leave what went before !
' My wife fled i' the company of a priest,
' Spent two days and two nights alone with him :
' Leave what came after ! ' He is hard to throw.
Moreover priests are merely flesh and blood ;   830
When we get weakness, and no guilt beside,
We have no such great ill-fortune : finding grey,
We gladly call that white which might be black,
Too used to the double-dye. So, if the priest
Moved by Pompilia's youth and beauty, gave
Way to the natural weakness. . . . Anyhow
Here be facts, charactery ; what they spell
Determine, and thence pick what sense you may !
There was a certain young bold handsome priest

Popular in the city, far and wide   840
Famed, for Arezzo 's but a little place,
As the best of good companions, gay and grave
At the decent minute ; settled in his stall,
Or sideling, lute on lap, by lady's couch,
Ever the courtly Canon : see in such
A star shall climb apace and culminate,
Have its due handbreadth of the heaven at Rome,
Though meanwhile pausing on Arezzo's edge,
As modest candle 'mid the mountain fog,
To rub off redness and rusticity   850
Ere it sweep chastened, gain the silver-sphere.
Whether through Guido's absence or what else,
This Caponsacchi, favourite of the town,
Was yet no friend of his nor free o' the house,
Though both moved in the regular magnates' march—
Each must observe the other's tread and halt
At church, saloon, theatre, house of play.
Who could help noticing the husband's slouch,
The black of his brow—or miss the news that buzzed
Of how the little solitary wife   860
Wept and looked out of window all day long ?
What need of minute search into such springs
As start men, set o' the move ?—machinery
Old as earth, obvious as the noonday sun.
Why, take men as they come,—an instance now,—
Of all those who have simply gone to see
Pompilia on her deathbed since four days,
Half at the least are, call it how you please,
In love with her—I don't except the priests
Nor even the old confessor whose eyes run   870
Over at what he styles his sister's voice
Who died so early and weaned him from the world.
Well, had they viewed her ere the paleness pushed
The last o' the red o' the rose away, while yet
Some hand, adventurous 'twixt the wind and her,
Might let the life run back and raise the flower
Rich with reward up to the guardian's face,—
Would they have kept that hand employed the
     same
At fumbling on with prayer-book pages ? No !
Men are men : why then need I say one word   880
More than this, that our man the Canon here
Saw, pitied, loved Pompilia ?

This is why ;
This startling why : that Caponsacchi's self—
Whom foes and friends alike avouch, for good
Or ill, a man of truth whate'er betide,
Intrepid altogether, reckless too
How his own fame and fortune, tossed to the winds,
Suffer by any turn the adventure take,   889
Nay, more—not thrusting, like a badge to hide,
'Twixt shirt and skin a joy which shown is shame—
But flirting flag-like i' the face o' the world
This tell-tale kerchief, this conspicuous love
For the lady,—oh, called innocent love, I know !
Only, such scarlet fiery innocence
As most men would try muffle up in shade,—
—'Tis strange then that this else abashless mouth
Should yet maintain, for truth's sake which is God's,
That it was not he made the first advance,
That, even ere word had passed between the two,
Pompilia penned him letters, passionate prayers,
If not love, then so simulating love   902
That he, no novice to the taste of thyme,
Turned from such over-luscious honey-clot
At end o' the flower, and would not lend his lip
Till . . but the tale here frankly outsoars faith :
There must be falsehood somewhere. For her part,
Pompilia quietly constantly avers
She never penned a letter in her life
Nor to the Canon nor any other man,   910
Being incompetent to write and read :
Nor had she ever uttered word to him, nor he
To her till that same evening when they met,
She on her window-terrace, he beneath
I' the public street, as was their fateful chance,
And she adjured him in the name of God
Find out and bring to pass where, when and how
Escape with him to Rome might be contrived.
Means found, plan laid and time fixed, she avers,
And heart assured to heart in loyalty,   920
All at an impulse ! All extemporized
As in romance-books ! Is that credible ?
Well, yes : as she avers this with calm mouth
Dying, I do think ' Credible ! ' you'd cry—
Did not the priest's voice come to break the spell :
They questioned him apart, as the custom is,

When first the matter made a noise at Rome,
And he, calm, constant then as she is now,
For truth's sake did assert and reassert
Those letters called him to her and he came,   930
—Which damns the story credible otherwise.
Why should this man,—mad to devote himself,
Careless what comes of his own fame, the first,—
Be studious thus to publish and declare
Just what the lightest nature loves to hide,
Nor screen a lady from the byword's laugh
' First spoke the lady, last the cavalier ! '
—I say,—why should the man tell truth just here
When graceful lying meets such ready shrift ?
Or is there a first moment for a priest   940
As for a woman, when invaded shame
Must have its first and last excuse to show ?
Do both contrive love's entry in the mind
Shall look, i' the manner of it, a surprise,
That after, once the flag o' the fort hauled down,
Effrontery may sink drawbridge, open gate,
Welcome and entertain the conqueror ?
Or what do you say to a touch of the devil's worst ?
Can it be that the husband, he who wrote
The letter to his brother I told you of,   950
I' the name of her it meant to criminate,—
What if he wrote those letters to the priest ?
Further the priest says, when it first befell,
This folly o' the letters, that he checked the flow,
Put them back lightly each with its reply.
Here again vexes new discrepancy :
There never reached her eye a word from him ;
He did write but she could not read—she could
Burn what offended wifehood, womanhood,
So did burn : never bade him come to her,   960
Yet when it proved he must come, let him come,
And when he did come though uncalled, she spoke
Prompt by an inspiration : thus it was.
Will you go somewhat back to understand ?

When first, pursuant to his plan, there sprang,
Like an uncaged beast, Guido's cruelty
On the weak shoulders of his wife, she cried
To those whom law appoints resource for such,
The secular guardian—that 's the Governor,   969

And the Archbishop,—that's the spiritual guide,
And prayed them take the claws from out her flesh.
Now, this is ever the ill consequence
Of being noble, poor and difficult,
Ungainly, yet too great to disregard,—
That the born peers and friends hereditary
Though disinclined to help from their own store
The opprobrious wight, put penny in his poke
From purse of theirs or leave the door ajar
When he goes wistful by at dinner-time,—
Yet, if his needs conduct him where they sit   980
Smugly in office, judge this, bishop that,
Dispensers of the shine and shade o' the place—
And if, the friend's door shut and purse undrawn,
The potentate may find the office-hall
Do as good service at no cost—give help
By-the-bye, pay up traditional dues at once
Just through a feather-weight too much i' the scale,
A finger-tip forgot at the balance-tongue,—
Why, only churls refuse, or Molinists.
Thus when, in the first roughness of surprise   990
At Guido's wolf-face whence the sheepskin fell,
The frightened couple, all bewilderment,
Rushed to the Governor,—who else rights wrong ?
Told him their tale of wrong and craved redress—
Why, then the Governor woke up to the fact
That Guido was a friend of old, poor Count !—
So, promptly paid his tribute, promised the pair,
Wholesome chastisement should soon cure their
    qualms
Next time they came and prated and told lies :
Which stopped all prating, sent them dumb to Rome.
Well, now it was Pompilia's turn to try :   1001
The troubles pressing on her, as I said,
Three times she rushed, maddened by misery,
To the other mighty man, sobbed out her prayer
At footstool of the Archbishop—fast the friend
Of her husband also ! Oh, good friends of yore !
So, the Archbishop, not to be outdone
By the Governor, break custom more than he,
Thrice bade the foolish woman stop her tongue,
Unloosed her hands from harassing his gout,   1010
Coached her and carried her to the Count again,
—His old friend should be master in his house,

Rule his wife and correct her faults at need !
Well, driven from post to pillar in this wise,
She, as a last resource, betook herself
To one, should be no family-friend at least,
A simple friar o' the city ; confessed to him,
Then told how fierce temptation of release
By self-dealt death was busy with her soul,   1019
And urged that he put this in words, write plain
For one who could not write, set down her prayer
That Pietro and Violante, parent-like
If somehow not her parents, should for love
Come save her, pluck from out the flame the brand
Themselves had thoughtlessly thrust in so deep
To send gay-coloured sparkles up and cheer
Their seat at the chimney-corner. The good friar
Promised as much at the moment ; but, alack,
Night brings discretion : he was no one's friend,
Yet presently found he could not turn about   1030
Nor take a step i' the case and fail to tread
On someone's toe who either was a friend,
Or a friend's friend, or friend's friend thrice-removed,
And woe to friar by whom offences come !
So, the course being plain,—with a general sigh
At matrimony the profound mistake,—
He threw reluctantly the business up,
Having his other penitents to mind.

If then, all outlets thus secured save one,
At last she took to the open, stood and stared   1040
With her wan face to see where God might wait—
And there found Caponsacchi wait as well
For the precious something at perdition's edge,
He only was predestinate to save,—
And if they recognized in a critical flash
From the zenith, each the other, her need of him,
His need of . . say, a woman to perish for,
The regular way o' the world, yet break no vow,
Do no harm save to himself,—if this were thus ?
How do you say ? It were improbable ;   1050
So is the legend of my patron-saint.

Anyhow, whether, as Guido states the case,
Pompilia,—like a starving wretch i' the street
Who stops and rifles the first passenger

In the great right of an excessive wrong,—
Did somehow call this stranger and he came,—
Or whether the strange sudden interview
Blazed as when star and star must needs go close
Till each hurts each and there is loss in heaven—
Whatever way in this strange world it was,—   1060
Pompilia and Caponsacchi met, in fine,
She at her window, he i' the street beneath,
And understood each other at first look.

All was determined and performed at once.
And on a certain April evening, late
I' the month, this girl of sixteen, bride and wife
Three years and over,—she who hitherto
Had never taken twenty steps in Rome
Beyond the church, pinned to her mother's gown,
Nor, in Arezzo, knew her way through street   1070
Except what led to the Archbishop's door,—
Such an one rose up in the dark, laid hand
On what came first, clothes and a trinket or two,
Belongings of her own in the old day,—
Stole from the side o' the sleeping spouse—who knows?
Sleeping perhaps, silent for certain,—slid
Ghost-like from great dark room to great dark room,
In through the tapestries and out again
And onward, unembarrassed as a fate,
Descended staircase, gained last door of all,   1080
Sent it wide open at first push of palm,
And there stood, first time, last and only time,
At liberty, alone in the open street,—
Unquestioned, unmolested found herself
At the city gate, by Caponsacchi's side,
Hope there, joy there, life and all good again,
The carriage there, the convoy there, light there
Broadening into a full blaze at Rome
And breaking small what long miles lay between ;
Up she sprang, in he followed, they were safe.   1090

The husband quotes this for incredible,
All of the story from first word to last :
Sees the priest's hand throughout upholding hers,
Traces his foot to the alcove, that night,
Whither and whence blindfold he knew the way,
Proficient in all craft and stealthiness ;

E

And cites for proof a servant, eye that watched
And ear that opened to purse secrets up,
A woman-spy,—suborned to give and take
Letters and tokens, do the work of shame   1100
The more adroitly that herself, who helped
Communion thus between a tainted pair,
Had long since been a leper thick in spot,
A common trull o' the town : she witnessed all,
Helped many meetings, partings, took her wage
And then told Guido the whole matter.   Lies !
The woman's life confutes her word,—her word
Confutes itself : ' Thus, thus and thus I lied.'
' And thus, no question, still you lie,' we say.

' Ay, but at last, e'en have it how you will,   1110
' Whatever the means, whatever the way, explodes
' The consummation '—the accusers shriek :
' Here is the wife avowedly found in flight,
' And the companion of her flight, a priest ;
' She flies her husband, he the church his spouse :
' What is this ? '

                        Wife and priest alike reply
' This is the simple thing it claims to be,
' A course we took for life and honour's sake,
' Very strange, very justifiable.'   1120
She says, ' God put it in my head to fly,
' As when the martin migrates : autumn claps
' Her hands, cries " Winter's coming, will be here
' " Off with you ere the white teeth overtake !
' " Flee ! " So I fled : this friend was the warm day,
' The south wind and whatever favours flight ;
' I took the favour, had the help, how else ?
' And so we did fly rapidly all night,
' All day, all night—a longer night—again,
' And then another day, longest of days,   1130
' And all the while, whether we fled or stopped,
' I scarce know how or why, one thought filled both,
' " Fly and arrive ! " So long as I found strength
' I talked with my companion, told him much,
' Knowing that he knew more, knew me, knew God
' And God's disposal of me,—but the sense
' O' the blessed flight absorbed me in the main,
' And speech became mere talking through a sleep,

' Till at the end of that last longest night
' In a red daybreak, when we reached an inn   1140
' And my companion whispered " Next stage—
      Rome ! "
' Sudden the weak flesh fell like piled-up cards,
' All the frail fabric at a finger's touch,
' And prostrate the poor soul too, and I said
' " But though Count Guido were a furlong off,
' " Just on me, I must stop and rest awhile ! "
' Then something like a white wave o' the sea
' Broke o'er my brain and buried me in sleep
' Blessedly, till it ebbed and left me loose,
' And where was I found but on a strange bed   1150
' In a strange room like hell, roaring with noise,
' Ruddy with flame, and filled with men, in front
' Whom but the man you call my husband, ay—
' Count Guido once more between heaven and me,
' For there my heaven stood, my salvation, yes—
' That Caponsacchi all my heaven of help,
' Helpless himself, held prisoner in the hands
' Of men who looked up in my husband's face
' To take the fate thence he should signify,
' Just as the way was at Arezzo : then,   1160
' Not for my sake but his who had helped me—
' I sprang up, reached him with one bound, and seized
' The sword o' the felon, trembling at his side,
' Fit creature of a coward, unsheathed the thing
' And would have pinned him through the poison-bag
' To the wall and left him there to palpitate,
' As you serve scorpions, but men interposed—
' Disarmed me, gave his life to him again
' That he might take mine and the other lives,
' And he has done so. I submit myself ! '   1170
The priest says—oh, and in the main result
The facts asseverate, he truly says,
As to the very act and deed of him,
However you mistrust the mind o' the man—
The flight was just for flight's sake, no pretext
For aught except to set Pompilia free :
He says ' I cite the husband's self's worst charge
' In proof of my best word for both of us.
' Be it conceded that so many times
' We took our pleasure in his palace : then,   1180
' What need to fly at all ?—or flying no less,

' What need to outrage the lips sick and white
' Of a woman, and bring ruin down beside,
' By halting when Rome lay one stage beyond ? '
So does he vindicate Pompilia's fame,
Confirm her story in all points but one—
This ; that, so fleeing and so breathing forth
Her last strength in the prayer to halt awhile,
She makes confusion of the reddening white
Which was the sunset when her strength gave way,
And the next sunrise and its whitening red   1191
Which she revived in when her husband came :
She mixes both times, morn and eve, in one,
Having lived through a blank of night 'twixt each
Though dead-asleep, unaware as a corpse,
She on the bed above ; her friend below
Watched in the doorway of the inn the while,
Stood i' the red o' the morn, that she mistakes,
In act to rouse and quicken the tardy crew
And hurry out the horses, have the stage   1200
Over, the last league, reach Rome and be safe :
When up came Guido.
                          Guido's tale begins—
How he and his whole household, drunk to death
By some enchanted potion, poppied drugs
Plied by the wife, lay powerless in gross sleep
And left the spoilers unimpeded way,
Could not shake off their poison and pursue,
Till noontide, then made shift to get on horse
And did pursue : which means, he took his time,
Pressed on no more than lingered after, step   1211
By step, just making sure o' the fugitives,
Till at the nick of time, he saw his chance,
Seized it, came up with and surprised the pair.
How he must needs have gnawn lip and gnashed teeth,
Taking successively at tower and town,
Village and roadside, still the same report
' Yes, such a pair arrived an hour ago,
' Sat in the carriage just where your horse stands,
' While we got horses ready,—turned deaf ear   1220
' To all entreaty they would even alight ;
' Counted the minutes and resumed their course.'
Would they indeed escape, arrive at Rome,
Leave no least loop to let damnation through,
And foil him of his captured infamy,

Prize of guilt proved and perfect ? So it seemed :
Till, oh the happy chance, at last stage, Rome
But two short hours off, Castelnuovo reached,
The guardian angel gave reluctant place,
Satan stepped forward with alacrity,   1230
Pompilia's flesh and blood succumbed, perforce
A halt was, and her husband had his will.
Perdue he couched, counted out hour by hour
Till he should spy in the east a signal-streak—
Night had been, morrow was, triumph would be.
Do you see the plan deliciously complete ?
The rush upon the unsuspecting sleep,
The easy execution, the outcry
Over the deed ' Take notice all the world !
' These two dead bodies, locked still in embrace,—
' The man is Caponsacchi and a priest,   1241
' The woman is my wife : they fled me late,
' Thus have I found and you behold them thus,
' And may judge me : do you approve or no ? '

Success did seem not so improbable,
But that already Satan's laugh was heard,
His black back turned on Guido—left i' the lurch
Or rather, baulked of suit and service now,
That he improve on both by one deed more,
Burn up the better at no distant day,   1250
Body and soul one holocaust to hell.
Anyhow, of this natural consequence
Did just the last link of the long chain snap :
For his eruption was o' the priest, alive
And alert, calm, resolute and formidable,
Not the least look of fear in that broad brow—
One not to be disposed of by surprise,
And armed moreover—who had guessed as much ?
Yes, there stood he in secular costume
Complete from head to heel, with sword at side,
He seemed to know the trick of perfectly.   1261
There was no prompt suppression of the man
As he said calmly ' I have saved your wife
' From death ; there was no other way but this ;
' Of what do I defraud you except death ?
' Charge any wrong beyond, I answer it.'
Guido, the valorous, had met his match,
Was forced to demand help instead of fight,

Bid the authorities o' the place lend aid
And make the best of a broken matter so.   1270
They soon obeyed the summons—I suppose,
Apprised and ready, or not far to seek—
Laid hands on Caponsacchi, found in fault,
A priest yet flagrantly accoutred thus,—
Then, to make good Count Guido's further charge,
Proceeded, prisoner made lead the way,
In a crowd, upstairs to the chamber-door
Where wax-white, dead asleep, deep beyond dream,
As the priest laid her, lay Pompilia yet.

And as he mounted step and step with the crowd
How I see Guido taking heart again !   1281
He knew his wife so well and the way of her—
How at the outbreak she would shroud her shame
In hell's heart, would it mercifully yawn—
How, failing that, her forehead to his foot,
She would crouch silent till the great doom fell,
Leave him triumphant with the crowd to see !
Guilt motionless or writhing like a worm ?
No ! Second misadventure, this worm turned,
I told you : would have slain him on the spot   1290
With his own weapon, but they seized her hands :
Leaving her tongue free, as it tolled the knell
Of Guido's hope so lively late.   The past
Took quite another shape now.   She who shrieked
' At least and for ever I am mine and God's,
' Thanks to his liberating angel Death—
' Never again degraded to be yours
' The ignoble noble, the unmanly man,
' The beast below the beast in brutishness ! '—
This was the froward child, ' the restif lamb   1300
' Used to be cherished in his breast,' he groaned—
' Eat from his hand and drink from out his cup,
' The while his fingers pushed their loving way
' Through curl on curl of that soft coat—alas,
' And she all silverly baaed gratitude
' While meditating mischief ! '—and so forth.
He must invent another story now !
The ins and outs o' the rooms were searched : he
          found
Or showed for found the abominable prize—
Love-letters from his wife who cannot write,   1310

Love-letters in reply o' the priest—thank God !—
Who can write and confront his character
With this, and prove the false thing forged throughout :
Spitting whereat, he needs must spatter who
But Guido's self ?—that forged and falsified
One letter called Pompilia's, past dispute :
Then why not these to make sure still more sure ?

So was the case concluded then and there :
Guido preferred his charges in due form,
Called on the law to adjudicate, consigned   1320
The accused ones to the Prefect of the place.
(Oh mouse-birth of that mountain-like revenge !)
And so to his own place betook himself
After the spring that failed,—the wildcat's way.
The captured parties were conveyed to Rome ;
Investigation followed here i' the court—
Soon to review the fruit of its own work,
From then to now being eight months and no more.
Guido kept out of sight and safe at home :
The Abate, brother Paolo, helped most   1330
At words when deeds were out of question, pushed
Nearest the purple, best played deputy,
So, pleaded, Guido's representative
At the court shall soon try Guido's self,—what 's more,
The court that also took—I told you, Sir—
That statement of the couple, how a cheat
Had been i' the birth of the babe, no child of theirs.
That was the prelude ; this, the play's first act :
Whereof we wait what comes, crown, close of all.

Well, the result was something of a shade   1340
On the parties thus accused,—how otherwise ?
Shade, but with shine as unmistakable.
Each had a prompt defence : Pompilia first—
' Earth was made hell to me who did no harm :
' I only could emerge one way from hell
' By catching at the one hand held me, so
' I caught at it and thereby stepped to heaven :
' If that be wrong, do with me what you will ! '
Then Caponsacchi with a grave grand sweep
O' the arm as though his soul warned baseness off—
' If as a man, then much more as a priest   1351
' I hold me bound to help weak innocence :

' If so my worldly reputation burst,
' Being the bubble it is, why, burst it may :
' Blame I can bear though not blameworthiness.
' But use your sense first, see if the miscreant here
' The man who tortured thus the woman, thus
' Have not both laid the trap and fixed the lure
' Over the pit should bury body and soul !
' His facts are lies : his letters are the fact—   1360
' An infiltration flavoured with himself !
' As for the fancies—whether . . . what is it you say ?
' The lady loves me, whether I love her
' In the forbidden sense of your surmise,—
' If, with the midday blaze of truth above,
' The unlidded eye of God awake, aware,
' You needs must pry about and track the course
' Of each stray beam of light may traverse earth,
' To the night's sun and Lucifer himself,
' Do so, at other time, in other place,   1370
' Not now nor here !   Enough that first to last
' I never touched her lip nor she my hand
' Nor either of us thought a thought, much less
' Spoke a word which the Virgin might not hear.
' Be that your question, thus I answer it.'

Then the court had to make its mind up, spoke.
' It is a thorny question, and a tale
' Hard to believe, but not impossible :
' Who can be absolute for either side ?
' A middle course is happily open yet.   1380
' Here has a blot surprised the social blank,—
' Whether through favour, feebleness or fault,
' No matter, leprosy has touched our robe
' And we're unclean and must be purified.
' Here is a wife makes holiday from home,
' A priest caught playing truant to his church,
' In masquerade moreover : both allege
' Enough excuse to stop our lifted scourge
' Which else would heavily fall. On the other hand,
' Here is a husband, ay and man of mark,   1390
' Who comes complaining here, demands redress
' As if he were the pattern of desert—
' The while those plaguy allegations frown,
' Forbid we grant him the redress he seeks.
' To all men be our moderation known !

Amato Idolo mio.

Sento le cose, che vi sono occorse, io non l'hò per male, mentre lei dice, che non si puol fare dormire mia Madre, mentre stà male, e non beue vino, e perciò non possa dormire. Puol essere, che in questi giorni guarisca, pure glie lo farrò auuisato, &c.

Fedele Amante
Amarilli.

Adorato, riuerito, amato mio Core.

Mi confondo in tante lodi &c. mi scriua più spesso, che puole. Circa il Dottore, lei m'offonde in dirmi, che io tornerò ad amar lui; Vi dico, che se nascesse al Mondo vn Sole, non hò Cuore per altra Piaga; mà chi mal fà, mal pensa &c. In quanto à quello, che vuol sapere del *Vino*, vi dico, che è rosso per hora: mà più in quà non sò, come sarà; mà ve lo farò auuisato, mandandoui mille, e mille, e mille, e millioni di baci, resto.

Questa sera venite ad vn' hora di notte, che vi voglio parlare, e tossite quando sete sotto la finestra.

Amarilli.

La Sgrana perche non poteua dire, come dite quì, che era di latte, che lei è nera più di mè, se fussi voi vi potria dire Auorio, come vi chiamo Io; Auertite, che la sera non sia il Geloso, e non io, però io tossirò, se non sentite tossire non vi mouete. Vi faccio sapere, che il Sig. Guido và fuora, ci starà più giorni; Però la prego venire la sera quasi ad vn hora di notte, e come sete sotto la fenestra, tossite, e fermateui vn poco, acciò io non sbagli. Lui và fuori Lunedì mattina &c.

Carissimo, meritissimo mio Amore, mio Bene.

Rendo infinite gratie della Rosalinda &c. Vorrei sapere, che cenni mi fece per la via del Poggio &c. e non perche io voglia far proua del vostro Amore, che sò molto bene, che sete costante quanto mè, e però io non voglio far queste proue &c. siche voi non potete dire, che io non vi voglia più bene, *perche tutto quello, che voleuo al Signor Guido è volto à voi, che lo meritate.*

Amarilli.

Ado-

THE FORGED ASSIGNATION

' Rewarding none while compensating each,
' Hurting all round though harming nobody,
' Husband, wife, priest, scot-free not one shall 'scape,
' Yet priest, wife, husband, boast the unbroken head
' From application of our excellent oil :   1400
' So that, whatever be the fact, in fine,
' It makes no miss of justice in a sort.
' First, let the husband stomach as he may,
' His wife shall neither be returned him, no—
' Nor branded, whipped and caged, but just consigned
' To a convent and the quietude she craves ;
' So is he rid of his domestic plague :
· What better thing can happen to a man ?
' Next, let the priest retire—unshent, unshamed,
' Unpunished as for perpetrating crime,   1410
' But relegated (not imprisoned, Sirs !)
' Sent for three years to clarify his youth
' At Civita, a rest by the way to Rome :
' There let his life skim off its last of lees
' Nor keep this dubious colour.   Judged the cause :
' All parties may retire, content, we hope.'
That 's Rome's way, the traditional road of law ;
Whither it leads is what remains to tell.

The priest went to his relegation-place,
The wife to her convent, brother Paolo   1420
To the arms of brother Guido with the news
And this beside—his charge was countercharged ;
The Comparini, his old brace of hates,
Were breathed and vigilant and venomous now—
Had shot a second bolt where the first stuck,
And followed up the pending dowry-suit
By a procedure should release the wife
From so much of the marriage-bond as barred
Escape when Guido turned the screw too much
On his wife's flesh and blood, as husband may.   1430
No more defence, she turned and made attack,
Claimed now divorce from bed and board, in short :
Pleaded such subtle strokes of cruelty,
Such slow sure siege laid to her body and soul,
As, proved,—and proofs seemed coming thick and
          fast,—
Would gain both freedom and the dowry back
Even should the first suit leave them in his grasp

So urged the Comparini for the wife.
Guido had gained not one of the good things
He grasped at by his creditable plan   1440
O' the flight and following and the rest : the suit
That smouldered late was fanned to fury new,
This adjunct came to help with fiercer fire,
While he had got himself a quite new plague—
Found the world's face an universal grin
At this last best of the Hundred Merry Tales
Of how a young and spritely clerk devised
To carry off a spouse that moped too much,
And cured her of the vapours in a trice :
And how the husband, playing Vulcan's part,   1450
Told by the Sun, started in hot pursuit
To catch the lovers, and came halting up,
Cast his net and then called the Gods to see
The convicts in their rosy impudence—
Whereat said Mercury ' Would that I were Mars ! '
Oh it was rare, and naughty all the same !
Brief, the wife's courage and cunning,—the priest's
    show
Of chivalry and adroitness,—last not least,
The husband—how he ne'er showed teeth at all,
Whose bark had promised biting ; but just sneaked
Back to his kennel, tail 'twixt legs, as 't were,— 1461
All this was hard to gulp down and digest.
So pays the devil his liegeman, brass for gold.
But this was at Arezzo : here in Rome
Brave Paolo bore up against it all—
Battled it out, nor wanting to himself
Nor Guido nor the House whose weight he bore
Pillar-like, not by force of arm but brain.
He knew his Rome, what wheels we set to work ;
Plied influential folk, pressed to the ear   1470
Of the efficacious purple, pushed his way
To the old Pope's self,—past decency indeed,—
Praying him take the matter in his hands
Out of the regular court's incompetence ;
But times are changed and nephews out of date
And favouritism unfashionable : the Pope
Said ' Render Cæsar what is Cæsar's due ! '
As for the Comparini's counter-plea,
He met that by a counter-plea again,
Made Guido claim divorce—with help so far   1480

By the trial's issue : for, why punishment
However slight unless for guiltiness
However slender ?—and a molehill serves
Much as a mountain of offence this way.
So was he gathering strength on every side
And growing more and more to menace—when
All of a terrible moment came the blow
That beat down Paolo's fence, ended the play
O' the foil and brought Mannaia on the stage. —1489

Five months had passed now since Pompilia's flight,
Months spent in peace among the Convert nuns :
This,—being, as it seemed, for Guido's sake
Solely, what pride might call imprisonment
And quote as something gained, to friends at home,—
This naturally was at Guido's charge :
Grudge it he might, but penitential fare,
Prayers, preachings, who but he defrayed the cost ?
So, Paolo dropped, as proxy, doit by doit
Like heart's blood, till—what 's here ? What notice
    comes ?
The Convent's self makes application bland   1500
That, since Pompilia's health is fast o' the wane,
She may have leave to go combine her cure
Of soul with cure of body, mend her mind
Together with her thin arms and sunk eyes
That want fresh air outside the convent-wall,
Say in a friendly house,—and which so fit
As a certain villa in the Pauline way,
That happens to hold Pietro and his wife,
The natural guardians ?   ' Oh, and shift the care
' You shift the cost, too ; Pietro pays in turn,   1510
' And lightens Guido of a load !   And then,
' Villa or convent, two names for one thing,
' Always the sojourn means imprisonment,
' *Domum pro carcere*—nowise we relax,
' Nothing abate : how answers Paolo ? '
                         You,
What would you answer ?   All so smooth and fair,
Even Paul's astuteness sniffed no harm i' the world.
He authorized the transfer, saw it made
And, two months after, reaped the fruit of the same,
Having to sit down, rack his brain and find   1521
What phrase should serve him best to notify

Our Guido that by happy providence
A son and heir, a babe was born to him
I' the villa,—go tell sympathizing friends!
Yes, such had been Pompilia's privilege:
She, when she fled, was one month gone with child,
Known to herself or unknown, either way
Availing to explain (say men of art)
The strange and passionate precipitance   1530
Of maiden startled into motherhood
Which changes body and soul by nature's law.
So when the she-dove breeds, strange yearnings come
For the unknown shelter by undreamed-of shores,
And there is born a blood-pulse in her heart
To fight if needs be, though with flap of wing,
For the wool-flock or the fur-tuft, though a hawk
Contest the prize,—wherefore, she knows not yet.
Anyhow, thus to Guido came the news.
' I shall have quitted Rome ere you arrive   1540
' To take the one step left,'—wrote Paolo.
Then did the winch o' the winepress of all hate,
Vanity, disappointment, grudge and greed,
Take the last turn that screws out pure revenge
With a bright bubble at the brim beside—
By an heir's birth he was assured at once
O' the main prize, all the money in dispute:
Pompilia's dowry might revert to her
Or stay with him as law's caprice should point,—
But now—now—what was Pietro's shall be hers,
What was hers shall remain her own,—if hers,   1551
Why then,—oh, not her husband's but—her heir's!
That heir being his too, all grew his at last
By this road or by that road, since they join.
Before, why, push he Pietro out o' the world,—
The current of the money stopped, you see,
Pompilia being proved no Pietro's child:
Or let it be Pompilia's life he quenched,
Again the current of the money stopped,—
Guido debarred his rights as husband soon,   1560
So the new process threatened ;—now, the chance,
Now, the resplendent minute! Clear the earth,
Cleanse the house, let the three but disappear
A child remains, depositary of all,
That Guido may enjoy his own again!
Repair all losses by a master-stroke,

Wipe out the past, all done and left undone,
Swell the good present to best evermore,
Die into new life, which let blood baptize !

So, i' the blue of a sudden sulphur-blaze,   1570
And why there was one step to take at Rome,
And why he should not meet with Paolo there,
He saw—the ins and outs to the heart of hell—
And took the straight line thither swift and sure.
He rushed to Vittiano, found four sons o' the soil,
Brutes of his breeding, with one spark i' the clod
That served for a soul, the looking up to him
Or aught called Franceschini as life, death,
Heaven, hell,—lord paramount, assembled these,
Harangued, equipped, instructed, pressed each clod
With his will's imprint ; then took horse, plied spur,
And so arrived, all five of them, at Rome   1582
On Christmas-Eve, and forthwith found themselves
Installed i' the vacancy and solitude
Left them by Paolo, the considerate man
Who, good as his word, disappeared at once
As if to leave the stage free. A whole week
Did Guido spend in study of his part,
Then played it fearless of a failure. One,
Struck the year's clock whereof the hours are days,
And off was rung o' the little wheels the chime   1591
' Good will on earth and peace to man : ' but, two,
Proceeded the same bell and, evening come,
The dreadful five felt finger-wise their way
Across the town by blind cuts and black turns
To the little lone suburban villa ; knocked—
' Who may be outside ? ' called a well-known voice.
' A friend of Caponsacchi's bringing friends
' A letter.'
              That 's a test, the excusers say :
Ay, and a test conclusive, I return.   1600
What ? Had that name brought touch of guilt or
      taste
Of fear with it, aught to dash the present joy
With memory of the sorrow just at end,—
She, happy in her parents' arms at length
With the new blessing of the two weeks' babe,—
How had that name's announcement moved the wife ?
Or, as the other slanders circulate,

Were Caponsacchi no rare visitant
On nights and days whither safe harbour lured,
What bait had been i' the name to ope the door ?
The promise of a letter ?   Stealthy guests   1611
Have secret watchwords, private entrances :
The man's own self might have been found inside
And all the scheme made frustrate by a word.
No : but since Guido knew, none knew so well,
The man had never since returned to Rome
Nor seen the wife's face more than villa's front,
So, could not be at hand to warn or save,—
For that, he took this sure way to the end.

' Come in,' bade poor Violante cheerfully,   1620
Drawing the door-bolt : that death was the first,
Stabbed through and through.   Pietro, close on her
     heels,
Set up a cry—' Let me confess myself !
' Grant but confession ! '   Cold steel was the grant.
Then came Pompilia's turn.
                         Then they escaped.
The noise o' the slaughter roused the neighbourhood.
They had forgotten just the one thing more
Which saves i' the circumstance, the ticket to-wit
Which puts post-horses at a traveller's use :   1630
So, all on foot, desperate through the dark
Reeled they like drunkards along open road,
Accomplished a prodigious twenty miles
Homeward, and gained Baccano very near,
Stumbled at last, deaf, dumb, blind through the
     feat,
Into a grange and, one dead heap, slept there
Till the pursuers hard upon their trace
Reached them and took them, red from head to
     heel,
And brought them to the prison where they lie.
The couple were laid i' the church two days ago,
And the wife lives yet by miracle.
                         All is told.   1642
You hardly need ask what Count Guido says,
Since something he must say.   ' I own the deed—'
(He cannot choose,—but—) ' I declare the same
' Just and inevitable,—since no way else
' Was left me, but by this of taking life,

‘ To save my honour which is more than life.
‘ I exercised a husband’s rights.’   To which
The answer is as prompt—‘ There was no fault   1650
‘ In any one o’ the three to punish thus :
‘ Neither i’ the wife, who kept all faith to you,
‘ Nor in the parents, whom yourself first duped,
‘ Robbed and maltreated, then turned out of doors.
‘ You wronged and they endured wrong ;   yours the
    fault.
‘ Next, had endurance overpassed the mark
‘ And turned resentment needing remedy,—
‘ Nay, put the absurd impossible case, for once—
‘ You were all blameless of the blame alleged
‘ And they blameworthy where you fix all blame,
‘ Still, why this violation of the law ?   1661
‘ Yourself elected law should take its course,
‘ Avenge wrong, or show vengeance not your right ;
‘ Why, only when the balance in law’s hand
‘ Trembles against you and inclines the way
‘ O’ the other party, do you make protest,
‘ Renounce arbitrament, flying out of court,
‘ And crying “ Honour’s hurt the sword must cure ” ?
‘ Aha, and so i’ the middle of each suit
‘ Trying i’ the courts,—and you had three in play
‘ With an appeal to the Pope’s self beside,—   1671
‘ What, you may chop and change and right your
    wrongs
‘ Leaving the law to lag as she thinks fit ? ’

That were too temptingly commodious, Count !
One would have still a remedy in reserve
Should reach the safest oldest sinner, you see !
One’s honour forsooth ?   Does that take hurt alone
From the extreme outrage ?   I who have no wife,
Being yet sensitive in my degree
As Guido,—must discover hurt elsewhere   1680
Which, half compounded-for in days gone by,
May profitably break out now afresh,
Need cure from my own expeditious hands.
The lie that was, as it were, imputed me
When you objected to my contract’s clause,—
The theft as good as, one may say, alleged,
When you, co-heir in a will, excepted, Sir,
To my administration of effects,

—Aha, do you think law disposed of these ?
My honour 's touched and shall deal death around ¡
Count, that were too commodious, I repeat !   1691
If any law be imperative on us all,
Of all are you the enemy : out with you
From the common light and air and life of man !

IV

TERTIUM QUID

TRUE, Excellency—as his Highness says,
Though she 's not dead yet, she 's as good as stretched
Symmetrical beside the other two ;
Though he 's not judged yet, he 's the same as judged,
So do the facts abound and superabound :
And nothing hinders, now, we lift the case
Out of the shade into the shine, allow
Qualified persons to pronounce at last,
Nay, edge in an authoritative word
Between this rabble's-brabble of dolts and fools   10
Who make up reasonless unreasoning Rome.
' Now for the Trial ! ' they roar : ' the Trial to test
' The truth, weigh husband and weigh wife alike
' I' the scales of law, make one scale kick the beam ! '
Law 's a machine from which, to please the mob,
Truth the divinity must needs descend
And clear things at the play's fifth act—aha !
Hammer into their noddles who was who
And what was what.   I tell the simpletons
' Could law be competent to such a feat   20
' 'T were done already : what begins next week
' Is end o' the Trial, last link of a chain
' Whereof the first was forged three years ago
' When law addressed herself to set wrong right,
' And proved so slow in taking the first step
' That ever some new grievance,—tort, retort,
' On one or the other side,—o'ertook i' the game,
' Retarded sentence, till this deed of death
' Is thrown in, as it were, last bale to boat
' Crammed to the edge with cargo—or passengers ?
' " *Trecentos inseris : ohe, jam satis est !*   31
' " *Huc appelle !* "—passengers, the word must be.'
Long since, the boat was loaded to my eyes.
To hear the rabble and brabble, you 'd call the case
Fused and confused past human finding out.
One calls the square round, t' other the round square—

And pardonably in that first surprise
O' the blood that fell and splashed the diagram :
But now we 've used our eyes to the violent hue
Can't we look through the crimson and trace lines ?
It makes a man despair of history,   41
Eusebius and the established fact—fig's end !
Oh, give the fools their Trial, rattle away
With the leash of lawyers, two on either side—
One barks, one bites,—Masters Arcangeli
And Spreti,—that 's the husband's ultimate hope
Against the Fisc and the other kind of Fisc,
Bound to do barking for the wife : bow—wow !
Why, Excellency, we and his Highness here
Would settle the matter as sufficiently   50
As ever will Advocate This and Fiscal That
And Judge the Other, with even—a word and a wink—
We well know who for ultimate arbiter.
Let us beware o' the basset-table—lest
We jog the elbow of Her Eminence,
Jostle his cards,—he 'll rap you out a . . st !
By the window-seat ! And here 's the Marquis too !
Indulge me but a moment : if I fail
—Favoured with such an audience, understand !—
To set things right, why, class me with the mob   60
As understander of the mind of man !

The mob,—now, that 's just how the error comes !
Bethink you that you have to deal with *plebs,*
The commonalty ; this is an episode
In burgess-life,—why seek to aggrandize,
Idealize, denaturalize the class ?
People talk just as if they had to do
With a noble pair that . . Excellency, your ear !
Stoop to me, Highness,—listen and look yourselves !

This Pietro, this Violante, live their life   70
At Rome in the easy way that 's far from worst
Even for their betters,—themselves love themselves,
Spend their own oil in feeding their own lamp
That their own faces may grow bright thereby.
They get to fifty and over : how 's the lamp ?
Full to the depth o' the wick,—moneys so much ;
And also with a remnant,—so much more
Of moneys,—which there 's no consuming now,

But, when the wick shall moulder out some day,
Failing fresh twist of tow to use up dregs,   80
Will lie a prize for the passer-by,—to-wit
Anyone that can prove himself the heir,
Seeing, the couple are wanting in a child :
Meantime their wick swims in the safe broad bowl
O' the middle rank,—not raised a beacon's height
For wind to ravage, nor swung till lamp graze ground
As watchman's cresset, he pokes here and there,
Going his rounds to probe the ruts i' the road
Or fish the luck o' the puddle.   Pietro's soul
Was satisfied when crony smirked, ' No wine   90
' Like Pietro's, and he drinks it every day ! '
His wife's heart swelled her boddice, joyed its fill
When neighbours turned heads wistfully at church,
Sighed at the load of lace that came to pray.
Well, having got through fifty years of flare,
They burn out so, indulge so their dear selves,
That Pietro finds himself in debt at last,
As he were any lordling of us all :
And, for the dark begins to creep on day,
Creditors grow uneasy, talk aside,   100
Take counsel, then importune all at once.
For if the good fat rosy careless man,
Who has not laid a ducat by, decease—
Let the lamp fall, no heir at hand to catch—
Why, being childless, there 's a spilth i' the street
O' the remnant, there 's a scramble for the dregs
By the stranger : so, they grant him no long day
But come in a body, clamour to be paid.

What 's his resource ?   He asks and straight obtains
The customary largess, dole dealt out   110
To, what we call our ' poor dear shame-faced ones,'
In secret once a month to spare the shame
O' the slothful and the spendthrift,—pauper-saints
The Pope puts meat i' the mouth of, ravens they,
And providence he—just what the mob admires !
That is, instead of putting a prompt foot
On selfish worthless human slugs whose slime
Has failed to lubricate their path in life,
Why, the Pope picks the first ripe fruit that falls
And gracious puts it in the vermin's way.   120
Pietro could never save a dollar ?   Straight

He must be subsidized at our expense :
And for his wife—the harmless household sheep
One ought not to see harassed in her age—
Judge, by the way she bore adversity,
O' the patient nature you ask pity for !
How long, now, would the roughest marketman,
Handling the creatures huddled to the knife,
Harass a mutton ere she made a mouth
Or menaced biting ? Yet the poor sheep here,   130
Violante, the old innocent burgess-wife,
In her first difficulty showed great teeth
Fit to crunch up and swallow a good round crime.
She meditates the tenure of the Trust,
Fidei commissum is the lawyer-phrase,
These funds that only want an heir to take—
Goes o'er the gamut o' the creditor's cry
By semitones from whine to snarl high up
And growl down low, one scale in sundry keys,—
Pauses with a little compunction for the face   140
Of Pietro frustrate of its ancient cheer,—
Never a bottle now for friend at need,—
Comes to a stop on her own frittered lace
And neighbourly condolences thereat,
Then makes her mind up, sees the thing to do :
And so, deliberately snaps house-book clasp,
Posts off to vespers, missal beneath arm,
Passes the proper San Lorenzo by,
Dives down a little lane to the left, is lost
In a labyrinth of dwellings best unnamed,   150
Selects a certain blind one, black at base,
Blinking at top,—the sign of we know what,—
One candle in a casement set to wink
Streetward, do service to no shrine inside,—
Mounts thither by the filthy flight of stairs,
Holding the cord by the wall, to the tip-top,
Gropes for the door i' the dark, ajar of course,
Raps, opens, enters in : up starts a thing
Naked as needs be—' What, you rogue, 't is you ?
' Back,—how can I have taken a farthing yet ?   160
' Mercy on me, poor sinner that I am !
' Here's . . why, I took you for Madonna's self
' With all that sudden swirl of silk i' the place !
' What may your pleasure be, my bonny dame ? '
Your Excellency supplies aught left obscure ?

One of those women that abound in Rome,
Whose needs oblige them eke out one poor trade
By another vile one : her ostensible work
Was washing clothes, out in the open air
At the cistern by Citorio ; but true trade—   170
Whispering to idlers when they stopped and praised
The ankles she let liberally shine
In kneeling at the slab by the fountain-side,
That there was plenty more to criticize
At home, that eve, i' the house where candle blinked
Decorously above, and all was done
I' the holy fear of God and cheap beside.
Violante, now, had seen this woman wash,
Noticed and envied her propitious shape,
Tracked her home to her house-top, noted too,   180
And now was come to tempt her and propose
A bargain far more shameful than the first
Which trafficked her virginity away
For a melon and three pauls at twelve years old.
Five minutes' talk with this poor child of Eve,
Struck was the bargain, business at an end—
' Then, six months hence, that person whom you trust,
' Comes, fetches whatsoever babe it be ;
' I keep the price and secret, you the babe,
' Paying beside for mass to make all straight :   190
' Meantime, I pouch the earnest-money-piece.'

Down stairs again goes fumbling by the rope
Violante, triumphing in a flourish of fire
From her own brain, self-lit by such success,—
Gains church in time for the ' *Magnificat* '
And gives forth ' My reproof is taken away,
' And blessed shall mankind proclaim me now,'
So that the officiating priest turns round
To see who proffers the obstreperous praise :
Then home to Pietro, the enraptured-much   200
But puzzled-more when told the wondrous news—
How orisons and works of charity,
(Beside that pair of pinners and a coif,
Birth-day surprise last Wednesday was five weeks)
Had borne fruit in the Autumn of his life,—
They, or the Orvieto in a double dose.
Anyhow, she must keep house next six months,
Lie on the settle, avoid the three-legged stool,

And, chiefly, not be crossed in wish or whim,
And the result was like to be an heir.   210

Accordingly, when time was come about,
He found himself the sire indeed of this
Francesca Vittoria Pompilia and the rest
O' the names whereby he sealed her his next day.
A crime complete in its way is here, I hope ?
Lies to God, lies to man, every way lies
To nature and civility and the mode :
Flat robbery of the proper heirs thus foiled
O' the due succession,—and, what followed thence,
Robbery of God, through the confessor's ear   220
Debarred the most note-worthy incident
When all else done and undone twelve month through
Was put in evidence at Easter-time.
All other peccadillos !—but this one
To the priest who comes next day to dine with us ?
'T were inexpedient ; decency forbade.

Is so far clear ?   You know Violante now,
Compute her capability of crime
By this authentic instance ?   Black hard cold
Crime like a stone you kick up with your foot   230
I' the middle of a field ?

                        I thought as much.
But now, a question,—how long does it lie,
The bad and barren bit of stuff you kick,
Before encroached on and encompassed round
With minute moss, weed, wild-flower—made alive
By worm, and fly, and foot of the free bird ?
Your Highness,—healthy minds let bygones be,
Leave old crimes to grow young and virtuous-like
I' the sun and air ; so time treats ugly deeds :   240
They take the natural blessing of all change.
There was the joy o' the husband silly-sooth,
The softening of the wife's old wicked heart.
Virtues to right and left, profusely paid
If so they might compensate the saved sin.
And then the sudden existence, dewy-dear,
O' the rose above the dungheap, the pure child
As good as new created, since withdrawn
From the horror of the pre-appointed lot   249

With the unknown father and the mother known
Too well,—some fourteen years of squalid youth,
And then libertinage, disease, the grave—
Hell in life here, hereafter life in hell :
Look at that horror and this soft repose !
Why, moralist, the sin has saved a soul !
Then, even the palpable grievance to the heirs—
'Faith, this was no frank setting hand to throat
And robbing a man, but . . Excellency, by your leave,
How did you get that marvel of a gem,
The sapphire with the Graces grand and Greek ?
The story is, stooping to pick a stone   261
From the pathway through a vineyard—no-man's-
    land—
To pelt a sparrow with, you chanced on this :
Why now, do those five clowns o' the family
O' the vinedresser digest their porridge worse
That not one keeps it in his goatskin pouch
To do flints'-service with the tinder-box ?
Do-n't cheat me, do n't cheat you, do n't cheat a
    friend !
But are you so hard on who jostles just
A stranger with no natural sort of claim   270
To the havings and the holdings (here 's the point)
Unless by misadventure, and defect
Of that which ought to be—nay, which there 's none
Would dare so much as wish to profit by—
Since who dares put in just so many words
' May Pietro fail to have a child, please God !
' So shall his house and goods belong to me,
' The sooner that his heart will pine betimes ' ?
Well then, God do n't please, nor his heart shall pine !
Because he has a child at last, you see,   280
Or selfsame thing as though a child it were,
He thinks, whose sole concern it is to think :
If he accepts it why should you demur ?

Moreover, say that certain sin there seem,
The proper process of unsinning sin
Is to begin well-doing somehow else.
Pietro,—remember, with no sin at all
I' the substitution,—why, this gift of God
Flung in his lap from over Paradise
Steadied him in a moment, set him straight   290

On the good path he had been straying from.
Henceforward no more wilfulness and waste,
Cuppings, carousings,—these a sponge wiped out.
All sort of self-denial was easy now
For the child's sake, the chatelaine to be,
Who must want much and might want who knows
    what ?
And so, the debts were paid, habits reformed,
Expense curtailed, the dowry set to grow.
As for the wife,—I said, hers the whole sin :   299
So, hers the exemplary penance. 'T was a text
Whereon folk preached and praised, the district
    through :
' Oh, make us happy and you make us good !
' It all comes of God giving her a child :
' Such graces follow God's best earthly gift ! '

Here you put by my guard, pass to my heart
By the home-thrust—' There 's a lie at base of all.'
Why, thou exact Prince, is it a pearl or no,
Yon globe upon the Principessa's neck ?
That great round glory of pellucid stuff,
A fish secreted round a grain of grit !   310
Do you call it worthless for the worthless core ?
(She do n't, who well knows what she changed for it !)
So, to our brace of burgesses again !
You see so far i' the story, who was right,
Who wrong, who neither, do n't you ? What, you
    do n't ?
Eh ? Well, admit there 's somewhat dark i' the case,
Let 's on—the rest shall clear, I promise you.
Leap over a dozen years : you find, these passed,
An old good easy creditable sire,
A careful housewife's beaming bustling face,   320
Both wrapped up in the love of their one child,
The strange tall pale beautiful creature grown
Lily-like out o' the cleft i' the sun-smit rock
To bow its white miraculous birth of buds
I' the way of wandering Joseph and his spouse,—
So painters fancy : here it was a fact.
And this their lily,—could they but transplant
And set in vase to stand by Solomon's porch
'Twixt lion and lion !—this Pompilia of theirs,
Could they see worthily married, well bestowed   330

In house and home ! And why despair of this
With Rome to choose from, save the topmost rank ?
Themselves would help the choice with heart and soul,
Throw their late savings in a common heap
Should go with the dowry, to be followed in time
By the heritage legitimately hers :
And when such paragon was found and fixed,
Why, they might chant their ' *Nunc dimittis* ' straight.

Indeed the prize was simply full to a fault ;
Exorbitant for the suitor they should seek,　　　340
And social class to choose among, these cits.
Yet there 's a latitude : exceptional white
Amid the general brown o' the species, lurks
A burgess nearly an aristocrat,
Legitimately in reach : look out for him !
What banker, merchant, has seen better days,
What second-rate painter a-pushing up,
Poet a-slipping down, shall bid the best
For this young beauty with the thumping purse ?
Alack, had it been but one of such as these　　　350
So like the real thing they may pass for it,
All had gone well ! Unluckily fate must needs
It proved to be the impossible thing itself ;
The truth and not the sham : hence ruin to them all.

For, Guido Franceschini was the head
Of an old family in Arezzo, old
To that degree they could afford be poor
Better than most : the case is common too.
Out of the vast door 'scutcheoned overhead,
Creeps out a serving-man on Saturdays　　　360
To cater for the week,—turns up anon
I' the market, chaffering for the lamb's least leg,
Or the quarter-fowl, less entrails, claws and comb :
Then back again with prize,—a liver begged
Into the bargain, gizzard overlooked,—
He 's mincing these to give the beans a taste,
When, at your knock, he leaves the simmering soup,
Waits on the curious stranger-visitant,
Napkin in half-wiped hand, to show the rooms,
Point pictures out have hung their hundred years,
' Priceless,' he tells you,—puts in his place at once
The man of money : yes, you 're banker-king　　　372

Or merchant-kaiser, wallow in your wealth
While patron, the house-master, can't afford
To stop our ceiling-hole that rain so rots—
But he 's the man of mark, and there 's his shield,
And yonder 's the famed Rafael, first in kind,
The painter painted for his grandfather—
You have paid a paul to see : ' Good morning, Sir ! '
Such is the law of compensation.   Here   380
The poverty was getting too acute ;
There gaped so many noble mouths to feed,
Beans must suffice unflavoured of the fowl.
The mother,—hers would be a spun-out life
I' the nature of things ; the sisters had done well
And married men of reasonable rank :
But that sort of illumination stops,
Throws back no heat upon the parent-hearth.
The family instinct felt out for its fire
To the Church,—the Church traditionally helps   390
A second son : and such was Paolo,
Established here at Rome these thirty years,
Who played the regular game,—priest and Abate,
Made friends, owned house and land, became of use
To a personage : his course lay clear enough.
The youngest caught the sympathetic flame,
And, though unfledged wings kept him still i' the cage,
Yet he shot up to be a Canon, so
Clung to the higher perch and crowed in hope.
Even our Guido, eldest brother, went   400
As far i' the way o' the Church as safety seemed,
He being Head o' the House, ordained to wive,—
So, could but dally with an Order or two
And testify good-will i' the cause : he clipt
His top-hair and thus far affected Christ,
But main promotion must fall otherwise,
Though still from the side o' the Church : and here
        was he
At Rome, since first youth, worn threadbare of soul
By forty-six years' rubbing on hard life,
Getting fast tired o' the game whose word is—'Wait ! '
When one day,—he too having his Cardinal   411
To serve in some ambiguous sort, as serve
To draw the coach the plumes o' the horses' heads,—
The Cardinal saw fit to dispense with him,
Ride with one plume the less ; and off it dropped.

Guido thus left,—with a youth spent in vain
And not a penny in purse to show for it,
Advised with Paolo, bent no doubt in chafe
The black brows somewhat formidably the while.
' Where is the good I came to get at Rome ? 420
' Where the repayment of the servitude
' To a purple popinjay, whose feet I kiss,
' Knowing his father wiped the shoes of mine ? '

' Patience,' pats Paolo the recalcitrant—
' You have not had, so far, the proper luck,
' Nor do my gains suffice to keep us both :
' A modest competency is mine, not more.
' You are the Count however, yours the style,
' Heirdom and state,—you can't expect all good.
' Had I, now, held your hand of cards . . well, well—
' What 's yet unplayed, I 'll look at, by your leave,
' Over your shoulder,—I who made my game, 432
' Let 's see, if I can't help to handle yours.
' Fie on you, all the Honours in your fist,
'Countship, Householdship,—how have you misdealt!
' Why, in the first place, they will marry a man !
' *Notum tonsoribus !* To the Tonsor then !
' Come, clear your looks, and choose your freshest suit,
' And, after function's done with, down we go
' To the woman-dealer in perukes, a wench 440
' I and some others settled in the shop
' At Place Colonna : she 's an oracle. Hmm !
' " Dear, 'tis my brother : brother, 'tis my dear.
' " Dear, give us counsel ! Whom do you suggest
' " As properest party in the quarter round,
' " For the Count here ?—he is minded to take wife,
' " And further tells me he intends to slip
' " Twenty zecchines under the bottom-scalp
' " Of his old wig when he sends it to revive
' " For the wedding : and I add a trifle too. 450
' " You know what personage I'm potent with." '
And so plumped out Pompilia's name the first.
She told them of the household and its ways,
The easy husband and the shrewder wife
In Via Vittoria,—how the tall young girl,
With hair black as yon patch and eyes as big
As yon pomander to make freckles fly,
Would have so much for certain, and so much more

In likelihood,—why, it suited, slipt as smooth
As the Pope's pantoufle does on the Pope's foot.
' I'll to the husband ! ' Guido ups and cries.   461
' Ay, so you 'd play your last court-card, no doubt ! '
Puts Paolo in with a groan—' Only, you see,
' 'Tis I, this time, that supervise your lead.
' Priests play with women, maids, wives, mothers,—
        why ?
' These play with men and take them off our hands.
' Did I come, counsel with some cut-beard gruff
' Or rather this sleek young-old barberess ?
' Go, brother, stand you rapt in the ante-room
' Of Her Efficacity my Cardinal   470
' For an hour,—he likes to have lord-suitors lounge,—
' While I betake myself to the grey mare,
' The better horse,—how wise the people's word !—
' And wait on Madam Violante.'
                                      Said and done.
He was at Via Vittoria in three skips :
Proposed at once to fill up the one want
O' the burgess-family which, wealthy enough,
And comfortable to heart's desire, yet crouched
Outside a gate to heaven,—locked, bolted, barred,
Whereof Count Guido had a key he kept   481
Under his pillow, but Pompilia's hand
Might slide behind his neck and pilfer thence.
The key was fairy ; mention of it, made
Violante feel the thing shoot one sharp ray
That reached the heart o' the woman. ' I assent :
' Yours be Pompilia, hers and ours that key
' To all the glories of the greater life !
' There 's Pietro to convince : leave that to me ! '

Then was the matter broached to Pietro ; then   490
Did Pietro make demand and get response
That in the Countship was a truth, but in
The counting up of the Count's cash, a lie :
He thereupon stroked grave his chin, looked great,
Declined the honour. Then the wife wiped one—
Winked with the other eye turned Paolo-ward,
Whispered Pompilia, stole to church at eve,
Found Guido there and got the marriage done,
And finally begged pardon at the feet
Of her dear lord and master. Whereupon   500

Quoth Pietro—' Let us make the best of things ! '
' I knew your love would license us,' quoth she :
Quoth Paolo once more, ' Mothers, wives and maids,
' These be the tools wherewith priests manage men.'

Now, here take breath and ask,—which bird o' the
    brace
Decoyed the other into clapnet ? Who
Was fool, who knave ? Neither and both, perchance.
There was a bargain mentally proposed
On each side, straight and plain and fair enough ;
Mind knew its own mind : but when mind must speak,
The bargain have expression in plain terms,   511
There was the blunder incident to words,
And in the clumsy process, fair turned foul.
The straight backbone-thought of the crooked speech
Were just—' I Guido truck my name and rank
' For so much money and youth and female charms.'—
' We Pietro and Violante give our child
' And wealth to you for a rise i' the world thereby.'
Such naked truth while chambered in the brain
Shocks nowise : walk it forth by way of tongue,—
Out on the cynical unseemliness !   521
Hence was the need, on either side, of a lie
To serve as decent wrappage : so, Guido gives
Money for money,—and they, bride for groom,
Having, he, not a doit, they, not a child
Honestly theirs, but this poor waif and stray.
According to the words, each cheated each ;
But in the inexpressive barter of thoughts,
Each did give and did take the thing designed,
The rank on this side and the cash on that—   530
Attained the object of the traffic, so.
The way of the world, the daily bargain struck
In the first market ! Why sells Jack his ware ?
' For the sake of serving an old customer.'
Why does Jill buy it ? ' Simply not to break
' A custom, pass the old stall the first time.'
Why, you know where the gist is of the exchange :
Each sees a profit, throws the fine words in.
Don't be too hard o' the pair ! Had each pretence
Been simultaneously discovered, stripped   540
From off the body o' the transaction, just
As when a cook . . will Excellency forgive ?

Strips away those long loose superfluous legs
From either side the crayfish, leaving folk
A meal all meat henceforth, no garnishry,
(With your respect, Prince !)—balance had been kept,
No party blamed the other,—so, starting fair,
All subsequent fence of wrong returned by wrong
I' the matrimonial thrust and parry, at least
Had followed on equal terms.   But, as it chanced,
One party had the advantage, saw the cheat   551
Of the other first and kept its own concealed :
And the luck o' the first discovery fell, beside,
To the least adroit and self-possessed o' the pair.
'Twas foolish Pietro and his wife saw first
The nobleman was penniless, and screamed
' We are cheated ! '

                    Such unprofitable noise
Angers at all times : but when those who plague,
Do it from inside your own house and home,   560
Gnats which yourself have closed the curtain round,
Noise goes too near the brain and makes you mad.
The gnats say, Guido used the candle-flame
Unfairly,—worsened that first bad of his,
By practise of all kind of cruelty
To oust them and suppress the wail and whine,—
That speedily he so scared and bullied them,
Fain were they, long before five months were out,
To beg him grant, from what was once their wealth,
Just so much as would help them back to Rome   570
Where, when they had finished paying the last doit
O' the dowry, they might beg from door to door.
So say the Comparini—as if it were
In pure resentment for this worse than bad,
That then Violante, feeling conscience prick,
Confessed her substitution of the child
Whence all the harm came,—and that Pietro first
Bethought him of advantage to himself
I' the deed, as part revenge, part remedy
For all miscalculation in the pact.   580

On the other hand ' Not so ! ' Guido retorts—
' I am the wronged, solely, from first to last,
' Who gave the dignity I engaged to give,
' Which was, is, cannot but continue gain.

' My being poor was a bye-circumstance,
' Miscalculated piece of untowardness,
' Might end to-morrow did heaven's windows ope,
' Or uncle die and leave me his estate.
' You should have put up with the minor flaw,   589
' Getting the main prize of the jewel.   If wealth,
' Not rank, had been prime object in your thoughts,
' Why not have taken the butcher's son, the boy
' O' the baker or candlestick-maker ?   In all the rest,
' It was yourselves broke compact and played false,
' And made a life in common impossible.
' Show me the stipulation of our bond
' That you should make your profit of being inside
' My house, to hustle and edge me out o' the same,
' First make a laughing-stock of mine and me,
' Then round us in the ears from morn to night   600
' (Because we show wry faces at your mirth)
' That you are robbed, starved, beaten and what not !
' You fled a hell of your own lighting-up,
' Pay for your own miscalculation too :
' You thought nobility, gained at any price,
' Would suit and satisfy,—find the mistake,
' And now retaliate, not on yourselves, but me.
' And how ?   By telling me, i' the face of the world,
' I it is have been cheated all this while,
' Abominably and irreparably,—my name   610
' Given to a cur-cast mongrel, a drab's brat,
' A beggar's bye-blow,—thus depriving me
' Of what yourselves allege the whole and sole
' Aim on my part i' the marriage,—money to-wit.
' This thrust I have to parry by a guard
' Which leaves me open to a counter-thrust
' On the other side,—no way but there 's a pass
' Clean through me.   If I prove, as I hope to do,
' There 's not one truth in this your odious tale
' O' the buying, selling, substituting—prove   620
' Your daughter was and is your daughter,—well,
' And her dowry hers and therefore mine,—what
    then ?
' Why, where 's the appropriate punishment for this
' Enormous lie hatched for mere malice' sake
' To ruin me ?   Is that a wrong or no ?
' And if I try revenge for remedy,
' Can I well make it strong and bitter enough ? '

.

I anticipate however—only ask,   628
Which of the two here sinned most ?   A nice point !
Which brownness is least black,—decide who can,
Wager-by-battle-of-cheating !   What do you say,
Highness ?   Suppose, your Excellency, we leave
The question at this stage, proceed to the next,
Both parties step out, fight their prize upon,
In the eye o' the world ?
        They brandish law 'gainst law ;
The grinding of such blades, each parry of each,
Throws terrible sparks off, over and above the thrusts,
And makes more sinister the fight, to the eye,
Than the very wounds that follow.   Beside the tale
Which the Comparini have to re-assert,   641
They needs must write, print, publish all abroad
The straitnesses of Guido's household life—
The petty nothings we bear privately
But break down under when fools flock around.
What is it all to the facts o' the couple's case,
How helps it prove Pompilia not their child,
If Guido's mother, brother, kith and kin
Fare ill, lie hard, lack clothes, lack fire, lack food ?
That 's one more wrong than needs.   650

           On the other hand,
Guido,—whose cue is to dispute the truth
O' the tale, reject the shame it throws on him,—
He may retaliate, fight his foe in turn
And welcome, we allow.   Ay, but he can't !
He 's at home, only acts by proxy here :
Law may meet law,—but all the gibes and jeers,
The superfluity of naughtiness,
Those libels on his House,—how reach at them ?
Two hateful faces, grinning all a-glow,   660
Not only make parade of spoil they filched,
But foul him from the height of a tower, you see.
Unluckily temptation is at hand—
To take revenge on a trifle overlooked,
A pet lamb they have left in reach outside,
Whose first bleat, when he plucks the wool away,
Will strike the grinners grave : his wife remains
Who, four months earlier, some thirteen years old,
Never a mile away from mother's house
And petted to the height of her desire,   670

Was told one morning that her fate was come,
She must be married—just as, a month before,
Her mother told her she must comb her hair
And twist her curls into one knot behind.
These fools forgot their pet lamb, fed with flowers,
Then 'ticed as usual by the bit of cake,
Out of the bower into the butchery.
Plague her, he plagues them threefold : but how
    plague ?
The world may have its word to say to that :
You can't do some things with impunity.   680
What remains . . well, it is an ugly thought . .
But that he drive herself to plague herself—
Herself disgrace herself and so disgrace
Who seek to disgrace Guido ?   .

                          There's the clue
To what else seems gratuitously vile,
If, as is said, from this time forth the rack
Was tried upon Pompilia : 't was to wrench
Her limbs into exposure that brings shame.
The aim o' the cruelty being so crueller still,   690
That cruelty almost grows compassion's self
Could one attribute it to mere return
O' the parents' outrage, wrong avenging wrong.
They see in this a deeper deadlier aim,
Not to vex just a body they held dear,
But blacken too a soul they boasted white,
And show the world their saint in a lover's arms,
No matter how driven thither,—so they say.

On the other hand, so much is easily said,
And Guido lacks not an apologist.   700
The pair had nobody but themselves to blame,
Being selfish beasts throughout, no less, no more :
—Cared for themselves, their supposed good, nought
    else,
And brought about the marriage ; good proved bad,
As little they cared for her its victim—nay,
Meant she should stay behind and take the chance,
If haply they might wriggle themselves free.
They baited their own hook to catch a fish
With this poor worm, failed o' the prize, and then
Sought how to unbait tackle, let worm float   710
                          F

Or sink, amuse the monster while they 'scaped.
Under the best stars Hymen brings above,
Had all been honesty on either side,
A common sincere effort to good end,
Still, this would prove a difficult problem, Prince !
—Given, a fair wife, aged thirteen years,
A husband poor, care-bitten, sorrow-sunk,
Little, long-nosed, bush-bearded, lantern-jawed,
Forty-six-years full,—place the two grown one,
She, cut off sheer from every natural aid,   720
In a strange town with no familiar face—
He, in his own parade-ground or retreat
As need were, free from challenge, much less check
To an irritated, disappointed will—
How evolve happiness from such a match ?
'T were hard to serve up a congenial dish
Out of these ill-agreeing morsels, Duke,
By the best exercise of the cook's craft,
Best interspersion of spice, salt and sweet !
But let two ghastly scullions concoct mess   730
With brimstone, pitch, vitriol and devil's-dung—
Throw in abuse o' the man, his body and soul,
Kith, kin and generation, shake all slab
At Rome, Arezzo, for the world to nose,
Then end by publishing, for fiend's arch-prank,
That, over and above sauce to the meat's self,
Why, even the meat, bedevilled thus in dish,
Was never a pheasant but a carrion-crow—
Prince, what will then the natural loathing be ?
What wonder if this ?—the compound plague o' the
        pair   740
Pricked Guido,—not to take the course they hoped,
That is, submit him to their statement's truth,
Accept its obvious promise of relief,
And thrust them out of doors the girl again
Since the girl's dowry would not enter there,
—Quit of the one if baulked of the other : no !
Rather did rage and hate so work in him,
Their product proved the horrible conceit
That he should plot and plan and bring to pass
His wife might, of her own free will and deed,   750
Relieve him of her presence, get her gone,
And yet leave all the dowry safe behind,
Confirmed his own henceforward past dispute,

While blotting out, as by a belch of hell,
Their triumph in her misery and death.

You see, the man was Aretine, had touch
O' the subtle air that breeds the subtle wit ;
Was noble too, of old blood thrice-refined
That shrinks from clownish coarseness in disgust :
Allow that such an one may take revenge,　　　760
You do n't expect he 'll catch up stone and fling,
Or try cross-buttock, or whirl quarter-staff ?
Instead of the honest drubbing clowns bestow,
When out of temper at the dinner spoilt,
On meddling mother-in-law and tiresome wife,—
Substitute for the clown a nobleman,
And you have Guido, practising, 't is said,
Unmitigably from the very first,
The finer vengeance : this, they say, the fact
O' the famous letter shows—the writing traced　　770
At Guido's instance by the timid wife
Over the pencilled words himself writ first—
Wherein she, who could neither write nor read,
Was made unblushingly declare a tale
To the brother, the Abate then in Rome,
How her putative parents had impressed,
On their departure, their enjoinment ; bade
' We being safely arrived here, follow, you !
' Poison your husband, rob, set fire to all,
' And then by means o' the gallant you procure　　780
' With ease, by helpful eye and ready tongue,
' The brave youth ready to dare, do and die,
' You shall run off and merrily reach Rome
' Where we may live like flies in honey-pot : '—
Such being exact the programme of the course
Imputed her as carried to effect.

They also say,—to keep her straight therein,
All sort of torture was piled, pain on pain,
On either side Pompilia's path of life,
Built round about and over against by fear,　　790
Circumvallated month by month, and week
By week, and day by day, and hour by hour,
Close, closer and yet closer still with pain,
No outlet from the encroaching pain save just
Where stood one saviour like a piece of heaven,

Hell's arms would strain round but for this blue gap
She, they say further, first tried every chink,
Every imaginable break i' the fire,
As way of escape : ran to the Commissary,
Who bade her not malign his friend her spouse ;   800
Flung herself thrice at the Archbishop's feet,
Where three times the Archbishop let her lie,
Spend her whole sorrow and sob full heart forth,
And then took up the slight load from the ground
And bore it back for husband to chastise,—
Mildly of course,—but natural right is right.
So went she slipping ever yet catching at help,
Missing the high till come to lowest and last,
No more than a certain friar of mean degree,
Who heard her story in confession, wept,   810
Crossed himself, showed the man within the monk.
' Then, will you save me, you the one i' the world ?
' I cannot even write my woes, nor put
' My prayer for help in words a friend may read,—
' I no more own a coin than have an hour
' Free of observance,—I was watched to church,
' Am watched now, shall be watched back presently,—
' How buy the skill of scribe i' the market-place ?
' Pray you, write down and send whatever I say
' O' the need I have my parents take me hence ! '   820
The good man rubbed his eyes and could not choose—
Let her dictate her letter in such a sense
That parents, to save breaking down a wall,
Might lift her over : she went back, heaven in her
        heart.
Then the good man took counsel of his couch,
Woke and thought twice, the second thought the best :
' Here am I, foolish body that I be,
' Caught all but pushing, teaching, who but I,
' My betters their plain duty,—what, I dare
' Help a case the Archbishop would not help,   830
' Mend matters, peradventure, God loves mar ?
' What hath the married life but strifes and plagues
' For proper dispensation ?   So a fool
' Once touched the ark,—poor Hophni that I am !
' Oh married ones, much rather should I bid,
' In patience all of ye possess your souls !
' This life is brief and troubles die with it :
' Where were the prick to soar up homeward else ? '

So saying, he burnt the letter he had writ,
Said *Ave* for her intention, in its place,   840
Took snuff and comfort, and had done with all.
Then the grim arms stretched yet a little more
And each touched each, all but one streak i' the midst,
Whereat stood Caponsacchi, who cried, ' This way,
' Out by me ! Hesitate one moment more
' And the fire shuts out me and shuts in you !
' Here my hand holds you life out ! ' Whereupon
She clasped the hand, which closed on hers and drew
Pompilia out o' the circle now complete.
Whose fault or shame but Guido's ?—ask her friends.

But then this is the wife's—Pompilia's tale—   851
Eve's . . . no, not Eve's, since Eve, to speak the truth,
Was hardly fallen (our candour might pronounce)
So much of paradisal nature, Eve's,
When simply saying in her own defence
' The serpent tempted me and I did eat.'
Her daughters ever since prefer to urge
' Adam so starved me I was fain accept
' The apple any serpent pushed my way.'
What an elaborate theory have we here,   860
Ingeniously nursed up, pretentiously
Brought forth, pushed forward amid trumpet-blast,
To account for the thawing of an icicle,
Show us there needed Ætna vomit flame
Ere run the crystal into dew-drops ! Else,
How, unless hell broke loose to cause the step,
How could a married lady go astray ?
Bless the fools ! And 't is just this way they are
     blessed,
And the world wags still,—because fools are sure
—Oh, not of my wife nor your daughter ! No !
But of their own : the case is altered quite.   871
Look now,—last week, the lady we all love,—
Daughter o' the couple we all venerate,
Wife of the husband we all cap before,
Mother o' the babes we all breathe blessings on,—
Was caught in converse with a negro page.
Hell thawed that icicle, else ' Why was it—
' Why ? ' asked and echoed the fools. ' Because, you
     fools,—'
So did the dame's self answer, she who could,

With that fine candour only forthcoming   880
When 't is no odds whether withheld or no—
' Because my husband was the saint you say,
' And,—with that childish goodness, absurd faith,
' Stupid self-satisfaction, you so praise,—
' Saint to you, insupportable to me.
' Had he,—instead of calling me fine names,
' Lucretia and Susanna and so forth,
' And curtaining Correggio carefully
' Lest I be taught that Leda had two legs,—
' —But once never so little tweaked my nose   890
' For peeping through my fan at Carnival,
' Confessing thereby " I have no easy task—
' " I need use all my powers to hold you mine,
' " And then,—why 't is so doubtful if they serve,
' " That—take this, as an earnest of despair ! "
' Why, we were quits—I had wiped the harm away,
' Thought " The man fears me ! " and foregone
        revenge.'
We must not want all this elaborate work
To solve the problem why young fancy-and-flesh
Slips from the dull side of a spouse in years,   900
Betakes it to the breast of brisk-and-bold
Whose love-scrapes furnish talk for all the town !

Accordingly, one word on the other side
Tips over the piled-up fabric of a tale.
Guido says—that is, always, his friends say—
It is unlikely from the wickedness,
That any man treat any woman so.
The letter in question was her very own,
Unprompted and unaided : she could write—
As able to write as ready to sin, or free,   910
When there was danger, to deny both facts.
He bids you mark, herself from first to last
Attributes all the so-styled torture just
To jealousy,—jealousy of whom but just
This very Caponsacchi !   How suits here
This with the other alleged motive, Prince ?
Would Guido make a terror of the man
He meant should tempt the woman, as they charge ?
Do you fright your hare that you may catch your hare ?
Consider too, the charge was made and met   920
At the proper time and place where proofs were plain—

Heard patiently and disposed of thoroughly
By the highest powers, possessors of most light,
The Governor, for the law, and the Archbishop
For the gospel : which acknowledged primacies,
'T is impudently pleaded, he could warp
Into a tacit partnership with crime—
He being the while, believe their own account,
Impotent, penniless and miserable !   929
He further asks—Duke, note the knotty point !—
How he,—concede him skill to play such part
And drive his wife into a gallant's arms,—
Could bring the gallant to play his part too
And stand with arms so opportunely wide ?
How bring this Caponsacchi,—with whom, friends
And foes alike agree, throughout his life
He never interchanged a civil word
Nor lifted courteous cap to—how bend him,
To such observancy of beck and call,
—To undertake this strange and perilous feat   940
For the good of Guido, using, as the lure,
Pompilia whom, himself and she avouch,
He had nor spoken with nor seen, indeed,
Beyond sight in a public theatre,
When she wrote letters (she that could not write !)
The importunate shamelessly-protested love
Which brought him, though reluctant, to her feet,
And forced on him the plunge which, howsoe'er
She might swim up i' the whirl, must bury him
Under abysmal black : a priest contrive   950
No mitigable amour to be hushed up,
But open flight and noon-day infamy ?
Try and concoct defence for such revolt !
Take the wife's tale as true, say she was wronged,—
Pray, in what rubric of the breviary
Do you find it registered the part of a priest
That to right wrongs he skip from the church-door,
Go journeying with a woman that 's a wife,
And be pursued, o'ertaken and captured . . . how ?
In a lay-dress, playing the sentinel   960
Where the wife sleeps (says he who best should know)
And sleeping, sleepless, both have spent the night !
Could no one else be found to serve at need—
No woman—or if man, no safer sort
Than this not well-reputed turbulence ?

Then, look into his own account o' the case !
He, being the stranger and astonished one,
Yet received protestations of her love
From lady neither known nor cared about :
Love, so protested, bred in him disgust   970
After the wonder,—or incredulity,
Such impudence seeming impossible.
But, soon assured such impudence might be,
When he had seen with his own eyes at last
Letters thrown down to him i' the very street
From behind lattice where the lady lurked,
And read their passionate summons to her side—
Why then, a thousand thoughts swarmed up and in,—
How he had seen her once, a moment's space,
Observed she was so young and beautiful,   980
Heard everywhere report she suffered much
From a jealous husband thrice her age,—in short
There flashed the propriety, expediency
Of treating, trying might they come to terms,
—At all events, granting the interview
Prayed for, and so adapted to assist
Decision as to whether he advance,
Stand or retire, in his benevolent mood.
Therefore the interview befell at length ;
And at this one and only interview,   990
He saw the sole and single course to take—
Bade her dispose of him, head, heart and hand,
Did her behest and braved the consequence,
Not for the natural end, the love of man
For woman whether love be virtue or vice,
But, please you, altogether for pity's sake—
Pity of innocence and helplessness !
And how did he assure himself of both ?
Had he been the house-inmate, visitor,
Eye-witness of the described martyrdom,   1000
So, competent to pronounce its remedy
Ere rush on such extreme and desperate course,
Involving such enormity of harm,
Moreover, to the husband judged thus, doomed
And damned without a word in his defence ?
But no,—the truth was felt by instinct here !
—Process which saves a world of trouble and time,
And there 's his story : what do you say to it,
Trying its truth by your own instinct too,

Since that 's to be the expeditious mode ?   1010
'. And now, do hear my version,' Guido cries :
' I accept argument and inference both.
' It would indeed have been miraculous
' Had such a confidency sprung to birth
' With no more fanning from acquaintanceship
' Than here avowed by my wife and this priest.
' Only, it did not : you must substitute
' The old stale unromantic way of fault,
' The commonplace adventure, mere intrigue
' In the prose form with the unpoetic tricks,   1020
' Cheatings and lies : they used the hackney chair
' Satan jaunts forth with, shabby and serviceable,
' No gilded jimcrack-novelty from below,
' To bowl you along thither, swift and sure.
' That same officious go-between, the wench
' That gave and took the letters of the two,
' Now offers self and service back to me :
' Bears testimony to visits night by night
' When all was safe, the husband far and away,—
' To many a timely slipping out at large   1030
' By light o' the morning-star, ere he should wake.
' And when the fugitives were found at last,
' Why, with them were found also, to belie
' What protest they might make of innocence,
' All documents yet wanting, if need were,
' To establish guilt in them, disgrace in me—
' The chronicle o' the converse from its rise
' To culmination in this outrage : read !
' Letters from wife to priest, from priest to wife,—
' Here they are, read and say where they chime in
' With the other tale, superlative purity   1041
' O' the pair of saints ! I stand or fall by these.'

But then on the other side again,—how say
The pair of saints ? That not one word is theirs—
No syllable o' the batch or writ or sent
Or yet received by either of the two.
' Found,' says the priest, ' because he needed them,
' Failing all other proofs, to prove our fault :
' So, here they are, just as is natural.
' Oh yes—we had our missives, each of us !   1050
' Not these, but to the full as vile, no doubt :
' Hers as from me,—she could not read, so burnt,—

' Mine as from her,—I burnt because I read.
' Who forged and found them ?   *Cui profuerint !* '
(I take the phrase out of your Highness' mouth)
' He who would gain by her fault and my fall,
' The trickster, schemer and pretender—he
' Whose whole career was lie entailing lie
' Sought to be sealed truth by the worst lie last ! '

Guido rejoins—' Did the other end o' the tale   1060
' Match this beginning !   'Tis alleged I prove
' A murderer at the end, a man of force
' Prompt, indiscriminate, effectual :   good !
' Then what need all this trifling woman's-work,
' Letters and embassies and weak intrigue,
' When will and power were mine to end at once
' Safely and surely ?   Murder had come first
' Not last with such a man, assure yourselves !
' The silent *acquetta*, stilling at command—
' A drop a day i' the wine or soup, the dose,—   1070
' The shattering beam that breaks above the bed
' And beats out brains, with nobody to blame
' Except the wormy age which eats even oak,—
' Nay, the staunch steel or trusty cord,—who cares
' I' the blind old palace, a pitfall at each step,
' With none to see, much more to interpose
' O' the two, three creeping house-dog-servant-things
' Born mine and bred mine ?—had I willed gross death,
' I had found nearer paths to thrust him prey   1079
' Than this that goes meandering here and there
' Through half the world and calls down in its course
' Notice and noise,—hate, vengeance, should it fail,
' Derision and contempt though it succeed !
' Moreover, what o' the future son and heir ?
' The unborn babe about to be called mine,—
' What end in heaping all this shame on him,
' Were I indifferent to my own black share ?
' Would I have tried these crookednesses, say,
' Willing and able to effect the straight ? '

' Ay, would you ! '—one may hear the priest retort,
' Being as you are, i' the stock, a man of guile,   1091
' And ruffianism but an added graft.
' You, a born coward, try a coward's arms,
' Trick and chicane,—and only when these fail

' Does violence follow, and like fox you bite
' Caught out in stealing. Also, the disgrace
' You hardly shrunk at, wholly shrivelled her :
' You plunged her thin white delicate hand i' the flame
' Along with your coarse horny brutish fist, 1099
' Held them a second there, then drew out both
' —Yours roughed a little, hers ruined through and
   through.
' Your hurt would heal forthwith at ointment's touch—
' Namely, succession to the inheritance
' Which bolder crime had lost you : let things change,
' The birth o' the boy warrant the bolder crime,
' Why, murder was determined, dared and done.
' For me,' the priest proceeds with his reply,
' The look o' the thing, the chances of mistake,
' All were against me,—that, I knew the first :
' But, knowing also what my duty was, 1110
' I did it : I must look to men more skilled
' I' the reading hearts than ever was the world.'

Highness, decide ! Pronounce, Her Excellency !
Or . . . even leave this argument in doubt,
Account it a fit matter, taken up
With all its faces, manifold enough,
To put upon—what fronts us, the next stage,
Next legal process !—Guido, in pursuit,
Coming up with the fugitives at the inn,
Caused both to be arrested then and there 1120
And sent to Rome for judgment on the case—
Thither, with all his armoury of proofs
Betook himself, and there we 'll meet him now,
Waiting the further issue.
       Here some smile
' And never let him henceforth dare to plead,—
' Of all pleas and excuses in the world
' For any deed hereafter to be done,—
' His irrepressible wrath at honour's wound !
' Passion and madness irrepressible ? 1130
' Why, Count and cavalier, the husband comes
' And catches foe i' the very act of shame :
' There 's man to man,—nature must have her way,—
' We look he should have cleared things on the spot.
' Yes, then, indeed—even tho' it prove he erred—
' Though the ambiguous first appearance, mount

' Of solid injury, melt soon to mist,
' Still,—had he slain the lover and the wife—
' Or, since she was a woman and his wife,
' Slain him, but stript her naked to the skin   1140
' Or at best left no more of an attire
' Than patch sufficient to pin paper to,
' Some one love-letter, infamy and all,
' As passport to the Paphos fit for such,
' Safe-conduct to her natural home the stews,—
' Good !   One had recognized the power o' the pulse.
' But when he stands, the stock-fish,—sticks to law—
' Offers the hole in his heart, all fresh and warm,
' For scrivener's pen to poke and play about—
' Can stand, can stare, can tell his beads perhaps,
' Oh, let us hear no syllable o' the rage !   1151
' Such rage were a convenient afterthought
' For one who would have shown his teeth belike,
' Exhibited unbridled rage enough,
' Had but the priest been found, as was to hope,
' In serge, not silk, with crucifix, not sword :
' Whereas the grey innocuous grub, of yore,
' Had hatched a hornet, tickle to the touch,
' The priest was metamorphosed into knight.
' And even the timid wife, whose cue was—shriek,
' Bury her brow beneath his trampling foot,—   1161
' She too sprang at him like a pythoness :
' So, gulp down rage, passion must be postponed,
' Calm be the word !   Well, our word is—we brand
' This part o' the business, howsoever the rest
' Befall.'
                ' Nay,' interpose as prompt his friends—
' This is the world's way !   So you adjudge reward
' To the forbearance and legality
' Yourselves begin by inculcating—ay,   1170
' Exacting from us all with knife at throat !
' This one wrong more you add to wrong's amount,—
' You publish all, with the kind comment here,
' " Its victim was too cowardly for revenge." '
Make it your own case,—you who stand apart !
The husband wakes one morn from heavy sleep,
With a taste of poppy in his mouth,—rubs eyes,
Finds his wife flown, his strong box ransacked too,
Follows as he best can, overtakes i' the end.
You bid him use his privilege : well, it seems   1180

He's scarce cool-blooded enough for the right move—
Does not shoot when the game were sure, but stands
Bewildered at the critical minute,—since
He has the first flash of the fact alone
To judge from, act with, not the steady lights
Of after-knowledge,—yours who stand at ease
To try conclusions : he 's in smother and smoke,
You outside, with explosion at an end :
The sulphur may be lightning or a squib—   1189
He 'll know in a minute, but till then, he doubts.
Back from what you know to what he knew not !
Hear the priest's lofty ' I am innocent,'
The wife's as resolute ' You are guilty ! '   Come !
Are you not staggered ?—pause, and you lose the move !
Nought left you but a low appeal to law,
' Coward ' tied to your tail for compliment !
Another consideration : have it your way !
Admit the worst : his courage failed the Count,
He 's cowardly like the best o' the burgesses
He 's grown incorporate with,—a very cur,   1200
Kick him from out your circle by all means !
Why, trundled down this reputable stair,
Still, the Church-door lies wide to take him in,
And the Court-porch also : in he sneaks to each,—
' Yes, I have lost my honour and my wife,
' And, being moreover an ignoble hound,
' I dare not jeopardize my life for them ! '
Religion and Law lean forward from their chairs,
' Well done, thou good and faithful servant ! '   Ay,
Not only applaud him that he scorned the world,
But punish should he dare do otherwise.   1211
If the case be clear or turbid,—you must say !

Thus, anyhow, it mounted to the stage
In the law-courts,—let 's see clearly from this point !—
Where the priest tells his story true or false,
And the wife her story, and the husband his,
All with result as happy as before.
The courts would nor condemn nor yet acquit
This, that or the other, in so distinct a sense
As end the strife to either's absolute loss :   1220
Pronounced, in place of something definite,
' Each of the parties, whether goat or sheep
' I' the main, has wool to show and hair to hide.

' Each has brought somehow trouble, is somehow cause
' Of pains enough,—even though no worse were proved.
' Here is a husband, cannot rule his wife
' Without provoking her to scream and scratch
' And scour the fields,—causelessly, it may be :
' Here is that wife,—who makes her sex our plague,
' Wedlock, our bugbear,—perhaps with cause enough :
' And here is the truant priest o' the trio, worst   1231
' Or best—each quality being conceivable.
' Let us impose a little mulct on each.
' We punish youth in state of pupilage
' Who talk at hours when youth is bound to sleep,
' Whether the prattle turn upon Saint Rose
' Or Donna Olimpia of the Vatican :
' 'T is talk, talked wisely or unwisely talked,
' I' the dormitory where to talk at all,
' Transgresses, and is mulct : as here we mean.   1240
' For the wife,—let her betake herself, for rest,
' After her run, to a House of Convertites—
' Keep there, as good as real imprisonment :
' Being sick and tired, she will recover so.
' For the priest, spritely strayer out of bounds,
' Who made Arezzo hot to hold him,—Rome
' Profits by his withdrawal from the scene.
' Let him be relegate to Civita,
' Circumscribed by its bounds till matters mend :
' There he at least lies out o' the way of harm   1250
' From foes—perhaps from the too friendly fair.
' And finally for the husband, whose rash rule
' Has but itself to blame for this ado,—
' If he be vexed that, in our judgments dealt,
' He fails obtain what he accounts his right,
' Let him go comforted with the thought, no less,
' That, turn each sentence howsoever he may,
' There 's satisfaction to extract therefrom.
' For, does he wish his wife proved innocent ?
' Well, she 's not guilty, he may safely urge,   1260
' Has missed the stripes dishonest wives endure—
' This being a fatherly pat o' the cheek, no more.
' Does he wish her guilty ?   Were she otherwise
' Would she be locked up, set to say her prayers,
' Prevented intercourse with the outside world,
' And that suspected priest in banishment,
' Whose portion is a further help i' the case ?

' Oh, ay, you all of you want the other thing,
' The extreme of law, some verdict neat, complete,—
' Either, the whole o' the dowry in your poke   1270
' With full release from the false wife, to boot,
' And heading, hanging for the priest, beside—
' Or, contrary, claim freedom for the wife,
' Repayment of each penny paid her spouse,
' Amends for the past, release for the future !   Such
' Is wisdom to the children of this world ;
' But we 've no mind, we children of the light,
' To miss the advantage of the golden mean,
' And push things to the steel point.'   Thus the courts.

Is it settled so far ?   Settled or disturbed,   1280
Console yourselves : 't is like . . . an instance, now !
You 've seen the puppets, of Place Navona, play,—
Punch and his mate,—how threats pass, blows are
        dealt,
And a crisis comes : the crowd or clap or hiss
Accordingly as disposed for man or wife—
When down the actors duck awhile perdue,
Donning what novel rag-and-feather trim
Best suits the next adventure, new effect :
And,—by the time the mob is on the move,
With something like a judgment *pro* and *con*,—   1290
There 's a whistle, up again the actors pop
In t' other tatter with fresh-tinseled staves,
To re-engage in one last worst fight more
Shall show, what you thought tragedy was farce.
Note, that the climax and the crown of things
Invariably is, the devil appears himself,
Armed and accoutred, horns and hoofs and tail !
Just so, nor otherwise it proved—you 'll see :
Move to the murder, never mind the rest !

Guido, at such a general duck-down,   1300
I' the breathing-space,—of wife to convent here,
Priest to his relegation, and himself
To Arezzo,—had resigned his part perforce
To brother Abate, who bustled, did his best,
Retrieved things somewhat, managed the three suits—
Since, it should seem, there were three suits-at-law
Behoved him look to, still, lest bad grow worse :
First civil suit,—the one the parents brought,

Impugning the legitimacy of his wife,
Affirming thence the nullity of her rights :   1310
This was before the Rota,—Molinès,
That 's judge there, made that notable decree
Which partly leaned to Guido, as I said,—
But Pietro had appealed against the same
To the very court will judge what we judge now—
Tommati and his fellows,—Suit the first.
Next civil suit,—demand on the wife's part
Of separation from the husband's bed
On plea of cruelty and risk to life—
Claims restitution of the dowry paid,   1320
Immunity from paying any more :
This second, the Vicegerent has to judge.
Third and last suit,—this time, a criminal one,—
Answer to, and protection from, both these,—
Guido's complaint of guilt against his wife
In the Tribunal of the Governor,
Venturini, also judge of the present cause.
Three suits of all importance plaguing him,
Beside a little private enterprise
Of Guido's,—essay at a shorter cut.   1330
For Paolo, knowing the right way at Rome,
Had, even while superintending these three suits
I' the regular way, each at its proper court,
Ingeniously made interest with the Pope
To set such tedious regular forms aside,
And, acting the supreme and ultimate judge,
Declare for the husband and against the wife.
Well, at such crisis and extreme of straits,
The man at bay, buffeted in this wise,
Happened the strangest accident of all.   1340
' Then,' sigh friends, ' the last feather broke his
        back,
' Made him forget all possible remedies
' Save one—he rushed to, as the sole relief
' From horror and the abominable thing.'
' Or rather,' laugh foes, ' then did there befall
' The luckiest of conceivable events,
' Most pregnant with impunity for him,
' Which henceforth turned the flank of all attack,
' And bade him do his wickedest and worst.'
—The wife's withdrawal from the Convertites,   1350
Visit to the villa where her parents lived,

And birth there of his babe. Divergence here !
I simply take the facts, ask what they show.

First comes this thunderclap of a surprise :
Then follow all the signs and silences
Premonitory of earthquake. Paolo first
Vanished, was swept off somewhere, lost to Rome :
(Wells dry up, while the sky is sunny and blue.)
Then Guido girds himself for enterprise,
Hies to Vittiano, counsels with his steward,   1360
Comes to terms with four peasants young and bold,
And starts for Rome the Holy, reaches her
At very holiest, for 't is Christmas Eve,
And makes straight for the Abate's dried-up font,
The lodge where Paolo ceased to work the pipes.
And then, rest taken, observation made
And plan completed, all in a grim week,
The five proceed in a body, reach the place,
—Pietro's, by the Paolina, silent, lone,
And stupefied by the propitious snow,—   1370
At one in the evening : knock : a voice ' Who's there ? '
' Friends with a letter from the priest your friend.'
At the door, straight smiles old Violante's self.
She falls,—her son-in-law stabs through and through,
Reaches thro' her at Pietro—' With your son
' This is the way to settle suits, good sire ! '
He bellows ' Mercy for heaven, not for earth !
' Leave to confess and save my sinful soul,
' Then do your pleasure on the body of me ! '
—' Nay, father, soul with body must take its chance ! '
He presently got his portion and lay still.   1381
And last, Pompilia rushes here and there
Like a dove among lightnings in her brake,
Falls also : Guido's, this last husband's-act.
He lifts her by the long dishevelled hair,
Holds her away at arms' length with one hand,
While the other tries if life come from the mouth—
Looks out his whole heart's hate on the shut eyes,
Draws a deep satisfied breath, ' So—dead at last ! '
Throws down the burthen on dead Pietro's knees,
And ends all with ' Let us away, my boys ! '   1391

And, as they left by one door, in at the other
Tumbled the neighbours—for the shrieks had pierced

To the mill and the grange, this cottage and that shed.
Soon followed the Public Force ; pursuit began
Though Guido had the start and chose the road :
So, that same night was he, with the other four,
Overtaken near Baccano,—where they sank
By the way-side, in some shelter meant for beasts,
And now lay heaped together, nuzzling swine,   1400
Each wrapped in bloody cloak, each grasping still
His unwiped weapon, sleeping all the same
The sleep o' the just,—a journey of twenty miles
Bringing just and unjust to a level, you see.
The only one i' the world that suffered aught
By the whole night's toil and trouble, flight and
      chase,
Was just the officer who took them, Head
O' the Public Force,—Patrizj, zealous soul,
Who, having duty to sustain the flesh,
Got heated, caught a fever and so died :   1410
A warning to the over-vigilant,
—Virtue in a chafe should change her linen quick,
Lest pleurisy get start of providence.
(That's for the Cardinal, and told, I think !)

Well, they bring back the company to Rome.
Says Guido, ' By your leave, I fain would ask
' How you found out 't was I who did the deed ?
' What put you on my trace, a foreigner,
' Supposed in Arezzo,—and assuredly safe   1419
' Except for an oversight : who told you, pray ? '
' Why, naturally your wife ! '   Down Guido drops
O' the horse he rode,—they have to steady and stay,
At either side the brute that bore him, bound,
So strange it seemed his wife should live and speak !
She had prayed—at least so people tell you now—
For but one thing to the Virgin for herself,
Not simply, as did Pietro 'mid the stabs,—
Time to confess and get her own soul saved—
But time to make the truth apparent, truth
For God's sake, lest men should believe a lie :   1430
Which seems to have been about the single prayer
She ever put up, that was granted her.
With this hope in her head, of telling truth,—
Being familiarized with pain, beside,—
She bore the stabbing to a certain pitch

Without a useless cry, was flung for dead
On Pietro's lap, and so attained her point.
Her friends subjoin this—have I done with them ?—
And cite the miracle of continued life
(She was not dead when I arrived just now)   1440
As attestation to her probity.

Does it strike your Excellency ?   Why, your Highness,
The self-command and even the final prayer,
Our candour must acknowledge explainable
As easily by the consciousness of guilt.
So, when they add that her confession runs
She was of wifehood one white innocence
In thought, word, act, from first of her short life
To last of it ; praying, i' the face of death,
That God forgive her other sins—not this,   1450
She is charged with and must die for, that she failed
Anyway to her husband : while thereon
Comments the old Religious—' So much good,
' Patience beneath enormity of ill,
' I hear to my confusion, woe is me,
' Sinner that I stand, shamed in the walk and gait
' I have practised and grown old in, by a child ! '—
Guido's friends shrug the shoulder, ' Just this same
' Prodigious absolute calm in the last hour
' Confirms us,—being the natural result   1460
' Of a life which proves consistent to the close.
' Having braved heaven and deceived earth through-
        out,
' She braves still and deceives still, gains thereby
' Two ends, she prizes beyond earth or heaven :
' First sets her lover free, imperilled sore
' By the new turn things take : he answers yet
' For the part he played : they have summoned him
        indeed :
' The past ripped up, he may be punished still :
' What better way of saving him than this ?
' Then,—thus she dies revenged to the uttermost
' On Guido, drags him with her in the dark,   1471
' The lower still the better, do you doubt ?
' Thus, two ways, does she love her love to the end,
' And hate her hate,—death, hell is no such price
' To pay for these,—lovers and haters hold.'
But there's another parry for the thrust.

' Confession,' cry folks—' a confession, think !
' Confession of the moribund is true ! '
Which of them, my wise friends ?   This public one,
Or the private other we shall never know ?   1480
The private may contain,—your casuists teach,—
The acknowledgment of, and the penitence for,
That other public one, so people say.
However it be,—we trench on delicate ground,
Her Eminence is peeping o'er the cards,—
Can one find nothing in behalf of this
Catastrophe ?   Deaf folks accuse the dumb !
You criticize the drunken reel, fool's-speech,
Maniacal gesture of the man,—we grant !
But who poured poison in his cup, we ask ?   1490
Recall the list of his excessive wrongs,
First cheated in his wife, robbed by her kin,
Rendered anon the laughing-stock o' the world
By the story, true or false, of his wife's birth,—
The last seal publicly apposed to shame
By the open flight of wife and priest,—why, Sirs,
Step out of Rome a furlong, would you know
What anotherguess tribunal than ours here,
Mere worldly Court without the help of grace,
Thinks of just that one incident o' the flight ?   1500
Guido preferred the same complaint before
The court at Arezzo, bar of the Granduke,—
In virtue of it being Tuscany
Where the offence had rise and flight began,—
Self-same complaint he made in the sequel here
Where the offence grew to the full, the flight
Ended : offence and flight, one fact judged twice
By two distinct tribunals,—what result ?
There was a sentence passed at the same time
By Arezzo and confirmed by the Granduke,   1510
Which nothing baulks of swift and sure effect
But absence of the guilty, (flight to Rome
Frees them from Tuscan jurisdiction now)
—Condemns the wife to the opprobrious doom
Of all whom law just lets escape from death.
The Stinche, House of Punishment, for life,—
That 's what the wife deserves in Tuscany :
Here, she deserves—remitting with a smile
To her father's house, main object of the flight !
The thief presented with the thing he steals !   1520

At this discrepancy of judgments—mad,
The man took on himself the office, judged ;
And the only argument against the use
O' the law he thus took into his own hands
Is . . what, I ask you ?—that, revenging wrong,
He did not revenge sooner, kill at first
Whom he killed last !   That is the final charge.
Sooner ?   What 's soon or late i' the case ?—ask we.
A wound i' the flesh no doubt wants prompt redress ;
It smarts a little to-day, well in a week,   1530
Forgotten in a month ; or never, or now, revenge !
But a wound to the soul ?   That rankles worse and
    worse.
Shall I comfort you, explaining—' Not this once
' But now it may be some five hundred times
' I called you ruffian, pandar, liar and rogue :
' The injury must be less by lapse of time ? '
The wrong is a wrong, one and immortal too,
And that you bore it those five hundred times,
Let it rankle unrevenged five hundred years,   1539
Is just five hundred wrongs the more and worse !
Men, plagued this fashion, get to explode this way,
If left no other.

                 ' But we left this man
' Many another way, and there's his fault,'
'T is answered—' He himself preferred our arm
' O' the law to fight his battle with.   No doubt
' We did not open him an armoury
' To pick and choose from, use, and then reject.
' He tries one weapon and fails,—he tries the next
' And next : he flourishes wit and common sense,
' They fail him,—he plies logic doughtily,   1551
' It fails him too,—thereon, discovers last
' He has been blind to the combustibles—
' That all the while he is a-glow with ire,
' Boiling with irrepressible rage, and so
' May try explosives and discard cold steel,—
' So hire assassins, plot, plan, execute !
' Is this the honest self-forgetting rage
' We are called to pardon ?   Does the furious bull
' Pick out four help-mates from the grazing herd
' And journey with them over hill and dale   1561
' Till he find his enemy ? '

        What rejoinder ? save
That friends accept our bull-similitude.
Bull-like,—the indiscriminate slaughter, rude
And reckless aggravation of revenge,
Were all i' the way o' the brute who never once
Ceases, amid all provocation more,
To bear in mind the first tormentor, first
Giver o' the wound that goaded him to fight : 1570
And, though a dozen follow and reinforce
The aggressor, wound in front and wound in flank,
Continues undisturbedly pursuit,
And only after prostrating his prize
Turns on the pettier, makes a general prey.
So Guido rushed against Violante, first
Author of all his wrongs, *fons et origo*
Malorum—increasingly drunk,—which justice done,
He finished with the rest. Do you blame a bull ?

In truth you look as puzzled as ere I preached !
How is that ? There are difficulties perhaps 1581
On any supposition, and either side.
Each party wants too much, claims sympathy
For its object of compassion, more than just.
Cry the wife's friends, ' O the enormous crime
' Caused by no provocation in the world ! '
' Was not the wife a little weak ? '—inquire—
' Punished extravagantly, if you please,
' But meriting a little punishment ?
' One treated inconsiderately, say, 1590
' Rather than one deserving not at all
' Treatment and discipline o' the harsher sort ? '
No, they must have her purity itself,
Quite angel,—and her parents angels too
Of an aged sort, immaculate, word and deed,
At all events, so seeming, till the fiend,
Even Guido, by his folly, forced from them
The untoward avowal of the trick o' the birth,
Would otherwise be safe and secret now.
Why, here you have the awfulest of crimes 1600
For nothing ! Hell broke loose on a butterfly !
A dragon born of rose-dew and the moon !
Yet here is the monster ! Why, he 's a mere man—
Born, bred and brought up in the usual way.
His mother loves him, still his brothers stick

To the good fellow of the boyish games ;
The Governor of his town knows and approves,
The Archbishop of the place knows and assists :
Here he has Cardinal This to vouch for the past,
Cardinal That to trust for the future,—match   1610
And marriage were a Cardinal's making,—in short,
What if a tragedy be acted here
Impossible for malice to improve,
And innocent Guido with his innocent four
Be added, all five, to the guilty three,
That we of these last days be edified
With one full taste o' the justice of the world ?

The long and the short is, truth is what I show :—
Undoubtedly no pains ought to be spared
To give the mob an inkling of our lights.   1620
It seems unduly harsh to put the man
To the torture, as I hear the court intends,
Though readiest way of twisting out the truth ;
He is noble, and he may be innocent :
On the other hand, if they exempt the man
(As it is also said they hesitate
On the fair ground, presumptive guilt is weak
I' the case of nobility and privilege),—
What crime that ever was, ever will be,
Deserves the torture ?   Then abolish it !   1630
You see the reduction *ad absurdum*, Sirs ?

Her Excellency must pronounce, in fine !
What, she prefers going and joining play ?
Her Highness finds it late, intends retire ?
I am of their mind : only, all this talk, talked,
'T was not for nothing that we talked, I hope ?
Both know as much about it, now, at least,
As all Rome : no particular thanks, I beg !
(You 'll see, I have not so advanced myself,
After my teaching the two idiots here !)   1640

V

COUNT GUIDO FRANCESCHINI

THANKS, Sir, but, should it please the reverend Court,
I feel I can stand somehow, half sit down
Without help, make shift to even speak, you see,
Fortified by the sip of . . . why, 't is wine,
Velletri,—and not vinegar and gall,
So changed and good the times grow ! Thanks, kind
    Sir !
Oh, but one sip 's enough ! I want my head
To save my neck, there 's work awaits me still.
How cautious and considerate . . . aie, aie, aie,
Not your fault, sweet Sir ! Come, you take to heart
An ordinary matter. Law is law.   11
Noblemen were exempt, the vulgar thought,
From racking, but, since law thinks otherwise,
I have been put to the rack : all 's over now,
And neither wrist—what men style, out of joint :
If any harm be, 't is the shoulder-blade,
The left one, that seems wrong i' the socket,—Sirs,
Much could not happen, I was quick to faint,
Being past my prime of life, and out of health.
In short I thank you,—yes, and mean the word.   20
Needs must the Court be slow to understand
How this quite novel form of taking pain,
This getting tortured merely in the flesh,
Amounts to almost an agreeable change
In my case, me fastidious, plied too much
With opposite treatment, used (forgive the joke)
To the rasp-tooth toying with this brain of mine,
And, in and out my heart, the play o' the probe.
Four years have I been operated on
I' the soul, do you see—its tense or tremulous part—
My self-respect, my care for a good name,   31
Pride in an old one, love of kindred—just
A mother, brothers, sisters, and the like,
That looked up to my face when days were dim,
And fancied they found light there—no one spot,

Foppishly sensitive, but has paid its pang.
That, and not this you now oblige me with,
That was the Vigil-torment, if you please !
The poor old noble House that drew the rags
O' the Franceschini's once superb array   40
Close round her, hoped to slink unchallenged by,—
Pluck off these ! Turn the drapery inside out
And teach the tittering town how scarlet wears !
Show men the lucklessness, the improvidence
Of the easy-natured Count before this Count,
The father I have some slight feeling for,
Who let the world slide, nor foresaw that friends
Then proud to cap and kiss the patron's shoe,
Would, when the purse he left held spider-webs,
Properly push his child to wall one day !   50
Mimic the tetchy humour, furtive glance
And brow where half was furious half fatigued,
O' the same son got to be of middle age,
Sour, saturnine,—your humble servant here,—
When things go cross and the young wife, he finds
Take to the window at a whistle's bid,
And yet demurs thereon, preposterous fool !—
Whereat the worthies judge he wants advice
And beg to civilly ask what 's evil here,
Perhaps remonstrate on the habit they deem   60
He 's given unduly to, of beating her
. . Oh, sure he beats her—why says John so else,
Who is cousin to George who is sib to Tecla's self
Who cooks the meal and combs the lady's hair ?
What ?   'T is my wrist you merely dislocate
For the future when you mean me martyrdom ?
—Let the old mother's economy alone,
How the brocade-strips saved o' the seamy side
O' the wedding-gown buy raiment for a year ?
—How she can dress and dish up—lordly dish   70
Fit for a duke, lamb's head and purtenance—
With her proud hands, feast household so a week ?
No word o' the wine rejoicing God and man
The less when three-parts water ?   Then, I say,
A trifle of torture to the flesh, like yours,
While soul is spared such foretaste of hell-fire,
Is naught.   But I curtail the catalogue
Through policy,—a rhetorician's trick,—
Because I would reserve some choicer points

O' the practice, more exactly parallel—   80
(Having an eye to climax) with what gift,
Eventual grace the Court may have in store
I' the way of plague—my crown of punishments.
When I am hanged or headed, time enough
To prove the tenderness of only that,
Mere heading, hanging,—not their counterpart,
Not demonstration public and precise
That I, having married the mongrel of a drab,
Am bound to grant that mongrel-brat, my wife,
Her mother's birthright-licence as is just,—   90
Let her sleep undisturbed, i' the family style,
Her sleep out in the embraces of a priest,
Nor disallow their bastard as my heir !
Your sole mistake,—dare I submit so much
To the reverend Court ?—has been in all this pains
To make a stone roll down hill,—rack and wrench
And rend a man to pieces, all for what ?
Why—make him ope mouth in his own defence,
Show cause for what he has done, the irregular deed,
(Since that he did it, scarce dispute can be)   100
And clear his fame a little, beside the luck
Of stopping even yet, if possible,
Discomfort to his flesh from noose or axe—
For that, out come the implements of law !
May it content my lords the gracious Court
To listen only half so patient-long
As I will in that sense profusely speak,
And—fie, they shall not call in screws to help !
I killed Pompilia Franceschini, Sirs ;
Killed too the Comparini, husband, wife,   110
Who called themselves, by a notorious lie,
Her father and her mother to ruin me.
There 's the irregular deed : you want no more
Than right interpretation of the same,
And truth so far—am I to understand ?
To that then, with convenient speed,—because
Now I consider,—yes, despite my boast,
There is an ailing in this omoplat
May clip my speech all too abruptly close,
Whatever the good-will in me.   Now for truth !   120

I' the name of the indivisible Trinity !
Will my lords, in the plentitude of their light,

Weigh well that all this trouble has come on me
Through my persistent treading in the paths
Where I was trained to go,—wearing that yoke
My shoulder was predestined to receive,
Born to the hereditary stoop and crease ?
Noble, I recognized my nobler still,
The Church, my suzerain ; no mock-mistress, she ;
The secular owned the spiritual : mates of mine   130
Have thrown their careless hoofs up at her call
' Forsake the clover and come drag my wain ! '
There they go cropping : I protruded nose
To halter, bent my back of docile beast,
And now am whealed, one wide wound all of me,
For being found at the eleventh hour o' the day
Padding the mill-track, not neck-deep in grass :
—My one fault, I am stiffened by my work,
—My one reward, I help the Court to smile !

I am representative of a great line,   140
One of the first of the old families
In Arezzo, ancientest of Tuscan towns.
When my worst foe is fain to challenge this,
His worst exception runs—not first in rank
But second, noble in the next degree
Only ; not malice' self maligns me more.
So, my lord opposite has composed, we know,
A marvel of a book, sustains the point
That Francis boasts the primacy 'mid saints ;
Yet not inaptly hath his argument   150
Obtained response from yon my other lord
In thesis published with the world's applause
—Rather 't is Dominic such post befits :
Why, at the worst, Francis stays Francis still,
Second in rank to Dominic it may be,
Still, very saintly, very like our Lord ;
And I at least descend from a Guido once
Homager to the Empire, nought below—
Of which account as proof that, none o' the line
Having a single gift beyond brave blood,   160
Or able to do aught but give, give, give
In blood and brain, in house and land and cash,
Not get and garner as the vulgar may,
We became poor as Francis or our Lord.
Be that as it likes you, Sirs,—whenever it chanced

Myself grew capable anyway of remark,
(Which was soon—penury makes wit premature)
This struck me, I was poor who should be rich
Or pay that fault to the world which trifles not
When lineage lacks the flag yet lifts the pole :   170
Therefore I must make move forthwith, transfer
My stranded self, born fish with gill and fin
Fit for the deep sea, now left flap bare-backed
In slush and sand, a show to crawlers vile
Reared of the low-tide and aright therein.
The enviable youth with the old name,
Wide chest, stout arms, sound brow and pricking
     veins,
A heartful of desire, man's natural load,
A brainful of belief, the noble's lot,—   179
All this life, cramped and gasping, high and dry
I' the wave's retreat,—the misery, good my lords,
Which made you merriment at Rome of late,—
It made me reason, rather—muse, demand
—Why our bare dropping palace, in the street
Where such-an-one whose grandfather sold tripe
Was adding to his purchased pile a fourth
Tall tower, could hardly show a turret sound ?
Why Countess Beatrice, whose son I am,
Cowered in the winter-time as she spun flax,
Blew on the earthen basket of live ash,   190
Instead of jaunting forth in coach and six
Like such-another widow who ne'er was wed ?
I asked my fellows, how came this about ?
' Why, Jack, the suttler's child, perhaps the camp's,
' Went to the wars, fought sturdily, took a town
' And got rewarded as was natural.
' She of the coach and six—excuse me there !
' Why, do n't you know the story of her friend ?
' A clown dressed vines on somebody's estate,
' His boy recoiled from muck, liked Latin more,
' Stuck to his pen and got to be a priest,   201
' Till one day . . do n't you mind that telling tract
' Against Molinos, the old Cardinal wrote ?
' He penned and dropped it in the patron's desk
' Who, deep in thought and absent much of mind,
' Licensed the thing, allowed it for his own ;
' Quick came promotion,—*suum cuique*, Count !
' Oh, he can pay for coach and six, be sure ! '

‘ —Well, let me go, do likewise : war 's the word—
‘ That way the Franceschini worked at first,   210
‘ I 'll take my turn, try soldiership.’—‘ What, you ?
‘ The eldest son and heir and prop o’ the house,
‘ So do you see your duty ? Here 's your post,
‘ Hard by the hearth and altar. (Roam from roof,
‘ This youngster, play the gipsy out of doors,
‘ And who keeps kith and kin that fall on us ?)
‘ Stand fast, stick tight, conserve your gods at home ! ’
‘ —Well then, the quiet course, the contrary trade !
‘ We had a cousin amongst us once was Pope,
‘ And minor glories manifold. Try the Church,   220
‘ The tonsure, and,—since heresy 's but half-slain
‘ Even by the Cardinal’s tract he thought he wrote,—
‘ Have at Molinos ! ’—‘ Have at a fool’s head !
‘ You a priest ? How were marriage possible ?
‘ There must be Franceschini till time ends—
‘ That 's your vocation. Make your brothers priests,
‘ Paul shall be porporate, and Girolamo step
‘ Red-stockinged in the presence when you choose,
‘ But save one Franceschini for the age !
‘ Be not the vine but dig and dung its root,   230
‘ Be not a priest but gird up priesthood’s loins,
‘ With one foot in Arezzo stride to Rome,
‘ Spend yourself there and bring the purchase back !
‘ Go hence to Rome, be guided ! ’

                So I was.
I turned alike from the hill-side zig-zag thread
Of way to the table-land a soldier takes,
Alike from the low-lying pasture-place
Where churchmen graze, recline and ruminate,
—Ventured to mount no platform like my lords   240
Who judge the world, bear brain I dare not brag—
But stationed me, might thus the expression serve,
As who should fetch and carry, come and go,
Meddle and make i’ the cause my lords love most—
The public weal, which hangs to the law, which holds
By the Church, which happens to be through God
    himself.
Humbly I helped the Church till here I stand,—
Or would stand but for the omoplat, you see !
Bidden qualify for Rome, I, having a field,
Went, sold it, laid the sum at Peter’s foot :   250

Which means—I settled home-accounts with speed,
Set apart just a modicum should suffice
To keep the villa's head above the waves
Of weed inundating its oil and wine,
And prop roof, stanchion wall o' the palace so
It should keep breath i' the body, hold its own
Amid the advance of neighbouring loftiness—
(People like building where they used to beg)—
Till succoured one day,—shared the residue
Between my mother and brothers and sisters there,
Black-eyed babe Donna This and Donna That,   261
As near to starving as might decently be,
—Left myself journey-charges, change of suit,
A purse to put i' the pocket of the Groom
O' the Chamber of the patron, and a glove
With a ring to it for the digits of the niece
Sure to be helpful in his household,—then
Started for Rome, and led the life prescribed.
Close to the Church, though clean of it, I assumed
Three or four orders of no consequence,   270
—They cast out evil spirits and exorcise,
For example ; bind a man to nothing more,
Give clerical savour to his layman's-salt,
Facilitate his claim to loaf and fish
Should miracle leave, beyond what feeds the flock,
Fragments to brim the basket of a friend—
While, for the world's sake, I rode, danced and gamed,
Quitted me like a courtier, measured mine
With whatsoever blade had fame in fence,
—Ready to let the basket go its round   280
Even though my turn was come to help myself,
Should Dives count on me at dinner-time
As just the understander of a joke
And not immoderate in repartee.
Utrique sic paratus, Sirs, I said
' Here,' (in the fortitude of years fifteen,
So good a pedagogue is penury)
' Here wait, do service,—serving and to serve !
' And, in due time, I nowise doubt at all,
' The recognition of my service comes.   290
' Next year I'm only sixteen. I can wait.'

I waited thirty years, may it please the Court :
Saw meanwhile many a denizen o' the dung

Hop, skip, jump o'er my shoulder, make him wings
And fly aloft,—succeed, in the usual phrase.
Everyone soon or late comes round by Rome :
Stand still here, you'll see all in turn succeed.
Why, look you, so and so, the physician here,
My father's lacquey's son we sent to school,
Doctored and dosed this Eminence and that,   300
Salved the last Pope his certain obstinate sore,
Soon bought land as became him, names it now :
I grasp bell at his griffin-guarded gate,
Traverse the half-mile avenue,—a term,
A cypress, and a statue, three and three,—
Deliver message from my Monsignor,
With varletry at lounge i' the vestibule
I 'm barred from, who bear mud upon my shoe.
My father's chaplain's nephew, Chamberlain,—
Nothing less, please you !—courteous all the same,
—He does not see me though I wait an hour   311
At his staircase-landing 'twixt the brace of busts,
A noseless Sylla, Marius maimed to match,
My father gave him for a hexastich
Made on my birth-day,—but he sends me down,
To make amends, that relic I prize most—
The unburnt end o' the very candle, Sirs,
Purfled with paint so prettily round and round,
He carried in such state last Peter's-day,—
In token I, his gentleman and squire,   320
Had held the bridle, walked his managed mule
Without a tittup the procession through.
Nay, the official,—one you know, sweet lords !—
Who drew the warrant for my transfer late
To the New Prisons from Tordinona,—he
Graciously had remembrance—' Francesc . . ha ?
' His sire, now—how a thing shall come about !—
' Paid me a dozen florins above the fee,
' For drawing deftly up a deed of sale   329
' When troubles fell so thick on him, good heart,
' And I was prompt and pushing ! By all means !
' At the New Prisons be it his son shall lie,—
' Anything for an old friend ! ' and thereat
Signed name with triple flourish underneath.
These were my fellows, such their fortunes now,
While I—kept fasts and feasts innumerable,
Matins and vespers, functions to no end

I' the train of Monsignor and Eminence,
As gentleman-squire, and for my zeal's reward
Have rarely missed a place at the table-foot   340
Except when some Ambassador, or such like,
Brought his own people.   Brief, one day I felt
The tick of time inside me, turning-point
And slight sense there was now enough of this :
That I was near my seventh climacteric,
Hard upon, if not over, the middle life,
And, although fed by the east-wind, fulsome-fine
With foretaste of the Land of Promise, still
My gorge gave symptom it might play me false ;
Better not press it further,—be content   350
With living and dying only a nobleman,
Who merely had a father great and rich,
Who simply had one greater and richer yet,
And so on back and back till first and best
Began i' the night ;   I finish in the day.
' The mother must be getting old,' I said ;
' The sisters are well wedded away, our name
' Can manage to pass a sister off, at need,
' And do for dowry : both my brothers thrive—
' Regular priests they are, nor, bat-like, 'bide   360
' 'Twixt flesh and fowl with neither privilege.
' My spare revenue must keep me and mine.
' I am tired : Arezzo's air is good to breathe ;
' Vittiano,—one limes flocks of thrushes there ;
' A leathern coat costs little and lasts long :
' Let me bid hope good-bye, content at home ! '
Thus, one day, I disbosomed me and bowed.
Whereat began the little buzz and thrill
O' the gazers round me ;   each face brightened up :
As when at your Casino, deep in dawn,   370
A gamester says at last, ' I play no more,
' Forego gain, acquiesce in loss, withdraw
' Anyhow : ' and the watchers of his ways,
A trifle struck compunctious at the word,
Yet sensible of relief, breathe free once more,
Break up the ring, venture polite advice—
' How, Sir ?   So scant of heart and hope indeed ?
' Retire with neither cross nor pile from play ?—
' So incurious, so short-casting ?—give your chance
' To a younger, stronger, bolder spirit belike,   380
' Just when luck turns and the fine throw sweeps all ? '

Such was the chorus : and its goodwill meant—
' See that the loser leave door handsomely !
' There 's an ill look,—it 's sinister, spoils sport,
' When an old bruised and battered year-by-year
' Fighter with fortune, not a penny in poke,
' Reels down the steps of our establishment
' And staggers on broad daylight and the world,
' In shagrag beard and doleful doublet, drops
' And breaks his heart on the outside : people prate
' " Such is the profit of a trip upstairs ! "   391
' Contrive he sidle forth, baulked of the blow
' Best dealt by way of moral, bidding down
' No curse but blessings rather on our heads
' For some poor prize he bears at tattered breast,
' Some palpable sort of kind of good to set
' Over and against the grievance : give him quick ! '
Whereon protested Paul, ' Go hang yourselves !
' Leave him to me.   Count Guido and brother of mine,
' A word in your ear ! Take courage since faint heart
' Ne'er won . . . aha, fair lady, do n't men say ? "' 401
' There 's a *sors*, there 's a right Virgilian dip !
' Do you see the happiness o' the hint ?   At worst,
' If the Church want no more of you, the Court
' No more, and the Camp as little, the ingrates,—come,
' Count you are counted : still you 've coat to back.
' Not cloth of gold and tissue, as we hoped,
' But cloth with sparks and spangles on its frieze
' From Camp, Court, Church, enough to make a shine,
' Entitle you to carry home a wife   410
' With the proper dowry, let the worst betide !
' Why, it was just a wife you meant to take ! '

Now, Paul's advice was weighty : priests should know :
And Paul apprised me, ere the week was out,
That Pietro and Violante, the easy pair,
The cits enough, with stomach to be more,
Had just the daughter and exact the sum
To truck for the quality of myself : ' She 's young,
' Pretty and rich : you 're noble, classic, choice.
' Is it to be a match ? '   ' A match,' said I.   420
Done ! He proposed all, I accepted all,
And we performed all.   So I said and did
Simply.   As simply followed, not at first
But with the outbreak of misfortune, still

G

One comment on the saying and doing—' What ?
' No blush at the avowal you dared buy
' A girl of age beseems your granddaughter,
' Like ox or ass ?   Are flesh and blood a ware ?
' Are heart and soul a chattel ? '
      Softly, Sirs !   430
Will the Court of its charity teach poor me
Anxious to learn, of any way i' the world,
Allowed by custom and convenience, save
This same which, taught from my youth up, I trod ?
Take me along with you ; where was the wrong step ?
If what I gave in barter, style and state
And all that hangs to Franceschinihood,
Were worthless,—why, society goes to ground,
Its rules are idiot's-rambling.   Honour of birth,—
If that thing has no value, cannot buy   440
Something with value of another sort,
You 've no reward nor punishment to give
I' the giving or the taking honour ; straight
Your social fabric, pinnacle to base,
Comes down a-clatter like a house of cards.
Get honour, and keep honour free from flaw,
Aim at still higher honour,—gabble o' the goose !
Go bid a second blockhead like myself
Spend fifty years in guarding bubbles of breath,
Soapsuds with air i' the belly, gilded brave, 450
Guarded and guided, all to break at touch
O' the first young girl's hand and first old fool's purse !
All my privation and endurance, all
Love, loyalty and labour dared and did,
Fiddle-de-dee !—why, doer and darer both,—
Count Guido Franceschini had hit the mark
Far better, spent his life with more effect,
As a dancer or a prizer, trades that pay !
On the other hand, bid this buffoonery cease,
Admit that honour is a privilege,   460
The question follows, privilege worth what ?
Why, worth the market-price,—now up, now down,
Just so with this as with all other ware :
Therefore essay the market, sell your name,
Style and condition to who buys them best !
' Does my name purchase,' had I dared inquire,
' Your niece, my lord ? ' there would have been rebuff
Though courtesy, your Lordship cannot else—

'Not altogether! Rank for rank may stand :
'But I have wealth beside, you—poverty;   470
'Your scale flies up there : bid a second bid,
'Rank too and wealth too!' Reasoned like your-
    self !
But was it to you I went with goods to sell ?
This time 'twas my scale quietly kissed the ground,
Mere rank against mere wealth—some youth beside,
Some beauty too, thrown into the bargain, just
As the buyer likes or lets alone. I thought
To deal o' the square : others find fault, it seems:
The thing is, those my offer most concerned,
Pietro, Violante, cried they fair or foul ?   480
What did they make o' the terms ? Preposterous
    terms ?
Why then accede so promptly, close with such
Nor take a minute to chaffer ? Bargain struck,
They straight grew bilious, wished their money back,
Repented them, no doubt : why, so did I,
So did your Lordship, if town-talk be true,
Of paying a full farm's worth for that piece
By Pietro of Cortona—probably
His scholar Ciro Ferri may have retouched—
You caring more for colour than design—   490
Getting a little tired of cupids too.
That 's incident to all the folk who buy !
I am charged, I know, with gilding fact by fraud ;
I falsified and fabricated, wrote
Myself down roughly richer than I prove,
Rendered a wrong revenue,—grant it all !
Mere grace, mere coquetry such fraud, I say :
A flourish round the figures of a sum
For fashion's sake, that deceives nobody.
The veritable back-bone, understood   500
Essence of this same bargain, blank and bare,
Being the exchange of quality for wealth,—
What may such fancy-flights be ? Flecks of oil
Flirted by chapmen where plain dealing grates.
I may have dripped a drop—' My name I sell ;
'Not but that I too boast my wealth '—as they,
'—We bring you riches ; still our ancestor
'Was hardly the rapscallion, folks saw flogged,
'But heir to we know who, were rights of force ! '
They knew and I knew where the back-bone lurked

I' the writhings of the bargain, lords, believe !   511
I paid down all engaged for, to a doit,
Delivered them just that which, their life long,
They hungered in the hearts of them to gain—
Incorporation with nobility thus
In word and deed : for that they gave me wealth.
But when they came to try their gain, my gift,
Quit Rome and qualify for Arezzo, take
The tone o' the new sphere that absorbed the old,
Put away gossip Jack and goody Joan   520
And go become familiar with the Great,
Greatness to touch and taste and handle now,—
Why, then,—they found that all was vanity,
Vexation, and what Solomon describes !
The old abundant city-fare was best,
The kindly warmth o' the commons, the glad clap
Of the equal on the shoulder, the frank grin
Of the underling at all so many spoons
Fire-new at neighbourly treat,—best, best and best
Beyond compare !—down to the loll itself   530
O' the pot-house settle,—better such a bench
Than the stiff crucifixion by my dais
Under the piece-meal damask canopy
With the coroneted coat of arms a-top !
Poverty and privation for pride's sake,
All they engaged to easily brave and bear,—
With the fit upon them and their brains a-work,—
Proved unendurable to the sobered sots.
A banished prince, now, will exude a juice
And salamander-like support the flame :   540
He dines on chestnuts, chucks the husks to help
The broil o' the brazier, pays the due baioc,
Goes off light-hearted : his grimace begins
At the funny humours of the christening-feast
Of friend the money-lender,—then he 's touched
By the flame and frizzles at the babe to kiss !
Here was the converse trial, opposite mind :
Here did a petty nature split on rock
Of vulgar wants predestinate for such—
One dish at supper and weak wine to boot !   550
The prince had grinned and borne : the citizen
     shrieked,
Summoned the neighbourhood to attest the wrong,
Made noisy protest he was murdered,—stoned

And burned and drowned and hanged,—then broke
    away,
He and his wife, to tell their Rome the rest.
And this you admire, you men o' the world, my lords ?
This moves compassion, makes you doubt my faith ?
Why, I appeal to . . sun and moon ? Not I !
Rather to Plautus, Terence, Boccaccio's Book,
My townsman, frank Ser Franco's merry Tales,— 560
To all who strip a vizard from a face,
A body from its padding, and a soul
From froth and ignorance it styles itself,—
If this be other than the daily hap
Of purblind greed that dog-like still drops bone,
Grasps shadow, and then howls the case is hard !

So much for them so far : now for myself,
My profit or loss i' the matter : married am I :
Text whereon friendly censors burst to preach.
Ay, at Rome even, long ere I was left   570
To regulate her life for my young bride
Alone at Arezzo, friendliness outbroke
(Sifting my future to predict its fault)
' Purchase and sale being thus so plain a point,
' How of a certain soul bound up, may-be,
' I' the barter with the body and money-bags ?
' From the bride's soul what is it you expect ? '
Why, loyalty and obedience,—wish and will
To settle and suit her fresh and plastic mind
To the novel, nor disadvantageous mould !   580
Father and mother shall the woman leave,
Cleave to the husband, be it for weal or woe :
There is the law : what sets this law aside
In my particular case ? My friends submit
' Guide, guardian, benefactor,—fee, faw, fum,
' The fact is you are forty-five years old,
' Nor very comely even for that age :
' Girls must have boys.' Why, let girls say so then,
Nor call the boys and men, who say the same,
Brute this and beast the other as they do !   590
Come, cards on table ! When you chaunt us next
Epithalamium full to overflow
With praise and glory of white womanhood,
The chaste and pure—troll no such lies o'er lip !
Put in their stead a crudity or two,

Such short and simple statement of the case
As youth chalks on our walls at spring of year !
No !   I shall still think nobler of the sex,
Believe a woman still may take a man
For the short period that his soul wears flesh,   600
And, for the soul's sake, understand the fault
Of armour frayed by fighting.   Tush, it tempts
One's tongue too much !   I 'll say—the law 's the law :
With a wife I look to find all wifeliness,
As when I buy, timber and twig, a tree—
I buy the song o' the nightingale inside.

Such was the pact :   Pompilia from the first
Broke it, refused from the beginning day
Either in body or soul to cleave to mine,
And published it forthwith to all the world.   610
No rupture,—you must join ere you can break,—
Before we had cohabited a month
She found I was a devil and no man,—
Made common cause with those who found as much,
Her parents, Pietro and Violante,—moved
Heaven and earth to the rescue of all three.
In four months' time, the time o' the parents' stay,
Arezzo was a-ringing, bells in a blaze,
With the unimaginable story rife
I' the mouth of man, woman and child—to-wit   620
My misdemeanour.   First the lighter side,
Ludicrous face of things,—how very poor
The Franceschini had become at last,
The meanness and the misery of each shift
To save a soldo, stretch and make ends meet.
Next, the more hateful aspect,—how myself
With cruelty beyond Caligula's
Had stripped and beaten, robbed and murdered them,
The good old couple, I decoyed, abused,
Plundered and then cast out, and happily so,   630
Since,—in due course the abominable comes,—
Woe worth the poor young wife left lonely here !
Repugnant in my person as my mind,
I sought,—was ever heard of such revenge ?
—To lure and bind her to so cursed a couch,
Such co-embrace with sulphur, snake and toad,
That she was fain to rush forth, call the stones
O' the common street to save her, not from hate

Of mine merely, but . . . must I burn my lips
With the blister of the lie ? . . the satyr-love   640
Of who but my own brother, the young priest,
Too long enforced to lenten fare belike,
Now tempted by the morsel tossed him full
I' the trencher where lay bread and herbs at best.
Mark, this yourselves say !—this, none disallows,
Was charged to me by the universal voice
At the instigation of my four-months' wife !—
And then you ask ' Such charges so preferred,
' (Truly or falsely, here concerns us not)
' Pricked you to punish now if not before ?—   650
' Did not the harshness double itself, the hate
' Harden ? ' I answer ' Have it your way and will ! '
Say my resentment grew apace : what then ?
Do you cry out on the marvel ?   When I find
That pure smooth egg which, laid within my nest,
Could not but hatch a comfort to us all,
Issues a cockatrice for me and mine,
Do you stare to see me stamp on it ?   Swans are soft :
Is it not clear that she you call my wife,
That any wife of any husband, caught   660
Whetting a sting like this against his breast,—
Speckled with fragments of the fresh-broke shell,
Married a month and making outcry thus,—
Proves a plague-prodigy to God and man ?
She married : what was it she married for,
Counted upon and meant to meet thereby ?
' Love ' suggests some one, ' love, a little word
' Whereof we have not heard one syllable.'
So, the Pompilia, child, girl, wife, in one,
Wanted the beating pulse, the rolling eye,   670
The frantic gesture, the devotion due
From Thyrsis to Neæra ! Guido's love—
Why not provençal roses in his shoe,
Plume to his cap, and trio of guitars
At casement, with a bravo close beside ?
Good things all these are, clearly claimable
When the fit price is paid the proper way.
Had it been some friend's wife, now, threw her fan
At my foot, with just this pretty scrap attached,
' Shame, death, damnation—fall these as they may,
' So I find you, for a minute ! Come this eve ! '   681
—Why, at such sweet self-sacrifice,—who knows ?

I might have fired up, found me at my post,
Ardent from head to heel, nor feared catch cough.
Nay, had some other friend's . . say, daughter, tripped
Upstairs and tumbled flat and frank on me,
Bareheaded and barefooted, with loose hair
And garments all at large,—cried ' Take me thus !
' Duke So-and-So, the greatest man in Rome—
' To escape his hand and heart have I broke bounds,
' Traversed the town and reached you ! '—Then, indeed,   691
The lady had not reached a man of ice !
I would have rummaged, ransacked at the word
Those old odd corners of an empty heart
For remnants of dim love the long disused,
And dusty crumblings of romance ! But here,
We talk of just a marriage, if you please—
The every-day conditions and no more ;
Where do these bind me to bestow one drop
Of blood shall dye my wife's true-love-knot pink ?
Pompilia was no pigeon, Venus' pet,   701
That shuffled from between her pressing paps
To sit on my rough shoulder,—but a hawk,
I bought at a hawk's price and carried home
To do hawk's service—at the Rotunda, say,
Where, six o' the callow nestlings in a row,
You pick and choose and pay the price for such.
I have paid my pound, await my penny's worth,
So, hoodwink, starve and properly train my bird,
And, should she prove a haggard,—twist her neck !
Did I not pay my name and style, my hope   711
And trust, my all ? Through spending these amiss
I am here ! 'T is scarce the gravity of the Court
Will blame me that I never piped a tune,
Treated my falcon-gentle like my finch.
The obligation I incurred was just
To practise mastery, prove my mastership :—
Pompilia's duty was—submit herself,
Afford me pleasure, perhaps cure my bile.
Am I to teach my lords what marriage means,   720
What God ordains thereby and man fulfils
Who, docile to the dictate, treads the house ?
My lords have chosen the happier part with Paul
And neither marry nor burn,—yet priestliness
Can find a parallel to the marriage-bond

In its own blessed special ordinance
Whereof indeed was marriage made the type :
The Church may show her insubordinate,
As marriage her refractory.   How of the Monk
Who finds the claustral regimen too sharp   730
After the first month's essay ?   What's the mode
With the Deacon who supports indifferently
The rod o' the Bishop when he tastes its smart
Full four weeks ?   Do you straightway slacken hold
Of the innocents, the all-unwary ones
Who, eager to profess, mistook their mind ?—
Remit a fast-day's rigour to the Monk
Who fancied Francis' manna meant roast quails,
Concede the Deacon sweet society,
He never thought the Levite-rule renounced,—   740
Or rather prescribe short chain and sharp scourge
Corrective of such peccant humours ?   This—
I take to be the Church's mode, and mine.
If I was over-harsh,—the worse i' the wife
Who did not win from harshness as she ought,
Wanted the patience and persuasion, lore
Of love, should cure me and console herself.
Put case that I mishandle, flurry and fright
My hawk through clumsiness in sportsmanship,
Twitch out five pens where plucking one would serve—
What, shall she bite and claw to mend the case ?   751
And, if you find I pluck five more for that,
Shall you weep ' How he roughs the turtle there ' ?

Such was the starting ; now of the further step.
In lieu of taking penance in good part,
The Monk, with hue and cry, summons a mob
To make a bonfire of the convent, say,—
And the Deacon's pretty piece of virtue (save
The ears o' the Court !   I try to save my head)
Instructed by the ingenuous postulant,   760
Taxes the Bishop with adultery, (mud
Needs must pair off with mud, and filth with filth)—
Such being my next experience : who knows not—
The couple, father and mother of my wife,
Returned to Rome, published before my lords,
Put into print, made circulate far and wide
That they had cheated me who cheated them ?
Pompilia, I supposed their daughter, drew

Breath first 'mid Rome's worst rankness, through the
    deed   769
Of a drab and a rogue, was bye-blow bastard-babe
Of a nameless strumpet, passed off, palmed on me
As the daughter with the dowry.   Daughter ?   Dirt
O' the kennel !   Dowry ?   Dust o' the street !   Nought
    more,
Nought less, nought else but—oh—ah—assuredly
A Franceschini and my very wife !
Now take this charge as you will, for false or true,—
This charge, preferred before your very selves
Who judge me now,—I pray you, adjudge again,
Classing it with the cheats or with the lies,
By which category I suffer most !   780
But of their reckoning, theirs who dealt with me
In either fashion,—I reserve my word,
Justify that in its place ; I am now to say,
Whichever point o' the charge might poison most,
Pompilia's duty was no doubtful one.
You put the protestation in her mouth
' Henceforward and forevermore, avaunt
' Ye fiends, who drop disguise and glare revealed
' In your own shape, no longer father mine
' Nor mother mine !   Too nakedly you hate   790
' Me whom you looked as if you loved once,—me
' Whom, whether true or false, your tale now damns,
' Divulged thus to my public infamy,
' Private perdition, absolute overthrow.
' For, hate my husband to your hearts' content,
' I, spoil and prey of you from first to last,
' I who have done you the blind service, lured
' The lion to your pitfall,—I, thus left
' To answer for my ignorant bleating there,   799
' I should have been remembered and withdrawn
' From the first o' the natural fury, not flung loose
' A proverb and a byeword men will mouth
' At the cross-way, in the corner, up and down
' Rome and Arezzo,—there, full in my face,
' If my lord, missing them and finding me,
' Content himself with casting his reproach
' To drop i' the street where such impostors die.
' Ah, but—that husband, what the wonder were !—
' If, far from casting thus away the rag
' Smeared with the plague, his hand had chanced upon,

'Sewn to his pillow by Locusta's wile,—   811
'Far from abolishing, root, stem and branch,
'The misgrowth of infectious mistletoe
'Foisted into his stock for honest graft,—
'If he, repudiate not, renounce nowise,
'But, guarding, guiding me, maintain my cause
'By making it his own, (what other way ?)
'—To keep my name for me, he call it his,
'Claim it of who would take it by their lie,—
'To save my wealth for me—or babe of mine   820
'Their lie was framed to beggar at the birth—
'He bid them loose grasp, give our gold again :
'Refuse to become partner with the pair
'Even in a game which, played adroitly, gives
'Its winner life's great wonderful new chance,—
'Of marrying, to-wit, a second time,—
'Ah, did he do thus, what a friend were he !
'Anger he might show,—who can stamp out flame
'Yet spread no black o' the brand ?—yet, rough albeit
'In the act, as whose bare feet feel embers scorch,
'What grace were his, what gratitude were mine ! '
Such protestation should have been my wife's.   832
Looking for this, do I exact too much ?
Why, here 's the,—word for word so much, no more,—
Avowal she made, her pure spontaneous speech
To my brother the Abate at first blush,
Ere the good impulse had begun to fade—
So did she make confession for the pair,
So pour forth praises in her own behalf.
'Ay, the false letter,' interpose my lords—   840
'The simulated writing,—'t was a trick :
'You traced the signs, she merely marked the same,
'The product was not hers but yours.'   Alack,
I want no more impulsion to tell truth
From the other trick, the torture inside there !
I confess all—let it be understood—
And deny nothing !   If I baffle you so,
Can so fence, in the plenitude of right,
That my poor lathen dagger puts aside
Each pass o' the Bilboa, beats you all the same,—
What matters inefficiency of blade ?   851
Mine and not hers the letter,—conceded, lords !
Impute to me that practice !—take as proved
I taught my wife her duty, made her see

What it behoved her see and say and do,
Feel in her heart and with her tongue declare,
And, whether sluggish or recalcitrant,
Forced her to take the right step, I myself
Marching in mere marital rectitude !
And who finds fault here, say the tale be true ?   860
Would not my lords commend the priest whose zeal
Seized on the sick, morose or moribund,
By the palsy-smitten finger, made it cross
His brow correctly at the critical time ?
—Or answered for the inarticulate babe
At baptism, in its stead declared the faith,
And saved what else would perish unprofessed ?
True, the incapable hand may rally yet,
Renounce the sign with renovated strength,—
The babe may grow up man and Molinist,—   870
And so Pompilia, set in the good path
And left to go alone there, soon might see
That too frank-forward, all too simple-strait
Her step was, and decline to tread the rough,
When here lay, tempting foot, the meadow-side,
And there the coppice called with singing-birds !
Soon she discovered she was young and fair,
That many in Arezzo knew as much,—
Yes, this next cup of bitterness, my lords,
Had to begin go filling, drop by drop,   880
Its measure up of full disgust for me,
Filtered into by every noisome drain—
Society's sink toward which all moisture runs.
Would not you prophesy—' She on whose brow is
        stamped
' The note of the imputation that we know,—
' Rightly or wrongly mothered with a whore,—
' Such an one, to disprove the frightful charge,
' What will she but exaggerate chastity,
' Err in excess of wifehood, as it were,
' Renounce even levities permitted youth,   890
' Though not youth struck to age by a thunderbolt ?
' Cry " wolf " i' the sheepfold, where 's the sheep dares
        bleat,
' Knowing the shepherd listens for a growl ? '
So you expect.   How did the devil decree ?
Why, my lords, just the contrary of course !
It was in the house from the window, at the church

From the hassock,—where the theatre lent its lodge,
Or staging for the public show left space,—
That still Pompilia needs must find herself
Launching her looks forth, letting looks reply   900
As arrows to a challenge ; on all sides
Ever new contribution to her lap,
Till one day, what is it knocks at my clenched teeth
But the cup full, curse-collected all for me ?
And I must needs drink, drink this gallant's praise,
That minion's prayer, the other fop's reproach,
And come at the dregs to—Caponsacchi ! Sirs,
I,—chin deep in a marsh of misery,
Struggling to extricate my name and fame
And fortune from the marsh would drown them all,
My face the sole unstrangled part of me,—   911
I must have this new gad-fly in that face,
Must free me from the attacking lover too !
Men say I battled ungracefully enough—
Was harsh, uncouth and ludicrous beyond
The proper part o' the husband : have it so !
Your lordships are considerate at least—
You order me to speak in my defence
Plainly, expect no quavering tuneful trills
As when you bid a singer solace you,—   920
Nor look that I shall give it, for a grace,
Stans pede in uno :—you remember well
In the one case, 't is a plainsong too severe,
This story of my wrongs,—and that I ache
And need a chair, in the other. Ask you me
Why, when I felt this trouble flap my face,
Already pricked with every shame could perch,—
When, with her parents, my wife plagued me too,—
Why I enforced not exhortation mild
To leave whore's-tricks and let my brows alone,   930
With mulct of comfits, promise of perfume ?

' Far from that ! No, you took the opposite course,
' Breathed threatenings, rage and slaughter ! ' What
      you will !
And the end has come, the doom is verily here,
Unhindered by the threatening. See fate's flare
Full on each face of the dead guilty three !
Look at them well, and now, lords, look at this !
Tell me : if on that day when I found first

That Caponsacchi thought the nearest way
To his church was some half-mile round by my door,
And that he so admired, shall I suppose,   941
The manner of the swallows' come-and-go
Between the props o' the window over-head,—
That window happening to be my wife's,—
As to stand gazing by the hour on high,
Of May-eves, while she sat and let him smile,—
If I,—instead of threatening, talking big,
Showing hair-powder, a prodigious pinch,
For poison in a bottle,—making believe
At desperate doings with a bauble-sword,   950
And other bugaboo-and-baby-work,—
Had, with the vulgarest household implement,
Calmly and quietly cut off, clean thro' bone,
But one joint of one finger of my wife,
Saying ' For listening to the serenade,
' Here's your ring-finger shorter a full third :
' Be certain I will slice away next joint,
' Next time that anybody underneath
' Seems somehow to be sauntering as he hoped
' A flower would eddy out of your hand to his   960
' While you please fidget with the branch above
' O' the rose-tree in the terrace ! '—had I done so,
Why, there had followed a quick sharp scream, some
        pain,
Much calling for plaister, damage to the dress,
A somewhat sulky countenance next day,
Perhaps reproaches,—but reflections too !
I don't hear much of harm that Malchus did
After the incident of the ear, my lords !
Saint Peter took the efficacious way ;
Malchus was sore but silenced for his life :   970
He did not hang himself i' the Potter's Field
Like Judas, who was trusted with the bag
And treated to sops after he proved a thief.
So, by this time, my true and obedient wife
Might have been telling beads with a gloved hand ;
Awkward a little at pricking hearts and darts
On sampler possibly, but well otherwise :
Not where Rome shudders now to see her lie.
I give that for the course a wise man takes ;
I took the other however, tried the fool's,   980
The lighter remedy, brandished rapier dread

With cork-ball at the tip, boxed Malchus' ear
Instead of severing the cartilage,
Called her a terrible nickname, and the like
And there an end : and what was the end of that ?
What was the good effect o' the gentle course ?
Why, one night I went drowsily to bed,
Dropped asleep suddenly, not suddenly woke,
But did wake with rough rousing and loud cry,
To find noon in my face, a crowd in my room,   990
Fumes in my brain, fire in my throat, my wife
Gone God knows whither,—rifled vesture-chest,
And ransacked money-coffer. ' What does it mean ? '
The servants had been drugged too, stared and
        yawned,
' It must be that our lady has eloped ! '
—' Whither and with whom ? '—' With whom but
        the Canon's self ?
' One recognizes Caponsacchi there ! '—
(By this time the admiring neighbourhood
Joined chorus round me while I rubbed my eyes)
' 'T is months since their intelligence began,—   1000
' A comedy the town was privy to,—
' He wrote and she wrote, she spoke, he replied,
' And going in and out your house last night
' Was easy work for one . . . to be plain with you . . .
' Accustomed to do both, at dusk and dawn
' When you were absent,—at the villa, you know,
' Where husbandry required the master-mind.
' Did not you know ? Why, we all knew, you see ! '
And presently, bit by bit, the full and true
Particulars of the tale were volunteered   1010
With all the breathless zeal of friendship—' Thus
' Matters were managed : at the seventh hour of
        night ' . . .
—' Later, at daybreak ' . . . ' Caponsacchi came ' . . .
—' While you and all your household slept like death,
' Drugged as your supper was with drowsy stuff ' . . .
—' And your own cousin Guillichini too—
' Either or both entered your dwelling-place,
' Plundered it at their pleasure, made prize of all,
' Including your wife . . .'—' Oh, your wife led the way,
' Out of doors, on to the gate . . .'—' But gates are shut,
' In a decent town, to darkness and such deeds : 1021
' They climbed the wall—your lady must be lithe—

' At the gap, the broken bit . . . '—' Torrione, true !
' To escape the questioning guard at the proper gate,
' Clemente, where at the inn, hard by, " the Horse,"
' Just outside, a calash in readiness
' Took the two principals, all alone at last,
' To gate San Spirito, which o'erlooks the road,
' Leads to Perugia, Rome and liberty.'
Bit by bit thus made-up mosaic-wise,   1030
Flat lay my fortune,—tesselated floor,
Imperishable tracery devils should foot
And frolic it on, around my broken gods,
Over my desecrated hearth.
                   So much
For the terrible effect of threatening, Sirs !

Well, this way I was shaken wide awake,
Doctored and drenched, somewhat unpoisoned so ;
Then, set on horseback and bid seek the lost,
I started alone, head of me, heart of me   1040
Fire, and each limb as languid . . . ah, sweet lords,
Bethink you !—poison-torture, try persuade
The next refractory Molinist with that ! . . .
Floundered thro' day and night, another day
And yet another night, and so at last,
As Lucifer kept falling to find hell,
Tumbled into the court-yard of an inn
At the end, and fell on whom I thought to find,
Even Caponsacchi,—what part once was priest,
Cast to the winds now with the cassock-rags :   1050
In cape and sword a cavalier confessed,
There stood he chiding dilatory grooms,
Chafing that only horseflesh and no team
Of eagles would supply the last relay,
Whirl him along the league, the one post more
Between the couple and Rome and liberty.
'T was dawn, the couple were rested in a sort,
And though the lady, tired,—the tenderer sex,—
Still lingered in her chamber,—to adjust
The limp hair, look for any blush astray,—   1060
She would descend in a twinkling,—' Have you out
' The horses therefore ! '
                So did I find my wife.
Is the case complete ?   Do your eyes here see with
    mine ?

Even the parties dared deny no one
Point out of all these points.
                    What follows next ?
' Why, that then was the time,' you interpose,
' Or then or never, while the fact was fresh,   1069
' To take the natural vengeance : there and thus
' They and you,—somebody had stuck a sword
' Beside you while he pushed you on your horse,—
' 'T was requisite to slay the couple, Count ! '
Just so my friends say—' Kill ! ' they cry in a breath,
Who presently, when matters grow to a head
And I do kill the offending ones indeed,—
When crime of theirs, only surmised before,
Is patent, proved indisputably now,—
When remedy for wrong, untried at the time,
Which law professes shall not fail a friend,   1080
Is thrice tried now, found threefold worse than null,—
When what might turn to transient shade, who knows ?
Solidifies into a blot which breaks
Hell's black off in pale flakes for fear of mine,—
Then, when I claim and take revenge—' So rash ? '
They cry—' so little reverence for the law ? '

Listen, my masters, and distinguish here !
At first, I called in law to act and help :
Seeing I did so, ' Why, 't is clear,' they cry,
' You shrank from gallant readiness and risk,   1090
' Were coward : the thing's inexplicable else.'
Sweet my lords, let the thing be ! I fall flat,
Play the reed, not the oak, to breath of man.
Only, inform my ignorance ! Say I stand
Convicted of the having been afraid,
Proved a poltroon, no lion but a lamb,—
Does that deprive me of my right of lamb
And give my fleece and flesh to the first wolf ?
Are eunuchs, women, children, shieldless quite
Against attack their own timidity tempts ?   1100
Cowardice were misfortune and no crime !
—Take it that way, since I am fallen so low
I scarce dare brush the fly that blows my face,
And thank the man who simply spits not there,—
Unless the Court be generous, comprehend
How one brought up at the very feet of law
As I, awaits the grave Gamaliel's nod

Ere he clench fist at outrage,—much less, stab !
—How, ready enough to rise at the right time,
I still could recognize no time mature   1110
Unsanctioned by a move o' the judgment-seat,
So, mute in misery, eyed my masters here
Motionless till the authoritative word
Pronounced amercement.   There 's the riddle solved :
This is just why I slew nor her nor him,
But called in law, law's delegate in the place,
And bade arrest the guilty couple, Sirs !
We had some trouble to do so—you have heard
They braved me,—he with arrogance and scorn,
She, with a volubility of curse,   1120
A conversancy in the skill of tooth
And claw to make suspicion seem absurd,
Nay, an alacrity to put to proof
At my own throat my own sword, teach me so
To try conclusions better the next time,—
Which did the proper service with the mob.
They never tried to put on mask at all :
Two avowed lovers forcibly torn apart,
Upbraid the tyrant as in a playhouse scene,
Ay, and with proper clapping and applause   1130
From the audience that enjoys the bold and free.
I kept still, said to myself, ' There 's law ! '   Anon
We searched the chamber where they passed the night,
Found what confirmed the worst was feared before,
However needless confirmation now—
The witches' circle intact, charms undisturbed
That raised the spirit and succubus,—letters, to-wit,
Love-laden, each the bag o' the bee that bore
Honey from lily and rose to Cupid's hive,—
Now, poetry in some rank blossom-burst,   1140
Now, prose,—' Come here, go there, wait such a while,
' He 's at the villa, now he 's back again :
' We are saved, we are lost, we are lovers all the same !
All in order, all complete,—even to a clue
To the drowsiness that happed so opportune—
No mystery, when I read ' Of all things, find
' What wine Sir Jealousy decides to drink—
' Red wine ?   Because a sleeping-potion, dust
' Dropped into white, discolours wine and shows.'

—' Oh, but we did not write a single word !   1150
    Somebody forged the letters in our name !—'

Both in a breath protested presently.
Aha, Sacchetti again !—' Dame,'—quoth the Duke,
' What meaneth this epistle, counsel me,
' I pick from out thy placket and peruse,
' Wherein my page averreth thou art white
' And warm and wonderful 'twixt pap and pap ? '
' Sir,' laughed the Lady ' 't is a counterfeit !
' Thy page did never stroke but Dian's breast,
' The pretty hound I nurture for thy sake :   1160
' To lie were losel,—by my fay, no more ! '
And no more say I too, and spare the Court.

Ah, the Court ! yes, I come to the Court's self ;
Such the case, so complete in fact and proof
I laid at the feet of law,—there sat my lords,
Here sit they now, so may they ever sit
In easier attitude than suits my haunch !
In this same chamber did I bare my sores
O' the soul and not the body,—shun no shame,
Shrink from no probing of the ulcerous part,   1170
Since confident in Nature,—which is God,—
That she who, for wise ends, concocts a plague,
Curbs, at the right time, the plague's virulence too :
Law renovates even Lazarus,—cures me !
Cæsar thou seekest ? To Cæsar thou shalt go !
Cæsar 's at Rome ; to Rome accordingly !

The case was soon decided : both weights, cast
I' the balance, vibrate, neither kicks the beam,
Here away, there away, this now and now that.
To every one o' my grievances law gave   1180
Redress, could purblind eye but see the point.
The wife stood a convicted runagate
From house and husband,—driven to such a course
By what she somehow took for cruelty,
Oppression and imperilment of life—
Not that such things were, but that so they seemed :
Therefore, the end conceded lawful, (since
To save life there 's no risk should stay our leap)
It follows that all means to the lawful end
Are lawful likewise,—poison, theft and flight.   1190
As for the priest's part, did he meddle or make,
Enough that he too thought life jeopardized ;
Concede him then the colour charity

Casts on a doubtful course,—if blackish white
Or whitish black, will charity hesitate ?
What did he else but act the precept out,
Leave, like a provident shepherd, his safe flock
To follow the single lamb and strayaway ?
Best hope so and think so,—that the ticklish time
I' the carriage, the tempting privacy, the last   1200
Somewhat ambiguous accident at the inn,
—All may bear explanation : may ? then, must !
The letters,—do they so incriminate ?
But what if the whole prove a prank o' the pen,
Flight of the fancy, none of theirs at all,
Bred of the vapours of my brain belike,
Or at worst mere exercise of scholar's-wit
In the courtly Caponsacchi : verse, convict ?
Did not Catullus write less seemly once ?
Yet *doctus* and unblemished he abides.   1210
Wherefore so ready to infer the worst ?
Still, I did righteously in bringing doubts
For the law to solve,—take the solution now !
' Seeing that the said associates, wife and priest,
' Bear themselves not without some touch of blame
' —Else why the pother, scandal and outcry
' Which trouble our peace and require chastisement ?
' We, for complicity in Pompilia's flight
' And deviation, and carnal intercourse
' With the same, do set aside and relegate   1220
' The Canon Caponsacchi for three years
' At Civita in the neighbourhood of Rome :
' And we consign Pompilia to the care
' Of a certain Sisterhood of penitents
' I' the city's self, expert to deal with such.'
Word for word, there's your judgment ! Read it, lords,
Re-utter your deliberate penalty
For the crime yourselves establish ! Your award—
Who chop a man's right-hand off at the wrist
For tracing with forefinger words in wine   1230
O' the table of a drinking-booth that bear
Interpretation as they mocked the Church !
—Who brand a woman black between the breasts
For sinning by connection with a Jew :
While for the Jew's self—pudency be dumb !
You mete out punishment such and such, yet so
Punish the adultery of wife and priest !
Take note of that, before the Molinists do

And read me right the riddle, since right must be !
While I stood rapt away with wonderment,   1240
Voices broke in upon my mood and muse.
' Do you sleep ? ' began the friends at either ear,
' The case is settled,—you willed it should be so—
' None of our counsel, always recollect !
' With law's award, budge !   Back into your place !
' Your betters shall arrange the rest for you.
' We 'll enter a new action, claim divorce :
' Your marriage was a cheat themselves allow :
' You erred i' the person,—might have married thus
' Your sister or your daughter unaware.   1250
' We 'll gain you, that way, liberty at least,
' Sure of so much by law's own showing.   Up
' And off with you and your unluckiness—
' Leave us to bury the blunder, sweep things smooth ! '
I was in humble frame of mind, be sure !
I bowed, betook me to my place again.
Station by station I retraced the road,
Touched at this hostel, passed this post-house by,
Where, fresh-remembered yet, the fugitives
Had risen to the heroic stature : still—   1260
' That was the bench they sat on,—there 's the board
' They took the meal at,—yonder garden-ground
' They leaned across the gate of,'—ever a word
O' the Helen and the Paris, with ' Ha ! you 're he,
' The . . . much-commiserated husband ? '   Step
By step, across the pelting, did I reach
Arezzo, underwent the archway's grin,
Traversed the length of sarcasm in the street,
Found myself in my horrible house once more,
And after a colloquy . . . no word assists !   1270
With the mother and the brothers, stiffened me
Strait out from head to foot as dead man does,
And, thus prepared for life as he for hell,
Marched to the public Square and met the world.
Apologize for the pincers, palliate screws ?
Ply me with such toy-trifles, I entreat !
Trust who has tried both sulphur and sops-in-wine !

I played the man as I best might, bade friends
Put non-essentials by and face the fact.
' What need to hang myself as you advise ?   1280
' The paramour is banished,—the ocean's width,

' Or the suburb's length,—to Ultima Thule, say,
' Or Proxima Civitas, what 's the odds of name
' And place ?   He 's banished, and the fact 's the thing.
' Why should law banish innocence an inch ?
' Here 's guilt then, what else do I care to know ?
' The adulteress lies imprisoned,—whether in a well
' With bricks above and a snake for company,
' Or tied by a garter to a bed-post,—much
' I mind what 's little,—least 's enough and to spare !
' The little fillip on the coward's cheek   1291
' Serves as though crab-tree cudgel broke his pate.
' Law has pronounced there 's punishment, less or
        more :
' And I take note o' the fact and use it thus—
' For the first flaw in the original bond,
' I claim release.   My contract was to wed
' The daughter of Pietro and Violante.   Both
' Protest they never had a child at all.
' Then I have never made a contract : good !
' Cancel me quick the thing pretended one.   1300
' I shall be free.   What matter if hurried over
' The harbour-boom by a great favouring tide,
' Or the last of a spent ripple that lifts and leaves ?
' The Abate is about it.   Laugh who wins !
' You shall not laugh me out of faith in law !
' I listen, through all your noise, to Rome ! '
                                        Rome spoke
In three months letters thence admonished me,
' Your plan for the divorce is all mistake.
' It would hold, now, had you, taking thought to wed
' Rachel of the blue eye and golden hair,   1311
' Found swarth-skinned Leah cumber couch next day :
' But Rachel, blue-eyed golden-haired aright,
' Proving to be only Laban's child, not Lot's,
' Remains yours all the same for ever more.
' No whit to the purpose is your plea : you err
' I' the person and the quality—nowise
' In the individual,—that 's the case in point !
' You go to the ground,—are met by a cross-suit
' For separation, of the Rachel here,   1320
' From bed and board,—she is the injured one,
' You did the wrong and have to answer it.
' As for the circumstance of imprisonment
' And colour it lends to this your new attack,

' Never fear, that point is considered too !
' The durance is already at an end ;
' The convent-quiet preyed upon her health,
' She is transferred now to her parents' house
' —No-parents, when that cheats and plunders you,
' But parentage again confessed in full,   1330
' When such confession pricks and plagues you more—
' As now—for, this their house is not the house
' In Via Vittoria wherein neighbours' watch
' Might incommode the freedom of your wife,
' But a certain villa smothered up in vines
' At the town's edge by the gate i' the Pauline way,
' Out of eye-reach, out of ear-shot, little and lone,
' Whither a friend,—at Civita, we hope,
' A good half-dozen-hours' ride off,—might, some eve,
' Betake himself, and whence ride back, some morn,
' Nobody the wiser : but be that as it may,   1341
' Do not afflict your brains with trifles now.
' You have still three suits to manage, all and each
' Ruinous truly should the event play false.
' It is indeed the likelier so to do,
' That brother Paul, your single prop and stay,
' After a vain attempt to bring the Pope
' To set aside procedures, sit himself
' And summarily use prerogative,
' Afford us the infallible finger's tact   1350
' To disentwine your tangle of affairs,
' Paul,—finding it moreover past his strength
' To stem the irruption, bear Rome's ridicule
' Of . . . since friends must speak . . . to be round with
    you . . .
' Of the old outwitted husband, wronged and wroth,
' Pitted against a brace of juveniles—
' A brisk priest who is versed in Ovid's art
' More than his Summa, and a gamesome wife
' Able to act Corinna without book,
' Beside the waggish parents who played dupes   1360
' To dupe the duper—(and truly divers scenes
' Of the Arezzo palace, tickle rib
' And tease eye till the tears come, so we laugh ;
' Nor wants the shock at the inn its comic force,
' And then the letters and poetry—*merum sal !*)
' —Paul, finally, in such a state of things,
' After a brief temptation to go jump

' And join the fishes in the Tiber, drowns
' Sorrow another and a wiser way :
' House and goods, he has sold all off, is gone,   1370
' Leaves Rome,—whether for France or Spain, who
        knows ?
' Or Britain almost divided from our orb.
' You have lost him anyhow.'
                                Now,—I see my lords
Shift in their seat,—would I could do the same !
They probably please expect my bile was moved
To purpose, nor much blame me : now, they judge,
The fiery titillation urged my flesh
Break through the bonds. By your pardon, no, sweet
        Sirs !
I got such missives in the public place ;   1380
When I sought home,—with such news, mounted stair
And sat at last in the sombre gallery,
('T was Autumn, the old mother in bed betimes,
Having to bear that cold, the finer frame
Of her daughter-in-law had found intolerable—
The brother, walking misery away
O' the mountain-side with dog and gun belike)
As I supped, ate the coarse bread, drank the wine
Weak once, now acrid with the toad's-head-squeeze,
My wife's bestowment, I broke silence thus :   1390
' Let me, a man, manfully meet the fact,
' Confront the worst o' the truth, end, and have peace !
' I am irremediably beaten here,—
' The gross illiterate vulgar couple,—bah !
' Why, they have measured forces, mastered mine,
' Made me their spoil and prey from first to last.
' They have got my name,—'t is nailed now fast to
        theirs,
' The child or changeling is anyway my wife ;
' Point by point as they plan they execute,
' They gain all, and I lose all—even to the lure   1400
' That led to loss,—they have the wealth again
' They hazarded awhile to hook me with,
' Have caught the fish and find the bait entire :
' They even have their child or changeling back
' To trade with, turn to account a second time.
' The brother, presumably might tell a tale
' Or give a warning,—he, too, flies the field,
' And with him vanish help and hope of help.

' They have caught me in the cavern where I fell,
' Covered my loudest cry for human aid   1410
' With this enormous paving-stone of shame.
' Well, are we demigods or merely clay ?
' Is success still attendant on desert ?
' Is this, we live on, heaven and the final state,
' Or earth which means probation to the end ?
' Why claim escape from man's predestined lot
' Of being beaten and baffled ?—God's decree,
' In which I, bowing bruised head, acquiesce.
' One of us Franceschini fell long since
' I' the Holy Land, betrayed, tradition runs,   1420
' To Paynims by the feigning of a girl
' He rushed to free from ravisher, and found
' Lay safe enough with friends in ambuscade
' Who flayed him while she clapped her hands and
    laughed :
' Let me end, falling by a like device.
' It will not be so hard. I am the last
' O' my line which will not suffer any more.
' I have attained to my full fifty years,
' (About the average of us all, 'tis said,
' Though it seems longer to the unlucky man)   1430
' —Lived through my share of life ; let all end here,
' Me and the house and grief and shame at once.
' Friends my informants,—I can bear your blow ! '
And I believe 't was in no unmeet match
For the stoic's mood, with something like a smile,
That, when morose December roused me next,
I took into my hand, broke seal to read
The new epistle from Rome.   ' All to no use !
' Whate'er the turn next injury take,' smiled I,
' Here 's one has chosen his part and knows his cue.
' I am done with, dead now ; strike away, good
    friends !   1441
' Are the three suits decided in a trice ?
' Against me,—there 's no question ! How does it go ?
' Is the parentage of my wife demonstrated
' Infamous to her wish ? Parades she now
' Loosed of the cincture that so irked the loin ?
' Is the last penny extracted from my purse
' To mulct me for demanding the first pound
' Was promised in return for value paid ?
' Has the priest, with nobody to court beside,   1450

' Courted the Muse in exile, hitched my hap
' Into a rattling ballad-rhyme which, bawled
' At tavern-doors, wakes rapture everywhere,
' And helps cheap wine down throat this Christmas
  time,
' Beating the bagpipes ? Any or all of these !
' As well, good friends, you cursed my palace here
' To its old cold stone face,—stuck your cap for crest
' Over the shield that 's extant in the Square,—
' Or spat on the statue's cheek, the impatient world
' Sees cumber tomb-top in our family church : 1460
' Let him creep under covert as I shall do,
' Half below-ground already indeed. Good-bye !
' My brothers are priests, and childless so ; that 's
  well—
' And, thank God most for this, no child leave I—
' None after me to bear till his heart break
' The being a Franceschini and my son ! '

' Nay,' said the letter, ' but you have just that !
' A babe, your veritable son and heir—
' Lawful,—'t is only eight months since your wife
' Left you,—so, son and heir, your babe was born
' Last Wednesday in the villa,—you see the cause
' For quitting Convent without beat of drum, 1472
' Stealing a hurried march to this retreat
' That 's not so savage as the Sisterhood
' To slips and stumbles : Pietro's heart is soft,
' Violante leans to pity's side,—the pair
' Ushered you into life a bouncing boy :
' And he 's already hidden away and safe
' From any claim on him you mean to make—
' They need him for themselves,—don 't fear, they
  know 1480
' The use o' the bantling,—the nerve thus laid bare
' To nip at, new and nice, with finger-nail ! '

Then I rose up like fire, and fire-like roared.
What, all is only beginning not ending now ?
The worm which wormed its way from skin through
  flesh
To the bone and there lay biting, did its best,
What, it goes on to scrape at the bone's self,
Will wind to inmost marrow and madden me ?

There 's to be yet my representative,
Another of the name shall keep displayed   1490
The flag with the ordure on it, brandish still
The broken sword has served to stir a jakes ?
Who will he be, how will you call the man ?
A Franceschini,—when who cut my purse,
Filched my name, hemmed me round, hustled me hard
As rogues at a fair some fool they strip i' the midst,
When these count gains, vaunt pillage presently :—
But a Caponsacchi, oh, be very sure !
When what demands its tribute of applause
Is the cunning and impudence o' the pair of cheats,
The lies and lust o' the mother, and the brave   1501
Bold carriage of the priest, worthily crowned
By a witness to his feat i' the following age,—
And how this three-fold cord could hook and fetch
And land leviathan that king of pride !
Or say, by some mad miracle of chance,
Is he indeed my flesh and blood, this babe ?
Was it because fate forged a link at last
Betwixt my wife and me, and both alike   1509
Found we had henceforth some one thing to love,
Was it when she could damn my soul indeed
She unlatched door, let all the devils o' the dark
Dance in on me to cover her escape ?
Why then, the surplusage of disgrace, the spilth
Over and above the measure of infamy,
Failing to take effect on my coarse flesh
Seasoned with scorn now, saturate with shame,—
Is saved to instil on and corrode the brow,
The baby-softness of my first-born child—
The child I had died to see though in a dream,   1520
The child I was bid strike out for, beat the wave
And baffle the tide of troubles where I swam,
So I might touch shore, lay down life at last
At the feet so dim and distant and divine
Of the apparition, as 't were Mary's babe
Had held, through night and storm, the torch aloft,—
Born now in very deed to bear this brand
On forehead and curse me who could not save !
Rather be the town-talk true, Square's jest, street's jeer
True, my own inmost heart's confession true,   1530
And he 's the priest's bastard and none of mine !
Ay, there was cause for flight, swift flight and sure !

The husband gets unruly, breaks all bounds
When he encounters some familiar face,
Fashion of feature, brow and eyes and lips
Where he least looked to find them,—time to fly !
This bastard then, a nest for him is made,
As the manner is of vermin, in my flesh—
Shall I let the filthy pest buzz, flap and sting,
Busy at my vitals and, nor hand nor foot   1540
Lift, but let be, lie still and rot resigned ?
No, I appeal to God,—what says Himself,
How lessons Nature when I look to learn ?
Why, that I am alive, am still a man
With brain and heart and tongue and right-hand too—
Nay, even with friends, in such a cause as this,
To right me if I fail to take my right.
No more of law ; a voice beyond the law
Enters my heart, *Quis est pro Domino ?*

Myself, in my own Vittiano, told the tale   1550
To my own serving-people summoned there :
Told the first half of it, scarce heard to end
By judges who got done with judgment quick
And clamoured to go execute her 'hest—
Who cried ' Not one of us that dig your soil
' And dress your vineyard, prune your olive-trees,
' But would have brained the man debauched our wife,
' And staked the wife whose lust allured the man,
' And paunched the Duke, had it been possible,
' Who ruled the land, yet barred us such revenge ! '
I fixed on the first whose eyes caught mine, some four,
Resolute youngsters with the heart still fresh,   1562
Filled my purse with the residue o' the coin
Uncaught-up by my wife whom haste made blind,
Donned the first rough and rural garb I found,
Took whatsoever weapon came to hand,
And out we flung and on we ran or reeled
Romeward, I have no memory of our way,
Only that, when at intervals the cloud
Of horror about me opened to let in life,   1570
I listened to some song in the ear, some snatch
Of a legend, relic of religion, stray
Fragment of record very strong and old
Of the first conscience, the anterior right,
The God's-gift to mankind, impulse to quench

The antagonistic spark of hell and tread
Satan and all his malice into dust,
Declare to the world the one law, right is right.
Then the cloud re-encompassed me, and so
I found myself, as on the wings of winds,   1580
Arrived : I was at Rome on Christmas Eve.

Festive bells—everywhere the Feast o' the Babe,
Joy upon earth, peace and good will to man !
I am baptized. I started and let drop
The dagger. ' Where is it, His promised peace ? '
Nine days o' the Birth-Feast did I pause and pray
To enter into no temptation more.
I bore the hateful house, my brother's once,
Deserted,—let the ghost of social joy   1589
Mock and make mouths at me from empty room
And idle door that missed the master's step,—
Bore the frank wonder of incredulous eyes,
As my own people watched without a word,
Waited, from where they huddled round the hearth
Black like all else, that nod so slow to come—
I stopped my ears even to the inner call
Of the dread duty, heard only the song
' Peace upon earth,' saw nothing but the face
O' the Holy Infant and the halo there
Able to cover yet another face   1600
Behind it, Satan's which I else should see.
But, day by day, joy waned and withered off :
The Babe's face, premature with peak and pine,
Sank into wrinkled ruinous old age,
Suffering and death, then mist-like disappeared,
And showed only the Cross at end of all,
Left nothing more to interpose 'twixt me
And the dread duty,—for the angel's song,
' Peace upon earth,' louder and louder pealed
' O Lord, how long, how long be unavenged ? '   1610
On the ninth day, this grew too much for man.
I started up—' Some end must be ! ' At once,
Silence : then, scratching like a death-watch-tick,
Slowly within my brain was syllabled,
' One more concession, one decisive way
' And but one, to determine thee the truth,—
' This way, in fine, I whisper in thy ear :
' Now doubt, anon decide, thereupon act ! '

' That is a way, thou whisperest in my ear !
' I doubt, I will decide, then act,' said I—   1620
Then beckoned my companions : ' Time is come ! '

And so, all yet uncertain save the will
To do right, and the daring aught save leave
Right undone, I did find myself at last
I' the dark before the villa with my friends,
And made the experiment, the final test,
Ultimate chance that ever was to be
For the wretchedness inside. I knocked—pronounced
The name, the predetermined touch for truth,
' What welcome for the wanderer ? Open straight—'
To the friend, physician, friar upon his rounds,   1631
Traveller belated, beggar lame and blind ?—
No, but—' to Caponsacchi ! '   And the door
Opened.
             And then,—why, even then, I think,
I' the minute that confirmed my worst of fears,
Surely,—I pray God that I think aright !—
Had but Pompilia's self, the tender thing
Who once was good and pure, was once my lamb
And lay in my bosom, had the well-known shape   1640
Fronted me in the door-way,—stood there faint
With the recent pang, perhaps, of giving birth
To what might, though by miracle, seem my child,—
Nay more, I will say, had even the aged fool
Pietro, the dotard, in whom folly and age
Wrought, more than enmity or malevolence,
To practice and conspire against my peace,—
Had either of these but opened, I had paused.
But it was she the hag, she that brought hell
For a dowry with her to her husband's house,   1650
She the mock-mother, she that made the match
And married me to perdition, spring and source
O' the fire inside me that boiled up from heart
To brain and hailed the Fury gave it birth,—
Violante Comparini, she it was,
With the old grin amid the wrinkles yet,
Opened : as if in turning from the Cross,
With trust to keep the sight and save my soul,
I had stumbled, first thing, on the serpent's head
Coiled with a leer at foot of it.   1660
                      There was the end !

Then was I rapt away by the impulse, one
Immeasurable everlasting wave of a need
To abolish that detested life. 'T was done :
You know the rest and how the folds o' the thing,
Twisting for help, involved the other two
More or less serpent-like : how I was mad,
Blind, stamped on all, the earth-worms with the asp,
And ended so.   You came on me that night,   1670
Your officers of justice,—caught the crime
In the first natural frenzy of remorse ?
Twenty miles off, sound sleeping as a child
On a cloak i' the straw which promised shelter first,
With the bloody arms beside me,—was it not so ?
Wherefore not ?   Why, how else should I be found ?
I was my own self, had my sense again,
My soul safe from the serpents.   I could sleep :
Indeed and, dear my lords, I shall sleep now,
Spite of my shoulder, in five minutes' space,   1680
When you dismiss me, having truth enough !
It is but a few days are passed, I find,
Since this adventure.   Do you tell me, four ?
Then the dead are scarce quiet where they lie,
Old Pietro, old Violante, side by side
At the church Lorenzo,—oh, they know it well !
So do I.   But my wife is still alive,
Has breath enough to tell her story yet,
Her way, which is not mine, no doubt at all.
And Caponsacchi, you have summoned him,—   1690
Was he so far to send for ?   Not at hand ?
I thought some few o' the stabs were in his heart,
Or had not been so lavish,—less had served.
Well, he too tells his story,—florid prose
As smooth as mine is rough.   You see, my lords,
There will be a lying intoxicating smoke
Born of the blood,—confusion probably,—
For lies breed lies—but all that rests with you !
The trial is no concern of mine ; with me
The main of the care is over : I at least   1700
Recognize who took that huge burthen off,
Let me begin to live again.   I did
God's bidding and man's duty, so, breathe free ;
Look you to the rest !   I heard Himself prescribe,
That great Physician, and dared lance the core

Of the bad ulcer ; and the rage abates,
I am myself and whole now : I prove cured
By the eyes that see, the ears that hear again,
The limbs that have relearned their youthful play,
The healthy taste of food and feel of clothes   1710
And taking to our common life once more,
All that now urges my defence from death.
The willingness to live, what means it else ?
Before,—but let the very action speak !
Judge for yourselves, what life seemed worth to me
Who, not by proxy but in person, pitched
Head-foremost into danger as a fool
That never cares if he can swim or no—
So he but find the bottom, braves the brook.
No man omits precaution, quite neglects   1720
Secrecy, safety, schemes not how retreat,
Having schemed he might advance. Did I so scheme ?
Why, with a warrant which 't is ask and have,
With horse thereby made mine without a word,
I had gained the frontier and slept safe that night.
Then, my companions,—call them what you please,
Slave or stipendiary,—what need of one
To me whose right-hand did its owner's work ?
Hire an assassin yet expose yourself ?
As well buy glove and then thrust naked hand   1730
I' the thorn-bush.   No, the wise man stays at home,
Sends only agents out, with pay to earn :
At home, when they come back,—he straight discards
Or else disowns.   Why use such tools at all
When a man's foes are of his house, like mine,
Sit at his board, sleep in his bed ?   Why noise,
When there 's the *acquetta* and the silent way ?
Clearly my life was valueless.

                              But now
Health is returned, and sanity of soul   1740
Nowise indifferent to the body's harm.
I find the instinct bids me save my life ;
My wits, too, rally round me ; I pick up
And use the arms that strewed the ground before,
Unnoticed or spurned aside : I take my stand,
Make my defence.   God shall not lose a life
May do Him further service, while I speak
And you hear, you my judges and last hope !

You are the law : 't is to the law I look.
I began life by hanging to the law, 1750
To the law it is I hang till life shall end.
My brother made appeal to the Pope, 't is true,
To stay proceedings, judge my cause himself
Nor trouble law,—some fondness of conceit
That rectitude, sagacity sufficed
The investigator in a case like mine,
Dispensed with the machine of law. The Pope
Knew better, set aside my brother's plea
And put me back to law,—referred the cause
Ad judices meos,—doubtlessly did well. 1760
Here, then, I clutch my judges,—I claim law—
Cry, by the higher law whereof your law
O' the land is humbly representative,—
Cry, on what point is it, where either accuse,
I fail to furnish you defence ? I stand
Acquitted, actually or virtually,
By every intermediate kind of court
That takes account of right or wrong in man,
Each unit in the series that begins 1769
With God's throne, ends with the tribunal here.
God breathes, not speaks, his verdicts, felt not heard,
Passed on successively to each court I call
Man's conscience, custom, manners, all that make
More and more effort to promulgate, mark
God's verdict in determinable words,
Till last come human jurists—solidify
Fluid result,—what 's fixable lies forged,
Statute,—the residue escapes in fume,
Yet hangs aloft, a cloud, as palpable
To the finer sense as word the legist welds. 1780
Justinian's Pandects only make precise
What simply sparkled in men's eyes before,
Twitched in their brow or quivered on their lip,
Waited the speech they called but would not come.
These courts then, whose decree your own confirms,—
Take my whole life, not this last act alone,
Look on it by the light reflected thence !
What has Society to charge me with ?
Come, unreservedly,—favour nor fear,—
I am Guido Franceschini, am I not ? 1790
You know the courses I was free to take ?
I took just that which let me serve the Church,

I gave it all my labour in body and soul
Till these broke down i' the service.   'Specify ? '
Well, my last patron was a Cardinal.
I left him unconvicted of a fault—
Was even helped, by way of gratitude,
Into the new life that I left him for,
This very misery of the marriage,—he
Made it, kind soul, so far as in him lay—   1800
Signed the deed where you yet may see his name.
He is gone to his reward,—dead, being my friend
Who could have helped here also,—that, of course !
So far, there 's my acquittal, I suppose.
Then comes the marriage itself—no question, lords,
Of the entire validity of that !
In the extremity of distress, 't is true,
For after-reasons, furnished abundantly,
I wished the thing invalid, went to you
Only some months since, set you duly forth   1810
My wrong and prayed your remedy, that a cheat
Should not have force to cheat my whole life long.
' Annul a marriage ?   'T is impossible !
' Though ring about your neck be brass not gold,
' Needs must it clasp, gangrene you all the same ! '
Well, let me have the benefit, just so far,
O' the fact announced,—my wife then is my wife,
I have allowance for a husband's right.
I am charged with passing right's due bound,—such
        acts
As I thought just, my wife called cruelty,   1820
Complained of in due form,—convoked no court
Of common gossipry, but took her wrongs—
And not once, but so long as patience served—
To the town's top, jurisdiction's pride of place,
To the Archbishop and the Governor.
These heard her charge with my reply, and found
That futile, this sufficient : they dismissed
The hysteric querulous rebel, and confirmed
Authority in its wholesome exercise,
They, with directest access to the facts.   1830
' —Ay, for it was their friendship favoured you,
' Hereditary alliance against a breach
' I' the social order : prejudice for the name
' Of Franceschini ! '—So I hear it said :
But not here.   You, lords, never will you say

' Such is the nullity of grace and truth,
' Such the corruption of the faith, such lapse
' Of law, such warrant have the Molinists
' For daring reprehend us as they do,—
' That we pronounce it just a common case,   1840
' Two dignitaries, each in his degree
' First, foremost, this the spiritual head, and that
' The secular arm o' the body politic,
' Should, for mere wrongs' love and injustice' sake,
' Side with, aid and abet in cruelty
' This broken beggarly noble,—bribed perhaps
' By his watered wine and mouldy crust of bread—
' Rather than that sweet tremulous flower-like wife
' Who kissed their hands and curled about their feet
' Looking the irresistible loveliness   1850
' In tears that takes man captive, turns ' . . . enough !
Do you blast your predecessors ?   What forbids
Posterity to trebly blast yourselves
Who set the example and instruct their tongue ?
You dreaded the crowd, succumbed to the popular cry,
Or else, would nowise seem defer thereto
And yield to public clamour though i' the right !
You ridded your eye of my unseemliness,
The noble whose misfortune wearied you,—
Or, what 's more probable, made common cause
With the cleric section, punished in myself   1861
Maladroit uncomplaisant laity,
Defective in behaviour to a priest
Who claimed the customary partnership
I' the house and the wife.   Lords, any lie will serve !
Look to it,—or allow me freed so far !

Then I proceed a step, come with clean hands
Thus far, re-tell the tale told eight months since.
The wife, you allow so far, I have not wronged,
Has fled my roof, plundered me and decamped   1870
In company with the priest her paramour :
And I give chase, came up with, caught the two
At the wayside inn where both had spent the night,
Found them in flagrant fault, and found as well,
By documents with name and plan and date,
The fault was furtive then that's flagrant now,
Their intercourse a long established crime.
I did not take the license law's self gives
To slay both criminals o' the spot at the time,

But held my hand,—preferred play prodigy   1880
Of patience which the world calls cowardice,
Rather than seem anticipate the law
And cast discredit on its organs,—you—
So, to your bar I brought both criminals,
And made my statement : heard their counter-charge
Nay,—their corroboration of my tale,
Nowise disputing its allegements, not
I' the main, not more than nature's decency
Compels men to keep silence in this kind,—
Only contending that the deeds avowed   1890
Would take another colour and bear excuse.
You were to judge between us ; so you did.
You disregard the excuse, you breathe away
The colour of innocence and leave guilt black,
' Guilty ' is the decision of the court,
And that I stand in consequence untouched,
One white integrity from head to heel.
Not guilty ?   Why then did you punish them ?
True, punishment has been inadequate—
'T is not I only, not my friends that joke,   1900
My foes that jeer, who echo ' inadequate '—
For, by a chance that comes to help for once,
The same case simultaneously was judged
At Arezzo, in the province of the Court
Where the crime had beginning but not end.
They then, deciding on but half o' the crime,
The effraction, robbery,—features of the fault
I never cared to dwell upon at Rome,—
What was it they adjudged as penalty
To Pompilia,—the one criminal o' the pair   1910
Amenable to their judgment, not the priest
Who is Rome's ?   Why, just imprisonment for life
I' the Stinche.   There was Tuscany's award
To a wife that robs her husband : you at Rome
Having to deal with adultery in a wife
And, in a priest, breach of the priestly vow,
Give gentle sequestration for a month
In a manageable Convent, then release,
You call imprisonment, in the very house
O' the very couple, the sole aim and end   1920
Of the culprits' crime was—there to reach and rest
And there take solace and defy me : well,—
This difference 'twixt their penalty and yours

Is immaterial : make your penalty less—
Merely that she should henceforth wear black gloves
And white fan, she who wore the opposite—
Why, all the same the fact o' the thing subsists.
Reconcile to your conscience as you may,
Be it on your own heads, you pronounced one half
O' the penalty for heinousness like hers   1930
And his, that 's for a fault at Carnival
Of comfit-pelting past discretion's law,
Or accident to handkerchief in Lent
Which falls perversely as a lady kneels
Abruptly, and but half conceals her neck !
I acquiesce for my part,—punished, though
By a pin-point scratch, means guilty : guilty means
—What have I been but innocent hitherto ?
Anyhow, here the offence, being punished, ends.

Ends ?—for you deemed so, did you not, sweet lords ?
That was throughout the veritable aim   1941
O' the sentence light or heavy,—to redress
Recognized wrong ?   You righted me, I think ?
Well then,—what if I, at this last of all,
Demonstrate you, as my whole pleading proves,
No particle of wrong received thereby
One atom of right ?—that cure grew worse disease ?
That in the process you call ' justice done '
All along you have nipped away just inch
By inch the creeping climbing length of plague   1950
Breaking my tree of life from root to branch,
And left me, after all and every act
Of your interference,—lightened of what load ?
At liberty wherein ?   Mere words and wind !
' Now I was saved, now I should feel no more
' The hot breath, find a respite from fixed eye
' And vibrant tongue ! '   Why, scarce your back was
        turned,
There was the reptile, that feigned death at first,
Renewing its detested spire and spire
Around me, rising to such heights of hate   1960
That, so far from mere purpose now to crush
And coil itself on the remains of me,
Body and mind, and there flesh fang content,
Its aim is now to evoke life from death,
Make me anew, satisfy in my son

The hunger I may feed but never sate,
Tormented on to perpetuity,—
My son, whom, dead, I shall know, understand,
Feel, hear, see, never more escape the sight
In heaven that 's turned to hell, or hell returned
(So, rather, say) to this same earth again,—   1971
Moulded into the image and made one,
Fashioned of soul as featured like in face,
First taught to laugh and lisp and stand and go
By that thief, poisoner and adulteress
I call Pompilia, he calls . . . sacred name,
Be unpronounced, be unpolluted here !
And last led up to the glory and prize of hate
By his . . foster-father, Caponsacchi's self,
The perjured priest, pink of conspirators,   1980
Tricksters and knaves, yet polished, superfine,
Manhood to model adolescence by . . .
Lords, look on me, declare,—when, what I show,
Is nothing more nor less than what you deemed
And doled me out for justice,—what did you say ?
For reparation, restitution and more,—
Will you not thank, praise, bid me to your breasts
For having done the thing you thought to do,
And thoroughly trampled out sin's life at last ?
I have heightened phrase to make your soft speech
       serve,   1990
Doubled the blow you but essayed to strike,
Carried into effect your mandate here
That else had fallen to ground : mere duty done,
Oversight of the master just supplied
By zeal i' the servant : I, being used to serve,
Have simply . . . what is it they charge me with ?
Blackened again, made legible once more
Your own decree, not permanently writ,
Rightly conceived but all too faintly traced,—
It reads efficient, now, comminatory,   2000
A terror to the wicked, answers so
The mood o' the magistrate, the mind of law.
Absolve, then, me, law's mere executant !
Protect your own defender,—save me, Sirs !
Give me my life, give me my liberty,
My good name and my civic rights again !
It would be too fond, too complacent play
Into the hands o' the devil, should we lose

The game here, I for God : a soldier-bee   2009
That yields his life, exenterate with the stroke
O' the sting that saves the hive.   I need that life,
Oh, never fear !   I 'll find life plenty use
Though it should last five years more, aches and all !
For, first thing, there's the mother's age to help—
Let her come break her heart upon my breast,
Not on the blank stone of my nameless tomb !
The fugitive brother has to be bidden back
To the old routine, repugnant to the tread,
Of daily suit and service to the Church,—
Thro' gibe and jest, those stones that Shimei flung !
Ay, and the spirit-broken youth at home,   2021
The awe-struck altar-ministrant, shall make
Amends for faith now palsied at the source,
Shall see truth yet triumphant, justice yet
A victor in the battle of this world !
Give me—for last, best gift, my son again,
Whom law makes mine,—I take him at your word,
Mine be he, by miraculous mercy, lords !
Let me lift up his youth and innocence
To purify my palace, room by room   2030
Purged of the memories, lend from his bright brow
Light to the old proud paladin my sire
Shrunk now for shame into the darkest shade
O' the tapestry, showed him once and shrouds him
     now !
Then may we,—strong from that rekindled smile,—
Go forward, face new times, the better day.
And when, in times made better through your brave
Decision now,—might but Utopia be !—
Rome rife with honest women and strong men,
Manners reformed, old habits back once more,   2040
Customs that recognize the standard worth,—
The wholesome household rule in force again,
Husbands once more God's representative,
Wives like the typical Spouse once more, and Priests
No longer men of Belial, with no aim
At leading silly women captive, but
Of rising to such duties as yours now,—
Then will I set my son at my right-hand
And tell his father's story to this point,
Adding ' The task seemed superhuman, still   2050
' I dared and did it, trusting God and law :

' And they approved of me : give praise to both ! '
And if, for answer, he shall stoop to kiss
My hand, and peradventure start thereat,—
I engage to smile ' That was an accident
' I' the necessary process,—just a trip
' O' the torture-irons in their search for truth,—
' Hardly misfortune, and no fault at all.'

VI

GIUSEPPE CAPONSACCHI

ANSWER you, Sirs ?   Do I understand aright ?
Have patience !   In this sudden smoke from hell,—
So things disguise themselves,—I cannot see
My own hand held thus broad before my face
And know it again.   Answer you ?   Then that means
Tell over twice what I, the first time, told
Six months ago : 't was here, I do believe,
Fronting you same three in this very room,
I stood and told you : yet now no one laughs,
Who then . . nay, dear my lords, but laugh you did,
As good as laugh, what in a judge we style   11
Laughter—no levity, nothing indecorous, lords !
Only,—I think I apprehend the mood :
There was the blameless shrug, permissible smirk,
The pen's pretence at play with the pursed mouth,
The titter stifled in the hollow palm
Which rubbed the eyebrow and caressed the nose,
When I first told my tale : they meant, you know,
' The sly one, all this we are bound believe !
' Well, he can say no other than what he says.   20
' We have been young, too,—come, there 's greater
      guilt !
' Let him but decently disembroil himself,
' Scramble from out the scrape nor move the mud,—
' We solid ones may risk a finger-stretch ! '
And now you sit as grave, stare as aghast
As if I were a phantom : now 't is—' Friend,
' Collect yourself ! '—no laughing matter more—
' Counsel the Court in this extremity,
' Tell us again ! '—tell that, for telling which,
I got the jocular piece of punishment,   30
Was sent to lounge a little in the place
Whence now of a sudden here you summon me
To take the intelligence from just—your lips

H 3

You, Judge Tommati, who then tittered most,—
That she I helped eight months since to escape
Her husband, is retaken by the same,
Three days ago, if I have seized your sense,—
(I being disallowed to interfere,
Meddle or make in a matter none of mine,
For you and law were guardians quite enough   40
O' the innocent, without a pert priest's help)—
And that he has butchered her accordingly,
As she foretold and as myself believed,—
And, so foretelling and believing so,
We were punished, both of us, the merry way :
Therefore, tell once again the tale ! For what ?
Pompilia is only dying while I speak !
Why does the mirth hang fire and miss the smile ?
My masters, there 's an old book, you should con
For strange adventures, applicable yet,   50
'T is stuffed with. Do you know that there was once
This thing : a multitude of worthy folk
Took recreation, watched a certain group
Of soldiery intent upon a game,—
How first they wrangled, but soon fell to play,
Threw dice,—the best diversion in the world.
A word in your ear,—they are now casting lots,
Ay, with that gesture quaint and cry uncouth,
For the coat of One murdered an hour ago !
I am a priest,—talk of what I have learned.   60
Pompilia is bleeding out her life belike,
Gasping away the latest breath of all,
This minute, while I talk—not while you laugh ?

Yet, being sobered now, what is it you ask
By way of explanation ? There 's the fact !
It seems to fill the universe with sight
And sound,—from the four corners of this earth
Tells itself over, to my sense at least.
But you may want it lower set i' the scale,—   69
Too vast, too close it clangs in the ear, perhaps ;
You 'd stand back just to comprehend it more :
Well then, let me, the hollow rock, condense
The voice o' the sea and wind, interpret you
The mystery of this murder. God above !
It is too paltry, such a transference
O' the storm's roar to the cranny of the stone !

This deed, you saw begin—why does its end
Surprise you ? Why should the event enforce
The lesson, we ourselves learned, she and I,   79
From the first o' the fact, and taught you, all in vain ?
This Guido from whose throat you took my grasp,
Was this man to be favoured, now, or feared,
Let do his will, or have his will restrained,
In the relation with Pompilia ?—say !
Did any other man need interpose
—Oh, though first comer, though as strange at the
     work
As fribble must be, coxcomb, fool that 's near
To knave as, say, a priest who fears the world—
Was he bound brave the peril, save the doomed,
Or go on, sing his snatch and pluck his flower,   90
Keep the straight path and let the victim die ?
I held so ; you decided otherwise,
Saw no such peril, therefore no such need
To stop song, loosen flower, and leave path : Law,
Law was aware and watching, would suffice,
Wanted no priest's intrusion, palpably
Pretence, too manifest a subterfuge !
Whereupon I, priest, coxcomb, fribble and fool,
Ensconced me in my corner, thus rebuked,
A kind of culprit, over-zealous hound   100
Kicked for his pains to kennel ; I gave place,
To you, and let the law reign paramount :
I left Pompilia to your watch and ward,
And now you point me—there and thus she lies !

Men, for the last time, what do you want with me ?
Is it,—you acknowledge, as it were, a use,
A profit in employing me ?—at length
I may conceivably help the august law ?
I am free to break the blow, next hawk that swoops
On next dove, nor miss much of good repute ?   110
Or what if this your summons, after all,
Be but the form of mere release, no more,
Which turns the key and lets the captive go ?
I have paid enough in person at Civita,
Am free,—what more need I concern me with ?
Thank you ! I am rehabilitated then,
A very reputable priest. But she—
The glory of life, the beauty of the world,

The splendour of heaven, . . . well, Sirs, does no one
    move ?
Do I speak ambiguously ? The glory, I say,   120
And the beauty, I say, and splendour, still say I,
Who, a priest, trained to live my whole life long
On beauty and splendour, solely at their source,
God,—have thus recognized my food in one,
You tell me, is fast dying while we talk,
Pompilia,—how does lenity to me,
Remit one death-bed pang to her ? Come, smile !
The proper wink at the hot-headed youth
Who lets his soul show, through transparent words,
The mundane love that 's sin and scandal too !   130
You are all struck acquiescent now, it seems :
It seems the oldest, gravest signor here,
Even the redoubtable Tommati, sits
Chop-fallen,—understands how law might take
Service like mine, of brain and heart and hand,
In good part.   Better late than never, law !
You understand of a sudden, gospel too
Has a claim here, may possibly pronounce
Consistent with my priesthood, worthy Christ,
That I endeavoured to save Pompilia ?   140

                        Then,
You were wrong, you see : that 's well to see, though
    late :
That 's all we may expect of man, this side
The grave : his good is—knowing he is bad :
Thus will it be with us when the books ope
And we stand at the bar on judgment-day.
Well then, I have a mind to speak, see cause
To relume the quenched flax by this dreadful light,
Burn my soul out in showing you the truth.
I heard, last time I stood here to be judged,   150
What is priest's-duty,—labour to pluck tares
And weed the corn of Molinism ; let me
Make you hear, this time, how, in such a case,
Man, be he in the priesthood or at plough,
Mindful of Christ or marching step by step
With . . . what 's his style, the other potentate
Who bids have courage and keep honour safe,
Nor let minuter admonition tease ?—
How he is bound, better or worse, to act.

Earth will not end through this misjudgment, no !
For you and the others like you sure to come,   161
Fresh work is sure to follow,—wickedness
That wants withstanding.   Many a man of blood,
Many a man of guile will clamour yet,
Bid you redress his grievance,—as he clutched
The prey, forsooth a stranger stepped between,
And there 's the good gripe in pure waste ! My part
Is done ; i' the doing it, I pass away
Out of the world.   I want no more with earth.
Let me, in heaven's name, use the very snuff   170
O' the taper in one last spark shall show truth
For a moment, show Pompilia who was true !
Not for her sake, but yours : if she is dead,
Oh, Sirs, she can be loved by none of you
Most or least priestly ! Saints, to do us good,
Must be in heaven, I seem to understand :
We never find them saints before, at least.
Be her first prayer then presently for you—
She has done the good to me . .
                              What is all this ?   180
There, I was born, have lived, shall die, a fool !
This is a foolish outset :—might with cause
Give colour to the very lie o' the man,
The murderer,—make as if I loved his wife,
In the way he called love.   He is the fool there !
Why, had there been in me the touch of taint,
I had picked up so much of knaves'-policy
As hide it, keep one hand pressed on the place
Suspected of a spot would damn us both.
Or no, not her !—not even if any of you   190
Dares think that I, i' the face of death, her death
That 's in my eyes and ears and brain and heart,
Lie,—if he does, let him ! I mean to say,
So he stop there, stay thought from smirching her
The snow-white soul that angels fear to take
Untenderly.   But, all the same, I know
I too am taintless, and I bare my breast.
You can 't think, men as you are, all of you,
But that, to hear thus suddenly such an end
Of such a wonderful white soul, that comes   200
Of a man and murderer calling the white black,
Must shake me, trouble and disadvantage.   Sirs,
Only seventeen !

Why, good and wise you are !
You might at the beginning stop my mouth :
So, none would be to speak for her, that knew.
I talk impertinently, and you bear,
All the same.   This it is to have to do
With honest hearts : they easily may err,
But in the main they wish well to the truth.   210
You are Christians ; somehow, no one ever plucked
A rag, even, from the body of the Lord,
To wear and mock with, but, despite himself,
He looked the greater and was the better.   Yes,
I shall go on now.   Does she need or not
I keep calm ?   Calm I 'll keep as monk that croons
Transcribing battle, earthquake, famine, plague,
From parchment to his cloister's chronicle.
Not one word more from the point now !

I begin.   220
Yes, I am one of your body and a priest.
Also I am a younger son o' the House
Oldest now, greatest once, in my birth-town
Arezzo, I recognize no equal there—
(I want all arguments, all sorts of arms
That seem to serve,—use this for a reason, wait !)
Not therefore thrust into the Church, because
O' the piece of bread one gets there.   We were first
Of Fiesole, that rings still with the fame
Of Capo-in-Sacco our progenitor :   230
When Florence ruined Fiesole, our folk
Migrated to the victor-city, and there
Flourished,—our palace and our tower attest,
In the Old Mercato,—this was years ago,
Four hundred, full,—no, it wants fourteen just.
Our arms are those of Fiesole itself,
The shield quartered with white and red : a branch
Are the Salviati of us, nothing more.
That were good help to the Church ?   But better still—
Not simply for the advantage of my birth   240
I' the way of the world, was I proposed for priest ;
But because there 's an illustration, late
I' the day, that 's loved and looked to as a saint
Still in Arezzo, he was bishop of,
Sixty years since : he spent to the last doit
His bishop's-revenue among the poor,

And used to tend the needy and the sick,
Barefoot, because of his humility.
He it was,—when the Granduke Ferdinand
Swore he would raze our city, plough the place   250
And sow it with salt, because we Aretines
Had tied a rope about the neck, to hale
The statue of his father from its base
For hate's sake,—he availed by prayers and tears
To pacify the Duke and save the town.
This was my father's father's brother.   You see,
For his sake, how it was I had a right
To the self-same office, bishop in the egg,
So, grew i' the garb and prattled in the school,
Was made expect, from infancy almost,   260
The proper mood o' the priest ; till time ran by
And brought the day when I must read the vows,
Declare the world renounced and undertake
To become priest and leave probation,—leap
Over the ledge into the other life,
Having gone trippingly hitherto up to the height
O'er the wan water.   Just a vow to read !

I stopped short awe-struck.   ' How shall holiest flesh
' Engage to keep such vow inviolate,   269
' How much less mine,—I know myself too weak,
' Unworthy !   Choose a worthier stronger man ! '
And the very Bishop smiled and stopped the mouth
In its mid-protestation.   ' Incapable ?
' Qualmish of conscience ?   Thou ingenuous boy !
' Clear up the clouds and cast thy scruples far !
' I satisfy thee there 's an easier sense
' Wherein to take such vow than suits the first
' Rough rigid reading.   Mark what makes all smooth,
' Nay, has been even a solace to myself !
' The Jews who needs must, in their synagogue,
' Utter sometimes the holy name of God,   281
' A thing their superstition boggles at,
' Pronounce aloud the ineffable sacrosanct,—
' How does their shrewdness help them ?   In this wise ;
' Another set of sounds they substitute,
' Jumble so consonants and vowels—how
' Should I know ?—that there grows from out the old
' Quite a new word that means the very same—
' And o'er the hard place slide they with a smile.

' Giuseppe Maria Caponsacchi mine,   290
' Nobody wants you in these latter days
' To prop the Church by breaking your back-bone,—
' As the necessary way was once, we know,
' When Diocletian flourished and his like ;
' That building of the buttress-work was done
' By martyrs and confessors : let it bide,
' Add not a brick, but, where you see a chink,
' Stick in a sprig of ivy or root a rose
' Shall make amends and beautify the pile !
' We profit as you were the painfullest   300
' O' the martyrs, and you prove yourself a match
' For the cruellest confessor ever was,
' If you march boldly up and take your stand
' Where their blood soaks, their bones yet strew the
        soil,
' And cry " Take notice, I the young and free
' " And well-to-do i' the world, thus leave the world,
' " Cast in my lot thus with no gay young world
' " But the grand old Church : she tempts me of the
        two ! "   308
' Renounce the world ?   Nay, keep and give it us !
' Let us have you, and boast of what you bring.
' We want the pick o' the earth to practise with,
' Not its offscouring, halt and deaf and blind
' In soul and body.   There 's a rubble-stone
' Unfit for the front o' the building, stuff to stow
' In a gap behind and keep us weather-tight ;
' There 's porphyry for the prominent place.   Good
        lack !
' Saint Paul has had enough and to spare, I trow,
' Of ragged run-away Onesimus :
' He wants the right-hand with the signet-ring
' Of King Agrippa, now, to shake and use.   320
' I have a heavy scholar cloistered up,
' Close under lock and key, kept at his task
' Of letting Fenelon know the fool he is,
' In a book I promise Christendom next Spring.
' Why, if he covets so much meat, the clown,
' As a lark's wing next Friday, or, any day,
' Diversion beyond catching his own fleas,
  He shall be properly swinged, I promise him.
' But you, who are so quite another paste
' Of a man,—do you obey me ?   Cultivate   320

' Assiduous, that superior gift you have
' Of making madrigals—(who told me ? Ah !)
' Get done a Marinesque Adoniad straight
' With a pulse o' the blood a-pricking, here and there,
' That I may tell the lady, " And he's ours ! " '

So I became a priest : those terms changed all,
I was good enough for that, nor cheated so ;
I could live thus and still hold head erect.
Now you see why I may have been before
A fribble and coxcomb, yet, as priest, break word
Nowise, to make you disbelieve me now.   341
I need that you should know my truth. Well, then,
According to prescription did I live,
—Conformed myself, both read the breviary
And wrote the rhymes, was punctual to my place
I' the Pieve, and as diligent at my post
Where beauty and fashion rule. I throve apace,
Sub-deacon, Canon, the authority
For delicate play at tarocs, and arbiter
O' the magnitude of fan-mounts : all the while   350
Wanting no whit the advantage of a hint
Benignant to the promising pupil,—thus :
' Enough attention to the Countess now,
' The young one ; 't is her mother rules the roast,
' We know where, and puts in a word : go pay
' Devoir to-morrow morning after mass !
' Break that rash promise to preach, Passion-week !
' Has it escaped you the Archbishop grunts
' And snuffles when one grieves to tell his Grace
' No soul dares treat the subject of the day   360
' Since his own masterly handling it (ha, ha !)
' Five years ago,—when somebody could help
' And touch up an odd phrase in time of need,
' (He, he !)—and somebody helps you, my son !
' Therefore, don't prove so indispensable
' At the Pieve, sit more loose i' the seat, nor grow
' A fixture by attendance morn and eve !
' Arezzo 's just a haven midway Rome—
' Rome 's the eventual harbour,—make for port,
' Crowd sail, crack cordage ! And your cargo be
' A polished presence, a genteel manner, wit   371
' At will, and tact at every pore of you !
' I sent our lump of learning, Brother Clout,

' And Father Slouch, our piece of piety,
' To see Rome and try suit the Cardinal.
' Thither they clump-clumped, beads and book in
        hand,
' And ever since 't is meat for man and maid
' How both flopped down, prayed blessing on bent pate
' Bald many an inch beyond the tonsure's need,
' Never once dreaming, the two moony dolts,   380
' There 's nothing moves his Eminence so much
' As—far from all this awe at sanctitude—
' Heads that wag, eyes that twinkle, modified mirth
' At the closet-lectures on the Latin tongue
' A lady learns so much by, we know where.
' Why, body o' Bacchus, you should crave his rule
' For pauses in the elegiac couplet, chasms
' Permissible only to Catullus ! There !
' Now go do duty : brisk, break Priscian's head
' By reading the day's office—there 's no help.   390
' You 've Ovid in your poke to plaster that ;
' Amen 's at the end of all : then sup with me ! '

    Well, after three or four years of this life,
In prosecution of my calling, I
Found myself at the theatre one night
With a brother Canon, in a mood and mind
Proper enough for the place, amused or no :
When I saw enter, stand, and seat herself
A lady, young, tall, beautiful, strange and sad.
It was as when, in our cathedral once,   400
As I got yawningly through matin-song
I saw *facchini* bear a burden up,
Base it on the high-altar, break away
A board or two, and leave the thing inside
Lofty and lone : and lo, when next I looked,
There was the Rafael ! I was still one stare,
When—' Nay, I'll make her give you back your
        gaze '—
Said Canon Conti ; and at the word he tossed
A paper-twist of comfits to her lap,
And dodged and in a trice was at my back   410
Nodding from over my shoulder. Then she turned,
Looked our way, smiled the beautiful sad strange
        smile.
' Is not she fair ? 'T is my new cousin,' said he :

' The fellow lurking there i' the black o' the box
' Is Guido, the old scapegrace : she 's his wife,
' Married three years since : how his Countship sulks !
' He has brought little back from Rome beside,
' After the bragging, bullying. A fair face,
' And—they do say—a pocket-full of gold
' When he can worry both her parents dead.   420
' I don 't go much there, for the chamber 's cold
' And the coffee pale. I got a turn at first
' Paying my duty,—I observed they crouched
' —The two old frightened family spectres, close
' In a corner, each on each like mouse on mouse
' I' the cat's cage : ever since, I stay at home.
' Hallo, there 's Guido, the black, mean and small,
' Bends his brows on us—please to bend your own
' On the shapely nether limbs of Light-skirts there
' By way of a diversion ! I was a fool   430
' To fling the sweetmeats. Prudence, for God's love !
' To-morrow I'll make my peace, e'en tell some fib,
' Try if I can't find means to take you there.'
That night and next day did the gaze endure,
Burnt to my brain, as sunbeam thro' shut eyes,
And not once changed the beautiful sad strange smile.
At vespers Conti leaned beside my seat
I' the choir,—part said, part sung—' *In ex-cel-sis—*
' All 's to no purpose : I have louted low,
' But he saw you staring—*quia sub*—do n't incline
' To know you nearer : him we would not hold   441
' For Hercules,—the man would lick your shoe
' If you and certain efficacious friends
' Managed him warily,—but there 's the wife :
' Spare her, because he beats her, as it is,
' She 's breaking her heart quite fast enough—*jam tu—*
' So, be you rational and make amends
' With little Light-skirts yonder—*in secula*
' *Secu-lo-o-o-o-rum.* Ah, you rogue ! Every one knows
' What great dame she makes jealous : one against one,
' Play, and win both ! '   451
                 Sirs, ere the week was out,
I saw and said to myself ' Light-skirts hides teeth
' Would make a dog sick,—the great dame shows spite
' Should drive a cat mad : 't is but poor work this—
' Counting one's fingers till the sonnet 's crowned.
' I doubt much if Marino really be

‘ A better bard than Dante after all.
‘ ’T is more amusing to go pace at eve
‘ I’ the Duomo,—watch the day’s last gleam outside
‘ Turn, as into a skirt of God’s own robe,   461
‘ Those lancet-windows’ jewelled miracle,—
‘ Than go eat the Archbishop’s ortolans,
‘ Digest his jokes.   Luckily Lent is near :
‘ Who cares to look will find me in my stall
‘ At the Pieve, constant to this faith at least—
‘ Never to write a canzonet any more.’

So, next week, ’t was my patron spoke abrupt,
In altered guise, ‘ Young man, can it be true ·
‘ That after all your promise of sound fruit,   470
‘ You have kept away from Countess young or old
‘ And gone play truant in church all day long ?
‘ Are you turning Molinist ? ’   I answered quick
‘ Sir, what if I turned Christian ?   It might be.
‘ The fact is, I am troubled in my mind,
‘ Beset and pressed hard by some novel thoughts.
‘ This your Arezzo is a limited world ;
‘ There ’s a strange Pope,—’t is said, a priest who
          thinks.
‘ Rome is the port, you say : to Rome I go.
‘ I will live alone, one does so in a crowd,   480
‘ And look into my heart a little.’   ‘ Lent
‘ Ended,’—I told friends,—‘ I shall go to Rome.’

    One evening I was sitting in a muse
Over the opened ‘ Summa,’ darkened round
By the mid-March twilight, thinking how my life
Had shaken under me,—broke short indeed
And showed the gap ’twixt what is, what should be,—
And into what abysm the soul may slip,
Leave aspiration here, achievement there,
Lacking omnipotence to connect extremes—   490
Thinking moreover . . oh, thinking, if you like,
How utterly dissociated was I
A priest and celibate, from the sad strange wife
Of Guido,—just as an instance to the point,
Nought more,—how I had a whole store of strengths
Eating into my heart, which craved employ,
And she, perhaps, need of a finger’s help,—
And yet there was no way in the wide world

To stretch out mine and so relieve myself—
How when the page o' the Summa preached its best,
Her smile kept glowing out of it, as to mock   501
The silence we could break by no one word,—
There came a tap without the chamber-door,
And a whisper, when I bade who tapped speak out,
And, in obedience to my summons, last
In glided a masked muffled mystery,
Laid lightly a letter on the opened book,
Then stood with folded arms and foot demure,
Pointing as if to mark the minutes' flight.

I took the letter, read to the effect   510
That she, I lately flung the comfits to,
Had a warm heart to give me in exchange,
And gave it,—loved me and confessed it thus,
And bade me render thanks by word of mouth,
Going that night to such a side o' the house
Where the small terrace overhangs a street
Blind and deserted, not the street in front :
Her husband being away, the surly patch,
At his villa of Vittiano.

          ' And you ? '—I asked :   520
' What may you be ? '—' Count Guido's kind of maid—
' Most of us have two functions in his house.
' We all hate him, the lady suffers much,
' 'T is just we show compassion, furnish aid,
' Specially since her choice is fixed so well.
' What answer may I bring to cheer the sweet
' Pompilia ? '

         Then I took a pen and wrote.
' No more of this ! That you are fair, I know :
' But other thoughts now occupy my mind.   530
' I should not thus have played the insensible
' Once on a time. What made you,—may one ask,—
' Marry your hideous husband ? 'T was a fault,
' And now you taste the fruit of it. Farewell.'

' There ! ' smiled I as she snatched it and was gone—
' There, let the jealous miscreant,—Guido's self,
' Whose mean soul grins through this transparent
     trick,—

' Be baulked so far, defrauded of his aim !
' What fund of satisfaction to the knave,
' Had I kicked this his messenger down stairs,   540
' Trussed to the middle of her impudence,
' Setting his heart at ease so ! No, indeed !
' There's the reply which he shall turn and twist
' At pleasure, snuff at till his brain grow drunk,
' As the bear does when he finds a scented glove
' That puzzles him,—a hand and yet no hand,
' Of other perfume than his own foul paw !
' Last month, I had doubtless chosen to play the dupe,
' Accepted the mock-invitation, kept
' The sham appointment, cudgel beneath cloak,   550
' Prepared myself to pull the appointer's self
' Out of the window from his hiding-place
' Behind the gown of this part-messenger
' Part-mistress who would personate the wife.
' Such had seemed once a jest permissible :
' Now, I am not i' the mood.'
                    Back next morn brought
The messenger, a second letter in hand.
' You are cruel, Thyrsis, and Myrtilla moans
' Neglected but adores you, makes request   560
' For mercy : why is it you dare not come ?
' Such virtue is scarce natural to your age :
' You must love someone else ; I hear you do,
' The Baron's daughter or the Advocate's wife,
' Or both,—all 's one, would you make me the third—
' I take the crumbs from table gratefully
' Nor grudge who feasts there. 'Faith, I blush and
        blaze !
' Yet if I break all bounds, there 's reason sure,
' Are you determinedly bent on Rome ?
' I am wretched here, a monster tortures me :   570
' Carry me with you ! Come and say you will !
' Concert this very evening ! Do not write !
' I am ever at the window of my room
' Over the terrace, at the *Ave*. Come ! '

I questioned—lifting half the woman's mask
To let her smile loose. ' So, you gave my line
' To the merry lady ? ' ' She kissed off the wax,
' And put what paper was not kissed away,
' In her bosom to go burn : but merry, no !

' She wept all night when evening brought no friend,
' Alone, the unkind missive at her breast ;   581
' Thus Philomel, the thorn at her breast too,
' Sings ' . . . ' Writes this second letter ? '   ' Even so !
' Then she may peep at vespers forth ? '—' What risk
' Do we run o' the husband ? '—' Ah,—no risk at all !
' He is more stupid even than jealous.   Ah—
' That was the reason ?   Why, the man 's away !
' Beside, his bugbear is that friend of yours,
' Fat little Canon Conti.   He fears him—
' How should he dream of you ?   I told you truth—
' He goes to the villa at Vittiano—'t is   591
' The time when Spring-sap rises in the vine—
' Spends the night there.   And then his wife 's a child,
' Does he think a child outwits him ?   A mere child :
' Yet so full grown, a dish for any duke.
' Do n't quarrel longer with such cates, but come ! '

I wrote ' In vain do you solicit me.
' I am a priest : and you are wedded wife,
' Whatever kind of brute your husband prove.
' I have scruples, in short.   Yet should you really show
' Sign at the window . . . but nay, best be good !
' My thoughts are elsewhere.'—' Take her that ! '
                              —' Again   603
' Let the incarnate meanness, cheat and spy,
' Mean to the marrow of him, make his heart
' His food, anticipate hell's worm once more !
' Let him watch shivering at the window—ay,
' And let this hybrid, this his light-of-love
' And lackey-of-lies,—a sage economy,—
' Paid with embracings for the rank brass coin,—
' Let her report and make him chuckle o'er   611
' The break-down of my resolution now,
' And lour at disappointment in good time !
' —So tantalize and so enrage by turns,
' Until the two fall each on the other like
' Two famished spiders, as the coveted fly
' That toys long, leaves their net and them at last ! '
And so the missives followed thick and fast
' For a month, say,—I still came at every turn   619
On the soft sly adder, endlong 'neath my tread.
I was met i' the street, made sign to in the church,
A slip was found i' the door-sill, scribbled word

'Twixt page and page o' the prayer-book in my place :
A crumpled thing dropped even before my feet,
Pushed through the blind, above the terrace-rail,
As I passed, by day, the very window once.
And ever from corners would be peering up
The messenger, with the self-same demand
' Obdurate still, no flesh but adamant ?   629
' Nothing to cure the wound, assuage the throe
' O' the sweetest lamb that ever loved a bear ? '
And ever my one answer in one tone—
' Go your ways, temptress ! Let a priest read, pray,
' Unplagued of vain talk, visions not for him !
' In the end, you 'll have your will and ruin me ! '

One day, a variation : thus I read :
' You have gained little by timidity.
' My husband has found out my love at length,
' Sees cousin Conti was the stalking-horse,
' And you the game he covered, poor fat soul !   640
' My husband is a formidable foe,
' Will stick at nothing to destroy you. Stand
' Prepared, or better, run till you reach Rome !
' I bade you visit me, when the last place
' My tyrant would have turned suspicious at,
' Or cared to seek you in, was . . why say, where ?
' But now all 's changed : beside, the season 's past
' At the villa,—wants the master's eye no more.
' Anyhow, I beseech you, stay away
' From the window ! He might well be posted there.'

I wrote—' You raise my courage, or call up   651
' My curiosity, who am but man.
' Tell him he owns the palace, not the street
' Under—that 's his and yours and mine alike.
' If it should please me pad the path this eve,
' Guido will have two troubles, first to get
' Into a rage and then get out again.
' Be cautious, though : at the *Ave !* '
                    You of the court !
When I stood question here and reached this point
O' the narrative,—search notes and see and say
If some one did not interpose with smile   662
And sneer, ' And prithee why so confident
' That the husband must, of all needs, not the wife,

' Fabricate thus,—what if the lady loved ?
' What if she wrote the letters ? '
                                  Learned Sir,
I told you there 's a picture in our church.
Well, if a low-browed verger sidled up
Bringing me, like a blotch, on his prod's point,   670
A transfixed scorpion, let the reptile writhe,
And then said, ' See a thing that Rafael made—
' This venom issued from Madonna's mouth ! '—
I should reply, ' Rather, the soul of you
' Has issued from your body, like from like,
' By way of the ordure-corner ! '
                                  But no less,
I tired of the same black teasing lie
Obtruded thus at every turn ; the pest
Was far too near the picture, anyhow :   680
One does Madonna service, making clowns
Remove their dung-heap from the sacristy.
' I will to the window, as he tempts,' said I :
' Yes, whom the easy love has failed allure,
' This new bait of adventure may,—he thinks.
' While the imprisoned lady keeps afar,
' There will they lie in ambush, heads alert,
' Kith, kin, and Count mustered to bite my heel.
' No mother nor brother viper of the brood
' Shall scuttle off without the instructive bruise ! '

So, I went : crossed street and street : ' The next
     street's turn,   691
' I stand beneath the terrace, see, above,
' The black of the ambush-window. Then, in place
' Of hand's throw of soft prelude over lute
' And cough that clears way for the ditty last,'—
I began to laugh already—' he will have
' " Out of the hole you hide in, on to the front,
' " Count Guido Franceschini, show yourself !
' " Hear what a man thinks of a thing like you,
' " And after, take this foulness in your face ! "   700

The words lay living on my lip, I made
The one turn more—and there at the window stood,
Framed in its black square length, with lamp in hand,
Pompilia ; the same great, grave, griefful air
As stands i' the dusk, on altar that I know,

Left alone with one moonbeam in her cell,
Our Lady of all the Sorrows.   Ere I knelt—
Assured myself that she was flesh and blood—
She had looked one look and vanished.
                    I thought—' Just so :
' It was herself, they have set her there to watch—
' Stationed to see some wedding-band go by,   712
' On fair pretence that she must bless the bride,
' Or wait some funeral with friends wind past,
' And crave peace for the corpse that claims its due.
' She never dreams they used her for a snare,
' And now withdraw the bait has served its turn.
' Well done, the husband, who shall fare the worse ! '
And on my lip again was—' Out with thee,
' Guido ! '   When all at once she re-appeared ;   720
But, this time, on the terrace overhead,
So close above me, she could almost touch
My head if she bent down ; and she did bend,
While I stood still as stone, all eye, all ear.

She began—' You have sent me letters, Sir :
' I have read none, I can neither read nor write ;
' But she you gave them to, a woman here,
' One of the people in whose power I am,
' Partly explained their sense, I think, to me
' Obliged to listen while she inculcates   730
' That you, a priest, can dare love me, a wife,
' Desire to live or die as I shall bid,
' (She makes me listen if I will or no)
' Because you saw my face a single time.
' It cannot be she says the thing you mean ;
' Such wickedness were deadly to us both :
' But good true love would help me now so much—
' I tell myself, you may mean good and true.
' You offer me, I seem to understand,
' Because I am in poverty and starve,   740
' Much money, where one piece would save my life.
' The silver cup upon the altar-cloth
' Is neither yours to give nor mine to take ;
' But I might take one bit of bread therefrom,
' Since I am starving, and return the rest,
' Yet do no harm : this is my very case.
' I am in that strait, I may not abstain
' From so much of assistance as would bring

' The guilt of theft on neither you nor me ;
' But no superfluous particle of aid.   750
' I think, if you will let me state my case,
' Even had you been so fancy-fevered here,
' Not your sound self, you must grow healthy now—
' Care only to bestow what I can take.
' That it is only you in the wide world,
' Knowing me nor in thought nor word nor deed,
' Who, all unprompted save by your own heart,
' Come proffering assistance now,—were strange
' But that my whole life is so strange : as strange
' It is, my husband whom I have not wronged   760
' Should hate and harm me.   For his own soul's sake,
' Hinder the harm !   But there is something more,
' And that the strangest : it has got to be
' Somehow for my sake too, and yet not mine,
' —This is a riddle—for some kind of sake
' Not any clearer to myself than you,
' And yet as certain as that I draw breath,—
' I would fain live, not die—oh no, not die !
' My case is, I was dwelling happily
' At Rome with those dear Comparini, called   770
' Father and mother to me ; when at once
' I found I had become Count Guido's wife :
' Who then, not waiting for a moment, changed
' Into a fury of fire, if once he was
' Merely a man : his face threw fire at mine,
' He laid a hand on me that burned all peace,
' All joy, all hope, and last all fear away,
' Dipping the bough of life, so pleasant once,
' In fire which shrivelled leaf and bud alike,
' Burning not only present life but past,   780
' Which you might think was safe beyond his reach.
' He reached it, though, since that beloved pair,
' My father once, my mother all those years,
' That loved me so, now say I dreamed a dream
' And bid me wake, henceforth no child of theirs,
' Never in all the time their child at all.
' Do you understand ?   I cannot : yet so it is.
' Just so I say of you that proffer help :
' I cannot understand what prompts your soul,
' I simply needs must see that it is so,   790
' Only one strange and wonderful thing more.
' They came here with me, those two dear ones, kept

' All the old love up, till my husband, till
' His people here so tortured them, they fled.
' And now, is it because I grow in flesh
' And spirit one with him their torturer,
' That they, renouncing him, must cast off me ?
' If I were graced by God to have a child,
' Could I one day deny God graced me so ?   779
' Then, since my husband hates me, I shall break
' No law that reigns in this fell house of hate,
' By using—letting have effect so much
' Of hate as hides me from that whole of hate,
' Would take my life which I want and must have—
' Just as I take from your excess of love
' Enough to save my life with, all I need.
' The Archbishop said to murder me were sin :
' My leaving Guido were a kind of death
' With no sin,—more death, he must answer for.
' Hear now what death to him and life to you   810
' I wish to pay and owe.   Take me to Rome !
' You go to Rome, the servant makes me hear.
' Take me as you would take a dog, I think,
' Masterless left for strangers to maltreat :
' Take me home like that—leave me in the house
' Where the father and the mother are ; and soon
' They'll come to know and call me by my name,
' Their child once more, since child I am, for all
' They now forget me, which is the worst o' the
          dream—   819
' And the way to end dreams is to break them, stand,
' Walk, go : then help me to stand, walk and go !
' The Governor said the strong should help the weak :
' You know how weak the strongest women are.
' How could I find my way there by myself ?
' I cannot even call out, make them hear—
' Just as in dreams : I have tried and proved the fact.
' I have told this story and more to good great men,
' The Archbishop and the Governor : they smiled.
' " Stop your mouth, fair one ! "—presently they
          frowned,
' " Get you gone, disengage you from our feet ! "   830
' I went in my despair to an old priest,
' Only a friar, no great man like these two,
' But good, the Augustinian, people name
' Romano,—he confessed me two months since :

' He fears God, why then needs he fear the world ?
' And when he questioned how it came about
' That I was found in danger of a sin—
' Despair of any help from providence,—
' " Since, though your husband outrage you," said he,
' " That is a case too common, the wives die   840
' " Or live, but do not sin so deep as this "—
' Then I told—what I never will tell you—
' How, worse than husband's hate, I had to bear
' The love,—soliciting to shame called love,—
' Of his brother,—the young idle priest i' the house
' With only the devil to meet there.   " This is grave —
' " Yes, we must interfere : I counsel,—write
' " To those who used to be your parents once,
' " Of dangers here, bid them convey you hence ! "
' " But," said I, " when I neither read nor write ? "
' Then he took pity and promised " I will write."   851
' If he did so,—why, they are dumb or dead :
' Either they give no credit to the tale,
' Or else, wrapped wholly up in their own joy
' Of such escape, they care not who cries, still
' I' the clutches.   Anyhow, no word arrives.
' All such extravagance and dreadfulness
' Seems incident to dreaming, cured one way,—
' Wake me !   The letter I received this morn,
' Said—if the woman spoke your very sense—   860
' " You would die for me : " I can believe it now :
' For now the dream gets to involve yourself.
' First of all, you seemed wicked and not good,
' In writing me those letters : you came in
' Like a thief upon me.   I this morning said
' In my extremity, entreat the thief !
' Try if he have in him no honest touch !
' A thief might save me from a murderer.
' 'T was a thief said the last kind word to Christ :
' Christ took the kindness and forgave the theft :
' And so did I prepare what I now say.   871
' But now, that you stand and I see your face,
' Though you have never uttered word yet,—well,
    I know,
' Here too has been dream-work, delusion too,
' And that at no time, you with the eyes here,
' Ever intended to do wrong by me,
' Nor wrote such letters therefore.   It is false,

' And you are true, have been true, will be true.
' To Rome then,—when is it you take me there ?
' Each minute lost is mortal. When ?—I ask.'   880

I answered ' It shall be when it can be.
' I will go hence and do your pleasure, find
' The sure and speedy means of travel, then
' Come back and take you to your friends in Rome.
' There wants a carriage, money and the rest,—
' A day's work by to-morrow at this time.
' How shall I see you and assure escape ? '

She replied, ' Pass, to-morrow at this hour.
' If I am at the open window, well :
' If I am absent, drop a handkerchief   890
' And walk by ! I shall see from where I watch,
' And know that all is done. Return next eve,
' And next, and so till we can meet and speak ! '
' To-morrow at this hour I pass,' said I.
She was withdrawn.
                              Here is another point
I bid you pause at. When I told thus far,
Someone said, subtly, ' Here at least was found
' Your confidence in error,—you perceived
' The spirit of the letters, in a sort,   900
' Had been the lady's, if the body should be
' Supplied by Guido : say, he forged them all !
' Here was the unforged fact—she sent for you,
' Spontaneously elected you to help,
' —What men call, loved you : Guido read her mind,
' Gave it expression to assure the world
' The case was just as he foresaw : he wrote,
' She spoke.'
                              Sirs, that first simile serves still,—
That falsehood of a scorpion hatched, I say,   910
Nowhere i' the world but in Madonna's mouth.
Go on ! Suppose, that falsehood foiled, next eve
Pictured Madonna raised her painted hand,
Fixed the face Rafael bent above the Babe,
On my face as I flung me at her feet :
Such miracle vouchsafed and manifest,
Would that prove the first lying tale was true ?
Pompilia spoke, and I at once received,
Accepted my own fact, my miracle

Self-authorised and self-explained,—she chose   920
To summon me and signify her choice.
Afterward,—oh ! I gave a passing glance
To a certain ugly cloud-shape, goblin-shred
Of hell-smoke hurrying past the splendid moon
Out now to tolerate no darkness more,
And saw right through the thing that tried to pass
For truth and solid, not an empty lie :
' So, he not only forged the words for her
' But words for me, made letters he called mine :
' What I sent, he retained, gave these in place,   930
' All by the mistress-messenger ! As I
' Recognized her, at potency of truth,
' So she, by the crystalline soul, knew me,
' Never mistook the signs. Enough of this—
' Let the wraith go to nothingness again,
' Here is the orb, have only thought for her ! '

' Thought ? ' nay, Sirs, what shall follow was not
         thought :
I have thought sometimes, and thought long and hard.
I have stood before, gone round a serious thing,
Tasked my whole mind to touch and clasp it close,
As I stretch forth my arm to touch this bar.   941
God and man, and what duty I owe both,—
I dare to say I have confronted these
In thought : but no such faculty helped here.
I put forth no thought,—powerless, all that night
I paced the city : it was the first Spring.
By the invasion I lay passive to,
In rushed new things, the old were rapt away ;
Alike abolished—the imprisonment   949
Of the outside air, the inside weight o' the world
That pulled me down. Death meant, to spurn the
         ground,
Soar to the sky,—die well and you do that.
The very immolation made the bliss ;
Death was the heart of life, and all the harm
My folly had crouched to avoid, now proved a veil
Hiding all gain my wisdom strove to grasp :
As if the intense centre of the flame
Should turn a heaven to that devoted fly
Which hitherto, sophist alike and sage,
Saint Thomas with his sober grey goose-quill,   960

And sinner Plato by Cephisian reed,
Would fain, pretending just the insect's good,
Whisk off, drive back, consign to shade again.
Into another state, under new rule
I knew myself was passing swift and sure ;
Whereof the initiatory pang approached,
Felicitous annoy, as bitter-sweet
As when the virgin-band, the victors chaste,
Feel at the end the earthly garments drop,
And rise with something of a rosy shame   970
Into immortal nakedness : so I
Lay, and let come the proper throe would thrill
Into the ecstacy and outthrob pain.

I' the grey of dawn it was I found myself
Facing the pillared front o' the Pieve—mine,
My church : it seemed to say for the first time
' But am not I the Bride, the mystic love
' O' the Lamb, who took thy plighted troth, my priest,
' To fold thy warm heart on my heart of stone
' And freeze thee nor unfasten any more ?   980
' This is a fleshly woman,—let the free
' Bestow their life-blood, thou art pulseless now ! '
See ! Day by day I had risen and left this church
At the signal waved me by some foolish fan,
With half a curse and half a pitying smile
For the monk I stumbled over in my haste,
Prostrate and corpse-like at the altar-foot
Intent on his *corona :* then the church
Was ready with her quip, if word conduced,
To quicken my pace nor stop for prating—' There !
' Be thankful you are no such ninny, go   991
' Rather to teach a black-eyed novice cards
' Than gabble Latin and protrude that nose
' Smoothed to a sheep's through no brains and much
        faith ! '
That sort of incentive ! Now the church changed
        tone—
Now, when I found out first that life and death
Are means to an end, that passion uses both,
Indisputably mistress of the man
Whose form of worship is self-sacrifice—   999
Now, from the stone lungs sighed the scrannel voice
' Leave that live passion, come be dead with me ! '

As if, i' the fabled garden, I had gone 1002
On great adventure, plucked in ignorance
Hedge-fruit, and feasted to satiety,
Laughing at such high fame for hips and haws,
And scorned the achievement : then come all at once
O' the prize o' the place, the thing of perfect gold,
The apple's self : and, scarce my eye on that,
Was 'ware as well o' the seven-fold dragon's watch.

Sirs, I obeyed. Obedience was too strange,— 1010
This new thing that had been struck into me
By the look o' the lady,—to dare disobey
The first authoritative word. 'T was God's.
I had been lifted to the level of her,
Could take such sounds into my sense. I said
' We two are cognizant o' the Master now ;
' It is she bids me bow the head : how true,
' I am a priest ! I see the function here ;
' I thought the other way self-sacrifice :
' This is the true, seals up the perfect sum. 1020
' I pay it, sit down, silently obey.'

So, I went home. Dawn broke, noon broadened, I—
I sat stone-still, let time run over me.
The sun slanted into my room, had reached
The west. I opened book,—Aquinas blazed
With one black name only on the white page.
I looked up, saw the sunset : vespers rang :
' She counts the minutes till I keep my word
' And come say all is ready. I am a priest.
' Duty to God is duty to her : I think 1030
' God, who created her, will save her too
' Some new way, by one miracle the more,
' Without me. Then, prayer may avail perhaps.'
I went to my own place i' the Pieve, read
The office : I was back at home again
Sitting i' the dark. ' Could she but know—but know
' That, were there good in this distinct from God's,
' Really good as it reached her, though procured
' By a sin of mine,—I should sin : God forgives.
' She knows it is no fear withholds me : fear ? 1040
' Of what ? Suspense here is the terrible thing.
' If she should, as she counts the minutes, come
' On the fantastic notion that I fear

I

' The world now, fear the Archbishop, fear perhaps
' Count Guido, he who, having forged the lies,
' May wait the work, attend the effect,—I fear
' The sword of Guido ! Let God see to that—
' Hating lies, let not her believe a lie ! '

Again the morning found me. ' I will work,
' Tie down my foolish thoughts. Thank God so far !
' I have saved her from a scandal, stopped the tongues
' Had broken else into a cackle and hiss   1052
' Around the noble name. Duty is still
' Wisdom : I have been wise.' So the day wore.

At evening—' But, achieving victory,
' I must not blink the priest's peculiar part,
' Nor shrink to counsel, comfort : priest and friend—
' How do we discontinue to be friends ?
' I will go minister, advise her seek
' Help at the source,—above all, not despair :   1060
' There may be other happier help at hand.
' I hope it,—wherefore then neglect to say ? '

There she stood—leaned there, for the second time,
Over the terrace, looked at me, then spoke :
' Why is it you have suffered me to stay
' Breaking my heart two days more than was need ?
' Why delay help, your own heart yearns to give ?
' You are again here, in the self-same mind,
' I see here, steadfast in the face of you,—
' You grudge to do no one thing that I ask.   1070
' Why then is nothing done ? You know my need.
' Still, through God's pity on me, there is time
' And one day more : shall I be saved or no ? '
I answered—' Lady, waste no thought, no word
' Even to forgive me ! Care for what I care—
' Only ! Now follow me as I were fate !
' Leave this house in the dark to-morrow night,
' Just before daybreak :—there 's new moon this eve—
' It sets, and then begins the solid black.
' Descend, proceed to the Torrione, step   1080
' Over the low dilapidated wall,
' Take San Clemente, there 's no other gate
' Unguarded at the hour : some paces thence
' An inn stands ; cross to it ; I shall be there.'

She answered, ' If I can but find the way.
' But I shall find it.   Go now ! '

                        I did go,
Took rapidly the route myself prescribed,
Stopped at Torrione, climbed the ruined place,
Proved that the gate was practicable, reached   1090
The inn, no eye, despite the dark, could miss,
Knocked there and entered, made the host secure :
' With Caponsacchi it is ask and have ;
' I know my betters.   Are you bound for Rome ?
' I get swift horse and trusty man,' said he.

Then I retraced my steps, was found once more
In my own house for the last time :   there lay
The broad pale opened Summa.   ' Shut his book,
' There 's other showing !   'T was a Thomas too
' Obtained,—more favoured than his namesake here,—
' A gift, tied faith fast, foiled the tug of doubt,—
' Our Lady's girdle ;   down he saw it drop   1102
' As she ascended into heaven, they say :
' He kept that safe and bade all doubt adieu.
' I too have seen a lady and hold a grace.'

I know not how the night passed :   morning broke :
Presently came my servant.   ' Sir, this eve—
' Do you forget ? '   I started.—' How forget ?
' What is it you know ? '—' With due submission, Sir,
' This being last Monday in the month but one   1110
' And a vigil, since to-morrow is Saint George,
' And feast day, and moreover day for copes,
' And Canon Conti now away a month,
' And Canon Crispi sour because, forsooth,
' You let him sulk in stall and bear the brunt
' Of the octave . . . Well, Sir, 'tis important ! '
                             ' True !
' Hearken, I have to start for Rome this night.
' No word, lest Crispi overboil and burst !
' Provide me with a laic dress !   Throw dust   1120
' I' the Canon's eye, stop his tongue's scandal so !
' See there 's a sword in case of accident.'
I knew the knave, the knave knew me.

                       And thus
Through each familiar hindrance of the day

Did I make steadily for its hour and end,—
Felt time's old barrier-growth of right and fit
Give way through all its twines, and let me go ;
Use and wont recognized the excepted man,
Let speed the special service,—and I sped   1130
Till, at the dead between midnight and morn,
There was I at the goal, before the gate,
With a tune in the ears, low leading up to loud,
A light in the eyes, faint that would soon be flare,
Ever some spiritual witness new and new
In faster frequence, crowding solitude
To watch the way o' the warfare,—till, at last,
When the ecstatic minute must bring birth,
Began a whiteness in the distance, waxed
Whiter and whiter, near grew and more near,   1140
Till it was she : there did Pompilia come :
The white I saw shine through her was her soul's,
Certainly, for the body was one black,
Black from head down to foot.   She did not speak,
Glided into the carriage,—so a cloud
Gathers the moon up.   ' By San Spirito,
' To Rome, as if the road burned underneath !
' Reach Rome, then hold my head in pledge, I pay
' The run and the risk to heart's content ! '   Just that,
I said,—then, in another tick of time,   1150
Sprang, was beside her, she and I alone.

So it began, our flight thro' dusk to clear,
Through day and night and day again to night
Once more, and to last dreadful dawn of all.
Sirs, how should I lie quiet in my grave
Unless you suffer me wring, drop by drop,
My brain dry, make a riddance of the drench
Of minutes with a memory in each,
Recorded motion, breath or look of hers,   1159
Which poured forth would present you one pure glass,
Mirror you plain,—as God's sea, glassed in gold,
His saints,—the perfect soul Pompilia ?   Men,
You must know that a man gets drunk with truth
Stagnant inside him !   Oh, they 've killed her, Sirs !
Can I be calm ?
              Calmly !   Each incident
Proves, I maintain, that action of the flight
For the true thing it was.   The first faint scratch

O' the stone will test its nature, teach its worth
To idiots who name Parian, coprolite.   1170
After all, I shall give no glare—at best
Only display you certain scattered lights
Lamping the rush and roll of the abyss—
Nothing but here and there a fire-point pricks
Wavelet from wavelet : well !
                        For the first hour
We both were silent in the night, I know :
Sometimes I did not see nor understand.
Blackness engulphed me,—partial stupor, say—
Then I would break way, breathe through the surprise,
And be aware again, and see who sat   1181
In the dark vest with the white face and hands.
I said to myself—' I have caught it, I conceive
' The mind o' the mystery : 't is the way they wake
' And wait, two martyrs somewhere in a tomb
' Each by each as their blessing was to die ;
' Some signal they are promised and expect,
' When to arise before the trumpet scares :
' So, through the whole course of the world they wait
' The last day, but so fearless and so safe !   1190
' No otherwise, in safety and not fear,
' I lie, because she lies too by my side.'
You know this is not love, Sirs,—it is faith,
The feeling that there 's God, he reigns and rules
Out of this low world : that is all ; no harm !
At times she drew a soft sigh—music seemed
Always to hover just above her lips
Not settle,—break a silence music too.

In the determined morning, I first found
Her head erect, her face turned full to me,   1200
Her soul intent on mine through two wide eyes.
I answered them.   ' You are saved hitherto.
' We have passed Perugia,—gone round by the wood
' Not through, I seem to think,—and opposite
' I know Assisi ; this is holy ground.'
Then she resumed.   ' How long since we both left
' Arezzo ? '—' Years—and certain hours beside.'

It was at . . . ah, but I forget the names !
'T is a mere post-house and a hovel or two,—
I left the carriage and got bread and wine   1210

And brought it her.—' Does it detain to eat ? '
' —They stay perforce, change horses,—therefore eat !
' We lose no minute : we arrive, be sure ! '
She said—I know not where—there 's a great hill
Close over, and the stream has lost its bridge,
One fords it. She began—' I have heard say
' Of some sick body that my mother knew,
' 'T was no good sign when in a limb diseased
' All the pain suddenly departs,—as if
' The guardian angel discontinued pain   1220
' Because the hope of cure was gone at last :
' The limb will not again exert itself,
' It needs be pained no longer : so with me,
' —My soul whence all the pain is past at once :
' All pain must be to work some good in the end,
' True, this I feel now, this may be that good,
' Pain was because of,—otherwise, I fear ! '

She said,—a long while later in the day,
When I had let the silence be,—abrupt—   1229
' Have you a mother ? '—' She died, I was born.'
' A sister then ? '—' No sister.'—' Who was it—
' What woman were you used to serve this way,
' Be kind to, till I called you and you came ? '
I did not like that word. Soon afterward—
' Tell me, are men unhappy, in some kind
' Of mere unhappiness at being men,
' As women suffer, being womanish ?
' Have you, now, some unhappiness, I mean,
' Born of what may be man's strength overmuch,
' To match the undue susceptibility,   1240
' The sense at every pore when hate is close ?
' It hurts us if a baby hides its face
' Or child strikes at us punily, calls names
' Or makes a mouth,—much more if stranger men
' Laugh or frown,—just as that were much to bear !
' Yet rocks split,—and the blow-ball does no more,
' Quivers to feathery nothing at a touch ;
' And strength may have its drawback, weakness
    scapes.'   1248

Once she asked ' What is it that made you smile,
' At the great gate with the eagles and the snakes,
' Where the company entered, 't is a long time since ? '

' —Forgive—I think you would not understand :
' Ah, but you ask me,—therefore, it was this.
' That was a certain bishop's villa-gate,
' I knew it by the eagles,—and at once
' Remembered this same bishop was just he
' People of old were wont to bid me please
' If I would catch preferment : so, I smiled
' Because an impulse came to me, a whim—
' What if I prayed the prelate leave to speak,   1260
' Began upon him in his presence-hall
' —" What, still at work so grey and obsolete ?
' " Still rocheted and mitred more or less ?
' " Do n't you feel all that out of fashion now ?
' " I find out when the day of things is done ! " '

At eve we heard the *angelus* : she turned—
' I told you I can neither read nor write.
' My life stopped with the play-time ; I will learn,
' If I begin to live again : but you—   1269
' Who are a priest—wherefore do you not read
' The service at this hour ?   Read Gabriel's song,
' The lesson, and then read the little prayer
' To Raphael, proper for us travellers ! '
I did not like that, neither, but I read.

When we stopped at Foligno it was dark.
The people of the post came out with lights :
The driver said, ' This time to-morrow, may
' Saints only help, relays continue good,
' Nor robbers hinder, we arrive at Rome.'
I urged,—' Why tax your strength a second night ?
' Trust me, alight here and take brief repose !   1281
' We are out of harm's reach, past pursuit : go sleep
' If but an hour !   I keep watch, guard the while
' Here in the doorway.'   But her whole face changed,
The misery grew again about her mouth,
The eyes burned up from faintness, like the fawn's
Tired to death in the thicket, when she feels
The probing spear o' the huntsman.   ' Oh, no stay ! '
She cried, in the fawn's cry, ' On to Rome, on, on—
' Unless 't is you who fear,—which cannot be ! '

We did go on all night ; but at its close   1291
She was troubled, restless, moaned low, talked at whiles

To herself, her brow on quiver with the dream :
Once, wide awake, she menaced, at arms' length
Waved away something—' Never again with you !
' My soul is mine, my body is my soul's :
' You and I are divided ever more
' In soul and body : get you gone ! '   Then I—
' Why, in my whole life I have never prayed !
' Oh, if the God, that only can, would help !   1300
' Am I his priest with power to cast out fiends ?
' Let God arise and all his enemies
' Be scattered ! '   By morn, there was peace, no sigh
Out of the deep sleep.

                When she woke at last,
I answered the first look—' Scarce twelve hours more,
' Then, Rome !   There probably was no pursuit,
' There cannot now be peril :   bear up brave !
' Just some twelve hours to press through to the prize—
' Then, no more of the terrible journey ! '   ' Then,
' No more o' the journey :   if it might but last !
' Always, my life-long, thus to journey still !   1312
' It is the interruption that I dread,—
' With no dread, ever to be here and thus !
' Never to see a face nor hear a voice !
' Yours is no voice ;   you speak when you are dumb ;
' Nor face, I see it in the dark.   I want
' No face nor voice that change and grow unkind.'
That I liked, that was the best thing she said.

In the broad day, I dared entreat, ' Descend ! '   1320
I told a woman, at the garden-gate
By the post-house, white and pleasant in the sun,
' It is my sister,—talk with her apart !
' She is married and unhappy, you perceive ;
' I take her home because her head is hurt ;
' Comfort her as you women understand ! '
So, there I left them by the garden-wall,
Paced the road, then bade put the horses to,
Came back, and there she sat :   close to her knee,
A black-eyed child still held the bowl of milk,   1330
Wondered to see how little she could drink,
And in her arms the woman's infant lay.
She smiled at me ' How much good this has done !
' This is a whole night's rest and how much more !

' I can proceed now, though I wish to stay.
' How do you call that tree with the thick top
' That holds in all its leafy green and gold
' The sun now like an immense egg of fire ? '
(It was a million-leaved mimosa.)   ' Take
' The babe away from me and let me go ! '   1340
And in the carriage ' Still a day, my friend !
' And perhaps half a night, the woman fears.
' I pray it finish since it cannot last.
' There may be more misfortune at the close,
' And where will you be ?   God suffice me then ! '
And presently—for there was a roadside-shrine—
' When I was taken first to my own church
' Lorenzo in Lucina, being a girl,
' And bid confess my faults, I interposed   1349
' " But teach me what fault to confess and know ! "
' So, the priest said—" You should bethink yourself :
' " Each human being needs must have done wrong ! "
' Now, be you candid and no priest but friend—
' Were I surprised and killed here on the spot,
' A runaway from husband and his home,
' Do you account it were in sin I died ?
' My husband used to seem to harm me, not . . .
' Not on pretence he punished sin of mine,
' Nor for sin's sake and lust of cruelty,
' But as I heard him bid a farming-man   1360
' At the villa take a lamb once to the wood
' And there ill-treat it, meaning that the wolf
' Should hear its cries, and so come, quick be caught,
' Enticed to the trap : he practised thus with me
' That so, whatever were his gain thereby,
' Others than I might become prey and spoil.
' Had it been only between our two selves,—
' His pleasure and my pain,—why, pleasure him
' By dying, nor such need to make a coil !
' But this was worth an effort, that my pain   1370
' Should not become a snare, prove pain threefold
' To other people—strangers—or unborn—
' How should I know ? I sought release from that—
' I think, or else from,—dare I say, some cause
' Such as is put into a tree, which turns
' Away from the northwind with what nest it holds,—
' The woman said that trees so turn : now, friend,
' Tell me, because I cannot trust myself !

I 3

' You are a man : what have I done amiss ? '
You must conceive my answer,—I forget—   1380
Taken up wholly with the thought, perhaps,
This time she might have said,—might, did not say—
' You are a priest.'   She said, ' my friend.'
                              Day wore,
We passed the places, somehow the calm went,
Again the restless eyes began to rove
In new fear of the foe mine could not see :
She wandered in her mind,—addressed me once
' Gaetano ! '—that is not my name : whose name ?
I grew alarmed, my head seemed turning too :   1390
I quickened pace with promise now, now threat :
Bade drive and drive, nor any stopping more.
' Too deep i' the thick of the struggle, struggle through!
' Then drench her in repose though death's self pour
' The plenitude of quiet,—help us, God,
' Whom the winds carry ! '

                         Suddenly I saw
The old tower, and the little white-walled clump
Of buildings and the cypress-tree or two,—
' Already Castelnuovo—Rome ! ' I cried,   1400
' As good as Rome,—Rome is the next stage, think !
' This is where travellers' hearts are wont to beat.
' Say you are saved, sweet lady ! '   Up she woke.
The sky was fierce with colour from the sun
Setting.   She screamed out, ' No, I must not die !
' Take me no farther, I should die : stay here !
' I have more life to save than mine ! '
                              She swooned.
We seemed safe : what was it foreboded so ?
Out of the coach into the inn I bore   1410
The motionless and breathless pure and pale
Pompilia,—bore her through a pitying group
And laid her on a couch, still calm and cured
By deep sleep of all woes at once.   The host
Was urgent ' Let her stay an hour or two !
' Leave her to us, all will be right by morn ! '
Oh, my foreboding !   But I could not choose.

I paced the passage, kept watch all night long.
I listened,—not one movement, not one sigh.   1419
' Fear not : she sleeps so sound ! ' they said—but I

Feared, all the same, kept fearing more and more,
Found myself throb with fear from head to foot,
Filled with a sense of such impending woe,
That, at first pause of night, pretence of gray,
I made my mind up it was morn.—' Reach Rome,
' Lest hell reach her !   A dozen miles to make,
' Another long breath, and we emerge ! '   I stood
I' the court-yard, roused the sleepy grooms.   ' Have
        out
' Carriage and horse, give haste, take gold ! '—said I.
While they made ready in the doubtful morn,—
'T was the last minute,—needs must I ascend   1431
And break her sleep ; I turned to go.
                                  And there
Faced me Count Guido, there posed the mean man
As master,—took the field, encamped his rights,
Challenged the world : there leered new triumph, there
Scowled the old malice in the visage bad
And black o' the scamp.   Soon triumph suppled the
        tongue
A little, malice glued to his dry throat,
And he part howled, part hissed . . . oh, how he kept
Well out o' the way, at arm's length and to spare !—
' My salutation to your priestship !   What ?   1442
' Matutinal, busy with book so soon
' Of an April day that 's damp as tears that now
' Deluge Arezzo at its darling's flight ?—
' 'T is unfair, wrongs feminity at large,
' To let a single dame monopolize
' A heart the whole sex claims, should share alike :
' Therefore I overtake you, Canon !   Come !
' The lady,—could you leave her side so soon ?
' You have not yet experienced at her hands   1451
' My treatment, you lay down undrugged, I see !.
' Hence this alertness—hence no death-in-life
' Like what held arms fast when she stole from mine.
' To be sure, you took the solace and repose
' That first night at Foligno !—news abound
' O' the road by this time,—men regaled me much,
' As past them I came halting after you,
' Vulcan pursuing Mars, as poets sing,—
' Still at the last here pant I, but arrive,   1460
' Vulcan—and not without my Cyclops too,
' The Commissary and the unpoisoned arm

‘ O’ the Civil Force, should Mars turn mutineer.
‘ Enough of fooling : capture the culprits, friend !
‘ Here is the lover in the smart disguise
‘ With the sword,—he is a priest, so mine lies still :
‘ There upstairs hides my wife the runaway,
‘ His leman : the two plotted, poisoned first,
‘ Plundered me after, and eloped thus far   1469
‘ Where now you find them.   Do your duty quick !
‘ Arrest and hold him ! That ’s done : now catch her ! ’
During this speech of that man,—well, I stood
Away, as he managed,—still, I stood as near
The throat of him,—with these two hands, my own,—
As now I stand near yours, Sir,—one quick spring,
One great good satisfying gripe, and lo !
There had he lain abolished with his lie,
Creation purged o’ the miscreate, man redeemed,
A spittle wiped off from the face of God !
I, in some measure, seek a poor excuse   1480
For what I left undone, in just this fact
That my first feeling at the speech I quote
Was—not of what a blasphemy was dared,
Not what a bag of venomed purulence
Was split and noisome,—but how splendidly
Mirthful, what ludicrous a lie was launched !
Would Molière’s self wish more than hear such man
Call, claim such woman for his own, his wife,
Even though, in due amazement at the boast,
He had stammered, she moreover was divine ?   1490
She to be his,—were hardly less absurd
Than that he took her name into his mouth,
Licked, and then let it go again, the beast,
Signed with his slaver.   Oh, she poisoned him,
Plundered him, and the rest !   Well, what I wished
Was, that he would but go on, say once more
So to the world, and get his meed of men,
The fist’s reply to the filth.   And while I mused,
The minute, oh the misery, was gone !
On either idle hand of me there stood   1500
Really an officer, nor laughed i’ the least.
They rendered justice to his reason, laid
Logic to heart, as ’t were submitted them
‘ Twice two makes four.’
                    ‘ And now, catch her ! ’—he cried.
That sobered me.   ‘ Let myself lead the way—

' Ere you arrest me, who am somebody,
' And, as you hear, a priest and privileged,—
' To the lady's chamber ! I presume you—men
' Expert, instructed how to find out truth,   1510
' Familiar with the guise of guilt. Detect
' Guilt on her face when it meets mine, then judge
' Between us and the mad dog howling there ! '
Up we all went together, in they broke
O' the chamber late my chapel. There she lay,
Composed as when I laid her, that last eve,
O' the couch, still breathless, motionless, sleep's self.
Wax-white, seraphic, saturate with the sun
O' the morning that now flooded from the front
And filled the window with a light like blood.   1520
' Behold the poisoner, the adulteress,
' —And feigning sleep too ! Seize, bind ! '—Guido
    hissed.

She started up, stood erect, face to face
With the husband : back he fell, was buttressed there
By the window all a-flame with morning-red,
He the black figure, the opprobrious blur
Against all peace and joy and light and life.
' Away from between me and hell ! '—she cried :
' Hell for me, no embracing any more !
' I am God's, I love God, God—whose knees I clasp,
' Whose utterly most just award I take,   1531
' But bear no more love-making devils : hence ! '
I may have made an effort to reach her side
From where I stood i' the door-way,—anyhow
I found the arms, I wanted, pinioned fast,
Was powerless in the clutch to left and right
O' the rabble pouring in, rascality
Enlisted, rampant on the side of hearth
Home and the husband,—pay in prospect too !
They heaped themselves upon me.—' Ha !—and him
' Also you outrage ? Him, too, my sole friend,   1541
' Guardian and saviour ? That I baulk you of,
' Since—see how God can help at last and worst ! '
She sprung at the sword that hung beside him, seized,
Drew, brandished it, the sunrise burned for joy
O' the blade, ' Die,' cried she, ' devil, in God's name ! '
Ah, but they all closed round her, twelve to one,
—The unmanly men, no woman-mother made,

Spawned somehow !   Dead-white and disarmed she
  lay.
No matter for the sword, her word sufficed   1550
To spike the coward through and through : he shook,
Could only spit between the teeth—' You see ?
' You hear ? Bear witness, then ! Write down ... but,
  no—
' Carry these criminals to the prison-house,
' For first thing ! I begin my search meanwhile
' After the stolen effects, gold, jewels, plate,
' Money and clothes, they robbed me of and fled :
' With no few amorous pieces, verse and prose,
' I have much reason to expect to find.'

When I saw, that,—no more than the first mad speech,
Made out the speaker mad and a laughing-stock,
So neither did this next device explode   1562
One listener's indignation,—that a scribe
Did sit down, set himself to write indeed,
And sundry knaves began to peer and pry
In corner and hole,—that Guido, wiping brow
And getting him a countenance, was fast
Losing his fear, beginning to strut free
O' the stage of his exploit, snuff here, sniff there,—
I took the truth in, guessed sufficiently   1570
The service for the moment—' What I say,
' Slight at your peril ! We are aliens here,
' My adversary and I, called noble both ;
' I am the nobler, and a name men know.
' I could refer our cause to our own court
' In our own country, but prefer appeal
' To the nearer jurisdiction.   Being a priest,
' Though in a secular garb,—for reasons good
' I shall adduce in due time to my peers,—
' I demand that the Church I serve, decide   1580
' Between us, right the slandered lady there.
' A Tuscan noble, I might claim the Duke :
' A priest, I rather choose the Church,—bid Rome
' Cover the wronged with her inviolate shield.'

There was no refusing this : they bore me off,
They bore her off, to separate cells o' the same
Ignoble prison, and, separate, thence to Rome.
Pompilia's face, then and thus, looked on me

The last time in this life : not one sight since,
Never another sight to be ! And yet   1590
I thought I had saved her.   I appealed to Rome :
It seems I simply sent her to her death.
You tell me she is dying now, or dead ;
I cannot bring myself to quite believe
This is a place you torture people in :
What if this your intelligence were just
A subtlety, an honest wile to work
On a man at unawares ?   'T were worthy you.
No, Sirs, I cannot have the lady dead !
That erect form, flashing brow, fulgurant eye,   1600
That voice immortal (oh, that voice of hers !)
That vision in the blood-red day-break—that
Leap to life of the pale electric sword
Angels go armed with,—that was not the last
O' the lady !   Come, I see through it, you find—
Know the manœuvre !   Also herself said
I had saved her : do you dare say she spoke false ?
Let me see for myself if it be so !   1608
Though she were dying, a priest might be of use,
The more when he 's a friend too,—she called me
Far beyond ' friend '.   Come, let me see her—indeed
It is my duty, being a priest : I hope
I stand confessed, established, proved a priest ?
My punishment had motive that, a priest
I, in a laic garb, a mundane mode,
Did what were harmlessly done otherwise.
I never touched her with my finger-tip
Except to carry her to the couch, that eve,
Against my heart, beneath my head, bowed low,
As we priests carry the paten : that is why   1620
—To get leave and go see her of your grace—
I have told you this whole story over again.
Do I deserve grace ?   For I might lock lips,
Laugh at your jurisdiction : what have you
To do with me in the matter ?   I suppose
You hardly think I donned a bravo's dress
To have a hand in the new crime ; on the old,
Judgment 's delivered, penalty imposed,
I was chained fast at Civita hand and foot—
She had only you to trust to, you and Rome,   1630
Rome and the Church, and no pert meddling priest
Two days ago, when Guido, with the right,

Hacked her to pieces.   One might well be wroth ;
I have been patient, done my best to help :
I come from Civita and punishment
As friend of the court—and for pure friendship's sake
Have told my tale to the end,—nay, not the end—
For, wait—I'll end—not leave you that excuse !

When we were parted,—shall I go on there ?
I was presently brought to Rome—yes, here I stood
Opposite yonder very crucifix—   1641
And there sat you and you, Sirs, quite the same.
I heard charge, and bore question, and told tale
Noted down in the book there,—turn and see
If, by one jot or tittle, I vary now !
I' the colour the tale takes, there 's change perhaps ;
'T is natural, since the sky is different,
Eclipse in the air now ;   still, the outline stays.
I showed you how it came to be my part
To save the lady.   Then your clerk produced   1650
Papers, a pack of stupid and impure
Banalities called letters about love—
Love, indeed,—I could teach who styled them so,
Better, I think, though priest and loveless both !
' —How was it that a wife, young, innocent,
' And stranger to your person, wrote this page ? '—
' —She wrote it when the Holy Father wrote
' The bestiality that posts thro' Rome,
' Put in his mouth by Pasquin.'—' Nor perhaps
' Did you return these answers, verse and prose,
' Signed, sealed and sent the lady ?   There 's your
         hand ! '   1661
' —This precious piece of verse, I really judge
' Is meant to copy my own character,
' A clumsy mimic ;   and this other prose,
' Not so much even ;   both rank forgery :
' Verse, quotha ?   Bembo's verse !   When Saint John
         wrote
' The tract " De Tribus ", I wrote this to match.'
' —How came it, then, the documents were found
' At the inn on your departure ? '—' I opine,
' Because there were no documents to find   1670
' In my presence,—you must hide before you find.
' Who forged them, hardly practised in my view ;
' Who found them, waited till I turned my back.'

' —And what of the clandestine visits paid,
' Nocturnal passage in and out.the house
' With its lord absent ?   'T is alleged you climbed . . .'
' —Flew on a broomstick to the man i' the moon !
' Who witnessed or will testify this trash ? '
' —The trusty servant, Margherita's self,
' Even she who brought you letters, you confess,
' And, you confess, took letters in reply :   1681
' Forget not we have knowledge of the facts ! '
' —Sirs, who have knowledge of the facts, defray
' The expenditure of wit I waste in vain,
' Trying to find out just one fact of all !
' She who brought letters from who could not write,
' And took back letters to who could not read,—
' Who was that messenger, of your charity ? '
' —Well, so far favours you.the circumstance
' That this same messenger . . . how shall we say ? . . .
' *Sub imputatione meretricis*   1691
' *Laborat*,—which makes accusation null :
' We waive this woman's :—nought makes void the
      next.
' Borsi, called Venerino, he who drove,
' O' the first night when you fled away, at length
' Deposes to your kissings in the coach,
' —Frequent, frenetic . . .'   ' When deposed he so ? '
' After some weeks of sharp imprisonment . . .'
' —Granted by friend the Governor, I engage—'
' —For his participation in your flight !   1700
' At length his obduracy melting made
' The avowal mentioned . . .' 'Was dismissed forthwith
' To liberty, poor knave, for recompense.
' Sirs, give what credit to the lie you can !
' For me, no word in my defence I speak,
' And God shall argue for the lady ! '
                                                    So
Did I stand question, and make answer, still
With the same result of smiling disbelief,
Polite impossibility of faith   1710
In such affected virtue in a priest ;
But a showing fair play, an indulgence, even,
To one no worse than others after all—
Who had not brought disgrace to the order, played
Discreetly, ruffled gown nor ripped the cloth
In a bungling game at romps : I have told you, Sirs—

If I pretended simply to be pure
Honest and Christian in the case,—absurd !
As well go boast myself above the needs
O' the human nature, careless how meat smells,   1720
Wine tastes,—a saint above the smack !   But once
Abate my crest, own flaws i' the flesh, agree
To go with the herd, be hog no more nor less,
Why, hogs in common herd have common rights—
I must not be unduly borne upon,
Who had just romanced a little, sown wild oats,
But 'scaped without a scandal, flagrant fault.
My name helped to a mirthful circumstance :
' Joseph ' would do well to amend his plea :
Undoubtedly—some toying with the wife,   1730
But as for ruffian violence and rape,
Potiphar pressed too much on the other side !
The intrigue, the elopement, the disguise,—well
        charged !
The letters and verse looked hardly like the truth.
Your apprehension was—of guilt enough
To be compatible with innocence,
So, punished best a little and not too much.
Had I struck Guido Franceschini's face,
You had counselled me withdraw for my own sake,
Baulk him of bravo-hiring.   Friends came round,
Congratulated, ' Nobody mistakes !   1741
' The pettiness o' the forfeiture defines
' The peccadillo : Guido gets his share :
' His wife is free of husband and hook-nose,
' The mouldy viands and the mother-in-law.
' To Civita with you and amuse the time,
' Travesty us " *De Raptu Helenæ* ! "
' A funny figure must the husband cut
' When the wife makes him skip,—too ticklish, eh ?
' Do it in Latin, not the Vulgar, then !   1750
' Scazons—we'll copy and send his Eminence !
' Mind—one iambus in the final foot !
' He 'll rectify it, be your friend for life ! '
Oh, Sirs, depend on me for much new light
Thrown on the justice and religion here
By this proceeding, much fresh food for thought !

And I was just set down to study these
In relegation, two short days ago,

Admiring how you read the rules, when, clap,
A thunder comes into my solitude—   1760
I am caught up in a whirlwind and cast here,
Told of a sudden, in this room where so late
You dealt out law adroitly, that those scales,
I meekly bowed to, took my allotment from,
Guido has snatched at, broken in your hands,
Metes to himself the murder of his wife,
Full measure, pressed down, running over now !
Can I assist to an explanation ?—Yes,
I rise in your esteem, sagacious Sirs,
Stand up a renderer of reasons, not   1770
'The officious priest would personate Saint George
For a mock Princess in undragoned days.
What, the blood startles you ? What, after all
The priest who needs must carry sword on thigh
May find imperative use for it ? Then, there was
A Princess, was a dragon belching flame,
And should have been a Saint George also ? Then,
There might be worse schemes than to break the
    bonds
At Arezzo, lead her by the little hand,
Till she reached Rome, and let her try to live ?   1780
But you were the law and the gospel,—would one
    please
Stand back, allow your faculty elbow-room ?
You blind guides who must needs lead eyes that see !
Fools, alike ignorant of man and God !
What was there here should have perplexed your wit
For a wink of the owl-eyes of you ? How miss,'
    then,
What 's now forced on you by this flare of fact—
As if Saint Peter failed to recognize
Nero as no apostle, John or James,
Till someone burned a martyr, made a torch   1790
O' the blood and fat to show his features by !
Could you fail read this cartulary aright
On head and front of Franceschini there,
Large-lettered like hell's masterpiece of print,—
That he, from the beginning pricked at heart
By some lust, letch of hate against his wife,
Plotted to plague her into overt sin
And shame, would slay Pompilia body and soul,
And save his mean self—miserably caught   1799

I' the quagmire of his own tricks, cheats and lies ?
—That himself wrote those papers,—from himself
To himself,—which, i' the name of me and her,
His mistress-messenger gave her and me,
Touching us with such pustules of the soul
That she and I might take the taint, be shown
To the world and shuddered over, speckled so ?
—That the agent put her sense into my words,
Made substitution of the thing she hoped,
For the thing she had and held, its opposite,   1809
While the husband in the background bit his lips
At each fresh failure of his precious plot ?
—That when at the last we did rush each on each,
By no chance but because God willed it so—
The spark of truth was struck from out our souls—
Made all of me, descried in the first glance,
Seem fair and honest and permissible love
O' the good and true—as the first glance told me
There was no duty patent in the world
Like daring try be good and true myself,   1819
Leaving the shows of things to the Lord of Show
And Prince o' the Power of the Air.   Our very flight,
Even to its most ambiguous circumstance,
Irrefragably proved how futile, false . . .
Why, men—men and not boys—boys and not babes—
Babes and not beasts—beasts and not stocks and
        stones !—
Had the liar's lie been true one pin-point speck,
Were I the accepted suitor, free o' the place,
Disposer of the time, to come at a call
And go at a wink as who should say me nay,—
What need of flight, what were the gain therefrom
But just damnation, failure or success ?   1831
Damnation pure and simple to her the wife
And me the priest—who bartered private bliss
For public reprobation, the safe shade
For the sunshine which men see to pelt me by :
What other advantage,—we who led the days
And nights alone i' the house,—was flight to find ?
In our whole journey did we stop an hour,
Diverge a foot from strait road till we reached
Or would have reached—but for that fate of ours—
The father and mother, in the eye of Rome,   1841
The eye of yourselves we made aware of us

At the first fall of misfortune ?   And indeed
You did so far give sanction to our flight,
Confirm its purpose, as lend helping hand,
Deliver up Pompilia not to him
She fled, but those the flight was ventured for.
Why then could you, who stopped short, not go on
One poor step more, and justify the means,
Having allowed the end ?—not see and say   1850
' Here 's the exceptional conduct that should claim
' To be exceptionally judged on rules
' Which, understood, make no exception here '—
Why play instead into the devil's hands
By dealing so ambiguously as gave
Guido the power to intervene like me,
Prove one exception more ? I saved his wife
Against law : against law he slays her now :
Deal with him !

              I have done with being judged.   1860
I stand here guiltless in thought, word and deed,
To the point that I apprise you,—in contempt
For all misapprehending ignorance
O' the human heart, much more the mind of Christ,—
That I assuredly did bow, was blessed
By the revelation of Pompilia.   There !
Such is the final fact I fling you, Sirs,
To mouth and mumble and misinterpret : there !
' The priest 's in love,' have it the vulgar way !
Unpriest me, rend the rags o' the vestment, do—
Degrade deep, disenfranchise all you dare—   1871
Remove me from the midst, no longer priest
And fit companion for the like of you—
Your gay Abati with the well-turned leg
And rose i' the hat-rim, Canons, cross at neck
And silk mask in the pocket of the gown,
Brisk bishops with the world's musk still unbrushed
From the rochet ; I 'll no more of these good things :
There 's a crack somewhere, something that 's unsound
I' the rattle !   1880

              For Pompilia—be advised,
Build churches, go pray !   You will find me there,
I know, if you come,—and you will come, I know.
Why, there 's a Judge weeping !   Did not I say

You were good and true at bottom ? You see the
    truth—
I am glad I helped you : she helped me just so.

But for Count Guido,—you must counsel there !
I bow my head, bend to the very dust,
Break myself up in shame of faultiness.
I had him one whole moment, as I said—   1890
As I remember, as will never out
O' the thoughts of me,—I had him in arm's reach
There,—as you stand, Sir, now you cease to sit,—
I could have killed him ere he killed his wife,
And did not : he went off alive and well
And then effected this last feat—through me !
Me—not through you—dismiss that fear ! 'T was you
Hindered me staying here to save her,—not
From leaving you and going back to him
And doing service in Arezzo. Come,   1900
Instruct me in procedure ! I conceive—
In all due self-abasement might I speak—
How you will deal with Guido : oh, not death !
Death, if it let her life be : otherwise
Not death,—your lights will teach you clearer ! I
Certainly have an instinct of my own
I' the matter : bear with me and weigh its worth !
Let us go away—leave Guido all alone
Back on the world again that knows him now !
I think he will be found (indulge so far !)   1910
Not to die so much as slide out of life,
Pushed by the general horror and common hate
Low, lower,—left o' the very ledge of things,
I seem to see him catch convulsively
One by one at all honest forms of life,
At reason, order, decency and use—
To cramp him and get foothold by at least ;
And still they disengage them from his clutch.
' What, you are he, then, had Pompilia once
' And so forwent her ? Take not up with us ! '   1920
And thus I see him slowly and surely edged
Off all the table-land whence life upsprings
Aspiring to be immortality,
As the snake, hatched on hill-top by mischance,
Despite his wriggling, slips, slides, slidders down
Hill-side, lies low and prostrate on the smooth

Level of the outer place, lapsed in the vale :
So I lose Guido in the loneliness,
Silence and dusk, till at the doleful end,
At the horizontal line, creation's verge,   1930
From what just is to absolute nothingness—
Lo, what is this he meets, strains onward still ?
What other man deep further in the fate,
Who, turning at the prize of a footfall
To flatter him and promise fellowship,
Discovers in the act a frightful face—
Judas, made monstrous by much solitude !
The two are at one now]   Let them love their love
That bites and claws like hate, or hate their hate
That mops and mows and makes as it were love !
There, let them each tear each in devil's-fun,   1941
Or fondle this the other while malice aches—
Both teach, both learn detestability !
Kiss him the kiss, Iscariot ! Pay that back,
That smatch o' the slaver blistering on your lip—
By the better trick, the insult he spared Christ—
Lure him the lure o' the letters, Aretine !
Lick him o'er slimy-smooth with jelly-filth
O' the verse-and-prose pollution in love's guise !
The cockatrice is with the basilisk !   1950
There let them grapple, denizens o' the dark,
Foes or friends, but indissolubly bound,
In their one spot out of the ken of God
Or care of man, for ever and ever more !

Why, Sirs, what 's this ? Why, this is sorry and
    strange !—
Futility, divagation : this from me
Bound to be rational, justify an act
Of sober man !—whereas, being moved so much,
I give you cause to doubt the lady's mind :
A pretty sarcasm for the world ! I fear   1960
You do her wit injustice,—all through me !
Like my fate all through,—ineffective help !
A poor rash advocate I prove myself.
You might be angry with good cause : but sure
At the advocate,—only at the undue zeal
That spoils the force of his own plea, I think ?
My part was just to tell you how things stand,
State facts and not be flustered at their fume.

But then 't is a priest speaks : as for love,—no !
If you let buzz a vulgar fly like that   1970
About your brains, as if I loved, forsooth,
Indeed, Sirs, you do wrong !   We had no thought
Of such infatuation, she and I :
There are many points that prove it : do be just !
I told you,—at one little roadside-place
I spent a good half-hour, paced to and fro
The garden ; just to leave her free awhile,
I plucked a handful of Spring herb and bloom :
I might have sat beside her on the bench   1979
Where the children were : I wish the thing had been,
Indeed : the event could not be worse, you know :
One more half-hour of her saved ! She 's dead now,
        Sirs !
While I was running on at such a rate,
Friends should have plucked me by the sleeve : I went
Too much o' the trivial outside of her face
And the purity that shone there—plain to me,
Not to you, what more natural ?   Nor am I
Infatuated,—oh, I saw, be sure !
Her brow had not the right line, leaned too much,
Painters would say ; they like the straight-up Greek :
This seemed bent somewhat with an invisible crown
Of martyr and saint, not such as art approves.   1992
And how the dark orbs dwelt deep underneath,
Looked out of such a sad sweet heaven on me—
The lips, compressed a little, came forward too,
Careful for a whole world of sin and pain.
That was the face, her husband makes his plea,
He sought just to disfigure,—no offence
Beyond that ! Sirs, let us be rational !
He needs must vindicate his honour,—ay,   2000
Yet shirks, the coward, in a clown's disguise,
Away from the scene, endeavours to escape.
Now, had he done so, slain and left no trace
O' the slayer,—what were vindicated, pray ?
You had found his wife disfigured or a corpse,
For what and by whom ?   It is too palpable !
Then, here 's another point involving law :
I use this argument to show you meant
No calumny against us by that title
O' the sentence,—liars try to twist it so :   2010
What penalty it bore, I had to pay

Till further proof should follow of innocence—
Probationis ob defectum,—proof ?
How could you get proof without trying us ?
You went through the preliminary form,
Stopped there, contrived this sentence to amuse
The adversary.   If the title ran
For more than fault imputed and not proved,
That was a simple penman's error, else
A slip i' the phrase,—as when we say of you   2020
' Charged with injustice '—which may either be
Or not be,—'t is a name that sticks meanwhile.
Another relevant matter :   fool that I am !
Not what I wish true, yet a point friends urge :
It is not true,—yet, since friends think it helps,—
She only tried me when some others failed—
Began with Conti, whom I told you of,
And Guillichini, Guido's kinsfolk both,
And when abandoned by them, not before,
Turned to me.   That 's conclusive why she turned.
Much good they got by the happy cowardice !   2031
Conti is dead, poisoned a month ago :
Does that much strike you as a sin ?   Not much,
After the present murder,—one mark more
On the Moor's skin,—what is black by blacker still ?
Conti had come here and told truth.   And so
With Guillichini ;   he 's condemned of course
To the galleys, as a friend in this affair,
Tried and condemned for no one thing i' the world,
A fortnight since by who but the Governor ?—
The just judge, who refused Pompilia help   2041
At first blush, being her husband's friend, you know.
There are two tales to suit the separate courts,
Arezzo and Rome :   he tells you here, we fled
Alone, unhelped,—lays stress on the main fault,
The spiritual sin, Rome looks to :   but elsewhere
He likes best we should break in, steal, bear off,
Be fit to brand and pillory and flog—
That 's the charge goes to the heart of the Governor :
If these unpriest me, you and I may yet   2050
Converse, Vincenzo Marzi-Medici !
Oh, Sirs, there are worse men than you I say !
More easily duped, I mean ;   this stupid lie,
Its liar never dared propound in Rome,
He gets Arezzo to receive,—nay more,

Gets Florence and the Duke to authorise !
This is their Rota's sentence, their Granduke
Signs and seals !   Rome for me henceforward—Rome,
Where better men are,—most of all, that man
The Augustinian of the Hospital,   2060
Who writes the letter,—he confessed, he says,
Many a dying person, never one
So sweet and true and pure and beautiful.
A good man !   Will you make him Pope one day ?
Not that he is not good too, this we have—
But old,—else he would have his word to speak,
His truth to teach the world : I thirst for truth,
But shall not drink it till I reach the source.

Sirs, I am quiet again.   You see, we are
So very pitiable, she and I,   2070
Who had conceivably been otherwise.
Forget distemperature and idle heat !
Apart from truth's sake, what 's to move so much ?
Pompilia will be presently with God ;
I am, on earth, as good as out of it,
A relegated priest ; when exile ends,
I mean to do my duty and live long.
She and I are mere strangers now : but priests
Should study passion ; how else cure mankind,
Who come for help in passionate extremes ?   2080
I do but play with an imagined life
Of who, unfettered by a vow, unblessed
By the higher call,—since you will have it so,—
Leads it companioned by the woman there.
To live, and see her learn, and learn by her,
Out of the low obscure and petty world—
Or only see one purpose and one will
Evolve themselves i' the world, change wrong to right :
To have to do with nothing but the true,
The good, the eternal—and these, not alone   2090
In the main current of the general life,
But small experiences of every day,
Concerns of the particular hearth and home :
To learn not only by a comet's rush
But a rose's birth,—not by the grandeur, God—
But the comfort, Christ.   All this, how far away !
Mere delectation, meet for a minute's dream !—
Just as a drudging student trims his lamp,

Opens his Plutarch, puts him in the place
Of Roman, Grecian ; draws the patched gown close,
Dreams, 'Thus should I fight, save or rule the world!'—
Then smilingly, contentedly, awakes   2102
To the old solitary nothingness.
So I, from such communion, pass content . . .

O great, just, good God !   Miserable me !

POMPILIA

I AM just seventeen years and five months old,
And, if I lived one day more, three full weeks ;
'T is writ so in the church's register,
Lorenzo in Lucina, all my names
At length, so many names for one poor child,
—Francesca Camilla Vittoria Angela
Pompilia Comparini,—laughable !
Also 't is writ that I was married there
Four years ago : and they will add, I hope,
When they insert my death, a word or two,—   10
Omitting all about the mode of death,—
This, in its place, this which one cares to know,
That I had been a mother of a son
Exactly two weeks. It will be through grace
O' the Curate, not through any claim I have ;
Because the boy was born at, so baptized
Close to, the Villa, in the proper church :
A pretty church, I say no word against,
Yet stranger-like,—while this Lorenzo seems
My own particular place, I always say.   20
I used to wonder, when I stood scarce high
As the bed here, what the marble lion meant,
With half his body rushing from the wall,
Eating the figure of a prostrate man—
(To the right, it is, of entry by the door)
An ominous sign to one baptized like me,
Married, and to be buried there, I hope.
And they should add, to have my life complete,
He is a boy and Gaetan by name—
Gaetano, for a reason,—if the friar   30
Don Celestine will ask this grace for me
Of Curate Ottoboni : he it was
Baptized me : he remembers my whole life
As I do his grey hair.

          All these few things
I know are true,—will you remember them ?

Because time flies. The surgeon cared for me,
To count my wounds,—twenty-two dagger-wounds,
Five deadly, but I do not suffer much—
Or too much pain,—and am to die to-night. 40

Oh how good God is that my babe was born,
—Better than born, baptized and hid away
Before this happened, safe from being hurt !
That had been sin God could not well forgive :
He was too young to smile and save himself.
When they took, two days after he was born,
My babe away from me to be baptized
And hidden awhile, for fear his foe should find,—
The country-woman, used to nursing babes, 49
Said ' Why take on so ? where is the great loss ?
' These next three weeks he will but sleep and feed,
' Only begin to smile at the month's end ;
' He would not know you, if you kept him here,
' Sooner than that ; so, spend three merry weeks
' Snug in the Villa, getting strong and stout,
' And then I bring him back to be your own,
' And both of you may steal to—we know where ! '
The month—there wants of it two weeks this day !
Still, I half fancied when I heard the knock
At the Villa in the dusk, it might prove she— 60
Come to say ' Since he smiles before the time,
' Why should I cheat you out of one good hour ?
' Back I have brought him ; speak to him and judge ! '
Now I shall never see him ; what is worse,
When he grows up and gets to be my age,
He will seem hardly more than a great boy ;
And if he asks ' What was my mother like ? '
People may answer ' Like girls of seventeen '—
And how can he but think of this and that,
Lucias, Marias, Sofias, who titter or blush 70
When he regards them as such boys may do ?
Therefore I wish some one will please to say
I looked already old though I was young ;
Do I not . . say, if you are by to speak . .
Look nearer twenty ? No more like, at least,
Girls who look arch or redden when boys laugh,
Than the poor Virgin that I used to know
At our street-corner in a lonely niche,—
The babe, that sat upon her knees, broke off,—

Thin white glazed clay, you pitied her the more :
She, not the gay ones, always got my rose.   81

How happy those are who know how to write !
Such could write what their son should read in time,
Had they a whole day to live out like me.
Also my name is not a common name,
' Pompilia,' and may help to keep apart
A little the thing I am from what girls are.
But then how far away, how hard to find
Will anything about me have become,
Even if the boy bethink himself and ask !   90
No father that he ever knew at all,
Nor ever had—no, never had, I say !
That is the truth,—nor any mother left,
Out of the little two weeks that she lived,
Fit for such memory as might assist :
As good too as no family, no name,
Not even poor old Pietro's name, nor hers,
Poor kind unwise Violante, since it seems
They must not be my parents any more.
That is why something put it in my head   100
To call the boy ' Gaetano '—no old name
For sorrow's sake ; I looked up to the sky
And took a new saint to begin anew.
One who has only been made saint—how long ?
Twenty-five years : so, carefuller, perhaps,
To guard a namesake than those old saints grow,
Tired out by this time,—see my own five saints !

On second thoughts, I hope he will regard
The history of me as what someone dreamed,
And get to disbelieve it at the last :   110
Since to myself it dwindles fast to that,
Sheer dreaming and impossibility,—
Just in four days too ! All the seventeen years,
Not once did a suspicion visit me
How very different a lot is mine
From any other woman's in the world.
The reason must be, 't was by step and step
It got to grow so terrible and strange :
These strange woes stole on tiptoe, as it were,
Into my neighbourhood and privacy,   120
Sat down where I sat, laid them where I lay ;

And I was found familiarised with fear,
When friends broke in, held up a torch and cried
' Why, you Pompilia in the cavern thus,
' How comes that arm of yours about a wolf ?
' And the soft length,—lies in and out your feet
' And laps you round the knee,—a snake it is ! '
And so on.

     Well, and they are right enough,
By the torch they hold up now : for first, observe,
I never had a father,—no, nor yet   131
A mother : my own boy can say at least
' I had a mother whom I kept two weeks ! '
Not I, who little used to doubt . . *I* doubt
Good Pietro, kind Violante, gave me birth ?
They loved me always as I love my babe
(—Nearly so, that is—quite so could not be—)
Did for me all I meant to do for him,
Till one surprising day, three years ago,
They both declared, at Rome, before some judge .
In some court where the people flocked to hear,
That really I had never been their child,   142
Was a mere castaway, the careless crime
Of an unknown man, the crime and care too much
Of a woman known too well,—little to these,
Therefore, of whom I was the flesh and blood :
What then to Pietro and Violante, both
No more my relatives than you or you ?
Nothing to them ! You know what they declared.

So with my husband,—just such a surprise, 150
Such a mistake, in that relationship !
Everyone says that husbands love their wives,
Guard them and guide them, give them happiness ;
'Tis duty, law, pleasure, religion : well,
You see how much of this comes true in mine !
People indeed would fain have somehow proved
He was no husband : but he did not hear,
Or would not wait, and so has killed us all.
Then there is . . only let me name one more !
There is the friend,—men will not ask about, 160
But tell untruths of, and give nicknames to,
And think my lover, most surprise of all !
Do only hear, it is the priest they mean,

Giuseppe Caponsacchi : a priest—love,
And love me ! Well, yet people think he did.
I am married, he has taken priestly vows,
They know that, and yet go on, say, the same,
' Yes, how he loves you ! ' ' That was love '—they say,
When anything is answered that they ask :
Or else ' No wonder you love him '—they say.   170
Then they shake heads, pity much, scarcely blame—
As if we neither of us lacked excuse,
And anyhow are punished to the full,
And downright love atones for everything !
Nay, I heard read-out in the public court
Before the judge, in presence of my friends,
Letters 't was said the priest had sent to me,
And other letters sent him by myself,
We being lovers !

                              Listen what this is like !   180
When I was a mere child, my mother . . that 's
Violante, you must let me call her so
Nor waste time, trying to unlearn the word, . . .
She brought a neighbour's child of my own age
To play with me of rainy afternoons ;
And, since there hung a tapestry on the wall,
We two agreed to find each other out
Among the figures. ' Tisbe, that is you,
' With half-moon on your hair-knot, spear in hand,
' Flying, but no wings, only the great scarf   190
' Blown to a bluish rainbow at your back :
' Call off your hound and leave the stag alone ! '
' —And there are you, Pompilia, such green leaves
' Flourishing out of your five finger-ends,
' And all the rest of you so brown and rough :
' Why is it you are turned a sort of tree ? '
You know the figures never were ourselves
Though we nicknamed them so. Thus, all my life,—
As well what was, as what, like this, was not,—
Looks old, fantastic and impossible :   200
I touch a fairy thing that fades and fades.
—Even to my babe ! I thought, when he was born,
Something began for once that would not end,
Nor change into a laugh at me, but stay
For evermore, eternally quite mine.
Well, so he is,—but yet they bore him off,

The third day, lest my husband should lay traps
And catch him, and by means of him catch me.
Since they have saved him so, it was well done :
Yet thence comes such confusion of what was   210
With what will be,—that late seems long ago,
And, what years should bring round, already come,
Till even he withdraws into a dream
As the rest do : I fancy him grown great,
Strong, stern, a tall young man who tutors me,
Frowns with the others ' Poor imprudent child !
' Why did you venture out of the safe street ?
' Why go so far from help to that lone house ?
' Why open at the whisper and the knock ? '

Six days ago when it was New Year's-day,   220
We bent above the fire and talked of him,
What he should do when he was grown and great.
Violante, Pietro, each had given the arm
I leant on, to walk by, from couch to chair
And fireside,—laughed, as I lay safe at last,
' Pompilia's march from bed to board is made,
' Pompilia back again and with a babe,
' Shall one day lend his arm and help her walk ! '
Then we all wished each other more New Years.
Pietro began to scheme—' Our cause is gained ;   230
' The law is stronger than a wicked man :
' Let him henceforth go his way, leave us ours !
' We will avoid the city, tempt no more
' The greedy ones by feasting and parade,—
' Live at the other villa, we know where,
' Still farther off, and we can watch the babe
' Grow fast in the good air ; and wood is cheap
' And wine sincere outside the city gate.
' I still have two or three old friends will grope
' Their way along the mere half-mile of road,   240
' With staff and lantern on a moonless night
' When one needs talk : they'll find me, never fear,
' And I'll find them a flask of the old sort yet ! '
Violante said ' You chatter like a crow :
' Pompilia tires o' the tattle, and shall to bed :
' Do not too much the first day,—somewhat more
' To-morrow, and, the next, begin the cape
' And hood and coat ! I have spun wool enough.'
Oh what a happy friendly eve was that !

K

And, next day, about noon, out Pietro went—   250
He was so happy and would talk so much,
Until Violante pushed and laughed him forth
Sight-seeing in the cold,—' So much to see
' I' the churches ! Swathe your throat three times ! '
      she cried,
' And, above all, beware the slippery ways,
' And bring us all the news by supper-time ! '
He came back late, laid by cloak, staff and hat,
Powdered so thick with snow it made us laugh,
Rolled a great log upon the ash o' the hearth,
And bade Violante treat us to a flask,   260
Because he had obeyed her faithfully,
Gone sight-see through the seven, and found no church
To his mind like San Giovanni—' There 's the fold,
' And all the sheep together, big as cats !
' And such a shepherd, half the size of life,
' Starts up and hears the angel '—when, at the door,
A tap : we started up : you know the rest.

Pietro at least had done no harm, I know ;
Nor even Violante, so much harm as makes
Such revenge lawful. Certainly she erred—   270
Did wrong, how shall I dare say otherwise ?—
In telling that first falsehood, buying me
From my poor faulty mother at a price,
To pass off upon Pietro as his child :
If one should take my babe, give him a name,
Say he was not Gaetano and my own,
But that some other woman made his mouth
And hands and feet,—how very false were that !
No good could come of that ; and all harm did.
Yet if a stranger were to represent   280
' Needs must you either give your babe to me
' And let me call him mine for ever more,
' Or let your husband get him '—ah, my God,
That were a trial I refuse to face !
Well, just so here : it proved wrong but seemed right
To poor Violante—for there lay, she said,
My poor real dying mother in her rags,
Who put me from her with the life and all,
Poverty, pain, shame and disease at once,
To die the easier by what price I fetched—   290
Also (I hope) because I should be spared

Sorrow and sin,—why may not that have helped ?
My father,—he was no one, any one,—
The worse, the likelier,—call him,—he who came,
Was wicked for his pleasure, went his way,
And left no trace to track by ; there remained
Nothing but me, the unnecessary life,
To catch up or let fall,—and yet a thing
She could make happy, be made happy with,   299
This poor Violante,—who would frown thereat ?

Well, God, you see ! God plants us where we grow.
It is not that, because a bud is born
At a wild briar's end, full i' the wild beast's way,
We ought to pluck and put it out of reach
On the oak-tree top,—say, ' There the bud belongs ! '
She thought, moreover, real lies were—lies told
For harm's sake ; whereas this had good at heart,
Good for my mother, good for me, and good
For Pietro who was meant to love a babe,
And needed one to make his life of use,   310
Receive his house and land when he should die.
Wrong, wrong and always wrong ! how plainly wrong !
For see, this fault kept pricking, as faults do,
All the same at her heart,—this falsehood hatched,
She could not let it go nor keep it fast.
She told me so,—the first time I was found
Locked in her arms once more after the pain,
When the nuns let me leave them and go home,
And both of us cried all the cares away,—
This it was set her on to make amends,   320
This brought about the marriage—simply this !
Do let me speak for her you blame so much !
When Paul, my husband's brother, found me out,
Heard there was wealth for who should marry me,
So, came and made a speech to ask my hand
For Guido,—she, instead of piercing straight
Through the pretence to the ignoble truth,
Fancied she saw God's very finger point,
Designate just the time for planting me,
(The wild briar-slip she plucked to love and wear)
In soil where I could strike real root, and grow, 331
And get to be the thing I called myself :
For, wife and husband are one flesh, God says,
And I, whose parents seemed such and were none,

Should in a husband have a husband now,
Find nothing, this time, but was what it seemed,
—All truth and no confusion any more.
I know she meant all good to me, all pain
To herself,—since how could it be aught but pain,
To give me up, so, from her very breast,   340
The wilding flower-tree-branch that, all those years,
She had got used to feel for and find fixed ?
She meant well : has it been so ill i' the main ?
That is but fair to ask : one cannot judge
Of what has been the ill or well of life,
The day that one is dying,—sorrows change
Into not altogether sorrow-like ;
I do see strangeness but scarce misery,
Now it is over, and no danger more.
My child is safe ; there seems not so much pain.
It comes, most like, that I am just absolved,   351
Purged of the past, the foul in me, washed fair,—
One cannot both have and not have, you know,—
Being right now, I am happy and colour things.
Yes, every body that leaves life sees all
Softened and bettered : so with other sights :
To me at least was never evening yet
But seemed far beautifuller than its day,
For past is past.

                    There was a fancy came,   360
When somewhere, in the journey with my friend,
We stepped into a hovel to get food ;
And there began a yelp here, a bark there,—
Misunderstanding creatures that were wroth
And vexed themselves and us till we retired.
The hovel is life : no matter what dogs bit
Or cats scratched in the hovel I break from,
All outside is lone field, moon and such peace—
Flowing in, filling up as with a sea
Whereon comes Someone, walks fast on the white,
Jesus Christ's self, Don Celestine declares,   371
To meet me and calm all things back again.

Beside, up to my marriage, thirteen years
Were, each day, happy as the day was long :
This may have made the change too terrible.
I know that when Violante told me first

The cavalier,—she meant to bring next morn,
Whom I must also let take, kiss my hand,—
Would be at San Lorenzo the same eve
And marry me,—which over, we should go   380
Home both of us without him as before,
And, till she bade speak, I must hold my tongue,
Such being the correct way with girl-brides,
From whom one word would make a father blush,—
I know, I say, that when she told me this,
—Well, I no more saw sense in what she said
Than a lamb does in people clipping wool ;
Only lay down and let myself be clipped.
And when next day the cavalier who came
(Tisbe had told me that the slim young man   390
With wings at head, and wings at feet, and sword
Threatening a monster, in our tapestry,
Would eat a girl else,—was a cavalier)
When he proved Guido Franceschini,—old
And nothing like so tall as I myself,
Hook-nosed and yellow in a bush of beard,
Much like a thing I saw on a boy's wrist,
He called an owl and used for catching birds,—
And when he took my hand and made a smile—
Why, the uncomfortableness of it all   400
Seemed hardly more important in the case
Than,—when one gives you, say, a coin to spend,—
Its newness or its oldness ; if the piece
Weigh properly and buy you what you wish,
No matter whether you get grime or glare !
Men take the coin, return you grapes and figs.
Here, marriage was the coin, a dirty piece
Would purchase me the praise of those I loved :
About what else should I concern myself ?

So, hardly knowing what a husband meant,   410
I supposed this or any man would serve,
No whit the worse for being so uncouth :
For I was ill once and a doctor came
With a great ugly hat, no plume thereto,
Black jerkin and black buckles and black sword,
And white sharp beard over the ruff in front,
And oh so lean, so sour-faced and austere !—
Who felt my pulse, made me put out my tongue,
Then oped a phial, dripped a drop or two

Of a black bitter something,—I was cured !   420
What mattered the fierce beard or the grim face ?
It was the physic beautified the man,
Master Malpichi,—never met his match
In Rome, they said,—so ugly all the same !

However, I was hurried through a storm,
Next dark eve of December's deadest day—
How it rained !—through our street and the Lion's-
        mouth
And the bit of Corso,—cloaked round, covered close,
I was like something strange or contraband,—
Into blank San Lorenzo, up the aisle,   430
My mother keeping hold of me so tight,
I fancied we were come to see a corpse
Before the altar which she pulled me toward.
There we found waiting an unpleasant priest
Who proved the brother, not our parish friend,
But one with mischief-making mouth and eye,
Paul, whom I know since to my cost.   And then
I heard the heavy church-door lock out help
Behind us : for the customary warmth,
Two tapers shivered on the altar.   ' Quick—   440
' Lose no time ! '—cried the priest.   And straightway
        down
From . . . what 's behind the altar where he hid—
Hawk-nose and yellowness and bush and all,
Stepped Guido, caught my hand, and there was I
O' the chancel, and the priest had opened book,
Read here and there, made me say that and this,
And after, told me I was now a wife,
Honoured indeed, since Christ thus weds the Church,
And therefore turned he water into wine,
To show I should obey my spouse like Christ.   450
Then the two slipped aside and talked apart,
And I, silent and scared, got down again
And joined my mother who was weeping now.
Nobody seemed to mind us any more,
And both of us on tiptoe found our way
To the door which was unlocked by this, and wide.
When we were in the street, the rain had stopped,
All things looked better.   At our own house-door,
Violante whispered ' No one syllable   459
' To Pietro !   Girl-brides never breathe a word ! '

' —Well treated to a wetting, draggle-tails ! '
Laughed Pietro as he opened—' Very near
' You made me brave the gutter's roaring sea
' To carry off from roost old dove and young,
' Trussed up in church, the cote, by me, the kite !
' What do these priests mean, praying folk to death
' On stormy afternoons, with Christmas close
' To wash our sins off nor require the rain ? '
Violante gave my hand a timely squeeze,
Madonna saved me from immodest speech,   470
I kissed him and was quiet, being a bride.

When I saw nothing more, the next three weeks,
Of Guido—' Nor the Church sees Christ ' thought I :
' Nothing is changed however, wine is wine
' And water only water in our house.
' Nor did I see that ugly doctor since
' The cure of the illness : just as I was cured,
' I am married,—neither scarecrow will return.'

Three weeks, I chuckled—' How would Giulia stare,
' And Tecla smile and Tisbe laugh outright,   480
' Were it not impudent for brides to talk ! '—
Until one morning, as I sat and sang
At the broidery-frame alone i' the chamber,—loud
Voices, two, three together, sobbings too,
And my name, ' Guido,' ' Paolo,' flung like stones
From each to the other ! In I ran to see.
There stood the very Guido and the priest
With sly face,—formal but nowise afraid,—
While Pietro seemed all red and angry, scarce
Able to stutter out his wrath in words ;   490
And this it was that made my mother sob,
As he reproached her—' You have murdered us,
' Me and yourself and this our child beside ! '
Then Guido interposed ' Murdered or not,
' Be it enough your child is now my wife !
' I claim and come to take her.'   Paul put in,
' Consider—kinsman, dare I term you so ?—
' What is the good of your sagacity
' Except to counsel in a strait like this ?
' I guarantee the parties man and wife   500
' Whether you like or loathe it, bless or ban.
' May spilt milk be put back within the bowl—

' The done thing, undone ?   You, it is, we look
' For counsel to, you fitliest will advise !
' Since milk, though spilt and spoilt, does marble good,
' Better we down on knees and scrub the floor,
' Than sigh, " the waste would make a syllabub ! "
' Help us so turn disaster to account,
' So predispose the groom, he needs shall grace
' The bride with favour from the very first,   510
' Not begin marriage an embittered man ! '
He smiled,—the game so wholly in his hands !
While fast and faster sobbed Violante—' Ay,
' All of us murdered, past averting now !
' O my sin, O my secret ! ' and such like.

Then I began to half surmise the truth ;
Something had happened, low, mean, underhand,
False, and my mother was to blame, and I
To pity, whom all spoke of, none addressed :
I was the chattel that had caused a crime.   520
I stood mute,—those who tangled must untie
The embroilment.   Pietro cried ' Withdraw, my child !
' She is not helpful to the sacrifice
' At this stage,—do you want the victim by
' While you discuss the value of her blood ?
' For her sake, I consent to hear you talk :
' Go, child, and pray God help the innocent ! '

I did go and was praying God, when came
Violante, with eyes swollen and red enough,
But movement on her mouth for make-believe   530
Matters were somehow getting right again.
She bade me sit down by her side and hear.
' You are too young and cannot understand,
' Nor did your father understand at first.
' I wished to benefit all three of us,
' And when he failed to take my meaning,—why,
' I tried to have my way at unaware—
' Obtained him the advantage he refused.
' As if I put before him wholesome food
' Instead of broken victual,—he finds change   540
' I' the viands, never cares to reason why,
' But falls to blaming me, would fling the plate
' From window, scandalize the neighbourhood,
' Even while he smacks his lips,—men's way, my child!

' But either you have prayed him unperverse
' Or I have talked him back into his wits :
' And Paolo was a help in time of need,—
' Guido, not much—my child, the way of men !
' A priest is more a woman than a man,   549
' And Paul did wonders to persuade.   In short,
' Yes, he was wrong, your father sees and says ;
' My scheme was worth attempting : and bears fruit,
' Gives you a husband and a noble name,
' A palace and no end of pleasant things.
' What do you care about a handsome youth ?
' They are so volatile, and tease their wives !
' This is the kind of man to keep the house.
' We lose no daughter,—gain a son, that's all :
' For 'tis arranged we never separate,
' Nor miss, in our grey time of life, the tints   560
' Of you that colour eve to match with morn.
' In good or ill, we share and share alike,
' And cast our lots into a common lap,
' And all three die together as we lived !
' Only, at Arezzo,—that 's a Tuscan town,
' Not so large as this noisy Rome, no doubt,
' But older far and finer much, say folks,—
' In a great palace where you will be queen,
' Know the Archbishop and the Governor,
' And we see homage done you ere we die.   570
' Therefore, be good and pardon ! '—' Pardon what ?
' You know things, I am very ignorant :
' All is right if you only will not cry ! '

And so an end !   Because a blank begins
From when, at the word, she kissed me hard and hot,
And took me back to where my father leaned
Opposite Guido—who stood eyeing him,
As eyes the butcher the cast panting ox
That feels his fate is come, nor struggles more,—
While Paul looked archly on, pricked brow at whiles
With the pen-point as to punish triumph there,—
And said ' Count Guido, take your lawful wife   582
' Until death part you ! '

                    All since is one blank,
Over and ended ; a terrific dream.
It is the good of dreams—so soon they go !

Wake in a horror of heart-beats, you may—
Cry, ' The dread thing will never from my thoughts ! '
Still, a few daylight doses of plain life,
Cock-crow and sparrow-chirp, or bleat and bell   590
Of goats that trot by, tinkling, to be milked ;
And when you rub your eyes awake and wide,
Where is the harm o' the horror ?   Gone !   So here.
I know I wake,—but from what ?   Blank, I say !
This is the note of evil : for good lasts.
Even when Don Celestine bade ' Search and find !
' For your soul's sake, remember what is past,
' The better to forgive it,'—all in vain !
What was fast getting indistinct before,
Vanished outright.   By special grace perhaps,   600
Between that first calm and this last, four years
Vanish,—one quarter of my life, you know.
I am held up, amid the nothingness,
By one or two truths only—thence I hang,
And there I live,—the rest is death or dream,
All but those points of my support.   I think
Of what I saw at Rome once in the Square
O' the Spaniards, opposite the Spanish House :
There was a foreigner had trained a goat,
A shuddering white woman of a beast,   610
To climb up, stand straight on a pile of sticks
Put close, which gave the creature room enough :
When she was settled there he, one by one,
Took away all the sticks, left just the four
Whereon the little hoofs did really rest,
There she kept firm, all underneath was air.
So, what I hold by, are my prayer to God,
My hope, that came in answer to the prayer,
Some hand would interpose and save me—hand
Which proved to be my friend's hand : and,—best
     bliss,—   620
That fancy which began so faint at first,
That thrill of dawn's suffusion through my dark,
Which I perceive was promise of my child,
The light his unborn face sent long before,—
God's way of breaking the good news to flesh.
That is all left now of those four bad years.
Don Celestine urged ' But remember more !
' Other men's faults may help me find your own.
' I need the cruelty exposed, explained,

' Or how can I advise you to forgive ? '   620
He thought I could not properly forgive
Unless I ceased forgetting,—which is true :
For, bringing back reluctantly to mind
My husband's treatment of me,—by a light
That 's later than my life-time, I review
And comprehend much and imagine more,
And have but little to forgive at last.
For now,—be fair and say,—is it not true
He was ill-used and cheated of his hope
To get enriched by marriage ? Marriage gave   640
Me and no money, broke the compact so :
He had a right to ask me on those terms,
As Pietro and Violante to declare
They would not give me : so the bargain stood :
They broke it, and he felt himself aggrieved,
Became unkind with me to punish them.
They said 't was he began deception first,
Nor, in one point whereto he pledged himself,
Kept promise : what of that, suppose it were ?
Echoes die off, scarcely reverberate   650
For ever,—why should ill keep echoing ill,
And never let our ears have done with noise ?
Then my poor parents took the violent way
To thwart him,—he must needs retaliate,—wrong,
Wrong, and all wrong,—better say, all blind !
As I myself was, that is sure, who else
Had understood the mystery : for his wife
Was bound in some sort to help somehow there.
It seems as if I might have interposed,
Blunted the edge of their resentment so,   660
Since he vexed me because they first vexed him ;
' I will entreat them to desist, submit,
' Give him the money and be poor in peace,—
' Certainly not go tell the world : perhaps
' He will grow quiet with his gains.'
                                    Yes, say
Something to this effect and you do well !
But then you have to see first : I was blind.
That is the fruit of all such wormy ways,
The indirect, the unapproved of God :   670
You cannot find their author's end and aim,
Not even to substitute your good for bad,
Your open for the irregular ; you stand

Stupefied, profitless, as cow or sheep
That miss a man's mind ; anger him just twice
By trial at repairing the first fault.
Thus, when he blamed me, ' You are a coquette,
' A lure-owl posturing to attract birds,
' You look love-lures at theatre and church,　　679
' In walk, at window ! '—that, I knew, was false :
But why he charged me falsely, whither sought
To drive me by such charge,—how could I know ?
So, unaware, I only made things worse.
I tried to soothe him by abjuring walk,
Window, church, theatre, for good and all,
As if he had been in earnest : that, you know,
Was nothing like the object of his charge.
Yes, when I got my maid to supplicate
The priest, whose name she read when she would read
Those feigned false letters I was forced to hear　690
Though I could read no word of,—he should cease
Writing,—nay, if he minded prayer of mine,
Cease from so much as even pass the street
Whereon our house looked,—in my ignorance
I was just thwarting Guido's true intent ;
Which was, to bring about a wicked change
Of sport to earnest, tempt a thoughtless man
To write indeed, and pass the house, and more,
Till both of us were taken in a crime.
He ought not to have wished me thus act lies,　700
Simulate folly,—but,—wrong or right, the wish,—
I failed to apprehend its drift.　How plain
It follows,—if I fell into such fault,
He also may have overreached the mark,
Made mistake, by perversity of brain,
In the whole sad strange plot, this same intrigue
To make me and my friend unself ourselves,
Be other man and woman than we were !
Think it out, you who have the time ! for me,—
I cannot say less ; more I will not say.　710
Leave it to God to cover and undo !
Only, my dulness should not prove too much !
—Not prove that in a certain other point
Wherein my husband blamed me,—and you blame,
If I interpret smiles and shakes of head,—
I was dull too.　Oh, if I dared but speak !
Must I speak ?　I am blamed that I forwent

A way to make my husband's favour come.
That is true : I was firm, withstood, refused . . .
—Women as you are, how can I find the words ?

I felt there was just one thing Guido claimed   721
I had no right to give nor he to take ;
We being in estrangement, soul from soul :
Till, when I sought help, the Archbishop smiled,
Inquiring into privacies of life,
—Said I was blameable—(he stands for God)
Nowise entitled to exemption there.
Then I obeyed,—as surely had obeyed
Were the injunction ' Since your husband bids,
' Swallow the burning coal he proffers you ! '   730
But I did wrong, and he gave wrong advice
Though he were thrice Archbishop,—that, I know !—
Now I have got to die and see things clear
Remember I was barely twelve years old—
A child at marriage : I was let alone
For weeks, I told you, lived my child-life still
Even at Arezzo, when I woke and found
First . . . but I need not think of that again—
Over and ended ! Try and take the sense
Of what I signify, if it must be so.   740
After the first, my husband, for hate's sake,
Said one eve, when the simpler cruelty
Seemed somewhat dull at edge and fit to bear,
' We have been man and wife six months almost :
' How long is this your comedy to last ?
' Go this night to my chamber, not your own ! '
At which word, I did rush—most true the charge—
And gain the Archbishop's house—he stands for
      God—
And fall upon my knees and clasp his feet,
Praying him hinder what my estranged soul   750
Refused to bear, though patient of the rest :
' Place me within a convent,' I implored—
' Let me henceforward lead the virgin life
' You praise in Her you bid me imitate ! '
What did he answer ? ' Folly of ignorance !
' Know, daughter, circumstances make or mar
' Virginity,—'t is virtue or 't is vice.
' That which was glory in the Mother of God
' Had been, for instance, damnable in Eve

' Created to be mother of mankind.   760
' Had Eve, in answer to her Maker's speech
' " Be fruitful, multiply, replenish earth "—
' Pouted " But I choose rather to remain
' " Single "—why, she had spared herself forthwith
' Further probation by the apple and snake,
' Been pushed straight out of Paradise ! For see—
' If motherhood be qualified impure,
' I catch you making God command Eve sin !
' —A blasphemy so like these Molinists',
' I must suspect you dip into their books.'   770
Then he pursued ' 'T was in your covenant ! '

No ! There my husband never used deceit.
He never did by speech nor act imply
' Because of our souls' yearning that we meet
' And mix in soul through flesh, which yours and mine
' Wear and impress, and make their visible selves,
' —All which means, for the love of you and me,
' Let us become one flesh, being one soul ! '
He only stipulated for the wealth ;
Honest so far. But when he spoke as plain—   780
Dreadfully honest also—' Since our souls
' Stand each from each, a whole world's width between,
' Give me the fleshy vesture I can reach
' And rend and leave just fit for hell to burn ! '—
Why, in God's name, for Guido's soul's own sake
Imperilled by polluting mine,—I say,
I did resist ; would I had overcome !

My heart died out at the Archbishop's smile ;
—It seemed so stale and worn a way o' the world,
As though 't were nature frowning—' Here is Spring,
' The sun shines as he shone at Adam's fall,   791
' The earth requires that warmth reach everywhere :
' What, must your patch of snow be saved forsooth
' Because you rather fancy snow than flowers ? '
Something in this style he began with me.
Last he said, savagely for a good man,
' This explains why you call your husband harsh,
' Harsh to you, harsh to whom you love. God's
        Bread !
' The poor Count has to manage a mere child
' Whose parents leave untaught the simplest things

' Their duty was and privilege to teach,—   801
' Goodwives' instruction, gossips' lore : they laugh
' And leave the Count the task,—or leave it me ! '
Then I resolved to tell a frightful thing.
' I am not ignorant,—know what I say,
' Declaring this is sought for hate, not love.
' Sir, you may hear things like almighty God.
' I tell you that my housemate, yes—the priest
· My husband's brother, Canon Girolamo—
' Has taught me what depraved and misnamed love
' Means, and what outward signs denote the sin,
' For he solicits me and says he loves,   812
' The idle young priest with nought else to do.
' My husband sees this, knows this, and lets be.
' Is it your counsel I bear this beside ? '
' —More scandal, and against a priest this time !
' What, 't is the Canon now ? '—less snappishly—
' Rise up, my child, for such a child you are,
' The rod were too advanced a punishment !
' Let 's try the honeyed cake.   A parable !   820
' " Without a parable spake He not to them."
' There was a ripe round long black toothsome fruit,
' Even a flower-fig, the prime boast of May :
' And, to the tree, said . . . either the spirit o' the fig,
' Or, if we bring in men, the gardener,
' Archbishop of the orchard—had I time
' To try o' the two which fits in best : indeed
' It might be the Creator's self, but then
' The tree should bear an apple, I suppose,—
' Well, anyhow, one with authority said   830
' " Ripe fig, burst skin, regale the fig-pecker—
' " The bird whereof thou art a perquisite ! "
' " Nay," with a flounce, replied the restif fig,
' " I much prefer to keep my pulp myself :
' " He may go breakfastless and dinnerless,
' " Supperless of one crimson seed, for me ! "
' So, back she flopped into her bunch of leaves.
' He flew off, left her,—did the natural lord,—
' And lo, three hundred thousand bees and wasps
' Found her out, feasted on her to the shuck :   840
' Such gain the fig's that gave its bird no bite !
' The moral,—fools elude their proper lot,
' Tempt other fools, get ruined all alike.
' Therefore go home, embrace your husband quick !

' Which if his Canon brother chance to see,
' He will the sooner back to book again.'

So, home I did go : so, the worst befell :
So, I had proof the Archbishop was just man,
And hardly that, and certainly no more.
For, miserable consequence to me,   850
My husband's hatred waxed nor waned at all,
His brother's boldness grew effrontery soon,
And my last stay and comfort in myself
Was forced from me : henceforth I looked to God
Only, nor cared my desecrated soul
Should have fair walls, gay windows for the world.
God's glimmer, that came through the ruin-top,
Was witness why all lights were quenched inside :
Henceforth I asked God counsel, not mankind.

So, when I made the effort, saved myself,   860
They said—' No care to save appearance here !
' How cynic,—when, how wanton, were enough ! '
—Adding, it all came of my mother's life—
My own real mother, whom I never knew,
Who did wrong (if she needs must have done wrong)
Through being all her life, not my four years,
At mercy of the hateful,—every beast
O' the field was wont to break that fountain-fence,
Trample the silver into mud so murk
Heaven could not find itself reflected there,—   870
Now they cry ' Out on her, who, plashy pool,
' Bequeathed turbidity and bitterness
' To the daughter-stream where Guido dipt and
        drank ! '

Well, since she had to bear this brand—let me !
The rather do I understand her now,—
From my experience of what hate calls love,—
Much love might be in what their love called hate.
If she sold . . . what they call, sold . . . me her child—
I shall believe she hoped in her poor heart
That I at least might try be good and pure,   880
Begin to live untempted, not go doomed
And done with ere once found in fault, as she.
Oh and, my mother, it all came to this ?
Why should I trust those that speak ill of you,

When I mistrust who speaks even well of them ?
Why, since all bound to do me good, did harm,
May not you, seeming as you harmed me most,
Have meant to do most good—and feed your child
From bramble-bush, whom not one orchard-tree
But drew-back bough from, nor let one fruit fall ?
This it was for you sacrificed your babe ?   891
Gained just this, giving your heart's hope away
As I might give mine, loving it as you,
If ˙. . but that never could be asked of me !

There, enough ! I have my support again,
Again the knowledge that my babe was, is,
Will be mine only.   Him, by death, I give
Outright to God, without a further care,—
But not to any parent in the world,—
So to be safe : why is it we repine ?   900
What guardianship were safer could we choose ?
All human plans and projects come to nought,
My life, and what I know of other lives,
Prove that : no plan nor project ! God shall care !

And now you are not tired ?   How patient then
All of you,—Oh yes, patient this long while
Listening, and understanding, I am sure !
Four days ago, when I was sound and well
And like to live, no one would understand.
People were kind, but smiled ' And what of him,   910
' Your friend, whose tonsure, the rich dark-brown
          hides ?
' There, there !—your lover, do we dream he was ?
' A priest too—never were such naughtiness !
' Still, he thinks many a long think, never fear,
' After the shy pale lady,—lay so light
' For a moment in his arms, the lucky one ! '
And so on : wherefore should I blame you much ?
So we are made, such difference in minds,
Such difference too in eyes that see the minds !
That man, you misinterpret and misprise—   920
The glory of his nature, I had thought,
Shot itself out in white light, blazed the truth
Through every atom of his act with me :
Yet where I point you, through the chrystal shrine,
Purity in quintessence, one dew-drop,

You all descry a spider in the midst.
One says, ' The head of it is plain to see,'
And one, ' They are the feet by which I judge,'
All say, ' Those films were spun by nothing else.'

Then, I must lay my babe away with God,   930
Nor think of him again, for gratitude.
Yes, my last breath shall wholly spend itself
In one attempt more to disperse the stain,
The mist from other breath fond mouths have made,
About a lustrous and pellucid soul :
So that, when I am gone but sorrow stays,
And people need assurance in their doubt
If God yet have a servant, man a friend,
The weak a saviour and the vile a foe,—
Let him be present, by the name invoked,   940
Giuseppe-Maria Caponsacchi !

                                     There,
Strength comes already with the utterance !
I will remember once more for his sake
The sorrow : for he lives and is belied.
Could he be here, how he would speak for me !

I had been miserable three drear years
In that dread palace and lay passive now,
When I first learned there could be such a man.
Thus it fell : I was at a public play,   950
In the last days of Carnival last March,
Brought there I knew not why, but now know well.
My husband put me where I sat, in front ;
Then crouched down, breathed cold through me from
        behind,
Stationed i' the shadow,—none in front could see,—
I, it was, faced the stranger-throng beneath,
The crowd with upturned faces, eyes one stare,
Voices one buzz. I looked but to the stage,
Whereon two lovers sang and interchanged
' True life is only love, love only bliss :   960
' I love thee—thee I love ! ' then they embraced.
I looked thence to the ceiling and the walls,—
Over the crowd, those voices and those eyes,—
My thoughts went through the roof and out, to Rome
On wings of music, waft of measured words,—

Set me down there, a happy child again,
Sure that to-morrow would be festa-day,
Hearing my parents praise past festas more,
And seeing they were old if I was young,
Yet wondering why they still would end discourse
With ' We must soon go, you abide your time,   971
' And,—might we haply see the proper friend
' Throw his arm over you and make you safe ! '

Sudden I saw him ; into my lap there fell
A foolish twist of comfits, broke my dream
And brought me from the air and laid me low,
As ruined as the soaring bee that 's reached
(So Pietro told me at the Villa once)
By the dust-handful. There the comfits lay :
I looked to see who flung them, and I faced   980
This Caponsacchi, looking up in turn.
Ere I could reason out why, I felt sure,
Whoever flung them, his was not the hand,—
Up rose the round face and good-natured grin
Of him who, in effect, had played the prank,
From covert close beside the earnest face,—
Fat waggish Conti, friend of all the world.
He was my husband's cousin, privileged
To throw the thing : the other, silent, grave,
Solemn almost, saw me, as I saw him.   990

There is a psalm Don Celestine recites,
' Had I a dove's wings, how I fain would flee ! '
The psalm runs not ' I hope, I pray for wings,'—
Not ' If wings fall from heaven, I fix them fast,'—
Simply ' How good it were to fly and rest,
' Have hope now, and one day expect content !
' How well to do what I shall never do ! '
So I said ' Had there been a man like that,
' To lift me with his strength out of all strife
' Into the calm, how I could fly and rest !   1000
' I have a keeper in the garden here
' Whose sole employment is to strike me low
' If ever I, for solace, seek the sun.
' Life means with me successful feigning death,
' Lying stone-like, eluding notice so,
' Forgoing here the turf and there the sky.
' Suppose that man had been instead of this ! '

Presently Conti laughed into my ear,
—Had tripped up to the raised place where I sat—
' Cousin, I flung them brutishly and hard !   1010
' Because you must be hurt, to look austere
' As Caponsacchi yonder, my tall friend
' A-gazing now.   Ah, Guido, you so close ?
' Keep on your knees, do !   Beg her to forgive !
' My cornet battered like a cannon-ball.
' Good bye, I 'm gone ! '—nor waited the reply.

That night at supper, out my husband broke,
' Why was that throwing, that buffoonery ?
' Do you think I am your dupe ?   What man would
      dare
' Throw comfits in a stranger lady's lap ?   1020
' 'Twas knowledge of you bred such insolence
' In Caponsacchi ; he dared shoot the bolt,
' Using that Conti for his stalking-horse.
' How could you see him this once and no more,
' When he is always haunting hereabout
' At the street-corner or the palace-side,
' Publishing my shame and your impudence ?
' You are a wanton,—I a dupe, you think ?
' O Christ, what hinders that I kill her quick ? '
Whereat he drew his sword and feigned a thrust.

All this, now,—being not so strange to me,   1031
Used to such misconception day by day
And broken-in to bear,—I bore, this time,
More quietly than woman should perhaps ;
Repeated the mere truth and held my tongue.

Then he said, ' Since you play the ignorant,
' I shall instruct you.   This amour,—commenced
' Or finished or midway in act, all 's one,—
' 'Tis the town-talk ; so my revenge shall be.
' Does he presume because he is a priest ?   1040
' I warn him that the sword I wear shall pink
' His lily-scented cassock through and through,
' Next time I catch him underneath your eaves ! '

But he had threatened with the sword so oft
And, after all, not kept his promise.   All
I said was, ' Let God save the innocent !

' Moreover, death is far from a bad fate.
' I shall go pray for you and me, not him ;
' And then I look to sleep, come death or, worse,
' Life.'   So, I slept   1050

                 There may have elapsed a week,
When Margherita,—called my waiting-maid,
Whom it is said my husband found too fair—
Who stood and heard the charge and the reply,
Who never once would let the matter rest
From that night forward, but rang changes still
On this the thrust and that the shame, and how
Good cause for jealousy cures jealous fools,
And what a paragon was this same priest
She talked about until I stopped my ears,—   1060
She said, ' A week is gone ; you comb your hair,
' Then go mope in a corner, cheek on palm,
' Till night comes round again,—so, waste a week
' As if your husband menaced you in sport.
' Have not I some acquaintance with his tricks ?
' Oh no, he did not stab the serving-man
' Who made and sang the rhymes about me once !
' For why ?   They sent him to the wars next day.
' Nor poisoned he the foreigner, my friend,
' Who wagered on the whiteness of my breast,—
' The swarth skins of our city in dispute :   1071
' For, though he paid me proper compliment,
' The Count well knew he was besotted with
' Somebody else, a skin as black as ink,
' (As all the town knew save my foreigner)
' He found and wedded presently,—" Why need
' " Better revenge ? "—the Count asked.   But what 's
    here ?
' A priest, that does not fight, and cannot wed,
' Yet must be dealt with !   If the Count took fire
' For the poor pastime of a minute,—me—   1080
' What were the conflagration for yourself,
' Countess and lady-wife and all the rest ?
' The priest will perish ; you will grieve too late :
' So shall the city-ladies' handsomest
' Frankest and liberalest gentleman
' Die for you, to appease a scurvy dog
' Hanging 's too good for.   Is there no escape ?
' Were it not simple Christian charity

‘ To warn the priest be on his guard,—save him
‘ Assured death, save yourself from causing it ?
‘ I meet him in the street.　Give me a glove,　　1091
‘ A ring to show for token !　Mum's the word ! ’

I answered, ‘ If you were, as styled, my maid,
‘ I would command you : as you are, you say,
‘ My husband's intimate,—assist his wife
‘ Who can do nothing but entreat “ Be still ! ”
‘ Even if you speak truth and a crime is planned,
‘ Leave help to God as I am forced to do !
‘ There is no other course, or we should craze,
‘ Seeing such evil with no human cure.　　1100
‘ Reflect that God, who makes the storm desist,
‘ Can make an angry violent heart subside.
‘ Why should we venture teach Him governance ?
‘ Never address me on this subject more ! ’

Next night she said, ‘ But I went, all the same,
‘ —Ay, saw your Caponsacchi in his house,
‘ And come back stuffed with news I must outpour.
‘ I told him, “ Sir, my mistress is a stone :
‘ “ Why should you harm her for no good you get ?
‘ “ For you do harm her—prowl about our place　1110
‘ “ With the Count never distant half the street,
‘ “ Lurking at every corner, would you look !
‘ “ 'Tis certain she has witched you with a spell.
‘ “ Are there not other beauties at your beck ?
‘ “ We all know, Donna This and Monna That
‘ “ Die for a glance of yours, yet here you gaze !
‘ “ Go make them grateful, leave the stone its cold ! ”
‘ And he—oh, he turned first white and then red,
‘ And then—“ To her behest I bow myself,
‘ “ Whom I love with my body and my soul :　　1120
‘ “ Only, a word i' the bowing !　See, I write
‘ “ One little word, no harm to see or hear !
‘ “ Then, fear no further ! ”　This is what he wrote.
‘ I know you cannot read,—therefore, let me !
‘ “ *My idol* ! ” ’ . . . .

　　　　　But I took it from her hand
And tore it into shreds.　‘ Why join the rest
‘ Who harm me ?　Have I ever done you wrong ?
‘ People have told me 't is you wrong myself :

' Let it suffice I either feel no wrong   1130
' Or else forgive it,—yet you turn my foe !
' The others hunt me and you throw a noose ! '

She muttered, ' Have your wilful way ! ' I slept.

Whereupon . . no, I leave my husband out !
It is not to do him more hurt, I speak.
Let it suffice, when misery was most,
One day, I swooned and got a respite so.
She stooped as I was slowly coming to,
This Margherita, ever on my trace,
And whispered—' Caponsacchi ! '   1140

                              If I drowned,
But woke afloat i' the wave with upturned eyes,
And found their first sight was a star ! I turned—
For the first time, I let her have her will,
Heard passively,—' The imposthume at such head,
' One touch, one lancet-puncture would relieve,—
' And still no glance the good physician's way
' Who rids you of the torment in a trice !
' Still he writes letters you refuse to hear.
' He may prevent your husband, kill himself,   1150
' So desperate and all fordone is he !
' Just hear the pretty verse he made to-day !
' A sonnet from Mirtillo. " *Peerless fair* . . .'
' All poetry is difficult to read,
' —The sense of it is, anyhow, he seeks
' Leave to contrive you an escape from hell,
' And for that purpose asks an interview.
' I can write, I can grant it in your name,
' Or, what is better, lead you to his house.
' Your husband dashes you against the stones ;   1160
' This man would place each fragment in a shrine :
' You hate him, love your husband ! '

                              I returned,
' It is not true I love my husband,—no,
' Nor hate this man. I listen while you speak,
' —Assured that what you say is false, the same :
' Much as when once, to me a little child,
' A rough gaunt man in rags, with eyes on fire,
' A crowd of boys and idlers at his heels,

' Rushed as I crossed the Square, and held my head
' In his two hands, " Here's she will let me speak !
' " You little girl, whose eyes do good to mine,   1172
' " I am the Pope, am Sextus, now the Sixth ;
' " And that Twelfth Innocent, proclaimed to-day,
' " Is Lucifer disguised in human flesh !
' " The angels, met in conclave, crowned me ! "—thus
' He gibbered and I listened ; but I knew
' All was delusion, ere folks interposed
' " Unfasten him, the maniac ! "   Thus I know
' All your report of Caponsacchi false,   1180
' Folly or dreaming ; I have seen so much
' By that adventure at the spectacle,
' The face I fronted that one first, last time :
' He would belie it by such words and thoughts.
' Therefore while you profess to show him me,
' I ever see his own face.   Get you gone ! '

' —That will I, nor once open mouth again,—
' No, by Saint Joseph and the Holy Ghost !
' On your head be the damage, so adieu ! '
And so more days, more deeds I must forget,   1190
Till . . what a strange thing now is to declare !
Since I say anything, say all if true !
And how my life seems lengthened as to serve !
It may be idle or inopportune,
But, true ?—why, what was all I said but truth,
Even when I found that such as are untrue
Could only take the truth in through a lie ?
Now—I am speaking truth to the Truth's self :
God will lend credit to my words this time.

It had got half through April.   I arose   1200
One vivid daybreak,—who had gone to bed
In the old way my wont those last three years,
Careless until, the cup drained, I should die.
The last sound in my ear, the over-night,
Had been a something let drop on the sly
In prattle by Margherita, ' Soon enough
' Gaieties end, now Easter 's past : a week,
' And the Archbishop gets him back to Rome,—
' Everyone leaves the town for Rome, this Spring,—
' Even Caponsacchi, out of heart and hope,   1210
' Resigns himself and follows with the flock.'

I heard this drop and drop like rain outside
Fast-falling through the darkness while she spoke :
So had I heard with like indifference,
' And Michael's pair of wings will arrive first
' At Rome to introduce the company,
' Will bear him from our picture where he fights
' Satan,—expect to have that dragon loose
' And never a defender ! '—my sole thought   1219
Being still, as night came, ' Done, another day !
' How good to sleep and so get nearer death ! '—
When, what, first thing at daybreak, pierced the sleep
With a summons to me ?   Up I sprang alive,
Light in me, light without me, everywhere
Change !   A broad yellow sun-beam was let fall
From heaven to earth,—a sudden drawbridge lay,
Along which marched a myriad merry motes,
Mocking the flies that crossed them and recrossed
In rival dance, companions new-born too.
On the house-eaves, a dripping shag of weed   1230
Shook diamonds on each dull grey lattice-square,
As first one, then another bird leapt by,
And light was off, and lo was back again,
Always with one voice,—where are two such joys ?—
The blessed building-sparrow !   I stepped forth,
Stood on the terrace,—o'er the roofs, such sky !
My heart sang, ' I too am to go away,
' I too have something I must care about,
' Carry away with me to Rome, to Rome !   1239
' The bird brings hither sticks and hairs and wool,
' And nowhere else i' the world ; what fly breaks rank,
' Falls out of the procession that befits,
' From window here to window there, with all
' The world to choose,—so well he knows his course ?
' I have my purpose and my motive too,
' My march to Rome, like any bird or fly !
' Had I been dead !   How right to be alive !
' Last night I almost prayed for leave to die,
' Wished Guido all his pleasure with the sword   1249
' Or the poison,—poison, sword, was but a trick,
' Harmless, may God forgive him the poor jest !
' My life is charmed, will last till I reach Rome !
' Yesterday, but for the sin,—ah, nameless be
' The deed I could have dared against myself !
' Now—see if I will touch an unripe fruit,

' And risk the health I want to have and use !
' Not to live, now, would be the wickedness,—
' For life means to make haste and go to Rome
' And leave Arezzo, leave all woes at once ! '

Now, understand here, by no means mistake !   1260
Long ago had I tried to leave that house
When it seemed such procedure would stop sin ;
And still failed more the more I tried—at first
The Archbishop, as I told you,—next, our lord
The Governor,—indeed I found my way,
I went to the great palace where he rules,
Though I knew well 't was he who,—when I gave
A jewel or two, themselves had given me,
Back to my parents,—since they wanted bread,
They who had never let me want a nosegay,—he
Spoke of the jail for felons, if they kept   1271
What was first theirs, then mine, so doubly theirs,
Though all the while my husband's most of all !
I knew well who had spoke the word wrought this :
Yet, being in extremity, I fled
To the Governor, as I say,—scarce opened lip
When—the cold cruel snicker close behind—
Guido was on my trace, already there,
Exchanging nod and wink for shrug and smile,
And I—pushed back to him and, for my pains,   1280
Paid with . . but why remember what is past ?
I sought out a poor friar the people call
The Roman, and confessed my sin which came
Of their sin,—that fact could not be repressed,—
The frightfulness of my despair in God :
And, feeling, through the grate, his horror shake,
Implored him, ' Write for me who cannot write,
' Apprise my parents, make them rescue me !
' You bid me be courageous and trust God :   1289
' Do you in turn dare somewhat, trust and write
' " Dear friends, who used to be my parents once,
' " And now declare you have no part in me,
' " This is some riddle I want wit to solve,
' " Since you must love me with no difference.
' " Even suppose you altered,—there 's your hate,
' " To ask for : hate of you two dearest ones
' " I shall find liker love than love found here,
' " If husbands love their wives.   Take me away

' " And hate me as you do the gnats and fleas,   1299
' " Even the scorpions !   How I shall rejoice ! "
' Write that and save me ! '   And he promised—wrote
Or did not write ; things never changed at all :
He was not like the Augustinian here !
Last, in a desperation I appealed
To friends, whoever wished me better days,
To Guillichini, that 's of kin,—' What, I—
' Travel to Rome with you ?   A flying gout
' Bids me deny my heart and mind my leg ! '
Then I tried Conti, used to brave—laugh back
The louring thunder when his cousin scowled   1310
At me protected by his presence : ' You—
' Who well know what you cannot save me from,—
' Carry me off !   What frightens you, a priest ? '
He shook his head, looked grave—'Above my strength!
' Guido has claws that scratch, shows feline teeth ;
' A formidabler foe than I dare fret :
' Give me a dog to deal with, twice the size !
' Of course I am a priest and Canon too,
' But . . by the bye . . though both, not quite so bold,
' As he, my fellow-Canon, brother-priest,   1320
' The personage in such ill odour here
' Because of the reports—pure birth o' the brain—
' Our Caponsacchi, he's your true Saint George
' To slay the monster, set the Princess free,
' And have the whole High-Altar to himself :
' I always think so when I see that piece
' I' the Pieve, that 's his church and mine, you know :
' Though you drop eyes at mention of his name ! '

That name had got to take a half-grotesque
Half-ominous, wholly enigmatic sense,   1330
Like any bye-word, broken bit of song
Born with a meaning, changed by mouth and mouth
That mix it in a sneer or smile, as chance
Bids, till it now means naught but ugliness
And perhaps shame.

                    —All this intends to say,
That, over-night, the notion of escape
Had seemed distemper, dreaming ; and the name,—
Not the man, but the name of him, thus made
Into a mockery and disgrace,—why, she   1340

Who uttered it persistently, had laughed,
' I name his name, and there you start and wince
' As criminal from the red tongs' touch ! '—yet now,
Now, as I stood letting morn bathe me bright,
Choosing which butterfly should bear my news,—
The white, the brown one, or that tinier blue,—
The Margherita, I detested so,
In she came—' The fine day, the good Spring time !
' What, up and out at window ? That is best.
' No thought of Caponsacchi ?—who stood there
' All night on one leg, like the sentry crane,   1351
' Under the pelting of your water-spout—
' Looked last look at your lattice ere he leave
' Our city, bury his dead hope at Rome ?
' Ay, go to looking-glass and make you fine,
' While he may die ere touch one least loose hair
' You drag at with the comb in such a rage ! '

I turned—' Tell Caponsacchi he may come ! '

' Tell him to come ? Ah, but, for charity,   1359
' A truce to fooling ! Come ? What,—come this eve ?
' Peter and Paul ! But I see through the trick—
' Yes, come, and take a flower-pot on his head
' Flung from your terrace ! No joke, sincere truth ? '

How plainly I perceived hell flash and fade
O' the face of her,—the doubt that first paled joy,
Then, final reassurance I indeed
Was caught now, never to be free again !
What did I care ?—who felt myself of force
To play with the silk, and spurn the horsehair-springe.

' But—do you know that I have bade him come,
' And in your own name ? I presumed so much,   1371
' Knowing the thing you needed in your heart.
' But somehow—what had I to show in proof ?
' He would not come : half-promised, that was all,
' And wrote the letters you refused to read.
' What is the message that shall move him now ?

    After the Ave Maria, at first dark,
' I will be standing on the terrace, say ! '

' I would I had a good long lock of hair
' Should prove I was not lying ! Never mind ! ' 1380

Off she went—' May he not refuse, that's all—
' Fearing a trick ! '

    I answered, ' He will come.'
And, all day, I sent prayer like incense up
To God the strong, God the beneficent,
God ever mindful in all strife and strait,
Who, for our own good, makes the need extreme,
Till at the last He puts forth might and saves.
An old rhyme came into my head and rang
Of how a virgin, for the faith of God, 1390
Hid herself, from the Paynims that pursued,
In a cave's heart ; until a thunderstone,
Wrapped in a flame, revealed the couch and prey :
And they laughed—' Thanks to lightning, ours at
  last ! '
And she cried ' Wrath of God, assert His love !
' Servant of God, thou fire, befriend His child ! '
And lo, the fire she grasped at, fixed its flash,
Lay in her hand a calm cold dreadful sword
She brandished till pursuers strewed the ground,
So did the souls within them die away, 1400
As o'er the prostrate bodies, sworded, safe,
She walked forth to the solitudes and Christ :
So should I grasp the lightning and be saved !

And still, as the day wore, the trouble grew
Whereby I guessed there would be born a star,
Until at an intense throe of the dusk,
I started up, was pushed, I dare to say,
Out on the terrace, leaned and looked at last
Where the deliverer waited me : the same
Silent and solemn face, I first descried 1410
At the spectacle, confronted mine once more.

So was that minute twice vouchsafed me, so
The manhood, wasted then, was still at watch
To save me yet a second time : no change
Here, though all else changed in the changing world !

I spoke on the instant, as my duty bade,
In some such sense as this, whatever the phrase.

' Friend, foolish words were borne from you to me ;
' Your soul behind them is the pure strong wind,
' Not dust and feathers which its breath may bear :
' These to the witless seem the wind itself,   1421
' Since proving thus the first of it they feel.
' If by mischance you blew offence my way,
' The straws are dropt, the wind desists no whit,
' And how such strays were caught up in the street
' And took a motion from you, why inquire ?
' I speak to the strong soul, no weak disguise.
' If it be truth,—why should I doubt it truth ?—
' You serve God specially, as priests are bound,
' And care about me, stranger as I am,   1430
' So far as wish my good,—that miracle
' I take to intimate He wills you serve
' By saving me,—what else can He direct ?
' Here is the service.   Since a long while now,
' I am in course of being put to death :
' While death concerned nothing but me, I bowed
' The head and bade, in heart, my husband strike.
' Now I imperil something more, it seems,
' Something that 's trulier me than this myself,
' Something I trust in God and you to save.   1440
' You go to Rome, they tell me :   take me there,
' Put me back with my people ! '

                              He replied—
The first word I heard ever from his lips,
All himself in it,—an eternity
Of speech, to match the immeasurable depths
O' the soul that then broke silence—' I am yours.'

So did the star rise, soon to lead my step,
Lead on, nor pause before it should stand still   1449
Above the House o' the Babe,—my babe to be,
That knew me first and thus made me know him,
That had his right of life and claim on mine,
And would not let me die till he was born,
But pricked me at the heart to save us both,
Saying ' Have you the will ?   Leave God the way ! '
And the way was Caponsacchi—' mine,' thank God !
He was mine, he is mine, he will be mine.

No pause i' the leading and the light ! I know,
Next night there was a cloud came, and not he :

But I prayed through the darkness till it broke   1460
And let him shine.   The second night, he came.

' The plan is rash ; the project desperate :
' In such a flight needs must I risk your life,
' Give food for falsehood, folly or mistake,
' Ground for your husband's rancour and revenge '—
So he began again, with the same face.
I felt that, the same loyalty—one star
Turning now red that was so white before—
One service apprehended newly : just
A word of mine and there the white was back !   1470

' No, friend, for you will take me !   'Tis yourself
' Risk all, not I,—who let you, for I trust
' In the compensating great God : enough !
' I know you : when is it that you will come ? '

' To-morrow at the day's dawn.'   Then I heard
What I should do : how to prepare for flight
And where to fly.

                    That night my husband bade
' —You, whom I loathe, beware you break my sleep
' This whole night !   Couch beside me like the corpse
' I would you were ! '   The rest you know, I think—
How I found Caponsacchi and escaped.   1482

And this man, men call sinner ? Jesus Christ !
Of whom men said, with mouths Thyself mad'st once,
' He hath a devil '—say he was Thy saint,
My Caponsacchi !   Shield and show—unshroud
In Thine own time the glory of the soul
If aught obscure,—if ink-spot, from vile pens
Scribbling a charge against him—(I was glad
Then, for the first time, that I could not write)— 1490
Flirted his way, have flecked the blaze !

                         For me,
'Tis otherwise : let men take, sift my thoughts
—Thoughts I throw like the flax for sun to bleach !
I did think, do think, in the thought shall die,
That to have Caponsacchi for my guide,
Ever the face upturned to mine, the hand
Holding my hand across the world,—a sense

That reads, as only such can read, the mark
God sets on woman, signifying so   1500
She should—shall peradventure—be divine ;
Yet 'ware, the while, how weakness mars the print
And makes confusion, leaves the thing men see,
—Not this man,—who from his own soul, re-writes
The obliterated charter,—love and strength
Mending what's marred : ' So kneels a votarist,
' Weeds some poor waste traditionary plot
' Where shrine once was, where temple yet may be,
' Purging the place but worshipping the while,
' By faith and not by sight, sight clearest so,—   1510
' Such way the saints work,'—says Don Celestine.
But I, not privileged to see a saint
Of old when such walked earth with crown and palm,
If I call ' saint ' what saints call something else—
The saints must bear with me, impute the fault
To a soul i' the bud, so starved by ignorance,
Stinted of warmth, it will not blow this year
Nor recognize the orb which Spring-flowers know.
But if meanwhile some insect with a heart
Worth floods of lazy music, spendthrift joy—   1520
Some fire-fly renounced Spring for my dwarfed cup,
Crept close to me with lustre for the dark,
Comfort against the cold,—what though excess
Of comfort should miscall the creature—sun ?
What did the sun to hinder while harsh hands
Petal by petal, crude and colourless,
Tore me ?   This one heart brought me all the Spring !

Is all told ?   There's the journey : and where's time
To tell you how that heart burst out in shine ?
Yet certain points do press on me too hard.   1530
Each place must have a name, though I forget :
How strange it was—there where the plain begins
And the small river mitigates its flow—
When eve was fading fast, and my soul sank,
And he divined what surge of bitterness,
In overtaking me, would float me back
Whence I was carried by the striding day—
So,—' This grey place was famous once,' said he—
And he began that legend of the place
As if in answer to the unspoken fear,   1540
And told me all about a brave man dead,

Which lifted me and let my soul go on !
How did he know too,—at that town's approach
By the rock-side,—that in coming near the signs,
Of life, the house-roofs and the church and tower
I saw the old boundary and wall o' the world
Rise plain as ever round me, hard and cold,
As if the broken circlet joined again,
Tightened itself about me with no break,—
As if the town would turn Arezzo's self,—   1550
The husband there,—the friends my enemies,
All ranged against me, not an avenue
I try, but would be blocked and drive me back
On him,—this other, . . oh the heart in that !
Did not he find, bring, put into my arms
A new-born babe ?—and I saw faces beam
Of the young mother proud to teach me joy,
And gossips round expecting my surprise
At the sudden hole through earth that lets in heaven.
I could believe himself by his strong will   1560
Had woven around me what I thought the world
We went along in, every circumstance,
Towns, flowers and faces, all things helped so well !
For, through the journey, was it natural
Such comfort should arise from first to last ?
As I look back, all is one milky way ;
Still bettered more, the more remembered, so
Do new stars bud while I but search for old,
And fill all gaps i' the glory, and grow him—
Him I now see make the shine everywhere.   1570
Even at the last when the bewildered flesh,
The cloud of weariness about my soul
Clogging too heavily, sucked down all sense,—
Still its last voice was, ' He will watch and care ;
' Let the strength go, I am content : he stays ! '
I doubt not he did stay and care for all—
From that sick minute when the head swam round,
And the eyes looked their last and died on him,
As in his arms he caught me and, you say,
Carried me in, that tragical red eve,   1580
And laid me where I next returned to life
In the other red of morning, two red plates
That crushed together, crushed the time between,
And are since then a solid fire to me,—
When in, my dreadful husband and the world

Broke,—and I saw him, master, by hell's right
And saw my angel helplessly held back
By guards that helped the malice—the lamb prone,
The serpent towering and triumphant—then
Came all the strength back in a sudden swell,   1590
I did for once see right, do right, give tongue
The adequate protest : for a worm must turn
If it would have its wrong observed by God.
I did spring up, attempt to thrust aside
That ice-block 'twixt the sun and me, lay low
The neutralizer of all good and truth.
If I sinned so,—never obey voice more
O' the Just and Terrible, who bids us—' Bear ! '
Not—' Stand by, bear to see my angels bear ! '
I am clear it was on impulse to serve God   1600
Not save myself,—no—nor my child unborn !
Had I else waited patiently till now ?—
Who saw my old kind parents, silly-sooth
And too much trustful, for their worst of faults,
Cheated, brow-beaten, stripped and starved, cast out
Into the kennel : I remonstrated,
Then sank to silence, for,—their woes at end,
Themselves gone,—only I was left to plague.
If only I was threatened and belied,
What matter ? I could bear it and did bear ;   1610
It was a comfort, still one lot for all :
They were not persecuted for my sake
And I, estranged, the single happy one.
But when at last, all by myself I stood
Obeying the clear voice which bade me rise,
Not for my own sake but my babe unborn,
And take the angel's hand was sent to help—
And found the old adversary athwart the path—
Not my hand simply struck from the angel's, but
The very angel's self made foul i' the face   1620
By the fiend who struck there,—that I would not bear,
That only I resisted ! So, my first
And last resistance was invincible.
Prayers move God ; threats, and nothing else, move
     men !
I must have prayed a man as he were God
When I implored the Governor to right
My parents' wrongs : the answer was a smile.
The Archbishop,—did I clasp his feet enough,

Hide my face hotly on them, while I told   1629
More than I dared make my own mother know ?
The profit was—compassion and a jest.
This time, the foolish prayers were done with, right
Used might, and solemnized the sport at once.
All was against the combat : vantage, mine ?
The runaway avowed, the accomplice-wife,
In company with the plan-contriving priest ?
Yet, shame thus rank and patent, I struck, bare,
At foe from head to foot in magic mail,
And off it withered, cobweb-armoury   1639
Against the lightning ! 'T was truth singed the lies
And saved me, not the vain sword nor weak speech !

You see, I will not have the service fail !
I say, the angel saved me : I am safe !
Others may want and wish, I wish nor want
One point o' the circle plainer, where I stand
Traced round about with white to front the world.
What of the calumny I came across,
What o' the way to the end ?—the end crowns all.
The judges judged aright i' the main, gave me
The uttermost of my heart's desire, a truce   1650
From torture and Arezzo, balm for hurt
With the quiet nuns,—God recompense the good !
Who said and sang away the ugly past.
And, when my final fortune was revealed,
What safety while, amid my parents' arms,
My babe was given me ! Yes, he saved my babe :
It would not have peeped forth, the bird-like thing,
Through that Arezzo noise and trouble : back
Had it returned nor ever let me see !
But the sweet peace cured all, and let me live   1660
And give my bird the life among the leaves
God meant him ! Weeks and months of quietude,
I could lie in such peace and learn so much—
Begin the task, I see how needful now,
Of understanding somewhat of my past,—
Know life a little, I should leave so soon.
Therefore, because this man restored my soul,
All has been right ; I have gained my gain, enjoyed
As well as suffered,—nay, got foretaste too
Of better life beginning where this ends—   1670
All through the breathing-while allowed me thus,

Which let good premonitions reach my soul
Unthwarted, and benignant influence flow
And interpenetrate and change my heart,
Uncrossed by what was wicked,—nay, unkind.
For, as the weakness of my time drew nigh,
Nobody did me one disservice more,
Spoke coldly or looked strangely, broke the love
I lay in the arms of, till my boy was born,
Born all in love, with nought to spoil the bliss   1680
A whole long fortnight : in a life like mine
A fortnight filled with bliss is long and much.
All women are not mothers of a boy,
Though they live twice the length of my whole life,
And, as they fancy, happily all the same.
There I lay, then, all my great fortnight long,
As if it would continue, broaden out
Happily more and more, and lead to heaven :
Christmas before me,—was not that a chance ?
I never realized God's birth before—   1690
How he grew likest God in being born.
This time I felt like Mary, had my babe
Lying a little on my breast like hers.
So all went on till, just four days ago—
The night and the tap.

                        O it shall be success
To the whole of our poor family !   My friends
. . Nay, father and mother,—give me back my word !
They have been rudely stripped of life, disgraced
Like children who must needs go clothed too fine,
Carry the garb of Carnival in Lent :   1701
If they too much affected frippery,
They have been punished and submit themselves,
Say no word : all is over, they see God
Who will not be extreme to mark their fault
Or He had granted respite : they are safe.

For that most woeful man my husband once,
Who, needing respite, still draws vital breath,
I—pardon him ?   So far as lies in me,
I give him for his good the life he takes,   1710
Praying the world will therefore acquiesce.
Let him make God amends,—none, none to me
Who thank him rather that, whereas strange fate

Mockingly styled him husband and me wife,
Himself this way at least pronounced divorce,
Blotted the marriage-bond : this blood of mine
Flies forth exultingly at any door,
Washes the parchment white, and thanks the blow.
We shall not meet in this world nor the next,
But where will God be absent ? In His face   1720
Is light, but in His shadow healing too :
Let Guido touch the shadow and be healed !
And as my presence was importunate,—
My earthly good, temptation and a snare,—
Nothing about me but drew somehow down
His hate upon me,—somewhat so excused
Therefore, since hate was thus the truth of him,—
May my evanishment for evermore
Help further to relieve the heart that cast
Such object of its natural loathing forth !   1730
So he was made ; he nowise made himself :
I could not love him, but his mother did.
His soul has never lain beside my soul ;
But for the unresisting body,—thanks !
He burned that garment spotted by the flesh !
Whatever he touched is rightly ruined : plague
It caught, and disinfection it had craved
Still but for Guido ; I am saved through him
So as by fire ; to him—thanks and farewell !   1739

Even for my babe, my boy, there 's safety thence—
From the sudden death of me, I mean : we poor
Weak souls, how we endeavour to be strong !
I was already using up my life,—
This portion, now, should do him such a good,
This other go to keep off such an ill !
The great life ; see, a breath and it is gone !
So is detached, so left all by itself
The little life, the fact which means so much.
Shall not God stoop the kindlier to His work,
His marvel of creation, foot would crush,   1750
Now that the hand He trusted to receive
And hold it, lets the treasure fall perforce ?
The better ; He shall have in orphanage
His own way all the clearlier : if my babe
Outlive the hour—and he has lived two weeks—
It is through God who knows I am not by.

Who is it makes the soft gold hair turn black,
And sets the tongue, might lie so long at rest,
Trying to talk ?   Let us leave God alone !
Why should I doubt He will explain in time   1760
What I feel now, but fail to find the words ?
My babe nor was, nor is, nor yet shall be
Count Guido Franceschini's child at all—
Only his mother's, born of love not hate !
So shall I have my rights in after-time.
It seems absurd, impossible to-day ;
So seems so much else not explained but known.

Ah !   Friends, I thank and bless you every one !
No more now : I withdraw from earth and man
To my own soul, compose myself for God.   1770

Well, and there is more !   Yes, my end of breath
Shall bear away my soul in being true !
He is still here, not outside with the world,
Here, here, I have him in his rightful place !
'T is now, when I am most upon the move,
I feel for what I verily find—again
The face, again the eyes, again, through all,
The heart and its immeasurable love
Of my one friend, my only, all my own,
Who put his breast between the spears and me.   1780
Ever with Caponsacchi !   Otherwise
Here alone would be failure, loss to me—
How much more loss to him, with life debarred
From giving life, love locked from love's display,
The   day-star   stopped   its   task   that   makes   night
      morn !
O lover of my life, O soldier-saint,
No work begun shall ever pause for death !
Love will be helpful to me more and more
I' the coming course, the new path I must tread,
My weak hand in thy strong hand, strong for that !
Tell him that if I seem without him now,   1791
That's the world's insight !   Oh, he understands !
He is at Civita—do I once doubt
The world again is holding us apart ?
He had been here, displayed in my behalf
The broad brow that reverberates the truth,

And flashed the word God gave him, back to man !
I know where the free soul is flown !   My fate
Will have been hard for even him to bear :
Let it confirm him in the trust of God,   1800
Showing how holily he dared the deed !
And, for the rest,—say, from the deed, no touch
Of harm came, but all good, all happiness,
Not one faint fleck of failure !   Why explain ?
What I see, oh, he sees and how much more !
Tell him,—I know not wherefore the true word
Should fade and fall unuttered at the last—
It was the name of him I sprang to meet
When came the knock, the summons and the end.
' My great heart, my strong hand are back again ! '
I would have sprung to these, beckoning across   1811
Murder and hell gigantic and distinct
O' the threshold, posted to exclude me heaven :
He is ordained to call and I to come !
Do not the dead wear flowers when dressed for
     God ?
Say,—I am all in flowers from head to foot !
Say,—not one flower of all he said and did,
Might seem to flit unnoticed, fade unknown,
But dropped a seed has grown a balsam-tree
Whereof the blossoming perfumes the place   1820
At this supreme of moments !   He is a priest ;
He cannot marry therefore, which is right :
I think he would not marry if he could.
Marriage on earth seems such a counterfeit,
Mere imitation of the inimitable :
In heaven we have the real and true and sure.
'T is there they neither marry nor are given
In marriage but are as the angels :   right,
Oh how right that is, how like Jesus Christ
To say that !   Marriage-making for the earth,   1830
With gold so much,—birth, power, repute so much,
Or beauty, youth so much, in lack of these !
Be as the angels rather, who, apart,
Know themselves into one, are found at length
Married, but marry never, no, nor give
In marriage ;   they are man and wife at once
When the true time is :   here we have to wait
Not so long neither !   Could we by a wish
Have what we will and get the future now,

Would we wish aught done undone in the past ?
So, let him wait God's instant men call years :   1841
Meantime hold hard by truth and his great soul,
Do out the duty !   Through such souls alone
God stooping shows sufficient of His light
For us i' the dark to rise by.   And I rise.

VIII

DOMINUS HYACINTHUS DE ARCHANGELIS,

PAUPERUM PROCURATOR

AH, my Giacinto, he 's no ruddy rogue,
Is not Cinone ?   What, to-day we 're eight ?
Seven and one 's eight, I hope, old curly-pate !
—Branches me out his verb-tree on the slate,
Amo —as —avi —atum —are —ans,
Up to *—aturus,* person, tense, and mood,
Quies me cum subjunctivo (I could cry)
And chews Corderius with his morning crust !
Look eight years onward, and he 's perched, he 's
    perched,
Dapper and deft on stool beside this chair,   10
Cinozzo, Cinoncello, who but he ?
—Trying his milk-teeth on some crusty case
Like this, papa shall triturate full soon
To smooth Papinianian pulp !
                It trots
Already through my head, though noon be now,
Does supper-time and what belongs to eve.
Dispose, O Don, o' the day, first work then play !
—The proverb bids.   And ' then ' means, won't we
    hold
Our little yearly lovesome frolic feast,   20
Cinuolo's birth-night, Cinicello's own,
That makes gruff January grin perforce !
For too contagious grows the mirth, the warmth
Escaping from so many hearts at once—
When the good wife, buxom and bonny yet,
Jokes the hale grandsire,—such are just the sort
To go off suddenly,—he who hides the key
O' the box beneath his pillow every night,—
Which box may hold a parchment (some one thinks)
Will show a scribbled something like a name   30
' Cinino, Ciniccino,' near the end,
          L 3

' To whom I give and I bequeath my lands,
' Estates, tenements, hereditaments,
' When I decease as honest grandsire ought : '
Wherefore—yet this one time again perhaps—
Sha'n't my Orvieto fuddle his old nose !
Then, uncles, one or the other, well i' the world,
May—drop in, merely?—trudge through rain and wind,
Rather ! The smell-feasts rouse them at the hint
There 's cookery in a certain dwelling-place !   40
Gossips, too, each with keepsake in his poke,
Will pick the way, thrid lane by lantern-light,
And so find door, put galligaskin off
At entry of a decent domicile
Cornered in snug Condotti,—all for love,
All to crush cup with Cinucciatolo !
                              Well,
Let others climb the heights o' the court, the camp !
How vain are chambering and wantonness,
Revel and rout and pleasures that make mad !   50
Commend me to home-joy, the family board,
Altar and hearth ! These, with a brisk career,
A source of honest profit and good fame,
Just so much work as keeps the brain from rust,
Just so much play as lets the heart expand,
Honouring God and serving man,—I say,
These are reality, and all else,—flutt,
Nutshell and naught,—thank Flaccus for the phrase !
Suppose I had been Fisc, yet bachelor !   59

Why, work with a will, then ! Wherefore lazy now ?
Turn up the hour-glass, whence no sand-grain slips
But should have done its duty to the saint
O' the day, the son and heir that 's eight years old !
Let law come dimple Cinoncino's cheek,
And Latin dumple Cinarello's chin,
The while we spread him fine and toss him flat
This pulp that makes the pancake, trim our mass
Of matter into Argument the First,
Prime Pleading in defence of our accused,
Which, once a-waft on paper wing, shall soar,   70
Shall signalise before applausive Rome
What study, and mayhap some mother-wit,
Can do toward making Master fop and Fisc
Old bachelor Bottinius bite his thumb.

Now, how good God is ! How falls plumb to point
This murder, gives me Guido to defend
Now, of all days i' the year, just when the boy
Verges on Virgil, reaches the right age
For some such illustration from his sire,
Stimulus to himself ! One might wait years   80
And never find the chance which now finds me !
The fact is, there 's a blessing on the hearth,
A special providence for fatherhood !
Here 's a man, and what 's more, a noble, kills
—Not sneakingly but almost with parade—
Wife's father and wife's mother and wife's self
That 's mother's self of son and heir (like mine !)
—And here stand I, the favoured advocate,
Who pluck this flower o' the field, no Solomon
Was ever clothed in glorious gold to match,   90
And set the same in Cinoncino's cap !
I defend Guido and his comrades—I !
Pray God, I keep me humble : not to me—
Non nobis, Domine, sed tibi laus !
How the fop chuckled when they made him Fisc !
We 'll beat you, my Bottinius, all for love,
All for our tribute to Cinotto's day !
Why, 'sbuddikins, old Innocent himself
May rub his eyes at the bustle,—ask ' What's this
' Rolling from out the rostrum, as a gust   100
' O' the *Pro Milone* had been prisoned there,
' And rattled Rome awake ? ' Awaken Rome,
How can the Pope doze on in decency ?
He needs must wake up also, speak his word,
Have his opinion like the rest of Rome,
About this huge, this hurly-burly case :
He wants who can excogitate the truth,
Give the result in speech, plain black and white,
To mumble in the mouth and make his own
—A little changed, good man, a little changed !   110
No matter, so his gratitude be moved,
By when my Giacintino gets of age,
Mindful of who thus helped him at a pinch,
Archangelus *Procurator Pauperum—*
And proved Hortensius *Redivivus !*
                                        Whew !
To earn the *Est-est,* merit the minced herb
That mollifies the liver's leathery slice,

With here a goose-foot, there a cock's-comb stuck,
Cemented in an element of cheese !   120
I doubt if dainties do the grandsire good :
Last June he had a sort of strangling . . . bah !
He 's his own master, and his will is made.
So, liver fizz, law flit and Latin fly
As we rub hands o'er dish by way of grace !
May I lose cause if I vent one word more
Except,—with fresh-cut quill we ink the white,—
P-r-o-pro Guidone et Sociis.   There !

Count Guido married—or, in Latin due,
What ?   *Duxit in uxorem ?*—commonplace !   130
T'œdas jugales iniit, subiit,—ha !
He underwent the matrimonial torch ?
Connubio stabili sibi junxit,—hum !
In stable bond of marriage bound his own ?
That 's clear of any modern taint : and yet . . .

Virgil is little help to who writes prose.
He shall attack me Terence with the dawn,
Shall Cinuccino !   Mum, mind business, Sir !
Thus circumstantially evolve we facts,
Ita se habet ideo series facti :   140
He wedded,—ah, with owls for augury !
Nupserat, heu sinistris avibus,
One of the blood Arezzo boasts her best,
Dominus Guido, nobili genere ortus,
Pompiliæ . . .

                But the version afterward !
Curb we this ardour !   Notes alone, to-day,
The speech to-morrow and the Latin last :
Such was the rule in Farinacci's time.
Indeed I hitched it into verse and good.
Unluckily, law quite absorbs a man,   150
Or else I think I too had poetized.
' Law is the pork substratum of the fry,
' Goose-foot and cock's-comb are Latinity,'—
And in this case, if circumstance assist,
We 'll garnish law with idiom, never fear !
Out-of-the-way events extend our scope :
For instance, when Bottini brings his charge,
' That letter which you say Pompilia wrote,
' To criminate her parents and herself

' And disengage her husband from the coil,— 160
' That, Guido Franceschini wrote, say we :
' Because Pompilia could nor read nor write,
' Therefore he pencilled her such letter first,
' Then made her trace in ink the same again.'
—Ha, my Bottini, have I thee on hip ?
How will he turn this nor break Tully's pate ?
' *Existimandum* ' (do n't I hear the dog !)
' *Quod Guido designaverit elementa*
' *Dictæ epistolæ, quæ fuerint*
' *(Superinducto ab ea calamo)* 170
' *Notata atramento* '—there 's a style !—
' *Quia ipsa scribere nesciebat.*' Boh !
Now, my turn ! Either, *Insulse* !—I outburst,
Stupidly put ! Inane is the response,
Inanis est responsio, or the like—
To-wit, that each of all those characters,
Quod singula elementa epistolæ,
Had first of all been traced for her by him,
Fuerant per eum prius designata,
And then, the ink applied a-top of that, 180
Et deinde, superinducto calamo,
The piece, she says, became her handiwork,
Per eam, efformata, ut ipsa asserit.
Inane were such response ! (a second time :)
Her husband outlined her the whole, forsooth ?
Vir ejus lineabat epistolam ?
What, she confesses that she wrote the thing,
Fatetur eam scripsisse, (scorn that scathes !)
That she might pay obedience to her lord ?
Ut viro obtemperaret, apices 190
(Here repeat charge with proper varied phrase)
Eo designante, ipsaque calamum
Super inducente ? By such argument,
Ita pariter, she seeks to show the same,
(Ay, by Saint Joseph and what saints you please)
Epistolam ostendit, medius fidius,
No voluntary deed but fruit of force !
Non voluntarie sed coacte scriptam !
That 's the way to write Latin, friend my Fisc !
Bottini is a beast, one barbarous : 200
Look out for him when he attempts to say
' Armed with a pistol, Guido followed her ! '
Will not I be beforehand with my Fisc,

Cut away phrase by phrase from underfoot !
Guido Pompiliam—Guido thus his wife
Following with igneous engine, shall I have ?
Armis munitus igneis persequens—
Arma sulphurea gestans, sulphury arms,
Or, might one style a pistol—popping-piece ?
Armatus breviori sclopulo ?   210
We 'll let him have been armed so, though it make
Somewhat against us : I had thought to own—
Provided with a simple travelling-sword,
Ense solummodo viatorio
Instructus : but we 'll grant the pistol here :
Better we lost the cause than lacked the gird
At the Fisc's Latin, lost the Judge's laugh !
It 's Venturini that decides for style.
Tommati rather goes upon the law.
So, as to law,—   220

                    Ah, but with law ne'er hope
To level the fellow,—do n't I know his trick !
How he draws up, ducks under, twists aside !
He 's a lean-gutted hectic rascal, fine
As pale-haired red-eyed ferret which pretends
'T is ermine, pure soft snow from tail to snout.
He eludes law by piteous looks aloft,
Lets Latin glance off as he makes appeal
To the saint that 's somewhere in the ceiling-top,—
Do you suppose that I do n't see the beast ?   230
Plague of the ermine-vermin !   For it takes,
It takes, and here 's the fellow Fisc, you see,
And Judge, you 'll not be long in seeing next !
Confound the fop—he 's now at work like me :
Enter his study, as I seem to do,
Hear him read out his writing to himself !
I know he writes as if he spoke : I hear
The hoarse shrill throat, see shut eyes, neck shot-forth,
—I see him strain on tiptoe, soar and pour
Eloquence out, nor stay nor stint at all—   240
Perorate in the air, and so, to press
With the product !   What abuse of type is here !
He 'll keep clear of my cast, my logic-throw,
Let argument slide, and then deliver swift
Some bowl from quite an unguessed point of stand—
Having the luck o' the last word, the reply !

A plaguy cast, a mortifying stroke :
You face a fellow—cries ' So, there you stand ?
' But I discourteous jump clean o'er your head !
' You play ship-carpenter, not pilot so,—   250
' Stop rat-holes, while a sea sweeps through the breach,—
' Hammer and fortify at puny points !
' Do, clamp and tenon, make all tight and safe !
' 'Tis here and here and here you ship a sea,
' No good of your stopped leaks and littleness ! '

Yet what do I name ' little and a leak ? '
The main defence o' the murder 's used to death,
By this time, dry bare bones, no scrap to pick :
Safer I worked at the new, the unforeseen,
The nice bye-stroke, the fine and improvised,   260
Point that can titillate the brain o' the Bench
Torpid with over-teaching, by this time !
As if Tommati, that has heard, reheard
And heard again, first this side and then that,—
Guido and Pietro, Pietro and Guido din
And deafen, full three years, at each long ear,—
Do n't want amusement for instruction now,
Won't rather feel a flea run o'er his ribs,
Than a daw settle heavily on his head !
Oh, I was young and had the trick of fence,   270
Knew subtle pass and push with careless right—
The left arm ever quietly behind back
With the dagger in 't : not both hands to blade :
Puff and blow, put the strength out, Blunderbore !
That 's my subordinate, young Spreti, now,
Pedant and prig,—he 'll pant away at proof,
That 's his way !

                    Now for mine—to rub some life
Into one's choppy fingers this cold day !
I trust Cinuzzo ties on tippet, guards   280
The precious throat on which so much depends !
Guido must be all goose-flesh in his hole,
Despite the prison-straw : bad Carnival
For captives ! no sliced fry for him, poor Count !

Carnival-time,—another providence !
The town a-swarm with strangers to amuse,
To edify, to give one's name and fame

In charge of, till they find, some future day,
Cintino come and claim it, his name too,
Pledge of the pleasantness they owe papa—   290
Who else was it, cured Rome of her great qualms,
When she must needs have her own judgment ?—ay
Since all her topping wits had set to work,
Pronounced already on the case : mere boys,
Twice Cineruggiolo's age and half his sense,
As good as tell me, when I cross the court,
' Master Arcangeli ! ' (plucking at my gown)
' We can predict, we comprehend your play,
' We 'll help you save your client.'   Tra-la-la !
I 've travelled ground, from childhood till this hour,
To have the town anticipate my track !   301
The old fox takes the plain and velvet path,
The young hound's predilection,—prints the dew,
Do n't he, to suit their pulpy pads of paw ?
No !   Burying nose deep down i' the briery bush,
Thus I defend Count Guido.
                              Where are we weak ?
First, which is foremost in advantage too,
Our murder,—we call, killing,—is a fact
Confessed, defended, made a boast of : good !   310
To think the Fisc claimed use of torture here,
And got thereby avowal plump and plain
That gives me just the chance I wanted,—scope
Not for brute-force but ingenuity,
Explaining matters, not denying them !
One may dispute,—as I am bound to do,
And shall,—validity of process here :
Inasmuch as a noble is exempt
From torture which plebeians undergo
In such a case : for law is lenient, lax,   320
Remits the torture to a nobleman
Unless suspicion be of twice the strength
Attaches to a man born vulgarly :
We do n't card silk with comb that dresses wool.
Moreover, 'twas severity undue
In this case, even had the lord been lout.
What utters, on this head, our oracle,
Our Farinacci, my Gamaliel erst,
In those immortal ' Questions ' ?   What I quote :
' Of all the tools at Law's disposal, sure   330
' That named *Vigiliarum* is the best—

' That is, the worst—to whoso has to bear :
' Lasting, as it may do, from some seven hours
' To ten, (beyond ten, we 've no precedent ;
' Certain have touched their ten but, bah, they
    died !)
' It does so efficaciously convince
' That,—speaking by much observation here,—
' Out of each hundred cases, by my count,
' Never I knew of patients beyond four
' Withstand its taste, or less than ninety-six   340
' End by succumbing : only martyrs four,
' Of obstinate silence, guilty or no,—against
' Ninety-six full confessors, innocent
' Or otherwise,—so shrewd a tool have we ! '
No marvel either : in unwary hands,
Death on the spot is no rare consequence :
As indeed all but happened in this case
To one of ourselves, our young tough peasant-friend
The accomplice called Baldeschi : they were rough,
Dosed him with torture as you drench a horse,   350
Not modify your treatment to a man :
So, two successive days he fainted dead,
And only on the third essay, gave up,
Confessed like flesh and blood. We could reclaim,—
Blockhead Bottini giving cause enough !
But no,—we 'll take it as spontaneously
Confessed : we 'll have the murder beyond doubt.
Ah, fortunate (the poet's word reversed)
Inasmuch as we know our happiness !
Had the antagonist left dubiety,   360
Here were we proving murder a mere myth,
And Guido innocent, ignorant, absent,—ay,
Absent ! He was—why, where should Christian be ?—
Engaged in visiting his proper church,
The duty of us all at Christmas-time ;
When Caponsacchi, the seducer, stung
To madness by his relegation, cast
About him and contrived a remedy :
To stave off what opprobrium broke afresh,
By the birth o' the babe, on him the imputed sire,
He came and quietly sought to smother up   371
His shame and theirs together,—killed the three,
And fled—(go seek him where you please to search)—
Just at the moment, Guido, touched by grace,

Devotions ended, hastened to the spot,
Meaning to pardon his convicted wife,
' Neither do I condemn thee, go in peace ! '—
Who thus arrived i' the nick of time to catch
The charge o' the killing, though great-heartedly
He came but to forgive and bring to life.   380
Doubt ye the force of Christmas on the soul ?
' Is thine eye evil because mine is good ? '

So, doubtless, had I needed argue here ·
But for the full confession round and sound !
Thus would you have some kingly alchemist,—
Whose concern should not be with proving brass
Transmutable to gold, but triumphing,
Rather, above his gold changed out of brass,
Not vulgarly to the mere sight and touch,
But in the idea, the spiritual display,   390
Proud apparition buoyed by winged words
Hovering above its birth-place in the brain,—
Here would you have this excellent personage
Forced, by the gross need, to gird apron round,
Plant forge, light fire, ply bellows,—in a word,
Demonstrate—when a faulty pipkin's crack
May disconcert you his presumptive truth !
Here were I hanging to the testimony
Of one of these poor rustics—four, ye Gods !
Whom the first taste of friend the Fiscal's cord   400
Might drive into undoing my whole speech,
Shaming truth so !
                          I wonder, all the same,
Not so much at those peasants' lack of heart ;
But—Guido Franceschini, nobleman,
Bear pain no better !   Everybody knows
It used once, when my father was a boy,
To form a proper, nay, important point
I' the education of our well-born youth,
To take the torture handsomely at need,   410
Without confessing in this clownish guise.
Each noble had his rack for private use,
And would, for the diversion of a guest,
Bid it be set up in the yard of arms,
To take thereon his hour of exercise,—
Command the varletry stretch, strain their best,
While friends looked on, admired my lord could smile

'Mid tugging which had caused an ox to roar.
Men are no longer men !

            —And advocates   420
No longer Farinacci, let men add,
If I one more time fly from point proposed !
So, *Vindicatio*,—here begins the same !—
Honoris causa ; so we make our stand :
Honour in us had injury, we shall prove.
Or if we fail to prove such injury
More than misprision of the fact,—what then ?
It is enough, authorities declare,
If the result, the deed in question now,
Be caused by confidence that injury   430
Is veritable and no figment : since,
What, though proved fancy afterward, seemed fact
At the time, they argue shall excuse result.
That which we do, persuaded of good cause
For what we do, hold justifiable !—
The casuists bid : man, bound to do his best,
They would not have him leave that best undone
And mean to do the worst,—though fuller light
Show best was worst and worst would have been best.
Act by the present light, they ask of man.   440
Ultra quod hic non agitur, besides
It is not anyway our business here,
De probatione adulterii,
To prove what we thought crime was crime indeed,
Ad irrogandam poenam, and require
Its punishment : such nowise do we seek :
Sed ad effectum, but 't is our concern,
Excusandi, here to simply find excuse,
Occisorem, for who did the killing-work,
Et ad illius defensionem, (mark   450
The difference !) and defend the man, just that.
Quo casu levior probatio
Exuberaret, to which end far lighter proof
Suffices than the prior case would claim :
It should be always harder to convict,
In short, than to establish innocence.
Therefore we shall demonstrate first of all
That Honour is a gift of God to man
Precious beyond compare,—which natural sense
Of human rectitude and purity,—   460

Which white, man's soul is born with, brooks no touch :
Therefore, the sensitivest spot of all,
Woundable by a wafture breathed from black,
Is,—honour within honour, like the eye
Centred i' the ball,—the honour of our wife.
Touch us o' the pupil of our honour, then,
Not actually,—since so you slay outright,—
But by a gesture simulating touch,
Presumable mere menace of such taint,—
This were our warrant for eruptive ire   470
' To whose dominion I impose no end.'

(Virgil, now, should not be too difficult
To Cinoncino,—say the early books . . . .
Pen, truce to further gambols ! *Poscimur !*)

Nor can revenge of injury done here
To the honour proved the life and soul of us,
Be too excessive, too extravagant :
Such wrong seeks and must have complete revenge.
Show we this, first, on the mere natural ground :
Begin at the beginning, and proceed   480
Incontrovertibly.   Theodoric,
In an apt sentence Cassiodorus cites,
Propounds for basis of all household law—
I hardly recollect it, but it ends,
' Bird mates with bird, beast genders with his like,
' And brooks no interference : ' bird and beast ?
The very insects . . . if they wive or no,
How dare I say when Aristotle doubts ?
But the presumption is they likewise wive,
At least the nobler sorts ; for take the bee   490
As instance,—copying King Solomon,—
Why that displeasure of the bee to aught
That savours of incontinency, makes
The unchaste a very horror to the hive ?
Whence comes it bees obtain the epithet
Of *castæ apes ?* notably ' the chaste ' ?
Because, ingeniously saith Scaliger,
(The young one—see his book of Table-talk)
' Such is their hatred of immodest act,
' They fall upon the offender, sting to death.'   500
I mind a passage much confirmative
I' the Idyllist (though I read him Latinized)

' Why ' asks a shepherd, ' is this bank unfit
' For celebration of our vernal loves ? '
' Oh swain,' returns the wiser shepherdess,
' Bees swarm here, and would quick resent our
       warmth ! '
Only cold-blooded fish lack instinct here,
Nor gain nor guard connubiality :
But beasts, quadrupedal, mammiferous,
Do credit to their beasthood : witness him,   510
That Ælian cites, the noble elephant,
(Or if not Ælian, somebody as sage)
Who seeing much offence beneath his nose,
His master's friend exceed in courtesy
The due allowance to that master's wife,
Taught them good manners and killed both at once,
Making his master and all men admire.
Indubitably, then, that master's self
Favoured by circumstance, had done the same
Or else stood clear rebuked by his own beast.   520
Adeo, ut qui honorem spernit, thus,
Who values his own honour not a straw,—
Et non recuperare curat, nor
Labours by might and main to salve its wound,
Se ulciscendo, by revenging him,
Nil differat a belluis, is a brute,
Quinimo irrationabilior
Ipsismet belluis, nay, contrariwise,
Much more irrational than brutes themselves,
Should be considered, *reputetur !* How ?   530
If a poor animal feel honour smart,
Taught by blind instinct nature plants in him,
Shall man,—confessed creation's master-stroke,
Nay, intellectual glory, nay, a god,
Nay, of the nature of my Judges here,—
Shall man prove the insensible, the block,
The blot o' the earth he crawls on to disgrace ?
(Come, that 's both solid and poetic)—man
Derogate, live for the low tastes alone,
Mean creeping cares about the animal life ?   540

May Gigia have remembered, nothing stings
Fried liver out of its monotony
Of richness like a root of fennel, chopped
Fine with the parsley : parsley-sprigs, I said—

Was there need I should say ' and fennel too ' ?
But no, she cannot have been so obtuse !
To our argument !   The fennel will be chopped.

From beast to man next mount we—ay, but, mind,
Still mere man, not yet Christian,—that, in time !
Not too fast, mark you !   'Tis on Heathen grounds
We next defend our act :   then, fairly urge—   551
If this were done of old, in a green tree,
Allowed in the Spring rawness of our kind,
What may be licensed in the Autumn dry,
And ripe, the latter harvest-tide of man ?
If, with his poor and primitive half-lights,
The Pagan, whom our devils served for gods,
Could stigmatise the breach of marriage-vow
As that which blood, blood only might efface,—
Absolve the husband, outraged, whose revenge   560
Anticipated law, plied sword himself,—
How with the Christian in full blaze of day ?
Shall not he rather double penalty,
Multiply vengeance, than, degenerate,
Let privilege be minished, droop, decay ?
Therefore set forth at large the ancient law !
Superabundant the examples be
To pick and choose from.   The Athenian Code,
Solon's, the name is serviceable,—then,   569
The Laws of the Twelve Tables, that fifteenth,—
' Romulus ' likewise rolls out round and large.
The Julian ;   the Cornelian ;   Gracchus' Law :
So old a chime, the bells ring of themselves !
Spreti can set that going if he please,
I point you, for my part, the belfry out,
Intent to rise from dusk, *diluculum*,
Into the Christian day shall broaden next.

First, the fit compliment to His Holiness
Happily reigning :   then sustain the point—
All that was long ago declared as law .   580
By the early Revelation, stands confirmed
By Apostle and Evangelist and Saint,—
To-wit—that Honour is the supreme good.
Why should I baulk Saint Jerome of his phrase ?
Ubi honor non est, where no honour is,
Ibi contemptus est ; and where contempt,

.

Ibi injuria frequens ; and where that,
The frequent injury, *ibi et indignatio ;*
And where the indignation, *ibi quies
Nulla ;* and where there is no quietude,   590
Why, *ibi,* there, the mind is often cast
Down from the heights where it proposed to dwell,
Mens a proposito sæpe dejicitur.
And naturally the mind is so cast down,
Since harder 't is, *quum difficilius sit,*
Iram cohibere, to coerce one's wrath,
Quam miracula facere, than work miracles,—
Saint Gregory smiles in his First Dialogue :
Whence we infer, the ingenuous soul, the man
Who makes esteem of honour and repute,   600
Whenever honour and repute are touched,
Arrives at term of fury and despair,
Loses all guidance from the reason-check :
As in delirium, or a frenzy-fit,
Nor fury nor despair he satiates,—no,
Not even if he attain the impossible,
O'erturn the hinges of the universe
To annihilate—not whoso caused the smart
Solely, the author simply of his pain,
But the place, the memory, *vituperii,*   610
O' the shame and scorn : *quia,*—says Solomon,
(The Holy Spirit speaking by his mouth
In Proverbs, the sixth chapter near the end)
—Because, the zeal and fury of a man,
Zelus et furor viri, will not spare,
Non parcet, in the day of his revenge,
In die vindictæ, nor will acquiesce,
Nec acquiescet, through a person's prayers,
Cujusdam precibus,—nec suscipiet,
Nor yet take, *pro redemptione,* for   620
Redemption, *dona plurium,* gifts of friends,
Nor money-payment to compound for ache.
Who recognises not my client's case ?
Whereto, as strangely consentaneous here,
Adduce Saint Bernard in the Epistle writ
To Robertulus, his nephew : Too much grief,
Dolor quippe nimius non deliberat,
Does not excogitate propriety,
Non verecundatur, nor knows shame at all,
Non consulit rationem, nor consults   630

Reason, *non dignitatis metuit*
Damnum, nor dreads the loss of dignity ;
Modum et ordinem, order and the mode,
Ignorat, it ignores : why, trait for trait,
Was ever portrait limned so like the life ?
(By Cavalier Maratta, shall I say ?
I hear he 's first in reputation now.)
Yes, that of Samson in the Sacred Text :
That 's not so much the portrait as the man !
Samson in Gaza was the antetype   640
Of Guido at Rome : for note the Nazarite !
Blinded he was,—an easy thing to bear,
Intrepidly he took imprisonment,
Gyves, stripes and daily labour at the mill :
But when he found himself, i' the public place,
Destined to make the common people sport,
Disdain burned up with such an impetus
I' the breast of him that, all of him on fire,
Moriatur, roared he, let my soul's self die,
Anima mea, with the Philistines !   650
So, pulled down pillar, roof, and death and all,
Multosque plures interfecit, ay,
And many more he killed thus, *moriens,*
Dying, *quam vivus,* than in his whole life,
Occiderat, he ever killed before.
Are these things writ for no example, Sirs ?
One instance more, and let me see who doubts !
Our Lord Himself, made up of mansuetude,
Sealing the sum of sufferance up, received
Opprobrium, contumely and buffeting   660
Without complaint : but when He found Himself
Touched in His honour never so little for once,
Then outbroke indignation pent before—
' *Honorem meum nemini dabo !* ' ' No,
' My honour I to nobody will give ! '
And certainly the example so hath wrought,
That whosoever, at the proper worth,
Apprises worldly honour and repute,
Esteems it nobler to die honoured man
Beneath Mannaia, than live centuries   670
Disgraced in the eye o' the world. We find Saint Paul
No recreant to this faith delivered once :
' Far worthier were it that I died,' cries he,
Expedit mihi magis mori, ' than

' That anyone should make my glory void,'
Quam ut gloriam meam quis evacuet!
See, *ad Corinthienses :* whereupon
Saint Ambrose makes a comment with much fruit,
Doubtless my Judges long since laid to heart,
So I desist from bringing forward here—   680
(I can't quite recollect it.)

                                   Have I proved
Satis superque, both enough and to spare,
That Revelation old and new admits
The natural man may effervesce in ire,
O'erflood earth, o'erfroth heaven with foamy rage,
At the first puncture to his self-respect ?
Then, Sirs, this Christian dogma, this law-bud
Full-blown now, soon to bask the absolute flower
Of Papal doctrine in our blaze of day,—   690
Bethink you, shall we miss one promise-streak,
One doubtful birth of dawn crepuscular,
One dew-drop comfort to humanity,
Now that the chalice teems with noonday wine ?
Yea, argue Molinists who bar revenge—
Referring just to what makes out our case !
Under old dispensation, argue they,
The doom of the adulterous wife was death,
Stoning by Moses' law.   ' Nay, stone her not,
' Put her away ! ' next legislates our Lord ;   700
And last of all, ' Nor yet divorce a wife ! '
Ordains the Church, ' she typifies ourself,
The Bride no fault shall cause to fall from Christ.'
Then, as no jot nor tittle of the Law
Has passed away—which who presumes to doubt ?
As not one word of Christ is rendered vain—
Which, could it be though heaven and earth should
        pass ?
—Where do I find my proper punishment
For my adulterous wife, I humbly ask
Of my infallible Pope,—who now remits   710
Even the divorce allowed by Christ in lieu
Of lapidation Moses licensed me ?
The Gospel checks the Law which throws the stone,
The Church tears the divorce-bill Gospel grants,
The wife sins and enjoys impunity !
What profits me the fulness of the days,
The final dispensation, I demand,

Unless Law, Gospel and the Church subjoin
' But who hath barred thee primitive revenge,
' Which, like fire damped and dammed up, burns more
    fierce ?   720
' Use thou thy natural privilege of man,
' Else wert thou found like those old ingrate Jews,
' Despite the manna-banquet on the board,
' A-longing after melons, cucumbers
' And such like trash of Egypt left behind ! '
(There was one melon, had improved our soup,
But did not Cinoncino need the rind
To make a boat with ? So I seem to think.)

Law, Gospel and the Church—from these we leap
To the very last revealment, easy rule   730
Befitting the well-born and thorough-bred
O' the happy day we live in,—not the dark
O' the early rude and acorn-eating race.
' Behold,' quoth James, ' we bridle in a horse
' And turn his body as we would thereby ! '
Yea, but we change the bit to suit the growth,
And rasp our colt's jaw with a rugged spike
We hasten to remit our managed steed
Who wheels round at persuasion of a touch.
Civilization bows to decency,   740
The acknowledged use and wont, the manners,—mild
But yet imperative law,—which make the man.
Thus do we pay the proper compliment
To rank, and that society of Rome,
Hath so obliged us by its interest,
Taken our client's part instinctively,
As unaware defending its own cause.
What *dictum* doth Society lay down
I' the case of one who hath a faithless wife ?
Wherewithal should the husband cleanse his way ?
Be patient and forgive ? Oh, language fails— 751
Shrinks from depicturing his punishment !
For if wronged husband raise not hue and cry,
Quod si maritus de adulterio non
Conquereretur, he 's presumed a—foh !
Presumitur leno : so, complain he must.
But how complain ? At your tribunal, lords ?
Far weightier challenge suits your sense, I wot !
You sit not to have gentlemen propose

Questions gentility can itself discuss.   760
Did not you prove that to our brother Paul ?
The Abate, *quum judicialiter*
Prosequeretur, when he tried the law,
Guidonis causam, in Count Guido's case,
Accidit ipsi, this befell himself,
Quod risum moverit et cachinnos, that
He moved to mirth and cachinnation, all
Or nearly all, *fere in omnibus*
Etiam sensatis et cordatis, men
Strong-sensed, sound-hearted, nay, the very Court,
Ipsismet in judicibus, I might add,   771
Non tamen dicam. In a cause like this,
So multiplied were reasons *pro* and *con*,
Delicate, intertwisted and obscure,
That law were shamed to lend a finger-tip
To unravel, readjust the hopeless twine,
While, half-a-dozen steps outside the court,
There stood a foolish trifler with a tool
A-dangle to no purpose by his side,
Had clearly cut the tangle in a trice.   780
Asserunt enim unanimiter
Doctores, for the Doctors all assert,
That husbands, *quod mariti*, must be held
Viles, cornuti reputantur, vile
And branching forth a florid infamy,
Si propriis manibus, if with their own hands,
Non sumunt, they take not straightway revenge,
Vindictam, but expect the deed be done
By the Court—*expectant illam fieri*
Per judices, qui summopere rident, which   790
Gives an enormous guffaw for reply,
Et cachinnantur. For he ran away,
Deliquit enim, just that he might 'scape
The censure of both counsellors and crowd,
Ut vulgi et Doctorum evitaret
Censuram, and lest so he superadd
To loss of honour ignominy too,
Et sic ne istam quoque ignominiam
Amisso honori superadderet.
My lords, my lords, the inconsiderate step   800
Was—we referred ourselves to law at all !
Twit me not with, ' Law else had punished you ! '
Each punishment of the extra-legal step,

To which the high-born preferably revert,
Is ever for some oversight, some slip
I' the taking vengeance, not for vengeance' self.
A good thing done unhandsomely turns ill ;
And never yet lacked ill the law's rebuke.
For pregnant instance, let us contemplate
The luck of Leonardus,—see at large   810
Of Sicily's Decisions sixty-first.
This Leonard finds his wife is false : what then ?
He makes her own son snare her, and entice
Out of the town-walls to a private walk,
Wherein he slays her with commodity.
They find her body half-devoured by dogs :
Leonard is tried, convicted, punished, sent
To labour in the galleys seven years long :
Why ?   For the murder ?   Nay, but for the mode !
Malus modus occidendi, ruled the Court,   820
An ugly mode of killing, nothing more !
Another fructuous sample,—see ' *De Re*
' *Criminali*,' in Matthæus' divine piece.
Another husband, in no better plight,
Simulates absence, thereby tempts the wife ;
On whom he falls, out of sly ambuscade,
Backed by a brother of his, and both of them
Armed to the teeth with arms that law had blamed.
Nimis dolose, overwilily,
Fuisse operatum, was it worked,   830
Pronounced the law : had all been fairly done
Law had not found him worthy, as she did,
Of four years' exile.   Why cite more ?   Enough
Is good as a feast—(unless a birthday-feast
For one's Cinuccio : so, we'll finish here)
My lords, we rather need defend ourselves
Inasmuch as for a twinkling of an eye
We hesitatingly appealed to law,—
Rather than deny that, on mature advice,
We blushingly bethought us, bade revenge   840
Back to the simple proper private way
Of decent self-dealt gentlemanly death.
Judges, there is the law, and this beside,
The testimony !   Look to it !
                                        Pause and breathe !
So far is only too plain ; we must watch,
Bottini will scarce hazard an attack

Here : let 's anticipate the fellow's play,
And guard the weaker places—warily ask,
What if considerations of a sort,   850
Reasons of a kind, arise from out the strange
Peculiar unforseen new circumstance
Of this our (candour owns) abnormal act,
To bar the right of us revenging so ?
' Impunity were otherwise your meed :
' Go slay your wife and welcome,'—may be urged,—
' But why the innocent old couple slay,
' Pietro, Violante ?   You may do enough,
' Not too much, not exceed the golden mean :
' Neither brute-beast nor Pagan, Gentile, Jew,   860
' Nor Christian, no nor votarist of the mode,
' Were free at all to push revenge so far ! '

No, indeed ?   Why, thou very sciolist !
The actual wrong, Pompilia seemed to do,
Was virtual wrong done by the parents here—
Imposing her upon us as their child—
Themselves allow : then, her fault was their fault,
Her punishment be theirs accordingly !
But wait a little, sneak not off so soon !
Was this cheat solely harm to Guido, pray ?   870
The precious couple you call innocent,—
Why, they were felons that law failed to clutch,
Qui ut fraudarent, who that they might rob,
Legitime vocatos, folks law called,
Ad fidei commissum, true heirs to the Trust,
Partum supposuerunt, feigned this birth,
Immemores reos factos esse, blind
To the fact that, guilty, they incurred thereby,
Ultimi supplicii, hanging or aught worse.
Do you blame us that we turn law's instruments
Not mere self-seekers,—mind the public weal,   881
Nor make the private good our sole concern ?
That having—shall I say—secured a thief,
Not simply we recover from his pouch
The stolen article our property,
But also pounce upon our neighbour's purse
We opportunely find reposing there,
And do him justice while we right ourselves ?
He owes us, for our part, a drubbing say,
But owes our neighbour just a dance i' the air   890

Under the gallows : so we throttle him.
The neighbour 's Law, the couple are the Thief,
We are the over-ready to help Law—
Zeal of her house hath eaten us up : for which,
Can it be, Law intends to eat up us,
Crudum Priamum, devour poor Priam raw,
('T was Jupiter's own joke) with babes to boot,
Priamique pisinnos, in Homeric phrase ?
Shame !——and so ends the period prettily.

But even,—prove the pair not culpable,   900
Free as unborn babe from connivance at,
Participation in, their daughter's fault :
Ours the mistake.   Is that a rare event ?
Non semel, it is anything but rare,
In contingentia facti, that by chance,
Impunes evaserunt, go scot-free,
Qui, such well-meaning people as ourselves,
Justo dolore moti, who aggrieved
With cause, *apposuerunt manus,* lay
Rough hands, *in innocentes,* on wrong heads.   910
Cite we an illustrative case in point :
Mulier Smirnea quœdam, good my lords,
A gentlewoman lived in Smyrna once,
Virum et filium ex eo conceptum, who
Both husband and her son begot by him,
Killed, *interfecerat, ex quo,* because,
Vir filium suum perdiderat, her spouse
Had been beforehand with her, killed her son,
Matrimonii primi, of a previous bed.
Deinde accusata, then accused,   920
Apud Dolabellam, before him that sat
Proconsul, *nec duabus cœdibus*
Comtaminatam liberare, nor
To liberate a woman doubly-dyed
With murder, *voluit,* made he up his mind,
Nec condemnare, nor to doom to death,
Justo dolore impulsam, one impelled
By just grief, *sed remisit,* but sent her up
Ad Areopagum, to the Hill of Mars,
Sapientissimorum judicum   930
Coetum, to that assembly of the sage
Paralleled only by my judges here ;
Ubi, cognito de causa, where, the cause

Well weighed, *responsum est*, they gave reply,
Ut ipsa et accusator, that both sides
O' the suit, *redirent*, should come back again,
Post centum annos, after a hundred years,
For judgment ; *et sic*, by which sage decree,
Duplici parricidio rea, one
Convicted of a double parricide,   940
Quamvis etiam innocentem, though in truth
Out of the pair, one innocent at least
She, *occidisset*, plainly had put to death,
Undequaque, yet she altogether 'scaped,
Evasit impunis.   See the case at length
In Valerius, fittingly styled *Maximus*,
That eighth book of his Memorable Facts.
Nor Cyriacus cites beside the mark :
Similiter uxor quœ mandaverat,
Just so, a lady who had taken care,   950
Homicidium viri, that her lord be killed,
Ex denegatione debiti,
For denegation of a certain debt,
Ma'rimonialis, he was loth to pay,
Fuit pecuniaria mulcta, was
Amerced in a pecuniary mulct,
Punita, et ad pœnam, and to pains,
Temporalem, for a certain space of time,
In monasterio, in a convent.

                          Ay,   960
In monasterio !   How he manages
In with the ablative, the accusative !
I had hoped to have hitched the villain into verse
For a gift, this very day, a complete list
O' the prepositions each with proper case,
Telling a story, long was in my head.
What prepositions take the accusative ?
Ad to or at—*who saw the cat ?*—down to
Ob, for, because of, *keep her claws off !* Ah,
Law in a man takes the whole liberty !   970
The muse is fettered,—just as Ovid found !

And now, sea widens and the coast is clear.
What of the dubious act you bade excuse ?
Surely things brighten, brighten, till at length
Remains—so far from act that needs defence—

Apology to make for act delayed
One minute, let alone eight mortal months
Of hesitation !   ' Why procrastinate ? '
(Out with it my Bottinius, ease thyself !)
' Right, promptly done, is twice right : right delayed
' Turns wrong.   We grant you should have killed your
          wife,   981
' But on the moment, at the meeting her
' In company with the priest : then did the tongue
' O' the Brazen Head give licence, " Time is now ! "
' You make your mind up : " Time is past " it peals.
' Friend, you are competent to mastery
' O' the passions that confessedly explain
' An outbreak,—yet allow an interval,
' And then break out as if time's clock still clanged.
' You have forfeited your chance, and flat you fall
' Into the commonplace category   991
' Of men bound to go softly all their days,
' Obeying law.'

              Now, which way make response ?
What was the answer Guido gave, himself ?
—That so to argue came of ignorance
How honour bears a wound : ' For, wound,' said he,
' My body, and the smart is worst at first :
' While, wound my soul where honour sits and rules,
' Longer the sufferance, stronger grows the pain,
' 'T is *ex incontinenti*, fresh as first.'   1001
But try another tack, calm common sense
By way of contrast : as—Too true, my lords !
We did demur, awhile did hesitate :
Yet husband sure should let a scruple speak
Ere he slay wife,—for his own safety, lords !
Carpers abound in this misjudging world.
Moreover, there 's a nicety in law
That seems to justify them should they carp :
Suppose the source of injury a son,—   1010
Father may slay such son yet run no risk :
Why graced with such a privilege ?   Because
A father so incensed with his own child,
Or must have reason, or believe he has :
Quia semper, seeing that in such event,
Presumitur, the law is bound suppose,
Quod capiat pater, that the sire must take,

Bonum consilium pro filio,
The best course as to what befits his boy,
Through instinct, *ex instinctu,* of mere love,   1020
Amoris, and, *paterni,* fatherhood ;
Quam confidentiam, which confidence,
Non habet, law declines to entertain,
De viro, of the husband : where has he
An instinct that compels him love his wife ?
Rather is he presumably her foe :
So, let him ponder long in this bad world
Ere do the simplest act of justice.

                                    But
Again—and here we brush Bottini's breast—   1030
Object you, ' See the danger of delay !
' Suppose a man murdered my friend last month :
' Had I come up and killed him for his pains
' In rage, I had done right, allows the law :
' I meet him now and kill him in cold blood,
' I do wrong, equally allows the law :
' Wherein do actions differ, yours and mine ? '
In plenitudine intellectus es ?
Hast thy wits, Fisc ?   To take such slayer's life,
Returns it life to thy slain friend at all ?   1040
Had he stolen ring instead of stabbing friend,—
To-day, to-morrow or next century,
Meeting the thief, thy ring upon his thumb,
Thou justifiably hadst wrung it thence :
So, couldst thou wrench thy friend's life back again,
Though prisoned in the bosom of his foe,
Why, law would look complacent on thy rush.
Our case is, that the thing we lost, we found :
The honour, we were robbed of eight months since,
Being recoverable at any day   1050
By death of the delinquent.   Go thy ways !
Ere thou hast learned law, will be much to do,
As said the rustic while he shod the goose.

Nay, if you urge me, interval was none !
From the inn to the villa—blank or else a bar
Of adverse and contrarious incident
Solid between us and our just revenge !
What with the priest who flourishes his blade,
The wife who like a fury flings at us,

                    M

The crowd—and then the capture, the appeal   1060
To Rome, the journey there, the journey thence,
The shelter at the House of Convertites,
The visits to the Villa, and so forth,
Where was one minute left us all this while
To put in execution that revenge
We planned o' the instant ?—as it were, plumped down
A round sound egg, o' the spot, some eight months
    since
Rome, more propitious than our nest, should hatch !
Object not, ' You reached Rome on Christmas-eve,
' And, despite liberty to act at once,   1070
' Waited a week—indecorous delay ! '
Hath so the Molinism-canker, lords,
Eaten to the bone ?   Is no religion left ?
No care for aught held holy by the Church ?
What, would you have us skip and miss those Feasts
O' the Natal Time, must we go prosecute
Secular business on a sacred day ?
Should not the merest charity expect,
Setting our poor concerns aside for once,
We hurried to the song matutinal   1080
I' the Sistine, and pressed forward for the Mass
The Cardinal that 's Camerlengo chaunts,
Then rushed on to the blessing of the Hat
And Rapier, which the Pope sends to what prince
Has done most detriment to the Infidel—
And thereby whet our courage if 't were blunt ?
Meantime, allow we kept the house a week,
Suppose not we were idle in our mew :
Picture Count Guido raging here and there—
' " Money ? " I need none—" Friends ? "   The word
    is null.   1090
' Match me the white was on that shield of mine
' Borne at ' . . wherever might be shield to bear ;
' I see my grandsire, he who fought so well
' At ' . . here find out and put in time and place
Of what might be a fight his grandsire fought :
' I see this—I see that— '

          See to it all,
Or I shall scarce see lamb's fry in an hour !
—Nod to the uncle, as I bid advance   1099
The smoking dish, ' This, for your tender teeth !

' Behoves us care a little for our kin—
' You, Sir,—who care so much for cousinship
' As come to your poor loving nephew's feast ! '
He has the reversion of a long lease yet—
Land to bequeath !   He loves lamb's fry, I know !

Here fall to be considered those same six
Qualities ;   what Bottini needs must call
So many aggravations of our crime,
Parasite-growth upon mere murder's back.
We summarily might dispose of such   1110
By some off-hand and jaunty fling, some skit—
' So, since there 's proved no crime to aggravate,
' A fico for your aggravations, Fisc ! '
No,—handle mischief rather,—play with spells
Were meant to raise a spirit, and laugh the while
We show that did he rise we are his match !
Therefore, first aggravation :   we made up—
Over and above our simple murdering selves—
A regular assemblage of armed men,
Coadunatio armatorum,—ay,   1120
Unluckily it was the very judge
Who sits in judgment on our cause to-day
That passed the law as Governor of Rome :
' Four men armed,'—though for lawful purpose, mark !
Much more for an acknowledged crime,—' shall die.'
We five were armed to the teeth, meant murder too ?
Why, that 's the very point that saves us, Fisc !
Let me instruct you.   Crime nor done nor meant,—
You punish still who arm and congregate :
For why have used bad means to a good end ?   1130
Crime being meant not done,—you punish still
The means to crime, you haply pounce upon,
Though circumstance have baulked you of their end :
But crime not only compassed but complete,
Meant and done too ?   Why, since you have the end,
Be that your sole concern, nor mind those means
No longer to the purpose !   Murdered we ?
(—Which, that our luck was in the present case,
Quod contigisse in præsenti casu,
Is palpable, *manibus palpatum est*—)   1140
Make murder out against us, nothing less !
Of many crimes committed with a view
To one main crime, you overlook the less,

Intent upon the large.   Suppose a man
Having in view commission of a theft,
Climb the town-wall : 't is for the theft he hangs,
Suppose you can convict him of such theft,
Remitted whipping due to who climbs wall
For bravery or wantonness alone,
Just to dislodge a daw's nest and no more.   1150
So I interpret you the manly mind
Of him the Judge shall judge both you and me,—
O' the Governor, who, being no babe, my Fisc,
Cannot have blundered on ineptitude !

Next aggravation,—that the arms themselves
Were specially of such forbidden sort
Through shape or length or breadth, as, prompt, law
      plucks
From single hand of solitary man,
And makes him pay the carriage with his life :
Delatio armorum, arms against the rule,   1160
Contra formam constitutionis, of
Pope Alexander's blessed memory.
Such are the poignard with the double prong,
Horn-like, when tines make bold the antlered buck,
And all of brittle glass—for man to stab
And break off short and so let fragment stick
Fast in the flesh to baffle surgery :
And such the Genoese blade with hooks at edge
That did us service at the Villa here.
Sed parcat mihi tam eximius vir,   1170
But, let so rare a personage forgive,
Fisc, thy objection is a foppery !
Thy charge runs, that we killed three innocents :
Killed, dost see ?   Then, if killed, what matter how ?—
By stick or stone, by sword or dagger, tool
Long or tool short, round or triangular—
Poor folks, they find small comfort in a choice !
Means to an end, means to an end, my Fisc !
Nature cries out ' Take the first arms you find ! '
Furor ministrat arma :   where 's a stone ?   1180
Unde mi lapidem, where darts for me ?
Unde sagittas ?   But subdue the bard
And rationalize a little :   eight months since,
Had we, or had we not, incurred your blame
For letting 'scape unpunished this bad pair ?

I think I proved that in last paragraph !
Why did we so ?   Because our courage failed.
Wherefore ?   Through lack of arms to fight the foe :
We had no arms or merely lawful ones,
An unimportant sword and blunderbuss,   1190
Against a foe, pollent in potency,
The *amasius,* and our vixen of a wife.
Well then, how culpably do we gird loin
And once more undertake the high emprise,
Unless we load ourselves this second time
With handsome superfluity of arms,
Since better say ' too much ' than ' not enough '
And ' *plus non vitiat,*' too much does no harm,
Except in mathematics, sages say.
Gather instruction from the parable !   1200
At first we are advised—' A lad hath here
' Seven barley loaves and two small fishes : what
' Is that among so many ? '   Aptly asked :
But put that question twice and, quite as apt
The answer is ' Fragments, twelve baskets full ! '

And, while we speak of superabundance, fling
A word by the way to fools that cast their flout
On Guido—' Punishment exceeds offence :
' You might be just but you were cruel too ! '
If so you stigmatise the stern and strict,   1210
Still, he is not without excuse—may plead
Transgression of his mandate, over-zeal
O' the part of his companions : all he craved
Was, they should fray the faces of the three :
Solummodo fassus est, he owns no more,
Dedisse mandatum, than that he desired,
Ad sfrisiandum, dicam, that they hack
And hew, i' the customary phrase, his wife,
Uxorem tantum, and no harm beside.
If his instructions then be misconceived,   1220
Nay, disobeyed, impute you blame to him ?
Cite me no Panicollus to the point,
As adverse ! Oh, I quite expect his case—
How certain noble youths of Sicily
Having good reason to mistrust their wives,
Killed them and were absolved in consequence :
While others who had gone beyond the need
By mutilation of the paramour

(So Galba in the Horatian satire grieved)
—These were condemned to the galleys, as for guilt
Exceeding simple murder of a wife.   1231
But why ?   Because of ugliness, and not
Cruelty, in the said revenge, I trow !
Ex causa abscissionis partium ;
Quia nempe id facientes reputantur
Naturæ inimici, man revolts
Against such as the natural enemy.
Pray, grant to one who meant to slit the nose
And slash the cheek and slur the mouth, at most,
A somewhat more humane award than these !   1240
Objectum funditus corruit, flat you fall,
My Fisc !   I waste no kick on you but pass.

Third aggravation : that our act was done—
Not in the public street, where safety lies,
Not in the bye-place, caution may avoid,
Wood, cavern, desert, spots contrived for crime,—
But in the very house, home, nook and nest,
O' the victims, murdered in their dwelling-place,
In domo ac habitatione propria,
Where all presumably is peace and joy.   1250
The spider, crime, pronounce we twice a pest
When, creeping from congenial cottage, she
Taketh hold with her hands, to horrify
His household more, i' the palace of the king.
All three were housed and safe and confident.
Moreover, the permission that our wife
Should have at length *domum pro carcere,*
Her own abode in place of prison,—why,
We ourselves granted, by our other self
And proxy Paolo : did we make such grant,   1260
Meaning a lure ?—elude the vigilance
O' the jailor, lead her to commodious death,
While we ostensibly relented ?
                                            Ay,
Just so did we, nor otherwise, my Fisc !
Is vengeance lawful ?   We demand our right,
But find it will be questioned or refused
By jailor, turnkey, hangdog,—what know we ?
Pray, how is it we should conduct ourselves ?
To gain our private right—break public peace,   1270
Do you bid us ?—trouble order with our broils ?

Endanger . . shall I shrink to own . . ourselves ?—
Who want no broken head nor bloody nose
(While busied slitting noses, breaking heads)
From the first tipstaff shall please interfere !
Nam quicquid sit, for howsoever it be,
An de consensu nostro, if with leave
Or not, *a monasterio*, from the nuns,
Educta esset, she had been led forth,
Potuimus id dissimulare, we   1280
May well have granted leave in pure pretence,
Ut aditum habere, that thereby
An entry we might compass, a free move
Potuissemus, to her easy death,
Ad eam occidendam. Privacy
O' the hearth, and sanctitude of home, say you ?
Would you give man's abode more privilege
Than God's ?—for in the churches where He dwells,
In quibus assistit Regum Rex, by means
Of His essence, *per essentiam*, all the same,   1290
Et nihilominus, therein, *in eis*,
Ex justa via delinquens, whoso dares
To take a liberty on ground enough,
Is pardoned, *excusatur :* that 's our case—
Delinquent through befitting cause. You hold,
To punish a false wife in her own house
Is graver than, what happens every day,
To hale a debtor from his hiding-place
In church protected by the Sacrament ?
To this conclusion have I brought my Fisc ?   1300
Foxes have holes, and fowls o' the air their nests ;
Praise you the impiety that follows, Fisc ?
Shall false wife yet have where to lay her head ?
' *Contra Fiscum definitum est !* ' He's done,
' *Surge et scribe*,' make a note of it !
—If I may dally with Aquinas' word.

Or in the death-throe does he mutter still ?
Fourth aggravation, that we changed our garb,
And rusticized ourselves with uncouth hat,
Rough vest and goatskin wrappage ; murdered thus
Mutatione vestium, in disguise,   1311
Whereby mere murder got complexed with wile,
Turned *homicidium ex insidiis.* Fisc,
How often must I round thee in the ears—

All means are lawful to a lawful end ?
Concede he had the right to kill his wife :
The Count indulged in a travesty ; why ?
De illa ut vindictam sumeret,
That on her he might lawful vengeance take,
Commodius, with more ease, *et tutius,*   1320
And safelier : wants he warrant for the step ?
Read to thy profit how the Apostle once
For ease and safety, when Damascus raged,
Was let down in a basket by the wall,
To 'scape the malice of the governor
(Another sort of Governor boasts Rome !)
—Many are of opinion,—covered close,
Concealed with—what except that very cloak
He left behind at Troas afterward ?
I shall not add a syllable : Molinists may !   1330

Well, have we more to manage ?   Ay, indeed !
Fifth aggravation, that our wife reposed
Sub potestate judicis, beneath
Protection of the judge,—her house was styled
A prison, and his power became its guard
In lieu of wall and gate and bolt and bar.
This a tough point, shrewd, redoubtable :
Because we have to supplicate the judge
Shall overlook wrong done the judgment-seat.
Now, I might suffer my own nose be pulled,   1340
As man—but then as father . . if the Fisc
Touched one hair of my boy who held my hand
In confidence he could not come to harm
Crossing the Corso, at my own desire,
Going to see those bodies in the church—
What would you say to that, Don Hyacinth ?
This is the sole and single knotty point :
For, bid Tommati blink his interest,
You laud his magnanimity the while :
But baulk Tommati's office,—he talks big !   1350
' My predecessors in the place,—those sons
' O' the prophets that may hope succeed me here,—
' Shall I diminish their prerogative ?
' Count Guido Franceschini's honour !—well,
' Has the Governor of Rome none ? '

                              You perceive,
The cards are all against us.   Make a push,

Kick over table, as our gamesters do !
We, do you say, encroach upon the rights,
Deny the omnipotence o' the Judge forsooth ?   1360
We, who have only been from first to last
Intent on that his purpose should prevail,
Nay, more, at times, anticipating both
At risk of a rebuke ?

               But wait awhile !
Cannot we lump this with the sixth and last
Of the aggravations—that the Majesty
O' the Sovereign here received a wound, to-wit,
Læsa Majestas, since our violence
Was out of envy to the course of law,   1370
In odium litis ?   We cut short thereby
Three pending suits, promoted by ourselves
I' the main,—which worsens crime, *accedit ad
Exasperationem criminis !*

Yes, here the eruptive wrath with full effect !
How—did not indignation chain my tongue—
Could I repel this last, worst charge of all !
(There is a porcupine to barbacue ;
Gigia can jug a rabbit well enough,
With sour-sweet sauce and pine-pips ; but, good Lord,
Suppose the devil instigate the wench   1381
To stew, not roast him ?   Stew my porcupine ?
If she does, I know where his quills shall stick !
Come, I must go myself and see to things :
I cannot stay much longer stewing here)
Our stomach . . I mean, our soul—is stirred within,
And we want words.   We wounded Majesty ?
Fall under such a censure, we,—who yearned
So much that Majesty dispel the cloud
And shine on us with healing on its wings,   1390
We prayed the Pope, *Majestas'* very self,
To anticipate a little the tardy pack,
Bell us forth deep the authoritative bay
Should start the beagles into sudden yelp
Unisonous,—and, Gospel leading Law,
Grant there assemble in our own behoof
A Congregation, a particular Court,
A few picked friends of quality and place,

To hear the several matters in dispute,
Causes big, little and indifferent,   1400
Bred of our marriage like a mushroom-growth,
All at once (can one brush off such too soon ?)
And so with laudable dispatch decide
Whether we, in the main (to sink detail)
Were one the Church should hold fast or let go.
' What, take the credit from the Law ? ' you ask ?
Indeed, we did !   Law ducks to Gospel here :
Why should Law gain the glory and pronounce
A judgment shall immortalize the Pope ?
Yes : our self-abnegating policy   1410
Was Joab's—we would rouse our David's sloth,
Bid him encamp against a city, sack
A place whereto ourselves had long laid siege,
Lest, taking it at last, it take our name
And be not *Innocentinopolis.*
But no !   The modesty was in alarm,
The temperance refused to interfere,
Returned us our petition with the word
' *Ad judices suos,*' ' Leave him to his Judge ! '
As who should say—' Why trouble my repose ?   1420
' Why consult Peter in a simple case,
' Peter's wife's sister in her fever-fit
' Might solve as readily as the Apostle's self ?
' Are my Tribunals posed by aught so plain ?
' Hath not my Court a conscience ?   It is of age,
' Ask it ! '

                We do ask,—but, inspire reply
To the Court thou bidst me ask, as I have asked—
Oh thou, who vigilantly dost attend
To even the few, the ineffectual words   1430
Which rise from this our low and mundane sphere
Up to thy region out of smoke and noise,
Seeking corroboration from thy nod
Who art all justice—which means mercy too
In a low noisy smoky world like ours
Where Adam's sin made peccable his seed !
We venerate the father of the flock,
Whose last faint sands of life, the frittered gold,
Fall noiselessly, yet all too fast, o' the cone
And tapering heap of those collected years,—   1440
Never have these been hurried in their flow,

Though justice fain would jog reluctant arm,
In eagerness to take the forfeiture
Of guilty life : much less shall mercy sue
In vain that thou let innocence survive,
Precipitate no minim of the mass
O' the all-so precious moments of thy life,
By pushing Guido into death and doom !

(Our Cardinal engages read my speech :   1449
They say, the Pope has one half-hour, in twelve,
Of something like a moderate return
Of the intellectuals,—never much to lose !—
If I adroitly plant this passage there,
The Fisc will find himself forestalled, I think,
Though he stand, beat till the old ear-drum break !
—Ah, boy of my own bowels, Hyacinth,
Wilt ever catch the knack,—requite the pains
Of poor papa, become proficient too
I' the how and why and when—the time to laugh,
The time to weep, the time, again, to pray,   1460
And all the times prescribed by Holy Writ ?
Well, well, we fathers can but care, but cast
Our bread upon the waters !)
                                        In a word,
These secondary charges go to ground,
Since secondary, so superfluous,—motes
Quite from the main point : we did all and some,
Little and much, adjunct and principal,
Causa honoris. Is there such a cause
As the sake of honour ? By that sole test try   1470
Our action, nor demand if more or less,
Because of the action's mode, we merit blame
Or may-be deserve praise. The Court decides.
Is the end lawful ? It allows the means :
What we may do we may with safety do,
And what means ' safety ' we ourselves must judge.
Put case a person wrongs me past dispute :
If my legitimate vengeance be a blow,
Mistrusting my bare arm can deal the same,
I claim co-operation of a stick ;   1480
Doubtful if stick be tough, I crave a sword ;
Diffident of ability in fence,
I fee a friend, a swordsman to assist :
Take one—who may be coward, fool or knave—

Why not take fifty ?—and if these exceed
I' the due degree of drubbing, whom accuse
But the first author of the aforesaid wrong
Who put poor me to such a world of pains ?
Surgery would have just excised a wart ;
The patient made such pother, struggled so   1490
That the sharp instrument sliced nose and all.
Taunt us not that our friends performed for pay !
For us, enough were simple honour's sake :
Give country clowns the dirt they comprehend,
The piece of gold !   Our reasons, which suffice
Ourselves, be ours alone ; our piece of gold
Be, to the rustic, reason and to spare !
We must translate our motives like our speech
Into the lower phrase that suits the sense
O' the limitedly apprehensive.   Let   1500
Each level have its language !   Heaven speaks first
To the angel, then the angel tames the word
Down to the ear of Tobit : he, in turn,
Diminishes the message to his dog,
And finally that dog finds how the flea
(Which else, importunate, might check his speed)
Shall learn its hunger must have holiday,—
How many varied sorts of language here,
Each following each with pace to match the step,
Haud passibus æquis !   1510

                    Talking of which flea
Reminds me I must put in special word
For the poor humble following,—the four friends,
Sicarii, our assassins in your charge.
Ourselves are safe in your approval now :
Yet must we care for our companions, plead
The cause o' the poor, the friends (of old-world faith)
Who are in tribulation for our sake.
Pauperum Procurator is my style :
I stand forth as the poor man's advocate :   1520
And when we treat of what concerns the poor,
Et cum agatur de pauperibus,
In bondage, *carceratis,* for their sake,
In eorum causis, natural piety,
Pietas, ever ought to win the day,
Triumphare debet, quia ipsi sunt,
Because those very paupers constitute,

Thesaurus Christi, all the wealth of Christ.
Nevertheless I shall not hold you long
With multiplicity of proofs, nor burn   1530
Candle at noon-tide, clarify the clear.
There beams a case refulgent from our books—
Castrensis, Butringarius, everywhere
I find it burn to dissipate the dark.
'T is this : a husband had a friend, which friend
Seemed to him over-friendly with his wife
In thought and purpose,—I pretend no more.
To justify suspicion or dispel,
He bids his wife make show of giving heed,
Semblance of sympathy—propose, in fine,   1540
A secret meeting in a private place.
The friend, enticed thus, finds an ambuscade,
To-wit, the husband posted with a pack
Of other friends, who fall upon the first
And beat his love and life out both at once.
These friends were brought to question for their help.
Law ruled ' The husband being in the right,
' Who helped him in the right can scarce be wrong '—
Opinio, an opinion every way,
Multum tenenda cordi, heart should hold !   1550
When the inferiors follow as befits
The lead o' the principal, they change their name,
And, *non dicuntur*, are no longer called
His mandatories, *mandatorii*,
But helpmates, *sed auxiliatores ;* since
To that degree does honour' sake lend aid,
Adeo honoris causa est efficax,
That not alone, *non solum*, does it pour
Itself out, *se diffundat*, on mere friends,
We bring to do our bidding of this sort,   1560
In mandatorios simplices, but sucks
Along with it in wide and generous whirl,
Sed etiam assassinii qualitate
Qualificatos, people qualified
By the quality of assassination's self,
Dare I make use of such neologism,
Ut utar verbo.

          Haste we to conclude :
Of the other points that favour, leave some few
For Spreti ; such as the delinquents' youth :   1570

One of them falls short, by some months, of age
Fit to be managed by the gallows ; two
May plead exemption from our law's award,
Being foreigners, subjects of the Granduke—
I spare that bone to Spreti and reserve
Myself the juicier breast of argument—
Flinging the breast-blade i' the face o' the Fisc,
Who furnished me the tid-bit : he must needs
Play off his armoury and rack the clowns,—
And they, at instance of the rack, confessed   1580
All four unanimously did resolve,—
That night o' the murder, in brief minutes snatched
Behind the back of Guido as he fled,—
That, since he had not kept his promise, paid
The money for the murder on the spot,
And, reaching home again, might even ignore
The past or pay it in improper coin,
They one and all resolved, these hopeful friends,
They would inaugurate the morrow's light,
Having recruited strength with needful rest,   1590
By killing Guido as he lay asleep
Pillowed by wallet which contained their fee.

I thank the Fisc for knowledge of this fact :
What fact could hope to make more manifest
Their rectitude, Guido's integrity ?
For who fails recognise apparent here,
That these poor rustics bore no envy, hate,
Malice nor yet uncharitableness
Against the people they had put to death ?
In them, did such an act reward itself ?   1600
All done was to deserve their simple pay,
Obtain the bread they earned by sweat of brow :
Missing this pay, they missed of everything—
Hence claimed it, even at expense of life
To their own lord, so little warped were they
By prepossession, such the absolute
Instinct of equity in rustic souls !
While he the Count, the cultivated mind,
He, wholly rapt in his serene regard
Of honour, as who contemplates the sun   1610
And hardly minds what tapers blink below,
He, dreaming of no argument for death
Except the vengeance worthy noble hearts,

Would he so desecrate the deed forsooth,
Vulgarise vengeance, as defray its cost
By money dug out of the dirty earth,
Mere irritant, in Maro's phrase, to ill ?
What though he lured base hinds by lucre's hope,—
The only motive they could masticate,   1619
Milk for babes, not strong meat which men require ?
The deed done, those coarse hands were soiled enough,
He spared them the pollution of the pay.
So much for the allegement, thine, my Fisc,
Quo nil absurdius, than which nought more mad,
Excogitari potest, may be squeezed
From out the cogitative brain of thee !

And now, thou excellent the Governor !
(Push to the peroration) *cæterum*
Enixe supplico, I strive in prayer,
Ut dominis meis, that unto the Court,   1630
Benigna fronte, with a gracious brow,
Et oculis serenis, and mild eyes,
Perpendere placeat, it may please them weigh,
Quod dominus Guido, that our noble Count,
Occidit, did the killing in dispute,
Ut ejus honor tumulatus, that
The honour of him buried fathom-deep
In infamy, *in infamia*, might arise,
Resurgeret, as ghosts break sepulchre !
Occidit, for he killed, *uxorem*, wife,   1640
Quia illi fuit, since she was to him,
Opprobrio, a disgrace and nothing more !
Et genitores, killed her parents too,
Qui, who, *postposita verecundia*,
Having thrown off all sort of decency,
Filiam repudiarunt, had renounced
Their daughter, *atque declarare non*
Erubuerunt, nor felt blush tinge cheek,
Declaring, *meretricis genitam*
Esse, she was the offspring of a drab,   1650
Ut ipse dehonestaretur, just
That so himself might lose his social rank !
Cujus mentem, and which daughter's heart and soul,
They, *perverterunt*, turned from the right course,
Et ad illicitos amores non
Dumtaxat pellexerunt, and to love

Not simply did alluringly incite,
Sed vi obedientiæ, but by force
O' the duty, *filialis*, daughters owe,
Coegerunt, forced and drove her to the deed : 1660
Occidit, I repeat he killed the clan,
Ne scilicet amplius in dedecore,
Lest peradventure longer life might trail,
Viveret, link by link his turpitude,
Invisus consanguineis, hateful so
To kith and kindred, *a nobilibus*
Notatus, shunned by men of quality,
Relictus ab amicis, left i' the lurch
By friends, *ab omnibus derisus*, turned
A common hack-block to try edge of jokes. 1670
Occidit, and he killed them here in Rome,
In Urbe, the Eternal City, Sirs,
Nempe quæ alias spectata est,
The appropriate theatre which witnessed once,
Matronam nobilem, Lucretia's self,
Abluere pudicitiæ maculas,
Wash off the spots of her pudicity,
Sanguine proprio, with her own pure blood ;
Quæ vidit, and which city also saw,
Patrem, Virginius, *undequaque*, quite, 1680
Impunem, with no sort of punishment,
Nor, *et non illaudatum*, lacking praise,
Sed polluentem parricidio,
Imbrue his hands with butchery, *filiæ,*
Of chaste Virginia, to avoid a rape,
Ne raperetur ad stupra ; so to heart,
Tanti illi cordi fuit, did he take,
Suspicio, the mere fancy men might have,
Honoris amittendi, of fame's loss,
Ut potius voluerit filia 1690
Orbari, that he chose to lose his child,
Quam illa incederet, rather than she walk
The ways an, *inhonesta*, child disgraced,
Licet non sponte, though against her will.
Occidit—killed them, I reiterate—
In propria domo, in their own abode,
Ut adultera et parentes, that each wretch,
Conscii agnoscerent, might both see and say,
Nullum locum, there's no· place, *nullumque esse*
Asylum, nor yet refuge of escape, 1700

Impenetrabilem, shall serve as bar,
Honori læso, to the wounded one
In honour ; *neve ibi opprobria*
Continuarentur, killed them on the spot
Moreover, dreading lest within those walls
The opprobrium peradventure be prolonged,
Et domus quæ testis fuit turpium,
And that the domicile which witnessed crime,
Esset et pœnæ, might watch punishment :
Occidit, killed, I round you in the ears,   1710
Quia alio modo, since by other mode,
Non poterat ejus existimatio,
There was no possibility his fame,
Læsa, gashed griesly, *tam enormiter*,
Ducere cicatrices, might be healed :
Occidit ut exemplum præberet
Uxoribus, killed her so to lesson wives
Jura conjugii, that the marriage-oath,
Esse servanda, must be kept henceforth :
Occidit denique, killed her, in a word,   1720
Ut pro posse honestus viveret,
That he, please God, might creditably live,
Sin minus, but if fate willed otherwise,
Proprii honoris, of his outraged fame,
Offensi, by Mannaja, if you please,
Commiseranda victima caderet,
The pitiable victim he should fall !

Done ! I' the rough, i' the rough ! But done ! And, lo,
Landed and stranded lies my very own,
My miracle, my monster of defence—   1730
Leviathan into the nose whereof
I have put fish-hook, pierced his jaw with thorn,
And given him to my maidens for a play !
I' the rough,—to-morrow I review my piece,
Tame here and there undue floridity,—
It 's hard : you have to plead before these priests
And poke at them with Scripture, or you pass
For heathen and, what's worse, for ignorant
O' the quality o' the Court and what it likes
By way of illustration of the law :   1740
To-morrow stick in this, and throw out that,
And, having first ecclesiasticized,
Regularize the whole, next emphasize,

Then latinize and lastly Cicero-ize,
Giving my Fisc his finish.   There 's my speech—
And where 's my fry, and family and friends ?
Where 's that old Hyacinth I mean to hug
Till he cries out, ' *Jam satis !* Let me breathe ! '
Oh, what an evening have I earned to-day !
Hail, ye true pleasures, all the rest are false !   1750
Oh, the old mother, oh, the fattish wife !
Rogue Hyacinth shall put on paper toque,
And wrap himself around with mamma's veil
Done up to imitate papa's black robe,
(I 'm in the secret of the comedy,—
Part of the program leaked out long ago !)
And call himself the Advocate o' the Poor,
Mimic Don father that defends the Count,
And for reward shall have a small full glass
Of manly red rosolio to himself,   1760
—Always provided that he conjugate
Bibo, I drink, correctly—nor be found
Make the *perfectum, bipsi*, as last year !
How the ambitious do so harden heart
As lightly hold by these home-sanctitudes,
To me is matter of bewilderment—
Bewilderment !   Because ambition's range
Is nowise tethered by domestic tie :
Am I refused an outlet from my home
To the world's stage ?—whereon a man should play
The man in public, vigilant for law,   1771
Zealous for truth, a credit to his kind,
Nay,—through the talent so employed as yield
The Lord his own again with usury,—
A satisfaction, yea, to God Himself !
Well, I have modelled me by Agur's wish,
' Remove far from me vanity and lies,
' Feed me with food convenient for me ! '   What
I' the world should a wise man require beyond ?
Can I but coax the good fat little wife   1780
To tell her fool of a father of the prank
His scapegrace nephew played this time last year
At Carnival,—he could not choose, I think,
But modify that inconsiderate gift
O' the cup and cover (somewhere in the will
Under the pillow, someone seems to guess)
—Correct that clause in favour of a boy

The trifle ought to grace with name engraved
(Would look so well produced in years to come
To pledge a memory when poor papa   1790
Latin and law are long since laid at rest)
Hyacintho dono dedit avus,—why,
The wife should get a necklace for her pains,
The very pearls that made Violante proud,
And Pietro pawned for half their value once,—
Redeemable by somebody—*ne sit*
Marita quæ rotundioribus
Onusta mammis . . . baccis ambulet,
Her bosom shall display the big round balls,
No braver should be borne by wedded wife !   1800
With which Horatian promise I conclude.
Into the pigeon-hole with thee, my speech !
Off and away, first work then play, play, play !
Bottini, burn your books, you blazing ass !
Sing ' Tra-la-la, for, lambkins, we must live ! '

JURIS DOCTOR JOHANNES-
BAPTISTA BOTTINIUS,

FISCI ET REV. CAM. APOSTOL. ADVOCATUS

HAD I God's leave, how I would alter things !
If I might read instead of print my speech,—
Ay, and enliven speech with many a flower
Refuses obstinately blow in print
As wildings planted in a prim parterre,—
This scurvy room were turned an immense hall ;
Opposite, fifty judges in a row ;
This side and that of me, for audience—Rome :
And, where yon window is, the Pope should be—
Watch, curtained, but yet visibly enough.   10
A buzz of expectation !   Through the crowd,
Jingling his chain and stumping with his staff,
Up comes an usher, louts him low, ' The Court
' Requires the allocution of the Fisc ! '
I rise, I bend, I look about me, pause
O'er the hushed multitude : I count—One, two—

Have ye seen, Judges, have ye, lights of law,—
When it may hap some painter, much in vogue
Throughout our city nutritive of arts,
Ye summon to a task shall test his worth,   20
And manufacture, as he knows and can,
A work may decorate a palace-wall,
Afford my lords their Holy Family,—
Hath it escaped the acumen of the Court
How such a painter sets himself to paint ?
Suppose that Joseph, Mary and her Babe
A-journeying to Egypt prove the piece :
Why, first he sedulously practiseth,
This painter,—girding loin and lighting lamp,—

Romana Homicidij cùm qualitate.

Ill.^{me} & Reu.^{me} Dñe. Quoniam (vt auditum_ fuit) præcipua defensio Domini Franceschini inquisiti consistit in prætensa Causa honoris, ob quam motus fuerit ad delinquendum Fisci propterea partes sunt huius insubsistentiam ostendere , vt debita pœna plectatur adeo atrox, & enorme delictum . .

Examinanda itaque assumo fundamenta, quibus asserta honoris Causa inniti potest, fugam scilicet infelicis Vxoris à Domo Viri, vna cum Canonico Caponsacco , cum quo in Hospitio Castri Noui capta fuit, & prætensas litteras amatorias in Processu super dicta fuga,& deuiatione insertas ex quibus prætensa Vxoris inhonestas desumitur cum alia cumulata in dicto processu , sint omninò læuia, vel æquiuoca, vel non probata , vt etiam colligi potest ex dimissione Francisca Vxoris cum sola cautione de habendo Domum pro Carcere , & D. Canonici cum triennali relegatione in Ciuitate Vetula , quæ vtique ostendit nullam fuisse à Fisco in eodem Processu acquisitam legitimam probationem inhonestatis , & prætensæ violationis fidei coniugalis , de qua fuerat per inquisitum delata .

Et quidem ex defensionibus tunc factis , immò ex ipso Processu luculenter apparuit iustissima causa , ob quam infelix Puella mota fuit ad arripiendam fugam , à Domo Viri , vt ad proprios lares remearet, & apud Parentes quietam, & tutam vitam traduceret. Notoriæ quippe sunt altercationes statim exortæ ob rei familiaris angustiam inter dictos miserrimæ Puellæ Parentes, & Inquisitum, eiusque matrem, & fratres ijsdem frustra lugentibus se fuisse deceptos sub specie non infimæ opulentiæ ob suppositum_ annuum redditum scut. 1700. qui prorsus insubsistens detectus fuit adeout dum moram in Domo Sponsi inquisiti traxerunt in Ciuitate Aretij adeò malè ab ipso eiusque Consanguineis habiti fuerint , vt post paucos menses ab eadem recedere , ac ad Vrbem redire coacti sint totoque tempore , quo conuixerunt continuè inter ipsos viguerint contentiones , & quærimoniæ , ob iustum dolorem deceptionis, quam passi fuerant excitatæ , vt constat ex Epistolis Abbatis Pauli Franceschini eas præsupponentibus ad defensam ponderatis per D. Procuratorem Charitatis , & indicantibus malum animum, vsque tunc aduersus infelices Parentes conceptum , & signanter in illa scripta 6. Martij ibi : *Torno à scriuere à V.S. che non voglio imitarlo nel modo di scriuere non essendo da par suo seminare certe parole nelle lettere, che meriterebbero risposte di fatti, è non di parole , e queste sono offensiue à segno , che le conseruo per suo rimprouero, e mortificatione: & intra ibi: che se lei ci darà de guai(che non credo mai) non ne resterebbe esente ne pur lei:* sufficiens autem ex Epistolis resultat probatio , vt monent *Gabriel tit. de confess. con-cluf. 1.*

A

On what may nourish eye, make facile hand ;   30
Getteth him studies (styled by draughtsmen so)
From some assistant corpse of Jew or Turk
Or, haply, Molinist, he cuts and carves,—
This Luca or this Carlo or the like :
To him the bones their inmost secret yield,
Each notch and nodule signify their use,
On him the muscles turn, in triple tier,
And pleasantly entreat the entrusted man,—
' Familiarize thee with our play that lifts
' Thus, and thus lowers again, leg, arm and foot ! '
—Ensuring due correctness in the nude.   41
Which done, is all done ?   Not a whit, ye know !
He,—to art's surface rising from her depth,—
If some flax-polled soft-bearded sire be found,
May simulate a Joseph, (happy chance !)
Limneth exact each wrinkle of the brow,
Loseth no involution, cheek or chap,
Till lo, in black and white, the senior lives !
Is it a young and comely peasant-nurse
That poseth ? (be the phrase accorded me !)   50
Each feminine delight of florid lip,
Eyes brimming o'er and brow bowed down with love,
Marmoreal neck and bosom uberous,—
Glad on the paper in a trice they go
To help his notion of the Mother-Maid :
Methinks I see it, chalk a little stumped !
Yea and her babe—that flexure of soft limbs,
That budding face imbued with dewy sleep,
Contribute each an excellence to Christ.
Nay, since he humbly lent companionship,   60
Even the poor ass, unpanniered and elate
Stands, perks an ear up, he a model too ;
While clouted shoon, staff, scrip and water-gourd,—
Aught may betoken travel, heat and haste,—
No jot nor tittle of these but in its turn
Ministers to perfection of the piece :
Till now, such piece before him, part by part,—
Such prelude ended,—pause our painter may,
Submit his fifty studies one by one,   69
And in some sort boast ' I have served my lords.'

But what ?   And hath he painted once this while ?
Or when ye cry ' Produce the thing required,

' Show us our picture shall rejoice its niche,
' Thy Journey through the Desert done in oils ! '—
What, doth he fall to shuffling 'mid his sheets,
Fumbling for first this, then the other fact
Consigned to paper,—' studies,' bear the term !—
And stretch a canvas, mix a pot of paste,
And fasten here a head and there a tail,
(The ass hath one, my Judges !) so dove-tail   80
Or, rather, ass-tail in, piece sorrily out—
By bits of reproduction of the life—
The picture, the expected Family ?
I trow not ! do I miss with my conceit
The mark, my lords ?—not so my lords were served !
Rather your artist turns abrupt from these,
And preferably buries him and broods
(Quite away from aught vulgar and extern)
On the inner spectrum, filtered through the eye,
His brain-deposit, bred of many a drop,   90
E pluribus unum : and the wiser he !
For in that brain,—their fancy sees at work,
Could my lords peep indulged,—results alone,
Not processes which nourish the result,
Would they discover and appreciate,—life
Fed by digestion, not raw food itself,
No gobbets but smooth comfortable chyme
Secreted from each snapped-up crudity,—
Less distinct, part by part, but in the whole
Truer to the subject,—the main central truth   100
And soul o' the picture, would my Judges spy,—
Not those mere fragmentary studied facts
Which answer to the outward frame and flesh—
Not this nose, not that eyebrow, the other fact
Of man's staff, woman's stole or infant's clout,
But lo, a spirit-birth conceived of flesh,
Truth rare and real, not transcripts, fact and false.
The studies—for his pupils and himself !
The picture be for our eximious Rome
And—who knows ?—satisfy its Governor,   110
Whose new wing to the villa he hath bought
(God give him joy of it) by Capena, soon
('T is bruited) shall be glowing with the brush
Of who hath long surpassed the Florentine,
The Urbinate and . . . what if I dared add,
Even his master, yea the Cortonese,—

I mean the accomplished Ciro Ferri, Sirs !
(—Did not he die ?   I'll see before I print.)

End we exordium, Phœbus plucks my ear !
Thus then, just so and no whit otherwise,   120
Have I,—engaged as I were Ciro's self,
To paint a parallel, a Family,
The patriarch Pietro with his wise old wife
To boot (as if one introduced Saint Anne
By bold conjecture to complete the group)
And juvenile Pompilia with her babe,
Who, seeking safety in the wilderness,
Were all surprised by Herod, while outstretched
In sleep beneath a palm-tree by a spring,
And killed,—the very circumstance I paint,   130
Moving the pity and terror of my lords—
Exactly so have I, a month at least,
Your Fiscal, made me cognizant of facts,
Searched out, pried into, pressed the meaning forth
Of every piece of evidence in point,
How bloody Herod slew these innocents,—
Until the glad result is gained, the group
Demonstrably presented in detail,
Their slumber and his onslaught,—like as life.
Yea and, availing me of help allowed   140
By law, discreet provision lest my lords
Be too much troubled by effrontery,—
The rack, law plies suspected crime withal—
(Law that hath listened while the lyrist sang
' Lene tormentum ingenio admoves,'
Gently thou joggest by a twinge the wit,
' Plerumque duro,' else were slow to blab !)
Through this concession my full cup runs o'er :
The guilty owns his guilt without reserve.
Therefore by part and part I clutch my case   150
Which, in entirety now,—momentous task,—
My lords demand, so render them I must,
Since, one poor pleading more and I have done.
But shall I ply my papers, play my proofs,
Parade my studies, fifty in a row,
As though the Court were yet in pupilage
And not the artist's ultimate appeal ?
Much rather let me soar the height prescribed
And, bowing low, proffer my picture's self !

No more of proof, disproof,—such virtue was,   160
Such vice was never in Pompilia, now !
Far better say ' Behold Pompilia ! '—(for
I leave the family as unmanageable,
And stick to just one portrait, but life-size.)
Hath calumny imputed to the fair
A blemish, mole on cheek or wart on chin,
Much more, blind hidden horrors best unnamed ?
Shall I descend to prove you, point by point,
Never was knock-knee known nor splay-foot found
In Phryne ? (I must let the portrait go,   170
Content me with the model, I believe)—
—I prove this ? An indignant sweep of hand,
Dash at and doing away with drapery,
And,—use your eyes, Athenians, smooth she smiles !
Or,—since my client can no longer smile,
And more appropriate instances abound,—
What is this Tale of Tarquin, how the slave
Was caught by him, preferred to Collatine ?
Thou, even from thy corpse-clothes virginal,
Look'st the lie dead, Lucretia !   180
                Thus at least
I, by the guidance of antiquity,
(Our one infallible guide) now operate,
Sure that the innocency shown is safe ;
Sure, too, that, while I plead, the echoes cry
(Lend my weak voice thy trump, sonorous Fame !)
' Monstrosity the Phrynean shape shall mar,
' Lucretia's soul comport with Tarquin's lie,
' When thistles grow on vines or thorns yield figs,
' Or oblique sentence leave this judgment-seat ! ' 190

A great theme : may my strength be adequate !
For—paint Pompilia, dares my feebleness ?
How did I unaware engage so much
—Find myself undertaking to produce
A faultless nature in a flawless form ?
What 's here ? Oh, turn aside nor dare the blaze
Of such a crown, such constellation, say,
As jewels here thy front, Humanity !
First, infancy, pellucid as a pearl ;
Then, childhood—stone which, dew-drop at the first,
(An old conjecture) sucks, by dint of gaze,   201
Blue from the sky and turns to sapphire so :

Yet both these gems eclipsed by, last and best,
Womanliness and wifehood opaline,
Its milk-white pallor,—chastity,—suffused
With here and there a tint and hint of flame,—
Desire,—the lapidary loves to find.
Such jewels bind conspicuously thy brow,
Pompilia, infant, child, maid, woman, wife—
Crown the ideal in our earth at last !   210
What should a faculty like mine do here ?
Close eyes, or else, the rashlier hurry hand !

Which is to say,—lose no time but begin !
Sermocinando ne declamem, Sirs,
Ultra clepsydram, as our preachers say,
Lest I exceed my hour-glass.   Whereupon,
As Flaccus prompts, I dare the epic plunge—
Begin at once with marriage, up till when
Little or nothing would arrest your love,
In the easeful life o' the lady ; lamb and lamb,   220
How do they differ ?   Know one, you know all
Manners of maidenhood : mere maiden she.
And since all lambs are like in more than fleece,
Prepare to find that, lamb-like, she too frisks—
O' the weaker sex, my lords, the weaker sex !
To whom, the Teian teaches us, for gift,
Not   strength,—man's   dower,—but   beauty,   nature
        gave,
' Beauty in lieu of spears, in lieu of shields ! '
And what is beauty's sure concomitant,
Nay, intimate essential character,   230
But melting wiles, deliciousest deceits,
The whole redoubted armoury of love ?
Therefore of vernal pranks, dishevellings
O' the hair of youth that dances April in,
And easily-imagined Hebe-slips
O'er sward which May makes over-smooth for foot—
These shall we pry into ?—or wiselier wink,
Though numerous and dear they may have been ?

For lo, advancing Hymen and his pomp !
Discedunt nunc amores, loves, farewell !   240
Maneat amor, let love, the sole, remain !
Farewell to dewiness and prime of life !
Remains the rough determined day : dance done,

To work, with plough and harrow! What comes
    next ?
'Tis Guido henceforth guides Pompilia's step,
Cries ' No more friskings o'er the foodful glebe,
' Else, 'ware the whip ! ' Accordingly,—first crack
O' the thong,—we hear that his young wife was barred,
Cohibita fuit, from the old free life,
Vitam liberiorem ducere.   250
Demur we ? Nowise : heifer brave the hind ?
We seek not there should lapse the natural law,
The proper piety to lord and king
And husband : let the heifer bear the yoke !
Only, I crave he cast not patience off,
This hind ; for deem you she endures the whip,
Nor winces at the goad, nay, restive, kicks ?
What if the adversary's charge be just,
And all untowardly she pursue her way
With groan and grunt, though hind strike ne'er so
    hard ?   260
If petulant remonstrance made appeal,
Unseasonable, o'erprotracted,—if
Importunate challenge taxed the public ear
When silence more decorously had served
For protestation,—if Pompilian plaint
Wrought but to aggravate Guidonian ire,—
Why, such mishaps, ungainly though they be,
Ever companion change, are incident
To altered modes and novelty of life :
The philosophic mind expects no less,   270
Smilingly knows and names the crisis, sits
Waiting till old things go and new arrive.
Therefore, I hold a husband but inept
Who turns impatient at such transit-time,
As if this running from the rod would last !

Since, even while I speak, the end is reached
Success awaits the soon-disheartened man,
The parents turn their backs and leave the house,
The wife may wail but none shall intervene,
He hath attained his object, groom and bride   280
Partake the nuptial bower no soul to see,
Old things are passed and all again is new,
Over and gone the obstacles to peace,
Novorum—tenderly the Mantuan turns

The expression, some such purpose in his eye—
Nascitur ordo ! Every storm is laid,
And forth from plain each pleasant herb may peep,
Each bloom of wifehood in abeyance late :
(Confer a passage in the Canticles.)

But what if, as 't is wont with plant and wife,   290
Flowers,—after a suppression to good end,
Still, when they do spring forth,—sprout here, spread
    there,
Anywhere likelier than beneath the foot
O' the lawful good-man gardener of the ground ?
He dug and dibbled, sowed and watered,—still
'T is a chance wayfarer shall pluck the increase.
Just so, respecting persons not too much,
The lady, foes allege, put forth each charm
And proper floweret of feminity
To whosoever had a nose to smell   300
Or breast to deck : what if the charge be true ?
The fault were graver had she looked with choice,
Fastidiously appointed who should grasp,
Who, in the whole town, go without the prize !
To nobody she destined donative,
But, first come was first served, the accuser saith :
Put case her sort of . . in this kind . . escapes
Were many and oft and indiscriminate—
Impute ye as the action were prepense,
The gift particular, arguing malice so ?   310
Which butterfly of the wide air shall brag
' I was preferred to Guido '—when 't is clear
The cup, he quaffs at, lay with olent breast
Open to gnat, midge, bee and moth as well ?
One chalice entertained the company ;
And if its peevish lord object the more,
Mistake, misname such bounty in a wife,
Haste we to advertise him—charm of cheek,
Lustre of eye, allowance of the lip,
All womanly components in a spouse,   320
These are no household-bread each stranger's bite
Leaves by so much diminished for the mouth
O' the master of the house at supper-time :
But rather like a lump of spice they lie,
Morsel of myrrh, which scents the neighbourhood
Yet greets its lord no lighter by a grain.

Nay, even so, he shall be satisfied !
Concede we there was reason in his wrong,
Grant we his grievance and content the man !
For lo, Pompilia, she submits herself ;   330
Ere three revolving years have crowned their course,
Off and away she puts this same reproach
Of lavish bounty, inconsiderate gift
O' the sweets of wifehood stored to other ends :
No longer shall he blame ' She none excludes,'
But substitute ' She laudably sees all,
' Searches the best out and selects the same.'
For who is here, long sought and latest found,
Waiting his turn unmoved amid the whirl,
' *Constans in levitate*,'—Ha, my lords ?   340
Calm in his levity,—indulge the quip !—
Since 't is a levite bears the bell away,
Parades him henceforth as Pompilia's choice.
'T is no ignoble object, husband !   Doubt'st ?
When here comes tripping Flaccus with his phrase
' Trust me, no miscreant singled from the mob,
' *Crede non illum tibi de scelesta*
' *Plebe delectum*,' but a man of mark,
A priest, dost hear ?   Why then, submit thyself !
Priest, ay and very phœnix of such fowl,   350
Well-born, of culture, young and vigorous,
Comely too, since precise the precept points—
On the selected levite be there found
Nor mole nor scar nor blemish, lest the mind
Come all uncandid through the thwarting flesh !
Was not the son of Jesse ruddy, sleek,
Pleasant to look on, pleasant every way ?
Since well he smote the harp and sweetly sang,
And danced till Abigail came out to see,
And seeing smiled and smiling ministered   360
The raisin-cluster and the cake of figs,
With ready meal refreshed the gifted youth,
Till Nabal, who was absent shearing sheep,
Felt heart sink, took to bed (discreetly done—
They might have been beforehand with him else)
And died—would Guido had behaved as well !
But ah, the faith of early days is gone,
Heu prisca fides !   Nothing died in him
Save courtesy, good sense and proper trust,
Which, when they ebb from souls they should o'erflow,

Discover stub, weed, sludge and ugliness.   371
(The Pope, you know, is Neapolitan
And relishes a sea-side simile.)
Deserted by each charitable wave,
Guido, left high and dry, shows jealous now !
Jealous avouched, paraded : tax the fool
With any peccadillo, he responds
' Truly I beat my wife through jealousy,
' Imprisoned her and punished otherwise,
' Being jealous : now would threaten, sword in hand,
' Now manage to mix poison in her sight,   381
' And so forth : jealously I dealt, in fine.'
Concede the fact and what remains to prove ?
Have I to teach my masters what effect
Hath jealousy and how, befooling men,
It makes false true, abuses eye and ear,
Turns the mist adamantine, loads with sound
Silence, and into void and vacancy
Crowds a whole phalanx of conspiring foes ?
Therefore who owns ' I watched with jealousy   390
' My wife ' adds ' for no reason in the world ! '
What need that who says ' madman ' should remark
' The thing he thought a serpent proved an eel ? '—
Perchance the right Comacchian, six foot length,
And not an inch too long for that same pie
(Master Arcangeli has heard of such)
Whose succulence makes fasting bearable ;
Meant to regale some moody splenetic
Who pleases to mistake the donor's gift,
And spies—I know not what Lernæan snake   400
I' the luscious Lenten creature, stamps forsooth
The dainty in the dust.

                              Enough !   Prepare,
His lunes announced, for downright lunacy !
Insanit homo, threat succeeds to threat,
And blow redoubles blow,—his wife, the block.
But, if a block, shall not she jar the hand
That buffets her ?   The injurious idle stone
Rebounds and fits the head of him who flung.
Causeless rage breeds, i' the wife now, rageful cause,
Tyranny wakes rebellion from its sleep.   411
Rebellion, say I ?—rather, self-defence,
Laudable wish to live and see good days,

Pricks our Pompilia on to fly the foe
By any means, at any price,—nay, more,
Nay, most of all, i' the very interest
Of the foe that, baffled of his blind desire
At any price, is truliest victor so.
Shall he effect his crime and lose his soul ?
No, dictates duty to a loving wife.   420
Far better that the unconsummate blow,
Adroitly baulked by her, should back again,
Correctively admonish his own pate !

Crime then,—the Court is with me ?—she must crush ;
How crush it ?   By all efficacious means ;
And these,—why, what in woman should they be ?
' With horns the bull, with teeth the lion fights,
' To woman,' quoth the lyrist quoted late,
' Nor teeth, nor horns, but beauty, Nature gave ! '
Pretty i' the Pagan !   Who dares blame the use
Of the armoury thus allowed for natural,—   431
Exclaim against a seeming-dubious play
O' the sole permitted weapon, spear and shield
Alike, resorted to i' the circumstance
By poor Pompilia ?   Grant she somewhat plied
Arts that allure, the magic nod and wink,
The witchery of gesture, spell of word,
Whereby the likelier to enlist this friend,
Yet stranger, as a champion on her side ?   439
Such, being but mere man, ('t was all she knew),
Must be made sure by beauty's silken bond,
The weakness that subdues the strong, and bows
Wisdom alike and folly.   Grant the tale
O' the husband, which is false, for proved and true
To the letter,—or the letters, I should say,
The abominations he professed to find
And fix upon Pompilia and the priest,—
Allow them hers—for though she could not write,
In early days of Eve-like innocence   449
That plucked no apple from the knowledge-tree,
Yet, at the Serpent's word, Eve plucks and eats
And knows—especially how to read and write :
And so Pompilia,—as the move o' the maw,
Quoth Persius, makes a parrot bid ' Good-day ! '
A crow salute the concave, and a pie
Endeavour at proficiency in speech,—

So she, through hunger after fellowship,
May well have learned, though late, to play the scribe :
As indeed, there 's one letter on the list
Explicitly declares did happen here.   460
' You thought my letters could be none of mine,'
She tells her parents—' mine, who wanted skill ;
' But now I have the skill, and write, you see ! '
She needed write love-letters, so she learned,
' *Negatas artifex sequi voces* '—though
This letter nowise 'scapes the common lot,
But lies i' the condemnation of the rest,
Found by the husband's self who forged them all.
Yet, for the sacredness of argument,
For this once an exemption shall it plead—   470
Anything, anything to let the wheels
Of argument run glibly to their goal !
Concede she wrote (which were preposterous)
This and the other epistle,—what of it ?
Where does the figment touch her candid fame ?
Being in peril of her life—' my life,
' Not an hour's purchase,' as the letter runs,—
And having but one stay in this extreme,
And out of the wide world a single friend—
What could she other than resort to him,   480
And how with any hope resort but thus ?
Shall modesty dare bid a stranger brave
Danger, disgrace, nay death in her behalf—
Think to entice the sternness of the steel
Save by the magnet moves the manly mind ?
—Most of all when such mind is hampered so
By growth of circumstance athwart the life
O' the natural man, that decency forbids
He stoop and take the common privilege,
Say frank ' I love,' as all the vulgar do.   490
A man is wedded to philosophy,
Married to statesmanship ; a man is old ;
A man is fettered by the foolishness
He took for wisdom and talked ten years since ;
A man is, like our friend the Canon here,
A priest, and wicked if he break his vow :
He dare to love, who may be Pope one day ?
Suppose this man could love, though, all the same—
From what embarrassment she sets him free   499
Should one, a woman he could love, speak first—

' 'T is I who break reserve, begin appeal,
' Confess that, whether you love me or no,
' I love you ! '   What an ease to dignity,
What help of pride from the hard high-backed chair
Down to the carpet where the kittens bask,
All under the pretence of gratitude !

From all which, I deduce—the lady here
Was bound to proffer nothing short of love
To the priest whose service was to save her.   What ?
Shall she propose him lucre, dust o' the mine,   510
Rubbish o' the rock, some diamond, muckworms prize,
Or pearl secreted by a sickly fish ?
Scarcely !   She caters for a generous taste.
'T is love shall beckon, beauty bid to breast,
Till all the Samson sink into the snare !
Because, permit the end—permit therewith
Means to the end !
                          How say you, good my lords ?
I hope you heard my adversary ring
The changes on this precept : now, let me   520
Reverse the peal !   *Quia dato licito fine,*
Ad illum assequendum ordinata
Non sunt damnanda media,—licit end
Enough was the escape from death, I hope,
To legalize the means illicit else
Of feigned love, false allurement, fancied fact.
Thus Venus losing Cupid on a day,
(See that *Idyllium Moschi*) seeking help,
In the anxiety of motherhood,
Allowably promised ' Who shall bring report   530
' Where he is wandered to, my winged babe,
' I give him for reward a nectared kiss ;
' But who brings safely back the truant's self,
' His be a super-sweet makes kiss seem cold ! '
Are not these things writ for example-sake ?

To such permitted motive, then, refer
All those professions, else were hard explain,
Of hope, fear, jealousy, and the rest of love !
He is Myrtillus, Amaryllis she,
She burns, he freezes,—all a mere device   540
To catch and keep the man may save her life,
Whom otherwise nor catches she nor keeps !

Worst, once, is best now : in all faith, she feigns :
Feigning,—the liker innocence to guilt,
The truer to the life is what she feigns !
How if Ulysses,—when, for public good
He sunk particular qualms and played the spy,
Entered Troy's hostile gate in beggar's garb—
How if he first had boggled at this clout,
Grown dainty o'er that clack-dish ?   Grime is grace
To whoso gropes amid the dung for gold.   551

Hence, beyond promises, we praise each proof
That promise was not simply made to break,—
No moonshine-structure meant to fade at dawn :
So call—(proofs consequent and requisite)—
What enemies allege of—more than words,
Deeds—meeting at the window, twilight-tryst,
Nocturnal entertainment in the dim
Old labyrinthine palace ; lies, we know—
Inventions we, long since, turned inside out.   560
Would such external semblance of intrigue
Demonstrate that intrigue must lurk perdue ?
Does every hazel-sheath disclose a nut ?
He were a Molinist who dared maintain
That midnight meetings in a screened alcove
Must argue folly in a matron—since
So would he bring a slur on Judith's self,
Commended beyond women that she lured
The lustful to destruction through his lust.
Pompilia took not Judith's liberty,   570
No faulchion find you in her hand to smite,—
No damsel to convey the head in dish,
Of Holophernes,—style the Canon so—
Or is it the Count ?   If I entangle me
With my similitudes,—if wax wings melt,
And earthward down I drop, not mine the fault :
Blame your beneficence, O Court, O sun,
Whereof the beamy smile affects my flight !
What matter, so Pompilia's fame revive
I' the warmth that proves the bane of Icarus ?   580

Yea, we have shown it lawful, necessary
Pompilia leave her husband, seek the house
O' the parents : and because 'twixt home and home
Lies a long road with many a danger rife,

Lions by the way and serpents in the path,
To rob and ravish,—much behoves she keep
Each shadow of suspicion from fair fame,
For her own sake much, but for his sake more,
The ingrate husband !   Evidence shall be,   589
Some witness to the world how white she walks
I' the mire she wanders through ere Rome she reach.
And who so proper witness as a priest ?
Gainsay ye ?   Let me hear who dares gainsay !
I hope we still can punish heretics !
' Give me the man ' I say with him of Gath,
' That we may fight together ! '   None, I think :
The priest is granted me.

                      Then, if a priest,
One juvenile and potent : else, mayhap,
That dragon, our Saint George would slay, slays him.
And should fair face accompany strong hand,   601
The more complete equipment : nothing mars
Work, else praiseworthy, like a bodily flaw
I' the worker : as 't is said Saint Paul himself
Deplored the check o' the puny presence, still
Cheating his fulmination of its flash,
Albeit the bolt therein went true to oak.
Therefore the agent, as prescribed, she takes,—
A priest, juvenile, potent, handsome too,—
In all obedience : ' good,' you grant again.   610
Do you ?   I would ye were the husband, lords !
How prompt and facile might departure be !
How boldly would Pompilia and the priest
March out of door, spread flag at beat of drum,
But that inapprehensive Guido grants
Neither premiss nor yet conclusion here,
And, purblind, dreads a bear in every bush !
For his own quietude and comfort, then,
Means must be found for flight in masquerade   619
At hour when all things sleep.—' Save jealousy ! '
Right, judges !   Therefore shall the lady's wit
Supply the boon thwart nature baulks him of,
And do him service with the potent drug
(Helen's nepenthe, as my lords opine)
Shall respite blessedly each frittered nerve
O' the much-enduring man : accordingly,
There lies he, duly dosed and sound asleep,

Relieved of woes, or real or raved about.
While soft she leaves his side, he shall not wake ;
Nor stop who steals away to join her friend,   630
Nor do him mischief should he catch that friend
Intent on more than friendly office,—nay,
Nor get himself raw head and bones laid bare
In payment of his apparition !
                         Thus
Would I defend the step,—were the thing true
Which is a fable,—see my former speech,—
That Guido slept (who never slept a wink)
Through treachery, an opiate from his wife,
Who not so much as knew what opiates mean.   640

Now she may start : but hist,—a stoppage still !
A journey is an enterprise which costs !
As in campaigns, we fight and others pay,
Suis expensis, nemo militat.
'T is Guido's self we guard from accident,
Ensuring safety to Pompilia, versed
Nowise in misadventures by the way,
Hard riding and rough quarters, the rude fare,
The unready host.   What magic mitigates
Each plague of travel to the unpractised wife ?   650
Money, sweet Sirs !   And were the fiction fact,
She helped herself thereto with liberal hand
From out the husband's store,—what fitter use
Was ever husband's money destined to ?
With bag and baggage thus did Dido once
Decamp,—for more authority, a queen !

So is she fairly on her route at last,
Prepared for either fortune : nay and if
The priest, now all a-glow with enterprise,
Cool somewhat presently when fades the flush   660
O' the first adventure, clouded o'er belike
By doubts, misgivings how the day may die,
Though born with such auroral brilliance,—if
The brow seem over-pensive and the lip
'Gin lag and lose the prattle lightsome late,—
Vanquished by tedium of a prolonged jaunt
In a close carriage o'er a jolting road,
With only one young female substitute
For seventeen other Canons of ripe age

Were wont to keep him company in church,— 670
Shall not Pompilia haste to dissipate
The silent cloud that, gathering, bodes her bale ?—
Prop the irresoluteness may portend
Suspension of the project, check the flight,
Bring ruin on them both ?—use every means,
Since means to the end are lawful ?   What i' the way
Of wile should have allowance like a kiss
Sagely and sisterly administered,
Sororia saltem oscula ?   We find
Such was the remedy her wit applied 680
To each incipient scruple of the priest,
If we believe,—as, while my wit is mine
I cannot,—what the driver testifies,
Borsi, called Venerino, the mere tool
Of Guido and his friend the Governor,—
The avowal I proved wrung from out the wretch,
After long rotting in imprisonment,
As price of liberty and favour : long
They tempted, he at last succumbed, and lo
Counted them out full tale each kiss required,— 690
' The journey was one long embrace,' quoth he.
Still, though we should believe the driver's lie,
Nor even admit as probable excuse,
Right reading of the riddle,—as I urged
In my first argument, with fruit perhaps—
That what the owl-like eyes (at back of head !)
O' the driver, drowsed by driving night and day,
Supposed a vulgar interchange of love,
This was but innocent jog of head 'gainst head,
Cheek meeting jowl as apple may touch pear 700
From branch and branch contiguous in the wind,
When Autumn blusters and the orchard rocks.
The rapid run and the rough road were cause
O' the casual ambiguity, no harm
I' the world to eyes awake and penetrative.
Yet,—not to grasp a truth I can forego
And safely fight without and conquer still,—
Say, she kissed him, and he kissed her again !
Such osculation was a potent means,
A very efficacious help, no doubt : 710
This with a third part of her nectar did
Venus imbue : why should Pompilia fling
The poet's declaration in his teeth ?—

Pause to employ what,—since it had success,
And kept the priest her servant to the end,—
We must presume of energy enough,
No whit superfluous, so permissible ?

The goal is gained : day, night and yet a day
Have run their round : a long and devious road
Is traversed,—many manners, various men   720
Passed in review, what cities did they see,
What hamlets mark, what profitable food
For after-meditation cull and store !
Till Rome, that Rome whereof—this voice,
Would it might make our Molinists observe,
That she is built upon a rock nor shall
Their powers prevail against her !—Rome, I say,
Is all but reached ; one stage more and they stop
Saved : pluck up heart, ye pair, and forward, then !

Ah, Nature—baffled she recurs, alas !   730
Nature imperiously exacts her due,
Spirit is willing but the flesh is weak,
Pompilia needs must acquiesce and swoon,
Give hopes alike and fears a breathing-while.
The innocent sleep soundly : sound she sleeps.
So let her slumber, then, unguarded save
By her own chastity, a triple mail,
And his good hand whose stalwart arms have borne
The sweet and senseless burthen like a babe
From coach to couch,—the serviceable man !   740
Nay, what and if he gazed rewardedly
On the pale beauty prisoned in embrace,
Stooped over, stole a balmy breath perhaps
For more assurance sleep was not decease—
‘ Ut vidi,’ ‘ how I saw ! ’ succeeded by
‘ Ut perii,’ ‘ how I sudden lost my brains ! ’
—What harm ensued to her unconscious quite ?
For, curiosity—how natural !
Importunateness—what a privilege   749
In the ardent sex !   And why curb ardour here ?
How can the priest but pity whom he saved ?
And pity is how near to love, and love
How neighbourly to unreasonableness !
And for love’s object, whether love were sage
Or foolish, could Pompilia know or care,

Being still sound asleep, as I premised ?
Thus the philosopher absorbed by thought,
Even Archimedes, busy o'er a book
The while besiegers sacked his Syracuse,
Was ignorant of the imminence o' the point   760
O' the sword till it surprised him : let it stab,
And never knew himself was dead at all.
So sleep thou on, secure whate'er betide !
For thou, too, hast thy problem hard to solve—
How so much beauty is compatible
With so much innocence !

                    Fit place, methinks,
While in this task she rosily is lost,
To treat of and repel objection here
Which,—frivolous, I grant,—but, still misgives   770
My mind, it may have flitted, gadfly-like,
And teazed the Court at times—as if, all said
And done, there still seemed, one might nearly say,
In a certain acceptation, somewhat more
Of what may pass for insincerity,
Falsehood, throughout the course Pompilia took,
Than befits Christian.   Pagans held, we know,
We always ought to aim at good and truth,
Not always put one thing in the same words :
Non idem semper dicere sed spectare   780
Debemus.   But the Pagan yoke was light ;
' Lie not at all,' the exacter precept bids :
Each least lie breaks the law,—is sin, ye hold.
I humble me, but venture to submit—
What prevents sin, itself is sinless, sure :
And sin, which hinders sin of deeper dye,
Softens itself away by contrast so.
Conceive me !   Little sin, by none at all,
Were properly condemned for great : but great,
By greater, dwindles into small again.   790
Now, what is greatest sin of womanhood ?
That which unwomans it, abolishes
The nature of the woman,—impudence.
Who contradicts me here ?   Concede me, then,
Whatever friendly fault may interpose
To save the sex from self-abolishment
Is three-parts on the way to virtue's rank !
Now, what is taxed here as duplicity,

Feint, wile and trick,—admitted for the nonce,—
What worse do one and all than interpose,   800
Hold, as it were, a deprecating hand,
Statuesquely, in the Medicean mode,
Before some shame which modesty would veil ?
Who blames the gesture prettily perverse ?
Thus,—lest ye miss a point illustrative,—
Admit the husband's calumny—allow
That the wife, having penned the epistle fraught
With horrors, charge on charge of crime, she heaped
O' the head of Pietro and Violante—(still
Presumed her parents)—and despatched the thing
To their arch-enemy Paolo, through free choice   811
And no sort of compulsion in the world—
Put case that she discards simplicity
For craft, denies the voluntary act,
Declares herself a passive instrument
I' the hands of Guido ; duped by knavery,
She traced the characters, she could not write,
And took on trust the unread sense which, read,
Were recognized but to be spurned at once.
Allow this calumny, I reiterate !   820
Who is so dull as wonder at the pose
Of our Pompilia in the circumstance ?
Who sees not that the too-ingenuous soul,
Repugnant even at a duty done
Which brought beneath too scrutinizing glare
The misdemeanours,—buried in the dark,—
Of the authors of her being, she believed,—
Stung to the quick at her impulsive deed,
And willing to repair what harm it worked,
She—wise in this beyond what Nero proved,   830
Who, when needs were the candid juvenile
Should sign the warrant, doom the guilty dead,
' Would I had never learned to write,' quoth he !
—Pompilia rose above the Roman, cried
' To read or write I never learned at all ! '
O splendidly mendacious !

                            But time fleets :
Let us not linger : hurry to the end,
Since end does flight and all disastrously.
Beware ye blame desert for unsuccess,   840
Disparage each expedient else to praise,

Call failure folly !   Man's best effort fails.
After ten years' resistance Troy fell flat :
Could valour save a town, Troy still had stood.
Pompilia came off halting in no point
Of courage, conduct, the long journey through :
But nature sank exhausted at the close,
And, as I said, she swooned and slept all night.
Morn breaks and brings the husband : we assist
At the spectacle.   Discovery succeeds.   850
Ha, how is this ?   What moonstruck rage is here ?
Though we confess to partial frailty now,
To error in a woman and a wife,
Is 't by the rough way she shall be reclaimed ?
Who bursts upon her chambered privacy ?
What crowd profanes the chaste *cubiculum ?*
What outcries and lewd laughter, scurril gibe
And ribald jest to scare the ministrant
Good angels that commerce with souls in sleep ?
Why, had the worst crowned Guido to his wish,   860
Confirmed his most irrational surmise,
Yet there be bounds to man's emotion, checks
To an immoderate astonishment.
'T is decent horror, regulated wrath,
Befit our dispensation : have we back
The old Pagan licence ?   Shall a Vulcan clap
His net o' the sudden and expose the pair
To the unquenchable universal mirth ?
A feat, antiquity saw scandal in
So clearly, that the nauseous tale thereof—   870
Demodocus his nugatory song—
Hath ever been concluded modern stuff
Impossible to the mouth of the grave Muse,
So, foisted into that Eighth Odyssey
By some impertinent pickthank.   O thou fool,
Count Guido Franceschini, what were gained
By publishing thy shame thus to the world ?
Were all the precepts of the wise a waste—
Bred in thee not one touch of reverence ?
Why, say thy wife—admonish we the fool,—   880
Were false, and thou bid chronicle thy shame,
Much rather should thy teeth bite out thy tongue,
Dumb lip consort with desecrated brow,
Silence become historiographer,
And thou—thine own Cornelius Tacitus !

But virtue, barred, still leaps the barrier, lords !
—Still, moon-like, penetrates the encroaching mist
And bursts, all broad and bare, on night, ye know !
Surprised, then, in the garb of truth, perhaps,
Pompilia, thus opposed, breaks obstacle,   890
Springs to her feet, and stands Thalassian-pure,
Confronts the foe,—nay, catches at his sword
And tries to kill the intruder, he complains.
Why, so she gave her lord his lesson back,
Crowned him, this time, the virtuous woman's way,
With an exact obedience ; he brought sword,
She drew the same, since swords are meant to draw.
Tell not me 't is sharp play with tools on edge !
It was the husband chose the weapon here.
Why did not he inaugurate the game   900
With some gentility of apophthegm
Still pregnant on the philosophic page,
Some captivating cadence still a-lisp
O' the poet's lyre ?   Such spells subdue the surge,
Make tame the tempest, much more mitigate
The passions of the mind, and probably
Had moved Pompilia to a smiling blush.
No, he must needs prefer the argument
O' the blow : and she obeyed, in duty bound,
Returned him buffet ratiocinative—   910
Ay, in the reasoner's own interest,
For wife must follow whither husband leads,
Vindicate honour as himself prescribes,
Save him the very way himself bids save !
No question but who jumps into a quag
Should stretch forth hand and pray one ' Pull me out
' By the hand ! ' such were the customary cry :
But Guido pleased to bid ' Leave hand alone !
' Join both feet, rather, jump upon my head,
' I extricate myself by the rebound ! '   920
And dutifully as enjoined she jumped—
Drew his own sword and menaced his own life,
Anything to content a wilful spouse.

And so he was contented—one must do
Justice to the expedient which succeeds,
Strange as it seem : at flourish of the blade,
The crowd drew back, stood breathless and abashed,
Then murmured ' This should be no wanton wife,

' No conscience-stricken creature, caught i' the act,
' And patiently awaiting our first stone : 930
' But a poor hard-pressed all-bewildered thing,
' Has rushed so far, misguidedly perhaps,
' Meaning no more harm than a frightened sheep.
' She sought for aid ; and if she made mistake
' I' the man could aid most, why—so mortals do :
' Even the blessed Magdalen mistook
' Far less forgiveably : consult the place—
' Supposing him to be the gardener,
' " Sir," said she, and so following.' Why more words ?
Forthwith the wife is pronounced innocent : 940
What would the husband more than gain his cause,
And find that honour flash in the world's eye,
His apprehension was lest soil had smirched ?

So, happily the adventure comes to close
Whereon my fat opponent grounds his charge
Preposterous : at mid-day he groans ' How dark ! '
Listen to me, thou Archangelic swine !
Where is the ambiguity to blame,
The flaw to find in our Pompilia ? Safe 949
She stands, see ! Does thy comment follow quick
' Safe, inasmuch as at the end proposed ;
' But thither she picked way by devious path—
' Stands dirtied, no dubiety at all !
' I recognize success, yet, all the same,
' Importunately will suggestion prick—
' What, had Pompilia gained the right to boast
' " No devious path, no doubtful patch was mine,
' " I saved my head nor sacrificed my foot ? "
' Why, being in a peril, show mistrust
' Of the angels set to guard the innocent ? 960
' Why rather hold by obvious vulgar help
' Of stratagem and subterfuge, excused
' Somewhat, but still no less a foil, a fault,
' Since low with high, and good with bad is linked ?
' Methinks I view some ancient bas-relief.
' There stands Hesione thrust out by Troy,
' Her father's hand has chained her to a crag,
' Her mother's from the virgin plucked the vest,
' At a safe distance both distressful watch,
' While near and nearer comes the snorting orc. 970
' I look that, white and perfect to the end,

' She wait till Jove despatch some demigod ;
' Not that,—impatient of celestial club
' Alcmena's son should brandish at the beast,—
' She daub, disguise her dainty limbs with pitch,
' And so elude the purblind monster !   Ay,
' The trick succeeds, but 't is an ugly trick,
' Where needs have been no trick ! '

                My answer ?   Faugh !
Nimis incongrue !   Too absurdly put !   980
Sententiam ego teneo contrariam,
Trick, I maintain, had no alternative.
The heavens were bound with brass,—Jove far at
    feast
(No feast like that thou didst not ask me to,
Arcangeli,—I heard of thy regale !)
With the unblamed Æthiop,—Hercules spun wool
I' the lap of Omphale, while Virtue shrieked—
The brute came paddling all the faster.   You
Of Troy, who stood at distance, where 's the aid
You offered in the extremity ?   Most and least,   990
Gentle and simple, here the Governor,
There the Archbishop, everywhere the friends,
Shook heads and waited for a miracle,
Or went their way, left Virtue to her fate.
Just this one rough and ready man leapt forth !
—Was found, sole anti-Fabius (dare I say)
To restore things, with no delay at all,
Qui, haud cunctando, rem restituit !   He,
He only, Caponsacchi 'mid a crowd,
Caught Virtue up, carried Pompilia off   1000
Thro' the gaping impotence of sympathy
In ranged Arezzo :   what you take for pitch,
Is nothing worse, belike, than black and blue,
Mere evanescent proof that hardy hands
Did yeoman's service, cared not where the gripe
Was more than duly energetic :   bruised,
She smarts a little, but her bones are saved
A fracture, and her skin will soon show sleek.
How it disgusts when weakness, false-refined,
Censures the honest rude effective strength,— 1010
When sickly dreamers of the impossible
Decry plain sturdiness which does the feat
With eyes wide open !

                         Did occasion serve,
I could illustrate, if my lords allow ;
Quid vetat, what forbids, I aptly ask
With Horace, that I give my anger vent,
While I let breathe, no less, and recreate
The gravity of my Judges, by a tale—
A case in point—what though an apologue   1020
Graced by tradition,—possibly a fact ?
Tradition must precede all scripture, words
Serve as our warrant ere our books can be :
So, to tradition back we needs must go
For any fact's authority : and this
Hath lived so far (like jewel hid in muck)
O' the page of that old lying vanity
Called ' Sepher Toldoth Yeschu : ' God be praised,
I read no Hebrew,—take the thing on trust :
But I believe the writer meant no good   1030
(Blind as he was to truth in some respects)
To our pestiferous and schismatic . . well,
My lords' conjecture be the touchstone, show
The thing for what it is !   The author lacks
Discretion, and his zeal exceeds : but zeal,—
How rare in our degenerate day !   Enough !
Here is the story,—fear not, I shall chop
And change a little, else my Jew would press
All too unmannerly before the Court.

It happened once,—begins this foolish Jew,   1040
Pretending to write Christian history,—
That three, held greatest, best and worst of men,
Peter and John and Judas, spent a day
In toil and travel through the country-side
On some sufficient business—I suspect,
Suppression of some Molinism i' the bud.
Foot-sore and hungry, dropping with fatigue,
They reached by nightfall a poor lonely grange,
Hostel or inn : so, knocked and entered there.
' Your pleasure, great ones ? '—' Shelter, rest and
        food ! '   1050
For shelter, there was one bare room above ;
For rest therein, three beds of bundled straw :
For food, one wretched starveling fowl, no more—
Meat for one mouth, but mockery for three.
' You have my utmost.'   How should supper serve ?

Peter broke silence.   ' To the spit with fowl !
' And while 't is cooking, sleep !—since beds there be,
' And, so far, satisfaction of a want.
' Sleep we an hour, awake at supper-time,
' Then each of us narrate the dream he had,   1060
' And he whose dream shall prove the happiest, point
' The clearliest out the dreamer as ordained
' Beyond his fellows to receive the fowl,
' Him let our shares be cheerful tribute to,
' His the entire meal, may it do him good ! '
Who could dispute so plain a consequence ?
So said, so done : each hurried to his straw,
Slept his hour's-sleep and dreamed his dream, and
        woke.
' I,' commenced John, ' dreamed that I gained the
        prize
' We all aspire to : the proud place was mine,   1070
' Throughout the earth and to the end of time
' I was the Loved Disciple : mine the meal ! '
' But I,' proceeded Peter, ' dreamed, a word
' Gave me the headship of our company,
' Made me the Vicar and Vice-regent, gave
' The keys of Heaven and Hell into my hand,
' And o'er the earth, dominion : mine the meal ! '
' While I,' submitted in soft under-tone
The Iscariot—sense of his unworthiness
Turning each eye up to the inmost white—   1080
With long-drawn sigh, yet letting both lips smack,
' I have had just the pitifullest dream
' That ever proved man meanest of his mates,
' And born foot-washer and foot-wiper, nay
' Foot-kisser to each comrade of you all !
' I dreamed I dreamed : and in that mimic dream
' (Impalpable to dream as dream to fact)
' Methought I meanly chose to sleep no wink
' But wait until I heard my brethren breathe ;   1089
' Then stole from couch, slipped noiseless to the door,
' Slid downstairs, furtively approached the hearth,
' Found the fowl duly brown, both back and breast,
' Hissing in harmony with the cricket's chirp,
' Grilled to a point ; said no grace but fell to,
' Nor finished till the skeleton lay bare.
' In penitence for which ignoble dream,
' Lo, I renounce my portion cheerfully !

' Fie on the flesh—be mine the ethereal gust,
' And yours the sublunary sustenance !
' See, that whate'er be left, ye give the poor ! '   1100
Down the two scuttled, one on other's heel,
Stung by a fell surmise ; and found, alack,
A goodly savour, both the drumstick-bones,
And that which henceforth took the appropriate name
O' the merry-thought, in memory of the fact
That to keep wide awake is our best dream.

So,—as was said once of Thucydides
And his sole joke, ' The lion, lo, hath laughed ! '—
Just so, the Governor and all that 's great
I' the city, never meant that Innocence   1110
Should starve thus while Authority sat at meat.
They meant to fling a bone at banquet's end,
Wished well to our Pompilia—in their dreams,
Nor bore the secular sword in vain—asleep :
Just so the Archbishop and all good like him
Went to bed meaning to pour oil and wine
I' the wounds of her, next day,—but long ere day,
They had burned the one and drunk the other : while
Just so, again, contrariwise, the priest
Sustained poor Nature in extremity   1120
By stuffing barley-bread into her mouth,
Saving Pompilia (grant the parallel)
By the plain homely and straightforward way
Taught him by common-sense.   Let others shriek
' Oh what refined expedients did we dream
' Proved us the only fit to help the fair ! '
He cried ' A carriage waits, jump in with me ! '

And now, this application pardoned, lords,—
This recreative pause and breathing-while,—
Back to beseemingness and gravity !   1130
For Law steps in : Guido appeals to Law,
Demands she arbitrate,—does well for once.
O Law, of thee how neatly was it said
By that old Sophocles, thou hast thy seat
I' the very breast of Jove, no meanlier throned !
Here is a piece of work now, hitherto
Begun and carried on, concluded near,
Without an eye-glance cast thy sceptre's way ;
And, lo the stumbling and discomfiture !

Well may you call them ' lawless,' means men take
To extricate themselves through mother-wit   1141
When tangled haply in the toils of life !
Guido would try conclusions with his foe,
Whoe'er the foe was and whate'er the offence ;
He would recover certain dowry-dues :
Instead of asking Law to lend a hand,
What pother of sword drawn and pistol cocked,
What peddling with forged letters and paid spies,
Politic circumvention !—all to end
As it began—by loss of the fool's head,   1150
First in a figure, presently in a fact.
It is a lesson to mankind at large.
How other were the end, would men be sage
And bear confidingly each quarrel straight,
O Law, to thy recipient mother-knees !
How would the children light come and prompt go,
This, with a red-cheeked apple for reward,
The other, peradventure red-cheeked too
I' the rear, by taste of birch for punishment.
No foolish brawling murders any more !   1160
Peace for the household, practice for the Fisc,
And plenty for the exchequer of my lords !
Too much to hope, in this world : in the next,
Who knows ?   Since, why should sit the Twelve
      enthroned
To judge the tribes, unless the tribes be judged ?
And 't is impossible but offences come :
So, all 's one lawsuit, all one long leet day !

Forgive me this digression—that I stand
Entranced awhile at Law's first beam, outbreak
O' the business, when the Count's good angel bade
' Put up thy sword, born enemy to the ear,   1171
' And let Law listen to thy difference ! '
And Law does listen and compose the strife,
Settle the suit, how wisely and how well !
On our Pompilia, faultless to a fault,
Law bends a brow maternally severe,
Implies the worth of perfect chastity,
By fancying the flaw she cannot find.
Superfluous sifting snow, nor helps nor harms :
'T is safe to censure levity in youth,   1180
Tax womanhood with indiscretion, sure !

Since toys, permissible to-day, become
Follies to-morrow : prattle shocks in church :
And that curt skirt which lets a maiden skip,
The matron changes for a trailing robe.
Mothers may risk thus much with half-shut eyes
Nodding above their spindles by the fire,
On the chance to hit some hidden fault, else safe.
Just so, Law hazarded a punishment—
If applicable to the circumstance,   1190
Why, well—if not so apposite, well too.
' Quit the gay range o' the world,' I hear her cry,
' Enter, in lieu, the penitential pound :
' Exchange the gauds of pomp for ashes, dust :—
' Leave each mollitious haunt of luxury,
' The golden-garnished silken-couched alcove,
' The many-columned terrace that so tempts
' Feminine soul put foot forth, nor stop ear
' To fluttering joy of lover's serenade,
' Leave these for cellular seclusion ; mask   1200
' And dance no more, but fast and pray ; avaunt—
' Be burned, thy wicked townsman's sonnet-book !
' Welcome, mild hymnal by . . . some better scribe !
' For the warm arms, were wont enfold thy flesh,
' Let wire-shirt plough and whip-cord discipline ! '
If such an exhortation proved, perchance,
Inapplicable, words bestowed in waste,
What harm, since law has store, can spend nor miss ?

And so, our paragon submits herself,
Goes at command into the holy house   1210
And, also at command, comes out again :
For, could the effect of such obedience prove
Too certain, too immediate ?   Being healed,
Go blaze abroad the matter, blessed one !
Art thou sound forthwith ?   Speedily vacate
The step by pool-side, leave Bethesda free
To patients plentifully posted round,
Since the whole need not the physician !   Brief,
She may betake her to her parents' place.
Welcome her, father, with wide arms once more,
Motion her, mother, to thy breast again !   1221
For why ?   The law relinquishes its charge,
Grants to your dwelling-place a prison's style,
But gives you back Pompilia ; golden days,

Redeunt Saturnia regna !   Six weeks slip,
And she is domiciled in house and home
As though she thence had never budged at all.
And thither let the husband, joyous—ay,
But contrite also—quick betake himself,
Proud that his dove which lay among the pots   1230
Hath mued those dingy feathers,—moulted now,
Shows silver bosom clothed with yellow gold.
Quick, he shall tempt her to the perch she fled,
Bid to domestic bliss the truant back !

O let him not delay !   Time fleets how fast,
And opportunity, the irrevocable,
Once flown will flout him !   Is the furrow traced ?
If field with corn ye fail preoccupy,
Darnel for wheat and thistle-beards for grain,
Infelix lolium, carduus horridus,   1240
Will grow apace in combination prompt,
Defraud the husbandman of his desire.
Already—hist—what murmurs 'monish now
The laggard ?—doubtful, nay, fantastic bruit
Of such an apparition, such return
Interdum, to anticipate the spouse,
Of Caponsacchi's very self !   'T is said
When nights are lone and company is rare,
His visitations brighten winter up.
If so they did—which nowise I believe—   1250
How can I ?—proof abounding that the priest,
Once fairly at his relegation-place
Never once left it—still, admit he stole
A midnight march, would fain see friend again,
Find matter for instruction in the past,
Renew the old adventure in such chat
As cheers a fireside !   He was lonely too,
He, too, must need his recreative hour.
Should it amaze the philosophic mind
If one, was wont the empurpled cup to quaff,   1260
Have feminine society at will,
Being debarred abruptly from all drink
Save at the spring which Adam used for wine,
Dread harm to just the health he hoped to guard,
And, meaning abstinence, gain malady ?
Ask Tozzi, now physician to the Pope !
' Little by little break '—(I hear he bids

Master Arcangeli my antagonist,
Who loves good cheer—and may indulge too much—
So I explain the logic of the plea   1270
Wherewith he opened our proceedings late)—
' Little by little break a habit, Don !
' Become necessity to feeble flesh ! '
And thus, nocturnal taste of intercourse
(Which never happened,—but, suppose it did)
May have been used to dishabituate
By sip and sip this drainer to the dregs
O' the draught of conversation,—heady stuff,
Brewage which broached, it took two days and nights
To properly discuss o' the journey, Sirs !   1280
Such is the second-nature, men call use,
That undelightful objects get to charm
Instead of chafe : the daily colocynth
Tickles the palate by repeated dose,
Old sores scratch kindly, the ass makes a push,
Although the mill-yoke-wound be smarting yet,
For mill-door bolted on a holiday—
And must we marvel if the impulse urge
To talk the old story over now and then,
The hopes and fears, the stoppage and the haste,—
Subjects of colloquy to surfeit once ?   1291
' Here did you bid me twine a rosy wreath ! '
' And there you paid my lips a compliment ! '
' There you admired the tower could be so tall ! '
' And there you likened that of Lebanon
' To the nose o' the beloved ! '—Trifles—still,
' *Forsan et hæc olim*,'—such trifles serve
To make the minutes pass in winter-time.

Husband, return then, I re-counsel thee !
For, finally, of all glad circumstance   1300
Should make a prompt return imperative,
What i' the world awaits thee, dost suppose ?
O' the sudden, as good gifts are wont befall,
What is the hap of the unconscious Count ?
That which lights bonfire and sets cask a-tilt,
Dissolves the stubborn'st heart in jollity.
O admirable, there is born a babe,
A son, an heir, a Franceschini last
And best o' the stock ! Pompilia, thine the palm !
Repaying incredulity with faith,   1310

Ungenerous thrift of each marital debt
With bounty in profuse expenditure,
Pompilia will not have the old year end
Without a present shall ring in the new—
Bestows upon her parsimonious lord
An infant for the apple of his eye,
Core of his heart, and crown completing life,
The *summum bonum* of the earthly lot !
' We,' saith ingeniously the sage, ' are born
' Solely that others may be born of us.'   1320
So, father, take thy child, for thine that child,
Oh nothing doubt !   In wedlock born, law holds
Baseness impossible, since ' *filius est*
' *Quem nuptiæ demonstrant,*' twits the text
Whoever dares to doubt.

                              Yet doubt he dares !
O faith where art thou flown from out the world ?
Already on what an age of doubt we fall !
Instead of each disputing for the prize,
The babe is bandied here from that to this.   1330
Whose the babe ?   ' *Cujum pecus* ? ' Guido's lamb ?
' *An Meliboei ?* '   Nay, but of the priest !
' *Non sed Ægonis !* '   Someone must be sire :
And who shall say, in such a puzzling strait,
If there were not vouchsafed some miracle
To the wife who had been harassed and abused
More than enough by Guido's family
For non-production of the promised fruit
Of marriage ?   What if Nature, I demand,
Touched to the quick by taunts upon her sloth,   1340
Had roused herself, put forth recondite power,
Bestowed this birth to vindicate her sway ?
Like to the favour, Maro memorized,
Was granted Aristæus when his hive
Lay empty of the swarm, not one more bee—
Not one more babe to Franceschini's house—
And lo, a new birth filled the air with joy,
Sprung from the bowels of the generous steed !
Just so a son and heir rejoiced the Count !
Spontaneous generation, need I prove   1350
Were facile feat to Nature at a pinch ?
Let whoso doubts, steep horsehair certain weeks,
In water, there will be produced a snake ;

A second product of the horse, which horse
Happens to be the representative—
Now that I think on 't—of Arezzo's self
The very city our conception blessed !
Is not a prancing horse the City-arms ?
What sane eye sees not such coincidence ?
Cur ego, boast thou, my Pompilia, then,   1360
Desperem fieri sine conjuge
Mater—how well the Ovidian distich suits !—
Et parere intacto dummodo
Casta viro ? but language baffles here.
Note, further, as to mark the prodigy,
The babe in question neither took the name
Of Guido, from the sire presumptive, nor
Giuseppe, from the sire potential, but
Gaetano—last saint of the hierarchy,
And newest namer for a thing so new :   1370
What other motive could have prompted choice ?

Therefore be peace again : exult, ye hills !
Ye vales rejoicingly break forth in song !
Incipe, parve puer, begin, small boy,
Risu cognoscere patrem, with a smile
To recognize thy parent !   Nor do thou
Boggle, oh parent, to return the grace—
Nec anceps hære, pater, puero
Cognoscendo—one might well eke out the prayer !
In vain !   The perverse Guido doubts his eyes,   1380
Distrusts assurance, lets the devil drive ;
Because his house is swept and garnished now,
He, having summoned seven like himself,
Must hurry thither, knock and enter in,
And make the last worse than the first, indeed !
Is he content ?   We are.   No further blame
O' the man and murder !   They were stigmatized
Befittingly : the Court heard long ago
My mind o' the matter, which, outpouring full,
Has long since swept, like surge i' the simile   1390
Of Homer, overborne both dyke and dam,
And whelmed alike client and advocate :
His fate is sealed, his life as good as gone,
On him I am not tempted to waste word.
Yet though my purpose holds,—which was and is
And solely shall be to the very end,

To draw the true *effigiem* of a saint,
Do justice to perfection in the sex,—
Yet, let not some gross pamperer o' the flesh
And niggard in the spirit's nourishment,   1400
Whose feeding hath offuscated his wit
Rather than law,—he never had, to lose—
Let not such advocate object to me
I leave my proper function of attack !
' What 's this to Bacchus ? '—(in the classic phrase,
Well used, for once) he hiccups probably.
O Advocate o' the Poor, thou born to make
Their blessing void—*beati pauperes !*
By painting saintship I depicture sin,
Beside the pearl, I prove how black the jet,   1410
And through Pompilia's virtue, Guido's crime.

Back to her, then,—with but one beauty more,
End we our argument,—one crowning grace
Pre-eminent 'mid agony and death.
For to the last Pompilia played her part,
Used the right means to the permissible end,
And, wily as an eel that stirs the mud
Thick overhead, so baffling spearman's thrust,
She, while he stabbed her, simulated death,
Delayed, for his sake, the catastrophe,   1420
Obtained herself a respite, four days' grace,
Whereby she told her story to the world,
Enabled me to make the present speech,
And, by a full confession, saved her soul.

Yet hold, even here would malice leer its last,
Gurgle its choaked remonstrance : snake, hiss free !
Oh, that 's the objection ?   And to whom ?—not
    her
But me, forsooth—as, in the very act
Of both confession and, what followed close,
Subsequent talk, chatter and gossipry,   1430
Babble to sympathizing he and she
Whoever chose besiege her dying bed,—
As this were found at variance with my tale,
Falsified all I have adduced for truth,
Admitted not one peccadillo here,
Pretended to perfection, first and last,
O' the whole procedure—perfect in the end,

Perfect i' the means, perfect in everything,
Leaving a lawyer nothing to excuse,
Reason away and show his skill about !   1440
—A flight, impossible to Adamic flesh,
Just to be fancied, scarcely to be wished,
And, anyhow, unpleadable in court !
' How reconcile ' gasps Malice ' that with this ? '

Your ' this,' friend, is extraneous to the law,
Comes of men's outside meddling, the unskilled
Interposition of such fools as press
Out of their province.   Must I speak my mind ?
Far better had Pompilia died o' the spot   1449
Than found a tongue to wag and shame the law,
Shame most of all herself,—did friendship fail,
And advocacy lie less on the alert.
Listen how these protect her to the end !
Do I credit the alleged narration ?   No !
Lied our Pompilia then, to laud herself ?
Still, no ;—clear up what seems discrepancy ?
The means abound,—art 's long, though time is
      short,
So, keeping me in compass, all I urge
Is—since, confession at the point of death,
Nam in articulo mortis, with the Church   1460
Passes for statement honest and sincere,
Nemo presumitur reus esse,—then,
If sure that all affirmed would be believed,
'T was charity, in one so circumstanced,
To spend her last breath in one effort more
For universal good of friend and foe,
And,—by pretending utter innocence,
Nay, freedom from each foible we forgive,—
Re-integrate—not solely her own fame,
But do the like kind office for the priest   1470
Whom the crude truth might treat less courteously,
Indeed, expose to peril, abbreviate
The life and long career of usefulness
Presumably before him : while her lord,
Whose fleeting life is forfeit to the law,—
What mercy to the culprit if, by just
The gift of such a full certificate
Of his immitigable guiltiness,
She stifled in him the absurd conceit

Of murder as it were a mere revenge !   1480
—Stopped confirmation of that jealousy
Which, had she but acknowledged the first flaw,
The faintest foible, might embolden him
To battle with his judge, baulk penitence,
Bar preparation for impending fate.
Whereas, persuade him he has slain a saint
Who sinned not in the little she did sin,
You urge him all the brisklier to repent
Of most and least and aught and everything !
Next,—if this view of mine, content ye not,   1490
Lords, nor excuse the genial falsehood here,
'T is come to our *Triarii*, last resource,
We fall back on the inexpugnable,
Submit you,—she confessed before she talked !
The sacrament obliterates the sin :
What is not,—was not, in a certain sense.
Let Molinists distinguish, ' Souls washed white
' Were red once, still show pinkish to the eye ! '
We say, abolishment is nothingness
And nothingness has neither head nor tail   1500
End nor beginning ;—better estimate
Exorbitantly, than disparage aught
Of the efficacity of the act, I hope !

Solvuntur tabulæ ?   May we laugh and go ?
Well,—not before (in filial gratitude
To Law, who, mighty mother, waves adieu)
We take on us to vindicate Law's self—
For,—yea, Sirs,—curb the start, curtail the stare !—
Remains that we apologize for haste
I' the Law, our lady who here bristles up   1510
' And my procedure ?   Did the Court mistake ?
' (Which were indeed a misery to think)
' Did not my sentence in the former stage
' O' the business bear a title plain enough ?
' *Decretum* '—I translate it word for word—
' " Decreed : the priest, for his complicity
' " I' the flight and deviation of the dame,
' " As well as for unlawful intercourse,
' " Is banished three years : " crime and penalty,
' Declared alike.   If he be taxed with guilt   1520
' How can you call Pompilia innocent ?
' If they be innocent, have I been just ? '

Gently, O mother, judge men !—whose mistake
Is in the poor misapprehensiveness.
The *Titulus* a-top of your decree
Was but to ticket there the kind of charge
You in good time would arbitrate upon.
Title is one thing,—arbitration's self,
Probatio, quite another possibly.
Subsistit, there holds good the old response,   1530
Responsio tradita, we must not stick,
Quod non sit attendendus Titulus,
To the Title, *sed Probatio*, but to Proof,
Resultans ex processu, and result
O' the Trial, and the style of punishment,
Et pœna per sententiam imposita ;
All is tentative, till the sentence come,
Mere indication of what men expect,
And nowise an assurance they shall find.
Lords, what if we permissibly relax   1540
The tense bow, as the law-god Phœbus bids,
Relieve our gravity at close of speech ?
I traverse Rome, feel thirsty, need a draught,
Look for a wine-shop, find it by the bough
Projecting as to say ' Here wine is sold ! '
So much I know,—' sold : ' but what sort of wine ?
Strong, weak, sweet, sour, home-made or foreign drink?
That much must I discover by myself.
' Wine is sold,' quoth the bough, ' but good or bad,
' Find, and inform us when you smack your lips ! '
Exactly so, Law hangs her title forth,   1551
To show she entertains you with such case
About such crime : come in ! she pours, you quaff.
You find the Priest good liquor in the main,
But heady and provocative of brawls.
Remand the residue to flask once more,
Lay it low where it may deposit lees,
I' the cellar : thence produce it presently,
Three years the brighter and the better !

                     Thus,   1560
Law's son, have I bestowed my filial help,
And thus I end, *tenax proposito ;*
Point to point as I purposed have I drawn
Pompilia, and implied as terribly
Guido : so, gazing, let the world crown Law—

Able once more, despite my impotence,
And helped by the acumen of the Court,
To eliminate, display, make triumph truth !
What other prize than truth were worth the pains ?

There 's my oration—much exceeds in length   1570
That famed Panegyric of Isocrates,
They say it took him fifteen years to pen.
But all those ancients could say anything !
He put in just what rushed into his head,
While I shall have to prune and pare and print.
This comes of being born in modern times
With priests for auditory.   Still, it pays.

THE POPE

Like to Ahasuerus, that shrewd prince,
I will begin,—as is, these seven years now,
My daily wont,—and read a History
(Written by one whose deft right hand was dust
To the last digit, ages ere my birth)
Of all my predecessors, Popes of Rome :
For though mine ancient early dropped the pen,
Yet others picked it up and wrote it dry,
Since of the making books there is no end.
And so I have the Papacy complete   10
From Peter first to Alexander last ;
Can question each and take instruction so.
Have I to dare,—I ask, how dared this Pope ?
To suffer ?   Suchanone, how suffered he ?
Being about to judge, as now, I seek
How judged once, well or ill, some other Pope ;
Study some signal judgment that subsists
To blaze on, or else blot, the page which seals
The sum up of what gain or loss to God
Came of His one more Vicar in the world.   20
So, do I find example, rule of life ;
So, square and set in order the next page,
Shall be stretched smooth o'er my own funeral cyst.

Eight hundred years exact before the year
I was made Pope, men made Formosus Pope,
Say Sigebert and other chroniclers.
Ere I confirm or quash the Trial here
Of Guido Franceschini and his friends,
Read,—how there was a ghastly Trial once
Of a dead man by a live man, and both, Popes :   30
Thus—in the antique penman's very phrase.

' Then Stephen, Pope and seventh of the name,
' Cried out, in synod as he sat in state,

‘ While choler quivered on his brow and beard,
‘ “ Come into court, Formosus, thou lost wretch,
‘ “ That claimedst to be late the Pope as I ! ”

‘ And at the word, the great door of the church
‘ Flew wide, and in they brought Formosus’ self,
‘ The body of him, dead, even as embalmed
‘ And buried duly in the Vatican   40
‘ Eight months before, exhumed thus for the nonce.
‘ They set it, that dead body of a Pope,
‘ Clothed in pontific vesture now again,
‘ Upright on Peter’s chair as if alive.
‘ And Stephen, springing up, cried furiously
‘ “ Bishop of Porto, wherefore didst presume
‘ “ To leave that see and take this Roman see,
‘ “ Exchange the lesser for the greater see,
‘ “ —A thing against the canons of the Church ? ”

‘ Then one, (a Deacon who, observing forms,   50
‘ Was placed by Stephen to repel the charge,
‘ Be advocate and mouthpiece of the corpse)
‘ Spoke as he dared, set stammeringly forth
‘ With white lips and dry tongue,—as but a youth,
‘ For frightful was the corpse-face to behold,—
‘ How nowise lacked there precedent for this.
‘ But when, for his last precedent of all,
‘ Emboldened by the Spirit, out he blurts
‘ “ And, Holy Father, didst not thou thyself
‘ “ Vacate the lesser for the greater see,   c0
‘ “ Half a year since change Arago for Rome ? ”
‘ “ —Ye have the sin’s defence now, synod mine ! ”
‘ Shrieks Stephen in a beastly froth of rage :
‘ “ Judge now betwixt him dead and me alive !
‘ “ Hath he intruded or do I pretend ?
‘ “ Judge, judge ! ”—breaks wavelike one whole foam
     of wrath.

‘ Whereupon they, being friends and followers,
‘ Said “ Ay, thou art Christ’s Vicar, and not he !
‘ “ Away with what is frightful to behold !
‘ “ This act was uncanonic and a fault.”   70

‘ Then, swallowed up in rage, Stephen exclaimed
‘ “ So, guilty !   So, remains I punish guilt !

' " He is unpoped, and all he did I damn :
' " The Bishop, that ordained him, I degrade :
' " Depose to laics those he raised to priests :
' " What they have wrought is mischief nor shall stand,
' " It is confusion, let it vex no more !
' " Since I revoke, annul and abrogate
' " All his decrees in all kinds : they are void !
' " In token whereof and warning to the world,   80
' " Strip me yon miscreant of those robes usurped,
' " And clothe him with vile serge befitting such !
' " Then hale the carrion to the market-place ;
' " Let the town-hangman chop from his right hand
' " Those same three fingers which he blessed withal ;
' " Next cut the head off, once was crowned forsooth :
' " And last go fling all, fingers, head and trunk,
' " In Tiber that my Christian fish may sup ! "
' —Either because of IXΘYΣ which means Fish
' And very aptly symbolizes Christ,   90
' Or else because the Pope is Fisherman
' And seals with Fisher's-signet.   Anyway,
' So said, so done : himself, to see it done,
' Following the corpse, they trailed from street to street
' Till into Tiber wave they threw the thing.
' The people, crowded on the banks to see,
' Were loud or mute, wept or laughed, cursed or jeered,
' According as the deed addressed their sense ;
' A scandal verily : and out spake a Jew
' " Wot ye your Christ had vexed our Herod thus ? "

' Now when, Formosus being dead a year,   101
' His judge Pope Stephen tasted death in turn,
' Made captive by the mob and strangled straight,
' Romanus, his successor for a month,
' Did make protest Formosus was with God,
' Holy, just, true in thought and word and deed.
' Next Theodore, who reigned but twenty days,
' Therein convoked a synod, whose decree
' Did reinstate, repope the late unpoped,
' And do away with Stephen as accursed.   110
' So that when presently certain fisher-folk
' (As if the queasy river could not hold
' Its swallowed Jonas, but discharged the meal)
' Produced the timely product of their nets,
' The mutilated man, Formosus,—saved

' From putrefaction by the embalmer's spice,
' Or, as some said, by sanctity of flesh,—
' " Why, lay the body again " bade Theodore
' " Among his predecessors, in the church
' " And burial-place of Peter ! " which was done. 120
' " And " addeth Luitprand " many of repute,
' " Pious and still alive, avouch to me
' " That as they bore the body up the aisle
' " The saints in imaged row bowed each his head
' " For welcome to a brother-saint come back."
' As for Romanus and this Theodore,
' These two Popes, through the brief reign granted
    each,
' Could but initiate what John came to close
' And give the final stamp to : he it was,
' Ninth of the name, (I follow the best guides)   130
' Who,—in full synod at Ravenna held
' With Bishops seventy-four, and present too
' Eude King of France with his Archbishopry,—
' Did condemn Stephen, anathematize
' The disinterment, and make all blots blank.
' " For," argueth here Auxilius in a place
' *De Ordinationibus*, " precedents
' " Had been, no lack, before Formosus long,
' " Of Bishops so transferred from see to see,—
' " Marinus, for example " : read the tract.   140

' But, after John, came Sergius, reaffirmed
' The right of Stephen, cursed Formosus, nay
' Cast out, some say, his corpse a second time.
' And here,—because the matter went to ground,
' Fretted by new griefs, other cares of the age,—
' Here is the last pronouncing of the Church,
' Her sentence that subsists unto this day.
' Yet constantly opinion hath prevailed
' I' the Church, Formosus was a holy man.'

Which of the judgments was infallible ?   150
Which of my predecessors spoke for God ?
And what availed Formosus that this cursed,
That blessed, and then this other cursed again ?
' Fear ye not those whose power can kill the body
' And not the soul,' saith Christ ' but rather those
' Can cast both soul and body into hell ! '

John judged thus in Eight Hundred Ninety Eight,
Exact eight hundred years ago to-day
When, sitting in his stead, Vice-gerent here,
I must give judgment on my own behoof.   160
So worked the predecessor : now, my turn !

In God's name !   Once more on this earth of God's,
While twilight lasts and time wherein to work,
I take His staff with my uncertain hand,
And stay my six and fourscore years, my due
Labour and sorrow, on His judgment-seat,
And forthwith think, speak, act, in place of Him—
The Pope for Christ.   Once more appeal is made
From man's assize to mine : I sit and see
Another poor weak trembling human wretch   170
Pushed by his fellows, who pretend the right,
Up to the gulf which, where I gaze, begins
From this world to the next,—gives way and way,
Just on the edge over the awful dark :
With nothing to arrest him but my feet.
He catches at me with convulsive face,
Cries ' Leave to live the natural minute more ! '
While hollowly the avengers echo ' Leave ?
' None !   So has he exceeded man's due share
' In man's fit licence, wrung by Adam's fall,   180
' To sin and yet not surely die,—that we,
' All of us sinful, all with need of grace,
' All chary of our life,—the minute more
' Or minute less of grace which saves a soul,—
' Bound to make common cause with who craves time,
' —We yet protest against the exorbitance
' Of sin in this one sinner, and demand
' That his poor sole remaining piece of time
' Be plucked from out his clutch : put him to death !
' Punish him now !   As for the weal or woe   190
' Hereafter, God grant mercy !   Man be just,
' Nor let the felon boast he went scot-free ! '
And I am bound, the solitary judge,
To weigh the worth, decide upon the plea,
And either hold a hand out, or withdraw
A foot and let the wretch drift to the fall.
Ay, and while thus I dally, dare perchance
Put fancies for a comfort 'twixt this calm
And yonder passion that I have to bear,—

As if reprieve were possible for both   200
Prisoner and Pope,—how easy were reprieve !
A touch o' the hand-bell here, a hasty word
To those who wait, and wonder they wait long,
I' the passage there, and I should gain the life !—
Yea, though I flatter me with fancy thus,
I know it is but nature's craven-trick.
The case is over, judgment at an end,
And all things done now and irrevocable :
A mere dead man is Franceschini here,
Even as Formosus centuries ago.   210
I have worn through this sombre wintry day,
With winter in my soul beyond the world's,
Over these dismalest of documents
Which drew night down on me ere eve befell,—
Pleadings and counter-pleadings, figure of fact
Beside fact's self, these summaries to-wit,—
How certain three were slain by certain five :
I read here why it was, and how it went,
And how the chief o' the five preferred excuse,
And how law rather chose defence should lie,—   220
What argument he urged by wary word
When free to play off wile, start subterfuge,
And what the unguarded groan told, torture's feat
When law grew brutal, outbroke, overbore
And glutted hunger on the truth, at last,—
No matter for the flesh and blood between.
All 's a clear rede and no more riddle now.
Truth, nowhere, lies yet everywhere in these—
Not absolutely in a portion, yet
Evolvable from the whole : evolved at last   230
Painfully, held tenaciously by me.
Therefore there is not any doubt to clear
When I shall write the brief word presently
And chink the hand-bell, which I pause to do.
Irresolute ?   Not I more than the mound
With the pine-trees on it yonder ! Some surmise,
Perchance, that since man's wit is fallible,
Mine may fail here ?   Suppose it so,—what then ?
Say,—Guido, I count guilty, there 's no babe
So guiltless, for I misconceive the man !   240
What 's in the chance should move me from my mind ?
If, as I walk in a rough country-side,
Peasants of mine cry ' Thou art he can help,

' Lord of the land and counted wise to boot :
' Look at our brother, strangling in his foam,
' He fell so where we find him,—prove thy worth ! '
I may presume, pronounce, ' A frenzy-fit,
' A falling-sickness or a fever-stroke !
' Breathe a vein, copiously let blood at once ! '
So perishes the patient, and anon　　　　　　　250
I hear my peasants—' All was error, lord !
' Our story, thy prescription : for there crawled
' In due time from our hapless brother's breast
' The serpent which had stung him : bleeding slew
' Whom a prompt cordial had restored to health.'
What other should I say than ' God so willed :
' Mankind is ignorant, a man am I :
' Call ignorance my sorrow not my sin ! '
So and not otherwise, in after-time,
If some acuter wit, fresh probing, sound　　　　260
This multifarious mass of words and deeds
Deeper, and reach through guilt to innocence,
I shall face Guido's ghost nor blench a jot.
' God who set me to judge thee, meted out
' So much of judging faculty, no more :
' Ask Him if I was slack in use thereof ! '
I hold a heavier fault imputable
inasmuch as I changed a chaplain once,
For no cause,—no, if I must bare my heart,—
Save that he snuffled somewhat saying mass.　　270
For I am ware it is the seed of act,
God holds appraising in His hollow palm,
Not act grown great thence on the world below,
Leafage and branchage, vulgar eyes admire.
Therefore I stand on my integrity,
Nor fear at all : and if I hesitate,
It is because I need to breathe awhile,
Rest, as the human right allows, review
Intent the little seeds of act, the tree,—　　　279
The thought, to clothe in deed, and give the world
At chink of bell and push of arrased door.

O pale departure, dim disgrace of day !
Winter 's in wane, his vengeful worst art thou,
To dash the boldness of advancing March !
Thy chill persistent rain has purged our streets
Of gossipry ; pert tongue and idle ear

By this, consort 'neath archway, portico.
But wheresoe'er Rome gathers in the grey,
Two names now snap and flash from mouth to mouth—
(Sparks, flint and steel strike) Guido and the Pope.
By this same hour to morrow eve—aha,   291
How do they call him ?—the sagacious Swede
Who finds by figures how the chances prove,
Why one comes rather than another thing,
As, say, such dots turn up by throw of dice,
Or, if we dip in Virgil here and there
And prick for such a verse, when such shall point.
Take this Swede, tell him, hiding name and rank,
Two men are in our city this dull eve ;
One doomed to death,—but hundreds in such plight
Slip aside, clean escape by leave of law   301
Which leans to mercy in this latter time ;
Moreover in the plenitude of life
Is he, with strength of limb and brain adroit,
Presumably of service here : beside,
The man is noble, backed by nobler friends :
Nay, for who wish him well, the city's self
Makes common cause with the house-magistrate,
The lord of hearth and home, domestic judge
Who ruled his own and let men cavil. Die ? 310
He 'll bribe a gaoler or break prison first !
Nay, a sedition may be helpful, give
Hint to the mob to batter wall, burn gate,
And bid the favourite malefactor march.
Calculate now these chances of escape !
' It is not probable, but well may be.'
Again, there is another man, weighed now
By twice eight years beyond the seven-times ten,
Appointed overweight to break our branch. 319
And this man's loaded branch lifts, more than snow,
All the world's cark and care, though a bird's nest
Were a superfluous burthen : notably
Hath he been pressed, as if his age were youth,
From to-day's dawn till now that day departs,
Trying one question with true sweat of soul
' Shall the said doomed man fitlier die or live ? '
When a straw swallowed in his posset, stool
Stumbled on where his path lies, any puff
That 's incident to such a smoking flax,
Hurries the natural end and quenches him ! 330

Now calculate, thou sage, the chances here,
Say, which shall die the sooner, this or that ?
' That, possibly, this in all likelihood.'
I thought so : yet thou tripp'st, my foreign friend !
No, it will be quite otherwise,—to-day
Is Guido's last : my term is yet to run.

But say the Swede were right, and I forthwith
Acknowledge a prompt summons and lie dead :
Why, then I stand already in God's face
And hear ' Since by its fruit a tree is judged,   340
' Show me thy fruit, the latest act of thine !
' For in the last is summed the first and all,—
' What thy life last put heart and soul into,
' There shall I taste thy product.'   I must plead
This condemnation of a man to-day.

Not so !   Expect nor question nor reply
At what we figure as God's judgment-bar !
None of this vile way by the barren words
Which, more than any deed, characterize
Man as made subject to a curse : no speech—   350
That still bursts o'er some lie which lurks inside,
As the split skin across the coppery snake,
And most denotes man ! since, in all beside,
In hate or lust or guile or unbelief,
Out of some core of truth the excrescence comes,
And, in the last resort, the man may urge
' So was I made, a weak thing that gave way
' To truth, to impulse only strong since true,
' And hated, lusted, used guile, forwent faith.'
But when man walks the garden of this world   360
For his own solace, and, unchecked by law,
Speaks or keeps silence as himself sees fit,
Without the least incumbency to lie,
—Why, can he tell you what a rose is like,
Or how the birds fly, and not slip to false
Though truth serve better ?   Man must tell his mate
Of you, me and himself, knowing he lies,
Knowing his fellow knows the same,—will think
' He lies, it is the method of a man ! '
And yet will speak for answer ' It is truth '   370
To him who shall rejoin ' Again a lie ! '
Therefore this filthy rags of speech, this coil

Of statement, comment, query and response,
Tatters all too contaminate for use,
Have no renewing : He, the Truth, is, too,
The Word. We men, in our degree, may know
There, simply, instantaneously, as here
After long time and amid many lies,
Whatever we dare think we know indeed
—That I am I, as He is He,—what else ?   380
But be man's method for man's life at least !
Wherefore, Antonio Pignatelli, thou
My ancient self, who wast no Pope so long
But studied God and man, the many years
I' the school, i' the cloister, in the diocese
Domestic, legate-rule in foreign lands,—
Thou other force in those old busy days
Than this grey ultimate decrepitude,—
Yet sensible of fires that more and more
Visit a soul, in passage to the sky,   390
Left nakeder than when flesh-robe was new—
Thou, not Pope but the mere old man o' the world,
Supposed inquisitive and dispassionate,
Wilt thou, the one whose speech I somewhat trust,
Question the after-me, this self now Pope,
Hear his procedure, criticize his work ?
Wise in its generation is the world.

This is why Guido is found reprobate.
I see him furnished forth for his career,
On starting for the life-chance in our world,   400
With nearly all we count sufficient help :
Body and mind in balance, a sound frame,
A solid intellect : the wit to seek,
Wisdom to choose, and courage wherewithal
To deal with whatsoever circumstance
Should minister to man, make life succeed.
Oh, and much drawback ! what were earth without ?
Is this our ultimate stage, or starting-place
To try man's foot, if it will creep or climb,
'Mid obstacles in seeming, points that prove   410
Advantage for who vaults from low to high
And makes the stumbling-block a stepping-stone ?
So, Guido, born with appetite, lacks food,
Is poor, who yet could deftly play-off wealth,
Straitened, whose limbs are restless till at large :

And, as he eyes each outlet of the cirque,
The narrow penfold for probation, pines
After the good things just outside the grate,
With less monition, fainter conscience-twitch,
Rarer instinctive qualm at the first feel   420
Of the unseemly greed and grasp undue,
Than nature furnishes the main mankind,—
Making it harder to do wrong than right
The first time, careful lest the common ear
Break measure, miss the outstep of life's march.
Wherein I see a trial fair and fit
For one else too unfairly fenced about,
Set above sin, beyond his fellows here,
Guarded from the arch-tempter, all must fight,
By a great birth, traditionary name,   430
Diligent culture, choice companionship,
Above all, conversancy with the faith
Which puts forth for its base of doctrine just
' Man is born nowise to content himself
' But please God.'   He accepted such a rule,
Recognized man's obedience ; and the Church,
Which simply is such rule's embodiment,
He clave to, he held on by,—nay, indeed,
Near pushed inside of, deep as layman durst,
Professed so much of priesthood as might sue   440
For priest's-exemption where the layman sinned,—
Got his arm frocked which, bare, the law would bruise.
Hence, at this moment, what 's his last resource,
His extreme stay and utmost stretch of hope
But that,—convicted of such crime as law
Wipes not away save with a worldling's blood,—
Guido, the three-parts consecrate, may 'scape ?
Nay, the portentous brothers of the man
Are veritably priests, protected each
May do his murder in the Church's pale,   450
Abate Paul, Canon Girolamo !
This is the man proves irreligiousest
Of all mankind, religion's parasite !
This may forsooth plead dinned ear, jaded sense,
The vice o' the watcher who bides near the bell,
Sleeps sound because the clock is vigilant,
And cares not whether it be shade or shine,
Doling out day and night to all men else !
Why was the choice o' the man to niche himself

Perversely 'neath the tower where Time's own tongue
Thus undertakes to sermonize the world ?   461
Why, but because the solemn is safe too,
The belfry proves a fortress of a sort,
Has other uses than to teach the hour,
Turns sunscreen, paravent and ombrifuge
To whoso seeks a shelter in its pale,
—Ay, and attractive to unwary folk
Who gaze at storied portal, statued spire,
And go home with full head but empty purse
Nor dare suspect the sacristan the thief !   470
Shall Judas,—hard upon the donor's heel,
To filch the fragments of the basket,—plead
He was too near the preacher's mouth, nor sat
Attent with fifties in a company ?
No,—closer to promulgated decree,
Clearer the censure of default.   Proceed !

I find him bound, then, to begin life well ;
Fortified by propitious circumstance,
Great birth, good breeding, with the Church for guide.
How lives he ?   Cased thus in a coat of proof,   480
Mailed like a man-at-arms, though all the while
A puny starveling,—does the breast pant big,
The limb swell to the limit, emptiness
Strive to become solidity indeed ?
Rather, he shrinks up like the ambiguous fish,
Detaches flesh from shell and outside show,
And steals by moonlight (I have seen the thing)
In and out, now to prey and now to skulk.
Armour he boasts when a wave breaks on beach,
Or bird stoops for the prize : with peril nigh,—   490
The man of rank, the much-befriended man,
The man almost affiliate to the Church,
Such is to deal with, let the world beware !
Does the world recognize, pass prudently ?
Do tides abate and sea-fowl hunt i' the deep ?
Already is the slug from out its mew,
Ignobly faring with all loose and free,
Sand-fly and slush-worm at their garbage-feast,
A naked blotch no better than they all :
Guido has dropped nobility, slipped the Church,   500
Plays trickster if not cut-purse, body and soul
Prostrate among the filthy feeders—faugh !

And when Law takes him by surprise at last,
Catches the foul thing on its carrion-prey,
Behold, he points to shell left high and dry,
Pleads ' But the case out yonder is myself ! '
Nay, it is thou, Law prongs amid thy peers,
Congenial vermin ; that was none of thee,
Thine outside,—give it to the soldier-crab !

For I find this black mark impinge the man,   510
That he believes in just the vile of life.
Low instinct, base pretension, are these truth ?
Then, that aforesaid armour, probity
He figures in, is falsehood scale on scale ;
Honor and faith,—a lie and a disguise,
Probably for all livers in this world,
Certainly for himself !   All say good words
To who will hear, all do thereby bad deeds
To who must undergo ; so thrive mankind !
See this habitual creed exemplified   520
Most in the last deliberate act ; as last,
So, very sum and substance of the soul
Of him that planned and leaves one perfect piece,
The sin brought under jurisdiction now,
Even the marriage of the man : this act
I sever from his life as sample, show
For Guido's self, intend to test him by,
As, from a cup filled fairly at the fount,
By the components we decide enough
Or to let flow as late, or staunch the source.   530

He purposes this marriage, I remark,
On no one motive that should prompt thereto—
Farthest, by consequence, from ends alleged
Appropriate to the action ; so they were :
The best, he knew and feigned, the worst he took.
Not one permissible impulse moves the man,
From the mere liking of the eye and ear,
To the true longing of the heart that loves,
No trace of these : but all to instigate,
Is what sinks man past level of the brute,   540
Whose appetite if brutish is a truth.
All is the lust for money : to get gold,—
Why, lie, rob, if it must be, murder !   Make
Body and soul wring gold out, lured within

The clutch of hate by love, the trap's pretence !
What good else get from bodies and from souls ?
This got, there were some life to lead thereby,
—What, where or how, appreciate those who tell
How the toad lives : it lives,—enough for me !
To get this good,—with but a groan or so,   550
Then, silence of the victims,—were the feat.
He foresaw, made a picture in his mind,—
Of father and mother stunned and echoless
To the blow, as they lie staring at fate's jaws
Their folly danced into, till the woe fell ;
Edged in a month by strenuous cruelty
From even the poor nook whence they watched the
          wolf
Feast on their heart, the lamb-like child his prey ;
Plundered to the last remnant of their wealth,
(What daily pittance pleased the plunderer dole)   560
Hunted forth to go hide head, starve and die,
So leave the pale awe-stricken wife, past hope
Of help i' the world now, mute and motionless,
His slave, his chattel, to use and then destroy :
All this, he bent mind how to bring about,
Put this in act and life, as painted plain,
And have success, the crown of earthly good,
In this particular enterprise of man,
A marriage—undertaken in God's face
With all those lies so opposite God's truth,   570
For ends so other than man's end.

                             Thus schemes
Guido, and thus would carry out his scheme :
But when an obstacle first blocks the path,
When he finds there is no monopoly
Of lies and trick i' the tricking lying world,—
That sorry timid natures, even this sort
O' the Comparini, want nor trick nor lie
Proper to the kind,—that as the gor-crow treats
The bramble-finch so treats the finch the moth,   580
And the great Guido is minutely matched
By this same couple,—whether true or false
The revelation of Pompilia's birth,
Which in a moment brings his scheme to nought,—
Then, he is piqued, advances yet a stage,
Leaves the low region to the finch and fly,

Soars to the zenith whence the fiercer fowl
May dare the inimitable swoop. I see.
He draws now on the curious crime, the fine
Felicity and flower of wickedness ;   590
Determines, by the utmost exercise
Of violence, made safe and sure by craft,
To satiate malice, pluck one last arch-pang
From the parents, else would triumph out of reach,
By punishing their child, within reach yet,
Who nowise could have wronged, thought, word or
     deed,
I' the matter that now moves him. So plans he,
Always subordinating (note the point !)
Revenge, the manlier sin, to interest
The meaner,—would pluck pang forth, but unclench
No gripe in the act, let fall no money-piece.   601
Hence a plan for so plaguing, body and soul,
His wife, so putting, day by day and hour by hour,
The untried torture to the untouched place,
As must precipitate an end foreseen,
Goad her into some plain revolt, most like
Plunge upon patent suicidal shame,
Death to herself, damnation by rebound
To those whose hearts he, holding hers, holds still :
Such a plan as, in its completeness, shall   610
Ruin the three together and alike,
Yet leave himself in luck and liberty,
No claim renounced, no right a forfeiture,
His person unendangered, his good fame
Without a flaw, his pristine worth intact,—
While they, with all their claims and rights that cling,
Shall forthwith crumble off him every side,
Scorched into dust, a plaything for the winds.
As when, in our Campagna, there is fired
The nest-like work that lets a peasant house ;   620
And, as the thatch burns here, there, everywhere,
Even to the ivy and wild vine, that bound
And blessed the hut where men were happy once,
There rises gradual, black amid the blaze,
Some grim and unscathed nucleus of the nest,—
Some old malicious tower, some obscene tomb
They thought a temple in their ignorance,
And clung about and thought to lean upon—
There laughs it o'er their ravage,—where are they ?

So did his cruelty burn life about,   630
And lay the ruin bare in dreadfulness,
Try the persistency of torment so
O' the wife, that, at some fierce extremity,
Some crisis brought about by fire and flame,
The patient stung to frenzy should break loose,
Fly anyhow, find refuge anywhere,
Even in the arms of who might front her first,
No monster but a man—while nature shrieked
' Or thus escape, or die ! '   The spasm arrived,
Not the escape by way of sin,—O God,   640
Who shall pluck sheep Thou holdest, from Thy hand ?
Therefore she lay resigned to die,—so far
The simple cruelty was foiled.   Why then,
Craft to the rescue, craft should supplement
Cruelty and show hell a masterpiece !
Hence this consummate lie, this love-intrigue,
Unmanly simulation of a sin,
With place and time and circumstance to suit—
These letters false beyond all forgery—
Not just handwriting and mere authorship,   650
But false to body and soul they figure forth—
As though the man had cut out shape and shape
From fancies of that other Aretine,
To paste below—incorporate the filth
With cherub faces on a missal-page !

Whereby the man so far attains his end
That strange temptation is permitted,—see !
Pompilia, wife, and Caponsacchi, priest,
Are brought together as nor priest nor wife
Should stand, and there is passion in the place,   660
Power in the air for evil as for good,
Promptings from heaven and hell, as if the stars
Fought in their courses for a fate to be.
Thus stand the wife and priest, a spectacle,
I doubt not, to unseen assemblage there.
No lamp will mark that window for a shrine,
No tablet signalize the terrace, teach
New generations which succeed the old,
The pavement of the street is holy ground ;
No bard describe in verse how Christ prevailed   670
And Satan fell like lightning !   Why repine ?
What does the world, told truth, but lie the more ?

A second time the plot is foiled ; nor, now,
By corresponding sin for countercheck,
No wile and trick to baffle trick and wile,—
The play of the parents !   Here the blot is blanched
By God's gift of a purity of soul
That will not take pollution, ermine-like
Armed from dishonour by its own soft snow.
Such was this gift of God who showed for once   680
How He would have the world go white : it seems
As a new attribute were born of each
Champion of truth, the priest and wife I praise,—
As a new safeguard sprang up in defence
Of their new noble nature : so a thorn
Comes to the aid of and completes the rose—
Courage to-wit, no woman's gift nor priest's,
I' the crisis ; might leaps vindicating right.
See how the strong aggressor, bad and bold,
With every vantage, preconcerts surprise,   690
Flies of a sudden at his victim's throat
In a byeway,—how fares he when face to face
With Caponsacchi ?   Who fights, who fears now ?
There quails Count Guido, armed to the chattering teeth,
Cowers at the steadfast eye and quiet word
O' the Canon at the Pieve !   There skulks crime
Behind law called in to back cowardice !
While out of the poor trampled worm the wife,
Springs up a serpent !

                              But anon of these !   700
Him I judge now,—of him proceed to note,
Failing the first, a second chance befriends
Guido, gives pause ere punishment arrive.
The law he called, comes, hears, adjudicates,
Nor does amiss i' the main,—secludes the wife
From the husband, respites the oppressed one, grants
Probation to the oppressor, could he know
The mercy of a minute's fiery purge !
The furnace-coals alike of public scorn,
Private remorse, heaped glowing on his head,   710
What if,—the force and guile, the ore's alloy,
Eliminate, his baser soul refined—
The lost be saved even yet, so as by fire ?
Let him, rebuked, go softly all his days
And, when no graver musings claim their due,

Meditate on a man's immense mistake
Who, fashioned to use feet and walk, deigns crawl—
Takes the unmanly means—ay, though to end
Man scarce should make for, would but reach thro'
     wrong,—
May sin, but must not needs shame manhood so :   720
Since fowlers hawk, shoot, nay and snare the game,
And yet eschew vile practice, nor find sport
In torch-light treachery or the luring owl.

But how hunts Guido ?   Why, the fraudful trap—
Late spurned to ruin by the indignant feet
Of fellows in the chase who loved fair play—
Here he picks up the fragments to the least,
Lades him and hies to the old lurking-place
Where haply he may patch again, refit
The mischief, file its blunted teeth anew,   730
Make sure, next time, a snap shall break the bone.
Craft, greed and violence complot revenge :
Craft, for its quota, schemes to bring about
And seize occasion and be safe withal :
Greed craves its act may work both far and near,
Crush the tree, branch and trunk and root beside,
Whichever twig or leaf arrests a streak
Of possible sunshine else would coin itself,
And drop down one more gold piece in the path.
Violence stipulates ' Advantage proved,   740
' And safety sure, be pain the overplus !
' Murder with jagged knife !   Cut but tear too !
' Foiled oft, starved long, glut malice for amends ! '
And, last, craft schemes,—scheme sorrowful and
     strange
As though the elements, whom mercy checked,
Had mustered hate for one eruption more,
One final deluge to surprise the Ark
Cradled and sleeping on its mountain-top :
The outbreak-signal—what but the dove's coos
Back with the olive in her bill for news   750
Sorrow was over ?   'T is an infant's birth,
Guido's first born, his son and heir, that gives
The occasion : other men cut free their souls
From care in such a case, fly up in thanks
To God, reach, recognize His love for once :
Guido cries ' Soul, at last the mire is thine !

' Lie there in likeness of a money-bag,
' This babe's birth so pins down past moving now,
' That I dare cut adrift the lives I late
' Scrupled to touch lest thou escape with them !   760
' These parents and their child my wife,—touch one
' Lose all !   Their rights determined on a head
' I could but hate, not harm, since from each hair
' Dangled a hope for me : now—chance and change !
' No right was in their child but passes now
' To that child's child and through such child to me.
' I am the father now,—come what, come will,
' I represent my child ; he comes between—
' Cuts sudden off the sunshine of this life   769
' From those three : why, the gold is in his curls !
' Not with old Pietro's, Violante's head,
' Not his grey horror, her more hideous black—
' Go these, devoted to the knife ! '
                                        'T is done :
Wherefore should mind misgive, heart hesitate ?
He calls to counsel, fashions certain four
Colourless natures counted clean till now,
—Rustic simplicity, uncorrupted youth,   778
Ignorant virtue !   Here 's the gold o' the prime
When Saturn ruled, shall shock our leaden day—
The clown abash the courtier !   Mark it, bards !
The courtier tries his hand on clownship here,
Speaks a word, names a crime, appoints a price,—
Just breathes on what, suffused with all himself,
Is red-hot henceforth past distinction now
I' the common glow of hell.   And thus they break
And blaze on us at Rome, Christ's Birthnight-eve !
Oh angels that sang erst ' On the earth, peace !
' To man, good will ! '—such peace finds earth to-day !
After the seventeen hundred years, so man   790
Wills good to man, so Guido makes complete
His murder ! what is it I said ?—cuts loose
Three lives that hitherto he suffered cling,
Simply because each served to nail secure,
By a corner of the money-bag, his soul,—
Therefore, lives sacred till the babe's first breath
O'erweights them in the balance,—off they fly !

So is the murder managed, sin conceived
To the full : and why not crowned with triumph too ?

Why must the sin, conceived thus, bring forth death ?
I note how, within hair's-breadth of escape,   801
Impunity and the thing supposed success,
Guido is found when the check comes, the change,
The monitory touch o' the tether—felt
By few, not marked by many, named by none
At the moment, only recognized aright
I' the fulness of the days, for God's, lest sin
Exceed the service, leap the line : such check—
A secret which this life finds hard to keep,
And, often guessed, is never quite revealed.   810
Guido must needs trip on a stumbling-block
Too vulgar, too absurdly plain i' the path !
Study this single oversight of care,
This hebetude that mars sagacity,
Forgetfulness of what the man best knew !
Here is a stranger who, with need to fly,
Needs but to ask and have the means of flight.
Why, the first urchin tells you, to leave Rome,
Get horses, you must show the warrant, just   819
The banal scrap, clerk's scribble, a fair word buys,
Or foul one, if a ducat sweeten word,—
And straight authority will back demand,
Give you the pick o' the post-house !—in such wise,
The resident at Rome for thirty years,
Guido, instructs a stranger !   And himself
Forgets just this poor paper scrap, wherewith
Armed, every door he knocks at opens wide
To save him : horsed and manned, with such advance
O' the hunt behind, why 't were the easy task
Of hours told on the fingers of one hand,   830
To reach the Tuscan Frontier, laugh at home,
Light-hearted with his fellows of the place,—
Prepared by that strange shameful judgment, that
Satire upon a sentence just pronounced
By the Rota and confirmed by the Granduke,—
Ready in a circle to receive their peer,
Appreciate his good story how, when Rome,
The Pope-King and the populace of priests
Made common cause with their confederate
The other priestling who seduced his wife,   840
He, all unaided, wiped out the affront
With decent bloodshed and could face his friends,
Frolic it in the world's eye.   Ay, such tale

Missed such applause, all by such oversight !
So, tired and footsore, those blood-flustered five
Went reeling on the road through dark and cold,
The few permissible miles, to sink at length,
Wallow and sleep in the first wayside straw,
As the other herd quenched, i' the wash o' the wave,
—Each swine, the devil inside him : so slept they,
And so were caught and caged—all through one trip,
Touch of the fool in Guido the astute !   852
He curses the omission, I surmise,
More than the murder. Why, thou fool and blind,
It is the mercy-stroke that stops thy fate,
Hamstrings and holds thee to thy hurt,—but how ?
On the edge o' the precipice ! One minute more,
Thou hadst gone farther and fared worse, my son,
Fathoms down on the flint and fire beneath !
Thy comrades each and all were of one mind   860
Straightway, thy murder done, to murder thee
In turn, because of promised pay withheld.
So, to the last, greed found itself at odds
With craft in thee, and, proving conqueror,
Had sent thee, the same night that crowned thy hope,
Thither where, this same day, I see thee not,
Nor, through God's mercy, need, to-morrow, see.

Such I find Guido, midmost blotch of black
Discernible in this group of clustered crimes
Huddling together in the cave they call   870
Their palace, outraged day thus penetrates.
Around him ranged, now close and now remote,
Prominent or obscure to meet the needs
O' the mage and master, I detect each shape
Subsidiary i' the scene nor loathed the less,
All alike coloured, all descried akin
By one and the same pitchy furnace stirred
At the centre : see, they lick the master's hand,—
This fox-faced horrible priest, this brother-brute
The Abate,—why, mere wolfishness looks well,   880
Guido stands honest in the red o' the flame,
Beside this yellow that would pass for white,
This Guido, all craft but no violence,
This copier of the mien and gait and garb
Of Peter and Paul, that he may go disguised,
Rob halt and lame, sick folk i' the temple-porch !

Armed with religion, fortified by law,
A man of peace, who trims the midnight lamp
And turns the classic page—and all for craft,
All to work harm with, yet incur no scratch !   890
While Guido brings the struggle to a close,
Paul steps back the due distance, clear o' the trap
He builds and baits. Guido I catch and judge ;
Paul is past reach in this world and my time :
That is a case reserved. Pass to the next,
The boy of the brood, the young Girolamo
Priest, Canon, and what more ? nor wolf nor fox,
But hybrid, neither craft nor violence
Wholly, part violence part craft : such cross
Tempts speculation—will both blend one day,   900
And prove hell's better product ? Or subside
And let the simple quality emerge,
Go on with Satan's service the old way ?
Meanwhile, what promise,—what performance too !
For there 's a new distinctive touch, I see,
Lust—lacking in the two—hell's own blue tint
That gives a character and marks the man
More than a match for yellow and red. Once more,
A case reserved : why should I doubt ? Then comes
The gaunt grey nightmare in the furthest smoke,
The hag that gave these three abortions birth,   911
Unmotherly mother and unwomanly
Woman, that near turns motherhood to shame
Womanliness to loathing : no one word,
No gesture to curb cruelty a whit
More than the she-pard thwarts her playsome whelps
Trying their milk-teeth on the soft o' the throat
O' the first fawn, flung, with those beseeching eyes,
Flat in the covert ! How should she but couch,
Lick the dry lips, unsheathe the blunted claw,   920
Catch 'twixt her placid eyewinks at what chance
Old bloody half-forgotten dream may flit,
Born when herself was novice to the taste,
The while she lets youth take its pleasure. Last,
These God-abandoned wretched lumps of life,
These four companions,—country-folk this time,
Not tainted by the unwholesome civic breath,
Much less the curse o' the court ! Mere striplings too,
Fit to do human nature justice still !
Surely when impudence in Guido's shape   930

Shall propose crime and proffer money's-worth
To these stout tall bright-eyed and black-haired boys,
The blood shall bound in answer to each cheek
Before the indignant outcry break from lip !
Are these i' the mood to murder, hardly loosed
From healthy autumn-finish, the ploughed glebe,
Grapes in the barrel, work at happy end,
And winter come with rest and Christmas play ?
How greet they Guido with his final task—
(As if he but proposed ' One vineyard more   940
' To dig, ere frost come, then relax indeed ! ')
' Anywhere, anyhow and anywhy,
' Murder me some three people, old and young,
' Ye never heard the names of,—and be paid
' So much ! '   And the whole four accede at once.
Demur ?   As cattle would, bid march or halt !
Is it some lingering habit, old fond faith
I' the lord of the land, instructs them,—birthright
        badge
Of feudal tenure claims its slaves again ?
Not so at all, thou noble human heart !   950
All is done purely for the pay,—which, earned,
And not forthcoming at the instant, makes
Religion heresy, and the lord o' the land
Fit subject for a murder in his turn.
The patron with cut throat and rifled purse,
Deposited i' the roadside-ditch, his due,
Nought hinders each good fellow trudging home,
The heavier by a piece or two in poke,
And so with new zest to the common life,
Mattock and spade, plough-tail and waggon-shaft,
Till some such other piece of luck betide,   961
Who knows ?   Since this is a mere start in life,
And none of them exceeds the twentieth year.

Nay, more i' the background, yet ?   Unnoticed forms
Claim to be classed, subordinately vile ?
Complacent lookers-on that laugh,—perchance
Shake head as their friend's horse-play grows too rough
With the mere child he manages amiss—
But would not interfere and make bad worse
For twice the fractious tears and prayers : thou know'st
Civility better, Marzi-Medici,   971
Governor for thy kinsman the Granduke !

Fit representative of law, man's lamp
I' the magistrate's grasp full-flare, no rushlight-end
Sputtering 'twixt thumb and finger of the priest !
Whose answer to these Comparini's cry
Is a threat,—whose remedy of Pompilia's wrong
A shrug o' the shoulder, a facetious word
Or wink, traditional with Tuscan wits,
To Guido in the doorway.   Laud to law !   980
The wife is pushed back to the husband, he
Who knows how these home-squabblings persecute
People who have the public good to mind,
And work best with a silence in the court !

Ah, but I save my word at least for thee,
Archbishop, who art under me in the Church,
As I am under God,—thou, chosen by both
To do the shepherd's office, feed the sheep—
How of this lamb that panted at thy foot
While the wolf pressed on her within crook's reach ?
Wast thou the hireling that did turn and flee ?   991
With thee at least anon the little word !

Such denizens o' the cave now cluster round
And heat the furnace sevenfold : time indeed
A bolt from heaven should cleave roof and clear place,
Transfix and show the world, suspiring flame,
The main offender, scar and brand the rest
Hurrying, each miscreant to his hole : then flood
And purify the scene with outside day—
Which yet, in the absolutest drench of dark,   1000
Ne'er wants a witness, some stray beauty-beam
To the despair of hell.

                    First of the first,
Such I pronounce Pompilia, then as now
Perfect in whiteness—stoop thou down, my child,
Give one good moment to the poor old Pope
Heart-sick at having all his world to blame—
Let me look at thee in the flesh as erst,
Let me enjoy the old clean linen garb,   1009
Not the new splendid vesture !   Armed and crowned,
Would Michael, yonder, be, nor crowned nor armed,
The less pre-eminent angel ?   Everywhere
I see in the world the intellect of man,

That sword, the energy his subtle spear,
The knowledge which defends him like a shield—
Everywhere ; but they make not up, I think,
The marvel of a soul like thine, earth's flower
She holds up to the softened gaze of God !
It was not given Pompilia to know much,
Speak much, to write a book, to move mankind,   1020
Be memorized by who records my time.
Yet if in purity and patience, if
In faith held fast despite the plucking fiend,
Safe like the signet-stone with the new name
That saints are known by,—if in right returned
For wrong, most pardon for worst injury,
If there be any virtue, any praise,—
Then will this woman-child have proved — who
      knows ?—
Just the one prize vouchsafed unworthy me,
Ten years a gardener of the untoward ground,   1030
I till,—this earth, my sweat and blood manure
All the long day that barrenly grows dusk :
At least one blossom makes me proud at eve
Born 'mid the briers of my enclosure !   Still
(Oh, here as elsewhere, nothingness of man !)
Those be the plants, imbedded yonder South
To mellow in the morning, those made fat
By the master's eye, that yield such timid leaf,
Uncertain bud, as product of his pains !
While—see how this mere chance-sown, cleft-nursed
      seed,   1040
That sprang up by the wayside 'neath the foot
Of the enemy, this breaks all into blaze,
Spreads itself, one wide glory of desire
To incorporate the whole great sun it loves
From the inch-height whence it looks and longs !   My
      flower,
My rose, I gather for the breast of God,
This I praise most in thee, where all I praise,
That having been obedient to the end
According to the light allotted, law
Prescribed thy life, still tried, still standing test,—
Dutiful to the foolish parents first,   1051
Submissive next to the bad husband,—nay,
Tolerant of those meaner miserable
That did his hests, eked out the dole of pain,—

Thou, patient thus, couldst rise from law to law,
The old to the new, promoted at one cry
O' the trump of God to the new service, not
To longer bear, but henceforth fight, be found
Sublime in new impatience with the foe !
Endure man and obey God : plant firm foot   1060
On neck of man, tread man into the hell
Meet for him, and obey God all the more !
Oh child that didst despise thy life so much
When it seemed only thine to keep or lose,
How the fine ear felt fall the first low word
' Value life, and preserve life for My sake ! '
Thou didst . . how shall I say ? . . receive so long
The standing ordinance of God on earth,
What wonder if the novel claim had clashed
With old requirement, seemed to supersede   1070
Too much the customary law ?   But, brave,
Thou at first prompting of what I call God,
And fools call Nature, didst hear, comprehend,
Accept the obligation laid on thee,
Mother elect, to save the unborn child,
As brute and bird do, reptile and the fly,
Ay and, I nothing doubt, even tree, shrub, plant
And flower o' the field, all in a common pact
To worthily defend that trust of trusts,
Life from the Ever Living :—didst resist—   1080
Anticipate the office that is mine—
And with his own sword stay the upraised arm,
The endeavour of the wicked, and defend
Him who,—again in my default,—was there
For visible providence : one less true than thou
To touch, i' the past, less practised in the right,
Approved so far in all docility
To all instruction,—how had such an one
Made scruple ' Is this motion a decree ? '
It was authentic to the experienced ear   1090
O' the good and faithful servant.   Go past me
And get thy praise,—and be not far to seek
Presently when I follow if I may !

And surely not so very much apart
Need I place thee, my warrior-priest,—in whom
What if I gain the other rose, the gold,
We grave to imitate God's miracle,

Greet monarchs with, good rose in its degree ?
Irregular noble scapegrace—son the same !
Faulty—and peradventure ours the fault   1100
Who still misteach, mislead, throw hook and line
Thinking to land leviathan forsooth,
Tame the scaled neck, play with him as a bird,
And bind him for our maidens !   Better bear
The King of Pride go wantoning awhile,
Unplagued by cord in nose and thorn in jaw,
Through deep to deep, followed by all that shine,
Churning the blackness hoary : He who made
The comely terror, He shall make the sword
To match that piece of netherstone his heart,   1110
Ay, nor miss praise thereby ; who else shut fire
I' the stone, to leap from mouth at sword's first stroke,
In lamps of love and faith, the chivalry
That dares the right and disregards alike
The yea and nay o' the world ?   Self-sacrifice,—
What if an idol took it ?   Ask the Church
Why she was wont to turn each Venus here,—
Poor Rome perversely lingered round, despite
Instruction, for the sake of purblind love,—
Into Madonna's shape, and waste no whit   1120
Of aught so rare on earth as gratitude !
All this sweet savour was not ours but thine,
Nard of the rock, a natural wealth we name
Incense, and treasure up as food for saints,
When flung to us—whose function was to give
Not find the costly perfume.   Do I smile ?
Nay, Caponsacchi, much I find amiss,
Blameworthy, punishable in this freak
Of thine, this youth prolonged though age was ripe,
This masquerade in sober day, with change   1130
Of motley too,—now hypocrite's-disguise,
Now fool's-costume : which lie was least like truth,
Which the ungainlier, more discordant garb
With that symmetric soul inside my son,
The churchman's or the worlding's,—let him judge,
Our Adversary who enjoys the task !
I rather chronicle the healthy rage,—
When the first moan broke from the martyr-maid
At that uncaging of the beasts,—made bare
My athlete on the instant, gave such good   1140
Great undisguised leap over post and pale

Right into the mid-cirque, free fighting-place.
There may have been rash stripping—every rag
Went to the winds,—infringement manifold
Of laws prescribed pudicity, I fear,
In this impulsive and prompt self-display !
Ever such tax comes of the foolish youth ;
Men mulct the wiser manhood, and suspect
No veritable star swims out of cloud :
Bear thou such imputation, undergo   1150
The penalty I nowise dare relax,—
Conventional chastisement and rebuke.
But for the outcome, the brave starry birth
Conciliating earth with all that cloud,
Thank heaven as I do ! Ay, such championship
Of God at first blush, such prompt cheery thud
Of glove on ground that answers ringingly
The challenge of the false knight,—watch we long,
And wait we vainly for its gallant like
From those appointed to the service, sworn   1160
His body-guard with pay and privilege—
White-cinct, because in white walks sanctity,
Red-socked, how else proclaim fine scorn of flesh,
Unchariness of blood when blood faith begs ?
Where are the men-at-arms with cross on coat ?
Aloof, bewraying their attire : whilst thou
In mask and motley, pledged to dance not fight,
Sprang'st forth the hero ! In thought, word and deed,
How throughout all thy warfare thou wast pure,
I find it easy to believe : and if   1170
At any fateful moment of the strange
Adventure, the strong passion of that strait,
Fear and surprise, may have revealed too much,—
As when a thundrous midnight, with black air
That burns, rain-drops that blister, breaks a spell,
Draws out the excessive virtue of some sheathed
Shut unsuspected flower that hoards and hides
Immensity of sweetness,—so, perchance,
Might the surprise and fear release too much
The perfect beauty of the body and soul   1180
Thou savedst in thy passion for God's sake,
He who is Pity : was the trial sore ?
Temptation sharp ? Thank God a second time !
Why comes temptation but for man to meet
And master and make crouch beneath his foot,

And so be pedestalled in triumph ?   Pray
' Lead us into no such temptations, Lord ! '
Yea, but, O Thou whose servants are the bold,
Lead such temptations by the head and hair,
Reluctant dragons, up to who dares fight,   1190
That so he may do battle and have praise !
Do I not see the praise ?—that while thy mates
Bound to deserve i' the matter, prove at need
Unprofitable through the very pains
We gave to train them well and start them fair,—
Are found too stiff, with standing ranked and ranged,
For onset in good earnest, too obtuse
Of ear, through iteration of command,
For catching quick the sense of the real cry,—   1199
Thou, whose sword-hand was used to strike the lute,
Whose sentry-station graced some wanton's gate,
Thou didst push forward and show mettle, shame
The laggards, and retrieve the day.   Well done !
Be glad thou hast let light into the world,
Through that irregular breach o' the boundary,—see
The same upon thy path and march assured,
Learning anew the use of soldiership,
Self-abnegation, freedom from all fear,
Loyalty to the life's end !   Ruminate,
Deserve the initiatory spasm,—once more   1210
Work, be unhappy but bear life, my son !

And troop you, somewhere 'twixt the best and worst,
Where crowd the indifferent product, all too poor
Makeshift, starved samples of humanity !
Father and mother, huddle there and hide !
A gracious eye may find you !   Foul and fair,
Sadly mixed natures : self-indulgent,—yet
Self-sacrificing too : how the love soars,
How the craft, avarice, vanity and spite
Sink again !   So they keep the middle course,   1220
Slide into silly crime at unaware,
Slip back upon the stupid virtue, stay
Nowhere enough for being classed, I hope
And fear.   Accept the swift and rueful death,
Taught, somewhat sternlier than is wont, what waits
The ambiguous creature,—how the one black tuft
Steadies the aim of the arrow just as well
As the wide faultless white on the bird's breast.

Nay, you were punished in the very part
That looked most pure of speck,—the honest love   1230
Betrayed you,—did love seem most worthy pains,
Challenge such purging, as ordained survive
When all the rest of you was done with ?   Go !
Never again elude the choice of tints !
White shall not neutralize the black, nor good
Compensate bad in man, absolve him so :
Life's business being just the terrible choice.

So do I see, pronounce on all and some
Grouped for my judgment now,—profess no doubt
While I pronounce : dark, difficult enough   1240
The human sphere, yet eyes grow sharp by use,
I find the truth, dispart the shine from shade,
As a mere man may, with no special touch
O' the lynx-gift in each ordinary orb :
Nay, if the popular notion class me right,
One of well nigh decayed intelligence,—
What of that ?   Through hard labour and good will,
And habitude that gives a blind man sight
At the practised finger-ends of him, I do
Discern, and dare decree in consequence,   1250
Whatever prove the peril of mistake.
Whence, then, this quite new quick cold thrill,—
        cloud-like,
This keen dread creeping from a quarter scarce
Suspected in the skies I nightly scan ?
What slacks the tense nerve, saps the wound-up spring
Of the act that should and shall be, sends the mount
And mass o' the whole man's-strength,—conglobed so
        late—
Shudderingly into dust, a moment's work ?
While I stand firm, go fearless, in this world,
For this life recognize and arbitrate,   1260
Touch and let stay, or else remove a thing,
Judge ' This is right, this object out of place,'
Candle in hand that helps me and to spare,—
What if a voice deride me, ' Perk and pry !
' Brighten each nook with thine intelligence !
' Play the good householder, ply man and maid
' With tasks prolonged into the midnight, test
' Their work and nowise stint of the due wage
' Each worthy worker : but with gyves and whip

' Pay thou misprision of a single point   1270
' Plain to thy happy self who lift'st the light,
' Lament'st the darkling,—bold to all beneath !
' What if thyself adventure, now the place
' Is purged so well ?   Leave pavement and mount roof,
' Look round thee for the light of the upper sky,
' The fire which lit thy fire which finds default
' In Guido Franceschini to his cost !
' What if, above in the domain of light,
' Thou miss the accustomed signs, remark eclipse ?
' Shalt thou still gaze on ground nor lift a lid,—   1280
' Steady in thy superb prerogative,
' Thy inch of inkling,—nor once face the doubt
' I' the sphere above thee, darkness to be felt ? '

Yet my poor spark had for its source, the sun ;
Thither I sent the great looks which compel
Light from its fount : all that I do and am
Comes from the truth, or seen or else surmised,
Remembered or divined, as mere man may :
I know just so, nor otherwise.   As I know,
I speak,—what should I know, then, and how speak
Were there a wild mistake of eye or brain   1291
In the recorded governance above ?
If my own breath, only, blew coal alight
I called celestial and the morning-star ?
I, who in this world act resolvedly,
Dispose of men, the body and the soul,
As they acknowledge or gainsay this light
I show them,—shall I too lack courage ?—leave
I, too, the post of me, like those I blame ?
Refuse, with kindred inconsistency,   1300
Grapple with danger whereby souls grow strong ?
I am near the end ; but still not at the end ;
All till the very end is trial in life :
At this stage is the trial of my soul
Danger to face, or danger to refuse ?
Shall I dare try the doubt now, or not dare ?

O Thou,—as represented here to me
In such conception as my soul allows,—
Under Thy measureless my atom width !—
Man's mind—what is it but a convex glass   1310
Wherein are gathered all the scattered points

Picked out of the immensity of sky,
To reunite there, be our heaven on earth,
Our known unknown, our God revealed to man ?
Existent somewhere, somehow, as a whole ;
Here, as a whole proportioned to our sense,—
There, (which is nowhere, speech must babble thus !)
In the absolute immensity, the whole
Appreciable solely by Thyself,—
Here, by the little mind of man, reduced   1320
To littleness that suits his faculty,
Appreciable too in the degree ;
Between Thee and ourselves—nay even, again,
Below us, to the extreme of the minute,
Appreciable by how many and what diverse
Modes of the life Thou makest be ! (why live
Except for love,—how love unless they know ?)
Each of them, only filling to the edge,
Insect or angel, his just length and breadth,
Due facet of reflection,—full, no less,   1330
Angel or insect, as Thou framedst things,—
I it is who have been appointed here
To represent Thee, in my turn, on earth,
Just as, if new philosophy know aught,
This one earth, out of all the multitude
Of peopled worlds, as stars are now supposed,—
Was chosen, and no sun-star of the swarm,
For stage and scene of Thy transcendent act
Beside which even the creation fades
Into a puny exercise of power.   1340
Choice of the world, choice of the thing I am,
Both emanate alike from the dread play
Of operation outside this our sphere
Where things are classed and counted small or great,—
Incomprehensibly the choice is Thine !
I therefore bow my head and take Thy place.
There is, beside the works, a tale of Thee
In the world's mouth which I find credible :
I love it with my heart : unsatisfied,
I try it with my reason, nor discept   1350
From any point I probe and pronounce sound.
Mind is not matter nor from matter, but
Above,—leave matter then, proceed with mind :
Man's be the mind recognized at the height,—
Leave the inferior minds and look at man.

Is he the strong, intelligent and good
Up to his own conceivable height ?   Nowise.
Enough o' the low,—soar the conceivable height,
Find cause to match the effect in evidence,
Works in the world, not man's, then God's ; leave
    man :
Conjecture of the worker by the work :   1361
Is there strength there ?—enough : intelligence ?
Ample : but goodness in a like degree ?
Not to the human eye in the present state,
This isoscele deficient in the base.
What lacks, then, of perfection fit for God
But just the instance which this tale supplies
Of love without a limit ?   So is strength,
So is intelligence ; then love is so,
Unlimited in its self-sacrifice :   1370
Then is the tale true and God shows complete.
Beyond the tale, I reach into the dark,
Feel what I cannot see, and still faith stands :
I can believe this dread machinery
Of sin and sorrow, would confound me else,
Devised,—all pain, at most expenditure
Of pain by Who devised pain,—to evolve,
By new machinery in counterpart,
The moral qualities of man—how else ?—
To make him love in turn and be beloved,   1380
Creative and self-sacrificing too,
And thus eventually God-like, (ay,
' I have said ye are Gods,'—shall it be said for
    nought ?)
Enable man to wring, from out all pain,
All pleasure for a common heritage
To all eternity : this may be surmised,
The other is revealed,—whether a fact,
Absolute, abstract, independent truth,
Historic, not reduced to suit man's mind,—
Or only truth reverberate, changed, made pass   1390
A spectrum into mind, the narrow eye,—
The same and not the same, else unconceived—
Though quite conceivable to the next grade
Above it in intelligence,—as truth
Easy to man were blindness to the beast
By parity of procedure,—the same truth
In a new form, but changed in either case :

What matter so the intelligence be filled ?
To the child, the sea is angry, for it roars ;　　1399
Frost bites, else why the tooth-like fret on face ?
Man makes acoustics deal with the sea's wrath,
Explains the choppy cheek by chymic law,—
To both, remains one and the same effect
On drum of ear and root of nose, change cause
Never so thoroughly : so our heart be struck,
What care I,—by God's gloved hand or the bare ?
Nor do I much perplex me with aught hard,
Dubious in the transmitting of the tale,—
No, nor with certain riddles set to solve.
This life is training and a passage ; pass,—　　1410
Still, we march over some flat obstacle
We made give way before us ; solid truth
In front of it, were motion for the world ?
The moral sense grows but by exercise.
'T is even as man grew probatively
Initiated in Godship, set to make
A fairer moral world than this he finds,
Guess now what shall be known hereafter.　Thus,
O' the present problem : as we see and speak,
A faultless creature is destroyed, and sin　　1420
Has had its way i' the world where God should rule.
Ay, but for this irrelevant circumstance
Of inquisition after blood, we see
Pompilia lost and Guido saved : how long ?
For his whole life : how much is that whole life ?
We are not babes, but know the minute's worth,
And feel that life is large and the world small,
So, wait till life have passed from out the world.

Neither does this astonish at the end,
That, whereas I can so receive and trust,　　1430
Men, made with hearts and souls the same as mine,
Reject and disbelieve,—subordinate
The future to the present,—sin, nor fear.
This I refer still to the foremost fact,
Life is probation and this earth no goal
But starting-point of man : compel him strive,
Which means, in man, as good as reach the goal,—
Why institute that race, his life, at all ?
But this does overwhelm me with surprise,
Touch me to terror,—not that faith, the pearl,　　1440

Should be let lie by fishers wanting food,—
Nor, seen and handled by a certain few
Critical and contemptuous, straight consigned
To shore and shingle for the pebble it proves,—
But that, when haply found and known and named
By the residue made rich for evermore,
These,—ay, these favoured ones, should in a trice
Turn, and with double zest go dredge for whelks,
Mud-worms that make the savoury soup.   Enough
O' the disbelievers, see the faithful few !   1450
How do the Christians here deport them, keep
Their robes of white unspotted by the world ?
What is this Aretine Archbishop, this
Man under me as I am under God,
This champion of the faith, I armed and decked,
Pushed forward, put upon a pinnacle,
To show the enemy his victor,—see !
What 's the best fighting when the couple close ?
Pompilia cries, ' Protect me from the fiend ! '
' No, for thy Guido is one heady, strong,   1460
' Dangerous to disquiet : let him bide !
' He needs some bone to mumble, help amuse
' The darkness of his den with : so, the fawn
' Which limps up bleeding to my foot and lies,
' —Come to me, daughter,—thus I throw him back ! '
Have we misjudged here, over-armed the knight,
Given gold and silk where the plain steel serves best,
Enfeebled whom we sought to fortify,
Made an archbishop and undone a saint ?
Well then, descend these heights, this pride of life,
Sit in the ashes with the barefoot monk   1471
Who long ago stamped out the worldly sparks.
Fasting and watching, stone cell and wire scourge,
—No such indulgence as unknits the strength—
These breed the tight nerve and tough cuticle,
Let the world's praise or blame run rillet-wise
Off the broad back and brawny breast, we know !
He meets the first cold sprinkle of the world
And shudders to the marrow, ' Save this child ?
' Oh, my superiors, oh, the Archbishop here !   1480
' Who was it dared lay hand upon the ark
' His betters saw fall nor put finger forth ?
' Great ones could help yet help not : why should
      small ?

' I break my promise : let her break her heart ! '
These are the Christians not the worldlings, not
The sceptics, who thus battle for the faith !
If foolish virgins disobey and sleep,
What wonder ?   But the wise that watch, this time
Sell lamps and buy lutes, exchange oil for wine,
The mystic Spouse betrays the Bridegroom here.
To our last resource, then !   Since all flesh is weak,
Bind weaknesses together, we get strength :   1492
The individual weighed, found wanting, try
Some institution, honest artifice
Whereby the units grow compact and firm :
Each props the other, and so stand is made
By our embodied cowards that grow brave.
The Monastery called of Convertites,
Meant to help women because these helped Christ,—
A thing existent only while it acts,   1500
Does as designed, else a nonentity,
For what is an idea unrealized ?—
Pompilia is consigned to these for help.
They do help ; they are prompt to testify
To her pure life and saintly dying days.
She dies, and lo, who seemed so poor, proves rich !
What does the body that lives through helpfulness
To women for Christ's sake ?   The kiss turns bite,
The dove's note changes to the crow's cry : judge !
' Seeing that this our Convent claims of right   1510
' What goods belong to those we succour, be
' The same proved women of dishonest life,—
' And seeing that this Trial made appear
' Pompilia was in such predicament,—
' The Convent hereupon pretends to said
' Succession of Pompilia, issues writ,
' And takes possession by the Fisc's advice.'
Such is their attestation to the cause
Of Christ, who had one saint at least, they hoped :
But, is a title-deed to filch, a corpse   1520
To slander, and an infant-heir to cheat ?
Christ must give up his gains then !   They unsay
All the fine speeches,—who was saint is whore.
Why, scripture yields no parallel for this !
The soldiers only threw dice for Christ's coat ;
We want another legend of the Twelve
Disputing if it was Christ's coat at all,

Claiming as prize the woof of price—for why ?
The Master was a thief, purloined the same,
Or paid for it out of the common bag !   1530
Can it be this is end and outcome, all
I take with me to show as stewardship's fruit,
The best yield of the latest time, this year
The seventeen-hundredth since God died for man ?
Is such effect proportionate to cause ?
And still the terror keeps on the increase
When I perceive . . how can I blink the fact ?
That the fault, the obduracy to good,
Lies not with the impracticable stuff
Whence man is made, his very nature's fault,   1540
As if it were of ice, the moon may gild
Not melt, or stone, 't was meant the sun should warm
Not make bear flowers,—nor ice nor stone to blame :
But it can melt, that ice, and bloom, that stone,
Impassible to rule of day and night !
This terrifies me, thus compelled perceive,
Whatever love and faith we looked should spring
At advent of the authoritative star,
Which yet lie sluggish, curdled at the source,—
These have leapt forth profusely in old time,   1550
These still respond with promptitude to-day,
At challenge of—what unacknowledged powers
O' the air, what uncommissioned meteors, warmth
By law, and light by rule should supersede ?
For see this priest, this Caponsacchi, stung
At the first summons,—' Help for honour's sake,
' Play the man, pity the oppressed ! '—no pause,
How does he lay about him in the midst,
Strike any foe, right wrong at any risk,
All blindness, bravery and obedience !—blind ?
Ay, as a man would be inside the sun,   1561
Delirious with the plenitude of light
Should interfuse him to the finger-ends—
Let him rush straight, and how shall he go wrong ?
Where are the Christians in their panoply ?
The loins we girt about with truth, the breasts
Righteousness plated round, the shield of faith,
The helmet of salvation, and that sword
O' the Spirit, even the word of God,—where these ?
Slunk into corners !   Oh, I hear at once   1570
Hubbub of protestation !   ' What, we monks

' We friars, of such an order, such a rule,
' Have not we fought, bled, left our martyr-mark
' At every point along the boundary-line
' 'Twixt true and false, religion and the world,
' Where this or the other dogma of our Church
' Called for defence ? '   And I, despite myself,
How can I but speak loud what truth speaks low,
' Or better than the best, or nothing serves !
' What boots deed, I can cap and cover straight
' With such another doughtiness to match,   1581
' Done at an instinct of the natural man ? '
Immolate body, sacrifice soul too,—
Do not these publicans the same ?   Outstrip !
Or else stop race, you boast runs neck and neck,
You with the wings, they with the feet,—for shame !
Oh, I remark your diligence and zeal !
Five years long, now, rounds faith into my ears,
' Help thou, or Christendom is done to death ! '
Five years since, in the Province of To-kien,   1590
Which is in China as some people know,
Maigrot, my Vicar Apostolic there,
Having a great qualm, issues a decree.
Alack, the converts use as God's name, not
Tien-chu but plain *Tien* or else mere *Shang-ti*,
As Jesuits please to fancy politic,
While, say Dominicans, it calls down fire,—
For *Tien* means heaven, and *Shang-ti*, supreme prince,
While *Tien-chu* means the lord of heaven : all cry,
' There is no business urgent for despatch   1600
' As that thou send a legate, specially
' Cardinal Tournon, straight to Pekin, there
' To settle and compose the difference ! '
So have I seen a potentate all fume
For some infringement of his realm's just right,
Some menace to a mud-built straw-thatched farm
O' the frontier, while inside the mainland lie,
Quite undisputed-for in solitude,
Whole cities plague may waste or famine sap :
What if the sun crumble, the sands encroach,   1610
While he looks on sublimely at his ease ?
How does their ruin touch the empire's bound ?

And is this little all that was to be ?
Where is the gloriously-decisive change,

The immeasurable metamorphosis
Of human clay to divine gold, we looked
Should, in some poor sort, justify the price ?
Had a mere adept of the Rosy Cross
Spent his life to consummate the Great Work,
Would not we start to see the stuff it touched   1620
Yield not a grain more than the vulgar got
By the old smelting-process years ago ?
If this were sad to see in just the sage
Who should profess so much, perform no more,
What is it when suspected in that Power
Who undertook to make and made the world,
Devised and did effect man, body and soul,
Ordained salvation for them both, and yet . .
Well, is the thing we see, salvation ?
                                                I   1630
Put no such dreadful question to myself,
Within whose circle of experience burns
The central truth, Power, Wisdom, Goodness,—
     God :
I must outlive a thing ere know it dead :
When I outlive the faith there is a sun,
When I lie, ashes to the very soul,—
Someone, not I, must wail above the heap,
' He died in dark whence never morn arose.'
While I see day succeed the deepest night—
How can I speak but as I know ?—my speech   1640
Must be, throughout the darkness, ' It will end : '
' The light that did burn, will burn!' Clouds obscure—
But for which obscuration all were bright ?
Too hastily concluded ! Sun-suffused,
A cloud may soothe the eye made blind by blaze,—
Better the very clarity of heaven :
The soft streaks are the beautiful and dear.
What but the weakness in a faith supplies
The incentive to humanity, no strength
Absolute, irresistible, comports ?   1650
How can man love but what he yearns to help ?
And that which men think weakness within strength,
But angels know for strength and stronger yet—
What were it else but the first things made new,
But repetition of the miracle,
The divine instance of self-sacrifice
That never ends and aye begins for man ?

So, never I miss footing in the maze,
No,—I have light nor fear the dark at all.

But are mankind not real, who pace outside   1660
My petty circle, the world measured me ?
And when they stumble even as I stand,
Have I a right to stop ears when they cry,
As they were phantoms, took the clouds for crags,
Tripped and fell, where the march of man might move ?
Beside, the cry is other than a ghost's,
When out of the old time there pleads some bard,
Philosopher, or both and—whispers not,
But words it boldly.   ' The inward work and worth
' Of any mind, what other mind may judge   1670
' Save God who only knows the thing He made,
' The veritable service He exacts ?
' It is the outward product men appraise.
' Behold, an engine hoists a tower aloft :
' " I looked that it should move the mountain too ! "
' Or else " Had just a turret toppled down,
' Success enough ! "—may say the Machinist
' Who knows what less or more result might be :
' But we, who see that done we cannot do,   1679
' " A feat beyond man's force," we men must say.
' Regard me and that shake I gave the world !
' I was born, not so long before Christ's birth,
' As Christ's birth haply did precede thy day,—
' But many a watch, before the star of dawn :
' Therefore I lived,—it is thy creed affirms,
' Pope Innocent, who art to answer me !—
' Under conditions, nowise to escape,
' Whereby salvation was impossible.
' Each impulse to achieve the good and fair,
' Each aspiration to the pure and true,   1690
' Being without a warrant or an aim,
' Was just as sterile a felicity
' As if the insect, born to spend his life
' Soaring his circles, stopped them to describe
' (Painfully motionless in the mid-air)
' Some word of weighty counsel for man's sake,
' Some " Know thyself " or " Take the golden mean ! "
' —Forwent his happy dance and the glad ray,
' Died half an hour the sooner and was dust.
' I, born to perish like the brutes, or worse,   1700

P

' Why not live brutishly, obey my law ?
' But I, of body as of soul complete,
' A gymnast at the games, philosopher
' I' the schools, who painted, and made music,—all
' Glories that met upon the tragic stage
' When the Third Poet's tread surprised the Two,—
' Whose lot fell in a land where life was great
' And sense went free and beauty lay profuse,
' I, untouched by one adverse circumstance,
' Adopted virtue as my rule of life,   1710
' Waived all reward, and loved for loving's sake,
' And, what my heart taught me, I taught the world,
' And have been teaching now two thousand years.
' Witness my work,—plays that should please, for-
        sooth !
' " They might please, they may displease, they shall
        teach,
' " For truth's sake," so I said, and did, and do.
' Five hundred years ere Paul spoke, Felix heard,—
' How much of temperance and righteousness,
' Judgment to come, did I find reason for,
' Corroborate with my strong style that spared   1720
' No sin, nor swerved the more from branding brow
' Because the sinner was called Zeus and God ?
' How nearly did I guess at that Paul knew ?
' How closely come, in what I represent
' As duty, to his doctrine yet a blank ?
' And as that limner not untruly limns
' Who draws an object round or square, which square
' Or round seems to the unassisted eye,
' Though Galileo's tube display the same
' Oval or oblong,—so, who controverts   1730
' I rendered rightly what proves wrongly wrought
' Beside Paul's picture ?   Mine was true for me.
' I saw that there are, first and above all,
' The hidden forces, blind necessities,
' Named Nature, but the thing's self unconceived :
' Then follow,—how dependent upon these,
' We know not, how imposed above ourselves,
' We well know,—what I name the gods, a power
' Various or one ; for great and strong and good
' Is there, and little, weak and bad there too,   1740
' Wisdom and folly : say, these make no God,—
' What is it else that rules outside man's self ?

' A fact then,—always, to the naked eye,—
' And, so, the one revealment possible
' Of what were unimagined else by man.
' Therefore, what gods do, man may criticize,
' Applaud, condemn,—how should he fear the truth ?
' But likewise have in awe because of power,
' Venerate for the main munificence,
' And give the doubtful deed its due excuse   1750
' From the acknowledged creature of a day
' To the Eternal and Divine.   Thus, bold
' Yet self-mistrusting, should man bear himself,
' Most assured on what now concerns him most—
' The law of his own life, the path he prints,—
' Which law is virtue and not vice, I say,—
' And least inquisitive where least search skills,
' I' the nature we best give the clouds to keep.
' What could I paint beyond a scheme like this
' Out of the fragmentary truths where light   1760
' Lay fitful in a tenebrific time ?
' You have the sunrise now, joins truth to truth,
' Shoots life and substance into death and void ;
' Themselves compose the whole we made before :
' The forces and necessity grow God,—
' The beings so contrarious that seemed gods,
' Prove just His operation manifold
' And multiform, translated, as must be,
' Into intelligible shape so far
' As suits our sense and sets us free to feel :   1770
' What if I let a child think, childhood-long,
' That lightning, I would have him spare his eye,
' Is a real arrow shot at naked orb ?
' The man knows more, but shuts his lids the same :
' Lightning's cause comprehends nor man nor child.
' Why then, my scheme, your better knowledge broke,
' Presently readjusts itself, the small
' Proportioned largelier, parts and whole named new :
' So much, no more two thousand years have done !
' Pope, dost thou dare pretend to punish me   1780
' For not descrying sunshine at midnight,
' Me who crept all-fours, found my way so far—
' While thou rewardest teachers of the truth,
' Who miss the plain way in the blaze of noon,—
' Though just a word from that strong style of mine,
' Grasped honestly in hand as guiding-staff,

' Had pricked them a sure path across the bog,
' That mire of cowardice and slush of lies
' Wherein I find them wallow in wide day ? '

How should I answer this Euripides ?   1790
Paul,—'t is a legend,—answered Seneca,
But that was in the day-spring ; noon is now
We have got too familiar with the light.
Shall I wish back once more that thrill of dawn ?
When the whole truth-touched man burned up, one
          fire ?
—Assured the trial, fiery, fierce, but fleet,
Would, from his little heap of ashes, lend
Wings to the conflagration of the world
Which Christ awaits ere He make all things new—
So should the frail become the perfect, rapt   1800
From glory of pain to glory of joy ; and so,
Even in the end,—the act renouncing earth,
Lands, houses, husbands, wives and children here,—
Begin that other act which finds all, lost,
Regained, in this time even, a hundredfold,
And, in the next time, feels the finite love
Blent and embalmed with its eternal life.
So does the sun ghastlily seem to sink
In those north parts, lean all but out of life,
Desist a dread mere breathing-stop, then slow   1810
Reassert day, begin the endless rise.
Was this too easy for our after-stage ?
Was such a lighting-up of faith, in life,
Only allowed initiate, set man's step
In the true way by help of the great glow ?
A way wherein it is ordained he walk,
Bearing to see the light from heaven still more
And more encroached on by the light of earth,
Tentatives earth puts forth to rival heaven,
Earthly incitements that mankind serve God   1820
For man's sole sake, not God's and therefore man's,
Till at last, who distinguishes the sun
From a mere Druid fire on a far mount ?
More praise to him who with his subtle prism
Shall decompose both beams and name the true.
In such sense, who is last proves first indeed ;
For how could saints and martyrs fail see truth
Streak the night's blackness ?   Who is faithful now,

Untwists heaven's pure white from the yellow flare
O' the world's gross torch, without a foil to help
Produce the Christian act, so possible   1831
When in the way stood Nero's cross and stake,—
So hard now that the world smiles ' Rightly done !
' It is the politic, the thrifty way,
' Will clearly make you in the end returns
' Beyond our fool's-sport and improvidence :
' We fools go thro' the cornfield of this life,
' Pluck ears to left and right and swallow raw,
' —Nay, tread, at pleasure, a sheaf underfoot,
' To get the better at some poppy-flower,—   1840
' Well aware we shall have so much wheat less
' In the eventual harvest : you meantime
' Waste not a spike,—the richlier will you reap !
' What then ? There will be always garnered meal
' Sufficient for our comfortable loaf,
' While you enjoy the undiminished prize ! '
Is it not this ignoble confidence,
Cowardly hardihood, that dulls and damps,
Makes the old heroism impossible ?

Unless . . what whispers me of times to come ?   1850
What if it be the mission of that age,
My death will usher into life, to shake
This torpor of assurance from our creed,
Re-introduce the doubt discarded, bring
The formidable danger back, we drove
Long ago to the distance and the dark ?
No wild beast now prowls round the infant camp ;
We have built wall and sleep in city safe :
But if the earthquake try the towers, that laugh
To think they once saw lions rule outside,   1860
Till man stand out again, pale, resolute,
Prepared to die,—that is, alive at last ?
As we broke up that old faith of the world,
Have we, next age, to break up this the new—
Faith, in the thing, grown faith in the report—
Whence need to bravely disbelieve report
Through increased faith in thing reports belie ?
Must we deny,—do they, these Molinists,
At peril of their body and their soul,—
Recognized truths, obedient to some truth   1870
Unrecognized yet, but perceptible ?—

Correct the portrait by the living face,
Man's God, by God's God in the mind of man ?
Then, for the few that rise to the new height,
The many that must sink to the old depth,
The multitude found fall away ! A few,
E'en ere the new law speak clear, keep the old,
Preserve the Christian level, call good good
And evil evil, (even though razed and blank
The old titles stand,) thro' custom, habitude,   1880
And all they may mistake for finer sense
O' the fact than reason warrants,—as before,
They hope perhaps, fear not impossibly.
Surely some one Pompilia in the world
Will say ' I know the right place by foot's feel,
' I took it and tread firm there ; wherefore change ? '
But what a multitude will fall, perchance,
Quite through the crumbling truth subjacent late,
Sink to the next discoverable base,
Rest upon human nature, take their stand   1890
On what is fact, the lust and pride of life !
The mass of men, whose very souls even now
Seem to need re-creating,—so they slink
Worm-like into the mud light now lays bare,—
Whose future we dispose of with shut eyes
' They are baptized,—grafted, the barren twigs,
' Into the living stock of Christ : may bear
' One day, till when they lie death-like, not dead,'—
Those who with all the aid of Christ lie thus,
How, without Christ, whither, unaided, sink ?   1900
What but to this rehearsed before my eyes ?
Do not we end, the century and I ?
The impatient antimasque treads close on kibe
O' the very masque's self it will mock,—on me,
Last lingering personage, the impatient mime
Pushes already,—will I block the way ?
Will my slow trail of garments ne'er leave space
For pantaloon, sock, plume and castanet ?
Here comes the first experimentalist
In the new order of things,—he plays a priest ;   1910
Does he take inspiration from the Church,
Directly make her rule his law of life ?
Not he : his own mere impulse guides the man—
Happily sometimes, since ourselves admit
He has danced, in gaiety of heart, i' the main

The right step in the maze we bade him foot.
What if his heart had prompted to break loose
And mar the measure ?   Why, we must submit
And thank the chance that brought him safely
  through.
Will he repeat the prodigy ?   Perhaps.   1920
Can he teach others how to quit themselves,
Prove why this step was right, while that were wrong ?
How should he ?   ' Ask your hearts as I asked mine,
' And get discreetly through the morrice so ;
' If your hearts misdirect you,—quit the stage,
' And make amends,—be there amends to make.'
Such is, for the Augustine that was once,
This Canon Caponsacchi we see now.
' And my heart answers to another tune,'
Puts in the Abate, second in the suite,   1930
' I have my taste too, and tread no such step !
' You choose the glorious life, and may, for me,
' Who like the lowest of life's appetites,—
' What you judge,—but the very truth of joy
' To my own apprehension which must judge.
' Call me knave and you get yourself called fool !
' I live for greed, ambition, lust, revenge ;
' Attain these ends by force, guile : hypocrite,
' To-day, perchance to-morrow recognized
' The rational man, the type of common sense.'   1940
There 's Loyola adapted to our time !
Under such guidance Guido plays his part,
He also influencing in due turn
These last clods where I track intelligence
By any glimmer, those four at his beck
Ready to murder any, and, at their own,
As ready to murder him,—these are the world !
And, first effect of the new cause of things,
There they lie also duly,—the old pair
Of the weak head and not so wicked heart,   1950
And the one Christian mother, wife and girl,—
—Which three gifts seem to make an angel up,—
The first foot of the dance is on their heads !

Still, I stand here, not off the stage though close
On the exit : and my last act, as my first,
I owe the scene, and Him who armed me thus
With Paul's sword as with Peter's key.   I smite

With my whole strength once more, then end my
    part,
Ending, so far as man may, this offence.
And when I raise my arm, what plucks my sleeve ?
Who stops me in the righteous function,—foe   1961
Or friend ?   O, still as ever, friends are they
Who, in the interest of outraged truth
Deprecate such rough handling of a lie !
The facts being proved and incontestable,
What is the last word I must listen to ?
Is it ' Spare yet a term this barren stock,
' We pray thee dig about and dung and dress
' Till he repent and bring forth fruit even yet ? '
Is it ' So poor and swift a punishment   1970
' Shall throw him out of life with all that sin ?
' Let mercy rather pile up pain on pain
' Till the flesh expiate what the soul pays else ? '
Nowise ! Remonstrance on all sides begins
Instruct me, there 's a new tribunal now
Higher than God's,—the educated man's !
Nice sense of honour in the human breast
Supersedes here the old coarse oracle—
Confirming handsomely a point or so
Wherein the predecessor worked aright   1980
By rule of thumb: as when Christ said,—when,
    where ?
Enough, I find it in a pleading here,—
' All other wrongs done, patiently I take :
' But touch my honour and the case is changed !
' I feel the due resentment,—*nemini*
' *Honorem trado*, is my quick retort.'
Right of Him, just as if pronounced to-day !
Still, should the old authority be mute,
Or doubtful, or in speaking clash with new,
The younger takes permission to decide.   1990
At last we have the instinct of the world
Ruling its household without tutelage,
And while the two laws, human and divine,
Have busied finger with this tangled case,
In the brisk junior pushes, cuts the knot,
Pronounces for acquittal. How it trips
Silverly o'er the tongue ! ' Remit the death !
' Forgive, . . well, in the old way, if thou please,
' Decency and the relics of routine

' Respected,—let the Count go free as air !   2000
' Since he may plead a priest's immunity,—
' The minor orders help enough for that,
' With Farinacci's licence,—who decides
' That the mere implication of such man,
' So privileged, in any cause, before
' Whatever court except the Spiritual,
' Straight quashes the procedure,—quash it, then !
' It proves a pretty loophole of escape
' Moreover, that, beside the patent fact
' O' the law's allowance, there 's involved the weal
' O' the Popedom : a son's privilege at stake,   2011
' Thou wilt pretend the Church's interest,
' Ignore all finer reasons to forgive !
' But herein lies the proper cogency—
' (Let thy friends teach thee while thou tellest beads)
' That in this case the spirit of culture speaks,
' Civilization is imperative.
' To her shall we remand all delicate points
' Henceforth, nor take irregular advice
' O' the sly, as heretofore : she used to hint   2020
' Apologies when law was out of sorts
' Because a saucy tongue was put to rest,
' An eye that roved was cured of arrogance :
' But why be forced to mumble under breath
' What soon shall be acknowledged the plain fact,
' Outspoken, say, in thy successor's time ?
' Methinks we see the golden age return !
' Civilization and the Emperor
' Succeed thy Christianity and Pope.
' One Emperor then, as one Pope now : meanwhile,
' She anticipates a little to tell thee " Take   2031
' " Count Guido's life, and sap society,
' " Whereof the main prop was, is, and shall prove
' " —Supremacy of husband over wife ! "
' Shall the man rule i' the house, or may his mate
' Because of any plea dispute the same ?
' Oh, pleas of all sorts shall abound, be sure,
' If once allowed validity,—for, harsh
' And savage, for, inept and silly-sooth,
' For, this and that, will the ingenious sex   2040
' Demonstrate the best master e'er graced slave :
' And there 's but one short way to end the coil,—
' By giving right and reason steadily
                    P 3

' To the man and master : then the wife submits.
' There it is broadly stated,—nor the time
' Admits we shift—a pillar ? nay, a stake
' Out of its place i' the tenement, one touch
' Whereto may send a shudder through the heap
' And bring it toppling on our heads perchance.
' Moreover, if this breed a qualm in thee,   2050
' Give thine own feelings play for once,—deal death ?
' Thou, whose own life winks o'er the socket-edge,
' Would'st thou it went out in such ugly snuff
' As dooming sons to death, though justice bade ?
' Why, on a certain feast, Barabbas' self
' Was set free not to cloud the general cheer.
' Neither shalt thou pollute thy Sabbath close !
' Mercy is safe and graceful.   How one hears
' The howl begin, scarce the three little taps
' O' the silver mallet ended on thy brow,—   2060
' " His last act was to sacrifice a Count
' " And thereby screen a scandal of the Church !
' " Guido condemned, the Canon justified
' " Of course,—delinquents of his cloth go free ! "
' And so the Luthers and the Calvins come,
' So thy hand helps Molinos to the chair
' Whence he may hold forth till doom's day on just
' These *petit-maître* priestlings, in the choir,
' *Sanctus et Benedictus*, with a brush
' Of soft guitar-strings that obey the thumb,   2070
' Touched by the bedside, for accompaniment !
' Does this give umbrage to a husband ?   Death
' To the fool, and to the priest impunity !
' But no impunity to any friend
' So simply over-loyal as these four
' Who made religion of their patron's cause,
' Believed in him and did his bidding straight,
' Asked not one question but laid down the lives
' This Pope took,—all four lives together made
' Just his own length of days,—so, dead they lie,
' As these were times when loyalty 's a drug,   2081
' And zeal in a subordinate too cheap
' And common to be saved when we spend life !
' Come, 't is too much good breath we waste in words :
' The pardon, Holy Father !   Spare grimace,
' Shrugs and reluctance !   Are not we the world,
' Bid thee, our Priam, let soft culture plead

' Hecuba-like, " *non tali* " (Virgil serves)
' " *Auxilio*," and the rest ! Enough, it works !
' The Pope relaxes, and the Prince is loth,   2090
' The father's bowels yearn, the man's will bends,
' Reply is apt. Our tears on tremble, hearts
' Big with a benediction, wait the word
' Shall circulate thro' the city in a trice,
' Set every window flaring, give each man
' O' the mob his torch to wave for gratitude.
' Pronounce it, for our breath and patience fail ! '

I will, Sirs : for a voice other than yours
Quickens my spirit. ' *Quis pro Domino ?*
' Who is upon the Lord's side ? ' asked the Count.
I, who write—   2101
                        ' On receipt of this command,
' Acquaint Count Guido and his fellows four
' They die to-morrow : could it be to-night,
' The better, but the work to do, takes time.
' Set with all diligence a scaffold up,
' Not in the customary place, by Bridge
' Saint Angelo, where die the common sort ;
' But since the man is noble, and his peers
' By predilection haunt the People's Square,   2110
' There let him be beheaded in the midst,
' And his companions hanged on either side :
' So shall the quality see, fear and learn.
' All which work takes time : till to-morrow, then,
' Let there be prayer incessant for the five ! '

For the main criminal I have no hope
Except in such a suddenness of fate.
I stood at Naples once, a night so dark
I could have scarce conjectured there was earth
Anywhere, sky or sea or world at all :   2120
But the night's black was burst through by a blaze—
Thunder struck blow on blow, earth groaned and
        bore,
Through her whole length of mountain visible :
There lay the city thick and plain with spires,
And, like a ghost disshrouded, white the sea.
So may the truth be flashed out by one blow,
And Guido see, one instant, and be saved.
Else I avert my face, nor follow him

Into that sad obscure sequestered state
Where God unmakes but to remake the soul   2130
He else made first in vain ; which must not be.
Enough, for I may die this very night
And how should I dare die, this man let live ?

Carry this forthwith to the Governor !

GUIDO

You are the Cardinal Acciaiuoli, and you,
Abate Panciatichi—two good Tuscan names :
Acciaiuoli—ah, your ancestor it was,
Built the huge battlemented convent-block
Over the little forky flashing Greve
That takes the quick turn at the foot o' the hill
Just as one first sees Florence : oh those days !
'T is Ema, though, the other rivulet,
The one-arched, brown brick bridge yawns over,—yes,
Gallop and go five minutes, and you gain   10
The Roman Gate from where the Ema 's bridged :
Kingfishers fly there : how I see the bend
O'erturreted by Certosa which he built,
That Senescal (we styled him) of your House !
I do adjure you, help me, Sirs !   My blood
Comes from as far a source : ought it to end
This way, by leakage through their scaffold-planks
Into Rome's sink where her red refuse runs ?
Sirs, I beseech you by blood-sympathy,
If there be any vile experiment   20
In the air,—if this your visit simply prove,
When all 's done, just a well-intentioned trick,
That tries for truth truer than truth itself,
By startling up a man, ere break of day,
To tell him he must die at sunset,—pshaw !
That man 's a Franceschini ; feel his pulse,
Laugh at your folly, and let 's all go sleep !
You have my last word,—innocent am I
As Innocent my Pope and murderer,
Innocent as a babe, as Mary's own,   30
As Mary's self,—I said, say and repeat,—
And why, then, should I die twelve hours hence ?   I—
Whom, not twelve hours ago, the gaoler bade
Turn to my straw-truss, settle and sleep sound
That I might wake the sooner, promptlier pay

His dues of meat-and-drink-indulgence, cross
His palm with fee of the good-hand, beside,
As gallants use who go at large again !
For why ?   All honest Rome approved my part ;
Whoever owned wife, sister, daughter,—nay,   40
Mistress,—had any shadow of any right
That looks like right, and, all the more resolved,
Held it with tooth and nail,—these manly men
Approved !   I being for Rome, Rome was for me !
Then, there 's the point reserved, the subterfuge
My lawyers held by, kept for last resource,
Firm should all else,—the impossible fancy !—fail,—
And sneaking burgess-spirit win the day :
The knaves !   One plea at least would hold, they
      laughed,
One grappling-iron scratch the bottom-rock   50
Even should the middle mud let anchor go—
And hook my cause on to the Clergy's,—plea
Which, even if law tipped off my hat and plume,
Would show my priestly tonsure, save me so,—
The Pope moreover, this old Innocent,
Being so meek and mild and merciful,
So fond o' the poor and so fatigued of earth,
So . . fifty thousand devils in deepest hell !
Why must he cure us of our strange conceit
Of the angel in man's likeness, that we loved   60
And looked should help us at a pinch ?   He help ?
He pardon ?   Here 's his mind and message—death,
Thank the good Pope !   Now, is he good in this,
Never mind, Christian,—no such stuff 's extant,—
But will my death do credit to his reign,
Show he both lived and let live, so was good ?
Cannot I live if he but like ?   ' The law ! '
Why, just the law gives him the very chance,
The precise leave to let my life alone,
Which the angelic soul of him (he says)   70
Yearns after !   Here they drop it in his palm,
My lawyers, capital o' the cursed kind,—
A life to take and hold and keep : but no !
He sighs, shakes head, refuses to shut hand,
Motions away the gift they bid him grasp,
And of the coyness comes that off I run
And down I go, he best knows whither,—mind,
He knows, and sets me rolling all the same !

Disinterested Vicar of our Lord,
This way he abrogates and disallows,   80
Nullifies and ignores,—reverts in fine
To the good and right, in detriment of me !
Talk away !   Will you have the naked truth ?
He 's sick of his life's supper,—swallowed lies :
So, hobbling bedward, needs must ease his maw
Just where I sit o' the door-sill.   Sir Abate,
Can you do nothing ?   Friends, we used to frisk :
What of this sudden slash in a friend's face,
This cut across our good companionship
That showed its front so gay when both were young ?
Were not we put into a beaten path,   91
Bid pace the world, we nobles born and bred,
The body of friends with each his scutcheon full
Of old achievement and impunity,—
Taking the laugh of morn and Sol's salute
As forth we fared, pricked on to breathe our steeds
And take equestrian sport over the green
Under the blue, across the crop,—what care ?
So we went prancing up hill and down dale,
In and out of the level and the straight,   100
By the bit of pleasant byeway, where was harm ?
Still Sol salutes me and the morning laughs :
I see my grandsire's hoof-prints,—point the spot
Where he drew rein, slipped saddle, and stabbed knave
For daring throw gibe—much less, stone—from pale.
Then back, and on, and up with the cavalcade ;
Just so wend we, now canter, now converse,
Till, 'mid the jauncing pride and jaunty port,
Something of a sudden jerks at somebody—
A dagger is out, a flashing cut and thrust,   110
Because I play some prank my grandsire played,
And here I sprawl : where is the company ?   Gone !
A trot and a trample ! only I lie trapped,
Writhe in a certain novel springe just set
By the good old Pope : I 'm first prize.   Warn me ?
     Why ?
Apprize me that the law o' the game is changed ?
Enough that I 'm a warning, as I writhe,
To all and each my fellows of the file,
And make law plain henceforward past mistake,
' For such a prank, death is the penalty ! '   120
Pope the Five Hundredth .. what do I know or care ?

Deputes your Eminence and Abateship
To announce that, twelve hours from this time, he needs
I just essay upon my body and soul
The virtue of his bran-new engine, prove
Represser of the pranksome !   I 'm the first !
Thanks.   Do you know what teeth you mean to try
The sharpness of, on this soft neck and throat ?
I know it,—I have seen and hate it,—ay,
As you shall, while I tell you : let me talk,   130
Or leave me, at your pleasure ! talk I must :
What is your visit but my lure to talk ?
You have a something to disclose ?—a smile,
At end of the forced sternness, means to mock
The heart-beats here ? I call your two hearts stone !
Is your charge to stay with me till I die ?
Be tacit as your bench, then !   Use your ears,
I use my tongue : how glibly yours will run
At pleasant supper-time . . God's curse ! . . to-night
When all the guests jump up, begin so brisk   140
' Welcome, his Eminence who shrived the wretch !
' Now we shall have the Abate's story ! '

                                        Life !
How I could spill this overplus of mine
Among those hoar-haired, shrunk-shanked, odds and ends
Of body and soul, old age is chewing dry !
Those windle-straws that stare while purblind death
Mows here, mows there, makes hay of juicy me,
And misses, just the bunch of withered weed,
Would brighten hell and streak its smoke with flame !
How the life I could shed yet never shrink,   151
Would drench their stalks with sap like grass in May !
Is it not terrible, I entreat you, Sirs ?
Such manifold and plenitudinous life,
Prompt at death's menace to give blow for threat,
Answer his ' Be thou not ! ' by ' Thus I am ! '—
Terrible so to be alive yet die ?

How I live, how I see ! so,—how I speak !
Lucidity of soul unlocks the lips :
I never had the words at will before.   160
How I see all my folly at a glance !

' A man requires a woman and a wife : '
There was my folly ; I believed the saw :
I knew that just myself concerned myself,
Yet needs must look for what I seemed to lack,
In a woman,—why, the woman 's in the man !
Fools we are, how we learn things when too late !
Overmuch life turns round my woman-side ;
The male and female in me, mixed before,
Settle of a sudden : I 'm my wife outright   170
In this unmanly appetite for truth,
This careless courage as to consequence,
This instantaneous sight through things and through,
This voluble rhetoric, if you please,—'t is she !
Here you have that Pompilia whom I slew,
Also the folly for which I slew her !
                                        Fool !
And, fool-like, what is it I wander from ?
What, of the sharpness of your iron tooth ?
Ah,—that I know the hateful thing : this way.   180
I chanced to stroll forth, many a good year gone,
One warm Spring eve in Rome, and unaware
Looking, mayhap, to count what stars were out,
Came on your huge axe in a frame, that falls
And so cuts off a man's head underneath,
Mannaia,—thus we made acquaintance first,
Out of the way, in a bye-part o' the town,
At the Mouth-of-Truth o' the river-side, you know :
One goes by the Capitol : and wherefore coy,
Retiring out of crowded noisy Rome ?   190
Because a very little time ago
It had done service, chopped off head from trunk,
Belonging to a fellow whose poor house
The thing had made a point to stand before.
Felice Whatsoever-was-the-name
Who stabled buffaloes and so gained bread,
(Our clowns unyoke them in the ground hard by)
And, after use of much improper speech,
Had struck at Duke Some-title-or-other's face,
Because he kidnapped, carried away and kept   200
Felice's sister that would sit and sing
I' the filthy doorway while she plaited fringe
To deck the brutes with,—on their gear it goes,—
The good girl with the velvet in her voice.
So did the Duke, so did Felice, so

Did Justice, intervening with her axe.
There the man-mutilating engine stood
At ease, both gay and grim, like a Swiss guard
Off duty,—purified itself as well,
Getting dry, sweet and proper for next week,—   210
And doing incidental good, 't was hoped
To the rough lesson-lacking populace
Who now and then, forsooth, must right their wrongs !
There stood the twelve-foot-square of scaffold, railed
Considerately round to elbow-height :
(Suppose an officer should tumble thence
And sprain his ankle and be lame a month,
Through starting when the axe fell and head too ?)
Railed likewise were the steps whereby 't was reached.
All of it painted red : red, in the midst,   220
Ran up two narrow tall beams barred across,
Since from the summit, some twelve feet to reach
The iron plate with the sharp shearing edge
Had . . slammed, jerked, shot or slid,—I shall find
    which !
There it lay quiet, fast in its fit place,
The wooden half-moon collar, now eclipsed
By the blade which blocked its curvature : apart,
The other half,—the under half-moon board
Which, helped by this, completes a neck's ombrace,——
Joined to a sort of desk that wheels aside   230
Out of the way when done with,—down you kneel,
In you 're wheeled, over you the other drops,
Tight you are clipped, whiz, there 's the blade on you,
Out trundles body, down flops head on floor,
And where 's your soul gone ?   That, too, I shall find !
This kneeling-place was red, red, never fear !
But only slimy-like with paint, not blood,
For why ? a decent pitcher stood at hand,
A broad dish to hold sawdust, and a broom
By some unnamed utensil,—scraper-rake,—   240
Each with a conscious air of duty done.
Underneath, loungers,—boys and some few men,—
Discoursed this platter and the other tool,
Just as, when grooms tie up and dress a steed,
Boys lounge and look on, and elucubrate
What the round brush is used for, what the square,—
So was explained—to me the skill-less man—
The manner of the grooming for next world

Undergone by Felice What's-his-name.   249
There 's no such lovely month in Rome as May—
May's crescent is no half-moon of red plank,
And came now tilting o'er the wave i' the west,
One greenish-golden sea, right 'twixt those bars
Of the engine—I began acquaintance with,
Understood, hated, hurried from before,
To have it out of sight and cleanse my soul !
Here it is all again, conserved for use :
Twelve hours hence I may know more, not hate worse.

That young May-moon-month !   Devils of the deep !
Was not a Pope then Pope as much as now ?   260
Used not he chirrup o'er the Merry Tales,
Chuckle,—his nephew so exact the wag
To play a jealous cullion such a trick
As wins the wife i' the pleasant story !   Well ?
Why do things change ?   Wherefore is Rome un-
          Romed ?
I tell you, ere Felice's corpse was cold,
The Duke, that night, threw wide his palace-doors,
Received the compliments o' the quality,
For justice done him,—bowed and smirked his best,
And in return passed round a pretty thing,   270
A portrait of Felice's sister's self,
Florid old rogue Albano's masterpiece,
As—better than virginity in rags—
Bouncing Europa on the back o' the bull :
They laughed and took their road the safelier home.
Ah, but times change, there 's quite another Pope,
I do the Duke's deed, take Felice's place,
And, being no Felice, lout and clout,
Stomach but ill the phrase ' I lose my head ! '   279
How euphemistic !   Lose what ?   Lose your ring,
Your snuff-box, tablets, kerchief !—but, your head ?
I learnt the process at an early age ;
'T was useful knowledge in those same old days,
To know the way a head is set on neck.
My fencing-master urged ' Would you excel ?
' Rest not content with mere bold give-and-guard,
' Nor pink the antagonist somehow-anyhow,—
' See me dissect a little, and know your game !
' Only anatomy makes a thrust the thing.'
Oh Cardinal, those lithe live necks of ours !   290

Here go the vertebræ, here's *Atlas*, here
Axis, and here the symphyses stop short,
So wisely and well,—as, o'er a corpse, we cant,—
And here 's the silver cord which . . . what 's our word ?
Depends from the gold bowl, which loosed (not ' lost ')
Lets us from heaven to hell,—one chop, we 're loose !
' And not much pain i' the process,' quoth the sage :
Who told him ?   Not Felice's ghost, I think !
Such ' losing ' is scarce Mother Nature's mode.
She fain would have cord ease itself away,   300
Worn to a thread by threescore years and ten,
Snap while we slumber : that seems bearable :
I 'm told one clot of blood extravasate
Ends one as certainly as Roland's sword,—
One drop of lymph suffused proves Oliver's mace,—
Intruding, either of the pleasant pair,
On the arachnoid tunic of my brain.
That 's Nature's way of loosing cord !—but Art,
How of Art's process with the engine here ?
When bowl and cord alike are crushed across,   310
Bored between, bruised through ?   Why, if Fagon's
        self,
The French Court's pride, that famed practitioner,
Would pass his cold pale lightning of a knife,
Pistoja-ware, adroit 'twixt joint and joint,
With just a ' See how facile, gentlefolks ! '—
The thing were not so bad to bear !   Brute force
Cuts as he comes, breaks in, breaks on, breaks out
O' the hard and soft of you : is that the same ?
A lithe snake thrids the hedge, makes throb no leaf :
A heavy ox sets chest to brier and branch,   320
Bursts somehow through, and leaves one hideous hole
Behind him !

                And why, why must this needs be ?
Oh, if men were but good !   They are not good,
Nowise like Peter : people called him rough,
But if, as I left Rome, I spoke the Saint,
—' *Petrus, quo vadis ?* '—doubtless, I should hear,
' To free the prisoner and forgive his fault !
' I plucked the absolute dead from God's own bar,
' And raised up Dorcas,—why not rescue thee ? '
What would cost one such nullifying word ?   331
If Innocent succeeds to Peter's place,

Let him think Peter's thought, speak Peter's speech !
I say, he is bound to it : friends, how say you ?
Concede I be all one bloodguiltiness
And mystery of murder in the flesh,
Why should that fact keep the Pope's mouth shut fast?
He execrates my crime,—good !—sees hell yawn
One inch from the red plank's end which I press,—
Nothing is better ! What's the consequence ? 340
How does a Pope proceed that knows his cue ?
Why, leaves me linger out my minute here,
Since close on death come judgment and the doom,
Nor cribs at dawn its pittance from a sheep
Destined ere dewfall to be butcher's-meat !
Think, Sirs, if I had done you any harm,
And you require the natural revenge,
Suppose, and so intend to poison me,
—Just as you take and slip into my draught
The paperful of powder that clears scores, 350
You notice on my brow a certain blue :
How you both overset the wine at once !
How you both smile ! ' Our enemy has the plague !
' Twelve hours hence he 'll be scraping his bones bare
' Of that intolerable flesh, and die,
' Frenzied with pain : no need for poison here !
' Step aside and enjoy the spectacle ! '
Tender for souls are you, Pope Innocent !
Christ's maxim is—one soul outweighs the world :
Respite me, save a soul, then, curse the world ! 360
' No,' venerable sire, I hear you smirk,
' No : for Christ's gospel changes names, not things,
' Renews the obsolete, does nothing more !
' Our fire-new gospel is retinkered law,
' Our mercy, justice,—Jove 's rechristened God,—
' Nay, whereas, in the popular conceit,
' 'T is pity that old harsh Law somehow limps,
' Lingers on earth, although Law's day be done,—
' Else would benignant Gospel interpose,
' Not furtively as now, but bold and frank 370
' O'erflutter us with healing in her wings,—
' Law is all harshness, Gospel were all love !—
' We like to put it, on the contrary,—
' Gospel takes up the rod which Law lets fall ;
' Mercy is vigilant when justice sleeps ;
' Does Law let Guido taste the Gospel-grace ?

‘ The secular arm allow the spiritual power
‘ To act for once ?—what compliment so fine
‘ As that the Gospel handsomely be harsh,   379
‘ Thrust back Law's victim on the nice and coy ? ’
Yes, you do say so,—else you would forgive
Me, whom Law dares not touch but tosses you !
Do n't think to put on the professional face !
You know what I know,—casuists as you are,
Each nerve must creep, each hair start, sting and
      stand,
At such illogical inconsequence !
Dear my friends, do but see !   A murder 's tried,
There are two parties to the cause : I 'm one,
—Defend myself, as somebody must do :
I have the best o' the battle : that 's a fact,   390
Simple fact,—fancies find no place beside :
What though half Rome condemned me ?   Half
      approved :
And, none disputes, the luck is mine at last,
All Rome, i' the main, acquits me : whereupon
What has the Pope to ask but ‘ How finds Law ? ’
‘ I find,’ replies Law, ‘ I have erred this while :
‘ Guilty or guiltless, Guido proves a priest,
‘ No layman : he is therefore yours, not mine :
‘ I bound him : loose him, you whose will is Christ's ! ’
And now what does this Vicar of the Lord,   400
Shepherd o' the flock,—one of whose charge bleats sore
For crook's help from the quag wherein it drowns ?
Law suffers him put forth the crumpled end,—
His pleasure is to turn staff, use the point,
And thrust the shuddering sheep he calls a wolf,
Back and back, down and down to where hell gapes !
‘ Guiltless,’ cries Law—‘ Guilty ’ corrects the Pope !
‘ Guilty,’ for the whim's sake !   ‘ Guilty,’ he somehow
      thinks,
And anyhow says : 't is truth ; he dares not lie !
Others should do the lying.   That 's the cause   410
Brings you both here : I ought in decency
Confess to you that I deserve my fate,
Am guilty, as the Pope thinks,—ay, to the end,
Keep up the jest, lie on, lie ever, lie
I' the latest gasp of me !   What reason, Sirs ?
Because to-morrow will succeed to-day
For you, though not for me : and if I stick

Still to the truth, declare with my last breath,
I die an innocent and murdered man,— 419
Why, there 's the tongue of Rome will wag a-pace
This time to-morrow,—do n't I hear the talk !
' So, to the last he proved impenitent ?
' Pagans have said as much of martyred saints !
' Law demurred, washed her hands of the whole case.
' Prince Somebody said this, Duke Something, that.
' Doubtless the man 's dead, dead enough, do n't fear !
' But, hang it, what if there have been a spice,
' A touch of . . eh ? You see, the Pope 's so old,
' Some of us add, obtuse,—age never slips
' The chance of shoving youth to face death first ! '
And so on. Therefore to suppress such talk 431
You two come here, entreat I tell you lies,
And end, the edifying way. I end,
Telling the truth ! Your self-styled shepherd thieves !
A thief—and how thieves hate the wolves we know :
Damage to theft, damage to thrift, all 's one !
The red hand is sworn foe of the black jaw !
That 's only natural, that 's right enough :
But why the wolf should compliment the thief 439
With the shepherd's title, bark out life in thanks,
And, spiteless, lick the prong that spits him,—eh,
Cardinal ? My Abate, scarcely thus !
There, let my sheepskin-garb, a curse on 't, go—
Leave my teeth free if I must show my shag !
Repent ? What good shall follow ? If I pass
Twelve hours repenting, will that fact hook fast
The thirteenth at the horrid dozen's end ?
If I fall forthwith at your feet, gnash, tear,
Foam, rave, to give your story the due grace,
Will that assist the engine half-way back 450
Into its hiding-house ?—boards, shaking now,
Bone against bone, like some old skeleton bat
That wants, now winter 's dead, to wake and prey !
Will howling put the spectre back to sleep ?
Ah, but I misconceive your object, Sirs !
Since I want new life like the creature,—life
Being done with here, begins i' the world away :
I shall next have ' Come, mortals, and be judged ! '
There 's but a minute betwixt this and then :
So, quick, be sorry since it saves my soul ! 460
Sirs, truth shall save it, since no lies assist !

Hear the truth, you, whatever you style yourselves,
Civilization and society !
Come, one good grapple, I with all the world !
Dying in cold blood is the desperate thing ;
The angry heart explodes, bears off in blaze
The indignant soul, and I 'm combustion-ripe.
Why, you intend to do your worst with me !
That 's in your eyes !   You dare no more than death,
And mean no less.   I must make up my mind !
So Pietro,—when I chased him here and there,   471
Morsel by morsel cut away the life
I loathed,—cried for just respite to confess
And save his soul :   much respite did I grant !
Why grant me respite who deserve my doom ?
Me—who engaged to play a prize, fight you,
Knowing your arms, and foil you, trick for trick,
At rapier-fence, your match and, may be, more.
I knew that if I chose sin certain sins,
Solace my lusts out of the regular way   480
Prescribed me, I should find you in the path,
Have to try skill with a redoubted foe ;
You would lunge, I would parry, and make end.
At last, occasion of a murder comes :
We cross blades, I, for all my brag, break guard,
And in goes the cold iron at my breast,
Out at my back, and end is made of me.
You stand confessed the adroiter swordsman,—ay,
But on your triumph you increase, it seems,
Want more of me than lying flat on face :   490
I ought to raise my ruined head, allege
Not simply I pushed worse blade o' the pair,
But my antagonist dispensed with steel !
There was no passage of arms, you looked me low,
With brow and eye abolished cut-and-thrust
Nor used the vulgar weapon !   This chance scratch,
This incidental hurt, this sort of hole
I' the heart of me ?   I stumbled, got it so !
Fell on my own sword as a bungler may !
Yourself proscribe such heathen tools, and trust
To the naked virtue :   it was virtue stood   501
Unarmed and awed me,—on my brow there burned
Crime out so plainly, intolerably, red,
That I was fain to cry—' Down to the dust
' With me, and bury there brow, brand and all ! '

Law had essayed the adventure,—but what 's Law ?
Morality exposed the Gorgon-shield !
Morality and Religion conquer me.
If Law sufficed would you come here, entreat
I supplement law, and confess forsooth ?   510
Did not the Trial show things plain enough ?
' Ah, but a word of the man's very self
' Would somehow put the keystone in its place
' And crown the arch ! ' Then take the word you
        want !

I say that, long ago, when things began,
All the world made agreement, such and such
Were pleasure-giving profit-bearing acts,
But henceforth extra-legal, nor to be :
You must not kill the man whose death would please
And profit you, unless his life stop yours   520
Plainly, and need so be put aside :
Get the thing by a public course, by law,
Only no private bloodshed as of old !
All of us, for the good of every one,
Renounced such licence and conformed to law :
Who breaks law, breaks pact, therefore, helps himself
To pleasure and profit over and above the due,
And must pay forfeit,—pain beyond his share :
For pleasure is the sole good in the world,
Anyone's pleasure turns to someone's pain,   530
So, let law watch for everyone,—say we,
Who call things wicked that give too much joy,
And nickname the reprisal, envy makes,
Punishment : quite right ! thus the world goes round.
I, being well aware such pact there was,
Who in my time have found advantage too
In law's observance and crime's penalty,—
Who, but for wholesome fear law bred in friends,
Had doubtless given example long ago,
Furnished forth some friend's pleasure with my pain,
And, by my death, pieced out his scanty life,—   541
I could not, for that foolish life of me,
Help risking law's infringement,—I broke bond,
And needs must pay price,—wherefore, here 's my
        head,
Flung with a flourish ! But, repentance too ?
But pure and simple sorrow for law's breach

Rather than blunderer's-ineptitude ?
Cardinal, no !   Abate, scarcely thus !
'T is the fault, not that I dared try a fall   549
With Law and straightway am found undermost,
But that I fail to see, above man's law,
God's precept you, the Christians recognize ?
Colly my cow !   Do n't fidget, Cardinal !
Abate, cross your breast and count your beads
And exorcize the devil, for here he stands
And stiffens in the bristly nape of neck,
Daring you drive him hence !   You, Christians both ?
I say, if ever was such faith at all
Born in the world, by your community
Suffered to live its little tick of time,   560
'T is dead of age now, ludicrously dead ;
Honour its ashes, if you be discreet,
In epitaph only !   For, concede its death,
Allow extinction, you may boast unchecked
What feats the thing did in a crazy land
At a fabulous epoch,—treat your faith, that way,
Just as you treat your relics :   ' Here 's a shred
' Of saintly flesh, a scrap of blessed bone,
' Raised King Cophetua, who was dead, to life
' In Mesopotamy twelve centuries since,   570
' Such was its virtue ! '   twangs the Sacristan,
Holding the shrine-box up, with hands like feet
Because of gout in every finger-joint :
Does he bethink him to reduce one knob,
Allay one twinge by touching what he vaunts ?
I think he half uncrooks fist to catch fee,
But, for the grace, the quality of cure,—
Cophetua was the man put that to proof !
Not otherwise, your faith is shrined and shown
And shamed at once :   you banter while you bow !
Do you dispute this ?   Come, a monster-laugh,   581
A madman's laugh, allowed his Carnival
Later ten days than when all Rome, but he,
Laughed at the candle-contest :   mine 's alight,
'T is just it sputter till the puff o' the Pope
End it to-morrow and the world turn Ash,
Come, thus I wave a wand and bring to pass
In a moment, in the twinkle of an eye,
What but that—feigning everywhere grows fact,
Professors turn possessors, realize   590

The faith they play with as a fancy now,
And bid it operate, have full effect
On every circumstance of life, to-day,
In Rome,—faith's flow set free at fountain-head !
Now, you 'll own, at this present when I speak,
Before I work the wonder, there 's no man
Woman or child in Rome, faith's fountain-head,
But might, if each were minded, realize
Conversely unbelief, faith's opposite—
Set it to work on life unflinchingly,   600
Yet give no symptom of an outward change :
Why should things change because men disbelieve ?
What 's incompatible, in the whited tomb,
With bones and rottenness one inch below ?
What saintly act is done in Rome to-day
But might be prompted by the devil,—' is '
I say not,—' has been, and again may be,'—
I do say, full i' the face o' the crucifix
You try to stop my mouth with !   Off with it !
Look in your own heart, if your soul have eyes ! 610
You shall see reason why, though faith were fled,
Unbelief still might work the wires and move
Man, the machine, to play a faithful part.
Preside your college, Cardinal, in your cape,
Or,—having got above his head, grown Pope,—
Abate, gird your loins and wash my feet !
Do you suppose I am at loss at all
Why you crook, why you cringe, why fast or feast ?
Praise, blame, sit, stand, lie or go !—all of it,
In each of you, purest unbelief may prompt,   620
And wit explain to who has eyes to see.
But, lo, I wave wand, make the false the true !
Here 's Rome believes in Christianity !
What an explosion, how the fragments fly
Of what was surface, mask and make-believe !
Begin now,—look at this Pope's-halberdier
In wasp-like black and yellow foolery !
He, doing duty at the corridor,
Wakes from a muse and stands convinced of sin !
Down he flings halbert, leaps the passage-length,
Pushes into the presence, pantingly   631
Submits the extreme peril of the case
To the Pope's self,—whom in the world beside ?—
And the Pope breaks talk with ambassador,

Bids aside bishop, wills the whole world wait
Till he secure that prize, outweighs the world,
A soul, relieve the sentry of his qualm !
His Altitude the Referendary,—
Robed right, and ready for the usher's word
To pay devoir,—is, of all times, just then   640
'Ware of a master-stroke of argument
Will cut the spinal cord . . ugh, ugh ! . . I mean,
Paralyse Molinism for evermore !
Straight he leaves lobby, trundles, two and two,
Down steps, to reach home, write if but a word
Shall end the impudence : he leaves who likes
Go pacify the Pope : there 's Christ to serve !
How otherwise would men display their zeal ?
If the same sentry had the least surmise
A powder-barrel 'neath the pavement lay   650
In neighbourhood with what might prove a match,
Meant to blow sky-high Pope and presence both—
Would he not break through courtiers, rank and
        file,
Bundle up, bear off and save body so,
O' the Pope, no matter for his priceless soul ?
There 's no fool's-freak here, nought to soundly swinge,
Only a man in earnest, you 'll so praise
And pay and prate about, that earth shall ring !
Had thought possessed the Referendary
His jewel-case at home was left ajar,   660
What would be wrong in running, robes awry,
To be beforehand with the pilferer ?
What talk then of indecent haste ?   Which means,
That both these, each in his degree, would do
Just that,—for a comparative nothing's sake,
And thereby gain approval and reward,—
Which, done for what Christ says is worth the world,
Procures the doer curses, cuffs and kicks.
I call such difference 'twixt act and act,
Sheer lunacy unless your truth on lip   670
Be recognized a lie in heart of you !
How do you all act, promptly or in doubt,
When there 's a guest poisoned at supper-time
And he sits chatting on with spot on cheek ?
' Pluck him by the skirt, and round him in the ears,
' Have at him by the beard, warn anyhow ! '
Good, and this other friend that 's cheat and thief

And dissolute,—go stop the devil's feast,
Withdraw him from the imminent hell-fire !   679
Why, for your life, you dare not tell your friend
' You lie, and I admonish you for Christ ! '
Who yet dare seek that same man at the Mass
To warn him—on his knees, and tinkle near,—
He left a cask a-tilt, a tap unturned,
The Trebbian running : what a grateful jump
Out of the Church rewards your vigilance !
Perform that self-same service just a thought
More maladroitly,—since a bishop sits
At function !—and he budges not, bites lip,—
' You see my case : how can I quit my post ?   690
' He has an eye to any such default.
' See to it, neighbour, I beseech your love ! '
He and you know the relative worth of things,
What is permissible or inopportune.
Contort your brows ! You know I speak the truth:
Gold is called gold, and dross called dross, i' the
        Book :
Gold you let lie and dross pick up and prize !
—Despite your muster of some fifty monks   698
And nuns a-maundering here and mumping there,
Who could, and on occasion would, spurn dross,
Clutch gold, and prove their faith a fact so far,—
I grant you ! Fifty times the number squeak
And gibber in the madhouse—firm of faith,
This fellow, that his nose supports the moon,
The other, that his straw hat crowns him Pope :
Does that prove all the world outside insane ?
Do fifty miracle-mongers match the mob
That acts on the frank faithless principle,
Born-baptized-and-bred Christian-atheists, each
With just as much a right to judge as you,—   710
As many senses in his soul, or nerves
I' neck of him as I,—whom, soul and sense,
Neck and nerve, you abolish presently,—
I being the unit in creation now
Who pay the Maker, in this speech of mine,
A creature's duty, spend my last of breath
In bearing witness, even by my worst fault
To the creature's obligation, absolute,
Perpetual : my worst fault protests, ' The faith
' Claims all of me : I would give all she claims,   720

' But for a spice of doubt : the risk 's too rash :
' Double or quits, I play, but, all or nought,
' Exceeds my courage : therefore, I descend
' To the next faith with no dubiety—
' Faith in the present life, made last as long
' And prove as full of pleasure as may hap,
' Whatever pain it cause the world.'   I 'm wrong ?
I 've had my life, whate'er I lose : I 'm right ?
I 've got the single good there was to gain.
Entire faith, or else complete unbelief,—   730
Aught between has my loathing and contempt,
Mine and God's also, doubtless : ask yourself,
Cardinal, where and how you like a man !
Why, either with your feet upon his head,
Confessed your caudatory, or at large
The stranger in the crowd who caps to you
But keeps his distance,—why should he presume ?
You want no hanger-on and dropper-off,
Now yours, and now not yours but quite his own,
According as the sky looks black or bright.   740
Just so I capped to and kept off from faith—
You promised trudge behind through fair and foul,
Yet leave i' the lurch at the first spit of rain.
Who holds to faith whenever rain begins ?
What does the father when his son lies dead,
The merchant when his money-bags take wing,
The politician whom a rival ousts ?
No case but has its conduct, faith prescribes :
Where 's the obedience that shall edify ?
Why, they laugh frankly in the face of faith   750
And take the natural course,—this rends his hair
Because his child is taken to God's breast,
That gnashes teeth and raves at loss of trash
Which rust corrupts and thieves break through and
     steal,
And this, enabled to inherit earth
Through meekness, curses till your blood runs cold !
Down they all drop to my low level, ease
Heart upon dungy earth that 's warm and soft,
And let who will, attempt the altitudes.
We have the prodigal son of heavenly sire,   760
Turning his nose up at the fatted calf,
Fain to fill belly with the husks we swine
Did eat by born depravity of taste !

Enough of the hypocrites.   But you, Sirs, you—
Who never budged from litter where I lay,
And buried snout i' the draff-box while I fed,
Cried amen to my creed's one article—
' Get pleasure, 'scape pain,—give your preference
' To the immediate good, for time is brief,
' And death ends good and ill and everything :   770
' What 's got is gained, what 's gained soon is gained
       twice,
' And,—inasmuch as faith gains most,—feign faith ! '
So did we brother-like pass word about :
—You, now,—like bloody drunkards but half-drunk,
Who fool men yet perceive men find them fools,
And that a titter gains the gravest mouth,—
O' the sudden you must needs re-introduce
Solemnity, must sober undue mirth
By a blow dealt your boon companion here
Who, using the old licence, dreamed of harm   780
No more than snow in harvest : yet it falls !
You check the merriment effectually
By pushing your abrupt machine i' the midst,
Making me Rome's example : blood for wine !
The general good needs that you chop and change !
I may dislike the hocus-pocus,—Rome,
The laughter-loving people, won't they stare
Chap-fallen !—while serious natures sermonize
' The magistrate, he beareth not the sword   789
' In vain ; who sins may taste its edge, we see ! '
Why my sin, drunkards ?   Where have I abused
Liberty, scandalized you all so much ?
Who called me, who crooked finger till I came,
Fool that I was, to join companionship ?
I knew my own mind, meant to live my life,
Elude your envy, or else make a stand,
Take my own part and sell you my life dear :
But it was ' Fie !   No prejudice in the world
' To the proper manly instinct !   Cast your lot
' Into our lap, one genius ruled our births,   800
' We 'll compass joy by concert ; take with us
' The regular irregular way i' the wood ;
' You 'll miss no game through riding breast by
       breast,
' In this preserve, the Church's park and pale,
' Rather than outside where the world is waste ! '

Come, if you said not that, did you say this ?
Give plain and terrible warning, ' Live, enjoy ?
' Such life begins in death and ends in hell !
' Dare you bid us assist you to your sins
' Who hurry sin and sinners from the earth ?   810
' No such delight for us, why then for you ?
' Leave earth, seek heaven or find its opposite ! '
Had you so warned me, not in lying words
But veritable deeds with tongues of flame,
That had been fair, that might have struck a man,
Silenced the squabble between soul and sense,
Compelled him make his mind up, take one course
Or the other, peradventure !—wrong or right,
Foolish or wise, you would have been at least
Sincere, no question,—forced me choose, indulge
Or else renounce my instincts, still play wolf   821
Or find my way submissive to the fold,
Be red-crossed on the fleece, one sheep the more.
But you as good as bade me wear sheep's wool
Over wolf's skin, suck blood and hide the noise
By mimicry of something like a bleat,—
Whence it comes that because, despite my care,
Because I smack my tongue too loud for once,
Drop baaing, here 's the village up in arms !
Have at the wolf's throat, you who hate the breed .
Oh, were it only open yet to choose—   831
One little time more—whether I 'd be free
Your foe, or subsidized your friend forsooth !
Should not you get a growl through the white
     fangs
In answer to your beckoning !   Cardinal,
Abate, managers o' the multitude,
I 'd turn your gloved hands to account, be sure !
You should manipulate the coarse rough mob :
'T is you I 'd deal directly with, not them,—
Using your fears : why touch the thing myself   840
When I could see you hunt and then cry ' Shares !
' Quarter the carcass or we quarrel ; come,
' Here 's the world ready to see justice done ! '
Oh, it had been a desperate game, but game
Wherein the winner's chance were worth the pains
To try conclusions !—at the worst, what 's worse
Than this Mannaia-machine, each minute's talk,
Helps push an inch the nearer me ?   Fool, fool !

You understand me and forgive, sweet Sirs ?
I blame you, tear my hair and tell my woe—   850
All 's but a flourish, figure of rhetoric !
One must try each expedient to save life.
One makes fools look foolisher fifty-fold
By putting in their place the wise like you
To take the full force of an argument
Would buffet their stolidity in vain.
If you should feel aggrieved by the mere wind
O' the blow that means to miss you and maul them,
That 's my success !   Is it not folly, now,
To say with folks, ' A plausible defence—   860
' We see through notwithstanding, and reject ? '
Reject the plausible they do, these fools,
Who never even make pretence to show
One point beyond its plausibility
In favour of the best belief they hold !
' Saint Somebody-or-other raised the dead : '
Did he ?   How do you come to know as much ?
' Know it, what need ?   The story 's plausible,
' Avouched for by a martyrologist,
' And why should good men sup on cheese and leeks
' On such a saint's day, if there were no saint ? '   871
I praise the wisdom of these fools, and straight
Tell them my story—' plausible, but false ! '
False, to be sure !   What else can story be
That runs—a young wife tired of an old spouse,
Found a priest whom she fled away with,—both
Took their full pleasure in the two-days' flight,
Which a grey-headed greyer-hearted pair,
(Whose best boast was, their life had been a lie)
Helped for the love they bore all liars.   Oh,   880
Here incredulity begins !   Indeed ?
Allow then, were no one point strictly true,
There 's that i' the tale might seem like truth at least
To the unlucky husband,—jaundiced patch,—
Jealousy maddens people, why not him ?
Say, he was maddened, so, forgivable !
Humanity pleads that though the wife were true,
The priest true, and the pair of liars true,
They might seem false to one man in the world !
A thousand gnats make up a serpent's sting,   890
And many sly soft stimulants to wrath
Compose a formidable wrong at last,

Q

That gets called easily by some one name
Not applicable to the single parts,
And so draws down a general revenge,
Excessive if you take crime, fault by fault.
Jealousy !   I have known a score of plays,
Were listened to and laughed at in my time
As like the everyday-life on all sides,
Wherein the husband, mad as a March hare,   900
Suspected all the world contrived his shame ;
What did the wife ?   The wife kissed both eyes blind,
Explained away ambiguous circumstance,
And while she held him captive by the hand,
Crowned his head,—you know what 's the mockery,—
By half her body behind the curtain.   That 's
Nature now !   That 's the subject of a piece
I saw in Vallombrosa Convent, made
Expressly to teach men what marriage was !
But say ' Just so did I misapprehend ! '   910
Or ' Just so she deceived me to my face ! '
And that 's pretence too easily seen through !
All those eyes of all husbands in all plays,
At stare like one expanded peacock-tail,
Are laughed at for pretending to be keen
While horn-blind : but the moment I step forth—
Oh, I must needs o' the sudden prove a lynx
And look the heart, that stone-wall, through and
        through !
Such an eye, God's may be,—not yours nor mine.

Yes, presently . . what hour is fleeting now ?   920
When you cut earth away from under me,
I shall be left alone with, pushed beneath
Some such an apparitional dread orb ;
I fancy it go filling up the void
Above my mote-self it devours, or what
Immensity please wreak on nothingness.
Just so I felt once, couching through the dark,
Hard by Vittiano ; young I was, and gay,
And wanting to trap fieldfares : first a spark
Tipped a bent, as a mere dew-globule might   930
Any stiff grass-stalk on the meadow,—this
Grew fiercer, flamed out full, and proved the sun.
What do I want with proverbs, precepts here ?
Away with man !   What shall I say to God ?

This, if I find the tongue and keep the mind—
' Do Thou wipe out the being of me, and smear
' This soul from off Thy white of things, I blot !
' I am one huge and sheer mistake,—whose fault ?
' Not mine at least, who did not make myself ! '
Someone declares my wife excused me so !   940
Perhaps she knew what argument to use.
Grind your teeth, Cardinal, Abate, writhe !
What else am I to cry out in my rage,
Unable to repent one particle
O' the past ?   Oh, how I wish some cold wise man
Would dig beneath the surface which you scrape,
Deal with the depths, pronounce on my desert
Groundedly !   I want simple sober sense,
That asks, before it finishes with a dog,
Who taught the dog that trick you hang him for ?
You both persist to call that act a crime,   951
Sense would call . . yes, I do assure you, Sirs, . .
A blunder !   At the worst, I stood in doubt
On cross-road, took one path of many paths :
It leads to the red thing, we all see now,
But nobody at first saw one primrose
In bank, one singing-bird in bush, the less,
To warn from wayfare : let me prove you that !
Put me back to the cross-road, start afresh !
Advise me when I take the first false step !   960
Give me my wife : how should I use my wife,
Love her or hate her ?   Prompt my action now !
There she stands, there she is alive and pale,
The thirteen-years'-old child, with milk for blood,
Pompilia Comparini, as at first,
Which first is only four brief years ago !
I stand too in the little ground-floor room
O' the father's house at Via Vittoria : see !
Her so-called mother,—one arm round the waist
O' the child to keep her from the toys—let fall,   970
At wonder I can live yet look so grim,—
Ushers her in, with deprecating wave
Of the other,—there she fronts me loose, at large,
Held only by the mother's finger-tip—
Struck dumb, for she was white enough before !
She eyes me with those frightened balls of black,
As heifer—the old simile comes pat—
Eyes tremblingly the altar and the priest :

The amazed look, all one insuppressive prayer,—
Might she but be set free as heretofore,   980
Have this cup leave her lips unblistered, bear
Any cross anywhither anyhow,
So but alone, so but apart from me !
You are touched ?   So am I, quite otherwise,
If 't is with pity.   I resent my wrong,
Being a man : we only show man's soul
Through man's flesh, she sees mine, it strikes her thus !
Is that attractive ?   To a youth perhaps—
Calf-creature, one-part boy to three-parts girl,
To whom it is a flattering novelty   990
That he, men use to motion from their path,
Can thus impose, thus terrify in turn
A chit whose terror shall be changed apace
To bliss unbearable when, grace and glow,
Prowess and pride descend the throne and touch
Esther in all that pretty tremble, cured
By the dove o' the sceptre !   But myself am old,
O' the wane at least, in all things : what do you say
To her who frankly thus confirms my doubt ?
I am past the prime, I scare the woman-world,   1000
Done-with that way : you like this piece of news ?
A little saucy rose-bud minx can strike
Death-damp into the breast of doughty king
Though 't were French Louis,—soul I understand,—
Saying, by gesture of repugnance, just
' Sire, you are regal, puissant and so forth,
' But—young you have been, are not, nor will be ! '
In vain the mother nods, winks, bustles up
' Count, girls incline to mature worth like you !
' As for Pompilia, what 's flesh, fish or fowl   1010
' To one who apprehends no difference,
' And would accept you even were you old
' As you are . . youngish by her father's side ?
' Trim but your beard a little, thin your bush
' Of eyebrow ; and for presence, portliness
' And decent gravity, you beat a boy ! '
Deceive you for a second, if you may,
In presence of the child that so loves age,
Whose neck writhes, cords itself against your kiss,
Whose hand you wring stark, rigid with despair !
Well, I resent this ; I am young in soul,   1021
Nor old in body,—thews and sinews here,—

Though the vile surface be not smooth as once,—
Far beyond the first wheelwork that went wrong
Through the untempered iron ere 't was proof :
I am the steel man worth ten times the crude,—
Would woman see what this declines to see,
Declines to say ' I see ',—the officious word
That makes the thing, pricks on the soul to shoot
New fire into the half-used cinder, flesh !   1030
Therefore 't is she begins with wronging me,
Who cannot but begin with hating her.
Our marriage follows : there we stand again !
Why do I laugh ?   Why, in the very gripe
O' the jaws of death's gigantic skull do I
Grin back his grin, make sport of my own pangs ?
Why from each clashing of his molars, ground
To make the devil bread from out my grist,
Leaps out a spark of mirth, a hellish toy ?
Take notice we are lovers in a church,   1040
Waiting the sacrament to make us one
And happy !   Just as bid, she bears herself,
Comes and kneels, rises, speaks, is silent,—goes :
So have I brought my horse, by word and blow,
To stand stock-still and front the fire he dreads.
How can I other than remember this,
Resent the very obedience ?   Gain thereby ?
Yes, I do gain my end and have my will,—
Thanks to whom ?   When the mother speaks the word,
She obeys it—even to enduring me !   1050
There had been compensation in revolt—
Revolt 's to quell : but martyrdom rehearsed,
But predetermined saintship for the sake
O' the mother ?—' Go ! ' thought I, ' we meet again ! '
Pass the next weeks of dumb contented death,
She lives,—wakes up, installed in house and home,
Is mine, mine all day-long, all night-long mine.
Good folks begin at me with open mouth
' Now, at least, reconcile the child to life !
' Study and make her love . . that is, endure   1060
' The . . hem ! the . . all of you though somewhat old,
' Till it amount to something, in her eye,
' As good as love, better a thousand times,—
' Since nature helps the woman in such strait,
' Makes passiveness her pleasure : failing which,
' What if you give up boys' and girls' fools'-play

' And go on to wise friendship all at once ?
' Those boys and girls kiss themselves cold, you know,
' Toy themselves tired and slink aside full soon
' To friendship, as they name satiety :   1070
' Thither go you and wait their coming ! '   Thanks,
Considerate advisers,—but, fair play !
Had you and I but started fair at first,
We, keeping fair, might reach it, neck by neck,
This blessed goal, whenever fate so please :
But why am I to miss the daisied mile
The course begins with, why obtain the dust
Of the end precisely at the starting-point ?
Why quaff life's cup blown free of all the beads,
The bright red froth wherein our beard should steep
Before our mouth essay the black o' the wine ?.   1081
Foolish, the love-fit ?   Let me prove it such
Like you, before like you I puff things clear !
' The best 's to come, no rapture but content !
' Not the first glory but a sober glow,
' Nor a spontaneous outburst in pure boon,
' So much as, gained by patience, care and toil ! '
Go preach that to your nephews, not to me
Who, tired i' the midway of my life, would stop
And take my first refreshment in a rose :   1090
What 's this coarse woolly hip, worn smooth of leaf,
You counsel I go plant in garden-pot,
Water with tears, manure with sweat and blood,
In confidence the seed shall germinate
And, for its very best, some far-off day,
Grow big, and blow me out a dog-rose bell ?
Why must your nephews begin breathing spice
O' the hundred-petalled Provence prodigy ?
Nay, more and worse,—would such my root bear rose—
Prove really flower and favourite, not the kind   1100
That 's queen, but those three leaves that make one cup
And hold the hedge-bird's breakfast,—then indeed
The prize though poor would pay the care and toil !
Respect we Nature that makes least as most,
Marvellous in the minim !   But this bud,
Bit through and burned black by the tempter's tooth,
This bloom whose best grace was the slug outside
And the wasp inside its bosom,—call you ' rose ' ?
Claim no immunity from a weed's fate
For the horrible present !   What you call my wife

I call a nullity in female shape,   1111
Vapid disgust, soon to be pungent plague,
When mixed with, made confusion and a curse
By two abominable nondescripts,
That father and that mother : think you see
The dreadful bronze our boast, we Aretines,
The Etruscan monster, the three-headed thing,
Bellerophon's foe !   How name you the whole beast ?
You choose to name the body from one head,
That of the simple kid which droops the eye,   1120
Hangs the neck and dies tenderly enough :
I rather see the griesly lion belch
Flame out i' the midst, the serpent writhe her rings,
Grafted into the common stock for tail,
And name the brute, Chimæra, which I slew !
How was there ever more to be—(concede
My wife's insipid harmless nullity)—
Dissociation from that pair of plagues—
That mother with her cunning and her cant—
The eyes with first their twinkle of conceit,   1130
Then, dropped to earth in mock-demureness,—now,
The smile self-satisfied from ear to ear,
Now, the prim pursed-up mouth's protruded lips,
With deferential duck, slow swing of head,
Tempting the sudden fist of man too much,—
That owl-like screw of lid and rock of ruff !
As for the father,—Cardinal, you know,
The kind of idiot !—rife are such in Rome,
But they wear velvet commonly, such fools,
At the end of life, can furnish forth young folk   1140
Who grin and bear with imbecility,
Since the stalled ass, the joker, sheds from jaw
Corn, in the joke, for those who laugh or starve :
But what say we to the same solemn beast
Wagging his ears and wishful of our pat,
When turned, with hide in holes and bones laid bare,
To forage for himself i' the waste o' the world,
Sir Dignity i' the dumps ?   Pat him ?   We drub
Self-knowledge, rather, into frowzy pate,
Teach Pietro to get trappings or go hang !   1150
Fancy this quondam oracle in vogue
At Via Vittoria, this personified
Authority when time was,—Pantaloon
Flaunting his tom-fool tawdry just the same

As if Ash-Wednesday were mid-Carnival !
That 's the extreme and unforgiveable
Of sins, as I account such.   Have you stooped
For your own ends to bestialize yourself
By flattery of a fellow of this stamp ?
The ends obtained, or else shown out of reach,   1160
He goes on, takes the flattery for pure truth,—
' You love and honour me, of course : what next ? '
What, but the trifle of the stabbing, friend ?—
Which taught you how one worships when the shrine
Has lost the relic that we bent before.
Angry ?   And how could I be otherwise ?
'T is plain : this pair of old pretentious fools
Meant to fool me : it happens, I fooled them.
Why could not these who sought to buy and sell
Me,—when they found themselves were bought and
     sold,
Make up their mind to the proved rule of right,   1171
Be chattel and not chapman any more ?
Miscalculation has its consequence ;
But when the shepherd crooks a sheep-like thing
And meaning to get wool, dislodges fleece
And finds the veritable wolf beneath,
(How that staunch image serves at every turn !)
Does he, by way of being politic,
Pluck the first whisker grimly visible ?—
Or rather grow in a trice all gratitude,   1180
Protest this sort-of-what-one-might-name sheep
Beats the old other curly-coated kind,
And shall share board and bed, if so it deign,
With its discoverer, like a royal ram ?
Ay, thus, with chattering teeth and knocking knees,
Would wisdom treat the adventure : these, forsooth,
Tried whisker-plucking, and so found what trap
The whisker kept perdue, two rows of teeth—
Sharp, as too late the prying fingers felt.
What would you have ?   The fools transgress, the
     fools   1190
Forthwith receive appropriate punishment :
They first insult me, I return the blow,
There follows noise enough : four hubbub months,
Now hue and cry, now whimpering and wail—
A perfect goose-yard cackle of complaint
Because I do not gild the geese their oats,—

I have enough of noise, ope wicket wide,
Sweep out the couple to go whine elsewhere,
Frightened a little, hurt in no respect,
And am just taking thought to breathe again,　　1200
Taste the sweet sudden silence all about,
When, there they are at it, the old noise I know,
At Rome i' the distance !　' What, begun once more ?
' Whine on, wail ever, 't is the loser's right ! '
But eh, what sort of voice grows on the wind ?
Triumph it sounds and no complaint at all !
And triumph it is !　My boast was premature :
The creatures, I turned forth, clapped wing and crew
Fighting-cock-fashion,—they had filched a pearl
From dung-heap, and might boast with cause enough !
I was defrauded of all bargained for,—　　1211
You know, the Pope knows, not a soul but knows
My dowry was derision, my gain—muck,
My wife, (the Church declared my flesh and blood)
The nameless bastard of a common whore :
My old name turned henceforth to . . shall I say
' He that received the ordure in his face ? '
And they who planned this wrong, performed this
　　　wrong,　　　　　　　　　　　　　　　　1218
And then revealed this wrong to the wide world,
Rounded myself in the ears with my own wrong,—
Why, these were . . note hell's lucky malice, now ! . .
These were just they, and they alone, could act
And publish in this wise their infamy,
Secure that men would in a breath believe
Compassionate and pardon them,—for why ?
They plainly were too stupid to invent,
Too simple to distinguish wrong from right,—
Inconscious agents they, the silly-sooth,
Of heaven's retributive justice on the strong
Proud cunning violent oppressor—me !　　1230
Follow them to their fate and help your best,
You Rome, Arezzo, foes called friends of mine,
They gave the good long laugh to at my cost !
Defray your share o' the cost since you partook
The entertainment !　Do !—assured the while,
That not one stab, I dealt to right and left,
But went the deeper for a fancy—this—
That each might do me two-fold service, find
A friend's face at the bottom of each wound,

And scratch its smirk a little !   1240
                                   Panciatichi !
There 's a report at Florence,—is it true ?—
That when your relative the Cardinal
Built, only the other day, that barrack-bulk,
The palace in Via Larga, someone picked
From out the street a saucy quip enough
That fell there from its day's flight through the town,
About the flat front and the windows wide
And ugly heap of cornice,—hitched the joke
Into a sonnet, signed his name thereto,   1250
And forthwith pinned on post the pleasantry.
For which he 's at the galleys, rowing now
Up to his waist in water,—just because
Panciatic and *lymphatic* rhymed so pat :
I hope, Sir, those who passed this joke on me
Were not unduly punished ?   What say you,
Prince of the Church, my patron ?   Nay, indeed !
I shall not dare insult your wits so much
As think this problem difficult to solve !
This Pietro and Violante, then, I say,   1260
These two ambiguous insects, changing name
And nature with the season's warmth or chill,—
Now, grovelled, grubbing toiling moiling ants,
A very synonym of thrift and peace,—
Anon, with lusty June to prick their heart,
Soared i' the air, winged flies for more offence,
Circled me, buzzed me deaf and stung me blind,
And stunk me dead with fetor in the face
Until I stopped the nuisance : there 's my crime !
Pity I did not suffer them subside   1270
Into some further shape and final form
Of execrable life ?   My masters, no !
I, by one blow, wisely cut short at once
Them and their transformations of disgust
In the snug little Villa out of hand.
' Grant me confession, give bare time for that ! '—
Shouted the sinner till his mouth was stopped.
His life confessed !—that was enough for me,
Who came to see that he did penance.   'S death !
Here 's a coil raised, a pother and for what ?   1280
Because strength, being provoked by weakness, fought
And conquered,—the world never heard the like !
Pah, how I spend my breath on them, as if

'T was their fate troubled me, too hard to range
Among the right and fit and proper things !

Ay, but Pompilia,—I await your word,—
She, unimpeached of crime, unimplicate
In folly, one of alien blood to these
I punish, why extend my claim, exact
Her portion of the penalty ? Yes, friends,   1290
I go too fast : the orator 's at fault :
Yes, ere I lay her, with your leave, by them
As she was laid at San Lorenzo late,
I ought to step back, lead her by degrees,
Recounting at each step some fresh offence,
Up to the red bed,—never fear, I will !
Gaze at her, where you place her, to begin,
Confound me with her gentleness and worth !
The horrible pair have fled and left her now,
She has her husband for her sole concern,   1300
His wife, the woman fashioned for his help,
Flesh of his flesh, bone of his bone, the bride
To groom as is the Church and Spouse, to Christ :
There she stands in his presence,—' Thy desire
' Shall be to the husband, o'er thee shall he rule ! '
—' Pompilia, who declare that you love God,
' You know who said that : then, desire my love,
' Yield me contentment and be ruled aright ! '
She sits up, she lies down, she comes and goes,
Kneels at the couch-side, overleans the sill   1310
O' the window, cold and pale and mute as stone,
Strong as stone also. ' Well, are they not fled ?
' Am I not left, am I not one for all ?
' Speak a word, drop a tear, detach a glance,
' Bless me or curse me of your own accord !
' Is it the ceiling only wants your soul,
' Is worth your eyes ? ' And then the eyes descend
And do look at me. Is it at the meal ?
' Speak ! ' she obeys, ' Be silent ! ' she obeys,
Counting the minutes till I cry ' Depart,'   1320
As brood-bird when you saunter past her eggs,
Departed, just the same through door and wall
I see the same stone strength of white despair.
And all this will be never otherwise !
Before, the parents' presence lent her life :
She could play off her sex's armoury,

Intreat, reproach, be female to my male,
Try all the shrieking doubles of the hare,
Go clamour to the Commissary, bid   1329
The Archbishop hold my hands and stop my tongue,
And yield fair sport so : but the tactics change,
The hare stands stock-still to enrage the hound !
Since that day when she learned she was no child
Of those she thought her parents,—that their trick
Had tricked me whom she thought sole trickster late,—
Why, I suppose she said within herself
' Then, no more struggle for my parents' sake,
' And, for my own sake, why needs struggle be ? '
But is there no third party to the pact ?
What of her husband's relish or dislike   1340
For this new game of giving up the game,
This worst offence of not offending more ?
I'll not believe but instinct wrought in this,
Set her on to conceive and execute
The preferable plague . . . how sure they probe,—
These jades, the sensitivest soft of man !
The long black hair was wound now in a wisp,—
Crowned sorrow better than the wild web late :
No more soiled dress, 'tis trimness triumphs now,
For how should malice go with negligence ?   1350
The frayed silk looked the fresher for her spite !
There was an end to springing out of bed,
Praying me, with face buried on my feet,
Be hindered of my pastime,—so an end
To my rejoinder, ' What, on the ground at last ?
' Vanquished in fight, a supplicant for life ?
' What if I raise you ? 'Ware the casting down
' When next you fight me ! ' Then, she lay there,
          mine :
Now, mine she is if I please wring her neck,—
A moment of disquiet, working eyes,   1360
Protruding tongue, a long sigh, then no more—
As if one killed the horse one could not ride !
Had I enjoined ' Cut off the hair ! '—why, snap
The scissors, and at once a yard or so
Had fluttered in black serpents to the floor :
But till I did enjoin it, how she combs,
Uncurls and draws out to the complete length,
Plaits, places the insulting rope on head
To be an eyesore past dishevelment !

Is all done ? Then sit still again and stare !   1370
I advise—no one think to bear that look
Of steady wrong, endured as steadily,
—Through what sustainment of deluding hope ?
Who is the friend i' the background that notes all ?
Who may come presently and close accounts ?
This self-possession to the uttermost,
How does it differ in aught, save degree,
From the terrible patience of God ?
            ' All which just means,   1379
' She did not love you ! ' Again the word is launched
And the fact fronts me ! What, you try the wards
With the true key and the dead lock flies ope ?
No, it sticks fast and leaves you fumbling still !
You have some fifty servants, Cardinal,—
Which of them loves you ? Which subordinate
But makes parade of such officiousness
That,—if there 's no love prompts it,—love, the sham,
Does twice the service done by love, the true.
God bless us liars, where 's one touch of truth
In what we tell the world, or world tells us,   1390
Of how we like each other ? All the same,
We calculate on word and deed, nor err,—
Bid such a man do such a loving act,
Sure of effect and negligent of cause,
Just as we bid a horse, with cluck of tongue,
Stretch his legs arch-wise, crouch his saddled back
To foot-reach of the stirrup—all for love,
And some for memory of the smart of switch
On the inside of the foreleg—what care we ?
Yet where 's the bond obliges horse to man   1400
Like that which binds fast wife to husband ? God
Laid down the law : gave man the brawny arm
And ball of fist—woman the beardless cheek
And proper place to suffer in the side :
Since it is he can strike, let her obey !
Can she feel no love ? Let her show the more,
Sham the worse, damn herself praiseworthily !
Who 's that soprano Rome went mad about
Last week while I lay rotting in my straw ?
The very jailor gossiped in his praise—   1410
How,—dressed up like Armida, though a man ;
And painted to look pretty, though a fright,—
He still made love so that the ladies swooned,

Being an eunuch. ' Ah, Rinaldo mine !
' But to breathe by thee while Jove slays us both ! '
All the poor bloodless creature never felt,
Si, do, re, mi, fa, squeak and squall—for what ?
Two gold zecchines the evening ! Here 's my slave,
Whose body and soul depend upon my nod,
Can't falter out the first note in the scale   1420
For her life ! Why blame me if I take the life ?
All women cannot give men love, forsooth !
No, nor all pullets lay the henwife eggs—
Whereat she bids them remedy the fault,
Brood on a chalk-ball : soon the nest is stocked—
Otherwise, to the plucking and the spit !
This wife of mine was of another mood—
Would not begin the lie that ends with truth,
Nor feign the love that brings real love about :
Wherefore I judged, sentenced and punished her.
But why particularize, defend the deed ?   1431
Say that I hated her for no one cause
Beyond my pleasure so to do,—what then ?
Just on as much incitement acts the world,
All of you ! Look and like ! You favour one,
Brow-beat another, leave alone a third,—
Why should you master natural caprice ?
Pure nature ! Try—plant elm by ash in file ;
Both unexceptionable trees enough,
They ought to overlean each other, pair   1440
At top and arch across the avenue
The whole path to the pleasaunce : do they so—
Or loathe, lie off abhorrent each from each ?
Lay the fault elsewhere, since we must have faults :
Mine shall have been,—seeing there 's ill in the end
Come of my course,—that I fare somehow worse
For the way I took,—my fault . . . . as God 's my judge
I see not where the fault lies, that 's the truth !
I ought . . oh, ought in my own interest
Have let the whole adventure go untried,   1450
This chance by marriage,—or else, trying it,
Ought to have turned it to account some one
O' the hundred otherwises ? Ay, my friend,
Easy to say, easy to do,—step right
Now you 've stepped left and stumbled on the thing,
—The red thing ! Doubt I any more than you
That practice makes man perfect ? Give again

The chance,—same marriage and no other wife,
Be sure I 'll edify you ! That 's because
I 'm practised, grown fit guide for Guido's self. 1460
You proffered guidance,—I know, none so well,—
You laid down law and rolled decorum out,
From pulpit-corner on the gospel-side,—
Wanted to make your great experience mine,
Save me the personal search and pains so : thanks !
Take your word on life's use ? When I take his—
The muzzled ox that treadeth out the corn,
Gone blind in padding round and round one path,—
As to the taste of green grass in the field !
What do you know o' the world that 's trodden flat
And salted sterile with your daily dung, 1471
Leavened into a lump of loathsomeness ?
Take your opinion of the modes of life,
The aims of life, life's triumph or defeat,
How to feel, how to scheme and how to do
Or else leave undone ? You preached long and loud
On high-days, ' Take our doctrine upon trust !
' Into the mill-house with you ! Grind our corn,
' Relish our chaff, and let the green grass grow ! '
I tried chaff, found I famished on such fare, 1480
So made this mad rush at the mill-house-door,
Buried my head up to the ears in dew,
Browsed on the best, for which you brain me, Sirs !
Be it so ! I conceived of life that way,
And still declare—life, without absolute use
Of the actual sweet therein, is death, not life.
Give me,—pay down,—not promise, which is air,—
Something that 's out of life and better still,
Make sure reward, make certain punishment,
Entice me, scare me,—I 'll forgo this life ; 1490
Otherwise, no !—the less that words, mere wind,
Would cheat me of some minutes while they plague.
The fulness of revenge here,—blame yourselves
For this eruption of the pent-up soul
You prisoned first and played with afterward !
' Deny myself ' meant simply pleasure you,
The sacred and superior, save the mark !
You,—whose stupidity and insolence
I must defer to, soothe at every turn,—
Whose swine-like snuffling greed and grunting lust
I had to wink at or help gratify,— 1501

While the same passions,—dared they perk in me,
Me, the immeasurably marked, by God,
Master of the whole world of such as you,—
I, boast such passions ?   'T was ' Suppress them
    straight !
' Or stay, we 'll pick and choose before destroy :
' Here 's wrath in you,—a serviceable sword,—
' Beat it into a ploughshare !   What 's this long
' Lance-like ambition ?   Forge a pruning-hook,
' May be of service when our vines grow tall !   1510
' But—sword used swordwise, spear thrust out as
    spear ?
' Anathema !   Suppression is the word ! '
My nature, when the outrage was too gross,
Widened itself an outlet over-wide
By way of answer ?—sought its own relief
With more of fire and brimstone than you wished ?
All your own doing : preachers, blame yourselves !

'Tis I preach while the hourglass runs and runs !
God keep me patient !   All I say just means—
My wife proved, whether by her fault or mine,—   1520
That 's immaterial,—a true stumbling-block
I' the way of me her husband : I but plied
The hatchet yourselves use to clear a path,
Was politic, played the game you warrant wins,
Plucked at law's robe a-rustle through the courts,
Bowed down to kiss divinity's buckled shoe
Cushioned i' the church : efforts all wide the aim !
Procedures to no purpose !   Then flashed truth !
The letter kills, the spirit keeps alive
In law and gospel : there be nods and winks   1530
Instruct a wise man to assist himself
In certain matters nor seek aid at all.
' Ask money of me,'—quoth the clownish saw,—
' And take my purse !   But,—speaking with respect,—
' Need you a solace for the troubled nose ?
' Let everybody wipe his own himself ! '
Sirs, tell me free and fair !   Had things gone well
At the wayside inn : had I surprised asleep
The runaways, as was so probable,
And pinned them each to other partridge-wise,
Through back and breast to breast and back, then bade
Bystanders witness if the spit, my sword,   1542

Were loaded with unlawful game for once—
Would you have interposed to damp the glow
Applauding me on every husband's cheek ?
Would you have checked the cry ' A judgment, see !
' A warning, note !   Be henceforth chaste, ye wives,
' Nor stray beyond your proper precinct, priests ! '
If you had, then your house against itself
Divides, nor stands your kingdom any more.   1550
Oh, why, why was it not ordained just so ?
Why fell not things out so nor otherwise ?
Ask that particular devil whose task it is
To trip the all-but-at perfection,—slur
The line o' the painter just where paint leaves off
And life begins,—puts ice into the ode
O' the poet while he cries ' Next stanza—fire ! '
Inscribes all human effort with one word,
Artistry's haunting curse, the Incomplete !
Being incomplete, the act escaped success.   1560
Easy to blame now !   Every fool can swear
To hole in net that held and slipped the fish.
But, treat my act with fair unjaundiced eye,
What was there wanting to a masterpiece
Except the luck that lies beyond a man ?
My way with the woman, now proved grossly wrong,
Just missed of being gravely grandly right
And making critics laugh o' the other side.
Do, for the poor obstructed artist's sake,
Go with him over that spoiled work once more !
Take only its first flower, the ended act   1571
Now in the dusty pod, dry and defunct !
I march to the Villa, and my men with me,
That evening, and we reach the door and stand.
I say . . no, it shoots through me lightning-like
While I pause, breathe, my hand upon the latch,
' Let me forebode !   Thus far, too much success :
' I want the natural failure—find it where ?
' Which thread will have to break and leave a loop
' I' the meshy combination, my brain's loom   1580
' Wove this long while and now next minute tests ?
' Of three that are to catch, two should go free,
' One must :   all three surprised,—impossible !
' Beside, I seek three and may chance on six,—
' This neighbour, t' other gossip,—the babe's birth
' Brings such to fireside and folks give them wine,—

' 'T is late : but when I break in presently
' One will 'be found outlingering the rest
' For promise of a posset,—one whose shout
' Would raise the dead down in the catacombs,   1590
' Much more the city-watch that goes its round.
' When did I ever turn adroitly up
' To sun some brick embedded in the soil,
' And with one blow crush all three scorpions there ?
' Or Pietro or Violante shambles off—
' It cannot be but I surprise my wife—
' If only she is stopped and stamped on, good !
' That shall suffice : more is improbable.
' Now I may knock ! '   And this once for my sake
The impossible was effected : I called king,   1600
Queen and knave in a sequence, and cards came,
All three, three only !   So, I had my way,
Did my deed : so, unbrokenly lay bare
Each tænia that had sucked me dry of juice,
At last outside me, not an inch of ring
Left now to writhe about and root itself
I' the heart all powerless for revenge !   Henceforth
I might thrive : these were drawn and dead and
          damned.
Oh Cardinal, the deep long sigh you heave
When the load 's off you, ringing as it runs   ● 1610
All the way down the serpent-stair to hell !
No doubt the fine delirium flustered me,
Turned my brain with the influx of success
As if the sole need now were to wave wand
And find doors fly wide,—wish and have my will,—
The rest o' the scheme would care for itself : escape ?
Easy enough were that, and poor beside !
It all but proved so,—ought to quite have proved,
Since, half the chances had sufficed, set free
Anyone, with his senses at command,   1620
From thrice the danger of my flight.   But, drunk,
Redundantly triumphant,—some reverse
Was sure to follow !   There 's no other way
Accounts for such prompt perfect failure then
And there on the instant.   Any day o' the week,
A ducat slid discreetly into palm
O' the mute post-master, while you whisper him—
How you the Count and certain four your knaves,
Have just been mauling who was malapert,

Suspect the kindred may prove troublesome,   1630
Therefore, want horses in a hurry,—that
And nothing more secures you any day
The pick o' the stable !   Yet I try the trick,
Double the bribe, call myself Duke for Count,
And say the dead man only was a Jew,
And for my pains find I am dealing just
With the one scrupulous fellow in all Rome—
Just this immaculate official stares,
Sees I want hat on head and sword in sheath,
Am splashed with other sort of wet than wine,   1640
Shrugs shoulder, puts my hand by, gold and all,
Stands on the strictness of the rule o' the road !
' Where 's the Permission ? '   Where 's the wretched
     rag
With the due seal and sign of Rome's Police,
To be had for asking, half-an-hour ago ?
' Gone ?   Get another, or no horses hence ! '
He dares not stop me, we five glare too grim,
But hinders,—hacks and hamstrings sure enough,
Gives me some twenty miles of miry road
More to march in the middle of that night   1650
Whereof the rough beginning taxed the strength
O' the youngsters, much more mine, such as you see,
Who had to think as well as act : dead-beat,
We gave in ere we reached the boundary
And safe spot out of this irrational Rome,—
Where, on dismounting from our steeds next day,
We had snapped our fingers at you, safe and sound,
Tuscans once more in blessed Tuscany,
Where the laws make allowance, understand
Civilized life and do its champions right !   1660
Witness the sentence of the Rota there,
Arezzo uttered, the Granduke confirmed,
One week before I acted on its hint,—
Giving friend Guillichini, for his love,
The galleys, and my wife your saint, Rome's saint,—
Rome manufactures saints enough to know,—
Seclusion at the Stinche for her life.
All this, that all but was, might·all have been,
Yet was not ! baulked by just a scrupulous knave
Whose palm was horn through handling horses' hoofs
And could not close upon my proffered gold !   1671
What say you to the spite of fortune ?   Well,

The worst 's in store : thus hindered, haled this way
To Rome again by hangdogs, whom find I
Here, still to fight with, but my pale frail wife ?
—Riddled with wounds by one not like to waste
The blows he dealt,—knowing anatomy,—
(I think I told you) one to pick and choose
The vital parts !   'T was learning all in vain !
She too must shimmer through the gloom o' the grave,
Come and confront me—not at judgement-seat   1681
Where I could twist her soul, as erst her flesh,
And turn her truth into a lie,—but there,
O' the death-bed, with God's hand between us both,
Striking me dumb, and helping her to speak,
Tell her own story her own way, and turn
My plausibility to nothingness !
Four whole days did Pompilia keep alive,
With the best surgery of Rome agape
At the miracle,—this cut, the other slash,   1690
And yet the life refusing to dislodge,
Four whole extravagant impossible days,
Till she had time to finish and persuade
Every man, every woman, every child
In Rome of what she would : the selfsame she
Who, but a year ago, had wrung her hands,
Reddened her eyes and beat her breasts, rehearsed
The whole game at Arezzo, nor availed
Thereby to move one heart or raise one hand !
When destiny intends you cards like these,   1700
What good of skill and preconcerted play ?
Had she been found dead, as I left her dead,
I should have told a tale brooked no reply :
You scarcely will suppose me found at fault
With that advantage !   ' What brings me to Rome ?
' Necessity to claim and take my wife :
' Better, to claim and take my new-born babe,—
' Strong in paternity a fortnight old,
' When 't is at strongest : warily I work,
' Knowing the machinations of my foe ;   1710
' I have companionship and use the night :
' I seek my wife and•child,—I find—no child
' But wife, in the embraces of that priest
' Who caused her to elope from me.   These two,
' Backed by the pander-pair who watch the while,
' Spring on me like so many tiger-cats,

' Glad of the chance to end the intruder.   I—
' What should I do but stand on my defence,
' Strike right, strike left, strike thick and threefold,
    slay,
' Not all—because the coward priest escapes.   1720
' Last, I escape, in fear of evil tongues,
' And having had my taste of Roman law.'
What 's disputable, refutable here ?—
Save by just this one ghost-thing half on earth,
Half out of it,—as if she held God's hand
While she leant back and looked her last at me,
Forgiving me (here monks begin to weep)
Oh, from her very soul, commending mine
To heavenly mercies which are infinite,—
While fixing fast my head beneath your knife !   1730
'T is fate not fortune !   All is of a piece !
What was it you informed me of my youths ?
My rustic four o' the family, soft swains,
What sweet surprise had they in store for me,
Those of my very household,—what did Law
Twist with her rack-and-cord-contrivance late
From out their bones and marrow ?   What but this—
Had no one of these several stumbling-blocks
Stopped me, they yet were cherishing a scheme,
All of their honest country homespun wit,   1740
To quietly next day at crow of cock,
Cut my own throat too, for their own behoof,
Seeing I had forgot to clear accounts
O' the instant, nowise slackened speed for that,—
And somehow never might find memory,
Once safe back in Arezzo, where things change,
And a court-lord needs mind no country lout.
Well, being the arch-offender, I die last,—
May, ere my head falls, have my eyesight free,
Nor miss them dangling high on either hand,   1750
Like scarecrows in a hemp-field, for their pains !

And then my Trial,—'t is my Trial that bites
Like a corrosive, so the cards are packed,
Dice loaded, and my life-stake tricked away !
Look at my lawyers, lacked they grace of law,
Latin or logic ?   Were not they fools to the height,
Fools to the depth, fools to the level between,
O' the foolishness set to decide the case ?

They feign, they flatter ; nowise does it skill,
Everything goes against me : deal each judge   1760
His dole of flattery and feigning,—why,
He turns and tries and snuffs and savours it,
As an old fly the sugar-grain, your gift ;
Then eyes your thumb and finger, brushes clean
The absurd old head of him, and whisks away,
Leaving your thumb and finger dirty.   Faugh !

And finally, after this long-drawn range
Of affront, failure, failure and affront,—
This path, twixt crosses leading to a skull,
Paced by me barefoot, bloodied by my palms   1770
From the entry to the end,—there 's light at length,
A cranny of escape,—appeal may be
To the old man, to the father, to the Pope,
For a little life—from one whose life is spent,
A little pity—from pity's source and seat,
A little indulgence to rank, privilege,
From one who is the thing personified,
Rank, privilege, indulgence, grown beyond
Earth's bearing, even, ask Jansenius else !
Still the same answer, still no other tune   1780
From the cicala perched at the tree-top
Than crickets noisy round the root,—'t is ' Die ! '
Bids Law—' Be damned ! ' adds Gospel,—nay,
No word so frank,—'t is rather, ' Save yourself ! '
The Pope subjoins—' Confess and be absolved !
' So shall my credit countervail your shame,
' And the world see I have not lost the knack
' Of trying all the spirits,—yours, my son,
' Wants but a fiery washing to emerge
' In clarity !   Come, cleanse you, ease the ache
' Of these old bones, refresh our bowels, boy ! '   1791
Do I mistake your mission from the Pope ?
Then, bear his Holiness the mind of me !
I do get strength from being thrust to wall,
Successively wrenched from pillar and from post
By this tenacious hate of fortune, hate
Of all things in, under, and above earth.
Warfare, begun this mean unmanly mode,
Does best to end so,—gives earth spectacle
Of a brave fighter who succumbs to odds   1800
That turn defeat to victory.   Stab, I fold

My mantle round me ! Rome approves my act :
Applauds the blow which costs me life but keeps
My honour spotless : Rome would praise no more
Had I fallen, say, some fifteen years ago,
Helping Vienna when our Aretines
Flocked to Duke Charles and fought Turk Mustafa ;
Nor would you two be trembling o'er my corpse
With all this exquisite solicitude.
Why is it that I make such suit to live ?   1810
The popular sympathy that 's round me now
Would break like bubble that o'er-domes a fly—
Pretty enough while he lies quiet there,
But let him want the air and ply the wing,
Why, it breaks and bespatters him, what else ?
Cardinal, if the Pope had pardoned me,
And I walked out of prison through the crowd,
It would not be your arm I should dare press !
Then, if I got safe to my place again,
How sad and sapless were the years to come ! 1820
I go my old ways and find things grown grey ;
You priests leer at me, old friends look askance ;
The mob 's in love, I 'll wager, to a man,
With my poor young good beauteous murdered wife :
For hearts require instruction how to beat,
And eyes, on warrant of the story, wax
Wanton at portraiture in white and black
Of dead Pompilia gracing ballad-sheet,
Which, had she died unmurdered and unsung,
Would never turn though she paced street as bare
As the mad penitent ladies do in France.   1831
My brothers quietly would edge me out
Of use and management of things called mine ;
Do I command ? ' You stretched command before ! '
Show anger ? ' Anger little helped you once ! '
Advise ? ' How managed you affairs of old ? '
My very mother, all the while they gird,
Turns eye up, gives confirmatory groan,—
For unsuccess, explain it how you will,
Disqualifies you, makes you doubt yourself, 1840
—Much more, is found decisive by your friends.
Beside, am I not fifty years of age ?
What new leap would a life take, checked like mine
I' the spring at outset ? Where 's my second chance ?
Ay, but the babe . . I had forgot my son,

My heir !   Now for a burst of gratitude !
There 's some appropriate service to intone,
Some *gaudeamus* and thanksgiving-psalm !
Old, I renew my youth in him, and poor
Possess a treasure,—is not that the phrase ?   1850
Only I must wait patient twenty years—
Nourishing all the while, as father ought,
The excrescence with my daily blood of life.
Does it respond to hope, such sacrifice,—
Grows the wen plump while I myself grow lean ?
Why, here 's my son and heir in evidence,
Who stronger, wiser, handsomer than I
By fifty years, relieves me of each load,—
Tames my hot horse, carries my heavy gun,
Courts my coy mistress,—has his apt advice   1860
On house-economy, expenditure,
And what not ?   All which good gifts and great growth
Because of my decline, he brings to bear
On Guido, but half apprehensive how
He cumbers earth, crosses the brisk young Count,
Who civilly would thrust him from the scene.
Contrariwise, does the blood-offering fail ?
There 's an ineptitude, one blank the more
Added to earth in semblance of my child ?
Then, this has been a costly piece of work,   1870
My life exchanged for his !—why he, not I,
Enjoy the world, if no more grace accrue ?
Dwarf me, what giant have you made of him ?
I do not dread the disobedient son—
I know how to suppress rebellion there,
Being not quite the fool my father was.
But grant the medium measure of a man,
The usual compromise 'twixt fool and sage,
—You know—the tolerably-obstinate,
The not-so-much-perverse but you may train,   1880
The true son-servant that, when parent bids
' Go work, son, in my vineyard ! ' makes reply
' I go, Sir ! '—Why, what profit in your son
Beyond the drudges you might subsidize,
Have the same work from at a paul the head ?
Look at those four young precious olive-plants
Reared at Vittiano,—not on flesh and blood,
These twenty years, but black bread and sour wine !
I bade them put forth tender branch, and hook

And hurt three enemies I had in Rome :   1890
They did my hest as unreluctantly,
At promise of a dollar, as a son
Adjured by mumping memories of the past !
No, nothing repays youth expended so—
Youth, I say, who am young still,—give but leave
To live my life out, to the last I 'd live
And die conceding age no right of youth !
It is the will runs the renewing nerve
Through flaccid flesh, would faint before the time.
Therefore no sort of use for son have I—   1900
Sick, not of life's feast but of steps to climb
To the house where life prepares her feast,—of means
To the end : for make the end attainable
Without the means,—my relish were like yours.
A man may have an appetite enough
For a whole dish of robins ready cooked,
And yet lack courage to face sleet, pad snow,
And snare sufficiency for supper.

                         Thus
The time's arrived when, ancient Roman-like,   1910
I am bound to fall on my own sword,—why not
Say—Tuscan-like, more ancient, better still ?
Will you hear truth can do no harm nor good ?
I think I never was at any time
A Christian, as you nickname all the world,
Me among others : truce to nonsense now !
Name me, a primitive religionist—
As should the aboriginary be
I boast myself, Etruscan, Aretine,   1919
One sprung,—your frigid Virgil's fieriest word,—
From fauns and nymphs, trunks and the heart of oak,
With,—for a visible divinity,—
The portent of a Jove Ægiochus
Descried 'mid clouds, lightning and thunder, couched
On topmost crag of your Capitoline—
'T is in the Seventh Æneid,—what, the Eighth ?
Right,—thanks, Abate,—though the Christian's dumb,
The Latinist 's vivacious in you yet !
I know my grandsire had our tapestry
Marked with the motto, 'neath a certain shield
His grandson presently will give some gules   1931
To vary azure.   First we fight for faiths,

But get to shake hands at the last of all :
Mine 's your faith too,—in Jove Ægiochus !
Nor do Greek gods, that serve as supplement,
Jar with the simpler scheme, if understood.
We want such intermediary race
To make communication possible ;
The real thing were too lofty, we too low,
Midway hang these : we feel their use so plain   1940
In linking height to depth, that we doff hat
And put no question nor pry narrowly
Into the nature hid behind the names.
We grudge no rite the fancy may demand ;
But never, more than needs, invent, refine,
Improve upon requirement, idly wise
Beyond the letter, teaching gods their trade,
Which is to teach us : we 'll obey when taught.
Why should we do our duty past the due ?   1949
When the sky darkens, Jove is wroth,—say prayer !
When the sun shines and Jove is glad,—sing psalm !
But wherefore pass prescription and devise
Blood-offering for sweat-service, lend the rod
A pungency through pickle of our own ?
Learned Abate,—no one teaches you
What Venus means and who 's Apollo here !
I spare you, Cardinal,—but, though you wince,
You know me, I know you, and both know that !
So, if Apollo bids us fast, we fast :
But where does Venus order we stop sense   1960
When Master Pietro rhymes a pleasantry ?
Give alms prescribed on Friday,—but, hold hand
Because your foe lies prostrate,—where 's the word
Explicit in the book debars revenge ?
The rationale of your scheme is just
' Pay toll here, there pursue your pleasure free ! '
So do.you turn to use the medium-powers,
Mars and Minerva, Bacchus and the rest,
And so are saved propitiating—what ?
What all good, all wise and all potent Jove   1970
Vexed by the very sins in man, himself
Made life's necessity when man he made ?
Irrational bunglers ! So, the living truth
Revealed to strike Pan dead, ducks low at last,
Prays leave to hold its own and live good days
Provided it go masque grotesquely, called

Christian not Pagan ?   Oh, you purged the sky
Of all gods save the One, the great and good,
Clapped hands and triumphed !   But the change came
    fast :
The inexorable need in man for life—   1980
Life,—you may mulct and minish to a grain
Out of the lump, so the grain left but live,—
Laughed at your substituting death for life,
And bade you do your worst,—which worst was done
—Pass that age styled the primitive and pure
When Saint this, Saint that, dutifully starved,
Froze, fought with beasts, was beaten and abused
And finally ridded of his flesh by fire,
Keeping the while unspotted from the world !—
Good : but next age, how goes the game, who gives
His life and emulates Saint that and this ?   1991
They mutiny, mutter who knows what excuse ?
In fine make up their minds to leave the new,
Stick to the old,—enjoy old liberty,
No prejudice, all the same, if so it please,
To the new profession : sin o' the sly, henceforth !
Let the law stand : the letter kills, what then ?
The spirit saves as unmistakeably.
Omniscience sees, Omnipotence could stop,
All-mercifulness pardons,—it must be,   2000
Frown law its fiercest, there 's a wink somewhere.

Such was the logic in this head of mine :
I, like the rest, wrote ' poison ' on my bread ;
But broke and ate :—said ' those that use the sword
' Shall perish by the same ; ' then stabbed my foe.
I stand on solid earth, not empty air :
Dislodge me, let your Pope's crook hale me hence !
Not he, nor you !   And I so pity both,
I 'll make the speech you want the wit to make :
' Count Guido, who reveal our mystery,   2010
' You trace all issues to the love of life :
' We have a life to love and guard, like you.
' Why did you put us upon self-defence ?
' You well knew what prompt pass-word would appease
' The sentry's ire when folk infringe his bounds,
' And yet kept mouth shut : do you wonder then
' If, in mere decency, he shot you dead ?
' He can't have people play such pranks as you

' Beneath his nose at noonday, who disdain
' To give him an excuse before the world,   2020
' By crying " I break rule to save our camp ! "
' Under the old rule, such offence were death ;
' And so had you heard Pontifex pronounce
' " Since you slay foe and violate the form,
' " That turns to murder, which were sacrifice
' " Had you, while, say, law-suiting him to death,
' " But raised an altar to the Unknown God,
' " Or else the Genius of the Vatican."
' Why then this pother ?—all because the Pope
' Doing his duty, cries " A foreigner,   2030
' " You scandalize the natives : here at Rome
' " *Romano vivitur more* : wise men, here,
' " Put the Church forward and efface themselves.
' " The fit defence had been,—you stamped on wheat,
' " Intending all the time to trample tares,—
' " Were fain extirpate, then, the heretic,
' " And now find, in your haste you slew a fool :
' " Nor Pietro, nor Violante, nor your wife
' " Meant to breed up your babe a Molinist !   2039
' " Whence you are duly contrite. Not one word
' " Of all this wisdom did you urge !—which slip
' " Death must atone for ! " '
                                   So, let death atone !
So ends mistake, so end mistakers !   end
Perhaps to recommence,—how should I know ?
Only, be sure, no punishment, no pain
Childish, preposterous, impossible,
But some such fate as Ovid could foresee,—
Byblis in fluvium, let the weak soul end
In water, *sed Lycaon in lupum*, but   2050
The strong become a wolf for evermore !
Change that Pompilia to a puny stream
Fit to reflect the daisies on its bank !
Let me turn wolf, be whole, and sate, for once,—
Wallow in what is now a wolfishness
Coerced too much by the humanity
That 's half of me as well !   Grow out of man,
Glut the wolf-nature,—what remains but grow
Into the man again, be man indeed
And all man ?   Do I ring the changes right ?   2060
Deformed, transformed, reformed, informed, con-
      formed !

The honest instinct, pent and crossed through life,
Let surge by death into a visible flow
Of rapture : as the strangled thread of flame
Painfully winds, annoying and annoyed,
Malignant and maligned, thro' stone and ore,
Till earth exclude the stranger : vented once,
It finds full play, is recognized a-top
Some mountain as no such abnormal birth.
Fire for the mount, the streamlet for the vale !   2070
Ay, of the water was that wife of mine—
Be it for good, be it for ill, no run
O' the red thread through that insignificance !
Again, how she is at me with those eyes !
Away with the empty stare !   Be holy still,
And stupid ever !   Occupy your patch
Of private snow that 's somewhere in what world
May now be growing icy round your head,
And aguish at your foot-print,—freeze not me,
Dare follow not another step I take,   2080
Not with so much as those detested eyes,
No, though they follow but to pray me pause
On the incline, earth's edge that 's next to hell !
None of your abnegation of revenge !
Fly at me frank, tug while I tear again !
There 's God, go tell Him, testify your worst !
Not she !   There was no touch in her of hate :
And it would prove her hell, if I reached mine !
To know I suffered, would still sadden her,
Do what the angels might to make amends !   2090
Therefore there 's either no such place as hell,
Or thence shall I be thrust forth, for her sake,
And thereby undergo three hells, not one—
I who, with outlet for escape to heaven,
Would tarry if such flight allowed my foe
To raise his head, relieved of that firm foot
Had pinned him to the fiery pavement else !
So am I made, ' who did not make myself : '
(How dared she rob my own lip of the word ?)
Beware me in what other world may be !—   2100
Pompilia, who have brought me to this pass !
All I know here, will I say there, and go
Beyond the saying with the deed.   Some use
There cannot but be for a mood like mine,
Implacable, persistent in revenge.

She maundered ' All is over and at end :
' I go my own road, go you where God will !
' Forgive you ? I forget you ! '   There 's the saint
That takes your taste, you other kind of men !
How you had loved her ! Guido wanted skill   2110
To value such a woman at her worth !
Properly the instructed criticize
' What 's here, you simpleton have tossed to take
' Its chance i' the gutter ?   This a daub, indeed ?
' Why, 't is a Rafael that you kicked to rags ! '
Perhaps so : some prefer the pure design :
Give me my gorge of colour, glut of gold
In a glory round the Virgin made for me !
Titian 's the man, not Monk Angelico
Who traces you some timid chalky ghost   2120
That turns the church into a charnel : ay,
Just such a pencil might depict my wife !
She,—since she, also, would not change herself,—
Why could not she come in some heart-shaped cloud,
Rainbowed about with riches, royalty
Rimming her round, as round the tintless lawn
Guardingly runs the selvage cloth of gold ?
I would have left the faint fine gauze untouched,
Needle-worked over with its lily and rose,
Let her bleach unmolested in the midst,   2130
Chill that selected solitary spot
Of quietude she pleased to think was life :
Purity, pallor grace the lawn no doubt
When there 's the costly bordure to unthread
And make again an ingot : but what 's grace
When you want meat and drink and clothes and fire ?
A tale comes to my mind that 's apposite—
Possibly true, probably false, a truth
Such as all truths we live by, Cardinal !
'T is said, a certain ancestor of mine   2140
Followed—whoever was the potentate,
To Paynimrie, and in some battle, broke
Through more than due allowance of the foe
And, risking much his own life, saved the lord's.
Battered and bruised, the Emperor scrambles up,
Rubs his eyes and looks round and sees my sire,
Picks a furze-sprig from out his hauberk-joint,
(Token how near the ground went majesty)
And says ' Take this, and, if thou get safe home,

' Plant the same in thy garden-ground to grow :
' Run thence an hour in a straight line, and stop :
' Describe a circle round (for central point)   2152
' The furze aforesaid, reaching every way
' The length of that hour's run : I give it thee,—
' The central point, to build a castle there,
' The circumjacent space, for fit demesne,
' The whole to be thy children's heritage,—
' Whom, for my sake, bid thou wear furze on cap ! '
Those are my arms : we turned the furze a tree
To show more, and the greyhound tied thereto,   2160
Straining to start, means swift and greedy both ;
He stands upon a triple mount of gold—
By Jove, then, he 's escaping from true gold
And trying to arrive at empty air !
Aha ! the fancy never crossed my mind !
My father used to tell me, and subjoin
' As for the castle, that took wings and flew :
' The broad lands,—why, to traverse them to-day
' Would task my gouty feet, though in my prime
' I doubt not I could stand and spit so far :   2170
' But for the furze, boy, fear no lack of that,
' So long as fortune leaves one field to grub !
' Wherefore hurra for furze and loyalty ! '
What may I mean, where may the lesson lurk ?
' Do not bestow on man by way of gift
' Furze without some substantial framework,—grace
' Of purity, a furze-sprig of a wife,
' To me, i' the thick of battle for my bread,
' Without some better dowry,—house and land ! '
No other gift than sordid muck ? Yes, Sir !   2180
Many more and much better. Give them me !
O those Olimpias bold, those Biancas brave,
That brought a husband will worth Ormuz' wealth !
Cried ' Thou being mine, why, what but thine am I ?
' Be thou to me law, right, wrong, heaven and hell !
' Let us blend souls, be thou in me to bid
' Two bodies work one pleasure ! What are these
' Called king, priest, father, mother, stranger, friend ?
' They fret thee or they frustrate ? Give the word—
' Be certain they shall frustrate nothing more !   2190
' And who is this young florid foolishness
' That holds thy fortune in his pigmy clutch,
' —Being a prince and potency, forsooth !—

' And hesitates to let the trifle go ?
' Let me but seal up eye, sing ear to sleep
' Sounder than Samson,—pounce thou on the prize
' Shall slip from off my breast, and down couch-side
' And on to floor, and far as my lord's feet—
' Where he stands in the shadow with the sword
' Waiting to see what Delilah dares do !   2200
' Is the youth fair ?   What is a man to me
' Who am thy call-bird ? Twist his neck—my dupe's,—
' Then take the breast shall turn a breast indeed ! '
Such women are there ; and they marry whom ?
Why, when a man has gone and hanged himself
Because of what he calls a wicked wife,—
See, if the turpitude, he makes his moan,
Be not mere excellence the fool ignores !
His monster is perfection, Circe, sent
Straight from the sun, with rod the idiot blames
As not an honest distaff to spin wool !   2211
O thou Lucrezia, is it long to wait
Yonder where all the gloom is in a glow
With thy suspected presence ?—virgin yet,
Virtuous again in face of what 's to teach—
Sin unimagined, unimaginable,—
I come to claim my bride,—thy Borgia's self
Not half the burning bridegroom I shall be !
Cardinal, take away your crucifix !
Abate, leave my lips alone, they bite !   2220
'T is vain you try to change, what should not change,
And cannot. I have bared, you bathe my heart—
It grows the stonier for your saving dew !
You steep the substance, you would lubricate,
In waters that but touch to petrify !

You too are petrifactions of a kind :
Move not a muscle that shows mercy ; rave
Another twelve hours, every word were waste !
I thought you would not slay impenitence,—
Teased first contrition from the man you slew,—   2230
I thought you had a conscience. Cardinal,
You know I am wronged!—wronged, say, and wronged
      maintain.
Was this strict inquisition made for blood
When first you showed us scarlet on your back,
Called to the College ? That straightforward way

To that legitimate end,—I think it passed
Over a scantling of heads brained, hearts broke,
Lives trodden into dust,—how otherwise ?
Such is the way o' the world, and so you walk :
Does memory haunt your pillow ?   Not a whit
God wills you never pace your garden-path   2241
One appetizing hour ere dinner-time
But your intrusion there treads out of life
An universe of happy innocent things :
Feel you remorse about that damsel-fly
Which buzzed so near your mouth and flapped your
       face,
You blotted it from being at a blow ?
It was a fly, you were a man, and more,
Lord of created things, so took your course.
Manliness, mind,—these are things fit to save,   2250
Fit to brush fly from : why, because I take
My course, must needs the Pope kill me ?—kill you !
Because this instrument he throws away
Is strong to serve a master : it were yours
To have and hold and get such good from out !
The Pope who dooms me, needs must die next year ;
I 'll tell you how the chances are supposed
For his successor : first the Chamberlain,
Old San Cesario,—Colloredo, next,—
Then, one, two, three, four, I refuse to name,   2260
After these, comes Altieri ; then come you—
Seventh on the list you are, unless . . ha, ha,
How can a dead hand give a friend a lift ?
Are you the person to despise the help
O' the head shall drop in pannier presently ?
So a child seesaws on or kicks away
The fulcrum-stone that 's all the sage requires
To fit his lever to and move the world.
Cardinal, I adjure you in God's name,
Save my life, fall at the Pope's feet, set forth   2270
Things your own fashion, not in words like these
Made for a sense like yours who apprehend !
Translate into the court-conventional
' Count Guido must not die, is innocent !
' Fair, be assured ! But what an he were foul,
' Blood-drenched and murder-crusted head to foot ?
' Spare one whose death insults the Emperor,
' And outrages the Louis you so love !

R

' He has friends who will avenge him ;   enemies
' Who hate the church now with impunity   2280
' Missing the old coercive :   would you send
' A soul straight to perdition, dying frank
' An atheist ? '   Go and say this, for God's sake !
—Why, you do n't think I hope you 'll say one word ?
Neither shall I persuade you from your stand
Nor you persuade me from my station :   take
Your crucifix away, I tell you twice !

Come, I am tired of silence !   Pause enough !
You have prayed :   I have gone inside my soul
And shut its door behind me :   't is your torch   2290
Makes the place dark,—the darkness let alone
Grows tolerable twilight,—one may grope
And get to guess at length and breadth and depth.
What is this fact I feel persuaded of—
This something like a foothold in the sea,
Although Saint Peter's bark scuds, billow-borne,
Leaves me to founder where it flung me first ?
Spite of your splashing, I am high and dry !
God takes his own part in each thing he made ;
Made for a reason, he conserves his work,   2300
Gives each its proper instinct of defence.
My lamblike wife could neither bark nor bite,
She bleated, bleated, till for pity pure,
The village roused it, ran with pole and prong
To the rescue, and behold the wolf 's at bay !
Shall he try bleating ?—or take turn or two,
Since the wolf owns to kinship with the fox,
And failing to escape the foe by these,
Give up attempt, die fighting quietly ?
The last bad blow that strikes fire in at eye   2310
And on to brain, and so out, life and all,
How can it but be cheated of a pang
While, fighting quietly, the jaws enjoy
Their re-embrace in mid back-bone they break,
After their weary work thro' the foes' flesh ?
That 's the wolf-nature.   Do n't mistake my trope !
The Cardinal is qualmish !   Eminence,
My fight is figurative, blows i' the air,
Brain-war with powers and principalities,
Spirit-bravado, no real fisticuffs !   2320
I shall not presently, when the knock comes,

Cling to this bench nor flee the hangman's face,
No, trust me ! I conceive worse lots than mine.
Whether it be the old contagious fit
And plague o' the prison have surprised me too,
The appropriate drunkenness of the death-hour
Creep on my sense, the work o' the wine and myrrh,—
I know not,—I begin to taste my strength,
Careless, gay even : what 's the worth of life ?
The Pope is dead, my murderous old man,   2330
For Tozzi told me so : and you, forsooth—
Why, you do n't think, Abate, do your best,
You 'll live a year more with that hacking cough
And blotch of crimson where the cheek 's a pit ?
Tozzi has got you also down in book.
Cardinal, only seventh of seventy near,
Is not one called Albano in the lot ?
Go eat your heart, you 'll never be a Pope !
Inform me, is it true you left your love,
A Pucci, for promotion in the church ?   2340
She 's more than in the church,—in the churchyard !
Plautilla Pucci, your affianced bride,
Has dust now in the eyes that held the love,—
And Martinez, suppose they make you Pope,
Stops that with *veto*,—so, enjoy yourself !
I see you all reel to the rock, you waves—
Some forthright, some describe a sinuous track,
Some crested, brilliantly with heads above,
Some in a strangled swirl sunk who knows how,
But all bound whither the main-current sets,   2350
Rockward, an end in foam for all of you !
What if I am o'ertaken, pushed to the front
By all you crowding smoother souls behind,
And reach, a minute sooner than was meant,
The boundary, whereon I break to mist ?
Go to ! the smoothest safest of you all,
Most perfect and compact wave in my train,
Spite of the blue tranquillity above,
Spite of the breadth before of lapsing peace
Where broods the halcyon and the fish leaps free,
Will presently begin to feel the prick   2361
At lazy heart, the push at torpid brain,
Will rock vertiginously in turn, and reel,
And, emulative, rush to death like me :
Later or sooner by a minute then,

So much for the untimeliness of death,—
And, as regards the manner that offends,
The rude and rough, I count the same for gain—
Be the act harsh and quick !   Undoubtedly
The soul 's condensed and, twice itself, expands
To burst thro' life, in alternation due,   2371
Into the other state whate'er it prove.
You never know what life means till you die :
Even throughout life, 't is death that makes life live,
Gives it whatever the significance.
For see, on your own ground and argument,
Suppose life had no death to fear, how find
A possibility of nobleness
In man, prevented daring any more ?
What 's love, what 's faith without a worst to dread ?
Lack-lustre jewelry ; but faith and love   2381
With death behind them bidding do or die—
Put such a foil at back, the sparkle 's born !
From out myself how the strange colours come !
Is there a new rule in another world ?
Be sure I shall resign myself : as here
I recognized no law I could not see,
There, what I see, I shall acknowledge too :
On earth I never took the Pope for God,
In heaven I shall scarce take God for the Pope.   2390
Unmanned, remade : I hold it probable—
With something changeless at the heart of me
To know me by, some nucleus that 's myself :
Accretions did it wrong ?   Away with them—
You soon shall see the use of fire !

                                        Till when,
All that was, is ; and must for ever be.
Nor is it in me to unhate my hates,—
I use up my last strength to strike once more
Old Pietro in the wine-house-gossip-face,   2400
To trample underfoot the whine and wile
Of that Violante,—and I grow one gorge
To loathingly reject Pompilia's pale
Poison my hasty hunger took for food.
A strong tree wants no wreaths about its trunk,
No cloying cups, no sickly sweet of scent,
But sustenance at root, a bucketful.
How else lived that Athenian who died so,

Drinking hot bull's-blood, fit for men like me ?
I lived and died a man, and take man's chance,
Honest and bold : right will be done to such.   2411

Who are these you have let descend my stair ?
Ha, their accursed psalm !   Lights at the sill !
Is it ' Open ' they dare bid you ?   Treachery !
Sirs, have I spoken one word all this while
Out of the world of words I had to say ?
Not one word !   All was folly—I laughed and mocked!
Sirs, my first true word, all truth and no lie,
Is—save me notwithstanding !   Life is all !
I was just stark mad,—let the madman live   2420
Pressed by as many chains as you please pile !
Do n't open !   Hold me from them !   I am yours,
I am the Granduke's—no, I am the Pope's !
Abate,—Cardinal,—Christ,—Maria,—God, . . .
Pompilia, will you let them murder me ?

XII

THE BOOK AND THE RING

HERE were the end, had anything an end :
Thus, lit and launched, up and up roared and soared
A rocket, till the key o' the vault was reached,
And wide heaven held, a breathless minute-space,
In brilliant usurpature : thus caught spark,
Rushed to the height, and hung at full of fame
Over men's upturned faces, ghastly thence,
Our glaring Guido : now decline must be.
In its explosion, you have seen his act,
By my power—may-be, judged it by your own,—
Or composite as good orbs prove, or crammed   11
With worse ingredients than the Wormwood Star.
The act, over and ended, falls and fades :
What was once seen, grows what is now described,
Then talked of, told about, a tinge the less
In every fresh transmission ; till it melts,
Trickles in silent orange or wan grey
Across our memory, dies and leaves all dark,
And presently we find the stars again.
Follow the main streaks, meditate the mode   20
Of brightness, how it hastes to blend with black !

After that February Twenty-Two,
Since our salvation, Sixteen-Ninety-Eight,
Of all reports that were, or may have been,
Concerning those the day killed or let live,
Four I count only. Take the first that comes.
A letter from a stranger, man of rank,
Venetian visitor at Rome,—who knows,
On what pretence of busy idleness ?
Thus he begins on evening of that day.   30

' Here are we at our end of Carnival ;
' Prodigious gaiety and monstrous mirth,
' And constant shift of entertaining show :
' With influx, from each quarter of the globe,

' Of strangers nowise wishful to be last
' I' the struggle for a good place presently
' When that befalls, fate cannot long defer.
' The old Pope totters on the verge o' the grave :
' You see, Malpichi understood far more
' Than Tozzi how to treat the ailments : age,   40
' No question, renders these inveterate.
' Cardinal Spada, actual Minister,
' Is possible Pope ; I wager on his head,
' Since those four entertainments of his niece
' Which set all Rome a-stare : Pope probably—
' Though Colloredo has his backers too,
' And San Cesario makes one doubt at times :
' Altieri will be Chamberlain at most.

' A week ago the sun was warm like May,
' And the old man took daily exercise   50
' Along the river-side ; he loves to see
' That Custom-house he built upon the bank,
' For, Naples-born, his tastes are maritime :
' But yesterday he had to keep in-doors
' Because of the outrageous rain that fell.
' On such days the good soul has fainting-fits,
' Or lies in stupor, scarcely makes believe
' Of minding business, fumbles at his beads.
' They say, the trust that keeps his heart alive
' Is that, by lasting till December next,   60
' He may hold Jubilee a second time,
' And, twice in one reign, ope the Holy Doors.
' By the way, somebody responsible
' Assures me that the King of France has writ
' Fresh orders : Fénelon will be condemned :
' The Cardinal makes a wry face enough,
' Having a love for the delinquent : still,
' He 's the ambassador, must press the point.
' Have you a wager too dependent here ?

' Now, from such matters to divert awhile,   70
' Hear of to-day's event which crowns the week,
' Casts all the other wagers into shade.
' Tell Dandolo I owe him fifty drops
' Of heart's blood in the shape of gold zecchines !
' The Pope has done his worst : I have to pay
' For the execution of the Count, by Jove !

' Two days since, I reported him as safe,
' Re-echoing the conviction of all Rome :
' Who could suspect the one deaf ear—the Pope's ?
' But prejudices grow insuperable,   80
' And that old enmity to Austria, that
' Passion for France and France's pageant-king
' (Of which, why pause to multiply the proofs
' Now scandalously rife in Europe's mouth ?)
' These fairly got the better in the man
' Of justice, prudence, and *esprit de corps.*
' And he persisted in the butchery.
' Also, 't is said that in his latest walk
' To that Dogana-by-the-Bank, he built,
' The crowd,—he suffers question, unrebuked,—   90
' Asked, " Whether murder was a privilege
' " Only reserved for nobles like the Count ? "
' And he was ever mindful of the mob.
' Martinez, the Cæsarian Minister,
' —Who used his best endeavours to spare blood,
' And strongly pleaded for the life " of one,"
' Urged he, "I may have dined at table with ! "—
' He will not soon forget the Pope's rebuff,
' —Feels the slight sensibly, I promise you !
' And but for the dissuasion of two eyes   100
' That make with him foul weather or fine day,
' He had abstained, nor graced the spectacle :
' As it was, barely would he condescend
' Look forth from the *palchetto* where he sat
' Under the Pincian : we shall hear of this !
' The substituting, too, the People's Square
' For the out-o'-the-way old quarter by the Bridge,
' Was meant as a conciliatory sop
' To the mob ; it gave one holiday the more.
' But the French Embassy might unfurl flag,—   110
' Still the good luck of France to fling a foe !
' Cardinal Bouillon triumphs properly !
' *Palchetti* were erected in the Place,
' And houses, at the edge of the Three Streets,
' Let their front windows at six dollars each :
' Anguisciola, that patron of the arts,
' Hired one ; our Envoy Contarini too.

' Now for the thing ; no sooner the decree
' Gone forth,—'t is four-and-twenty hours ago,—

' Than Acciaioli and Panciatichi,   120
' Old friends, indeed compatriots of the man,
' Being pitched on as the couple properest
' To intimate the sentence yesternight,
' Were closeted ere cock-crow with the Count.
' They both report their efforts to dispose
' The unhappy nobleman for ending well,
' Despite the natural sense of injury,
' Were crowned at last with a complete success :
' And when the Company of Death arrived
' At twenty-hours,—the way they reckon here,—
' We say, at sunset, after dinner-time,—   131
' The Count was led down, hoisted up on car,
' Last of the five, as heinousest, you know :
' Yet they allowed one whole car to each man.
' His intrepidity, nay, nonchalance,
' As up he stood and down he sat himself,
' Struck admiration into those who saw.
' Then the procession started, took the way
' From the New Prisons by the Pilgrim's Street,
' The street of the Governo, Pasquin's Street,   140
' (Where was stuck up, 'mid other epigrams,
' A quatrain . . but of all that, presently !)
' The Place Navona, the Pantheon's Place,
' Place of the Column, last the Corso's length,
' And so debouched thence at Mannaia's foot
' I' the Place o' the People.   As is evident,
' (Despite the malice,—plainly meant, I fear,
' By this abrupt change of locality,—
' The Square 's no such bad place to head and hang)
' We had the titillation as we sat   150
' Assembled, (quality in conclave, ha ?)
' Of, minute after minute, some report
' How the slow show was winding on its way.
' Now did a car run over, kill a man,
' Just opposite a pork-shop numbered Twelve :
' And bitter were the outcries of the mob
' Against the Pope : for, but that he forbids
' The Lottery, why, twelve were Tern Quatern !
' Now did a beggar by Saint Agnes, lame
' From his youth up, recover use of leg,   160
' Through prayer of Guido as he glanced that way :
' So that the crowd near crammed his hat with coin.
' Thus was kept up excitement to the last,

R 3

' —Not an abrupt out-bolting, as of yore,
' From Castle, over Bridge and on to block,
' And so all ended ere you well could wink !

' Guido was last to mount the scaffold-steps
' Here also, as atrociousest in crime.
' We hardly noticed how the peasants died,
' They dangled somehow soon to right and left,   170
' And we remained all ears and eyes, could give
' Ourselves to Guido undividedly,
' As he harangued the multitude beneath.
' He begged forgiveness on the part of God,
' And fair construction of his act from men,
' Whose suffrage he entreated for his soul,
' Suggesting that we should forthwith repeat
' A *Pater* and an *Ave*, with the hymn
' *Salve Regina Cœli*, for his sake.
' Which said, he turned to the confessor, crossed   180
' And reconciled himself, with decency,
' Oft glancing at Saint Mary's opposite
' Where they possess, and showed in shrine to-day,
' The blessed *Umbilicus* of our Lord,
' (A relic 't is believed no other church
' In Rome can boast of)—then rose up, as brisk
' Knelt down again, bent head, adapted neck,
' And, with the name of Jesus on his lips,
' Received the fatal blow.

                              ' The headsman showed   190
' The head to the populace.   Must I avouch
' We strangers own to disappointment here ?
' Report pronounced him fully six feet high,
' Youngish, considering his fifty years,
' And, if not handsome, dignified at least.
' Indeed, it was no face to please a wife !
' His friends say, this was caused by the costume :
' He wore the dress he did the murder in,
' That is, a *just-a-còrps* of russet serge,
' Black camisole, coarse cloak of baracan   200
' (So they style here the garb of goat's-hair cloth)
' White hat and cotton cap beneath, poor Count,
' Preservative against the evening dews .
' During the journey from Arezzo.   Well,
' So died the man, and so his end was peace ;

‘ Whence many a moral were to meditate.
‘ Spada,—you may bet Dandolo,—is Pope ?
‘ Now for the quatrain ! ’

                  No, friend, this will do !
You ’ve sputtered into sparks.   What streak comes
    next ?   210
A letter : Don Giacinto Arcangeli,
Doctor and Proctor, him I made you mark
Buckle to business in his study late,
The virtuous sire, the valiant for the truth,
Acquaints his correspondent,—Florentine,
By name Cencini, advocate as well,
Socius and brother-in-the-devil to match,—
A friend of Franceschini, anyhow,
And knit up with the bowels of the case,—
Acquaints him, (in this paper that I touch)   220
How their joint effort to obtain reprieve
For Guido had so nearly nicked the nine
And ninety and one over,—he would say,
At Tarocs,—or succeeded,—in our phrase.
To this Cencini's care I owe the Book,
The yellow thing I take and toss once more
—How will it be, my four-years’-intimate,
When thou and I part company anon ?—
’T was he, the ‘ whole position of the case,’
Pleading and summary, were put before ;   230
Discreetly in my Book he bound them all,
Adding some three epistles to the point.
Here is the first of these, part fresh as penned,
The sand, that dried the ink, not rubbed away,
Though penned the day whereof it tells the deed :
Part—extant just as plainly, you know where,
Whence came the other stuff, went, you know how,
To make the ring that's all but round and done.

‘ Late they arrived, too late, egregious Sir,
‘ Those same justificative points you urge   240
‘ Might benefit His Blessed Memory
‘ Count Guido Franceschini now with God :
‘ Since the Court,—to state things succinctly,—styled
‘ The Congregation of the Governor,

' Having resolved on Tuesday last our cause
' I' the guilty sense, with death for punishment,
' Spite of all pleas by me deducible
' In favour of said Blessed Memory,—
' I, with expenditure of pains enough,
' Obtained a respite, leave to claim and prove   250
' Exemption from the law's award,—alleged
' The power and privilege o' the Clericate :
' To which effect a courier was despatched.
' But ere an answer from Arezzo came,
' The Holiness of our Lord the Pope (prepare !)
' Judging it inexpedient to postpone
' The execution of such sentence passed,
' Saw fit, by his particular chirograph,
' To derogate, dispense with privilege,
' And wink at any hurt accruing thence   260
' To Mother Church through damage of her son ;
' Also, to overpass and set aside
' That other plea on score of tender age,
' Put forth by me to do Pasquini good,
' One of the four in trouble with our friend.
' So that all five, to-day, have suffered death
' With no distinction save in dying,—he,
' Decollated by way of privilege,
' The rest hanged decently and in order.   Thus
' Came the Count to his end of gallant man,   270
' Defunct in faith and exemplarity :
' Nor shall the shield of his great House lose shine,
' Nor its blue banner blush to red thereby.
' This, too, should yield sustainment to our hearts—
' He had commiseration and respect
' In his decease from universal Rome,
' *Quantum est hominum venustiorum,*
' The nice and cultivated everywhere :
' Though, in respect of me his advocate,
' Needs must I groan o'er my debility,   280
' Attribute the untoward event o' the strife
' To nothing but my own crass ignorance
' Which failed to set the valid reasons forth,
' Find fit excuse : such is the fate of war !
' May God compensate us the direful blow
' By future blessings on his family
' Whereof I lowly beg the next commands ;
' —Whereto, as humbly, I confirm myself . . . '

And so forth,—follow name and place and date :
On the next leaf—   290
     ' *Hactenus senioribus !*
' There, old fox, show the clients t' other side
' And keep this corner sacred, I beseech !
' You and your pleas and proofs were what folks
  call
' Pisan assistance, aid that comes too late,
' Saves a man dead as nail in post of door.
' Had I but time and space for narrative !   .
' What was the good of twenty Clericates
' When Somebody's thick headpiece once was bent
' On seeing Guido's drop into the bag ?   300
' How these old men like giving youth a push !
' So much the better : next push goes to him,
' And a new Pope begins the century.
' Much good I get by my superb defence !
' But argument is solid and subsists,
' While obstinacy and ineptitude
' Accompany the owner to his tomb ;
' What do I care how soon ?   Beside, folks see !
' Rome will have relished heartily the show,
' Yet understood the motives, never fear,   310
' Which caused the indecent change o' the People's
  Place
' To the People's Playground,—stigmatize the spite
' Which in a trice precipitated things !
' As oft the moribund will give a kick
' To show they are not absolutely dead,
' So feebleness i' the socket shoots its last,
' A spirt of violence for energy !

' But thou, Cencini, brother of my breast,
' O fox, whose home is 'mid the tender grape,
' Whose couch in Tuscany by Themis' throne,   320
' Subject to no such . . . but I shut my mouth
' Or only open it again to say,
' This pother and confusion fairly laid,
' My hands are empty and my satchel lank.
' Now then for both the Matrimonial Cause
' And the case of Gomez !   Serve them hot and hot !

' *Reliqua differamus in crastinum !*
' The impatient estafette cracks whip outside :

‘ Still, though the earth should swallow him who
    swears
‘ And me who make the mischief, in must slip   330
‘ —My boy, your godson, fat-chaps Hyacinth,
‘ Enjoyed the sight while Papa plodded here.
‘ I promised him, the rogue, a month ago,
‘ The day his birthday was, of all the days,
‘ That if I failed to save Count Guido’s head,
‘ Cinuccio should at least go see it chopped
‘ From trunk—“ So, latinize your thanks ! ” quoth I :
‘ “ That I prefer, *hoc malim*,” raps me out
‘ The rogue : you notice the subjunctive ?   Ah !
‘ Accordingly he sat there, bold in box,   340
‘ Proud as the Pope behind the peacock-fans :
‘ Whereon a certain lady-patroness
‘ For whom I manage things (my boy in front,
‘ Her Marquis sat the third in evidence ;
‘ Boys have no eyes nor ears save for the show)
‘ “ This time, Cintino,” was her sportive word,
‘ When whiz and thump went axe and mowed lay man,
‘ And folks could fall to the suspended chat,
‘ “ This time, you see, Bottini rules the roast,
‘ “ Nor can Papa with all his eloquence   350
‘ “ Be reckoned on to help as heretofore ! ”
‘ Whereat Cinone pouts ; then, sparkishly—
‘ “ Papa knew better than aggrieve his Pope,
‘ “ And baulk him of his grudge against our Count,
‘ “ Else he ’d have argued-off Bottini’s ” . . what ?
‘ “ His nose,”—the rogue ! well parried of the boy !
‘ He ’s long since out of Cæsar (eight years old)
‘ And as for tripping in Eutropius . . well,
‘ Reason the more that we strain every nerve
‘ To do him justice, mould a model-mouth,   360
‘ A Bartolus-cum-Baldo for next age :
‘ For that I purse the pieces, work the brain,
‘ And want both Gomez and the marriage-case,
‘ Success with which shall plaster aught of pate
‘ That ’s broken in me by Bottini’s flail,
‘ And bruise his own, belike, that wags and brags.
‘ *Adverti supplico humiliter*
‘ *Quod*, do n’t the fungus see, the fop divine
‘ That one hand drives two horses, left and right ?
‘ With this rein did I rescue from the ditch   370
‘ The fortune of our Franceschini, keep

' Unsplashed the credit of a noble House,
' And set the fashionable cause of Rome
' A-prancing till bystanders shouted " 'ware ! "
' The other rein's judicious management
' Suffered old Somebody to keep the pace,
' Hobblingly play the roadster : who but he
' Had his opinion, was not led by the nose
' In leash of quibbles strung to look like law !
' You 'll soon see,—when I go to pay devoir   380
' And compliment him on confuting me,—
' If, by a back-swing of the pendulum,
' Grace be not, thick and threefold, consequent !
' " I must decide as I see proper, Don !
' " The Pope, I have my inward lights for guide.
' " Had learning been the matter in dispute,
' " Could eloquence avail to gainsay fact,
' " Yours were the victory, be comforted ! "
' Cinuzzo will be gainer by it all.
' Quick then with Gomez, hot and hot next case ! '

Follows, a letter, takes the other side.   391
Tall blue-eyed Fisc whose head is capped with cloud,
Doctor Bottini,—to no matter who,
Writes on the Monday two days afterward.
Now shall the honest championship of right,
Crowned with success, enjoy at last, unblamed,
Moderate triumph !   Now shall eloquence
Poured forth in fancied floods for virtue's sake,
(The print is sorrowfully dyked and dammed,
But shows where fain the unbridled force would flow,
Finding a channel)—now shall this refresh   401
The thirsty donor with a drop or two !
Here has been truth at issue with a lie :
Let who gained truth the day have handsome pride
In his own prowess !   Eh ?   What ails the man ?

' Well, it is over, ends as I foresaw :
' Easily proved, Pompilia's innocence !
' Catch them entrusting Guido's guilt to me !
' I had, as usual, the plain truth to plead.
' I always knew the clearness of the stream   410
' Would show the fish so thoroughly, child might prong
' The clumsy monster : with no mud to splash,
' Small credit to lynx-eye and lightning-spear !

' This Guido,—(much sport he contrived to make,
' Who at first twist, preamble of the cord,
' Turned white, told all, like the poltroon he was !)—
' Finished, as you expect, a penitent,
' Fully confessed his crime, and made amends,
' And, edifying Rome last Saturday,
' Died like a saint, poor devil !   That 's the man
' The gods still give to my antagonist :   421
' Imagine how Arcangeli claps wing,
' And crows !   " Such formidable facts to face,
' " So naked to attack, my client here,
' " And yet I kept a month the Fisc at bay,
' " And in the end had foiled him of the prize
' " By this arch-stroke, this plea of privilege,
' " But that the Pope must gratify his whim,
' " Put in his word, poor old man,—let it pass ! "
—Such is the cue to which all Rome responds.   430
What with the plain truth given me to uphold,
And, should I let truth slip, the Pope at hand
To pick up, steady her on legs again,
My office turns a pleasantry indeed !
Not that the burly boaster did one jot
O' the little was to do—young Spreti's work !
But for him,—mannikin and dandiprat,
Mere candle-end and inch of cleverness
Stuck on Arcangeli's save-all,—but for him   439
The spruce young Spreti, what is bad were worse !

I looked that Rome should have the natural gird
At advocate with case that proves itself ;
I knew Arcangeli would grin and brag :
But what say you to one impertinence
Might move a man ?   That monk, you are to know,
That barefoot Augustinian whose report
O' the dying woman's words did detriment
To my best points it took the freshness from,
—That meddler preached to purpose yesterday
At San Lorenzo as a winding-up   450
O' the shows, have proved a treasure to the church.
Out comes his sermon smoking from the press :
Its text—" Let God be true, and every man
" A liar "—and its application, this,
The longest-winded of the paragraphs,
I straight unstitch, tear out and treat you with :

‘ ’T is piping hot and posts through Rome to-day.
‘ Remember it, as I engage to do !

‘ But if you rather be disposed to see
‘ In the result of the long trial here,—   460
‘ This dealing doom to guilt and doling praise
‘ To innocency,—any proof that truth
‘ May look for vindication from the world,
‘ Much will you have misread the signs, I say.
‘ God, who seems acquiescent in the main
‘ With those who add " So will He ever sleep "—
‘ Flutters their foolishness from time to time,
‘ Puts forth His right-hand recognizably ;
‘ Even as, to fools who deem He needs must right
‘ Wrong on the instant, as if earth were heaven,   470
‘ He wakes remonstrance—"Passive, Lord, how long ?"
‘ Because Pompilia’s purity prevails,
‘ Conclude you, all truth triumphs in the end ?
‘ So might those old inhabitants of the ark,
‘ Witnessing haply their dove’s safe return,
‘ Pronounce there was no danger all the while
‘ O’ the deluge, to the creature’s counterparts,
‘ Aught that beat wing i’ the world, was white or soft,—
‘ And that the lark, the thrush, the culver too,
‘ Might equally have traversed air, found earth,   480
‘ And brought back olive-branch in unharmed bill.
‘ Methinks I hear the Patriarch’s warning voice—
‘ " Though this one breast, by miracle, return,
‘ " No wave rolls by, in all the waste, but bears
‘ " Within it some dead dove-like thing as dear,
‘ " Beauty made blank and harmlessness destroyed ! "
‘ How many chaste and noble sister-fames
‘ Wanted the extricating hand, and lie
‘ Strangled, for one Pompilia proud above
‘ The welter, plucked from the world’s calumny,
‘ Stupidity, simplicity,—who cares ?   491

‘ Romans !   An elder race possessed your land
‘ Long ago, and a false faith lingered still,
‘ As shades do, though the morning-star be out.
‘ Doubtless, some pagan of the twilight-day
‘ Has often pointed to a cavern-mouth,
‘ Obnoxious to beholders, hard by Rome,
‘ And said,—nor he a bad man, no, nor fool,—

' Only a man, so, blind like all his mates,—
' " Here skulk in safety, lurk, defying law,   500
' " The devotees to execrable creed,
' " Adoring—with what culture . . Jove, avert
' " Thy vengeance from us worshippers of thee ! . .
' " What rites obscene—their idol-god, an Ass ! "
' So went the word forth, so acceptance found,
' So century re-echoed century,
' Cursed the accursed,—and so, from sire to son,
' You Romans cried " The offscourings of our race
' " Corrupt within the depths there : fitly, fiends
' " Perform a temple-service o'er the dead :   510
' " Child, gather garment round thee, pass nor pry ! "
' So groaned your generations : till the time
' Grew ripe, and lightning hath revealed, belike,—
' Thro' crevice peeped into by curious fear,—
' Some object even fear could recognize
' I' the place of spectres ; on the illumined wall,
' To-wit, some nook, tradition talks about,
' Narrow and short, a corpse's length, no more :
' And by it, in the due receptacle,
' The little rude brown lamp of earthenware,   520
' The cruse, was meant for flowers, but held the blood,
' The rough-scratched palm-branch, and the legend left
' *Pro Christo.*   Then the mystery lay clear :
' The abhorred one was a martyr all the time,
' A saint whereof earth was not worthy.   What ?
' Do you continue in the old belief ?
' Where blackness bides unbroke, must devils be ?
' Is it so certain, not another cell
' O' the myriad that make up the catacomb,
' Contains some saint a second flash would show ?
' Will you ascend into the light of day   531
' And, having recognized a martyr's shrine,
' Go join the votaries that gape around
' Each vulgar god that awes the market-place ?
' Be these the objects of your praising ?   See !
' In the outstretched right hand of Apollo, there,
' Is screened a scorpion : housed amid the folds
' Of Juno's mantle, lo, a cockatrice !
' Each statue of a god were fitlier styled
' Demon and devil.   Glorify no brass   540
' That shines like burnished gold in noonday glare,
' For fools !   Be otherwise instructed, you !

' And preferably ponder, ere ye pass,
' Each incident of this strange human play
' Privily acted on a theatre,
' Was deemed secure from every gaze but God's,—
' Till, of a sudden, earthquake lays wall low
' And lets the world see the wild work inside,
' And how, in petrifaction of surprise,
' The actors stand,—raised arm and planted foot,—
' Mouth as it made, eye as it evidenced,   551
' Despairing shriek, triumphant hate,—transfixed,
' Both he who takes and she who yields the life.

' As ye become spectators of this scene—
' Watch obscuration of a fame pearl-pure
' In vapoury films, enwoven circumstance,
' —A soul made weak by its pathetic want
' Of just the first apprenticeship to sin,
' Would thenceforth make the sinning soul secure
' From all foes save itself, that 's truliest foe,—   560
' For egg turned snake needs fear no serpentry,—
' As ye behold this web of circumstance
' Deepen the more for every thrill and throe,
' Convulsive effort to disperse the films
' And disenmesh the fame o' the martyr,—mark
' How all those means, the unfriended one pursues,
' To keep the treasure trusted to her breast,
' Each struggle in the flight from death to life,
' How all, by procuration of the powers
' Of darkness, are transformed,—no single ray,   570
' Shot forth to show and save the inmost star,
' But, passed as through hell's prism, proceeding black
' To the world that hates white : as ye watch, I say,
' Till dusk and such defacement grow eclipse
' By,—marvellous perversity of man !—
' The inadequacy and inaptitude
' Of that self-same machine, that very law
' Man vaunts, devised to dissipate the gloom,
' Rescue the drowning orb from calumny,
' —Hear law, appointed to defend the just,   580
' Submit, for best defence, that wickedness
' Was bred of flesh and innate with the bone
' Borne by Pompilia's spirit for a space,
' And no mere chance fault, passionate and brief :
' Finally, when ye find,—after this touch

' Of man's protection which intends to mar
' The last pin-point of light and damn the disc,—
' One wave of the hand of God amid the worlds
' Bid vapour vanish, darkness flee away,
' And leave the vexed star culminate in peace   590
' Approachable no more by earthly mist—
' What I call God's hand,—you, perhaps,—this chance
' Of the true instinct of an old good man
' Who happens to hate darkness and love light,—
' In whom too was the eye that saw, not dim,
' The natural force to do the thing he saw,
' Nowise abated,—both by miracle,—
' All this well pondered,—I demand assent
' To the enunciation of my text
' In face of one proof more that " God is true   600
' " And every man a liar "—that who trusts
' To human testimony for a fact
' Gets this sole fact—himself is proved a fool ;
' Man's speech being false, if but by consequence
' That only strength is true ; while man is weak,
' And, since truth seems reserved for heaven not earth,
' Should learn to love what he may speak one day.

' For me, the weary and the worn, who prompt
' To mirth or pity, as I move the mood,—
' A friar who glide unnoticed to the grave,   610
' Bare feet, coarse robe and rope-girt waist of mine,—
' I have long since renounced your world, ye know :
' Yet weigh the worth of worldly prize foregone,
' Disinterestedly judge this and that
' Good ye account good : but God tries the heart.
' Still, if you question me of my content
' At having put each human pleasure by,
' I answer, at the urgency of truth,
' As this world seems, I dare not say I know
' —Apart from Christ's assurance which decides—
' Whether I have not failed to taste some joy.   621
' For many a dream would fain perturb my choice—
' How love, in those the varied shapes, might show
' As glory, or as rapture, or as grace :
' How conversancy with the books that teach,
' The arts that help,—how, to grow great, in fine,
' Rather than simply good, and bring thereby
' Goodness to breathe and live, nor, born i' the brain,

' Die there,—how these and many another gift
' May well be precious though abjured by me.   630
' But, for one prize, best meed of mightiest man,
' Arch-object of ambition,—earthly praise,
' Repute o' the world, the flourish of loud trump,
' The softer social fluting,—Oh, for these,
' —No, my friends ! Fame,—that bubble which, world-wide
' Each blows and bids his neighbour lend a breath,
' That so he haply may behold thereon
' One more enlarged distorted false fool's-face,
' Until some glassy nothing grown as big
' Send by a touch the imperishable to suds,—   640
' No, in renouncing fame, the loss was light,
' Choosing obscurity, the chance was well ! '

Didst ever touch such ampollosity
As the man's own bubble, let alone its spite ?
What 's his speech for, but just the fame he flouts—
How he dares reprehend both high and low ?
Else had he turned the sentence ' God is true
' And every man a liar—save the Pope
' Happily reigning—my respects to him ! '
—So, rounded off the period. Molinism   650
Simple and pure ! To what pitch get we next ?
I find that, for first pleasant consequence,
Gomez, who had intended to appeal
From the absurd decision of the Court,
Declines, though plain enough his privilege,
To call on help from lawyers any more—
Resolves the liars may possess the world,
Till God have had sufficiency of both :
So may I whistle for my job and fee !

But, for this virulent and rabid monk,—   660
If law be an inadequate machine,
And advocacy, so much impotence,
We shall soon see, my blatant brother ! That 's
Exactly what I hope to show your sort !
For, by a veritable piece of luck,
True providence, you monks round period with,
All may be gloriously retrieved. Perpend !

That Monastery of the Convertites
Whereto the Court consigned Pompilia first,
—Observe, if convertite, why, sinner then,   670
Or where the pertinency of award ?—
And whither she was late returned to die,
—Still in their jurisdiction, mark again !—
That thrifty Sisterhood, for perquisite,
Claims every paul whereof may die possessed
Each sinner in the circuit of its walls.
Now, this Pompilia, seeing that by death
O' the couple, all their wealth devolved on her,
Straight utilized the respite ere decease
By regular conveyance of the goods   680
She thought her own, to will and to devise,—
Gave all to friends, Tighetti and the like,
In trust for him she held her son and heir,
Gaetano,—trust to end with infancy :
So willing and devising, since assured
The justice of the Court would presently
Confirm her in her rights and exculpate,
Re-integrate and rehabilitate—
Station as, through my pleading, now she stands.
But here 's the capital mistake : the Court   690
Found Guido guilty,—but pronounced no word
About the innocency of his wife :
I grounded charge on broader base, I hope !
No matter whether wife be true or false,
The husband must not push aside the law,
And punish of a sudden : that 's the point !
Gather from out my speech the contrary !
It follows that Pompilia, unrelieved
By formal sentence from imputed fault,
Remains unfit to have and to dispose   700
Of property, which law provides shall lapse :
Wherefore the Monastery claims its due.
And whose, pray, whose the office, but the Fisc's ?
Who but I institute procedure next
Against the person of dishonest life,
Pompilia, whom last week I sainted so ?
I, it is, teach the monk what scripture means,
And that the tongue should prove a two-edged sword,
No axe sharp one side, blunt the other way,
Like what amused the town at Guido's cost !   710
Astræa redux ! I've a second chance

Before the self-same Court o' the Governor
Who soon shall see volte-face and chop, change sides !
Accordingly, I charge you on your life,
Send me with all dispatch the judgement late
O' the Florence Rota Court, confirmative
O' the prior judgement at Arezzo, clenched
Again by the Granducal signature,
Wherein Pompilia is convicted, doomed,
And only destined to escape through flight   720
The proper punishment.   Send me the piece,—
I 'll work it !   And this foul-mouthed friar shall find
His Noah's-dove that brought the olive back,
Is turned into the other sooty scout,
The raven, Noah first of all put forth the ark,
And never came back, but ate carcasses !
No adequate machinery in law ?
No power of life and death i' the learned tongue ?
Methinks I am already at my speech,
Startle the world with ' Thou, Pompilia, thus ?   730
' How is the fine gold of the Temple dim ! '
And so forth.   But the courier bids me close,
And clip away one joke that runs through Rome,
Side by side with the sermon which I send—
How like the heartlessness of the old hunks
Arcangeli !   His Count is hardly cold,
His client whom his blunders sacrificed,
When somebody must needs describe the scene—
How the procession ended at the church
That boasts the famous relic : quoth our brute,   740
' Why, that's just Martial's phrase for "make an end"—
' *Ad umbilicum sic perventum est !* '
The callous dog,—let who will cut off head,
He cuts a joke, and cares no more than so !
I think my speech shall modify his mirth :
' How is the fine gold dim ! '—but send the piece !

Alack, Bottini, what is my next word
But death to all that hope ?   The Instrument
Is plain before me, print that ends my Book
With the definitive verdict of the Court,   750
Dated September, six months afterward,
(Such trouble and so long, the old Pope gave !)

' In restitution of the perfect fame
' Of dead Pompilia, *quondam* Guido's wife,
' And warrant to her representative
' Domenico Tighetti, barred hereby,
' While doing duty in his guardianship,
' From all molesting, all disquietude,
' Each perturbation and vexation brought
' Or threatened to be brought against the heir   760
' By the Most Venerable Convent called
' Saint Mary Magdalen o' the Convertites
' I' the Corso.'
                    Justice done a second time !
Well judged, Marc Antony, *Locum-tenens*
O' the Governor, a Venturini too !
For which I save thy name,—last of the list !

Next year but one, completing his nine years
Of rule in Rome, died Innocent my Pope
—By some accounts, on his accession-day.   770
If he thought doubt would do the next age good,
'T is pity he died unapprised what birth
His reign may boast of, be remembered by—
Terrible Pope, too, of a kind,—Voltaire.

And so an end of all i' the story.   Strain
Never so much my eyes, I miss the mark
There lived or died that Gaetano, child
Of Guido and Pompilia :   only find,
Immediately upon his father's death,
A record in the annals of the town   780
That Porzia, sister of our Guido, moved
The Priors of Arezzo and their head
Its Gonfalonier to give loyally
A public attestation to the right
O' the Franceschini to men's reverence—
Apparently because of the incident
O' the murder—there 's no mention made of crime,
But what else caused such urgency to cure
The mob, just then, of chronic greediness
For scandal, love of lying vanity,   790
And appetite to swallow crude reports
That bring annoyance to their betters ?—Bane
Which, here, was promptly met by antidote.
I like and shall translate the eloquence

latiùs deduƈtis &c. vigore decreti remiſſionis cauſæ faƈti ab Illu-
ſtriſſ., & Reuerendiſſ. D. Anditore SS. per aƈta Paſchaſij, de
quo in aƈtis &c. relata cauſa in Congregatione, & de voto eiuſ-
dem dicimus, pronunciamus, declaramus, ac diffinitiuè ſententi-
tiamùs ex nouiter deduƈtis NON CONSTARE DE DICTO
PRÆTENSO ADVLTERIO, & proptereà memoriam eiuſ-
dem Franciſcæ Pompiliæ OMNINO' reſtituendæ fore, & eſſe
priſtinæ famæ, & exiſtimationi, eumdemque D. Tighettum,
nomine, quo ſuprà, ex haƈtenus deduƈtis abſoluendum, & li-
berandum fore, & eſſe ab omnibus, & ſingulis inquietationibus,
& moleſtationibus, vexationibus, & perturbationibus harum
occaſione illatis, aut inferri comminatis, prout harum ſerie
reſtituimus, & reſpeƈtiuè abſoluimus, & liberamus, vt ſuprà, &
pro reſtituta, & reſpeƈtiuè abſoluto, & liberato haberi volu-
mus, & mandamus, & proceſſum, ſeù proceſſus quòſcumq; deſu-
per fabricatum, ſeù fabricatos eſſe abolendum, ſeù abolendos,
proùt abolemus, & caſſamus, perpetuum ſilentium eidem
Fiſco, & litis conſortibus imponendo; & ità Dicimus, pronunciamus, declaramus, ac diffinitiuè ſententiamus, non ſolùm
&c. ſed & omni &c.
Ità pronunciaui ego Marcus Antonius Venturinus Locumtenens.
Lata hac die 19. Auguſti 1698. præſentibus DD. Antonio Bernar-
dino Piceno, & Antonio Toparino de Caprarola Teſtibus &c.

Illuſtriſſimo Vrbis Gubernatore in Criminalibus, ſiue
Excellentiſſimo D. Venturino.

Citentur infraſcripti ad docendum de Appellatione, eiuſque legiti-
ma proſequutione primo pro prima ad p. d. Inſtante D. Dominico Tighetto hærede beneficiato quondam Franciſcæ Pompiliæ,
olim vxoris qu. Guidonis Franciſchini principali, ſiue &c.
           Charitas.
D. Ioannes Maria Serbuccius vti Procurator, & Dominus litis ef-
feƈtus diƈti qu. Guidonis Franceſchini exaduerſo principalis.
D. Franciſcus Paraccianus exaduerſo Procurator Venerabilis Mo-
naſterij, & Monialium Sanƈtæ Mariæ Magdalenæ Conuertita-
rum ad Curſum pro omni &c.
   Feci domi d. c. 31. Auguſti 1698. Molinellus.
Die prima Septembris 1698. Relatione faƈta comparuit R. D. Alexander Caſſar Procurator Subſtitutus Charitatis petijt, & obti-
nuit, vt ſupra.

Illuſtriſſimo Vrbis Gubernatore in Criminalibus, ſiue
Excellentiſſimo D. Venturino.

Citentur Infraſcripti ad docendum de appellatione, eiuſque legiti-
ma proſequutione, 2. pro 2. ad p. d. inſtante D. Dominico Tighetto Hærede Beneficiato quondam Franciſcæ Pompiliæ olim
vxoris quondam Guidonis Franceſchini principali ſiue &c.
           Charitas.

Of nearly the worst Latin ever writ :
' Since antique time whereof the memory
' Holds the beginning, to this present hour,
' Our Franceschini ever shone, and shine,
' Still i' the primary rank, supreme amid
' The lustres of Arezzo, proud to own   800
' In this great family—her flag-bearer,
' Guide of her steps and guardian against foe,—
' As in the first beginning, so to-day ! '
There, would you disbelieve stern History,
Trust rather to the babble of a bard ?
I thought, Arezzo, thou hadst fitter souls,
Petrarch,—nay, Buonarroti at a pinch,
To do thee credit as *vexillifer !*
Was it mere mirth the Patavinian meant,
Making thee out, in his veracious page,   810
Founded by Janus of the Double Face ?

Well, proving of such perfect parentage,
Our Gaetano, born of love and hate,
Did the babe live or die ?—one fain would find !
What were his fancies if he grew a man ?
Was he proud,—a true scion of the stock,—
Of bearing blazon, shall make bright my Book—
Shield, Azure, on a Triple Mountain, Or,
A Palm-tree, Proper, whereunto is tied
A Greyhound, Rampant, striving in the slips ?   820
Or did he love his mother, the base-born,
And fight i' the ranks, unnoticed by the world ?

Such, then, the final state o' the story. So
Did the Star Wormwood in a blazing fall
Frighten awhile the waters and lie lost :
So did this old woe fade from memory,
Till after, in the fulness of the days,
I needs must find an ember yet unquenched,
And, breathing, blow the spark to flame. It lives,
If precious be the soul of man to man.   830

So, British Public, who may like me yet,
(Marry and amen !) learn one lesson hence
Of many which whatever lives should teach :
This lesson, that our human speech is naught,
Our human testimony false, our fame
And human estimation words and wind.

Why take the artistic way to prove so much ?
Because, it is the glory and good of Art,
That Art remains the one way possible
Of speaking truth, to mouths like mine, at least.
How look a brother in the face and say   841
' Thy right is wrong, eyes hast thou yet art blind,
' Thine ears are stuffed and stopped, despite their
      length,
' And, oh, the foolishness thou countest faith ! '
Say this as silverly as tongue can troll—
The anger of the man may be endured,
The shrug, the disappointed eyes of him
Are not so bad to bear—but here 's the plague
That all this trouble comes of telling truth,
Which truth, by when it reaches him, looks false,
Seems to be just the thing it would supplant,   851
Nor recognizable by whom it left—
While falsehood would have done the work of truth.
But Art,—wherein man nowise speaks to men,
Only to mankind,—Art may tell a truth
Obliquely, do the thing shall breed the thought,
Nor wrong the thought, missing the mediate word.
So may you paint your picture, twice show truth,
Beyond mere imagery on the wall,—
So, note by note, bring music from your mind,   860
Deeper than ever the Andante dived,—
So write a book shall mean, beyond the facts,
Suffice the eye and save the soul beside.

And save the soul ! If this intent save mine,—
If the rough ore be rounded to a ring,
Render all duty which good ring should do,
And, failing grace, succeed in guardianship,—
Might mine but lie outside thine, Lyric Love,
Thy rare gold ring of verse (the poet praised)
Linking our England to his Italy !   870

THE END

OXFORD : HORACE HART
PRINTER TO THE UNIVERSITY

RETURN TO ➡ CIRCULATION DEPARTMENT
202 Main Library

LOAN PERIOD 1 HOME USE	2	3
4	5	6

ALL BOOKS MAY BE RECALLED AFTER 7 DAYS

1-month loans may be renewed by call
1-year loans may be recharged by bringing the books to the Circulation Desk
Renewals and recharges may be made 4 days prior to due date

DUE AS STAMPED BELOW

REC CIRC MAY 1 1985

UNIVERSITY OF CALIFORNIA, BERKELEY
BERKELEY, CA 94720

FORM NO. DD6, 60m, 1/83

ImTheStory.com

Personalized Classic Books in many genre's

Unique gift for kids, partners, friends, colleagues

Customize:

- • Character Names
- • Upload your own front/back cover images (optional)
- • Inscribe a personal message/dedication on the
  inside page (optional)

Customize many titles Including

- • Alice in Wonderland
- • Romeo and Juliet
- • The Wizard of Oz
- • A Christmas Carol
- • Dracula
- • Dr. Jekyll & Mr. Hyde
- • And more...

Emily's Adventures in Wonderland

Ryan & Julia